Plato the Teacher

Plato the Teacher

The Crisis of the Republic

William H. F. Altman

LEXINGTON BOOKS
Lanham • Boulder • New York • Toronto • Plymouth, UK

Published by Lexington Books
A wholly owned subsidiary of The Rowman & Littlefield Publishing Group, Inc.
4501 Forbes Boulevard, Suite 200, Lanham, Maryland 20706
http://www.lexingtonbooks.com

Estover Road, Plymouth PL6 7PY, United Kingdom

British Library Cataloguing in Publication Information Available

Library of Congress Cataloging-in-Publication Data
Altman, William H. F., 1955-
Plato the teacher : the crisis of The republic / William H.F. Altman.
pages cm
Includes bibliographical references and indexes.
ISBN 978-0-7391-7138-7 (cloth : alk. paper) -- ISBN 978-0-7391-7139-4 (electronic)
1. Plato. Republic. 2. Justice. 3. Teaching--Methodology. I. Title.
JC71.P6A53 2012
321'.07--dc23

2011046892

™ The paper used in this publication meets the minimum requirements of American National Standard for Information Sciences—Permanence of Paper for Printed Library Materials, ANSI/NISO Z39.48-1992.

Printed in the United States of America

in memoriam

Adeline Furness Altman

(1913-2010)

"But if something different manifests itself in the individual, we will return again to the state and test it there [πάλιν ἐπανιόντες ἐπὶ τὴν πόλιν βασανιοῦμεν] and it may be that, by examining them side by side and rubbing them against one another [παρ' ἄλληλα σκοποῦντες καὶ τρίβοντες] as it were from the fire sticks we may cause the spark of justice to flash forth [ὥσπερ ἐκ πυρείων ἐκλάμψαι ποιήσαιμεν τὴν δικαιοσύνην], and when it is thus revealed confirm it in our own minds."

Republic IV. 434e4-435a4; translation Paul Shorey.

"And how," said Thrasymachus, "shall I persuade you? For if you haven't been persuaded by what I was saying just now, what more can I do for you? Or should I insert my teaching [τὸν λόγον], betaking it into your soul?" "My God," was what I said, "Not you, indeed [μὴ σύ γε]."

Republic I. 345b5-8; translation mine.

"and this rule over children [ἡ τῶν παίδων ἀρχή], our not allowing them to be free until, as it were in a city, we will have established a polity [πολιτεία] within them and, by fostering what is best [τὸ βέλτιστον θεραπεύσαντες] by the same sort of thing in ourselves, have set up in its place a similar guardian and ruler [φύλακα ὅμοιον καὶ ἄρχοντα] in the child and then, indeed, we let it go free."

Republic IX. 590e2-591a3; Shorey translation modified.

Contents

Acknowledgements xi
Preface to *Plato the Teacher* xiii

An Introduction to Plato's *Republic*: Inside and Outside the Text 1

1 The First Words of Plato's Πολιτεία 37-76

§1. κατέβην 37
§2. χθές 46
§3. εἰς Πειραιᾶ 51
§4. μετὰ Γλαύκωνος 54
§5. τοῦ Ἀρίστωνος 65

2 Challenges 77-109

§6. Cephalus and the Meaning of Life 77
§7. Polemarchus Meets Appearance and Reality 82
§8. Thrasymachus and the City of Good Men Only 87
§9. Glaucon's Challenge to Socrates 101
§10. The Challenge of Adeimantus to Plato 105

3 The Shorter Way 111-169

§11. Introduction to Methodology 111
§12. Methodology II: Hypotheses 117
§13. Methodology III: Images 129
§14. Looking Out for Number One 142
§15. Making Friends with Thrasymachus 158

4 The Longer Way 171-243

§16. The Speech to the Guardians 171
§17. Justice and the Good on the Divided Line 181
§18. The Idea of the Good and Plato's Theory of Forms 185
§19. An Intellectual History of the Return 204
§20. Whistling a Tune on the Way Down 236

5 The Firesticks **245-289**

§21. 434d1-435a4 245
§22. Two Jobs for One Man: Beyond the Tripartite Soul 250
§23. The Third Wave of Paradox 257
§24. Plato's *Letters* 259
§25. Untimely Meditations on the Idea of Justice 275

6 Democracy and Education **291-358**

§26. Genetic Fictions 291
§27. The Equality of the Sexes 294
§28. Higher Education: Why the Good is not the One 305
§29. Reading Order Revisited 336
§30. The Age of Heroes 348

7 Choices **359-399**

§31. The Sewer of Romulus 359
§32. The Perfectly Bearable Lightness of Being 367
§33. Coming Up and Going Down 372
§34. Plato the Imitator 377
§35. Odysseus or Achilles? 382

Bibliography 401
Index 425
Index verborum 471
Index locorum 475
About the Author 489

Acknowledgements

In the case of a life's work, one's debts cannot be justly and easily reckoned. With her unique combination of mysticism and compassion, Adeline Furness was the ideal mother for a Platonist and it is thanks to her that the first time I read a Platonic dialogue—the *Meno*—I found it in a volume that also included Thomas Taylor's translation of *Alcibiades Major*. She also equipped me with an intellectual for a father and Oscar Altman not only introduced me to Plato and the classics but more importantly offered me the counter-ballast of Judaism to complement her own committed monism. I was assigned the *Meno* by Anne Yondorf and Stephen Morse during my senior year at Sidwell Friends and the uproarious comments of my best friend Sam Gordon about "bee-ness" and what "would seem to be the virtuous activity under the circumstances" ring in my ears to this day although he himself is long gone. Also gone is Elisabeth Young-Bruehl, with whom I read *Cratylus* in "Cosmos as Language"; her serious approach to the playful magic of Plato inspired me. Also inspiring was Victor Gourevitch, who made me yearn to learn Greek, and George Creeger who taught me that there was nothing more important to grasp than the difference between Plato and Aristotle. My professors at the University of Toronto schooled my passion: Wallace McLeod, Graeme Nicholson, George Edison, and above all Daniel DeMontmollin taught me the Classics although I will also never forget hearing T. M. Robinson translating Thucydides. Andreas Lehner hired me to teach History at Harwood Union and then allowed me to offer a course on Plato in 1982-83; this was the first and thus far my only attempt to teach all the dialogues in the proper reading order. The students in that seminar will live in my memory and it is a pleasure to record their names here: Dan Boyce, Cathy Boadway, Kate Hosford, Heather Harwood, Dan Finley, George Houston, Marc Wennberg, Brenda Buker, Larry Knowles, and Glenn Story; not only did each contribute to my understanding of various details but collectively they taught me that Plato, taught in order, was accessible to public high school students. My biggest regret here is that I did not yet grasp how *Laws* needs to be read; our day up on Camel's Hump would have been much more fun if I knew then what I know now. The National Endowment for the Humanities awarded me a grant to develop "Three Democracies" and it was this project that made me a Ciceronian; I am profoundly grateful to the NEH of that era for assisting secondary school teachers to implement their own scholarly projects. Not only in relation to the Cave and the *Alcibiades Major* but also to the course as a whole, the ninth-graders of Vermont's Mad River Valley responded vibrantly to Platonic pedagogy and many happy years of teaching the history of Athens and Rome have left their mark on this book. Champlain College offered me the chance to teach "Introduction to Philosophy" every semester between 1988 and 1995 and the present work grows directly out of those lectures; I am grateful to Dean David Huwiler and Weston Donehower for making this possible. But a considerable amount of the formative teaching and learning was unpaid and in particular, "the Academy Summer" of 1986 stands out: this was when I learned about the centrality of the mathematical monad among the five mathematical sciences thanks to the delightful company of Dan Finley, Heather Harwood, George Houston, Adam Lehner, Alice Meeker, and Danny Myers. Also invigorating were the three "Plato and the Bible" courses I offered in Montpelier and, amid many others, Tom and Jeff Dean, John Nelson, and Diane Villemaire have helped me grow as a thinker and Ciceronian Platonist. Although I have had many fine students, the finest proved to be my own sons, Philip and Elias; never have I been so challenged, motivated, and awe-struck. Above all others, you boys have been my touchstone and whenever I think of you, "my cup runneth over." But I cannot forget all the ninth-graders at Harwood who proved to me that Plato actually "worked," especially Seth Brunnell who woke up on the day when I was teaching the Cave. The older students I taught at Champlain, Wes Donehower Jr. in particular, also proved that Plato has not forgotten the art of changing lives. It is finally a crowning pleasure to thank my beautiful wife Zoraide: your support for, and belief in me has made this book possible, especially since it was in our beautiful green room on the Rua Anita Garibaldi in Floripa where it first hit me in the middle of the night that I could divide *Plato the Teacher* into three and begin writing the first volume immediately. Your quick grasp of Platonism has taught me more than you will ever know and here, again, my darling, my cup runneth over. Having decided to enter the world of academic publishing, I have incurred a whole new kind of debts and obligations; among those I want to thank are Michael Zank, John Ferrari, Mitch Miller, Victoria Wohl, Jill Frank, Allen Miller, Luc Brisson, Vladimir Suchan, Alan Gilbert, Kyriakos Demetriou, Ron Polansky, Edward Halper, Thornton Lockwood, Peter Minowitz, and Francisco Gonzalez. The philosophical wrestler Ernie Aleva and James Wood, friend of the *Philebus*, have been particularly lively interlocutors and Roslyn Weiss has modeled for me the best in the business as well as providing ongoing support, encouragement, and criticism. The staff at Alderman in Charlottesville has offered invaluable assistance and I am grateful to the Commonwealth of Virginia for granting its residents access to a great University's library. Finally, the professionals at Rowman & Littlefield and Lexington Books have been a delight: in addition to Joseph Parry, who got this particular ball rolling, it is a pleasure to thank Melissa Wilks, Alison Northridge, and Laura Reiter.

Lynchburg, Virginia
December 26, 2011

Preface to *Plato the Teacher*

For where the starting point [ἀρχὴ] is something the reasoner does not know, and the conclusion [τελευτὴ] and all that intervenes [τὰ μεταξὺ] is a tissue of things not really known, what possibility is there that assent in such cases can ever be converted into true knowledge or science?

Plato, *Republic* 533c3-6; Paul Shorey translation[1]

If someone were to reduce Plato to a system, he would render a great service to the human race.

G. W. Leibniz; Letter to Rémond[2]

When considered as a whole—of which this study of Plato's *Republic* is the principal part—*Plato the Teacher* constitutes an attempt to perform this service in a manner Leibniz almost certainly did not anticipate. The phrase "*réduire Platon en système*" strongly suggests that Leibniz did not consider the possibility that Plato's dialogues *already* constituted a system and it is probable that he believed the dialogue form in which they were written was detachable from a philosophic teaching that could, perhaps by that very detachment, be *reduced* to a system. Here, by contrast, the ongoing project is more expansive and involves recognizing Plato's dialogues, all thirty-five of them, as the now disparate and scattered elements (*disiecta membra*) of a once grand but permanently playful pedagogical system (σύνοψις at *R.* 537c2) that *Plato himself created*, a system that now depends on visualizing the dialogues as teaching tools and then, by following Plato's hints, rearranging them a certain order as the interlocking parts of a coherent curriculum. In an important sense, then, I am claiming that Plato is already that elusive "someone" desiderated by Leibniz; if this identification is unacceptable, someone else will, however reluctantly, be forced to take some responsibility for rendering this service. In any case, attempts to rediscover the

1. All references to *Republic* are based on S. R. Slings (ed.), *Platonis* Rempublicam (Oxford: Clarendon Press, 2003). References to Plato's other writings are based on John Burnet (ed.), *Platonis Opera* (Oxford: Clarendon Press, 1900-1907). Abbreviations for the dialogues are in conformity with Liddell and Scott (hereafter "LSJ").

2. Translation mine. See Giovanni Reale, *Toward a New Interpretation of Plato,* translated by John R. Catan and Richard Davies (Washington DC: Catholic University of America Press), 4n6 for the importance of this letter to the Tübingen School.

Reading Order of Plato's Dialogues were once common and the time is ripe to renew this project with modern means and classic common sense: the dialogues must be read as dialogues but not to the point of denying Plato's ongoing *intention* to educate those who read them. Unfortunately, it is not universally agreed that Plato used his dialogues as teaching tools.

Aside from the dialogues in general and *Republic* VII in particular, our best guide to the actual practice of Platonic pedagogy is the Seventh Letter. Plato's own ongoing desire (ἐπιθυμία at *Ep.* 325b1) to enter politics (*Ep.* 324b9-c1, 325a7-b1, and 325e1-2) was the Academy's *raison d'être*: inspired by nostalgia for the good old days (*Ep.* 324d7-8 and 325d3-4), well aware of the need for political allies (*Ep.* 325d1-2), and cognizant that the decay of the ancestral constitution made finding these difficult (*Ep.* 325d2-4), Plato chose the by no means easy task of "procuring for himself" (κτᾶσθαι) new ones (καινούς ἄλλους at *Ep.* 325d4-5); I take this to have been the Academy's original purpose. Plato's description of the education of Dion (*Ep.* 327a1-4) proves that the combination of theory and political practice was implicit and enduring in Plato's teaching while each reader must decide whether Plato was, as he claims, ignorant of the anti-tyrannical implications of his practical counsel (*Ep.* 327a4-5). In any case, Plato was by this time already an experienced educator; this is evident from his claim that Dion was not only "very quick to learn" (*Ep.* 327a6) but that "none of the youngsters I have ever happened upon" (*Ep.* 327b1; translations mine) could compare with him. As his keenest student, Dion was in a good position to explain the purport of Plato's teaching and, in the Seventh Letter, Plato permits him to do so: in begging his teacher to return to Sicily, Dion is in need

> of the arguments and the eloquence that I know you, more than others, could wield to turn the minds of young people [ἀνθρώπους νέους] to virtue and justice [ἐπὶ τὰ ἀγαθὰ καὶ τὰ δίκαια] so as to establish in all cases mutual friendship and alliance.[3]

Plato's Dion is familiar with the *Republic*: he alludes to the choice of lives (*Ep.* 327e1-2; cf. 334d8-e1)—origin of "the crisis of the *Republic*"—and, more decisively, he refers directly to the Third Wave of Paradox (*Ep.* 328a6-b1) where philosophers must acquire political power or kings must philosophize.[4] In addition to depicting Dion's familiarity with the *Republic*, Plato himself states while describing Dion's education that he was quick to learn "both with respect to other things and with respect to the discourses that by then had come into being through me [πρὸς τοὺς τότε ὑπ' ἐμοῦ λόγους γενόμενους]" (327a6-7; trans-

3. *Ep.* 328d6-e1 (L. A. Post translation modified); Plato is imagining the now dead Dion having made this speech (*Ep.* 328d4-329a5) while alive; cf. the speech of the Athenian Laws in *Crito*.

4. Plato explains the circumstances leading to his discovery of the Paradox (*Ep.* 325d1-326a7) and it is useful to compare its famous version at *R.* 473c11-d1 with what I take to be the more Academic formulation at *Ep.* 326a7-b4 paraphrased here.

lation mine) and these literally translated words I take to refer to the dialogues (cf. *Ep.* 363a6) that Plato had written by that time. While there is no way to know what dialogues Plato used to educate Dion, there is no doubt that the author of the Seventh Letter intends its readers to understand that *Republic* was one of them.

More important than the Seventh Letter is the evidence of the dialogues themselves when reconsidered with respect to reading order. As reconstructed here,[5] *Protagoras* is the beginning (ἀρχή) of the reading order of Plato's dialogues and its end (τελευτή) is *Phaedo*: the dialogues as a whole tell an entertaining story, primarily about Socrates, that begins before dawn and ends at nightfall. Within this story, Plato's *Republic* occupies the central place: it is eighteenth out of thirty-five. *Plato the Teacher* begins with *Republic* not because it is the first dialogue Plato intended the student to read but because it can be usefully considered, however inadequately from my perspective, in isolation: although necessarily preceded by *Cleitophon* and followed by *Timaeus*, Plato's *Republic* is a microcosm of the entire Platonic universe[6] and it is here that he has already indicated the kind of cosmologists he intends us to be (cf. *Phd.* 114d8-115a3). With a pedagogical reading of *Republic* in place, the dialogues that precede it can be shown to prepare the student to learn from it; with its lessons having been learned, Plato has prepared the student to meet the considerable challenges he will offer them in the difficult dialogues that lay ahead. This study of the *Republic* therefore has a double purpose: it introduces a broader project that will eventually encompass all of Plato's dialogues by means of a stand-alone account of his most important dialogue. Although this brief Preface naturally cannot defend that broader project, a sketch of the principles on which it depends and an overview of its results may be of some service to the reader.

In an important 1998 article,[7] Carol Poster—as part of "a methodological prolegomenon to Platonic hermeneutics"—classified four ways of ordering the Platonic dialogues, one of them designated "pedagogical order" and defined as "the order in which we should read or teach the dialogues." In accordance with the conception that guides the present project—a conception in which the indispensable role of Poster's "dramatic chronology" and "theoretical or metaphysical order" is guided throughout by pedagogical considerations—dialogues can

---

5. William H. F. Altman, "The Reading Order of Plato's Dialogues." *Phoenix* 64 nos. 1-2 (Winter 2010), 18-51.

6. As a whole my project will answer Diskin Clay, "Gaps in the 'Universe' of the Platonic Dialogues." *Proceedings of the Boston Area Colloquium in Ancient Philosophy* 3 (1987), 131-157. In the case of the *Cleitophon, Republic, Timaeus* and *Critias* tetralogy, consider 151: "The unwritten {*Philosopher*} and {*Hermocrates*} [I will reserve brackets for my own interpolations in quoted material] are great gaps in the universe of the Platonic dialogues, as is the missing conclusion of the *Critias* and the myth of Atlantis. These occupy vast interstellar spaces that are beyond the reach of even speculation." I will maintain that their absence is deliberate.

7. Carol Poster, "The Idea(s) of Order of Platonic Dialogues and Their Hermeneutic Consequences." *Phoenix* 52 nos. 3-4 (Autumn-Winter 1998), 282-298.

still be meaningfully classified as early, middle, and late but no longer with respect to Plato's development (hereafter "developmentalism"), the dominant paradigm of nineteenth- and twentieth-century Plato scholarship,[8] about which I am agnostic. By this I mean that the chronology of Platonic composition is no more relevant to reconstructing the reading order of Plato's dialogues than reconstructing that reading order was to nineteenth- and twentieth-century Plato scholarship. A reconstruction of the Platonic reading order offers no basis for denying the conclusions drawn from stylometric analysis and *vice versa*. Plato could have composed the dialogues in precisely the order presently accepted and gradually worked them into an evolving reading order of which even the initial conception may well have been a comparatively late development. It is only the conclusion tacitly but illegitimately derived from stylometric analysis that will be categorically rejected here: if stylometry can tell us what dialogues were composed after *Republic*, it cannot tell us how to read them.[9] Even if the assumption upon which stylometric analysis depends is correct and *Laws* was the last dialogue Plato wrote, this still proves nothing about the goal or τελός of Plato's thought in any philosophical sense.

As studies of Thrasyllus have shown,[10] our edition of Plato is inseparable from the search for the reading order of Plato's dialogues: the nine "tetralogies"—thirty-five dialogues and the *Letters* arranged in sets of four—constituted his version of it. It is instructive that the Neo-Platonist Albinus took Thrasyllus to task for the opening *Euthyphro*, *Apology*, *Crito*, and *Phaedo* quartet;[11] a long tradition of ancient attempts to reconstruct the Platonic reading order had been guided by what Poster calls "theoretical and metaphysical order" in sharp distinction to the "dramatic chronology" that guided Thrasyllus, albeit to a remarkably limited extent.[12] But neither of these two schools of thought privileged "pedagogical order" in the sense I propose. This can be illustrated with reference to *Alcibiades Major*: both camps accepted it as genuine but those who placed it first in the reading order—the camp hostile to the First Tetralogy of Thrasyl-

8. Poster, "The Idea(s)," 282 calls this "chronology of composition"; see also Jacob Howland, "Re-Reading Plato: The Problem of Platonic Chronology." *Phoenix* 45 no. 3 (Autumn 1991), 189-214.

9. Debra Nails, "Plato's "Middle" Cluster." *Phoenix* 48 no. 1 (Spring 1994), 62-67.

10. Michael Dunn, "The Organization of the Platonic Corpus Between the First and Second Century A.D." (Ph.D. dissertation, Yale University, 1974) and "Iamblichus, Thrasyllus, and the Reading order of the Platonic Dialogues." in R. Baine Harris (ed.), *Studies in Neoplatonism: Ancient and Modern, Volume I* (Albany: State University of New York, 1976). See also Harold Tarrant, *Thrasyllan Platonism* (Ithaca, NY: Cornell University Press, 1993).

11. H. Gregory Snyder, *Teachers and Texts in the Ancient World; Philosophers, Jews and Christians* (London: Routledge, 2000), 98-99.

12. See A. J. Festugière, "L'ordre de lecture des dialogues de Platon aux Ve/VIe siècles." *Museum Helveticum* 26 (1969), 281-296 and Jaap Mansfeld, *Prolegomena: Questions to be Settled Before the Study of an Author, or a Text* (Leiden: Brill, 1994), 64n111 and 67-68.

lus—did so for theoretical/metaphysical reasons, not pedagogical ones. Proclus,[13] for example, says nothing about the fact that its childlike and natural simplicity—if the teacher reads "Socrates," the student scarcely needs a script—makes *Alcibiades Major* the ideal place to begin guiding the neophyte.[14] The first principle of the reading order proposed here is that it is guided throughout by pedagogical considerations: to speak very roughly, the more difficult dialogues are to be read only after the preparation provided by easier and earlier ones, i.e., earlier with respect to a coherent curriculum rather than to "Plato's development."

This reconstruction project is therefore both old and new: it accomplishes an ancient objective with means not ably employed in antiquity. Precisely because most of those who sought the reading order in the past were guided by a Neo-Platonic contempt for the merely historical, they ignored the pedagogical advantages of "dramatic chronology" whereas a cycle of dialogues culminating in *Phaedo* tells a compelling story with a happy ending about a remarkable hero. As for Thrasyllus, the limits of his loyalty to "dramatic chronology" can be illustrated by the fact that he failed to interpolate *Sophist* and *Statesman* between *Euthyphro* and *Apology* in his First Tetralogy. Had he done so, he would have had no sound pedagogical reason for confronting neophytes with the difficult *Sophist* as their second dialogue. In short, placing *Phaedo* last not only provides a good ending for the story of Socrates but also ensures that complex dialogues like *Theaetetus*, *Sophist* and *Statesman* are read near the end of it. And it is certainly Plato's concern for effective pedagogy that explains the priority of the elementary *Alcibiades Major*.

It is probably no accident that a concern for reconstructing the Platonic reading order would disappear as soon as the *Alcibiades Major* was dropped from the canon.[15] Freed at last from the metaphysical baggage of Neo-

---

13. William O'Neill, (ed.), *Proclus:* Alcibiades I*; A Translation and Commentary* (The Hague: Martinus Nijhof, 1965), 1-4

14. W. A. Heidel, *Pseudo-Platonica* (Baltimore, MD: Johns Hopkins University Press, 1896), 62: "Furthermore, in its character as a primer of Platonism in regards to ethics and politics, *Alcibiades I* contains a greater number of distinctively Platonic thoughts than can be found in any number of even the greater single works of Plato. In this respect the dialogue may be pronounced *too* Platonic." Cf. W. K. C. Guthrie, *A History of Greek Philosophy*, Vol. III (Cambridge, UK: Cambridge University Press, 1969), 470: "a dialogue which, whether or not Plato wrote it, was aptly described by Burnet as 'designed as a sort of introduction to Socratic philosophy for beginners.'"

15. Conversely, it is renewed interest in the *Alcibiades Major*—see Gary Alan Scott, *Plato's Socrates as Educator* (Albany: State University of New York Press, 2000) and Nicholas Denyer (ed.), *Plato:* Alcibiades (Cambridge, UK: Cambridge University Press, 2001)—and the other athetized dialogues that has finally made it possible to renew the reading order question. John M. Cooper (ed.) and D. S. Hutchinson. *Plato, Complete Works; edited with an Introduction and Notes* (Chicago, IL: Hackett, 1997) not only makes all thirty-five dialogues widely available in English but also contains the following observation (x): "Thrasyllus' order appears to be determined by no single criterion but by

Platonism, any pedagogical justification for regarding *Alcibiades Major* as a wonderful way to introduce the student/reader to a Platonic dialogue immediately confronts the modern objection that it, along with a considerable (but now apparently shrinking) number of dialogues, isn't by Plato. The growing interest in *Cleitophon* is a case in point, especially because it affords an instance where my reconstruction coincides with that of Thrasyllus.[16] Considered alone, *Cleitophon* appears to be incomplete and inauthentic. But it is of great pedagogical importance when considered as an authentic introduction to *Republic*, as Thrasyllus too must have recognized.[17] The second principle of the Reading Order proposed here is that none of the thirty-five dialogues transmitted by Thrasyllus are to be considered inauthentic *a priori* and indeed a new criterion for authenticity will be employed: a dialogue is authentic when it is snugly joined—by dramatic, pedagogical, and/or theoretical/metaphysical considerations—between two other dialogues, the one that precedes and the one that follows it in the reconstructed Reading Order.

The third principle is that dramatic considerations are our best guide to the Platonic reading order and therefore trump more speculative principles in cases of conflict: the difficult *Protagoras* thus precedes the introductory *Alcibiades Major*. It will be observed that although both are present in the house of Callias, Socrates never speaks to Alcibiades in *Protagoras* while the *Alcibiades Major* represents their first actual conversation (*Alc. 1* 103a4). In that conversation, the otherwise befuddled Alcibiades evades (to his cost) a Socratic trap by means of a sophisticated trick (*Alc. 1* 111a1-3) used the day before by Protagoras (*Prt.* 327e3-328a1). But dramatic connections between dialogues need not always be chronological;[18] a much broader conception of dramatic detail will be employed here. For example, the *Menexenus* takes place after the *Lysis* with respect to "dramatic chronology"; Menexenus has grown up since his schooldays with Lysis. But as I have shown in another place,[19] there are pedagogical, theoretical,

---

several sometimes conflicting ones, though his arrangement may represent some more or less unified idea about the order in which the dialogues should be read and taught."

16. See my "Reading Order and Authenticity: The Place of *Theages* and *Cleitophon* in Platonic Pedagogy" (forthcoming in *Plato* 11).

17. Cf. Joseph Souilhé, *Platon; Oeuvres Complètes*, Volume 13.1 (Paris: Budé, 1949), 179. *Cleitophon* will be given consideration in the Introduction that follows.

18. Two recent studies arrange the dialogues with respect to their dramatic dates: Catherine H. Zuckert, *Plato's Philosophers: The Coherence of the Dialogues* (Chicago, IL: University of Chicago Press, 2009) and Laurence Lampert, *How Philosophy Became Socratic: A Study of Plato's* Protagoras, Charmides, *and* Republic (Chicago, IL: University of Chicago Press, 2010). For my reviews of these important books, see *Polis* 27 n. 1 (Summer 2010), 147-150 and *Polis* 28 n. 1 166-170 (Summer 2011). For a critique of ordering the dialogues exclusively by dramatic dates, see my "*Laches* Before *Charmides*: Fictive Chronology and Platonic Pedagogy." *Plato* 10 (November, 2010) at http://gramata.univ-paris1.fr/Plato/spip.php?page=imprimer&id_article=95 (accessed August 5, 2011).

19. Altman, "The Reading Order of Plato's Dialogues," sections §3 and §4.

and dramatic considerations that place *Lysis* after *Symposium* just as there are pedagogical, theoretical, dramatic, and indeed chronological considerations that place *Menexenus* before it. In neither case is the "dramatic" connection crudely chronological: the fact, for example, that Socrates leaves Agathon's house for the Lyceum (*Smp.* 223d10) and that the *Lysis* finds him *en route* thither (*Ly.* 203a1) is paradigmatic of the kind of intra-textual dramatic clue that guides my reconstruction.

With a title suggesting a beginning and a dramatic setting that wakes the dawn (*Prt.* 310a8; cf. *Phd.* 118e7-8), the *Protagoras* is both a difficult dialogue and a very vivid one: it brings to life the historical context for even the dullest student but would confuse even the brightest about a wide variety of important subjects.[20] A fourth principle of the reconstruction I have undertaken is that Plato employs "proleptic" composition:[21] he begins by confusing the student in an ultimately salutary manner, i.e., about things that it is pedagogically useful for the student to be confused. To give the most important example: the student who comes to *Republic* with *Protagoras* in mind—where piety may be the fifth virtue and virtue may have no parts (*Prt.* 349b1-3)—will be justly critical of the justice discovered in Book IV.

The fifth principle is the absolute centrality of *Republic*.[22] Although less accessible to those who have not recently completed the series of dialogues beginning with *Protagoras* and ending with *Cleitophon*, *Republic* VII contains the essence of Platonism; validating this claim is indeed the principal purpose of the present study. In accordance with an ongoing emphasis on Platonic pedagogy, Plato is understood here first and foremost as a teacher, a teacher with a school—the Academy—as well as a teaching. The dialogues are intended to transmit that teaching through (1) the dialectic represented in the dialogues, (2) dialectic between students about the dialogues, and (3)—this point is crucial for the reading order hypothesis—the inter-dialogue dialectic between the dialogues when read in the proper order. Most importantly, "(3)" reveals the *centrality* of (4) the decisive dialogue between Plato and the reader in *Republic* VII, leading to what I will call "the crisis of the *Republic*." Understanding Plato's pedagogy

---

20. See the brilliant "Conclusion" at W. K. C. Guthrie, *A History of Greek Philosophy*, Volume IV (Cambridge, UK: Cambridge University Press, 1975), 235.

21. The pioneer here is Charles H. Kahn; see in particular his "Did Plato Write Socratic Dialogues?" *Classical Quarterly* 31 (1981), 305-20, "Plato's *Charmides* and the Proleptic Reading of Socratic Dialogues." *Journal of Philosophy* 85 (1988), 541-549, and *Plato and the Socratic Dialogue: The Philosophical Use of Literary Form* (Cambridge, UK: Cambridge University Press, 1996).

22. For a recent statement of the scholarly consensus—notice also the claim that *Republic* "brings together all of Plato's prior work" (1)—see the editorial "Introduction" to Mark L. McPherran (ed.), *Plato's* Republic: *A Critical Guide* (Cambridge, UK: Cambridge University Press, 2010), 1-2: "The *Republic*, then, is justly celebrated as Plato's central text, and scholars continue to regard it as Plato's *magnum opus*." For a statement of the the minority view, see Julia Annas, *Platonic Ethics, Old and New* (Ithaca, NY: Cornell University Press, 1999), 95.

therefore depends on the recognition that there are three distinct classes of Platonic dialogue: *Republic*, the dialogues that prepare the way for *Republic*, and the dialogues that follow it in the Platonic reading order.

The basic principle underlying this classification is that Platonism, more or less as traditionally understood, can most easily be found in *Symposium*, *Republic*, and *Phaedo*.[23] In accordance with the importance of the visual revelation that is the Platonic Idea, these dialogues will here be called "visionary." It will likewise be seen that the Plato who emerges from the reconstructed reading order will closely resemble what used to be called "a Platonist." He is in any case both a philosopher and a teacher: a teacher who, while alive, taught others to philosophize and who—especially when the dialectical unity of his richly diverse curriculum[24] is recognized—continues to do just that through his writings. The present study will argue that the heart of his thought is "the Idea of the Good" and, in its light, the true philosopher's just return to the Cave. Certainly Plato's Socrates does not *know* (*Ap.* 21d7) that he knows nothing; his use of the dialogue form does not preclude the fact that he has a teaching.[25] Although each dialogue is a beautiful work of art, the principle that each dialogue must be understood without reference to any other—the principle of hermeneutic isolationism[26]—is antithetical to the project undertaken here. In full awareness that some may regard the following claim as an unwarranted "reduction," it is necessary to identify the view that Plato has a visionary teaching and that he expressed it in his dialogues as a sixth principle.

The seventh (and final) principle is more difficult to elucidate but is of utmost importance. To begin with, it identifies "testing" as a crucial element of Platonic pedagogy. For reasons to be explained later, I will use the neologism "basanistic," based on the Greek word for "touchstone" (cf. *Grg*. 486d1-7), as a technical term. There are three points that need to be made right away about "the basanistic element in Plato's dialogues": (1) along with *proleptic* and *visionary*, the *basanistic* element is best understood as one of three theoretical and hypothetical springboards (*R.* 511b6) toward hermeneutic clarity rather than as a rigid and exclusive technical term. (2) Although there is a meaningful sense in which a given dialogue can crudely be called proleptic, visionary, or basanistic, it is

23. Kahn, *Plato and the Socratic Dialogue*, 42 and 274.

24. Cicero, *Orator* 12.

25. *pace* Leo Strauss, "Plato" (1963) in Leo Strauss and Joseph Cropsey (eds.), *History of Political Philosophy*, third edition (Chicago, IL: University of Chicago Press, 1987), 33 followed by Michael Frede, "Plato's Arguments and the Dialogue Form" in James C. Klagge and Nicholas D. Smith eds., *Methods of Interpreting Plato and his Dialogues*, 201-219 (Oxford: Oxford University Press, 1992); for "knowledge of ignorance," see Leo Strauss, *Natural Right and History* (Chicago, IL: University of Chicago Press, 1953), 32 and *Studies in Platonic Political Philosophy* (Chicago, IL: University of Chicago Press, 1983), 42.

26. Gerald A. Press, "Principles of Dramatic and Non-dogmatic Plato Interpretation" and "Introduction" to Press (ed.), *Plato's Dialogues: New Studies and Interpretations* (Lanham, MD: Rowman & Littlefield, 1993), 109-11.

better to think of this triad as inter-related elements that can also be deployed in a single dialogue, or even in a single passage (as will be demonstrated in section §8 below). (3) The basanistic element is like a springboard in another sense, the same sense in which a good student actually learns from taking a well-constructed test. Plato deploys the basanistic element for a triple purpose: (a) to ensure that the student has grasped his visionary teaching, (b) to cause that teaching to leap from the text into the mind of the student (cf. epigraphs and *Ep.* 341c4-d2), and thus (c) to point the student to something even greater than what the teacher has already taught.

Beginning with *Timaeus*, the dialogues that follow *Republic* repeatedly expose the student to views that tend to undermine both its political and ontological teaching.[27] It is therefore no accident that the developmentalist paradigm has generally presented Plato as having abandoned the visionary teaching of his "middle dialogues";[28] this abandonment is real but its educational significance has been misunderstood. The important point is that the pedagogical coherence of the Platonic curriculum is *dialectical* and therefore does not preclude the possibility that the "late dialogues" are antithetical to what Plato has taught through Socrates in the *Republic*. To put it more simply: Plato perfected the use of the pedagogical technique that constitutes the theoretical basis of the true-false question. Only when students can spot and reject a deliberately created falsehood masquerading as the teacher's authoritative statement have they internalized the truth. In accordance with the new paradigm being introduced here, the entire post-*Republic* curriculum is not indicative of any change in Plato's thinking but rather demonstrates his magisterial use of basanistic pedagogy. An early indication of how Plato will test the reader can be found in what is missing from the summary of "the *Republic*" that Socrates gives early in *Timaeus*, beginning with the elision of the Third Wave of Paradox.[29] But Plato's basanistic pedagogy is so rigorous that it is not always enough to distinguish Socrates from Plato's other philosophers. A crucial instance of the basanistic is Socrates' erroneous insistence at *Phaedrus* 275d4-e5 on the mute incapacity of a written text to cre-

27. Richard Kraut usefully devotes consecutive sections to "Does Plato change his mind about forms?" and "Does Plato change his mind about politics?" in the online *Stanford Encyclopedia of Philosophy* at http://plato.stanford.edu/entries/plato/ (accessed August 5, 2011).

28. Cf. Kraut, "Plato": "If, on the other hand, we find that Timaeus or the Eleatic visitor talks about forms in a way that does not harmonize with the way Socrates conceives of those abstract objects, in the dialogues that assign him a central role as director of the conversation, then the most plausible explanation for these discrepancies is that Plato has changed his mind about the nature of these entities."

29. See the thoughtful comments of Peter Kalkavage, *Plato's* Timaeus (Newburyport, MA: Focus, 2001), 8-9: "In short, the speech Socrates agreed to give yesterday seems not to be the *Republic* but a pale image of the *Republic*—pale because philosophic virtue in its precise sense was missing, because man was present only as a political animal. . . .The abbreviated summary of the *Republic* signals the abbreviation of philosophy itself."

ate dialectic with the student/reader or to achieve anything more than "meaning one thing only, the same thing always." To begin with, every good book on Plato, by helping us see at least one passage in a new light, proves this judgment wrong; we have all, moreover, seen our understanding of Plato's texts in particular not only grow but change each time we read or teach them. It is unlikely that Plato, who created these texts, was unaware of this. The real dialogue is always between Plato and the student. The present study is devoted to bringing that dialogue into the open in the context of "the crisis of the *Republic*."

With respect to the overall project, then, the foregoing seven principles may be usefully simplified as follows: §1. Pedagogical Effectiveness: elementary dialogues precede complex ones, §2. New Criterion of Authenticity: each dialogue snug between two others, §3. Primacy of Dramatic Connections, often but not exclusively chronological, §4. Proleptic Composition: confusing students first in a pedagogically useful way. §5. Centrality of *Republic*: having been prepared (§4) for the Good and Justice, §6. Visionary Teaching: Plato revealed (§5) as teacher and "Platonist," §7. "Basanistic" Testing: students must reject falsehoods on the basis of §6. Finally, the results of the entire project may be of some interest:

Protagoras		*Timaeus*
Alcibiades Major		*Critias*
Alcibiades Minor		*Philebus*
Erastai		*Phaedrus*
Hippias Major		*Parmenides*
Hippias Minor		*Cratylus*
Ion		*Theaetetus*
Menexenus		*Euthyphro*
Symposium	*Republic*	*Sophist*
Lysis		*Statesman*
Euthydemus		*Apology of Socrates*
Laches		*Hipparchus*
Charmides		*Minos*
Gorgias		*Crito*
Theages		*Laws*
Meno		*Epinomis*
Cleitophon		*Phaedo*

It is my hope that should the present study be greeted with some interest, companion volumes will eventually follow it, treating respectively the dialogues that follow and precede *Republic* in the Reading Order of Plato's Dialogues.

An Introduction to Plato's *Republic*:

Inside and Outside the Text

It wouldn't even be called "Plato's *Republic*" without Cicero: the word "republic" derives from Latin and Aristocles the son of Ariston—he who preferred to be called "Plato"—named it his Πολιτεία.[1] This indicates from the start how much stands outside this famous text—the things between (τὰ μεταξύ) that text and us—mediating an English-speaking reader's entry into the fabulous riches it contains. In the case of Cicero's important role, this is a very good thing: Plato's *Republic* is not cheapened, distorted, nor diminished by the powerful influence[2] of this great Roman and, given that citizens of the United States of America still have a republic to lose, the traditional title for what would otherwise be "Plato's *Polity*" proves both provocative and timely. This was evidently true for Cicero's time as well. By anticipating the spiritual agonies of Catullus (559e9-560a2), the political promises of Catiline (566a1-2), the gangs of Clodius (564d6-e2), the assassination of C. Julius Caesar (566a11-b2), and even Ovid's post-Ciceronian poetic revenge on his adopted son,[3] Plato's *Republic* must have seemed to Cicero as if it had been written expressly for him and his contemporaries. And were it not for us, I would be tempted to claim that it had been.

For us, of course, we ourselves are the most obvious things standing outside the text, our world and our concerns, all of which might seem very distant from Plato's world. But halfway between Plato's Athens and our polity, albeit not in any crudely spatial or chronological sense, stands Rome's lost Republic, and, at its wave-smashed helm, Cicero: the statesman and philosopher whom I regard as Plato's best student *and rival* precisely because he, unlike the hypothesized

1. All references to *Republic* will hereafter be to the edition of S. R. Slings, cited by Stephanus numbers only. Unless otherwise noted, all translations from *Republic* will be those of Paul Shorey, *Plato's Republic*, as translator (Cambridge, MA: Harvard University Press, 1930 and 1935).

2. Cf. Malcolm Schofield, "Approaching the *Republic*" in Christopher Rowe and M. Schofield (eds.) in association with Simon Hornblower and Melissa Lane, *The Cambridge History of Greek and Roman Political Thought* (Cambridge, UK: Cambridge University Press, 2000), 199 and Terry Penner, "What is the Form of the Good the Form of? A Question about the Plot of the *Republic*" in Douglas Cairns, Fritz-Gregor Herrmann, and Terry Penner (eds.). *Pursuing the Good; Ethics and Metaphysics in Plato's* Republic, 15-41 (Edinburgh: University of Edinburgh Press, 2007), 21.

3. 573a8-b7 and 566c9-d2; cf. Ovid *Amores* 1.2.

Guardians of the imaginary City, *voluntarily* went back down into the Cave of political life and resisted tyranny there.[4] In accordance with what I will call "Justice" but in any case in accordance with the first and more difficult path circumscribed by the Third Wave of Paradox, Tullius Cicero was both philosopher and statesman and thus performed two jobs, for only one of which (474c1-2) he was by nature suited (433a5-6):

> He himself, however, besought his friends not to call him "orator" but "philosopher"; for having chosen philosophy as his *métier* [ἔργον], he employed rhetoric as a tool [ὀργάνῳ χρῆσθαι] for the needs of being political [πολιτευόμενος].[5]

Conventionally regarded as a teacher of rhetoric who recommended adding a tincture of philosophy to a polished orator's education,[6] Cicero is better understood as a philosopher who saw, from an early age,[7] the republican and philosophical necessity for the lover of wisdom to learn how to use rhetoric both skillfully and well. We would have neither "Plato's *Republic*" nor our own without Cicero,[8] the eloquent Platonist[9] whose polity did not give way to tyranny as long as he lived and whose Republic lived at least until he died, the year the rebellious Ovid was born.[10]

Cicero expressed the timeless and trans-national essence of Plato's *Republic* appropriately enough in his own *de Republica*: more specifically, he did this in the *Somnium Scipionis* ("The Dream of Scipio"). In the dream with which Cicero ends his *Republic*, Scipio finds himself in the heavens looking down upon the tiny spherical earth so far below. Bewildered by the heavenly music he hears, Scipio asks his Grandfather, vivid companion of his otherworldly dream, what it is that he is hearing; the old man explains what he hears and sees and, above all, what it is his duty to do next:

---

4. For "voluntarily" (*voluntate*) see Cicero *de Officiis* 1.28; for "rival" (*aemulus*) see Quintilian 10.123.

5. Plutarch *Cicero* 32.5 (translation mine); see also 4.1-2.

6. Cf. James M. May and Jakob Wisse, *Cicero:* On the Ideal Orator *(De Oratore)* (New York and Oxford: Oxford University Press, 2001), 11-12

7. Cicero *de Inventione* 1.1-5.

8. Gilbert Highet, *The Classical Tradition* (Oxford: Oxford University Press, 1947), 398-401 and 670n1 (quoting Camille Desmoulins): "Ces républicains étaient la plupart des jeunes gens qui, nourris de la lecture de Cicéron dans les colleges, s'y étaient passiones pour la liberté."

9. See my "Tullia's Secret Shrine: Birth and Death in Cicero's *de Finibus*." *Ancient Philosophy* 28 no. 2 (Fall 2008), 373-393; "Womanly Humanism in Cicero's *Tusculan Disputations*." *Transactions of the American Philological Association* 139 no. 2 (Autumn 2009), 411-445, and "The Truly False Basis of Cicero's Platonism." *McNeese Review* 40 (2010), 37-56.

10. Ovid *Tristia* 4.10.6. See also Plutarch *Life of Demosthenes* 3.3.

> But in order that you, Africanus, will be more keen to guard the Republic, consider this: for all of those who've preserved, aided, and improved their native land, certain is their special place in heaven, where they will—supremely happy—enjoy eternity forever. For there is nothing more delightful—at least regarding what transpires on the earth—to that highest God who rules the entire universe than the legislatures and assemblies of men conjoined by law which are called 'polities' or 'States.' And of these, those who are the steersmen and preservers—having departed from this place—return to it once again.[11]

Traditionally understood in terms of the final myth that Socrates entrusts to Er,[12] Scipio's Dream is in fact Cicero's version of the most important, memorable, and justly famous passage in Plato's *Republic*, indicated as such by its first word ("I went down"): the Allegory of the Cave.[13]

As befits an orator, Cicero creates an audible image of the Idea of the Good rather than the visible sun outside of the Cave as Plato's Socrates had: it is the Music of the Spheres (617b6-8) to whose blissful harmonies (*de Republica* 6.22) Scipio and "others who, with pre-eminent inspiration, have, during this human life, cultivated divine studies" (*alii qui praestantibus ingeniis in vita humana divina studia coluerunt*) must temporarily (*Rep.* 6.33) deny themselves audience by courageously returning as statesman (*Rep.* 6.17) to the tiny earth so far below, that cosmically insignificant (*Rep.* 6.25) but ethically crucial scene of danger, death (*Rep.* 6.16), and duty (*Rep.* 6.19). The philosopher leaves the visible world behind and rises to the eternally beautiful, then, convinced of the justice of the downward course—and blind to what the world regards as self-interest—returns to the shadows down below for the good of the state (*civitatis salus* at *Rep.* 6.16). It is tempting to say that while the most important thing that Plato's *Republic* obviously contains is the Allegory of the Cave, it is no less true to say that Plato's *Republic* also secretly contains the εἶδος (434d2) or Idea of Justice. What follows will show that these two statements say the same thing in two different ways. To put the point historically, this book is a Ciceronian reading of Plato's *Republic*, guided by Cicero's precept and inspired by Cicero's practice.[14]

---

11. Cicero, *de Republica* 6.17 (translation mine).

12. James E. G. Zetzel, *Cicero.* De Re Publica: *Selections* (Cambridge, UK: Cambridge University Press, 1995), 15 and 223-24 and J. G. F. Powell (ed.), *Cicero: On Friendship and the Dream of Scipio* (Oxford: Oxford University Press, 1990), 122-23 following Macrobius, *Commentary on the Dream of Scipio*, 1.1-2

13. *pace* Burkert, Walter. "Cicero als Platoniker und Skeptiker." *Gymnasium* 72 (1965), 175-200 at 198: "Unter allen Platonzitaten und Platonanklagen bei Cicero ist nie von dem die Rede, was für uns Zentrum der platonischen Philosophie zu halten geneigt sind: vom Höhlengleichnis." Hereafter all quotations from French and German will be translated.

14. Perhaps best understood in opposition to Terry Penner, "Platonic justice and what we mean by 'justice.'" *Plato* 5 (2005) at www.nd.edu/~plato/plato5issue/Penner.pdf (accessed August 6, 2011), which advances an argument (13) against using (Cicero's) "*Republic*" as title for Plato's dialogue based on the claim that the internal justice of "the Harmonious Man" (443c9-444a6)—"egoistic" and based entirely on "self-interest"

> Of course I'm also aware that I often seem to be saying original things when I'm saying very ancient ones (albeit having been unheard by most) and I confess myself to stand out as an orator—if that's what I am, or in any case, whatever else it is that I am [*aut etiam quicumque sim*]—not from the ministrations of the rhetoricians but from the open spaces of the Academy. For such is the *curricula* of many-leveled and conflicting dialogues [*curricula multiplicium variorumque sermonum*] in which the tracks of Plato have been principally impressed.[15]

It is highly significant that Cicero calls the dialogues of Plato *multiplex* or multi-leveled. To take the most relevant example: the Allegory of the Cave (514a2-517a6) appears not to contain Socrates' account of justice: Socrates appears to have already defined justice well before Book VII. Socrates appears to have discovered justice in Book IV and has applied the definition developed there (433a8-9) first to the City and then to the individual Man (443c5-d1). But it is also in Book IV that Socrates first reveals the existence of "a longer and fuller road" (435d3) and it is this revelation that makes Plato's *Republic* what Cicero calls "*multiplex*." Although Socrates never names it as such, there is also necessarily a Shorter Way and the first mention of the Longer Way, placed between the definitions of justice in the City and justice in the Man, reveals that there is a far less inadequate road to the knowledge he and his interlocutors are seeking *but that they are not presently traveling it* (435c9-d4). The object of their search is a persuasive proof from Socrates that it is better for those inter-

---

(34)—is "the *principal* subject matter of the dialogue." With Penner's insistence that justice for both Plato and Socrates is "this science of happiness in situations where there's temptation to think that *(trying to) take advantage of others (pleon echein) or to harm others* will maximize one's happiness" (35), cf. Cicero *De Officiis* 1.29 (translation Miller): "There are some also who, either from zeal in attending their own business or through some sort of aversion to their fellow men, claim that they are occupied solely with their own affairs, without seeming to themselves to be doing anyone any injury. But while they steer clear of the one kind of injustice [cf. 1.23: 'There are, on the one hand, two kinds of injustice—the one, on the part of those who inflict wrong, the other on the part of those who, when they can, do not shield from wrong those upon whom it is being inflicted'], they fall into the other: they are traitors to social life, for they contribute to it none of their interest, none of their effort, none of their means."

15. Cicero *Orator* 12 (translation mine); Elaine Fantham, *The Roman World of Cicero's* De Oratore (Oxford: Oxford University Press, 2004), 50n2 recommends translating *sermones* as "dialogues;" for *varius* as "conflicting" see *Oxford Latin Dictionary* §3. Note that the passage from *De Officiis* quoted in the previous note follows a passage where Cicero criticizes only *the superficial level* of *Republic* VII, a level in conflict with the philosopher's voluntary return to the Cave. Cf. Penner, "Platonic Justice," 73n51: "On the other hand, that the main line of the *Republic*'s account of justice does involve the just person seeking his or her own good seems to me undeniable (so that the best one can get from 519c-521b is the appearance of a certain unresolved tension in Plato's view)." The present reading aims for something *better*; i.e., something more in accordance with the Idea of the Good (cf. Penner at 71-72n49 on "the only thing good in itself").

locutors to choose to be just rather than unjust, regardless of any rewards or consequences in this world and beyond it.[16] Not every reading of Plato's *Republic* emphasizes the fact that *Republic* is first and foremost about a decision for justice as opposed to an ideal City, not every reading emphasizes that the dialogue is multiplex, containing as it does both Longer and Shorter Ways, and not every reading emphasizes the fact that the definitions of justice presented in *Republic* IV are discovered while following the latter. But a good reading must do all of these things and, in any case, the present reading emphasizes all three from the start.

Plato's *Republic* is a vivid book and is justly famous for its visual images of which the Cave is simply the most important. There is a memorable Ship (488a7-489a2) and a multi-headed beast (588c7-d1), a City of Good Men Only (347d2-6), and a city of simple god-fearing rustics (372a5-c2). For the mathematically inclined (as every reader of *Republic* must be) there is also a geometrical image of a Line divided into two sections, each of which is then divided into two sub-sections, all in accordance with the same ratio that defined the original division (509d6-8). The intimate and deliberately contrived connection between what Socrates never quite calls "the Shorter Way" and the Second Part of the Divided Line (510b4-511b2)[17] is *the interpretive foundation* for my reading of Plato's *Republic*. The second-highest part of the Line is the sub-section that Socrates allows to appear, for purposes of pedagogical clarity (510c1), to be comprehended by mathematics (510c2-511a2) but which in fact represents *any* investigation of intelligible (as opposed to visible) objects that must nevertheless make use of visual images of those objects (510b4-8 and 511a4-9) and is dependent on unquestioned assumptions. It is the coordination of the Second Part of the Divided Line with the Shorter Way (for so it will be called throughout although Socrates left it nameless) that proves the justice discovered in Book IV is not Plato's Justice.

The use of the capital "J" requires justification: in accordance with a multi-leveled text containing both a Shorter and a Longer Way, Socrates provides not only a single definition of justice (albeit applied separately to both City and Man) but also the intimation, adumbration, or indication of what will here be called "Justice." The explicit definition of justice in both City and Man announced in Book IV is based on a methodology whose inadequacy is stated in Book IV but not fully explained until Book VI where the Second Part of the Divided Line implicitly anatomizes the methodological essence and inadequacies of the Shorter Way, thus revealing the origin, nature, and limitations of the definition(s) of justice reached while following it. It is only by means of the Longer Way (504b2) that Justice will be discovered, and this book is an ongoing

16. The net result of the constraints imposed by Glaucon and Adeimantus, culminating at 367e1-5, and, it will be noted, absent from Cicero's *Somnium*; cf. *Rep*. 6.12.

17. It is third in order of presentation but will be called "the Second Part [of the Divided Line]" because when Socrates, having begun with the highest section, then links it with διάνοια at 511d8-e1, he explicitly calls it "the second."

justification for the view that Plato's actual conception of what we call "justice" is what will here be called "Justice" (as opposed to the two-fold justice of Man and City in Book IV) and which is best understood as the Idea of Justice. It is, for example, Justice that Cicero practiced by being both philosopher and statesman (and dying for it) in Rome. And the Justice that Socrates both practices and points to on the theoretical plane is, I will argue, eminently practical and political no less than philosophical and is, moreover, what leads to his trial, imprisonment, and death.[18] But Plato's *Republic* is not political in the sense that it has conventionally and traditionally been taken to be political; it paradoxically describes the ideal City only because Justice is necessarily the intersection of a philosopher with an unjust city. The resolution of this paradox is "the crisis of the *Republic*."

Even the most committed adherent of the view that Plato's *Republic* contains Plato's program for a perfect or best city—an idealistic political program of dubious practicality, possibility, or merit—must smile at the decision of a Neoplatonist to recreate it in Asia Minor during the reign of the Emperor Gallienus.[19] But even if it were not intended to be practical in this sense, the dialogue has traditionally been read as Plato's conception of an ideal if utopian state.[20] The inadequacy of this way of reading *Republic* is proved here by the coordination of the Second Part of the Divided Line with the Shorter Way, which is not to deny that there are many other good reasons to recognize this approach as inadequate—in particular, the fact that Socrates undertakes the construction of the City (369a1-369a8) in an attempt to prove to Adeimantus (367b3-6) and Glaucon that Justice is choiceworthy (360e1-3) both in and of itself (361c4-d3) and with respect to its consequences (358a1-3). The use of the capital "J" here is therefore important: it is not the justice revealed in Book IV that will persuade both of these young men: Glaucon in particular will require and recognize Justice (520e1). There is no doubt, then, that Plato's *Republic* is about a City—indeed about several of them—but a blueprint of Plato's ideal city is not to be found within this text or anywhere else in his writings, certainly not in *Statesman* and least of all in *Laws*.[21] Socrates' words and actions in *Republic* are guided by a determination to persuade others, some of them inside and (this claim is crucial) others *outside* the text, to choose Justice. In other words: Plato the Teacher is interested in persuading *the reader* to choose and act in accor-

---

18. *Phd.* 98e5-99a4 (Tredennick translation modified): "Because, by the dog, I fancy that these sinews and bones would have been in the neighborhood of Megara and Boeotia long ago—impelled by a conviction of what is best!—if I did not think it was more just [δικαιότερον] to submit to whatever penalty my country orders rather than take to my heels [φεύγειν] and run away." δικαιότερον is used in the same context at *Phd.* 98e4; with φεύγειν, cf. *Tht.* 176b1.

19. Porphyry *Life of Plotinus* 12.

20. E.g. Ernest Barker, *Greek Political Theory* (London: Methuen, 1918).

21. See my "A Tale of Two Drinking Parties: Plato's *Laws* in Context." *Polis* 27 no. 2 (Fall 2010), 240-264.

dance with Justice, not inspiring e.g. Plotinus to recreate the City that his Socrates merely uses in order to help him do so. Because Plato succeeded in the case of Cicero, the Roman is a better guide to Platonism than, for example, Speusippus, Plato's nephew and successor in the Academy.

But if a political program for an ideal City is not to be found in Plato's *Republic*, neither is Justice; although it is praised, promulgated, and practiced throughout Plato's *Republic*, the Idea of Justice is never explicitly named or defined as such. Readers must discover it for themselves. This explains why few of them have done so. Those who have will recognize in this student-centered pedagogy the essence of Plato's genius: as reflected in my title, he was a peerless teacher. How the man taught while encased in a body is a matter of informed speculation. But how he taught after he had died: this we can discover for ourselves in his dialogues. And it is such effective pedagogy, such a marvelous way of teaching, that it is difficult to believe that he would have taught any differently in person than by reading his dialogues aloud with his students, discussing those dialogues with them, and perhaps—this would constitute the aspect of his teaching that we cannot hope to reconstruct—discussing individual students in the context of his dialogues. Naturally nobody knows anything about the specific circumstances of any of this on an empirical basis and, especially for the third, we must rely entirely on our own experiences, imagination, and intuitions.

What can be known is that it is not only the dialogue between interlocutors that creates or circumscribes a Platonic dialogue. To be sure, the text contains a dialogue; dialogue is precisely what is to be found *inside* the text of Plato. But outside of the text is always the reader, and Plato the Teacher (for so he will be called) discovered a way to make the dialogue within the text burst the bonds of the written word and leap—"like a blaze kindled by a leaping spark" (*Ep.* 341c7-d1; translation Post)—outside of that text and become a second dialogue between the reader and his written dialogue. To put it another way: Plato created a written dialogue that provoked his reader's response,[22] revealed its purpose only to the reader who joined in the discussion, and opened its secrets only to the reader who experiences him- or herself as being directly addressed by the text. In other words, "dialogue" in Plato is not simply the imitated conversation between his interlocutors presented in the text. Indeed the thing within *Republic*

22. The clearest literary precedent for my reading of *Republic*—and even more so of *Laws* (see previous note)—is Stanley Fish, *Surprised by Sin: The Reader in* Paradise Lost, second edition (Cambridge, MA: Harvard University Press, 1997). But the use of "provoked" (and "provocation" generally) indicates that among currently active Plato scholars, I find the work of Mitchell Miller particularly congenial; cf. "Platonic Provocations: Reflections on the Soul and the Good in the *Republic*" in Dominic J. O'Meara (ed.), *Platonic Investigations*, 163-193 (Washington D.C.: Catholic University of America Press, 1995), 165: "There is, however, a second level of provocation and initiation as well: precisely by Socrates' exchange with his interlocutors, *Plato* challenges *us*, the listeners outside the dialogue."

upon which I have laid emphasis from the start is that it is multi-leveled and thus that it contains an ongoing dialogue of sorts between the Shorter and Longer Ways; only the reader who attends to that impersonal or rather methodological dialogue—and thereby realizes the hardly invisible inadequacy of the Shorter Way (444a5-6)—will find in the text the deliberate provocation that Plato placed there. A provocation *inside* the text combined with a reader's decision in response to that provocation *outside* of it; such is Plato's *Republic*. If it is a truism that there is no book without a reader, in the case of *Republic*, this becomes the golden truth: what is here called "the crisis of the *Republic*" takes "crisis" (κρίσις at 360d8, 361d5, 555b7) in the Greek sense: it is only by means of the reader's act of discriminating choice or *decision* in response to the deliberate provocation of *Republic* that yields Justice along the Longer Way.

How can Plato achieve this amazing result and provoke the reader's response in such a manner as to achieve his pedagogical purposes? These pages are devoted to explaining this complicated and brilliantly executed process. But three strategies among many may profitably be mentioned right away: to begin with, Socrates can follow a path that he knows and explicitly tells us is inadequate and this is what he does along the Shorter Way. Socrates can also use expressive but obscure language to suggest the existence of a more adequate path (434d1-435a4) and then leave it up to the reader to determine when it is that path upon which the dialogue, or even the reader's dialogue with the dialogue, is proceeding. The third way is more controversial: Socrates can say or write statements that neither Socrates nor Plato believe to be true (e.g. 347d6-8; see section §8) but which provoke the reader to discover the truth by responding to the merely apparent position of the author or speaker. Three examples of the use of *deliberate falsehood* in basanistic pedagogy (see Preface) may be usefully if cursorily sketched.

The first doesn't involve the reader at all but occurs entirely within the action as inscribed within another Platonic dialogue. In *Euthydemus*, Socrates makes a deliberately insulting prediction (*Euthd.* 297d1-2) that Ctesippus evidently takes to be directed at himself (*Euthd.* 303a6) and that paradoxically prompts the young man to prove the prediction wrong by behaving exactly the way Socrates actually wants him to behave, i.e., in a manner opposite to that which Socrates "predicted."[23] The second is more famous and its implications more far-reaching: Socrates' claim in *Phaedrus* that a written work inevitably maintains "a most majestic silence" (*Phdr.* 275d6; translation R. Hackforth) and therefore cannot achieve precisely the effect that Plato's *Republic* will here be shown to have actually achieved. Finally, Plato claims in his Seventh Letter that he has never composed a work about the most important subjects and will never do so in the future (*Ep.* 341c4-d2) while provocatively using words that echo the expressive, beautiful, and obscure language found in the crucial Firesticks passage of *Republic* IV (435a1-3), discussed in section §21 below.

23. See my "Leo Strauss and the *Euthydemus*" in *Classical Journal* 102 no. 4 (Winter 2007), 355-79, especially 371-75.

For the present, and taking advantage of the fact that Cicero enjoys less respect than Plato, a more detailed look at Cicero's use of Plato's provocative tricks will make the same point. In the dialogue found in Book II of his *Academica*,[24] a character he calls "Cicero,"[25] after asking about whom he could possibly speak with greater certainty, asserts that he imagines himself to have actually lived with Plato and Socrates and therefore, on the basis of the many conversations that have been recorded

> it is not possible to doubt [*dubitari non possit*] that nothing seemed to Socrates able to be known [*sciri posse*]; he excepted one thing only: to know him himself to know nothing [*scire se nihil se scire*], nothing more.[26]

To say next to nothing about the evidence, likewise contained in his *Academica*, that Cicero *knows* that not *all* of "the many conversations that have been recorded" feature a skeptical Socrates (note the use of "almost" or *fere* at *Academica* 1.16), and that he is fully aware that neither Xenophon nor Plato ever presents Socrates as stating that he *knows* himself to know nothing (cf. *Academica* 1.16 and *Ap.* 21d3-6),[27] Cicero emphasizes that Arcesilaus had taught that it would be impossible to *know* that one knows nothing if knowledge were impossible (*Academica* 1.45). As this passage indicates, then, Cicero is capable of making his "Cicero" contradict himself repeatedly in a very brief space of time:[28] obviously one cannot know that one knows absolutely nothing and that even if Socrates were correct in asserting that it was not possible to know anything—which he could not possibly be—it would necessarily remain possible for "Cicero" to doubt that Socrates had thought, let alone known, this.

Deliberate self-contradiction is a wonderful teaching device:[29] the literal minded will deny its very existence and duly (and dully) demonstrate that any-

---

24. What follows is treated in more detail—and in dialogue with Myles Burnyeat, "Antipater and Self-Refutation; Elusive Arguments in Cicero's *Academica*" in Brad Inwood and Jaap Mansfield (eds.). *Assent and Argument: Studies in Cicero's* Academic Books, 276-310 (Leiden: Brill, 1997)—in Altman, "The Truly False Basis of Cicero's Platonism," 46-48.

25. Julia Annas (ed.). *Cicero: On Moral Ends*, translated by Raphael Woolf (Cambridge UK: Cambridge University Press, 2001), xvi: "Although he [sc. the character in *de Finibus*] is called Cicero, he is not to be straightforwardly identified with the author Marcus Tullius Cicero."

26. Cicero *Academica* 2.74; translation mine.

27. See Richard Bett, "Socratic Ignorance" in Donald R. Morrison (ed.), *The Cambridge Companion to Socrates*, 215-236. (Cambridge, UK: Cambridge University Press, 2011), at 218-19. For Arcesilaus, see 365-67 (same volume) in A. A. Long, "Socrates in Later Greek Philosophy," 355-379.

28. See John Glucker, "Socrates in the Academic Books and Other Ciceronian Works" in Inwood and Mansfield, *Assent and Argument*, 69, Comments 1.

29. Cf. Leo Strauss, "Fârâbî's Plato" in *Louis Ginzberg Jubilee Volume*, 357-393 (New York: American Academy for Jewish Research, 1945), 369: "If he [sc. Fârâbî] understands by 'philosophy' in both cases the same thing, he flatly contradicts himself.

one who points to an author's deliberate self-contradictions cannot exclude the possibility that these were unintentional or that it is purely arbitrary to discriminate the deliberate and intentional provocation from the unconscious and inept mistake. The seeker after truth, by contrast, will enter the magic portal opened thereby with an alternately knowing, incredulous, and awestruck smile. In the case of Cicero, deliberate self-contradiction was intended to arouse his attentive readers from their *skeptical* slumbers no less effectively than David Hume later awakened Immanuel Kant from the dogmatic variety. And of course a writer of dialogues can easily create any number of dogmatists who contradict themselves as well (cf. Cicero *de Natura Deorum* 2.30, 2.46, and 2.77). But when Cicero allows his Crassus to observe that Plato never showed himself to be more eloquent than in the speech against rhetoric he placed in the mouth of Socrates in *Gorgias* (*de Oratore* 1.47), he proves the principal point: Plato is a peerless teacher and the essence of Platonic pedagogy is to provoke a carefully contrived moment of crisis (520c1) within the reader (520b5-c1) by means of paradox (473d3-5), inadequate surfaces (435c9-d2), intimations of hidden depths (435d2-3 and 434e4-435a4), as well as a series of deliberate self-contradictions (e.g., 347d6-8), out of which—"like a blaze kindled from a leaping spark"[30]—emerges Plato's teaching.

A great teacher will attract a great variety of students and those students will respond in a variety of ways (*Tusculan Disputations* 5.11) probably commensurate in number with the excitement that is great teaching. Plato's students include Aristotle, the Neoplatonists, and the Plato scholars of today. Not all of these will embrace what has traditionally been called "Platonism": some will refute it, others will embrace it in a bastard form, still others will question its very existence. Amidst this bewildering variety of critical responses, several must be noticed here. Naturally a book called *Plato the Teacher* must assert, and is indeed an implicit and ongoing assertion, that Plato had "a teaching." A formidable twentieth-century interpreter of Plato has denied this:[31] on the basis of the dialogue form, i.e., because Plato himself never said anything,[32] and a Socra-

This would not be altogether surprising. For, as we ought to have learned from Maimonides who knew his Fârâbî, contradictions are a normal pedagogic device of the genuine philosophers. In that case it would be incumbent upon the reader to find out by his own reflection, if guided by the author's intimations, which of the two contradictory statements was considered by the author to be true." Cf. Strauss, *Persecution and the Art*, 68-69. Lest such views be taken as Straussian, it deserves consideration that the pedagogical deployment of deliberate falsehood is the basis for the ubiquitous true/false question.

30. *Ep.* 341c7-8 (L.A. Post); cf. 435a1-2.

31. Strauss, "Plato," 33: "Strictly there is no Platonic teaching; at most there is the teaching of the men who are the chief characters in his dialogues. Why Plato proceeded in this manner is not easy to say. Perhaps he was doubtful whether there can be a philosophic teaching proper. Perhaps he, too, thought like his master Socrates that philosophy is in the last analysis knowledge of ignorance. "

32. Leo Strauss, *The Rebirth of Classic Political Rationalism*, edited by Thomas Pangle (Chicago: University of Chicago Press, 1989), 161: "In the case of Shakespeare,

tes who knows that he knows nothing (with no self-contradiction noted), Leo Strauss has nevertheless made possible a reading of Plato that involves carefully contrived surfaces and secrets lurking in the textual shadows. Meanwhile the Tübingen School, most ably represented by Hans Joachim Krämer,[33] have—on the basis of *Phaedrus*, the Seventh Letter, Aristotle's testimony, and the doxography relating to post-Plato Academy—called attention to the unwritten doctrines to which they claim Plato actually subscribed and which he taught: doctrines indicated but not to be found in his dialogues; a teaching indeed, but an extra-textual one.

Both of these positions get an important piece of the truth. It is my purpose to show that Plato does indeed have "a secret teaching" but that he never intended it to be a perfectly well kept secret: it is only partially hidden *in his dialogues* and Plato not only wanted his best students (among whom he did not number his immediate successors in the Academy) to discover it for themselves but saw to it that an attentive reader could and always will be able to discover it (as Cicero did) principally in *Republic*. There is therefore as much common ground with the Tübingen School to be found here as there is with Strauss: Plato's teaching is not simply within the text (in agreement with Tübingen), least of all on the surface of the text (in accordance with Strauss). It is the identification of an exoteric surface in Plato's text that constitutes Strauss's great contribution although here his own methods will be used to reverse his own inversion of Plato's *Republic*.[34] In other words: Strauss is right about the deliberately

for instance, who would dare to say that according to Shakespeare life is a tale told by an idiot, full of sound and fury, signifying nothing?" So also Frede, "Plato's Arguments," 214: "And finally we have to keep in mind that however the fictional questioner or respondent of the dialogue may be, nothing follows from this about the commitment of the author of the dialogue; Plato even in the least aporetic and most dogmatic dialogues remains at a radical distance from the views and arguments of the fictional character of the dialogue." Note 204-5 on Cicero.

33. See Reale, *New Interpretation*, xxiii-xxvi for an accessible overview. Foundational is Hans-Joachim Krämer, *Arete bei Platon und Aristoteles* (Heidelberg: C. Winter, 1959)

34. See Leo Strauss to Jacob Klein, New York City, February 16, 1939 at Strauss, *Gesammelte Schriften*. Bd. III, edited by Heinrich and Wiebke Meier (Stuttgart: J. B. Metzler, 2001), 567-68 (translation mine): "The *Republic* is *beginning* to become clear to me. My conjecture from the previous year, that its actual theme is the question of the relationship between the political and theoretical life, and that it is dedicated to a radical critique and condemnation of the political life, has proved completely right. It has therefore defined itself with utmost precision: the *Republic* is indeed an ironic justification [*Rechtfertigung*] of injustice [ἀδικία], for Philosophy *is* injustice—that comes out with wondrous clarity in the dialogue with Thrasymachus." A candid reader of Strauss, *The City and Man* will find no reason to imagine that Strauss changed his mind. Meanwhile, Klein should probably be viewed as straddling the difference between Tübingen and Strauss; the common ground between these two post-War schools of German Plato scholarship deserves further study.

inadequate surface in general—although his hostility to the Idea of the Good[35] prevents him from recognizing that this surface is the Shorter Way—but wrong about what the attentive student will find both below and above it, i.e., the Longer Way, the Good, and Justice. The Tübingen School is likewise correct that there is a teaching outside of the text but, following a deadpan or literalist reading of *Phaedrus* 275d4-e5,[36] they banish that teaching from the dialogues and misplace it in a lost lecture hall of the vanished Academy whereas it is actually located in the reader's response to a deliberately provocative text. On the other hand, the *Prinzipienlehre* they identify as Plato's esoteric teaching—a "protology" based on the One and Indefinite Dyad—is by no means a figment of their imagination and, especially in considering the post-*Republic* dialogues (see Preface), the project of the Tübingen School as well as the methods of Strauss will be radicalized before being used to reverse their conclusions.

Both Strauss and the scholars of Tübingen were German; at the risk of giving voice to Anglophonic parochialism, the more influential literature of the current scholarly mainstream is Anglo-American and this is a mixed blessing. English speakers, endowed by their language with an imperative to regard themselves as "sensible men" and indeed to accept as real that alone which "makes sense,"[37] ought not to reckon themselves, despite Shakespeare and our current political hegemony, as Plato's ideal interpreters by nature. For too many years, the "what is Plato trying to say here"[38] school has treated Plato's text as a series

35. Leo Strauss, *The City and Man* (Chicago, IL: University of Chicago Press, 1964), 119. This element of the Strauss-inspired scholarship reaches a *crescendo* (or *reductio ad absurdum*) at Lampert, *How Philosophy Became Socratic*, 353: "The short road leads to the bright and beautiful that secures the moral universe in the ruling principle of the Good." It is, of course, only the Longer Way that does so.

36. Reale, *New Interpretation*, 51-62 and Krämer, *Arete bei Platon und Aristoteles*, 393. This element of the Tübingen School reaches a *crescendo* (or *reductio ad absurdum*) at Thomas A. Szlezák, *Reading Plato*, translated by Graham Zanker (London: Routledge, 1999), 46 where the dialogues must become "a witty game which gave him [sc. Plato] great pleasure."

37. Cf. J. N. Findlay, *Plato: The Written and Unwritten Doctrines* (London: Routledge & Kegan Paul, 1974), 1: "The aim of this book is to make sense, in a comprehensively general manner, of a philosophy which seeks to make sense of every phenomenon, fact or side of reality that it considers, and also seeks to weave all its separate exercises of sense-making into a single, comprehensive fabric of sense, dependent throughout on the operations of a single unifying Principle or set of Principles."

38. Although primarily associated in my mind with Gregory Vlastos, with whom I studied Plato and from whose lips I often heard this expression, a textual example on the crucial matter may be found beginning in Nicholas Denyer, "Ethics in Plato's *Republic*" in Godfrey Vesey (ed.), *Philosophers Ancient and Modern*, 19-33 (Cambridge UK: Cambridge University Press, 1986), at 29: "Consider what he [sc. Plato] says in *Rep*. 519-520, a very awkward and unsatisfactory discussion of why philosophers who have enjoyed the course of intellectual activity and development that culminates in knowledge of the Good itself should expect to come back down into the cave and govern. . . . I suspect Plato can in fact do better than this awkward passage would suggest." After proposing his own

of arguments to be considered without regard to dramatic context, analyzed, frequently invalidated as fallacious, sophistical, or inadvertently flawed and, if one wished to be taken quite seriously, expressed in terms of the propositional calculus. On the other hand, the image of Plato as a logically unsophisticated and fuzzy-headed idealist can usefully be corrected by an all-American pragmatism: the truth of Plato's teaching turns out to be the student who puts it into practice, just as Cicero did. Moreover, an ongoing concern with "Plato's development" frequently makes traditional Anglophone scholarship extremely useful to the student of reading order.[39]

There is, in any case, a pervasively Platonic problem facing every academic who studies Plato, regardless of the language they may speak or the school to which they adhere: a problem implicit in the modern appropriation of the term "academic." Everyone knows that Socrates created a paradox about philosophers and kings (473c11-d3); it is crucial to grasp that the Third Wave of Paradox (472a3-4) not only asserts two ways to combine philosophy and ruling but also two distinct types of *personae non gratae*: political men who refuse to take philosophy seriously *and philosophers who refuse to participate in politics* (473d3-5; see section §22). It is not Plato's problem that the study of Plato is considered the exclusive preserve of those we call "academics" but it must be recognized as his plight: permanent residents of the ivory tower are not ideally placed to recognize Cicero's active and political response to the Cave as Platonic Justice. Making matters more difficult, the literature on Plato—to which this book is obviously just one more contribution—is already so voluminous that no Plato scholar could master it although no interpreter of Plato can be taken seriously without entering into a dialogue with it.

But Plato would not have required his students to engage in this dialogue even if had he known of this literature's existence and it is always worth asking oneself while reading books on Plato: "Would *Plato* be pleased with this book?" Along with Shakespeare's Cassius (*Julius Caesar* III. i. 111-2), Plato could easily have imagined (499c7-d6) the existence of our scholarship by asking: "How many ages hence will this our lofty scene be acted over? In states unborn, in accents yet unknown?" But the Anglophone scholarship of the last hundred years—a time period that deliberately excludes Adam and Burnet, Liddell and Scott[40]—is not the exclusive portal through which even the English-speaking

neutralist solution (see section §19), Denyer writes on 20: "This or something like it is the way that Plato should, I think, have resolved the difficulties posed for him by his assumption that what makes both a city and an individual just is a single feature present in both cases."

39. E.g., the sequential arrangement of *Cratylus* and *Theaetetus* suggested by David Sedley, *Plato's* Cratylus (Cambridge, UK: Cambridge University Press, 2003), 170-72.

40. Annas, *Platonic Ethics*, 95: "It is easy to remain unaware of the extent to which our attitude to it [sc. the *Republic*], as a political work, and as the obvious centerpiece of Plato's thought, derives from Victorian traditions, particularly that of Jowett." My debts to the British scholars of this period are innumerable, especially to Benjamin Jowett, James Adam, John Burnet, T. H. Heath, H. G. Dakyns, Lewis Campbell, and R. G. Bury

student of today must necessarily enter Plato's text. The real portal, of course, is only to be found in Attic Greek: Plato chooses his words carefully and without our careful attention to the words he uses, his teaching must remain obscure. But in return for sparing the reader a Hegelian accounting of current scholarship by which a variety of luminaries would be shown to be simultaneously necessary and inadequate stages on the dialectical path to my own views, I will likewise spare myself the necessity of carefully documenting or cursorily refuting every scholarly opinion that contradicts my own except on the most essential questions, e.g., the philosopher's voluntary return to the Cave (see section §19). As it happens, the coordination of the methodology described in the mathematical section of the Divided Line with the definitions of justice found in Book IV is original;[41] thus its far-reaching ramifications distance my findings, even the problems with which my reading must grapple, from those of previous Plato scholars to a considerable and not entirely unwelcome degree.

Consider the following passage by Francisco J. Gonzalez in a note about the Divided Line:

> The *Republic* as a whole is like one of those visible diagrams used by geometers to illustrate something invisible. It is precisely as an imitation of the ascent to the good that the dialogue is "hypothetical." Yet it must have been Plato's hope that we the readers would use the dialogue as a "springboard" and "footing" from which to engage in dialectic itself.[42]

The first sentence comes extremely close to my conception although in my case it is only the City constructed along the Shorter Way—not "the *Republic* as a

---

as well as to the immediate heirs of their erudition, humanity, and imperial self-assurance: A. E. Taylor, F. M. Cornford, W. K. C. Guthrie, and Mary Renault.

41. Not entirely original, of course. After quoting F. M. Cornford "Mathematics and Dialectic in the *Republic* VI.-VII. (II.)." *Mind* n.s. 41 no. 162 (April 1932), 173-190, 183: "If he [sc. Plato] stops short [sc. of the Good], his definitions of Justice and other ideas, though correct, will be analogous to a mathematical hypothesis," John Gould, *The Development of Plato's Ethics* (Cambridge, UK: Cambridge University Press, 1955), continues at 178-79: "From this point of view, διάνοια [sc. the faculty associated with the second or mathematical part of the Divided Line at 511d8-e1] may reach an understanding of any number of unrelated moral Forms, but cannot achieve complete ethical certainty until those forms are seen in relation both to one another, and to the origin of them all, the Good. This is, for instance, the situation reached in Book IV of the *Republic*, where four ἀρεταί have been defined but not so related; it accounts for the reference to the 'longer road.'" Even more explicit are 179: "ethical διάνοια, like mathematics, is still subject to the flaws for which it is criticized in the explanation of the line diagram" and 181: "We are intended to feel that, like διάνοια, these definitions [sc. of the virtues in Book IV] do not reach the heart of the matter." For a recent development, unfortunately at the expense of νόησις, see David N. McNeill, *An Image of the Soul in Speech: Plato and the Problem of Socrates* (University Park: Pennsylvania State University Press, 2010), 235-37.

42. Francisco J. Gonzalez, *Dialectic and Dialogue; Plato's Practice of Philosophical Inquiry* (Evanston, IL: Northwestern University Press, 1998), 374n69.

whole"—that chapter 3 will show is analogous to the geometrical diagrams Gonzalez mentions. And the third sentence anticipates another point of contact: the decisive role left for the reader to play. This element has recently been made even more conspicuous by Mitchell Miller in his "Beginning the 'Longer Way.'"

> The catalyzing idea of this chapter is that *Plato* intends the shortfall of Plato's presentation of the "longer way" as a pointed provocation to *us*, aimed at moving us to speak up and ask Socrates for a deeper introduction. Of course it will be up to us, mining the text as responsibly as possible, to discover this deeper Socratic position for ourselves.[43]

This, of course, anticipates my position to an even greater degree although I would need to substitute "shorter" for "longer" in the first sentence. In my reading, once the flawed methodology of the Shorter Way becomes clear, the reader uses *its* faulty methods and conclusions as a "springboard" and "footing" that leads directly to Justice on the Longer Way (cf. 511b2-c2).[44] To summarize: here the Longer Way does not fall short (*pace* Miller) but accomplishes its objective (albeit only within the reader) while *Republic* offers the reader something much less open-ended than an exhortation to pursue dialectic further outside of the text (*pace* Gonzalez) although its Shorter Way is precisely like a geometer's diagram. More important than any differences, however, is the shared emphasis on the reader's response to a deliberate "shortfall" in the text. This is a crucial aspect of what I call "Plato's basanistic pedagogy."

Before leaving Gonzalez behind, it is useful to draw attention to his early and important call for "a third way" in Platonic studies.[45] This is a very apt phrase and admits of several useful applications. To begin with, there is Gonzalez's own application of it: his "third way" avoids both the skeptical and doctrinal reading of Plato, i.e., either a Plato who, apparently like Socrates, knows nothing and thus arrives at no tangible results or, on the other hand, a Plato with

43. Mitchell Miller, "Beginning 'The Longer Way'" in G. R. F. Ferrari (ed.), *The Cambridge Companion to Plato's* Republic, 310-344 (Cambridge, UK: Cambridge University Press, 2007), 311.

44. Dominic Scott, "The *Republic*" in Gail Fine (ed.), *Oxford Handbook to Plato*, 360-382 (Oxford: Oxford University Press, 2008), at 367-69 refers to "the metaphysical defense" of justice, "not one that he [sc. Socrates] proffers directly" (369). Although this amounts to a defense of the Shorter Way's justice *via* the Forms *qua* objects of soul-simplifying *eros* (368), Scott does point further at 369: "The 'longer route' would require investigating the matter by reference to the Form of the Good—something that will take the trainee guardians in the ideal state many years to achieve [Note: I will call confining going back down into the Cave *to the Guardians* 'singularism'; see section §19]. In effect, this would be a much more thorough enterprise than the very provisional line of argument I have called the metaphysical defense." This "much more thorough enterprise" is undertaken below.

45. Francisco J. Gonzalez (ed.), *The Third Way: New Directions in Platonic Studies* (Lanham, MD: Rowman & Littlefield, 1995).

a variety of explicit doctrines.[46] Christopher Rowe has recently taken up this distinction and indeed embraced "the third way" albeit in a strictly negative sense.[47] This is a highly significant development because of quite another application of "the third way" conception: a third alternative to both the Anglo-American analytic tradition championed by Gregory Vlastos and Terence Irwin, and that of the Straussians. Rowe is a distinguished representative of the former school and it is noteworthy that he rejects developmentalism (i.e., a reading of Plato's dialogues based on their chronological order of composition), long a basic principle if not the foundation of the analytic approach.[48] Although Rowe never mentions Strauss, it is Strauss and his students who have assiduously evaded or dismissed the developmentalist approach, and a candid consideration of Plato studies in the late twentieth-century—even an anti-Straussian one[49]—would need to credit Strauss with originating this anti-developmental development visible in e.g., Rowe. Only a few innovative Plato scholars like John Ferrari, Roslyn Weiss, and Catherine Zuckert have somehow managed, while avoiding or ignoring developmentalism, to combine analytic clarity with Straussian attention to dramatic detail and it is to be hoped that this kind of "third way" will now become the wave of the future.

Another application of "the third way" is no less germane to my overall project. Mainstream emancipation from developmentalism as yet has no name but when it gets one, it will be confronted with the dilemma of situating itself between a unitarian reading of Plato, where all of the genuine dialogues are part of one consistent project,[50] and what might be called "hermeneutic isolationism," i.e., the view that each Platonic dialogue must be read on its own terms without reference to any other.[51] As a matter of logic as opposed to chronology, nineteenth- and twentieth-century developmentalism is actually "a third way" with respect to this dilemma: each dialogue reflected Plato's thought at the time it was written but the dialogues as a whole, arranged according to order of composition, reflect Plato's overall development; any given dialogue could then be considered in two different aspects, both temporarily isolationist and developmentally unitarian. As a matter of fact, however, developmentalism always tended toward the second alternative even if, or indeed precisely if, Plato had changed his views: dialogues were seldom read carefully in their own right and

46. Gonzalez, *The Third Way*, 12-13.

47. Christopher Rowe, *Plato and the Art of Philosophical Writing* (Cambridge, UK: Cambridge University Press, 2007), 6n14.

48. Rowe, *Plato and the Art*, 48-51.

49. See my *The German Stranger: Leo Strauss and National Socialism* (Lanham, MD: Lexington Books, 2011), 473-74 and 488-89.

50. Beginning in the United States with Paul Shorey, *The Unity of Plato's Thought* (Chicago IL: University of Chicago Press, 1903).

51. Despite the clarity of Press, "Principles," 109-11, there is no reason to question the claim at J. Angelo Corlett, "Interpreting Plato's Dialogues." *Classical Quarterly* (n.s.) 47 no. 2 (1997), 423-437 that Frede, "Plato's Arguments" lays the foundations for the doctrine; the latter is usefully discussed in Gonzalez, *The Third Way*, 159n6.

it was this fact—an extremely disrespectful way of reading carefully constructed works of art—that gave Strauss and his followers the opening they needed. While there seems to be some confusion among Straussians as to whether isolationism or some form of unitarianism is the best way to go,[52] non-Straussian post-developmentalists must now squarely face this dilemma. And there are inchoate indications that the preferred solution at the moment is an ordering of the dialogues not by chronology of Platonic composition but by dramatic or "fictive chronology,"[53] where *Parmenides*, with a young Socrates, stands first, *Phaedo* obviously last, and the Athenian Stranger becomes a doubly displaced person threatened with extinction.[54] Before this narrowly chronological approach—best understood as the equally time-bound and thus anachronistic after-life of a decayed nineteenth-century developmentalism—gathers too much steam, I am offering a pedagogical alternative. After all, what kind of teacher would introduce a student to Plato with *Parmenides* or *Laws*?[55]

As indicated in the Preface, my work considers all of Plato's dialogues as a well-ordered pedagogical program and aims to reconstruct the Reading Order of Plato's Dialogues, i.e., the order in which Plato the Teacher intended them to be heard, read, or taught. This reconstruction project represents a post-developmentalist approach although it would be more accurate to say, given that concern with reading order was widespread in antiquity, that it revives a pre-developmentalist position. Along with instances where fictive chronology is obvious (e.g., *Theaetetus*, *Euthyphro*, *Sophist*, *Statesman*, and *Apology*), a fresh way of looking at certain dramatic details (e.g., the fact that Socrates in *Symposium* leaves Agathon's for the Lyceum, destination of his journey at the start of *Lysis* and then scene of *Euthydemus*) discovers in them the clues that indicate reading order. Although non-Straussians erroneously regard attention to such details as distinctively Straussian,[56] the willingness of Straussians in particular to

---

52. For a unitarian approach in the Straussian tradition, see Joseph Cropsey, *Plato's World: Man's Place in the Cosmos* (Chicago, IL: University of Chicago Press, 1995); a discussion of *Cleitophon* later in this Introduction will indicate the countervailing pull of isolationism.

53. See Charles L. Griswold Jr., "*E Pluribus Unum*? On the Platonic 'Corpus.'" *Ancient Philosophy* 19 (1999), 361-97 at 387-90.

54. See Deborah Nails, *The People of Plato; A Prosopography of Plato and Other Socratics* (Indianapolis, IN: Hackett, 2002), 307-30, and Gerald A. Press, *Plato: A Guide for the Perplexed* (London: Continuum, 2007), 57 and 69. The tremendous value of *The People of Plato* is independent of its author's interest in fictive chronology although the latter has already proved influential; see Zuckert, *Plato's Philosophers*, 9n19.

55. This question points to the principal weakness of Zuckert's otherwise admirable and unquestionably path-breaking *Plato's Philosophers*. See Mark Blitz, *Plato's Political Philosophy* (Baltimore, MD: Johns Hopkins University Press, 2010), 275-77n8 for a useful overview of her impact and the present state of the question.

56. E.g. Christopher Gill, "Review of *The Phaedo: A Platonic Labyrinth* by Ronna Burger." *Classical Review* n.s. 36 n. 1 (1986), 141-142 at 141: "Straussian critics assume that the dialogues are formally cohesive wholes (in which even seemingly incidental

rehabilitate several dialogues dismissed as inauthentic beginning in the nineteenth century has unquestionably had a huge and salutary influence on my project.[57] As for Anglo-American influence, my primary debt is to the nuanced unitarianism of Charles S. Kahn. Despite the fact that he remains wedded to developmentalism,[58] his discovery of "proleptic composition" lays the foundation for much of my own work and will receive further consideration below (section §8). But between the Straussians and the Anglo-Americans, I must follow "a third way."[59] On the other hand, it really isn't very productive to think in terms of triangulating between these two modern approaches not only because reconstructing the reading order of Plato's dialogues is an ancient concern and Ciceronian Platonism isn't on anybody's radar screen today, but most importantly, because the majority of Straussians and Anglo-American developmentalists reject the view that Plato himself was ever (Strauss) or remained (developmentalism) what was once called "a Platonist" whereas my own work is dedicated precisely to vindicating Plato, from first to last, as a Platonist.[60] In section §5, I will

---

details serve a larger purpose) and that they are deliberately multivocal, being designed to yield deeper levels of meaning to more penetrating readers. These assumptions are not inherently implausible but the 'commentaries' on the dialogues produced by Straussian critics are usually quite impenetrable to non-Straussians." Gill's astute observations don't penetrate to the root of this impenetrability; cf. Leo Strauss, *Persecution and the Art of Writing* (Chicago, IL: University of Chicago Press, 1952), 36: "Exoteric literature presupposes that there are basic truths which would not be pronounced in public by any decent man, because they would do harm to many people, who having been hurt, would naturally be inclined to hurt in turn him who pronounces the unpleasant truths."

57. Beginning with Thomas L. Pangle L. (ed.). *The Roots of Platonic Political Philosophy: Ten Forgotten Socratic Dialogues, Translated, with Interpretive Essays* (Ithaca, NY: Cornell University Press, 1987).

58. Charles H. Kahn, "Response to Griswold." *Ancient Philosophy* 20 (2000), 189-193.

59. Well described at Walter Watson, "Dogma, Skepticism, and Dialogue" in Gonzalez, *The Third Way,* 189-210 at 203: "Both the skeptic and the dogmatist separate the independence of the dialogues from their systematic unity. The one sees them as independent and therefore not a system, the other as presenting a single doctrine and therefore as not independent. We need not suppose either that the autonomy of each dialogue precludes their unity as parts of a system or that their unity as parts of a system must take the form of a common doctrine that precludes their independence. The third way must here unite independence and systematic unity."

60. As opposed to a "nondogmatic" Plato; see Press, *Plato's Dialogues*, 1993, 5-6 and Victorino Tejera, "The Hellenistic Obliteration of Plato's Dialogism" in Press (ed.), *Plato's Dialogues*, at 132 who rejects "the pythagorizing idealism which is now called platonism" whereby "Socrates was turned into a dogmatist and Plato into a dull literalist unable to be logically consistent." My own approach leaves much of "Plato the Platonist" intact without making either Plato dully literal or Socrates a Pythagorean dogmatist; this results from attending to Plato's deliberate, dialectical, and pedagogical *inconsistency*. Cf. Gonzalez, *A Third Way*, 13: "This state of affairs [the limitations of both 'doctrinal' and 'nondoctrinal' interpretations of Plato] cannot but leave us wishing for some third alternative: an interpretation that, unlike the skeptical one, grants a positive content to

do my best to indicate what I mean by "Platonism" but for the present, it is enough to mention a characteristic insistence on the existence of an unchanging intelligible realm of Being as sharply distinguished from the ceaselessly changing visible realm of Becoming.

Chronological developmentalism inevitably undermines the timeless aspect of Platonism, precisely its most compelling feature from a Platonist's perspective. But a renewed capacity to see Plato as a Platonist is but one possible alternative arising from the incipient flight from developmentalism and unfortunately it is also one of the least likely. On the other hand, without loosening the grip of developmentalism, a revived Platonism is inconceivable rather than merely improbable. This is, indeed, a crucial point. The story of Plato's development and the arrangement of his dialogues with respect to chronology of composition created a Plato who *himself* evolved beyond Platonism; he may have been what is called "a Platonist" in certain of "the middle dialogues"—including *Republic*—but he outgrew it with age. In an intellectual climate where things like the timeless Idea of the Good, the Doctrine of Recollection, and the Immortality of the Soul—a fair catalogue of what has traditionally been regarded or recognized as Platonism—will never and can never "make sense" (cf. 610a9), it is therefore probably unreasonable to expect a rebirth of Platonism in the English-speaking world. In other words, even if developmentalism is jettisoned, the Anglo-American tradition of Plato studies is unlikely to be responsible for a genuine Platonic revival.[61] Little more is to be expected from the Straussians: they must not only follow their leader by embracing a Socrates who knows nothing can be known,[62] but must also reject, refute, or at least ignore the view that Plato taught the Ideas, the immortality of the Soul, or that knowledge is Recollection.[63] As long as there are Straussians, they will tend to regard traditional Platonism as nothing more than a pious fiction, a point of view not even temporarily embraced by Plato himself. From a Platonist's perspective, then, there is no need for triangulation between these poles: there is nothing to choose between the Straussian and Anglo-American—or, for that matter, between the analytic or continental—schools of anti-Platonism. And a middle ground between them

Plato's philosophy, and that, unlike the 'doctrinal' one, is able to show some necessary connection between this philosophy and the dialogue form. Is there such an alternative?"

61. As indicated by Rowe, *Plato and the Art*, 276n5: "That is [the note is attached to the statement 'the 'things in themselves' are accessible, by philosophical means, from where we are now'], there is little or nothing *other-worldly* about the Plato whose outlines I am sketching, despite his apparent adherence to the idea of the soul's immortality: that in a way commits him to the existence of another world, but if so, that other world hardly seems to be treated as more than a waiting-room for souls awaiting reincarnation."

62. First at "Cohen und Maimuni" (1931) in Leo Strauss, *Gesammelte Schriften*. Bd. II. Ed. Heinrich u. Wiebke Meier (Stuttgart: J. B. Metzler, 1997), 411; cf. Jacob Klein, *A Commentary on Plato's* Meno (Chicago, IL: University of Chicago Press, 1965), 23 for the suggestion of Platonic skepticism *via* Socratic ignorance. Cf. 337e4-7.

63. Cf. Strauss, "Fârâbî's Plato," 364, 371-72 and "the specific immunity of the commentator" at Strauss, *Persecution and the Art*, 14.

based on "Platonic anonymity"[64] can reveal Plato's intentions no better than any given story based on developmentalism about the evolution of Plato's "theory of X" that completely ignores his use of the dialogue form.

The preceding paragraphs will suffice to indicate in broad outlines the relationship between my approach and current scholarship. But here my own special problem arises: whatever it is that Platonism turns out to be, he did not begin teaching it in *Republic* and a concern for reading order shows that he carefully prepared the student/reader to receive that teaching well in advance. Although the present work is a stand-alone book on Plato's *Republic*, it is also intended to be something more (see Preface) and, in any case, a systematic approach to a new way of reading *Republic* requires some prior attention to the claim that Plato intended the student/reader to have read several other dialogues before *Republic* because there are critical moments in the text that presuppose the reader's familiarity with several of these "earlier" dialogues.

Given that two of them have, as their eponymous titles, young men who are mentioned in *Republic*, one might think that literary allusions of such an obvious kind would be entirely unproblematic; the problem becomes acute as soon as these titles are named: *Theages* and *Cleitophon*. In addition to developmentalism, nineteenth-century scholarship also gave rise to another important revolution in Platonic studies: the discovery or claim that certain dialogues attributed to him were not the genuine works of Plato.[65] In the present case, although neither *Cleitophon* nor *Theages* are considered authentic by the scholarly mainstream,[66] here again, as is the case with developmentalism, the tide is finally turning.[67] In another place, I argue for the authenticity of these two dialogues on

---

64. See Gerald A. Press (ed.), *Who Speaks for Plato? Studies in Platonic Anonymity* (Lanham, MD: Rowman & Littlefield, 2000), Charles L. Griswold Jr. (ed.), *Platonic Writings, Platonic Readings* (University Park, Pennsylvania State University Press, 2002), and E. N. Tigerstedt, *Interpreting Plato* (Uppsala: Almquist & Wiksell, 1977), which provides a good introduction at 98-99. This approach must be distinguished from Ludwig Edelstein, "Platonic Anonymity," *American Journal of Philology* 83 no. 1 (January1962), 1-22 who seems to have coined the term. Note that e.g. Jürgen Mittelstrass, "On Socratic Dialogue" in Griswold, *Platonic Writings*, has much to say about Plato even while asserting "Platonic anonymity."

65. Two first-rate overviews of this process are Kyriakos Demetriou, "Reconsidering the Platonic *Cleitophon*," *Polis* 17 (2000), 133-160 and Hayden Ausland, "On a Curious Platonic Dialogue," *Ancient Philosophy* 25 (2005), 403-425, at 417-21.

66. Conservative opinion is reflected at Rowe, *Plato and the Art*, 198-99 where twenty-six of the thirty-five dialogues edited by Thrasyllus are accepted as genuine. This excludes *Alcibiades Major*, *Alcibiades Minor*, *Erastai*, *Hippias Major*, *Theages*, *Cleitophon*, *Hipparchus*, *Minos*, and *Epinomis*. Rowe comments at 198n1: "Missing from the list are *Alcibiades I*, *Clitophon*, and *Hippias Major* (and one or more of the Letters) which in the view of some stand a fair chance of being genuine (not in my view), and numerous certainly spurious dialogues and other works that somehow found their way into the corpus."

67. See Jacques Bailly, *The Socratic* Theages; *Introduction, English Translation, Greek Text and Commentary* (Hildesheim: Georg Olms, 2004) and S. R. Slings, *Plato:*

the basis of their place in a reconstructed reading order.[68] But despite the considerable complications involved, this Introduction must conclude with some discussion of Plato's *Cleitophon*, regarded by Thrasyllus as the introduction to *Republic* and recognized as such by me. Discussion of *Cleitophon* is justified by the fact that all five of the dialogues immediately preceding *Republic* in my reconstructed Reading Order—*Charmides*, *Gorgias*, *Theages*, *Meno*, and *Cleitophon*—play important parts in *Republic* and must therefore be discussed at various places in this book. Of course it is only *Theages* and *Cleitophon* that create a serious problem, or indeed any problem at all: scholars writing about *Republic* habitually cite parallel or relevant passages from the other three dialogues (and many others) without methodological defense or comment. Indeed it is rather ironic that no conventional Plato scholar would feel the need to justify using a passage from *Charmides* (where Socrates defines temperance with the same formula he will apply to justice in *Republic* IV),[69] *Gorgias* (where he will claim that it is more shameful to inflict wrong that to suffer it), or *Meno* (where he introduces Recollection) in elucidating *Republic.*

The claim that there are some dialogues that Plato intends us to read before *Republic* is only marginally more important than its corollary claim that there are dialogues that Plato intended us to read only *after* reading *Republic.* It is primarily (but by no means exclusively) here that the technical term "basanistic," introduced in the Preface and based on Plato's favorite word for "test," will prove useful. When, for example, the Idea of the Good does not appear in a "later" dialogue (in either sense of that word) the reader should consider herself being tested in accordance with what I call "the Battle Hymn of the *Republic.*"

> "And is not this true of the good likewise—that the man who is unable to define in his discourse and distinguish and abstract from all other things the idea of the good, and who cannot, as it were in battle, running the gauntlet of all tests, and striving to examine everything by essential reality and not by opinion, hold on his way through all this without tripping in his reasoning—the man who lacks this power, you will say, does not really know the good itself or any particular good; but if he apprehends any adumbration of it, his contact with it is by opinion, not by knowledge; and dreaming and dozing through his present life, before he awakens here he will arrive at the house of Hades and fall asleep for ever? " "Yes, by Zeus," said he, "all this I will stoutly affirm."[70]

Clitophon (Cambridge, UK: Cambridge University Press, 1999), no doubt responsible for the presence of *Cleitophon* at Terence Irwin, "The Platonic Corpus" in Gail Fine (ed.), *Oxford Handbook to Plato*, 63-87 (Oxford: Oxford University Press, 2008), 75.

68. My "Reading Order and Authenticity: The Place of *Theages* and *Cleitophon* in Platonic Pedagogy" is forthcoming in *Plato: The electronic Journal of the International Plato Society* (2011).

69. See Gabriel Danzig, "True Justice in the *Republic.*" *Illinois Classical Studies* 23 (1998), 85-99.

70. 534b8-d2; I have modified Shorey's translation.

Challenging the reader to enter into an active dialogue with the text is essential to Plato's project as described here and the role of the basanistic element in Plato's *Republic* will receive detailed attention beginning in section §8. But it is important to understand from the beginning why a number of dialogues—including *Timaeus*, *Critias*, *Philebus*, *Phaedrus*, *Parmenides*, *Cratylus*, *Sophist*, *Statesman*, and *Laws*—are not and indeed should not be used to suggest that, e.g., Plato changed his mind about the centrality and absolute transcendence of the Idea of the Good. In the context of reading order, then, although *Protagoras* and *Meno* stand between *Republic* and us, these so-called "later" dialogues should not. But unfortunately they do, at least when taken to prove that Plato abandoned the idealism of his great "middle period" dialogues.

Although it will be illustrated for the time being only in the context of *Republic*, the discovery of a basanistic element in Platonic pedagogy is without doubt the most important conceptual breakthrough in *Plato the Teacher* as a whole. In the context of the *Republic*, it is the deliberate but deceptive inadequacy of the Shorter Way as revealed by its analogy with the Second Part of the Divided Line that constitutes the crucial example but there are many others. Given the central importance of this discovery to my own work, it is important to emphasize from the start that the historical or rather philosophical precedent for Plato's basanistic pedagogy is Parmenides' "Way of Opinion."[71] After the goddess has revealed "Truth" to the chariot-borne seeker, she commands him to learn more by hearing "the deceptive cosmos of my verses" (Parmenides 8.52; translation mine). This describes exactly what I claim Plato has done by placing the cosmological *Timaeus* immediately after *Republic* in the Reading Order of his dialogues; in Parmenides as well, a "likely" (Parmenides 8.60) but ultimately deceptive cosmology follows "The Way of Truth."[72] Although this line of argument cannot be fully developed in a stand-alone volume on the *Republic*, it is important to understand that I intend, in due course, to supplement the common view that Parmenides guided Plato to a conception of transcendent Being—a theme that will be developed in section §5 in the context of *Republic* V—with a new claim about the Parmenidean basis of Platonic pedagogy.

The influence Parmenides exercised on Plato hardly makes him unique: Plato's genius drew on many sources, not all of them strictly philosophical, and he frequently depends on his readers to be as familiar with those sources as he

---

71. Following the lead of G. E. L. Owen, "Eleatic Questions," *Classical Quarterly* (n.s.) 10 no. 1 (May 1960), 84-102, A. A. Long, "The Principles of Parmenides' Cosmology," *Phronesis* 8 no. 2 (1963), 90-107, and Alexander P. D. Mourelatos, *The Route of Parmenides*, revised and expanded edition (Las Vegas, NV: Parmenides Press, 2008). For further discussion, see section §25 below. References to the fragments of Parmenides will be in accordance with Mourelatos, 279-84, cited in accordance with the numeration of Diels-Kranz.

72. Thus I am deeply indebted to A. E. Taylor, *A Commentary on Plato's* Timaeus (Oxford: Clarendon Press, 1928), which famously argues that Timaeus does not speak for Plato. For a recent endorsement of Taylor's approach, see Zuckert, *Plato's Philosophers*, 475-81.

was. Some will find the claim that Plato expected the reader of *Republic* to have already read *Gorgias* and *Protagoras* debatable; what then will they say about the claim that he also expected them to have read Thucydides? It is tolerably obvious that he expected and indeed required his readers to know Homer and, as I will argue in section §30, Hesiod as well; this familiarity is actually a prerequisite for reading Plato well and not simply in the vague sense that it provides useful or even indispensable cultural context. As it happens, an interest in the reading order of Plato's dialogues has made me sensitive to the question of what other texts Plato the Teacher expected his students to have read before, in addition to, and in tandem with, his own writings. And in the process of these investigations, it has become obvious that serious students of Plato need to begin asking themselves—on the basis of evidence from the dialogues themselves—what kind of readers Plato anticipated having and what he actually expected those readers to have carefully read beforehand. And here a strong stand must be taken from the start against reading Plato as if he were only addressing—and only intended to address—his own contemporaries:[73] it is as mistaken to doubt that Plato considered his own writings to be "a possession into forever" (κτῆμά ἐς αἰεὶ; Thucydides 1.22.4) as it is to assume that he believed every literary work he had read or heard would share this distinction with his own magnificent dialogues.

It may therefore be useful to consider four categories of other writers from Plato's perspective: (1) the ancients, like Homer, Hesiod, and Parmenides whose immortality he clearly anticipated and upon which he both counted and depended, (2) roughly contemporary writers who would survive *along* with but independently of him, (3) those writers—both ancient and current—whom *he* set about to immortalize by making them indispensable prerequisites to his own work (Lysias comes to mind), and (4) those who would either not survive (*Ti.* 22c1-3) or do so in fragments (*Ion* 534d4-7). Whether he regarded Thucydides as belonging to the second or third category may be debatable; that he both anticipated and counted on Thucydides' literary immortality, along with his own, is not.[74]

The claim that Plato expected his writings to be "a possession for eternity" brings up the important question of Plato's Platonism in a very natural way: a philosophical commitment to the Idea of the Good as a metaphysical reality, enduring unchanged forever, inevitably promotes the long view. Thucydides realized that human events would continue to operate in accordance with some-

---

73. Danielle S. Allen, *Why Plato Wrote* (Chichester: Wiley-Blackwell, 2010) supports a claim of this kind; see 108: "Plato wrote to affect politics, and Athenian politics specifically." Although she clearly thinks some timeless value can be derived from reconsidering "the western world's first message man" (147), it is less because of what he wrote than why he wrote it (4): "I soon realized that asking and answering the question, 'Why did Plato write?" might provide us with philosophical and historical treasure."

74. These claims are more fully developed and defended in Section §4 (on *Menexenus*) of Altman, "The Reading Order of Plato's Dialogues."

thing unchanging; for the great historian, this would be human nature (see section §2). The details might change but as long as there were men, "such things or very similar ones will come to be again" (Thucydides 1.22.4; translation by Jowett). If Thucydides had good reason to believe that his book would last forever—and its uncanny prescience no less than its actual survival proves that he did—it is silly to think that Plato didn't have an even *better* reason to think the same about his: for what can be better than the Good? Whether human nature will remain the same, whether Thucydides or anyone else has grasped anything more than "the truth of its present appearance" (611c5), these become debatable propositions for the author of *Republic*; it is rather Being, that which does not merely appear but eternally is what it is, that alone exists and necessarily does so without changing. Aside from the reader, then, the most important thing to be sought both inside and outside the text of Plato's *Republic* is the Idea of the Good (see section §18): i.e., the essence of Platonism, the basis for the centrality of *Republic* in Platonic pedagogy, and thus the ultimate justification for beginning *Plato the Teacher* with a detailed and essentially independent account of *Republic* even if it isn't actually the first dialogue Plato intended his student/reader to have read/heard and cannot be fully appreciated without some consideration of its place in a larger pedagogical structure.

There are two texts in *Republic* about the Idea of the Good that I want to discuss in this Introduction even though they will receive further attention in the text that follows. The first is the famous claim that the Good is "beyond Being" (509b8). I understand this claim in the reflected light of Kant's "thing in itself." There is no Kantianism without "the thing in itself" but the very essence of Kant's thought is that it cannot become a basis for any possible experience and hence cannot be known in the way that we can know or experience other things. But it unquestionably exists, and does so outside of time and space; it cannot belong to the phenomenal, only to the noumenal realm. I take this to be a useful way to begin thinking about the words ἐπέκεινα τῆς οὐσιας ("beyond being").[75]

Objectionable enough in the case of Kant's "thing in itself," it would currently count as heresy—and there are, unfortunately, post-God heresies—to claim that Plato's Idea of the Good is the God of monotheistic revelation. But it would be an error of equally historic proportions to insist that it can't be. If it is an anachronism to say of Plato's Idea of the Good that it was intended by its exponent, defender, and discoverer to be an anticipation of God, it is also an anachronism to say that it must necessarily be something completely different from, exclusive of, and antithetical to that same God. When Plato's Socrates claims that the Good is "beyond Being," I consider that a pious way of saying that he doesn't know or cannot give an adequate account of that which is su-

75. It will eventually become necessary to address the rival claims of the Tübingen School; see in particular Hans Joachim Krämer, "ΕΠΕΚΕΙΝΑ ΤΗΣ ΟΥΣΙΑΣ; Zu Platon, *Politeia* 509 B," *Archiv für Geschichte der Philosophie* 51 (1969), 1-30.

preme, unique, and which truly is what it is, and thus is eternally *causa sui.*[76] Like "my Higher Power" in Alcoholics Anonymous, Plato's placement of the Good "beyond Being" defies any outsider's attempt to say precisely what utterly transcendent, unique, omnipotent entity it *cannot* be. It is therefore as unhistorical to insist that the Good is the God of Judeo-Christian-Muslim revelation (revealed only later or elsewhere) as it is to categorically deny that it could be (and would someday or elsewhere be revealed to be) that God. Despite the anti-theological prejudices of our own times, then, the parallels that leave the question eternally open must not be dogmatically rejected or despised. The metaphysical basis of Platonism is an ontology of that which truly is (477b11-12) and no matter how inconvenient it may be that the unspeakable name of the LORD is what *it* is, it nevertheless is what it is (*Exodus* 3:14).[77] And that which truly is—the ultimate basis of an ontology that looks beyond the merely apparent "being" of concrete particulars, of phenomenal experience, or, in a word, of Becoming—is what Socrates in *Republic* VI and VII calls "the Idea of the Good." Socrates calls it "beyond being" not because it is different from, exclusive of, and antithetical to what he will characterize as "Being" in Book VII. He calls it "beyond Being" because he does not wish even his own discussion of Being to determine or delimit our conception of the Good.[78]

---

76. James Adam (ed.), *The* Republic *of Plato* (Cambridge, UK: Cambridge University Press, 1902), vol. 2, 62, line 13 (on 509b): "The ὑπερουσιότης of the Good is merely Plato's way of saying that the first Principle of all existence must be self-derived." Cf. Guthrie, *History of Greek Philosophy* 4, 507: "It [sc. 'Goodness itself'] is the justification of its own existence." [Hereafter, citations to Adam will be of the form: *Republic of Plato*, 2.62] For an unusually bold attempt to annihilate the Good and not merely its transcendence, see Drew A. Hyland, "Against a Platonic 'Theory' of Forms" in William A. Welton (ed.), *Plato's Forms; Varieties of Interpretation*, 257-272 (Lanham, MD: Lexington Books, 2002) at 271: "For, as previously cited, the Idea of the Good, we are told, is 'beyond Being,' and intelligibility, although it is the ultimate source of the intelligibility available through the other Ideas. Moreover, it is something that, Socrates warns us, we can never adequately know. So although *Being* or the forms, is in principle intelligible in the 'light' of the Good, there is this mysterious entity or nonentity, explicitly *beyond Being*, the source of all Being, which is itself, apparently, not even in principle intelligible. How, one might well ask, could anyone possibly know this?"

77. Minucius Felix *Octavius* 18.8-10 (Rendell translation following Kerr): "'God cannot be seen—he is too bright for sight—he is too pure for touch; nor measured—for he is beyond all sense, infinite, measureless, his dimensions known to himself alone. Too narrow is our breast to take him in, therefore we can only measure him aright by calling him immeasurable. As I feel, so will I speak: he who thinks he knows the greatness of God makes it less; he who would not lessen it, knows it not [*qui non vult minuere, non novit*]. Seek not a name for God: God is his name.'" This is a far better explanation of "beyond Being" than that offered by Hyland in the previous note.

78. The most common Anglophone error is to assume that Socrates' refusal to discuss the Good necessarily proves that he is less able than someone else would be to do so; see Rowe, *Plato and the Art*, 221 and Donald R. Morrison, "The Utopian Character of Plato's Ideal City" in G. R. F. Ferrari (ed.), *The Cambridge Companion to Plato's* Re-

The second thing is what Socrates says when refusing Glaucon's praiseworthy request that he give an account of the Good: he can only give an account of "the offspring of the Good" (506e2). The identity of this offspring, like the meaning of "beyond Being," has been widely debated and it will continue to be.[79] Plato may be said to have provoked both of these debates deliberately and many thought-provoking accounts of Platonism—one is tempted to say that all thought-provoking accounts of Platonism—depend on at least one of these two crucial texts. But this is putting the cart before the horse: the meaning of these two texts is obscure and was intended to be so; grasping their meaning and import should therefore follow, not constitute—should confirm or challenge, not ground—one's conception of Platonism. But two approaches to the second of these must be rejected at the start: if we take the physical sun to be the only begotten offspring of the Good, then we are back in the phenomenal world and that isn't the proper place to insist that Platonism belongs;[80] an alternative to this approach will be presented in section §18. As for the more metaphysically inclined, the offspring of the Good could certainly be the One if the two are not considered one and the same; this solution—so crucial for the Tübingen School—will be discussed in section §25.

For the time being, the best solution is to profess ignorance about the meaning of "the offspring of the Good" until one has deduced its meaning from what it is that Socrates is actually doing—i.e., from that which Socrates actually wishes to discuss—in *Republic*. "But of what seems to be the offspring of the good and most nearly made in its likeness I am willing to speak if you too wish it, and otherwise to let the matter drop" (506e2-3). The reader will also note here the dependence of Socrates on Glaucon, i.e., on him who stands in the exact same place within the dialogue as the reader stands outside of it. And it is the

---

public, 232-255 (Cambridge, UK: Cambridge University Press, 2007) at 240. Preferable is Terence Irwin, *Plato's Ethics* (Oxford: Oxford University Press, 1995), 272-73.

79. Perhaps because of Anaxagoras, Socrates will show himself to be a public upholder of the sun's divinity at *Ap.* 26d1-3 but he will also do so in a somewhat more private setting, according to Alcibiades, at *Smp.* 220d4-5. Note that the claim that the Good is "beyond Being" (509b8) depends on the sun/Good connection—prepared by the "offspring of the Good" passage (506e2)—as implemented by the analogy at 509b2-10: the Good must be beyond οὐσία because the sun is beyond γένεσις. But Socrates' rejection of astronomy's claim to be "the study of the things above" (VII 529a9-10; translation mine) indicates that Socrates knows the sun belongs to the phenomenal world of Becoming and is not, as he falsely claims at 509b3, *beyond* it. For this reason, I am inclined to echo Glaucon's incredulous imprecation of Apollo at 509c1-2.

80. Cf. Hans-Georg Gadamer, *The Idea of the Good in Platonic-Aristotelian Philosophy*. Translated by P. Christopher Smith (New Haven, CT: Yale University Press, 1986), 118: "True reality, or 'being,' is one but nevertheless in all things." For Gadamer's relation to Tübingen, see Hans-Georg Gadamer, *Dialogue and Dialectic: Eight Hermeneutical Studies on Plato*, translated and with an introduction by P. Christopher Smith (New Haven, CT: Yale University Press, 1980). Cf. 530b7 and 532a1-d1, in particular the emendation proposed by Slings at 532c2.

reader to whom Socrates' proposal is congenial who need only ask: of what does Socrates self-evidently wish to speak? And this—at least on the night in question (for Glaucon) or in *Republic* as text (for its reader)—is evidently *justice*. It is by no means clear how justice can be considered "an offspring of the Good"; indeed, the justice discovered in accordance with the methods of the Shorter Way is unquestionably *not* its offspring as proved by the fact that it is discovered (Book IV) well before the first analogy of the Sun (Book VI). In fact, one of the principal clues about the Longer Way's shadowy Justice—as opposed to the Shorter Way's explicit account of justice in Book IV—is that it can, must, and will be shown to be "the offspring of the Good" precisely because the Longer Way revolves around the Good (504b1-505b1).

In summary: if the Idea of the Good could have been contained within the text, it would necessarily be the best and most important thing within that text. But it cannot be contained; the words ἐπέκεινα τῆς οὐσιας bear witness to its freedom from all containment. But so in a meaningful sense are we: both the Good and the reader stand outside the text although in intimate relationship with it. Like the Idea of the Good, the reader is both completely outside of the text and yet somehow, in a manner still to be determined, the decisive element presupposed within that text: without the reader *and* without the Good—both of them as it were "without" the text and yet somehow completing it—there is no Justice understood as "offspring of the good" (ἔκγονος τοῦ ἀγαθοῦ). In short, without both the Good and the reader, the text is incomplete.

The reader in question is, of course, all of us: the modern readers of Plato's *Republic*. Standing between the modern reader and the text, definitely outside of it but threatening to control access to it, is the modern scholarly literature, dominated, since the nineteenth-century, by those who not only would exclude the authenticity of *Cleitophon* and *Theages* but whose approach to reading Plato is guided by a chronological arrangement of Plato's dialogues predicated on the view that Plato's views changed over time and thus that even the creator of Platonism may well have abandoned it. As indicated above, learned voices have recently been raised against this domination in a useful and respectful way. But all of the relevant literature should be divided into two different classes: that which helps the modern reader to read Plato in his native Attic Greek and thus to understand his written word precisely as he wrote it, and, on the other hand, that which serves some other purpose, e.g., to elucidate Plato's Development, Plato's Theory of Ideas, Plato's Ideal City, or even, as is the case with the present work, Plato's *Republic*. The first of these classes—including Smythe's *Greek Grammar*, Denniston's *The Greek Particles*, Liddell and Scott, and the Adam commentary—unquestionably brings the reader closer to the text and regardless of philosophical content should be regarded as closer to Plato than the reader is, standing between the two on a higher rung on the ladder and usefully mediating the reader's ascent to the text. The other class does not necessarily do this and can safely be allowed to stand, as it were, *behind* the reader, ready as a support system should one need a team of experts who have tried to do what we as readers are trying to do: climb the ladder all the way up to Plato's beautiful and enigmatic text.

Consider this interpretive ladder also from the other end: looking down from the text of the *Republic*. Just as the modern English-speaking reader stands between Adam's commentary and *The Cambridge Companion to Plato* so also, as I have been trying to suggest, the text itself stands between the writings that Plato intended the reader to have already read before they began reading *Republic* and, on the other hand, the dialogues that he intended his students to read only after reading it. With a triad on the reader's end (the reader stands between necessary textual aids and the merely supporting interpretive literature) and another on the text's (the text stands between that which must be read beforehand and that which should be considered after), there remains another rung of the ladder to be inserted between them: the ancient scholars, mathematicians, and philosophers who can help the modern student/reader who wishes to enter Plato's world, many of whom probably saw themselves as doing precisely that; Plutarch springs to mind. The influence of Cicero has been emphasized from the start and Euclid too will play a role in due course. In addition to the ancient Platonists who may or may not have understood him, there are those who disagreed with Plato—Aristotle is of course the most important of these—and those who considered Plato and Aristotle to be compatible. Among many far greater names, some attention will be given here to Dionysius of Halicarnassus, who preserved for us the famous story about the opening words of Plato's *Republic* (*de Compositione Verborum* 3.16).

Under Plato's bed at the time of his death, Dionysius informs us, was found a tablet upon which the opening words of the *Republic* were written in a variety of different word orders. Dionysius records only the order of our text, beginning with the word κατέβην ("I went down"). This story—once "known to all philologists" (translation mine)—indicates two important things: that Plato regarded the opening words of his *Republic* as particularly significant and thus a fortiori that he regarded his *Republic* as particularly significant. The following study of Plato the Teacher—an account that begins with the opening words of the *Republic* (chapter 1)—is guided or rather supported by this anecdote from Dionysius, an anecdote that offers external evidence for a reading that nevertheless could have been deduced from internal evidence alone, especially because the opening words of great books generally prove to be highly significant. On the other hand, it is ungrateful to bite the hand that feeds you and perhaps the importance of Socrates' opening word, the word order of his opening phrase, and even the crucial place of *Republic* among Plato's writings,[81] may not have

81. In the light of Julia Annas, *An Introduction to Plato's* Republic (Oxford: Oxford University Press, 1981), a frequently cited introduction to Plato's *Republic*, the following passage at Annas, *Platonic Ethics* (1999), 95 is particularly noteworthy (emphasis mine): "If we try to jettison the assumptions that the *Republic* is a contribution to political theory, *and that it is obviously the most important and central of the dialogues*, the natural culmination of a development from the Socratic dialogues, and if we try to restore it to its

become known or at least as widely accepted were it not for Dionysius' decision to preserve this anecdote for our benefit. We would unquestionably be the poorer without it.

The same is true of Plato's *Cleitophon,* and this Introduction will conclude with discussion of this until recently neglected dialogue that precedes *Republic* in my reconstruction of the Reading Order of Plato's Dialogues. Considered in isolation, *Cleitophon* has heretofore seemed both incomplete and inauthentic. And this is precisely the point: the reading order hypothesis means that no dialogue must be considered in isolation. It is not difficult to identify "un-Platonic" elements in a dialogue where Socrates is attacked and offers no defense to the extra-legal "charges" brought against him. But Thrasyllus recognized that *Cleitophon* doesn't stand in isolation: his Eighth Tetralogy consists of *Cleitophon, Republic, Timaeus* and *Critias*. When *Republic* follows *Cleitophon,* it must be understood as Socrates' response to the charges brought against him in *Cleitophon.* In the context of reading order, then, *Cleitophon* should not only be recognized as the introduction to *Republic* but also its literary *provocation*. As paradoxical as it may sound, *Cleitophon* is authentic precisely because it is "un-Platonic." But before developing this claim, a glance at the current state of the problem will suggest why this little dialogue is making something of a comeback.

To begin with, then, there has long been "the riddle of the *Cleitophon.*"[82] While the only "riddle" for those scholars who athetize the dialogue involves discovering its author and determining that author's purpose, those who ascribe the dialogue to Plato must confront the riddle of "Socrates' Silence"[83] in the face

---

ancient place—one dialogue among many in which Plato develops an argument about the sufficiency of virtue for happiness—we shall have done a great deal to restore balance and proportion to our study of Plato's thought." Note that the claims of the Tübingen School likewise depend on valorizing the ancient reception of Plato; see e.g. Krämer, "ΕΠΕΚΕΙΝΑ," 28 and 30.

82. See Johannes Geffcken, "Das Rätsel des *Kleitophon.*" *Hermes* 68 no. 4 (1933), 429-439 followed by David L. Roochnik, "The Riddle of the *Cleitophon.*" *Ancient Philosophy* 4 (1984), 132-145.

83. Clifford Orwin, "The Case against Socrates: Plato's *Clitophon.*" *Canadian Journal of Political Science / Revue canadienne de science politique* 15 no. 4 (December 1982), 741-753 at 751, Jan Blits, "Socratic Teaching and Justice: Plato's *Cleitophon.*" *Interpretation* 13 no. 3 (September 1985), 321-334, at 321 and 334, Christopher Bruell, *On the Socratic Education; An Introduction to the Shorter Platonic Dialogues* (Lanham, MD: Rowman & Littlefield, 1999), 199, Mark Kremer, "Socratic Philosophy and the *Cleitophon.*" *The Review of Politics* 62 no. 3 (Summer 2000), 479-502 at 494, the same author's Clitophon*: On Socrates and the Modern Mind* (Lanham, MD: Rowman & Littlefield, 2004), 2, Arlene Saxonhouse, "The Socratic Silence in Plato's *Cleitophon.*" *Polis* 22 no. 1 (2005), 128-135, and Martin J. Plax, "Socrates' Silence in the *Cleitophon* and his *Apology* Speech." Paper presented at the Annual Meeting of the Midwest Political Science Association, April 18, 2006.

of "Cleitophon's Challenge."[84] Based on the reading order hypothesis, my approach is to solve "the riddle" by reading Plato's *Republic* as Socrates' response to Cleitophon's Challenge: I claim that Socrates' Silence is broken in *Republic* and therefore that *Cleitophon*, when read as an introduction to *Republic*, can be proved to have a genuine place among the dialogues of Plato.

In reviewing the work of previous scholars,[85] G. S. Bowe has usefully distinguished three ways of considering *Cleitophon* en route to defending the third: (1) as preceding *Republic* in a dramatic sense, (2) as following *Republic*, and (3) as independent of *Republic*.[86] Despite Bowe's "In Defense of *Clitophon*," I do not believe that the dialogue will ever be welcomed back into the canon on the basis of a stand-alone approach alone;[87] even if a new consensus pronounces it genuine, it would—much like *Critias*—probably be regarded as unfinished. Moreover, the fact that two of the three approaches distinguished by Bowe situate it in proximity to *Republic*, it seems unnatural to divorce them,[88] especially because hermeneutic isolationism (the claim that each of Plato's dialogues must be evaluated without reference to any other) is so easily refuted on the basis of dyads like *Timaeus-Critias* and *Sophist-Statesman*.[89] Indeed it is the implicit

---

84. Teruo Mishima, "Clitophon's Challenge and the Aporia of Socratic Protreptic." Paper presented at Cambridge University, September 21, 2010 and Hugh H. Benson (forthcoming), *Clitophon's Challenge: Platonic Dialectic and the Philosophical Method in Plato's Classical Dialogues* at http://www.ou.edu/ouphil/faculty/benson/benson.htm (accessed July 10, 2011); cf. Blits, "Socratic Teaching," 321 and 330.

85. G. S. Bowe, "In Defense of *Clitophon*." *Classical Philology* 102 no. 3 (July 2007), 245-264. Not only is this otherwise admirable piece no longer up to date, it does not address the prior Ausland, "Curious Dialogue" and Demetriou, "Reconsidering the Platonic *Cleitophon*." For the most recent bibliography, see Christopher Moore, "Socrates and Clitophon in the Platonic *Clitophon*" (unpublished draft of May 10, 2010) at https://webspace.utexas.edu/crm697/www/clitophon.pdf (accessed July 10, 2011).

86. Bowe, "Defense," 249; cf. 245. This scheme is preferable to the four-fold classification at Roochnik, "Riddle," 134; his (emphasis mine) "(4) The dialogue is a *self-contained* Platonic work and worthy of serious study," although it comes closest, leaves no room for the approach I am proposing; although I do not regard it as "self-contained," it is nevertheless a "Platonic work and worthy of serious study." For Roochnik, see 138.

87. Ficino, A. E. Taylor, Paul Shorey, and S. R. Slings are cited at Bowe, "Defense," 248 as examples of scholars who changed their minds on the authenticity of *Cleitophon*; this illustrates how little certainty exists on the question.

88. Consider the confusion of Hippolytus (the Christian apologist) who treated *Cleitophon* and *Republic* as one dialogue; Bowe, "Defense," 246. See also Saxonhouse, "Socratic Silence," 128: "clearly a companion piece to the *Republic*."

89. To say nothing of the *Alcibiades* and *Hippias* twins along with *Laws-Epinomis*. Bowe, "Defense," 253n42 rejects the authority of Thrasyllus for reading *Republic* after *Cleitophon* (as well as, presumably, for reading *Timaeus* after *Republic* and *Critias* after *Timaeus*) on the basis of the criticism of the tetralogical scheme found in George Grote, *Plato and the Other Companions of Sokrates* (London: J. Murray, 1865). Although I reject his organization by tetralogies—the first ignores, for example the *Sophist-Statesman* dyad interpolated between *Euthyphro* and *Apology*, and his decisions to split

application of this isolationist hermeneutic that makes the riddle of Socrates' Silence particularly difficult and pressing.[90] But Socrates' Silence in the face of Cleitophon's Challenge is likewise more difficult for those who favor "(2)" over "(1)": if Cleitophon's Challenge is not answered in *Republic*, then an explanation for Socrates' Silence must be found elsewhere, in some extra-textual—and thus even less likely—place. In addition to following the ancient indication provided by Thrasyllus, "(1)" has the advantage that it eliminates the problem of Socrates' Silence at the start: Socrates is *not* silent but because Cleitophon's Challenge is formidable, he will require the entire *Republic* to meet it just as he will require nine more books to meet the challenge offered by Glaucon and Adeimantus in *Republic* II.

In arguing for "(3)", Bowe advances arguments against both "(1)" and "(2)". Although there is more that could be said against "(2)",[91] it is his argument against "(1)" that is relevant here:[92]

> Those who take the dialogue as complete and authentic often place the *Clitophon* dramatically before the *Republic*. While this may seem to some to be a more natural order, it also leads to interpretations of the *Clitophon* that see Clitophon as going from bad to worse, based on a few remarks in *Republic* 1.[93]

Bowe's argument depends on the assumption that Plato crafted Socrates' account of Cleitophon in *Republic* I in accordance with historical verisimilitude rather than pedagogical effectiveness:[94] once the great monologue Socrates de-

---

some dyads (e.g. *Hipparchus* and *Minos*) while creating others (e.g., *Symposium* and *Phaedrus*), Thrasyllus gets the Eighth Tetralogy right.

90. See Kremer, *On Socrates and the Modern Mind*, ix: it was Nietzsche's critique of Plato that led him to *Cleitophon* and he "was unable to discover" in the *Cleitophon* (emphasis mine) "a Socrates worthy to be Nietzsche's antagonist *and even critic*."

91. Particularly with respect to Michael Davis, "On the Intention of Plato's *Cleitophon*." *Metis: Revue d'anthropologie du monde grec ancien* 13 (1998), 273-285 and Bruell, *Socratic Education*, 189-99; cf. Zuckert, *Plato's Philosophers*, 336n101.

92. The objection to "(1)" on the basis of "uneasiness" at Bruell, *Socratic Education*, 193 is particularly revealing but cannot be discussed here; see Altman, *The German Stranger*, 349-52 and 444. For a friendlier critique of Bruell's objection, see Kremer, "Socratic Philosophy," 492n20 and 500n28. It is, in any case, thanks to the lack of any clear guidance from Strauss himself that this quarrel between two able Straussians becomes possible; cf. the earlier contrast between Orwin and Roochnik.

93. Bowe, "Defense," 251; cf. the somewhat stronger statement at 249: "Those who take the dialogue as complete and authentic place the *Clitophon* dramatically ahead of the *Republic*." See Kremer, "Socratic Philosophy," for emphasis on the "movement" that Bowe calls "going from bad to worse."

94. Cf. Orwin, "The Case Against Socrates," 752: "As has been argued above, we need not take this ending to imply that Kleitophon has left Socrates speechless. It means merely that Socrates' reply is somehow beside the point, which fact requires interpretation. We learn from the *Republic*, however, that Kleitophon continues to frequent Thrasy-

livers is recognized as his *immediate* response to Cleitophon's Challenge,[95] Bowe's central objection to "(1)" becomes irrelevant. It is my hope that parental storytellers will immediately recognize from experience the efficacy of inserting their own child in the midst of a fiction. In other words: I am claiming that Cleitophon is the first-order imaginary audience for Socrates in Plato's *Republic*.[96] Socrates thereby breaks his silence, responds to Cleitophon's Challenge, and attempts to warn him off from Thrasymachus—to say nothing of the "relativism" or "positivism" that "Cleitophon" (i.e., the Cleitophon described by Socrates in *Republic*) defends in Book I[97]—all at the same time. To put it another way: I am claiming that the Cleitophon who appears in direct dialogue in *Cleitophon* is the actual Cleitophon whereas the Cleitophon whose words and actions Socrates narrates in *Republic* is a counter-factual "Cleitophon,"[98] con-

---

machus: whatever Socrates may have replied, it did not satisfy him." Comparable is Ausland, "Curious Dialogue," 416 (emphasis mine): "'He [sc. Cleitophon] thinks I'm [Ausland is imagining what Socrates might have said to himself] unwilling to give him more but I know I'm unable [cf. Richard Rutherford, *The Art of Plato: Ten Essays in Platonic Interpretation* (London: Duckworth, 1995), 100 and Jacques A. Bailly, *Plato's* Euthyphro *and* Clitophon (Newburyport, MA: Focus, 2003), 116]. Yet he also seems elated by his own rhetorical performance, so I had best not say anything just now. Perhaps *I'll take the next opportunity that arises* to converse in front of him with Thrasymachus and try to get beyond our usual quarrel."

95. Bowe, "Defense," 245n3 (emphases mine): "I do not mean to imply (in the case of *Republic* 1 and *Clitophon*) that we should think of this [sc. 'dramatic ordering'] as an *uninterrupted* dramatic order, although it is possible to do so *on some accounts*." I *am* implying this but Bowe does not address any other accounts that do so.

96. Plato's readers are his second-order audience; the rest of the fictional audience in the home of Cephalus could be reckoned his third-order audience.

97. Bowe, "Defense," 253 (emphasis mine): "If we accept that Roochnik's 'relativism' or Orwin's 'legal positivism' deserves no good response, we are left wondering why *the* Republic *provides such a good response to it*—why it provides a reason for believing that justice is higher than law and thus is not a matter of mere convention—or, as one might more traditionally say, why the *Republic* clearly defends φύσις against νόμος."

98. See Michael Davis, *The Soul of the Greeks: An Inquiry* (Chicago IL: University of Chicago Press, 2011), 159-173. After stating succinctly what I regard as the best solution at 160—"In one way, it seems obvious that the *Cleitophon* comes before the *Republic*. It poses the question to which the *Republic* is the answer"—Davis rejects it at 160-61 (emphasis mine): "What makes this scenario difficult is that Cleitophon is one of the characters present in the *Republic*; it would, of course, be odd for Socrates *to offer as new evidence a narration of a conversation in which Cleitophon was himself a participant.* Isn't it more reasonable, then, to assume that the events narrated in the *Republic* come after the events of the *Cleitophon*?" But on Davis's account of *Cleitophon*, Cleitophon does *exactly the same thing* that Davis claims it would "be odd for Socrates" to do: face to face with Socrates, Cleitophon makes Socrates his character by "inventing a speech" (165: "Has Cleitophon invented a Socratic speech and presented it to Socrates as his own?), a favor Socrates then returns in *Republic*, i.e., in his reply to Cleitophon. Note Davis's quotation marks around this fictional "Socrates" (twice), his "Cleitophon's Socrates" (166-67), and (at 166): "Cleitophon has Socrates reply to an imagined objection."

structed by Socrates for a pedagogical purpose, one who has already made the move "from bad to worse." In *Republic*, Socrates is therefore using an openly relativistic acolyte "Cleitophon" to tell the actual Cleitophon what will become of him if he follows up on his threat to devote himself to Thrasymachus.

If reading *Republic* as Socrates' immediate response to Cleitophon's Challenge disposes of Bowe's objections to "(2)", his defense of "(3)" strengthens my case for the reading order hypothesis. His defense rests on separating an "aporetic" Socrates from a "constructive" Socrates and reading *Cleitophon* as a constructive critique of the former and thus as a necessary propædeutic to the latter:

> For if the Socrates that Clitophon is criticizing in the *Clitophon* is the aporetic Socrates and not the constructive one, the reason for his silence is obvious—his work with Clitophon in this frame of mind and at this stage of development is over.[99]

This is likewise the way I read *Cleitophon*: its protagonist forces Socrates to break the kind of "silence"[100] that characterizes the aporetic dialogues that precede it in the Reading Order of Plato's Dialogues and this, in turn, offers Plato the excuse to create in his *Republic* a constructive answer to Cleitophon's Challenge. Given the totality of the Platonic dialogues, and particularly given his *Republic*, Bowe shows why Cleitophon's charge is false: "Socrates is only an impediment if one mistakes the aporetic Socrates for the constructive one."[101] In the same way, the more than Thrasymachean "Cleitophon" depicted by Socrates in *Republic* I is only an impediment to recognizing *Cleitophon* as an introduction to *Republic* if one mistakes the constructive Socrates for the aporetic one.[102]

This is exactly what Socrates' Cleitophon or "Cleitophon" does with Polemarchus at 340b6-7.

99. Bowe, "Defense," 261; cf. 259: "The idea that Clitophon's claims may make sense as a response to *Republic* 1, which is aporetic in form, but not to *Republic* 2-10 suggests that Clitophon is directing his remarks at the Socrates of the aporetic dialogues." Just as the real Cleitophon confronts the aporetic Socrates, the constructive Socrates constructs a counter-factual Cleitophon.

100. Bowe, "Defense," 263: "Socrates' silence at the end of the *Clitophon*, then, is best explained by the fact that the aporetic Socrates can do no more for Clitophon."

101. Bowe, "Defense," 263.

102. For a recent attempt to do this on a systematic basis, see Sandra Peterson, *Socrates and Philosophy in the Dialogues of Plato* (Cambridge, UK: Cambridge University Press, 2011). Although by no means allergic to discussing dialogues of dubious authenticity—cf. the discussion of *Lovers* at 201-5—Peterson unfortunately does not mention *Cleitophon*. Determined to prove that what Bowe calls "the constructive" Socrates does not exist and that "the apparently confident doctrinal Socrates" (i) is merely stating what his *interlocutors* believe to be suitable doctrine, she mentions the Divided Line (152 and 158) only in the context of the claim (158) that "Glaucon likes enumerations and correspondences and that Socrates very often addresses to Glaucon proposals that have a mathematical flavor." She does, however, leave an open place for the reader at 165.

To turn now to the dialogue itself, Cleitophon is willing to admit that the speeches of Socrates are "most valuable admonitions and most useful [προτρεπτικωτάτους τε . . . καὶ ὠφελιμωτάτους] literally capable of waking us up, as it were, out of our slumber."[103] But he wants "to hear what was to follow next." The phrase τὸ μετὰ ταῦτα ("that which comes after these things"; translation mine) is the *Leitmotiv* of the *Cleitophon* (*Clit.* 408c4, 408c9, and 408d7) and this makes sense once we realize that it is *Republic* that will do so. Now that he has been persuaded to seek virtue, Cleitophon wants to know how to practice it; he is therefore "inquiring what discourse might be the one after these [πυνθανόμενος τίς ὁ μετὰ ταῦτ' εἴη λόγος]" (*Clit.* 408c9). The λόγος we call "*Republic*" is the answer to Cleitophon's question and thus the Platonic response to Cleitophon's Challenge.

Just as the phrase ὁ μετὰ ταῦτα λόγος denominates *Republic*, the word "ταῦτα" refers to the *aporetic dialogues* the reader has already read before reading *Cleitophon*. At this point in his well-ordered pedagogical program (see Preface, figure 1), Plato employs Cleitophon to represent what any critical auditor/reader of the foregoing series of primarily aporetic/elenctic dialogues would understandably be feeling/seeking before reading/hearing *Republic*. In *Cleitophon*, then, Cleitophon is asking for *Republic*: begging for it, as it were:

> "I ask you, my very good Sirs, in what sense do we now accept the exhortation to virtue which Socrates has given us. Are we to regard it as all there is, and suppose it to be impossible to pursue the object [sc. virtue] further and grasp it fully [ἐπεξελθεῖν δὲ οὐκ ἔνι τῷ πράγματι καὶ λαβεῖν αὐτὸ τελέως]?" (*Clit.* 408d1-4).

From what Cleitophon (or any given student) can glean from the early dialogues—i.e., "early" with respect to reading order—it does not seem that he can either "grasp virtue fully" or put these lessons into practice (τῷ πράγματι). As Plato's paradigm for the committed student, Cleitophon not only wants to know what comes next, he wants to know what to *do* next. In lieu of answers, he sees only a disappointing alternative:

> and is this to be our lifelong task, just to exhort those who have not as yet been exhorted, and that they in turn should exhort others [τοὺς μήπω προτετραμμένους προτρέπειν, καὶ ἐκείνους αὖ ἑτέρους] (*Clit.* 408d5-6)

Is this all Socrates can offer his hearers (or Plato his readers): that they exhort others to leave behind false virtues and search for real ones?

> Or, when we have agreed that this is exactly what a man should do [τοῦτ' αὐτὸ ἀνθρώπῳ πρακτέον εἶναι] ought we to ask Socrates, and one another, the fur-

---

103. *Clit.* 408c2-4; unless noted, all translations from this dialogue are by Francisco J. Gonzalez in Cooper and Hutchinson, *Complete Dialogues*.

ther question [τὸ μετὰ τοῦτ' ἐπανερωτᾶν]: "What is the next step?" [τί τοὐντεῦθεν;] (*Clit.* 408d7-e2)

This is the crucial passage in *Cleitophon*, hereafter to be called "Cleitophon's Question," a description that applies better than the conventional but overly polemical "Cleitophon's Challenge." It is a *practical* question, most effectively distilled into the words: "What must be done?" (τί πρακτέον;). To the extent that *Republic* can easily be read, and has repeatedly been read since antiquity as a purely *theoretical* work[104]—i.e., Plato's program for an ideal city—its proximity to *Cleitophon* constitutes the best extra-textual reason for reading it differently. In this way, the reading order hypothesis allows a lesser dialogue like *Cleitophon* to play a significant role in elucidating the far more important dialogue that follows it.

In the present case, Cleitophon's Question will eventually receive its precise and triumphant answer at *Republic* 520c1: καταβατέον ("it is necessary to go [back] down"). When Plato's *Republic* is read as Socrates' answer to Cleitophon's Question, it becomes much easier to recognize that the obligatory καταβατέον, flagged as important by Socrates' opening word (κατέβην at 327a1), is addressed not only to the temporarily captious Guardians (520a7-8) as represented by their skilful spokesman Glaucon (519d8-9), but also to Cleitophon, whose τί τοὐντεῦθεν provokes it. And once the narrative frame has been broken by our awareness of Cleitophon's semi-textual presence as Socrates' first-order audience, Plato has opened the door to applying καταβατέον both to Glaucon and to us. When guided to Plato's Socratic answer by Cleitophon's Question, τὸ μετὰ ταῦτα tells any given reader/auditor precisely what comes next and, above all, where the philosopher must go from here: back down into the Cave of political life, as Cicero did.[105]

---

104. W. H. Stahl (ed. and trans.). *Macrobius,* Commentary on the Dream of Scipio. (New York: Columbia University Press, 1990), 81.

105. It is significant that Cicero (and many other ancient authorities) regarded Demosthenes as Plato's auditor; see A. E. Douglas (ed.), *M. Tulli Ciceronis* Brutus (Oxford: Clarendon Press, 1960), 100. An unusually detailed dismissal of this possibility can be found at P. A. Brunt, "Plato's Academy and Politics" in *Studies in Greek History and Thought*, 282-342 (Oxford: Clarendon Press, 1993), 300-1n52. But the tide may be turning; see Craig Cooper, "Philosophers, Politics, Academics: Demosthenes' Rhetorical Reputation in Antiquity" in Ian Worthington (ed.), *Demosthenes: Statesman and Orator*, 224-245 (London: Routledge, 2000) and Galen O. Rowe, "Two Responses by Isocrates to Demosthenes." *Historia* 51 n. 2 (2nd Qtr. 2002), 149-162 at 161 (last sentence): "Finally, the dispute between Demosthenes and Isocrates tends to corroborate the tradition that Demosthenes was one of Plato's students." And even though Allen, *Why Plato Wrote*, depends on the view that Demosthenes was combating Plato's influence (121), she has performed a useful service by bringing them together; cf. 122 ("The Athenian politicians Demosthenes and Aeschines were members of an elite who appear to have read Plato's dialogues, though without being members of the Academy") and 192-93n14. Cf. 554c4-10 with he agony of the young Demosthenes.

Plato's *Republic* offers any given Cleitophon—whether this be the Cleitophon of *Cleitophon*, Socrates' "Cleitophon" in *Republic*, or the reader—sufficient time and ample reason to change her or his position. It all depends on how powerfully a reader allows him- or herself to be affected by Plato through Socrates: the more powerfully the reader is affected, the less vehemently will he or she insist that Cleitophon could not have been converted by the moral and persuasive power of a Socratic speech. The same dilemma faces the reader of *Gorgias*: Callicles too falls silent in the wake of the just use of Socratic eloquence and Aristocles the son of Ariston, does not tell us in the dialogue what Callicles did next. Naturally the greatest of Socratic speeches—Plato's *Republic*—can stand on its own, i.e., without the introductory *Cleitophon*. But it need not be required to do so. *Cleitophon* can therefore easily be compared to the anecdote preserved by Dionysius: it is useful for understanding Plato's *Republic*. And as a first step in catching sight of Plato the Teacher, it is important to see how Cleitophon's Question: "What is the next step?" (τί τοὐντεῦθεν;), receives a definitive answer in that immortal λόγος whose first word, carefully chosen, is κατέβην.

Chapter One

The First Words of Plato's Πολιτεία

Section 1. κατέβην

Justice is discovered three times in Plato's *Republic* and the first of these is hidden in a most unlikely place. The first word of Book I— "κατέβην" ("I went down" from the verb καταβαίνειν; "to go down")—embodies Plato's complete and considered teaching about Justice, i.e., the dialogue's principal, overriding, and indeed its sole concern. Beautifully written though it is, filled to overflowing with literary, political, historical, athletic, musical, military, economic, mathematical, harmonic, logical, psychological, ontological, methodological, and pedagogical riches (a by no means complete list) to such an extent that it almost seems a blasphemy to say that any one thing is its principal concern, Plato's sole purpose is to persuade the reader—just as Socrates' sole purpose is to persuade Glaucon—to choose Justice. In retrospect, i.e., in the context of the Allegory of the Cave in Book VII,[1] Socrates' first word reveals that Justice is the philosopher's voluntary decision to Go Back Down into the Cave, instantiated in the first place by Socrates himself.[2]

Socrates never applies the expression "going back down into the Cave" to himself but he does use it while explaining what the thirty-five year-old Guardians (540a4-5 and 537d3) will be compelled to do by Glaucon after completing five years (539e2-3) of training in dialectic:

---

1. See Kenneth Dorter "Philosopher-Rulers: How Contemplation Becomes Action." *Ancient Philosophy* 21 (September 2001), 335-356, at 345n19: "Readers have often seen in the *Republic's* opening words, 'I went down', a reference to the philosopher's descent into the cave."

2. Socrates' descent to the Piraeus in the context of the Cave is also central for Eva Brann with Peter Kalkavage and Eric Salem, *The Music of the Republic: Essays on Socrates' Conversations and Plato's Writings* (Philadelphia, PA: Paul Dry, 2004); see 116-21, 213-16, and 244: "Socrates, by descending with Glaucon into the mythical setting of the Peiraic underworld, has shown him that he lives as one imprisoned in a mortal Hades. But this demonstration is itself a release, the first step of the rescue." See also Richard J. Klonoski, "The Preservation of Homeric Tradition: Heroic Re-Performance in the *Republic* and the *Odyssey*." *Clio* 22 (1993), 251-271, especially 259, 264-65, 266-68.

> "For after that, they will be obligated by you to go down [καταβιβαστέοι ἔσονταί σοι] back into the cave just mentioned [εἰς τὸ σπήλαιον πάλιν ἐκεῖνο], and will be required to rule [ἀναγκαστέοι ἄρχειν] both as concerns war and whatsoever are commands of youth so that they may not fall short of the others in experience either; and in these offices, too, they must be tested [βασανιστέοι] to see whether they will remain steadfast while being dragged in all directions or if they too will swerve somewhat." (539e3-540a2; translation mine)

Like the Latin gerundive (e.g. *agenda* as "the things that must be done"), Greek verbal adjectives (ending in the plural with -τέοι) necessarily convey *obligation*; it will be noted that there are three such words in this sentence. As already suggested in the discussion of Cleitophon's Question (see Introduction), the "crisis of the *Republic*" will be any given reader's voluntary choice to apply to her- or himself the obligation implicit in the verbal adjective derived directly from καταβαίνω and found but once in *Republic*: καταβατέον at 520c1 (see section §16). But here, the first of three verbal adjectives (καταβιβαστέοι) is derived from the causal form of the opening verb while the agent enforcing this obligation is Glaucon: since the Guardians will be sent back down into the Cave by Glaucon, their "going back down" is enforced, not voluntary. Since it is not a free choice, it cannot be Justice (cf. Cicero *de Officiis* 1.28). Even if the Guardians were philosophers—and what kind of philosopher needs to be compelled to seek out the Good?[3]—the application of compulsion necessarily distances them from Justice. While approximating Justice, the Guardians do not instantiate it.

It is precisely because the Guardians do not instantiate Justice that Socrates can use them—i.e., Plato can use Socrates' account of them—to illuminate what Justice is: the *action* of the Guardian may closely resemble Justice but the fact that it is not voluntary makes Justice *conspicuous by its absence*. The act the Guardians are *forced* to perform would be Justice if and only if they themselves freely chose to perform it. The fiction that it is Glaucon who will compel them to perform it reminds us that there is no one who can compel Glaucon himself to choose the life of Justice: if Glaucon decides to go back down into the Cave, that choice will be his alone. Plato's *Republic* may be said to be about what will be called "Glaucon's Choice": beginning at Book II, Socrates is responding to Glaucon's demand that Socrates persuade him—after explaining its nature and origin and proving that there are those who freely choose it—that the just life is choice-worthy for Glaucon himself (see section §9). Immediately outside of the text is the possibility that Socrates is speaking to Cleitophon and merely using Socrates' attempt to persuade Glaucon—the central fiction of Plato's *Republic* is, of course, Glaucon's Choice[4]—as a means to answering Cleitophon's Question. And even further outside of the text is the certainty that Plato is speaking to

3. 540a6-9; cf. Rachel Barney, "Eros and Necessity in the Ascent from the Cave." *Ancient Philosophy* 28 no. 2 (Fall 2008), 357-372.

4. Cf. Penner, "What is the Form of the Good the Form of?"

the reader and merely using Glaucon's Choice to prove that the life of Justice is choice-worthy for us as well. But Plato cannot persuade the reader—or, if you prefer, Socrates cannot persuade Glaucon—without recourse or reference to the most obvious, blatant, and well-known fiction in his *Republic*: the hypothetical City along with its imaginary Guardians (see chapter 3). These Guardians exist only within the argument that Socrates offers Glaucon and the rest of the auditors, and, unlike those auditors, they are *compelled* to do what Socrates wishes to persuade Glaucon, Cleitophon, and the reader to do *voluntarily*.

This is why the opening word of Socrates is so important: if Socrates did not present himself as having gone down in Book I—back down into the Cave, as the reader will eventually discover in Book VII—one might be inclined to believe that it was only the purely fictional Guardians who are compelled to do so: the opening κατέβην is the first, most significant, and indeed decisive piece of textual evidence that Plato intends the Allegory of the Cave to be applied to someone other than the imaginary Guardians of a non-existent City.[5] As his first word will suggest in retrospect, it is Socrates who dispels any given reader's ultimately self-serving illusion that it is only the Guardians of the imaginary City who are being told to do what Marcus Tullius Cicero did. This ultimately becomes clear when Socrates concludes the image of the Cave with a self-referential description of a person who chooses to return to it:

> "And consider this also," said I, "if such a one should go down again [εἰ πάλιν ὁ τοιοῦτος καταβὰς] and take his old place would he not get his eyes full of darkness, thus suddenly coming out of the sunlight?" "He would indeed." "Now if he should be required to contend [διαμιλλᾶσθαι] with these perpetual prisoners in 'evaluating' these shadows while his vision was still dim and before his eyes were accustomed to the dark—and this time required for habituation would not be very short—would he not provoke laughter, and would it not be said of him that he had returned from his journey aloft with his eyes ruined and that it was not worth while even to attempt the ascent? And if it were possible to lay hands on and to kill the man who tried to release them and lead them up [τὸν ἐπιχειροῦντα λύειν τε καὶ ἀνάγειν], would they not kill him?" "They certainly would," he said. (516e3-517a7)

5. Mitchell Miller, "Platonic Provocations: Reflections on the Soul and the Good in the *Republic*" in Dominic J. O'Meara (ed.), *Platonic Investigations*, 163-193 (Washington D.C.: Catholic University of America Press, 1995), 185: "The philosopher *par excellence*, he [sc. Socrates] has spent his life going down into the cave—whether this be the marketplace, a Callias' or an Agathon's house, or the Piraeus—and seeking out his 'likes' by relentless provocative elenchus." One should not press "likes" so far; a more combative Socrates emerges in Roslyn Weiss, *The Socratic Paradox and its Enemies* (Chicago, IL: University of Chicago Press, 2006), 2: "Plato's Socrates is a fighter." See also Roslyn Weiss, *Virtue in the Cave; Moral Inquiry in the* Meno (Oxford: Oxford University Press, 2001) and Dominic Scott, *Recollection and Experience; Plato's Theory of Learning and its Successors* (Cambridge, UK: Cambridge University Press, 1995), 48-50.

If we are unprepared to recognize a Socratic self-portrait on the spot,[6] the reference just a few moments later to "such a one" being compelled to contend in law courts quickly erases all doubt (517d7-e1). But Socrates has a good motive for not making the actual Allegory simply autobiographical:[7] Plato's purpose is not only to praise Socrates for his Justice but also to persuade us to emulate him by choosing it as well. Since those others need to know the worldly consequences of what they are choosing, Socrates is made to offer himself as an instantiation of Justice from the start.

It will be noted that there is no element of compulsion involved in the return to the Cave; "such a one," having already returned, will doubtless be compelled to contend with the Cave dwellers "in 'evaluating' these shadows." But only the one attempting "to release and lead them up" will face the murderous rage of the Cavemen and there is no indication whatsoever that either this attempt or the Return that makes it possible are involuntary in any way. In fact, the Return is simply stated (by the aorist participle καταβάς) and thus appears to be entirely unmotivated; the only hint about its motivation is supplied by considering what "such a one" does having returned: she attempts to lead others out. And it is worth considering with some care that the first thought of a Return to the Cave arises from the escapee's recollection of that first habitation and what passed for wisdom there: she will congratulate herself on the change but pity those who remain behind (516c4-6). But prior to her making this evaluation, it is the allegorical Sun that appears to have reminded her of her former habitation and this is very strange: the Good is conspicuously absent in the Cave. The fire that burns within it represents the visible sun (517b3).

> "And so, finally, I suppose, he would be able to look upon the sun itself and see its true nature, not by reflections in water or phantasms of it in an alien setting, but in and by itself in its own place." "Necessarily," he said. "And at this point he would infer and conclude that this it is that provides the seasons and the courses of the year and presides over all things in the visible region, and is in some sort the cause of all these things that they had seen [καὶ ἐκείνων ὧν σφεῖς ἑώρων τρόπον τινὰ πάντων αἴτιος]." "Obviously," he said, "that would be the next step." "Well then, if he recalled to mind his first habitation and what passed for wisdom there, and his fellow-bondsmen, do you not think that he would count himself happy in the change and pity them?" (516b4-c6)

6. Shorey, *Plato's Republic*, 2.129n"c": "An obvious allusion to the fate of Socrates." So also Adam, *Republic of Plato*, 2.94-95: "καὶ τὸν ἐπιχειροῦντα κτλ. is a manifest and touching allusion to the death of Socrates, whose fate was the most conspicuous example in Greek history of the principle here laid down."

7. Cf. Ruby Blondell, *The Play of Character in Plato's Dialogues* (Cambridge, UK: Cambridge University Press, 2002), 87: "But if Sokrates is the unique embodiment of the philosopher, and as such incomparable, this establishes a profoundly pessimistic, even tragic, outlook for the future of philosophy."

Up until this point, "such a one" has consistently been singular, as indeed he or she repeatedly is in this passage as well. But the use of the plural σφεῖς is responsible for the avoidance of a perfect non sequitur in the unlikely transition from the sun to the Cave: in some sense (τρόπον τινά) the sun is the cause (αἴτιος) even of all those things that *they* saw. Who are they? The plural points to those who remain in the Cave, no longer only the one who has emerged from it. It is somehow the ubiquitous and all-embracing causal influence of the sun—only now discovered by reasoning and made emphatic by Plato's placement of πάντων ("all things")—that reminds the philosopher of those who remain below in the Cave. More importantly, this discovery leads her to pity them for the exact same reason that she will consider herself happy. Once having been reminded of *them* by the Good, there is nevertheless absolutely nothing in the text—particularly if Homer's wily Odysseus is telling the truth about Achilles in Hades (see section §35) and if the words of Odysseus's Achilles apply to the Cave (516d4-7; cf. *Smp.* 180b4-5)—to explain why "such a one" would voluntarily return to such an undesirable place.

Justice resolves these difficulties. Having seen the causal influence of the Good, an influence that extends even into the Cave in a manner that seems to have nothing to do with any direct relation between the sun and the fire burning within it (see Introduction and section §18), the individual escapee realizes that the allegorical or figurative Sun, i.e., the Idea of the Good (517b8-c1) is somehow also the cause of all the things they saw down below (516b8-c2). This realization, it bears repeating, leads to both self-congratulation and pity for others (516c4-6). How strong, we must ask ourselves, must this Sun-inspired pity be? Fully aware of the paltry value of what passes for wisdom in the Cave (516c8-d4), that anything would be preferable to seeing things once again the way its prisoners see them (516d4-e2), that returning to the darkness from the light will make this impossible in any case (516e3-6), that one will nevertheless be compelled to compete with those who see far better in the dark (516e7-517a2), that one's long-lasting inability to compete with them will furnish clear and comical evidence that the upward course has destroyed one's own eyes and thus should not be undertaken by others (517a2-4)—an argument that effectively refutes the attempt "to release them and lead them up," Socrates' sole suggestion as to the return's ultimate purpose or final cause—and finally that, if somehow they might be able to take "such a one" in their hands (517a5-6), they would kill the one attempting to release them from their restraining chains (517a4-6). Only the philosophic reader's voluntary choice to instantiate this virtuous course of action—in perfect contempt of the possibility that one could actually fall into the murderous hands of the Cavemen—would show that they are following the downward course of Socrates and have therefore have chosen for themselves the life of Justice he embodied and has, thanks to Plato, modeled for them.

Since Plato's purpose in *Republic* is to persuade the reader to make Glaucon's Choice by choosing Justice, an extended conversation between Socrates and Glaucon is both textual analogue and the pedagogical provocation for an extra-textual dialogue between teacher/writer and student/reader. Indeed the well-prepared student/reader has already been encouraged to take the critical first step outside of Plato's text by seeing *Republic* as Socrates' answer to Cleitophon's Question. When considered alone, however, *Republic* revolves around Glaucon's Choice and all the student/reader need do is identify with Glaucon's open-minded demand for persuasive proof. But Glaucon is not Socrates' only interlocutor even within the strict confines of the discourse that begins with the word κατέβην. And it must be granted that for all of Plato's evident love for Glaucon (see section §4), he entrusts to his other brother Adeimantus the most beautiful expression of the literary conceit embodied in his *Republic*. In his attempt to persuade Socrates to stay in the Piraeus—Polemarchus had been inclined to playfully force him to do so (327c7-9)—Adeimantus tells Glaucon and Socrates, with evident and perfectly unself-conscious enthusiasm, of the torch-passing spectacle to be held later that evening.[8] Adeimantus captures the attention of Socrates to such an extent that even Polemarchus now drops the language of force and revealingly seconds him by giving four of his own reasons designed to persuade Socrates to stay. As things turn out, they will never (1) see the torch race on horseback, (2) experience the remainder of the all-night festival, (3) eat a proper dinner, or (4) be joined by other young men: the only thing they will do is (5) talk. But thanks to us—to Plato's concern (or pity) for us as expressed through Socrates' concern (or pity) for Cleitophon, Glaucon, Adeimantus, and Polemarchus—the torch is passed nevertheless and Adeimantus gets his way after all: λαμπάδια ἔχοντες διαδώσουσιν ἀλλήλοις.[9] The torch that will be passed is, of course, the Torch of Justice. It burns bright even in the darkest Cave or rather it cannot burn bright anywhere else. And it is among the shadows of the Cave that Plato justifies Socrates' opening word.

In "Plato on Why Mathematics is Good for the Soul," Myles Burnyeat shows us just how close to the Idea or εἶδος of Justice Plato is willing to let his Socrates take us in the *Republic*. The passage in question begins with this description of the philosopher's progress in the Allegory of the Cave:

> At the beginning, they meet puppets of the just (note the plural ἀγάλματα at 517d9); at the end the Good, which Socrates describes both as the cause of all

8. The relevant passage is 328a1-328b3: "'Do you mean to say,' interposed Adeimantus, 'that you haven't heard that there is to be a torchlight race this evening on horseback in honor of the Goddess?' 'On horseback?' said I. 'That is a new idea. Will they carry torches and pass them along to one another [λαμπάδια ἔχοντες διαδώσουσιν ἀλλήλοις] as they race with the horses, or how do you mean?' '[1] That's the way of it,' said Polemarchus, 'and, besides, [2] there is to be a night festival which will be worth seeing. For after [3] dinner we will get up and go out and see the sights [1 and 2 repeated] and [4] meet a lot of the lads there and [5] have good talk. So stay and do as we ask.' 'It looks as if we should have to stay,' said Glaucon. 'Well,' said I, 'if it so be, so be it.'"

9. "Having torches, they will pass them along, one to another" (translation mine). I suspect that it was James Adam's own wish to have the cover of his magisterial two-volume commentary adorned with a numismatic representation of this wonderful line. All students of Plato have abundant cause to regret the absence of Adam's Introduction.

things right and beautiful, and as that which anyone who is going to act wisely either in public or private life must know (517c).[10]

In fact, the encounter with the ἀγάλματα to which Burnyeat here refers occurs only when Socrates describes the philosopher's *return* to the Cave:

"And again, do you think it at all strange," said I, "if a man returning from divine contemplations [θείων . . . θεωριῶν] to the petty miseries of men [τὰ ἀνθρώπειά . . . κακὰ] cuts a sorry figure and appears most ridiculous, if, while still blinking through the gloom, and before he has become sufficiently accustomed to the environing darkness, he is compelled in courtrooms or elsewhere to contend about the shadows of justice or the images [περὶ τῶν τοῦ δικαίου σκιῶν ἢ ἀγαλμάτων] that cast the shadows and to wrangle in debate about the notions of these things in the minds of those who have never seen justice itself [αὐτὴν δικαιοσύνην]?" "It would be by no means strange," he said. (517d4-e2)

Returning from divine contemplations, the philosopher must contend with those who know only the ἀγάλματα that cast "the shadows of the just" while the philosopher has seen "justice itself." Here Burnyeat raises the all-important question: "They return having seen 'justice itself' (517e). But when?"[11] At this point in Socrates' narrative, the philosopher has only just seen the Idea of the Good (517b8-c4) and what follows from this vision in the text is the philosopher's perfectly understandable unwillingness to go back down.[12] By the time he describes how philosophers must "wrangle in debate," Socrates has given the reader no indication whatsoever of why the philosopher would return or rather *has already returned* to the Cave, only why one would not. The Platonic answer to the question Burnyeat is brilliant enough to raise but not quite simple enough

---

10. Myles Burnyeat, "Plato on Why Mathematics is Good for the Soul." *Proceedings of the British Academy* 103 (2000), 1-81 in Timothy Smiley (ed.), *Mathematics and Necessity; Essays in the History of Philosophy*, 46.

11. The elegant answer at Burnyeat, "Plato on Why Mathematics is Good," 46 is that "dialectical debate about the conceptual foundations of mathematics is itself, at a very abstract level, a debate about values like justice." Against Cornford, "Mathematics and Dialectic" (46n62)—who recognized how sharp the distinction between the First and Second parts of the Divided Line actually is—Burnyeat explains "Why Mathematics is Good for the Soul" by linking mathematics to "the Form of Justice." This linkage is probably inconsistent with his able defense (42; cf. the italicized "may" at 34) of Intermediates in the Divided Line (see section §25).

12. 517c6-d3: "'Come then,' I said, 'and join me in this further thought, and do not be surprised that those who have attained to this height are not willing to occupy themselves with the affairs of men [τὰ τῶν ἀνθρώπων πράττειν], but their souls ever feel the upward urge and the yearning for that sojourn above [ἀλλ' ἄνω ἀεὶ ἐπείγονται αὐτῶν αἱ ψυχαὶ διατρίβειν]. For this, I take it, is likely if in this point too the likeness of our image holds.' 'Yes, it is likely.'" This passage directly precedes the one quoted in the text above.

to answer is that the philosopher's decision to return to the Cave ipso facto presupposes "justice itself" and thus the philosopher who returns to the shadows has, by that very action, discovered the Idea of Justice.

It is now time to return to where this section began: "justice is discovered three times in Plato's *Republic*." The only explicit "discovery" of justice (i.e., in Book IV) is, for reasons that will emerge in chapter 3, deliberately inadequate. The first and third of them—this section's subject up until this point—depend entirely on the Cave and what is discovered in the Cave constitutes Justice only for those who begin to walk with confidence the Longer Way when it reappears at 504b1-d3. But justice (the capital 'J' will be reserved for the Longer Way's adumbration of the real thing, anticipated by κατέβην) is also discovered in between these two along the Shorter Way. In fact, the discovery of justice in Book IV—the only discovery recognized as such by most of Plato's readers—constitutes for all the others one of the most perfect jokes perpetrated by "the playful Plato."[13] The discovery that "justice in the City" is "each individual doing the job for which they are by nature suited" is surely one of the great anticlimaxes in world literature.[14] Has there ever been a good student who was not bitterly (if only secretly) disappointed with this trivial result? Without mercy, Plato's Socrates increases our sense of anticlimax by building up the reader's suspense with hunting imagery, picked up by Glaucon:

---

13. See William Chase Greene, "The Spirit of Comedy in Plato." *Harvard Studies in Classical Philology* 31 (1920), 63-123, G. J. de Vries, *Spel bij Plato* (Amsterdam: Noord-Hollandsche Uitg. Mij, 1949), and Gavin Ardley, "The Role of Play in the Philosophy of Plato." *Philosophy* 42 no. 161 (July 1967), 226-244, particularly at 240: "The serious and the playful are sisters. Through their association in contrariety, through the aporiai engendered thereby, the intelligence is set in motion. The proper handling of this ascending counterpoint is the key to education. The maintenance of the fugue is no easy matter; we so readily run after one contrary to the exclusion of the other." Paul Plass, "'Play' and Philosophic Detachment in Plato." *Transactions of the American Philological Association* 98 (1967), 343-364 usefully discusses "'playful' detachment from the lower, sensuous world" at 360.

14. 432e7-433b1: "'That is a tedious prologue,' he said, 'for an eager listener.' 'Listen then,' said I, 'and learn if there is anything in what I say. For what we laid down in the beginning as a universal requirement when we were founding our city, this I think, or some form of this, is justice. And what we did lay down, and often said, you recall, was that each one man must perform one social service in the state for which his nature is best adapted.' 'Yes, we said that.' 'And again that to do one's own business and not to be a busybody is justice, is a saying that we have heard from many and have often repeated [πολλάκις] ourselves.'" Shorey, *Plato's Republic* (1.368n"a") and Adam, *Republic of Plato* (1.239) admit that Socrates in fact *doesn't* say (or at any rate, hasn't said) this, at least about justice. But Adam notes that Socrates has done so in *Alc. 1* 127a14-c7. Only if the *Alcibiades Major* is genuine is Socrates speaking the truth here; the fact that this dialogue is so early in the Reading Order (see Preface) means that its contents *have* been discussed πολλάκις. A good guardian requires a good memory and the reading order hypothesis illustrates the methods by which Plato cultivated it in his students: they must repeatedly remember "early" dialogues, applying those lessons to what they are hearing.

> "And truly," said I, "it appears to be an inaccessible place, lying in deep shadows." "It certainly is a dark covert, not easy to beat up [δύσβατός γέ τις ὁ τόπος φαίνεται καὶ ἐπίσκιος: ἔστι γοῦν σκοτεινὸς καὶ δυσδιερεύνητος]."[15]

On the Longer Way, Justice *will* be found—literally "adumbrated"—in the "dark covert" of the Cave. Exaggerated to the point of comedy in the context of Book IV, these words are therefore a perfect prolepsis for what is to come; they *foreshadow* the Cave, as the sentence that provokes "the crisis of the *Republic*" makes perfectly clear:

> "'Down you must go [καταβατέον] then, each in his turn, to the habitation of the others and accustom yourselves to the observation of the obscure things [τὰ σκοτεινὰ] there.'"[16]

Only in Book VII, then, will Justice actually be found in a τόπος σκοτεινός ("dark place"); on the Shorter Way, the imagery is out of place. In addition to the descent to the shadows,[17] the difficulty of the ascent from the Cave (515e7) will correspond to δύσβατός at 432c8 while the δυσδιερεύνητος will also prove appropriate, as shown in section §16. Disguised as an ironic hunt in Book IV, this passage therefore becomes a comical but critical clue, particularly important because Socrates will do absolutely nothing in Book VII to alert the reader—aside, that is, from the towering excellence of the Allegory itself and the dialogue's opening word—that Justice is about to be found there. But no less than the third discovery of Justice (in the Cave of Book VII) is the first (the opening word of Book I) to be found in the second (the discovery of justice in the City in Book IV). And therefore, when Socrates finally catches sight of "it," he says something true about both the Shorter and the Longer Ways:

> "Why, all the time, bless your heart, the thing apparently was tumbling about our feet from the start and yet we couldn't see it, but were most ludicrous, like people who sometimes hunt for what they hold in their hands."[18]

Indeed, it was long before laying down the principle that "each would do one job" in Book II (369e3; cf. 369a3) that Socrates had said "κατέβην."

---

15. 432c8-9. The hunting image is made even more explicit as passage continues at 432c9-d4: "'But all the same on we must go.' 'Yes, on.' And I caught view and gave a hulloa and said, 'Glaucon, I think we have found its trail and I don't believe it will get away from us.'"

16. 520c1-3; with τὰ σκοτεινὰ, cf. 516e4.

17. The use of ἐπίσκιος ("shadowy") is likewise revealing: the shadows of the Cave are mentioned three times at 515a7, 515b9, and 515c2.

18. 432d8-e2. What Socrates *explicitly* means by saying "from the start" will be discussed in chapter 3.

Section 2. χθές

The second word of the *Republic* (and a perfect word to come second since it inevitably points us back to something earlier) is χθές ("yesterday"). This word constitutes another delicious joke, an ontological claim whose credibility depends in no small measure on Plato's literary genius, and, at least as far as I myself am concerned, nothing less than the literal truth expressed in the guise of metaphor. Let's start, after a momentary digression, with the first of these.

When asked in Book II (357d4) whether the just life is to be chosen on the basis (1) of itself or (2) of its results, Socrates replies it is to be chosen on the basis (3) of both of these reasons.[19] As it turns out, of course, he must (thanks to Glaucon) find a way to prove that it is to be chosen on the basis of "(1)" but not of either "(2)" or "(3)." It will probably come as no surprise to discover that I believe that writing *Plato the Teacher* constitutes in part my own attempt to practice Justice. And I am sure that it will become evident that I find spending time in Plato's company in the service of what I, at least, conceive Justice to be, to be a very pleasant task in and of itself: even if I knew that nobody would read these words in my lifetime, I would write them anyway. But I also write them for the sake of a reward: the opportunity to read the Πολιτεία aloud (in Greek) to a party of eager and knowledgeable graduate students who are willing to sit up all night in order to discover exactly how long it took for Socrates to tell the story of what he did the night before.[20] That is something I long to know by experience.

The delicious joke of the χθές would only become fully intelligible thereafter: for now, I can only conjecture. But even without any chronological exactitude, the playful Plato is asking us to believe that Socrates went down to the Piraeus yesterday, was detained there just as he was beginning to make his homeward journey, and was either forced or persuaded (the text leaves us in doubt about which)[21] to conduct a conversation about justice.[22] This conversation lasted well into the night and probably into the wee hours of the morning; perhaps a rooster crowed at the very moment that Socrates said: "Let's hire a

---

19. 358a1-3: "'In my opinion,' I said, 'it belongs in the fairest class, that which a man who is to be happy must love both for its own sake and for the results.'"

20. See Kent Moors, "The Argument Against a Dramatic Date for Plato's *Republic*," *Polis* 7 no. 1 (Spring 1987), 6-31 at 31n68: "taking from ten to fifteen hours to deliver orally." This valuable article argues persuasively that Plato intended *Republic* to be "timeless" (23). By extension, then, χθές refers to "all our yesterdays."

21. But see Mitchell Miller, "Beginning 'The Longer Way'" in G. R. F. Ferrari (ed.), *The Cambridge Companion to Plato's* Republic, 310-344 (Cambridge, UK: Cambridge University Press, 2007), 317: "His [sc. Socrates'] presence in the Piraeus—doubled 'now,' a fictional day later, by his indefatigable narration of the night's events to us—stands strikingly at odds with his account of the philosopher's reluctance to 'descend.' Is this tension significant?"

22. For the force/persuasion dyad, see 365d4-5; for voluntarily/under compulsion, see 399c2; for voluntarily/involuntarily, see 413a1.

herald" (580b9). In any case, after speaking all night, he finally made the journey home by walking the four kilometers up to Athens from the Piraeus and at some point during that day, was apparently asked (or was otherwise induced by a question like Cleitophon's) to account for his recent activities. At which point, he proceeded to narrate—in exhaustive but obviously not exhausting detail—the conversation as Plato has recorded it for us. The willingness of Socrates to repeat the conversation at length proves that he did so *willingly* both times and not as a result of being *forced* to do so. Of course the full dimensions of this joke remain unknown until I get my graduate students. Naturally we will be supplied with refreshments but probably not a dinner: drinks, chips, and a tasty salsa or dip should be sufficient to keep us going.

In response to what he calls "the City of Pigs" (372d5), Glaucon pointedly remarks on the absence of such "relish" ("ἄνευ ὄψου," is the expression he uses at 372c3). Socrates proceeds to pass him some (372c5-d4) but this leaves Glaucon unsatisfied. When Socrates asks him what is missing (372d7), he replies:

> "What is customary," he replied. "They must recline on couches [ἐπί τε κλινῶν], I presume, if they are not to be uncomfortable, and dine from tables and have dishes and sweetmeats such as are now in use." (372d8-e1)

There is no passage in the dialogue that a movie director, setting out to film *Republic*, would find more useful in bringing to life the scene in the well-appointed house of Polemarchus than this one. Are not our interlocutors, including Socrates himself, reclined on sofas (Shorey's Socrates will call them "beds" in Book X) even as they speak? If we are to believe that such a marathon of conversation actually took place once upon a time down in the Piraeus, we must certainly assume that all the participants were comfortably seated (or reclining), that they had plenty of food (certainly what we call today "finger-food") and something to drink, if only to "wet the whistle."

> and condiments just as they have today . . . and crackers [καὶ ὄψα ἅπερ καὶ οἱ νῦν ἔχουσι . . . καὶ τραγήματα]. (372e1; translation mine)

I like to imagine that Glaucon, having scrutinized the tasty morsel while saying "οἱ νῦν ἔχουσι," takes a bite immediately after he says "τραγήματα," having dipped it into the salsa at the word "ὄψα."

If we could allow *Republic* to become real to us just for a moment—if we could see Plato's beloved older[23] brother with that grinning, winning, smile on his handsome[24] face as he munches provocatively the tasty morsel—we would

23. But see Moors, "Against a Dramatic Date," 12-16.

24. In addition to inspiring poetry, Glaucon seems to be in love; consider his amendment at 468b13-c4. Socrates teases him at 474c8-475a4 because he knows that one particular boy or girl (cf. 468c2-3) presently engrosses Glaucon's erotic passions.

realize that Glaucon does not reject the City of Pigs because it is inadequate to his inordinate passions; he rejects it because he and his kind are not to be found in it. To realize *this* City would require legislating himself out of existence, and that is something he cannot and will not do. *Why should he?* Socrates is describing this City only because the son of Ariston has challenged the son of Sophroniscus and Phaenarete to persuade him that the life of Justice is better *for him*—better for Glaucon—than the life of injustice recommended by Thrasymachus. The reason that the City of Pigs cannot instruct Glaucon is not because it does not contain the fodder he desires: what it lacks is Glaucon himself.

These comments are germane to my second point about χθές, or rather to its second part: an ontological claim whose credibility depends in no small measure on Plato's literary genius. It is Glaucon's rejection of primitivism[25] (in the form of "the City of Pigs," the city with no "beds") that makes the scene down in the Piraeus seem ultra-modern. Just as a playwright uses "a play within a play" to increase the verisimilitude of those actors on the stage who watch it, so also does Plato heighten the modernity of his fictional actors, thereby emphasizing the reality of the χθές, by presenting them as being light-years removed from the primitive if natural conditions that later readers (i.e., us) might be inclined to attribute to those, like Glaucon and the rest, who, after all, lived some twenty-five hundred years before we did.

But rather than belabor the point—pleasant though such labor would be—that it is Plato's literary skill that creates the illusion that his *Republic* took place "yesterday," it is necessary to push on in the direction of the first part: the ontological claim on which the validity of χθές depends. This claim, of course, is that Plato regards the transcendent Idea of the Good—and consequently Justice as well, which, as a result of the Cave, has the distinction between Being and Becoming as the condition of its possibility—as perfectly timeless: what he has discovered about them remains as fresh and new as if it had been discovered only yesterday. Plutarch gives the classic definition of "the classic" when he describes the Parthenon and the other buildings on the Acropolis in his *Life of Pericles* and what he writes there applies perfectly to Plato's dialogues:

> Each one of them, in its beauty, was even then and at once antique; but in the freshness of its vigor it is, even to the present day, recent and newly wrought. Such is the bloom of perpetual newness, as it were, upon these works of his, which makes them ever to look untouched by time, as though the unfaltering breath of an ageless spirit had been infused into them.[26]

It is vain to inquire whether Plato achieved this amazing combination in his dialogues—I take it for granted that every reader will acknowledge *that* he

---

25. A. O. Lovejoy and George Boas, *Primitivism and Related Ideas in Antiquity* (Baltimore, MD: Johns Hopkins University Press, 1935), 155-56. The insightful comment at 156n2 reminds us that Justice does not require a three-class City, only justice does.

26. Plutarch *Pericles* 13.3; translation Bernadotte Perrin.

achieved it; not even the harshest critics of Plato deny that he was a great writer—because of his ontology or his historical circumstances, living as he did when the Parthenon had been built, as it were, only *yesterday*. The two are one and the same. The greatness of Athens, reflected in its glorious achievements, was the necessary precondition for seeing how far short it fell of its own ideals. The only Golden Age for human beings is the moment where the gap, *Kluft* (G. "cleft") or χωρισμός (Gk. "separation;" *Phd.* 67d9) between the achieved reality and the ideal becomes palpable and we are momentarily liberated from an unblinking allegiance to what are, after all, only the shadows of the Cave. The Parthenon, for example—matchless tribute to the Virgin Goddess armed with shield and spear—was both supremely beautiful and hideously ugly:[27] the outward sign of an inward and spiritual disgrace on the part of those who had once triumphed at Marathon and Salamis and all too soon would nuke the neutral island of Melos.[28]

The anachronism involved in claiming that the Athenians used a nuclear weapon against Melos in 416 B.C. is merely apparent. If the Athenians had had our bombs, they would have eventually used them. And, by the same tragic token, if we eventually use our bombs on e.g. Iran, we will be effectively "killing all the men on the island of Melos and selling the women and children into slavery" (Thucydides 5.116.4; Jowett). I might add that should this catastrophe occur, the United States will witness the return appearances of a Euripides to shame us with another *Trojan Women* and likewise of a numerous band of "the hymnists of tyranny" (568b8, translation mine), educated by Thrasymachus, to justify each and every one of our deadly decisions. I will here express my debt to F. M. Cornford: the opening paragraph of his 1933 lecture "Plato's Commonwealth" set me on the road to understanding χθές. Or perhaps it was the

27. As we know from Plutarch's *Pericles* 12.1-2, the money used to construct the great public buildings on the Acropolis was taken (without consulting its other members) from the common treasury of the Delian League, a defensive alliance (against a third Persian invasion) that stood revealed by this action as the Athenian Empire. "But that which brought most delightful adornment to Athens, and the greatest amazement to the rest of mankind; that which alone now testifies for Hellas that her ancient power and splendor, of which so much is told, was no idle fiction—I mean his construction of sacred edifices—this, more than all the public measures of Pericles, his enemies maligned and slandered. They cried out in the assemblies: 'The people has lost its fair fame and is in ill repute because it has removed the public moneys of the Hellenes from Delos into its own keeping, and that seemliest of all excuses which it had to urge against its accusers, to wit, that out of fear of the Barbarians it took the public funds from that sacred isle and was now guarding them in a stronghold, of this Pericles has robbed it. And surely Hellas is insulted with a dire insult and manifestly subjected to tyranny when she sees that, with her own enforced contributions for the war, we are gilding and bedizening our city, which, for all the world like a wanton woman, adds to her wardrobe precious stones and costly statues and temples worth their millions'" (Perrin translation).

28. Melos refused to join the Delian League and was destroyed (see Book V of Thucydides).

second paragraph, which is, in any case, (unlike the first, to which it revealingly refers) short enough to be quoted here in its entirety:

> That description (as perhaps you have guessed) was designed to leave you in doubt whether I was speaking of the history of Athens, from the struggle with Persia, through the golden age of Pericles, to the Peloponnesian War and the early manhood of Plato, or the history of England, from the struggle with Napoleon, through the golden age of Victoria, to the war of 1914 and the early manhood of the younger generation.[29]

It is the uncanny parallels between high Victorian or Edwardian Britain and Plato's Athens that explains why the Anglophone student of the *Republic* cannot take a serious step without James Adam, who published his magisterial commentary in 1902, at her side. In addition to Cornford, W. K. C. Guthrie, R. Hackforth, and E. R. Dodds would witness the whirlwind but they were only able to recognize it because of countless others like Jowett and Burnet, Liddell and Scott.[30]

If the United States of today are less refined and scholarly than Great Britain was a hundred years ago, we are also more democratic and far closer to the Iron Age of tyranny. There is little need, for example, for me to devote chapters or even pages to Thrasymachus: he is unquestionably alive and well (despite the sickness in his soul) and has already proved himself fully capable of advising our leaders in Washington. To be sure, it is thanks to Plato's ontology—his commitment to anchor his vision of Justice in the timeless berth of the eternal Idea—that gives him permission to write "χθές." Unlike Nietzsche, himself the successor of Callicles and Thrasymachus,[31] Plato embraces a metaphysical position that is perfectly consistent with offering us "untimely meditations." But it is only because Thucydides was right—"that such things, or very similar ones will come to be again"—that, at least for this American born in 1955, the conversation in the Piraeus *literally* took place only yesterday. Perhaps it is I who am the metaphor.

---

29. F. M. Cornford, *The Unwritten Philosophy and Other Essays*, edited with an Introductory Memoir by W. K. C. Guthrie (Cambridge, UK: Cambridge University Press, 1967), 47-48.

30. See John Glucker, "Plato in England; The Nineteenth Century and After" in Hermann Funke (ed.), *Utopie und Tradition; Platons Lehre vom Staat in der Moderne*, 149-210. (Würzberg: Königshausen & Neumann, 1987).

31. See the Appendix "Socrates, Callicles, and Nietzsche" in E. R. Dodds, *Plato,* Gorgias; *A Revised Text with Introduction and Commentary* (Oxford: Clarendon Press, 1959), 387-91. Nietzsche actually chose to mention neither, i.e., to conceal his debt. My *Friedrich Wilhelm Nietzsche: The Philosopher of the Second Reich* is forthcoming (2013) from Lexington Books.

Section 3. εἰς Πειραιᾶ

And so it happens that Socrates caught sight of no submarines or aircraft carriers when he went down εἰς Πειραιᾶ ("to Piraeus") nor did he find himself walking alongside any anti-missile installations. None of these had yet been invented in the fifth-century before Christ. But then again, the Spartans were not in possession of any siege equipment that could—as the Romans savagely, and with great technological sophistication, would—batter down the walls of their enemies. Even though the Spartans were as invincible on land as an armor division would be against infantry, the Long Walls that connected Athens to its bustling harbor were, for all intents and purposes, the anti-missile defense system of yesterday. And the sleek, swift, lethal three-banked battleships of mighty Athens—more than two hundred of them—were the carrier battle groups (accompanied by Marine expeditionary task forces) of their day. Down to the Piraeus—the Piraeus where the Navy berths its hellhounds—walked Socrates and Glaucon. The Great Fleet was the basis of Athenian power: the origin of her Empire, or, if you prefer, the Delian League. Kept in constant readiness for battle, these deadly triremes are attended by skilled technicians in their arsenals while, in both peace and war, the burly stevedores unload the known world's wealth on bustling wharves for consumption back up in Athens, only a yesterday away.

The battleships of Athens were not powered by nuclear reactors but neither did they depend on the ever-shifting winds: they were powered by rowers—farmers, fishermen, and myriad other things in peacetime—well-trained enough to turn those long cruisers on an obol and hurtle them, crushing waves to spray, in whatever direction their cybernauts might wish. These rowers were not slaves: they were the proletariat of Athens. The Fleet was the basis of the Athenian Empire but the citizen-rowers were the basis of the Fleet. And so it happened—after Themistocles' victory over the Persians at Salamis—that Athens became the world's first Democracy. It was not the knights on their curried chargers or even the brilliant bronzed hoplites of Marathon—the solid "yokemen" of hill-rolled Attica—that made mighty Athens possible: it was the many, the poor, the working-class. They claimed their share of the power they had freely given the violet-crowned city. Egalitarian democracy and imperial arrogance—not unlike Justice and its opposite—are inextricably linked down in the Piraeus: Piraeus, where the navy lies.

Plato does not tell us—as he did in the *Symposium*—exactly when *this* conversation occurred: when the literal "yesterday" of Socrates' descent took place. But he tells us enough: Justice is discussed in the context and against the backdrop of War.[32] It takes place sometime between the death of Pericles and the tragic departure of the Great Fleet for Sicily: the day that all Athens (except for Socrates, who was too sick from grief to go; see *Theages* 129c8-d2) "went down

32. The importance of this backdrop is ably treated in Jill Frank, "Wages of War: On Judgment in Plato's *Republic*." *Political Theory* 35 no. 4 (August 2007), 443-467.

to the Piraeus" for a much less healthy reason. Yes, it takes place, took place, had taken place, during the Great War:[33] during the first phase (431-421 B.C.) of what Thucydides has taught us to call "the Peloponnesian War."[34] Both Glaucon and his brother Adeimantus have just distinguished themselves in action near Megara (368a3): that's somewhat like saying a British soldier of the First World War has just returned from Ypres or an American sailor has recently been on active duty in the Persian Gulf.[35]

The Navy is the basis of Athens' ability to carry on this War and it is also an indirect cause of it. The justification for the Athenian Empire—as the Athenian Ambassador tells the Spartans in 432 B.C.—is that the strong naturally rule the weak.[36] Spartan fear of Athenian power is, according to Thucydides (1.88), the cause of the War. A more patriotic Athenian might say that it was the Spartan decision—instigated by the conniving Corinthians, smarting over Potidaea and Corcyra—to break the Treaty that caused it. Both are correct. The Navy makes possible the projection of Imperial Power and that power, like any power, brings both benefits and dangers to the one who possesses it. The *Republic* takes place at the epicenter of a great Empire's source of power, a power that will soon be misused with palpably disastrous results in Sicily (*Thg.* 129c8-d2) and, if Socrates is correct, is already being misused. Thrasymachus is the apologist not only for the Athenian Empire but for any crimes it may have or may eventually perpetrate.[37] To this extent, *Republic* is a wartime debate about War and

---

33. Thomas Mann, *The Magic Mountain*, translated by H. T. Lowe-Porter (New York: Alfred A. Knopf, 1927), v: "It takes place—or, rather, deliberately to avoid the present tense, it took place, and had taken place—in the long ago, in the old days, the days of the world before the Great War, in the beginning of which so much began that has scarcely yet left off beginning."

34. For a balanced discussion of the dramatic date of the dialogue, see Guthrie, *History of Greek Philosophy* IV, 438. To the extent that Debra Nails, "The Dramatic Date of Plato's *Republic*," *Classical Journal* 93 no. 4 (April-May 1998), 383-396 argues against a fixed date as distinguished from fragmenting the *Republic* in order to account for its chronological inconsistencies, it is useful. More dogmatic claims have recently been advanced by Lampert, *How Philosophy Became Socratic*, 405-11 who rests them on identifying "the goddess" as Bendis and the research of Christopher Planeaux, "The Date of Bendis' Entry into Attica," *Classical Journal* 96 no. 2 (December 2000-January 2001), 165-192.

35. See Thucydides 2.31.3 where Athenian invasions of Megara occur every year (κατὰ ἔτος).

36. Thucydides 1.72.2 (Dent): "It follows that it was not a very wonderful action, or contrary to the common practice of mankind, if we did accept an empire that was offered to us, and refused to give it up under the pressure of three of the strongest motives, fear, honor, and interest. And it was not we who set the example, for it has always been the law that the weaker should be subject to the stronger."

37. 351a7-b5: "'I wish, Thrasymachus, to consider it in some such fashion as this. A city, you would say, may be unjust and try to enslave other cities unjustly, have them enslaved and hold many of them in subjection.' 'Certainly,' he said; 'and this is what the best state will chiefly do, the state whose injustice is most complete.'"

Plato requires his readers to understand that it is the world of Thucydides that stands outside but in immediate juxtaposition with his own text (see Introduction). In short: *Republic* is a discussion of the use and abuse of power in a place of great power. In fact, it is a discussion of perfect Justice in a setting that is, for all intents and purposes, perfectly unjust or at least on the verge of becoming so.

Plato's decision to bring his discussion of Justice εἰς Πειραιᾶ raises the crucial question: how can we hope to discover justice in an unjust city? To which I respond: how can we discover that we don't know what justice is—the precondition of our searching for it[38]—in any other kind of place? We are all born in the Cave: we generally believe that "justice" is what Thrasymachus says that it is: whatever version of justice works to the advantage of the most powerful people in our native land. But something extraordinary happened in the Goddess of Wisdom's[39] storied city in the years after Marathon. It was precisely the gap, indeed the yawning abyss, between Athenian ideals and Athenian practice—two opposite things eternally conjoined notwithstanding in Athena's temple built from marble and from gold—that made Platonism possible. This doesn't mean that the truths expressed by Plato are merely relative to the historical conditions that actually engendered them. It means that fifth-century Athens was an excellent place in which to discover the timeless truth, not only in philosophy—as demonstrated by Socrates and Plato—but also in the achievements of Phidias and Pericles, of Xenophon, Thucydides, Aristophanes, Sophocles, Euripides, and Aeschylus. Naturally, one cannot take a step in the direction of contextualizing the *Republic* without grim-eyed Thucydides. But seeing Plato in relation to his time by means of Thucydides (and many others) does not in any

38. This crucial insight is introduced with utmost clarity (as befits its crucial importance for understanding the first thing about philosophy) after Alcibiades admits he can name no one who *taught* him justice in *Alc.1* 109e1-110c11 (Hutchinson): "*Alcibiades*: Don't you think I might know about justice and injustice in some other way? *Socrates*: Yes, you might—if you found it out. *Alcibiades*: Well, don't you think I might find it out? *Socrates*: Yes, of course—if you investigate the matter. *Alcibiades*: And don't you think I might investigate it? *Socrates*: Yes, I do—if you thought you didn't know." The trap into which Alcibiades—and every honest person—falls at *Alc.1* 106d4-5 (the far-reaching implications of the admission are consummated between *Alc.1* 109e1-110c11) is thus the basis for understanding (1) Socratic Ignorance, (2) Plato the Teacher (note the sublime faith of "Yes, of course—if you investigate the matter") and (3) fifth-century Athens. In the Golden Age of Pericles, no small number of Athenians realized that they did not know what justice really is. Alcibiades, of course, uses what he learned in the *Protagoras* (*Prt.* 327e3-328a1) to wiggle out of this salutary trap (*Alc.1* 111a1-4).

39. Or, to speak as an Athenian, simply: "the Goddess" (LSJ, θεός II; cf. *Ti.* 21a2). The fact that we have only the word of the Thracian Thrasymachus for identifying Socrates' "the Goddess" of 327a2 with the Thracian Bendis (354a10-11) has not received the critical attention it deserves; for a partial exception, see Lampert, *How Philosophy Became Socratic*, 243. The significance of Athena for understanding Athens has likewise received inadequate attention. A good place to begin the process of revision is Victoria Wohl, *Love Among the Ruins: The Erotics of Democracy in Classical Athens* (Princeton, NJ: Princeton University Press, 2002); see 33, 45, 83, and 188-203.

way diminish the timeless validity of his teaching. Both Thucydides and Plato aim to defeat what we now call "historicism": both aimed to create, and indeed succeeded in creating, a κτῆμά ἐς αἰεὶ ("a possession [sent forth] into forever").

> Perhaps for listeners, the non-mythic aspect of my histories is seeming rather less than pleasant. But for such of those who will wish to see clearly both the past and even the future—for someday, in accordance with the way of men, the near equivalent to things like these will come to be again—it will be enough to judge them useful. As a possession into eternity rather than as a prize-winner to hear today is it composed.[40]

Despite the sweet perfection of the other dialogues—either *singulatim* or in σύνοψις ("comprehensive survey" at 537c2)—it is the *Republic* that is and will forever remain Plato's κτῆμά ἐς αἰεὶ.

Not that we should we forget a host of lesser luminaries. In this section, for example, I have taken Isocrates[41] as my model. In the *Panegyricus*, he states his intention "to freshly revisit ancient deeds and to speak in classic style of things that have but recently occurred."[42] And without the orator Lysias (*Against Eratosthenes* 12 and 19), himself a member of the fictional audience down in the Piraeus, we would not know that his father Cephalus—in whose beautiful home the *Republic* takes place—was a weapons manufacturer, enriched by the War.

Section 4. μετὰ Γλαύκωνος

Like Cephalus (and Thrasymachus), Leo Strauss was not a native of the city where he made his mark. His influence has made it both easier and more difficult to see *Republic* for what it is, and that in three ways: (1) he makes it easier because he taught us how to read Plato: with careful attention to dramatic details, skepticism about developmentalism, and a willingness to take seriously dialogues rejected as spurious.[43] He (2) makes it more difficult because he delivers Plato over into the hands of Plato's enemies, primarily Nietzsche.[44] But (3) as I argued in the previous section (i.e., an unjust context is the necessary precondition for discovering justice), a deeply flawed reading of Plato's *Republic* is not without its uses. On balance then—and by a two-thirds majority—Strauss has made it easier to understand the *Republic*. To refute every false thing Strauss

40. Thucydides, 1.22.4 (translation mine).

41. The remarkable longevity of Isocrates is foundation upon which Gibbon constructs one of his Golden Paragraphs (in chapter 40), the one he devotes to fifth-century Athens on the occasion of Justinian's decision to close the schools of Athens.

42. Isocrates, *Panegyricus* 4.7, translation mine.

43. For developmentalism, see Strauss, *Classical Political Rationalism*, 154; for Strauss and the Platonic *dubia*, see Altman, *German Stranger*, 490n219.

44. Who is the fourth of "the four chief sources on which we depend if we wish to understand the thought of Socrates" (Strauss, *Classical Political Rationalism*, 103; cf. 177)? See my "Leo Strauss and the *Euthydemus*," 377n101.

says about it gives him far too much power: I will content myself to wrestle at close quarters (*Alc. 1* 107e5-6) with him and his students on only one: the significance of the words "μετὰ Γλαύκωνος" ("with Glaucon").

In Book V, Glaucon interrupts Socrates in order to demand an account of how the City could be realized. Strauss describes Glaucon's interruption at 471c3-e4 as follows:

> Socrates is not for long allowed to escape from his awesome duty to answer the question of the possibility of the just city. The manly or rather spirited Glaucon compels him to face that question. Perhaps we should say that by apparently escaping to the subject of war—a subject both easier in itself and more attractive to Glaucon than the communism regarding women and children—yet treating that subject according to the stern demands of justice and thus depriving it of much of its attractiveness, he compels Glaucon to compel him to return to the fundamental question.[45]

This interpretation of Glaucon's interruption is closely connected to Strauss's overall characterization of Glaucon as being spirited (θυμοειδής) and interested in war. Not only is this characterization picked up by other Straussians (like Seth Benardete[46] and Allan Bloom[47]) but is also found before Strauss in traditional commentators like James Adam.[48] A closer look at Glaucon's interruption at 471c4 serves as a starting-point for a re-evaluation of the view that Glaucon is best characterized as the personification of θυμός, "courage and erotic desire,"[49] or indeed of anything other than himself.[50]

---

45. Leo Strauss, *The City and Man* (Chicago, IL: University of Chicago Press, 1964), 118. The words "manly or rather spirited" are revealing: Socrates calls Glaucon the first but not the second at 357a3.

46. Seth Benardete, *Socrates' Second Sailing* (Chicago, IL: University of Chicago Press, 1989), 120-23. Glaucon's nature is here described (123) as being "divided apparently equally between the thumoeidetic and the erotic." He also writes there: "Glaucon's demand that the good city in speech be realized measures exactly the degree to which he has not understood *The Republic.*"

47. See the comments on Glaucon's interruption in "Interpretive Essay," Allan Bloom, *The Republic of Plato* (New York: Basic Books, 1968), at 388: "although Socrates provides some satisfactions to be derived from war for Glaucon's erotic and warlike temper, the general intention is to temper and humanize war." He describes Glaucon himself in more detail on 375: "surely his specific form of spiritedness leads him off to war in pursuit of satisfaction of desire for pleasure and victory." Indeed Bloom's characterization of Glaucon emphasizes desire (345-48). Moreover, his expression for the appetitive part of the soul is "the desiring part" (375).

48. Adam, *Republic of Plato*, 1.100 on 372d: "Glaucon, who is nothing if not θυμοειδής (Introd. #2)." It is a pity that we do not have the "Introduction" to which Adam here refers.

49. Strauss, *Classical Political Rationalism*, 171.

50. Glaucon is characterized in more flattering but equally one-sided terms by C. D. C. Reeve, *Philosopher-Kings* (Princeton, NJ: Princeton University Press, 1988) who

The suggestion that Glaucon finds the subject of war attractive puts Strauss and the Straussians[51] in the awkward position of needing to find a plausible reason why Glaucon would interrupt the discussion of a topic he finds attractive. Although Strauss's explanation[52] of this (i.e., that by discussing war "according to the stern demands of justice" Socrates deprives it of much of its attractiveness and thereby compels Glaucon to change the subject) is false, I do think that Strauss is on the right track (albeit for the wrong reasons) when he suggests that Socrates in some sense "compels Glaucon to compel him" to abandon the subject of war. I will show that there are at least three distinct ways in which Socrates could be said to provoke Glaucon's interruption.

The first provocation is inherent in the structure of the discussion of the Second Wave of Paradox. To begin with, Socrates explicitly skirts the issue of the possibility of implementing his proposals in the playful passage between 457e7 and 458b7. He does so after stating, over Glaucon's objection, that in the case of this Second Wave of Paradox, the possibility of putting his proposals into practice will be the chief topic of contention as opposed to the utility of those proposals (457d6-9). This deliberate postponement by Socrates is further emphasized by the fact that the First Wave of Paradox is discussed possibility first and utility second whereas this order is reversed in the case of the Second Wave. Socrates is deliberately saving what he regards as the most controversial subject for last. Although Glaucon astutely thinks the utility of the Second Wave

---

maintains that Glaucon (and Adeimantus) are to be understood as "philosophic men" (41) in contrast with "honor lovers" and "money-makers," and he fits all of the interlocutors of the *Republic* into this scheme (35). He also connects this typology to the tripartite soul, identifying Glaucon and Adimantus with reason (36) as opposed to "aspiration" (his translation for θυμός) personified by Thrasymachus. With Reeve for reason, Bernadette for θυμός, and Bloom (?) for desire, it would seem that the critics have covered all the bases looking for a way to fit poor Glaucon into the tripartite structure of the soul. Leon Craig, *The War Lover* (Toronto: University of Toronto Press, 1994) comes close to splitting the difference between two different soul-characterizations (reason and θυμός) with his identification of Glaucon as an isocratic timocrat (77 and 112f.) Perhaps the first effort to fit the interlocutors of *Republic* into a scheme of cities (and certainly the inspiration for Craig's approach) was made by Strauss, *City and Man*, 85 where he suggests that Glaucon may be identified with the aristocracy and states that he and Adimantus "belong at the very least to timocracy." One finds oneself yearning for the days when a scholar like Gottfried Stallbaum, *Platonis Opera Omnia* (Gotha: Hennings, Stallbaum 1858-1859), 3.1, cxviii, was satisfied with describing Glaucon (in comparison with Adimantus) in the following terms (translation mine): "even more than in Adeimantus, there is present in Glaucon a quickness, a greater force of mind, and vehemence" and letting it go at that. In fact, Glaucon is best understood as Plato's favorite among his two beloved elder brothers.

51. Benardete, *Second Sailing*, 120: "Glaucon becomes so impatient with Socrates' description of the restrained military practices of the city that he jumps over the issue of the possibility of communism to that of the regime." Cf. Bloom, *Republic of Plato*, 388-89.

52. Followed (rather slavishly, it seems to me) by Bloom and Benardete.

is more debatable than Socrates (457e1), there is no reason to think that Glaucon is not in agreement with Socrates from the start that the possibility of these proposals is a provocative and highly debatable subject and therefore one that he is eager to hear discussed.

In addition to (1) the deliberately provocative structure of the discussion of the Second Wave is (2) a more deliberate provocation at 466d5-7. Socrates speaks here as though the utility of his proposals has been sufficiently elucidated and he now must turn his attention to the possibility of such a community coming about. It is clear that Glaucon welcomes the transition to this topic (466d8) for he states that he was about to remind Socrates to discuss it. But Socrates, instead of doing so, launches into the subject of war with no attempt to prove that such a subject is anything more than a complete non sequitur. Such a non sequitur is all the more noteworthy because it is Socrates and not Glaucon who has just said that the logical topic to discuss next is the possibility of Socrates' proposals coming into being. And finally it is (3) the *manner* in which Socrates describes the City at war that constitutes the third and most revealing provocation for Glaucon to compel Socrates to return to the question of the possibility of the city. This provocation (if indeed it is only a single provocation and not several) will require more attention than the two already mentioned.

The point to be realized at the outset is that the discussion of war between Socrates and Glaucon takes place during an actual war (section §3). This is important because the specific proposals that Socrates makes about the City's conduct of war are closely connected with several important events of that actual War. In fact, the rules and regulations concerning warfare proposed by Socrates between 469b5 and 471c2 would, if actually put into practice, alter the Peloponnesian War beyond recognition, to say the very least.[53] To begin with, if the proposals of Socrates became realities, the Peloponnesian War would no longer be a "war" at all: as a conflict between Greeks, it would become, according to the Socratic argument (470b4-d2), merely a species of what he calls "faction." This change would not simply be semantic: it is the horrors of the Peloponnesian War, legislated out of existence by Socrates in the passage which immediately precedes Glaucon's interruption at 471c4, that give Glaucon a number of excellent reasons for wishing to see the City realized.

A particularly vivid example of such horrors is the fact that if the City were both possible and realized, it would eliminate what was certainly the most signal act[54] of injustice committed by Athens during the war: the destruction of Melos

53. Cf. what would be left of Homer's *Iliad* if the strictures of Socrates at 390e4-391a2 were applied to it. It is also noteworthy that none of the proposals made by Socrates between 469b5 and Glaucon's interruption at 471c4 have any clear connection with the Second Wave of Paradox.

54. For an ancient *testimonium* to the validity of this characterization, see Xenophon *Hellenica* 2.2.3.

in 416 B.C.[55] Two passages, one at 469b8-c1 and the other immediately before Glaucon's interruption (471a9-b5), make it clear that the enslavement of women and children would be eliminated if the City could be realized. I suggest that Glaucon, like Euripides in *The Trojan Women*, viewed the events on Melos (or the contemplation of similar actions in the case of Mytilene) as a tragedy for Athens and craved the realization of the City as an anodyne.

But comedy is even more instructive than tragedy for gaining a fuller understanding of Glaucon's interruption at 471c4: anti-war sentiment in Athens during the war is a central theme of many of the earlier comedies of Aristophanes. Especially among the noble families of Athens who owned extensive ancestral properties in Attica, the annual depredations of the Spartan invaders were a strong incentive to try to achieve peace. The Long Walls that connected Athens to the Piraeus protected the city and "the sinews of war" from the Spartans: the rest of Attica hardly fared as well. Although there is no direct evidence that Ariston and his sons (i.e., Glaucon, Adeimantus, and Plato himself) were anti-war, they were certainly nobles and doubtless landowners.[56] (In this context, it should be noted that although he never speaks, the son of Nicias himself[57] is present in the home of Cephalus.) It is not out of place to wonder how the ancestral property of Plato's family fared during the yearly invasions of Attica during the Peloponnesian War: a careful reading of Book V suggests that this was a crucial consideration for Glaucon.[58]

This line of thought is designed to prepare the reader for an investigation of Socrates' curious emphasis on the fact that if the City were realized, Greeks

---

55. Involved as it is with the thorny question of the dialogue's *exact* dramatic date, this line of argument runs the risk of becoming highly complex. Some critics (e.g. Guthrie, *History of Greek Philosophy* IV, 437-38; cf. Nails, *People of Plato*, 324-26) have argued for a dramatic date after 416, which would allow us to believe that Socrates has Melos in mind. What seems obvious is that Plato intends *the reader* to have Melos in mind while reading 471a11-b1 (especially the words ἀλλ' ὀλίγους ἀεὶ ἐχθροὺς τοὺς αἰτίους τῆς διαφορᾶς at 471b1). For those passionate about historical verisimilitude in Plato's dialogues, I would suggest that whether or not the events on Melos have occurred at the time of the conversation, the Mytilene Debate has already raised the possibility of such horrors. It bears repeating that Thrasymachus approves of such Athenian policies at 351b1-5.

56. Diogenes Laertius, *Lives of Eminent Philosophers* 3.1.

57. See 327c2. Niceratus is also mentioned in *La.* 200d1. Indeed *Laches* shows that Socrates was a friend of the well-known Athenian conservative and peacemaker. We can certainly infer that Glaucon is familiar with the arguments both for and against a continuation of the war. The fact that Glaucon distinguished himself περὶ τὴν Μεγαροῖ μάχην (368a3) should not be taken to prove that he could not be anti-war. The career of Siegfried Sassoon is a notable example of how one can be both anti-war and a war-hero.

58. We know from *Lives of Eminent Philosophers* 3.6 that Plato was of the deme Collytus, which was one of the urban demes—see David Whitehead, *The Demes of Attica* (Princeton, NJ: Princeton University Press), 1986—but this is no reason to doubt that his family, on both father's and mother's sides, owned extensive properties *outside* the walls of Athens.

would no longer burn the habitations and devastate the lands of their fellow Greeks (470a5-b1).[59] If Glaucon's family had been directly affected by the failure of the Spartans to conduct themselves "according to the stern demands of justice" (Strauss), it would constitute another and eminently human explanation of why he would want Socrates to show how the City could be realized. Such an explanation would constitute a long step toward seeing Glaucon as a real person (as he undoubtedly was to his brother Plato)[60] rather than as a personification of θυμός or indeed anything else.

Immediately after proscribing the practice of using captured weapons as dedicatory offerings (another clear reference to the Peloponnesian War),[61] Socrates brings up the matter of land and houses without any explanation of how this topic is connected with what he has just been discussing. Indeed its only connection with what precedes it is that both are practices witnessed during the Peloponnesian War that Socrates is proscribing for the City. He simply raises the question without stating any position in regard to it:

> "And in the matter of devastating the land of the Greeks and burning their houses, how will your soldiers deal with their enemies?" (470a5-7)

Glaucon responds that he would gladly hear Socrates' views on this question (470a8), which is certainly not surprising if we entertain that hypothesis that, as a member of a land-owning family of Attica, he is personally interested in the question. At any rate, he does not choose this moment to interrupt Socrates, as he might well have done given the opening provided by yet another Socratic non sequitur. His interest in the topic allows Socrates to continue:

> "In my view," said I, "they ought to do neither, but confine themselves to taking away the annual harvest. Shall I tell you why?" (470a9-b2)

59. Cf. Thucydides 2.23. On Plato's most general expression for laying waste the countryside (γῆν τέμνειν), which he uses at 471c1-2, see LSJ on τέμνειν (1775, IV.3; emphasis mine): "lay waste the country *by felling the fruit tress,* cutting the corn, etc." This expression is also used by Thucydides (see reference in LSJ).

60. The only explicit attempt to deny this self-evident proposition that I can discover is in Craig, *War Lover*, 367n1: "The only prudent assumption is that the characters portrayed in the dialogue (and whose relationship to Plato's actual brothers is unknown and unknowable) first of all serve his literary, that is, his politico-philosophical purpose as perfectly as he was capable of making them." Such a premise, I suppose, is Craig's justification (and presumably the justification of the other critics as well) for portraying Glaucon as a one-dimensional personification of, e.g., one part of the tripartite soul. Against this should be considered the "considerable amount of family pride" that Guthrie, *History of Greek Philosophy* IV, 11 perceptively discerns in Plato.

61. Notably the Spartan shields captured on Sphacteria in 425 B.C; see the *Knights* of Aristophanes.

When Glaucon responds in the affirmative, Socrates launches into an elaborate proof of this proposal.

Indeed it is important to note that some of the most important statements Socrates makes about the conduct of war are presented in the form of an argument to validate the proposition that Greeks should not devastate the lands of Greeks.[62] It is within this argument, for example, that Socrates renames conflicts between Greek cities "factions," refusing to call them wars (470c7-d2).[63] The fact that such conflicts exist is proof that Greece is suffering from a disease (470d1).[64] It is here that Socrates (or should we say Glaucon?) states for the first time that the City is Greek (470e4-5) and therefore "good and gentle" (470e6). Given the realities of the Peloponnesian War, such comments had more than a little irony and black humor to them. I would suggest that it is partly with these devices that Socrates "compels Glaucon to compel him to return to the fundamental question."

> "Will they not then regard any difference with Greeks who are their own people as a form of faction and refuse even to speak of it as war?" (471a1-2)

Such a question, given the context of the grim war then taking place, is tantamount to giving a description of a tasty dinner to a band of starving men. In all likelihood, all of the Athenians in the room are veterans; certainly Socrates, Glaucon and Adeimantus[65] are. Socrates is blithely legislating out of existence a War that is presently threatening their actual lives.[66] One wonders how the following statement would have affected Niceratus the son of Nicias:[67]

---

62. This argument (470b4-471c2) immediately precedes Glaucon's interruption.

63. καὶ στάσιν τὴν τοιαύτην ἔχθραν κλητέον is the exact expression used. Thucydides obviously calls it τὸν πόλεμον (1.1) as all his contemporaries did.

64. Note that Socrates says this in a present general conditional sentence: ὅταν τι τοιοῦτον δρῶσιν being the protasis. It will remain for Glaucon to make it explicit that such things are presently occurring in Greece. Socrates is elaborating his points in a general and (gallingly) theoretical style. As Smythe's *Greek Grammar* reports (#2337): "the conclusion holds true of any time or of all time." I imagine contemporaries would have found the κτῆμά ἐς αἰεὶ motif in Thucydides galling as well: does it not denigrate our recent sufferings to have them described in such general terms?

65. A military exploit of the brothers is mentioned in *Republic* itself at 368a3. The high-points of Socrates' military career are well known (see for example *Ap.* 28e1-3).

66. Presumably a blast of the trumpet could call them to arms at any moment. I would imagine that most of these young men were wealthy enough to serve in the cavalry; cf. 467d10-e4. See also Mary Renault, *The Last of the Wine* (New York: Pantheon Books, 1956). One wonders how many of them preferred notwithstanding to fight *as hoplites* when the expedition of 415 B.C. left for Sicily.

67. His father was the leader of the anti-war party and the architect of the Peace of Nicias in 421 B.C. A. E. Taylor, *Plato: The Man and his Work*, third edition (London: Methuen, 1929), 263 argued that 422-421 is the most likely dramatic date for the dialogue.

> "And they will conduct their quarrels always looking forward to reconciliation?" (471a4)

Socrates is here giving voice to the views of conservatives like Nicias for whom the war was a disastrous mistake because they simply did not feel implacable enmity toward their Spartan foes. Indeed Nicias himself must have been trusting in something like following when he surrendered in Sicily;[68] not as a chimerical proposal of a philosophical stargazer but as a practical political reality:

> "They will correct them, then, for their own good, not chastising them with a view of their enslavement or their destruction, but acting as correctors, not as enemies." (471a6-7)

It is at this point that Socrates returns the proposition he set out to prove at 470a9-b2. Note the relentless repetition with which Socrates reminds these young men not only of their city's crimes on Melos, but (perhaps more poignantly) of the scenes of their childhood: of the ruined farms of Attica and the trees of Acharnae they will climb no more:

> "They will not, being Greeks, ravage Greek territory nor burn habitations, and they will not admit that in any city all the population are their enemies, men, women, and children, but will say that only a few at any time are their foes, those, namely, who are to blame for the quarrel. And on these considerations they will not be willing to lay waste the soil, since the majority are their friends, nor to destroy the houses, but will carry the conflict only to the point of compelling the guilty to do justice by the pressure of the suffering of the innocent."[69]

That Glaucon's brother is accustomed to spending time in rural Attica is made explicit in Book VIII (at 563d1-2) where he bears witness to the deteriorated conditions then prevailing in the countryside. Is it simply democracy (as the context requires us to believe) that has created the conditions he has experienced

---

68. Thucydides 7.86. Plutarch says that Socrates predicted the expedition would lead to the destruction of Athens (*Life of Nicias* 13.6); this indicates little more than that Plutarch regarded *Theages* as genuine.

69. 471a9-b5. The words οἱ αἴτιοι ἀναγκασθῶσιν ὑπὸ τῶν ἀναιτίων ἀλγούντων δοῦναι δίκην (471b4-5) are, as I have already suggested, more reminiscent of Mytilene (see Thucydides 3.48, especially the distinction οὓς μὲν . . . τοὺς δ' ἄλλους than of Melos, although Socrates' earlier expression αλλ' ὀλίγους (471b1) could be compared to Thucydides 5.84. The notion of compelling the guilty to do the right thing *by the suffering of innocents* really doesn't fit either Melos or Mytilene particularly well. Perhaps we could take these general words to apply to the devastation of Attica; they seem to fit this situation best. In other words, Nicias and the anti-war landowners of Attica (the suffering innocents) can by vote or force (compel) Cleon and the democrats (the guilty) to make peace with Sparta (the right or just thing). But the expression "paying the penalty" (δοῦναι δίκην) seems most applicable to Mytilene.

in the country and of which Socrates himself is evidently aware?[70] If, as seems likely, the Spartans had wrought havoc with the ancestral properties of Glaucon's family in Attica, and if, as also seems probable, the well-informed Socrates (*Tht.* 144c5-8) was aware of the extent of that havoc, the emphasis that Socrates places on the devastation of fields and habitations would become a third and more poignant provocation for Glaucon to compel Socrates to show how the City could be realized.

Glaucon's response to this speech is important because it is the first time that either he or Socrates refers to the fact that the conduct that Socrates is proscribing is presently being practiced by Greeks against each other. In other words, it is the only explicit reference to the fact of the Peloponnesian War in the discussion of conduct during war.

> "I," he said, "agree that our citizens ought to deal with their Greek opponents on this wise, while treating barbarians as Greeks now treat Greeks."[71]

As far as Glaucon (and many commentators)[72] is concerned, the most important point being made by Socrates is his distinction between Greeks and barbarians. For Socrates, however, this distinction is only a premise in his lengthy argument that the soldiers of the City would not devastate the lands of Greeks and burn their houses, the proposition he first announced at 470a5-6. And thus, for the *fourth* time (470a5-6, 471a9-10, 471b2-3, and now at 471c1-2), Socrates reminds Glaucon that his real proposal *hits closer to home* than the comparatively abstract premise (i.e., that Greeks should not treat Greeks the way that they would treat barbarians) he has used to defend it:

> "Shall we lay down this law also, then, for our guardians, that they are not to lay waste the land or burn the houses?" (471c1-2)

---

70. Cf. the speech of Burgundy in Act V of *Henry V* which describes the effects of the Hundred Years War on France in somewhat similar terms (V.ii.59): "but grow like savages, as solders will." As for the speculative "trees of Acharnae" mentioned above, one might cite Sonnet 73.4: "Bare ruined choirs where late the sweet bird sang."

71. 471b6-8. ὡς νῦν οἱ Ἕλληνες πρὸς ἀλλήλους being the key expression and νῦν ("now") the key word (471b8). I cannot agree with Adam, *Republic of Plato*, who is, alas, confined to *asserting* at 1.325: "In any case "νῦν" should no doubt be referred to the time when Plato wrote these words, and not to the date of action of the dialogue. See also 'Introd.' #4." Once again, one has cause to lament the missing Introduction. We have already seen that Glaucon uses the word νῦν at 372e1 (section §2).

72. The Straussians pay a great deal of attention to the distinction made between Greek and barbarian, even though Strauss himself does not. See especially Bloom, *Republic of Plato*, 388-89: "At this point Socrates accepts the Greek, or conventional, distinction between Greek and barbarian. One should not, however, assume that he is limited by this horizon; he is speaking to Glaucon who is subject to such limitations." This doesn't seem to fit very well with Bloom's distinction—following Strauss, *City and Man*, 85-91—between Adeimantus, who relies on received opinion or convention, and Glaucon, who bases his argument on nature (342).

This is the speech of Socrates that immediately precedes Glaucon's interruption.

It seems to me that Strauss and the Straussians are completely off the mark when they suggest that Glaucon would find the subject of warfare more attractive if Socrates were not regulating it. This interpretation rests on a one-sided characterization of Glaucon as a "thumoeidetic man" who is therefore impatient with Socrates' treatment of warfare. Socrates is, to be sure, legislating out of existence many of the horrors of war. By never acknowledging that it is a specific War—the War that Glaucon and his contemporaries knew all too well—Strauss and the Straussians are backed into the corner of needing to find an explanation of why "the war-lover" doesn't want to talk about war any more. There is no reason to believe that Glaucon would find a description of the actual Peloponnesian War (a conversation with Thucydides, for example) to be a more attractive topic than the present conversation led by Socrates. Had he done so, however, he would not have had far to go to find one: the Peloponnesian War was doubtless the theme of many private conversations that neither Plato nor Thucydides nor anyone else have recorded for us.

In response to Strauss, I have shown that attention must be paid to the connection between the realization of the City and the events of the Peloponnesian War. The fact that Strauss himself does not do so is all the more unfortunate given that his book *The City and Man* includes a chapter on Thucydides. The important point to grasp is that if the City is possible and could be realized, the Peloponnesian War would ipso facto cease to exist. This gives Glaucon several important incentives to wish the City realized and thus to compel Socrates to discuss its possibility. To make some of these explicit: (1) Glaucon (like Nicias) may simply wish to see the end of the War in general, (2) Glaucon (like Euripides) may be one of those who will be (or was) appalled by the events on Melos (or the near miss earlier on Mytilene) and is looking for a way to escape such situations, and (3) Glaucon's sense of personal loss resulting from the Spartan depredations of Attica may have made Socrates' pronouncements about the devastation of farms and fields unbearably painful for him and thus have caused him not only to want to change the subject but to learn how to eliminate the conditions that have caused such losses to his city and himself. Any one of these possibilities—or all of them taken together—along with the structure of the Second Wave and the comment at 466d4-6, show that Socrates *provokes* Glaucon's interruption.

Indeed, the foregoing remarks might well be taken to mean that it is solely the provocations of Socrates that force Glaucon's interruption at 471c4. Socrates' role is indisputably important. Nevertheless it is Glaucon's interruption and his alone. Plato has gone out of his way to show how important this interruption is in *Timaeus* where there is no Glaucon to move the conversation forward toward the Idea of the Good.[73] Even more perhaps than Glaucon's next interruption at 506d1 (an interruption which is directly and explicitly connected to the

73. The summary of the previous day's discussion at *Ti.* 17c1-19b2 does not include the Third Wave of Paradox or, indeed, the discussion of the conduct of the War.

Idea of the Good), the interruption at 471c4—leading as it does to the subject of philosophy *via* the Third Wave of Paradox—takes us to the heart of Plato's *Republic.* Perhaps the greatest paradox involved here is that Glaucon's attempt to see the City made *visible* (i.e., both possible and actual) leads to a discussion of the realm of the purely *intelligible*; that Glaucon's pursuit of the City Immanent leads the conversation to the Idea Transcendent. Are we to explain this solely by showing the dexterity of Socrates in leading a philosophically limited Glaucon to the broad open spaces of Platonism?

To answer such a question would require on the spot a thorough investigation of the entire dialogue, and that is far beyond the scope of this section. Even an investigation of Glaucon's role in *Republic* is far too broad a topic at this point because without Glaucon, there would have been nothing except Book I: it seems clear that Plato wished to emphasize the point that Glaucon's question at the beginning of Book II is the only reason why the dialogue does not end with Book I. Indeed Plato gives us reason to believe that without his brother, there may not even have been that: It is Glaucon, using the verbal adjective μενετέον, who decides that "it is necessary to remain" down in the Piraeus at 328b2. Glaucon interrupts Socrates at 471c3 because of the City; as I showed in section §2 (on "the City of Pigs" at 372c3), he has already interrupted Socrates for the sake of the Man: i.e., for the sake of himself. He interrupts Socrates in Book V because he seeks to bridge the gap between the City, which Socrates has been describing at war, and Athens, the city of his birth, which is also at War. In so doing, he seeks *not so much the realization of the City as the end of the War.* It is the injustices committed and suffered by Athens during that war, systematically legislated out of existence by Socrates, that make Glaucon yearn for the realization of the City.

Glaucon (and the rest of the men in the room) are none other than the οἱ νῦν to whom he refers at 372e1:

> "They must recline on couches, I presume, if they are not to be uncomfortable, and dine from tables with condiments just as they have today [οἱ νῦν] and crackers." (327d7-9; Shorey modified)

They are not "reclined on rustic beds strewed with bryony and myrtle"[74] nor can they identify with those who are;[75] they are well-born Athenian gentlemen and citizen-soldiers whose city is rich, powerful, and presently at War, apparently in an effort keep itself so. The war is filled with horrors, and their city has committed and suffered many injustices; it will suffer and commit many more. Can they themselves, as individual men, practice justice? Do they even seek to do so?

74. 372b5; I have let stand one of Shorey's errors: there are no *beds*—they are merely reclining—in the City of Pigs.

75. Although he ignores 372b7-8, Allan Silverman, *The Dialectic of Essence: A Study of Plato's Metaphysics* (Princeton, NJ: Princeton University Press, 2002), 69 is illuminating on "the city of pigs."

This is the question that keeps them talking all through the night. This is the question that Socrates tries to persuade them to answer "yes!" This is the immortal question that was raised only because once upon a time a young man named Glaucon so desperately needed it answered.

Glaucon's apparent desire for relishes is really an expression of the sincerity of his attempt to become a just human being, even now, even while living in an unjust city. Thrasymachus, the foreign sycophant, praises Athens for its crimes; Glaucon, the native-born patriot and war-hero, recoils in horror from the crimes his city has committed even while mourning the injuries both he and it have suffered. It is because of his secret tears that Glaucon yearns, not just for himself, but also for Athens, to see how the City could be realized. If there is no going back to bryony and myrtle, not even a way to get back to the cherished country scenes of childhood, there may yet be a road that doesn't lead to Melos and the quarries of Syracuse.

Knowing that Athens did not find that road makes Glaucon all the more beautiful and good because he searched for it. The topic he wishes to discuss is simply the right conduct of his life, a topic than which no other is more important (336e7, 344e1-3, and 352d6-7). Applying the lessons he learns from Socrates down in the Piraeus may well be difficult. There would, however, have been no lessons taught there at all if Glaucon the son of Ariston had not been intent on applying them. In his immortal *Republic*, Plato shows his older brother as the kind of student every teacher would want: an intelligent and sensitive student, a questioner, and above all, the kind of human being who will not leave the lessons learned at the classroom door.

Section 5. τοῦ Ἀρίστωνος

Taken in isolation, the fifth and last of "the First Words of Plato's Πολιτεία" are ambiguous. It is not just because of Adeimantus that Glaucon isn't the only τοῦ Ἀρίστωνος ("[son of] Ariston") with whom we must reckon: it is now time to speak of Ariston's third, most famous, and yet also most elusive son: Plato. It has become a commonplace that we know nothing of Plato's own thoughts through his dialogues.[76] As a corrective to the old dispensation when Plato was taken to believe everything that one of his main characters said, this is without doubt salutary. But we now have entered a phase where the opposite extreme has become equally misleading: where Plato has become too detached from Socrates. For the most part, I will conform to the current conventions and analyze the *Republic* using "Socrates" as the active agent. But I reserve the right to speak of Plato's agency as well. *Republic* is, after all, his book; indeed, it is his masterpiece: the book he lives by. Moreover, *this* book is about Plato: *Plato the Teacher*.

76. Strauss, *Classical Political Rationalism*, 51-52.

We know more about Plato than we think we do. The two most important things we know about him—apart from (1) his writings—are that (2) he was a teacher and (3) that his real name was Aristocles the son of Ariston.[77] Since *Plato the Teacher* is an attempt to recover from "(1)" a few secrets pertaining to "(2)," it is the relationship between "Plato" and "Aristocles" that I will discuss here. To begin then: Aristocles the son of Ariston, despite having, as it were, the best of names (as it were, twice over), chose to be called by a *nickname*—something unusual if not unique in ancient philosophy—and that the nickname he allowed himself to be called was "Plato." Everybody knows—and his real name makes it crystal clear in any case—that Plato was of aristocratic birth and belonged to one of the most powerful families in the most powerful of cities.[78] Aristocles was by birth an aristocrat and was named as such. The name "Glaucon" suggests Athena's owl and "Adeimantus" is "the fearless one." But "Aristocles" fits Plato equally well: "he with the best reputation." Plato is the first philosopher whose writings survive complete; this fact alone speaks volumes about the high repute in which he has continuously been held by scholars ancient and modern. He is unquestionably the most famous of Ariston's sons. But it is not uncharacteristic of the man that he has kept the memory of his brothers green as well.

On the other hand, Plato's reputation has now fallen on dark days: in our democratic age, he is reputed to be an elitist, a hater of democracy, and an enemy of "the open society" and such, as his family name indicates, was he somehow born to be. He is both hated and loved by being so regarded, of course, but foes and friends alike agree—as I will try to show—on an illusion. In chapter 6, for example, the anti-democratic Plato will be discussed. For now, I'd like to point out that the very nickname "Plato" suggests that Aristocles, born to be the best of the best, evidently changed his point of view. What "haughty aristocratic prig" (as I. F. Stone was wont to call Plato) prefers to be called "Buffer"?[79] If nicknames were as common in Athens as they are in New Orleans, it would be another matter. But "Plato" is the only philosopher's nickname we know. Plato chose not to be called "Aristocles." It is *prima facie* obvious that Plato had a change of heart with respect to what he regarded as the best name for himself. The fact that his given name already meant "best" by the conventional aristocratic measure strongly suggests he came to use quite another kind of measure. Of Aristocles we can imagine Plato saying: "'Twas I; but 'tis not I. I do not shame to tell you the thing I was, since my conversion so sweetly tastes, being the thing I am" (*As You Like* IV.iii.135-7; cf. 613a1-2).

To the extent that there are any, the facts of the curious case of Plato's name change are found in Diogenes Laertius:

---

77. Serious attention to this important question can be found at Sedley, *Plato's* Cratylus, 21-23; he calls it "a remarkably neglected snippet of evidence."

78. See Nails, *People of Plato*, 243-50.

79. *pace* Sedley, *Plato's* Cratylus, 21-22: "Changing your name from Aristocles to Plato was a bit like changing it from Johnson to Jenkins."

> He had two brothers, Adeimantus and Glaucon, and a sister, Potone, who was the mother of Speusipppus. He was taught letters in the school of Dionysius, who is mentioned by him in the *Rivals*. And he learnt gymnastics under Ariston, the Argive wrestler. And from him he received the name of Plato on account of his robust figure, in place of his original name which was Aristocles, after his grandfather, as Alexander informs us in his *Successions* [*of Philosophers*]. But others affirm that he got the name Plato from the breadth of his style [πλατύτητα τῆς ἑρμενείας], or from the breadth of his forehead, as suggested by Neanthes. Others again affirmed that he wrestled in the Isthmian Games[80]

It will be seen that Diogenes Laertius gives three different stories about "Plato." The first and most likely version is that it was a nickname given to Aristocles by his wrestling coach. This seems very probable given what I know of wrestling coaches and the fascinating coincidence that the Argive's name was "Ariston." Perhaps the difficulty Aristocles—not only an excellent wrestler but the scion of one of Athens' most prominent families—would naturally encounter in calling his foreign-born wrestling coach by his father's name explains the nickname; perhaps young Aristocles, by submitting to being called "Plato," earned thereby the right to publicly call Ariston the Argive by some other name as well: given what I know of young athletes, I don't doubt that there was an alternative circulating the gymnasium. In any case, I believe that Plato was originally given the name "Plato" (1) in his youth, (2) by virtue of his body, and (3) by his wrestling coach.

I suggest that the name "Plato" came to have connotations for Plato that made it a better name for the man he really was than "Aristocles." Moreover, I suggest that given what we know of Platonism's pronounced tendency to separate the soul from the body (the χωρισμός of *Phd.* 67d9), and give pride of place to the soul,[81] it is likely that Plato believed "Plato" captured the truth about himself—about his soul, rather than his body—better than "Aristocles" did. In short, I would place myself among those who "affirm that he got the name 'Plato' from the breadth of his style [πλατύτητα τῆς ἑρμενείας]." I don't regard this second version identified by Diogenes as being in any way incompatible with the *palaestra* origins of "Plato" arising from Ariston the Argive, given, that is, the distinction between how the nickname first arose as opposed to why Plato allowed it to stick with him into later life. Note that the third version, the

80. *Lives of Eminent Philosophers* 3.4 (translation Hicks); note that Diogenes Laertius regards *Erastai* as a genuine work of Plato.

81. Nowhere more succinctly stated than at *Alc. 1* 129e3-130a4 (Hutchinson): "*Socrates*: Doesn't a man use his whole body, too? *Alcibiades*: Certainly. *Socrates*: And we agreed that the user is different from the thing used. *Alcibiades*: Yes. *Socrates*: So a man is different from his own body. *Alcibiades*: So it seems. Socrates: Then what *is* a man? *Alcibiades*: I don't know what to say. *Socrates*: Yes you do—say it's what uses the body. *Alcibiades*: Yes. *Socrates*: What else uses it except the soul? *Alcibiades*: Nothing else. *Socrates*: And doesn't the soul rule the body? *Alcibiades*: Yes."

mere suggestion of Neanthes, is a compromise between the first two in respect of the soul/body distinction: a broad forehead is often considered a physical manifestation of intellectual capacity. By placing Neanthes last and using the word "suggests," Diogenes himself suggests that Neanthes is offering a mere conjecture about "Plato." But the synthetic nature of that conjecture makes it worthy of mention: it plausibly fits the case, as busts of Plato show.

I propose an alternative synthesis to that of Neanthes by combining in a chronological development an origin based on the body with an evolving significance pertaining to the soul. In other words: what began as a physical description came to take on an intellectual or spiritual dimension, as "some affirm." Just as the phrase "πλατύτητα τῆς ἑρμενείας" admits of considerable "breadth of interpretation" (indeed that is the more literal translation of the Greek) so also does the "some" broaden still further "the breadth of interpretation" permitted to any one of us. Apparently there were ancient writers who offered conjectures about the intellectual or spiritual significance of the nickname "Plato." In other words, our primary source offers an ancient precedent for using considerable "breadth of interpretation" in explaining how Aristocles came to be Plato.

Before concluding this section with my own attempt to interpret the significance of "Plato" in the context of Platonism—and thereby to learn more about τοῦ Ἀρίστωνος—it is important to point out that Plato always remained Aristocles the son of Ariston in one important respect: he was a powerful man not only by virtue of what he had learned from Ariston the Argive. He was rich, forceful, and capable enough to have prevented himself from becoming known to posterity as "Plato" if he had wished to do so. In other words, we can be in no doubt—and this single fact justifies my earlier claim that "we know more about Plato than we think we do"—that Plato wanted to be known as "Plato." He had some reason, and I do not think it is too much to assert categorically that he had what *he* would have regarded as a good reason, for wishing to be known as Plato. If we only knew what Plato actually meant by "good," we would know more about the reasons he self-evidently had for changing his name. But then again, we *do* know what Plato regarded as the source of all good reasons: the Idea of the Good.

The heart of Platonism is the Idea of the Good.[82] His decision to allow his youthful nickname to stand, illustrates the heart of his philosophy perfectly:

---

82. 534b8-d1: "'And is not this true of the good likewise—that the man who is unable to define in his discourse and distinguish and abstract from all other things the aspect or idea of the good, and who cannot, as it were in battle, running the gauntlet of all tests, and striving to examine everything by essential reality and not by opinion, hold on his way through all this without tripping in his reasoning—the man who lacks this power, you will say, does not really know the good itself or any particular good; but if he apprehends any adumbration of it, his contact with it is by opinion, not by knowledge; and dreaming and dozing through his present life, before he awakens here he will arrive at the house of Hades and fall asleep for ever?' 'Yes, by Zeus,' said he, 'all this I will stoutly

without the Good, both "the better" and "the best" are meaningless terms. There is nothing that is better without the Good and there is nothing best except the Idea of the Good. The ease with which we habitually determine that one thing is "better" than another and that whatever we ourselves prefer is "the best" obscures—to the point of invisibility—the question of the Good. As the French say: "*Le meilleur est l'ennemi du bien*" ("The better is the enemy of the good"). Here—in our world—one thing may well *appear* to be better than another. But the Good upon which any "best" or "better" necessarily depends—i.e., the Idea of the Good—is *not* to be found here, not *in* or *of* this world. There can be nothing better than the Good and it alone is best. Everything that is not the Idea of the Good is equally not the Good: even "better" and "best" are meaningless terms except as logical echoes or consequences of the Good. The Idea of the Good is by so much, by so far and away, the best of things—it is so much better than everything and anything else—that in respect of what is truly better, everything besides the Good is equal: equally here (where the Good is not) and equally not the Good.

Before trying to connect this with "Plato," let me go back to the statement: "The heart of Plato's philosophy is the Idea of the Good." My willingness to state so baldly this highly debatable proposition constitutes not only a deliberate provocation, but even more importantly the basic premise for my account of what "Plato" means. I need this premise to make my case. The proof of the proposition that "the heart of Plato's philosophy is the Idea of the Good" can only arise, of course, from considering a variety of texts; this will be done in section §18. Nevertheless, it is possible even now to move into a middle ground between bald assertion and textual proof. This section's purpose is to delineate that middle ground.

First of all, let's rid the proposition of the metaphor: the basic point is something like: "Plato thought (or believed, or even knew) that the Idea of the Good is real." If we are prepared to believe that Plato had seen (or otherwise "believed in" or "knew to exist") the Idea of the Good, then it is obvious without proof (on the textual basis of his Πολιτεία) that "the heart of Plato's philosophy is the Idea of the Good." But because (1) it is most difficult to determine whether "believed in" or "knew to exist" is more accurate, (2) it is cumbersome to repeat this awkward but accurate formula, and (3) because the word "Idea"—itself a metaphor—has its etymological origin in vision, I will use here simply "Plato had seen," without prejudice to the problem raised in "(1)." Although this form of stating it is strong (i.e., it suggests "knowledge" rather than "belief") I have now defined "had seen" so as to allow the meaning of the phrase to vibrate between this strong sense and a sense as weak (but no weaker) as that expressed in: "Plato saw the necessity of believing in the Idea of the Good and therefore did so." The question that I want to raise is, then: are *we* prepared to believe that

---

affirm.'" Note the ghostly presence of both a championship wrestler and a discerning aristocrat in this passage. For analysis of "the Battle Hymn of the *Republic*," see sections §18 and §23.

Plato had seen the Idea of the Good? In other words, I'd like to take a closer look at those who deny my claim that "the heart of Plato's philosophy is the Idea of the Good."

This proposition admits of four possibilities given that *we* either believe or not and that *Plato* had either seen or he had not. Let's not quibble at this point about whether we ourselves know or believe that Plato had seen or had not seen and rest content with "we believe." The four possibilities are, therefore, (a) those who themselves believe in the Idea of the Good also believe that Plato had seen the Idea of the Good, (b) those who themselves believe in the Idea of the Good but do not believe that Plato had seen the Idea of the Good, (c) those who do not themselves believe in the Idea of the Good but do believe that Plato had seen (here, of course, in the weakest sense) the Idea of the Good, and (d) those who do not themselves believe in the Idea of the Good and do not believe that Plato had seen the Idea of the Good. Without any equivocation or mental reservation, I enroll myself in the first of these camps.

As for the other three groups with opinions on this subject, I reject the possibility that there exist any individuals who belong in "(b)": anyone who themselves believes in the Idea of the Good would be most uncharitable to deny that Plato too held such a belief. This leaves only "(c)" and "(d)". I regard "(c)" as a perfectly rational position and therefore completely entitled to the highest respect from one of Plato's friends. Although my book is written in part to persuade readers in this category that there may be more grounds for them to embrace Platonism than they had heretofore seen, every Platonist knows that not everybody is going to become a Platonist. For those who aren't Platonists, then, "(c)" is the position of the balanced scholar in the tradition of Aristotle: the one who is willing to take the word of Socrates in the *Republic* to be the considered position of Plato with respect to the Good and that, although they themselves don't find that word or position compelling, are perfectly happy to admit that Plato himself, at least while writing the *Republic*, held such views.

This leaves "(d)". Let me start by contrasting my position with theirs: I derived my belief in the Idea of the Good from Plato. A book entitled *Plato the Teacher* written by someone who was not Plato's student—i.e., had not been taught by him and therefore did not know what kind of teacher he was—would be a perfect waste of time to read. As Plato's student, I gladly confess that belief in the Idea of the Good has passed from Plato (through his immortal *Republic*) on down to me: in short, the priorities involved—chronological and otherwise—are all on his side. He is prior to me in time, he is the absolute ἀρχή of my opinions about the Good, and the influence all flows in a one-way direction: I wasn't a Platonist before I studied Plato and I wouldn't be one without him. Compare this condition with those who belong in "(d)."

In what direction flows the influence in the case of those who do not themselves believe in the Idea of the Good and who do not believe that Plato had seen the Idea of the Good? No one would be shameless enough to claim that they learned atheism, injustice, nihilism, the Will to Power, or, to state it more classically, Thrasymacheanism, from Plato's *Republic*. Those who were already atheists, nihilists, or students of Nietzsche have used Thrasymachus to show that Plato was one of them, which he wasn't and isn't. Since such thinkers are necessarily inclined to—indeed must—believe in "a secret Plato," perhaps they are most charitably understood as readers of Aristocles the son of Ariston. But Plato himself understood them (along with the "What is Plato trying to say here?" school of though that denies Plato any secrets whatsoever) less charitably: as "bald-headed tinkers" (495e5) who impose their own spiritual disabilities on what they still call "philosophy." Those who do not themselves believe in the Idea of the Good and who do not believe that Plato had seen the Idea of the Good are simply projecting[83] their own position onto Plato: they are reading their Modern views into this Ancient text.

With this in mind, let's return to the connection between "Plato" and "the Good." All other things beside the Good are equally not the Good and the Good is not to be found *here*. It is somehow elsewhere. It is invisible. It cannot be touched or physically grasped. We are separated from it, divided by some boundary from the place where *it* is. What is the limit-line beyond which is to be found the Good? What is it that divides us from the unseen Good? The answer to this question is found in the concept of division itself and it is the delineating boundary that is essential to all division. Consider the symbol of division: "÷". It consists of *three* elements: two separated points and the line that separates them. It is the dividing line that *divides* the divided into two separated things. It is for this reason that dualism always requires a third: the dividing line, the actual division between the two distinguished principles. The two things divided in Platonism—the Good *there* and us *here*—are divided precisely *by* Platonism; i.e., *by Plato*. We need only imagine the symbol for "division" in three dimensions to discover that "Plato" is not so much the one-dimensional line of the division symbol (÷) but rather a two-dimensional *plateau*.

At the risk of describing nothing more substantial than a dream,[84] I'd like to make some further use of this image in order to illustrate my conception of Pla-

83. Cf. Davis, *Soul of the Greeks*, 225-26: "Being mistaken is the engine that drives Diotima's ascent. We get what we longed for only to discover that it is not what we longed for. The peak of the ascent—*to kalon kath'auto*—is the beloved as so altogether other as to draw us completely outside ourselves [this sentence preserves the Ancient truth; the Modern projection now follows:]. In so doing, it provides us with the perfect projection of ourselves as what always goes outside of itself for the sake of itself. The beautiful-itself thus something like pure soul. Put a little perversely, one might say that *to kalon kath'auto* is perfectly unsatisfactory."

84. No one accorded a philosopher's dreams more value than the son of Ariston; consider 571d7-572a9; "'But when, I suppose, a man's condition is healthy [ὑγιεινῶς] and sober, and he goes to sleep after arousing his rational part and entertaining it with fair words [λόγων καλῶν] and thoughts, and attaining to clear self-consciousness [εἰς σύννοιαν αὐτὸς αὑτῷ ἀφικόμενος], while he has neither starved nor indulged to repletion his appetitive part [τὸ ἐπιθυμητικὸν], so that it may be lulled to sleep and not disturb the better part by its pleasure or pain, but may suffer that in isolated purity [αὐτὸ καθ' αὑτὸ μόνον καθαρὸν] to examine and reach out towards and apprehend some of

tonism. With "Plato" imagined as a two-dimensional but infinitely extended geometrical plane separating two points, let's imagine the northernmost of these points, dots, or circles as the well-rounded sphere of Parmenides.[85] Regardless of whether the goddess-guided chariot ascends or descends in Parmenides' "Truth,"[86] in the Platonic version of the story it is the ascent described in *Phaedrus*:[87] the highest soaring souls transgress the plateau dividing Becoming from Being going up and then falling back down at *Phaedrus* 247d5-4. Aside from the single but nevertheless three-dimensional sphere of "Truth," there is nothing else north of the plateau, not even the void of Democritus. In short, as in the conventional sign of division, there are still only three elements: the dividing line (albeit now re-imagined as an infinitely extended plane) and the two dots on either side of it, one of them the three-dimensional sphere of Parmenidean Being. South of the plateau is our visible world of Becoming in all its infinite diversity and divisibility, a world that can nevertheless be plausibly but inaccurately reconfigured or imagined as an equally well-rounded sphere by a physicist like Timaeus (cf. *Ti.* 33b4-5). It is necessarily difficult to say what Becoming *is* and therefore what it is like. Be that as it may be, the intervening plateau is not recognized as such when seen from any point south of it. Instead, it mirrors the world of Becoming below but does so in a purified or mathematical manner. The purification or rationalization of the infinite divisibility of its permanent flux by means of this mathematical mirror culminates in "the whole" of the physicists, i.e., the integrated universe or unique cosmos of the *Timaeus* or some equally but merely likely facsimile thereof. To the Platonist, by contrast, there is no such

---

the things unknown to it [ὃ μὴ οἶδεν], past [τι τῶν γεγονότων], present or future and when he has in like manner tamed his passionate part, and does not after a quarrel fall asleep with anger still awake within him, but if he has thus quieted the two elements in his soul and quickened the third, in which reason resides, and so goes to his rest, you are aware that in such case he is most likely to apprehend truth, and the visions of his dreams are least likely to be lawless.'" This passage contains the Platonic explanation of *déjà vu* as *the fulfillment of a forgotten prophetic dream*. If it be objected that this account of *déjà vu* isn't Plato's, then I'll be happy to claim it as my own. Note Plato's anticipation of Freud on: (1) the value of dreams, (2) the Oedipal Complex (569b7 and 571d1), and (3) the three parts of the soul (surely the 'Id' will be allowed to be Plato's τὸ ἐπιθυμητικὸν). See my "How to Interpret Cicero's Dialogue on Divination." *Interpretation* 35 no. 2 (Spring 2008), 105-121 at 109-10 for Cicero's treatment of this passage at *de Divinatione* 1.61-63.

85. B8.43-44; cf. Mourelatos, *Route of Parmenides*, 123-24 and John Palmer, *Parmenides and Presocratic Philosophy* (Oxford: Oxford University Press, 2009), 155-57.

86. For recent discussion, see M. Laura Gemelli Marciano, "Images and Experiences: At the Roots of Parmenides' *Aletheia*." *Ancient Philosophy* 28 (Spring 2008), 21-49. See also Mauro Tulli, "L'esortazione di Parmenide al sapere." *Materiali e discussioni per l'analisi dei testi classici* 31 (1993), 35-50.

87. Svetla Slaveva-Griffin, "Of Gods, Philosophers, and Charioteers: Content and Form in Parmenides' Proem and Plato's *Phaedrus*." *Transactions of the American Philological Association* 133 no. 2 (Autumn 2003), 227-253.

whole: this is also why Parmenides is generally thought to have no place in his thinking for the world of Becoming. In any case, much as a certain kind of two-dimensional image, if stared at with a temporary oblivion of conventional focus, suddenly, as it were, "goes" three-dimensional to our dazzled sight, so too the true philosopher eventually reaches a point when careful scrutiny of the reflected image of the world below in the south-side mirror of the plateau gives way to its sudden translucence. And at the very moment that the plane's translucence makes possible a first glimpse of the otherworldly "Truth," "Plato" too becomes visible for the first time *qua* transgressed "plateau."

The foregoing, then, offers some impression of what I take Platonism to be: the kind of otherworldly dualism that Nietzsche was still honest enough to hate. Three points about the image are particularly important: (1) it indicates the ontological "condition for the possibility of," but does not itself include or even suggest the all-important ethical dimension of Platonism, i.e., the obligation, having seen through the plateau, to go back down into a world of illusion for the sake of the greater Good, (2) it puts in its place the misguided attempt of cosmologists and other mystics to give the sensible world of Becoming a Being-like integrity it cannot possess, and (3) it begins to suggest the Parmenidean origins of Platonism. The second and third of these are conveniently brought together in the following passage from Alexander Mourelatos:

> The proofs of B8 culminated in the comparison of what-is with a "well-rounded sphere." As we saw in (ix) [in a table called "Similarities-with-a-Difference between "Doxa" and "Truth" on 248-49, (ix) juxtaposes two similar but different uses of πείρατα ("bounds," "bands," or "limits")], the comparison becomes reified in the "Doxa" [sc. the "Way of Opinion"]. The world is literally a gigantic physical sphere, or a nesting of rings: the "outermost boundary" has now become the shining "outermost heaven"; the "bands" or "bounds," which expressed the perfection or actuality of what is, have now been projected as physical "bands" (the rings or wheels of the stars).[88]

Parmenides reveals that that the constructions of the cosmologists re-enact a metaphysical unity foreign to their subject matter. Standing in opposition to mankind's yearning for unity—what I will call our "*Drang nach Einheit*"—Parmenides' division between "Truth" and "Doxa" itself demonstrates the limits of cosmology and monism. This division,[89] literary origin of the Platonic "plateau," is Parmenidean and so, as it turns out, is the pedagogy that tempts the student to ignore it by placing the deliberately truth-like deceptions of the "Way of Opinion" immediately after "Truth." Plato's advance on Parmenides is neither ontological nor pedagogical but ethical; hence the importance of "(1)" in

88. Mourelatos, *Route of Parmenides*, 250-51.

89. Cf. "la drastica lacerazione" (84) at Mauro Tulli, "Il rapporto di Parmenide con i πολλοί" in Graziano Arrighetti (ed.), *Ricerche di Filologia Classica IV: Poesia Greca*, 171-187 (Pisa: Giardini, 1995).

Platonism. But this passage from W. K. C. Guthrie indicates that the traditional view of Parmenides requires some revision:

> Plato modified the harsh dichotomy of Parmenides . . . by introducing an intermediate category between being and non-being, namely the world of becoming.[90]

Beginning with *Plato's Reception of Parmenides* (1999), John A. Palmer has inaugurated a new era in the study of Plato; the challenge he poses to "Guthrie's narrative"[91] in *Parmenides and Presocratic Philosophy* (2009) must likewise be of interest to all serious students of Greek Philosophy. As these titles indicate, Parmenides is at the center of Palmer's story. Especially with his account of Zeno and Melissus,[92] Palmer has shown how the strict monism that the tradition attributed to Parmenides himself arises from a series of misunderstandings. Particularly important in the present context is his discussion of *Republic* V;[93] he argues persuasively that Socrates' account of philosophy is Parmenidean and even more originally,[94] that Parmenides was, as it were, more Platonic than previously thought.[95] According to Palmer, Parmenides was not a "strict" but rather "a generous monist"[96] and thus made room for something that neither necessarily is nor that absolutely is not. To put it another way, Palmer's "modal interpretation"[97] of Parmenides makes room for what Plato called "Becoming" as "contingent being."[98] For this reason, placing "opinion" ("doxa") between knowledge of "what necessarily is and cannot not be" and ignorance of "what is not and cannot be" in *Republic* V (476e7-479e5) does not constitute Plato's advance on but rather his embrace of Parmenides.[99] Although Palmer's reading of

90. Guthrie, *History of Greek Philosophy* IV, 34.

91. Palmer, *Parmenides and Presocratic Philosophy*, 7-18.

92. Palmer, *Parmenides and Presocratic Philosophy*, ch. 5.

93. John A. Palmer, *Plato's Reception of Parmenides* (Oxford: Oxford University Press, 1999), ch. 4.

94. Cf. Ian Crystal, "Parmenidean Allusions in *Republic* V." *Ancient Philosophy* 16 (Fall 1996), 351-363.

95. Palmer, *Plato's Reception*, 82: "Where mortals have gone wrong, then, is not in believing that the world of ordinary experience exists but in assuming that it can constitute a proper object of knowledge. By now it should be clear that Plato will have found ample material in Parmenides that confirmed his own view of the status of the material world." This last sentence should warn the reader that my brief summary ignores the fact that Palmer's first book, as a contribution to reception studies, disclaims any "essentialist" reading of Parmenides (13-14). Cf. *Parmenides and Presocratic Philosophy*, 126-29.

96. Palmer, *Parmenides and Presocratic Philosophy*, 45-50 is programmatic.

97. See Palmer, *Parmenides and Presocratic Philosophy*, 93-100.

98. Palmer, *Parmenides and Presocratic Philosophy*, vi.

99. Palmer, *Plato's Reception*, 40-55. Palmer overlooks an important intersection between *Republic* V and the "Way of Opinion": at 478c12-13, Socrates remarks that opinion is "darker than knowledge but brighter than ignorance." In Parmenides, the fraudulent first "forms" of the "cosmos" are fire and night (B8.52-59). Crystal, "Par-

Parmenides' cosmology leaves something to be desired,[100] his claim that the attribution of a radical or Becoming-excluding monism to Parmenides springs from the eristic and sophistic reception of his thought is magisterial.[101]

Aristotle, who played a crucial role in the misunderstanding of Parmenides that Palmer seeks to deconstruct, famously identified the great influences on Plato as Cratylus (who familiarized him with the doctrines of Heraclitus), Socrates, and Pythagoras in *Metaphysics* A.6. What made it particularly easy for the Stagirite to ignore the influence of Parmenides on Plato was his own misunderstanding of the Eleatic, specifically his failure to distinguish the two parts of Parmenides' poem:

> All thinkers then agree in making the contraries principles, both those who describe the All as one and unmoved (for even Parmenides treats hot and cold as principles under the names of fire and earth) and those too who use the rare and the dense. The same is true of Democritus also, with his plenum and void, both of which exist, he says, the one as being, the other as not being.[102]

The fact that Aristotle links Parmenides and Democritus is this way demonstrates his misunderstanding of the relationship between "Truth" and "the Way of Opinion" in the poem of Parmenides. In the cosmological part, "fire and earth" function as the fraudulent first principles of a deliberately "deceptive cosmos of words"[103] (naturally Democritus, by contrast, aims to give an accurate picture of the physical world in the certainty that there is no other kind) while only the well-rounded sphere of Being revealed in "Truth" necessarily exists.

---

menidean Allusions" cites "B8.57-60" at 357 but does not remark that the significance of the parallel is that Plato's account of opinion echoes Parmenides' "Way of Opinion."

100. See Palmer, *Parmenides and Presocratic Philosophy*, 159-163; he responds to the approach I favor at 162 although I would replace Owen's "dialectical" with "pedagogical" in the passage quoted at 162n36. Also important is Rose Cherubin, "Light, Night, and the Opinions of Mortals: Parmenides B8.51-61 and B9." *Ancient Philosophy* 25 (Spring 2005), 1-23.

101. In particular, see "Melissus as Eristic" in Palmer, *Parmenides and Presocratic Philosophy*, 216-224 and John Palmer, "Melissus and Parmenides." *Oxford Studies in Ancient Philosophy* 26 (2004), 19-54.

102. *Physics* A.5 (188a18-23); translation R. P. Hardie and R. K. Gaye.

103. These are actually fire and night at Parmenides B8.56 and 59. The decisive impact of Parmenides, and in particular of his "Way of Opinion," on Plato's *Timaeus* is suggested but not developed by the astute question posed by Taylor, *Commentary*, 94n2: "Is it possible that it may have been a reminiscence of this very passage [at *Ti.* 31b6-8, Timaeus says: 'in beginning to construct the body of the all, the god proceeded to make it out of fire and earth' (translation Peter Kalkavage)] which led Aristotle into the loose statement that the two ['forms'] in Parmenides are ['fire'] and ['earth']?" In a work in progress, "Taylor's *Timaeus* and Plato's Parmenidean Pedagogy," I will validate Taylor's view that Timaeus does not speak for Plato—a view that has recently received support from Zuckert—and show how Parmenides' "Way of Opinion" was the prototype for the discourse of Timaeus, another κοσμός ἐπέων ἀπατηλός (Parmenides B8.52).

Having missed the pre-Platonic "plateau" dividing Parmenides' "cosmology" from "Truth," Aristotle lays the groundwork for the Tübingen School with his equally misguided deformation of Plato as a modified Pythagorean who made the One and Indefinite Dyad his cosmological first principles. Aristotle fails to grasp that neither Parmenides nor Plato were cosmologists because he fails to understand why both of them made a place for cosmology on the other side of "Truth."

Without the "plateau" defining this "other side," there is no Platonism.[104] And one of the principal advantages of the dualism inherent in the son of Ariston's "plateau" is that it does not run afoul of the problem of the One and the Many. Squarely confronting our *Drang nach Einheit*, Plato's solution to that ancient problem precludes any attempt to show that all of the *many* things are nevertheless *one*; indeed the visible world of the cosmos-creators is one only insofar as it is not something else: the Being that truly and necessarily is. Of course no account of Platonism is complete without ethical action in accordance with the Good, an action that has this dualism as the condition of its possibility, i.e., without the philosopher who has crossed the plateau going up who then chooses to cross it once again and thus can say along with Socrates: "κατέβην."

In conclusion: the etymology of "Plato" and "plateau" are the same: they derive from the same Greek word for "wide," "broad," "flat," and "level." Leaving the history of Greek Philosophy aside, an important first step is simply to pronounce "Plato" correctly. You can almost hear it when you say "Πλάτων" in Plato's native language, sounding the "ω" (omega) with that grand, rich, resonant "o" sound that the Greeks called "the big O," and then stretch it out—savor it a bit—as a long vowel in Greek should always be savored. This, then, constitutes my attempt to persuade the reader to rethink the meaning of Πλάτων as the true form, the reborn, Parmenidean, and Socratized version, of τοῦ Ἀρίστωνος.

---

104. Unfortunately, this is not accepted by Palmer; see *Parmenides and Presocratic Philosophy*, 335: "In the end, the spherical cosmos of the *Timaeus* modeled upon the intelligible living creature, and not the Forms, is the nearest analogue in Plato of What Is in Parmenides." Worse is 344-45: "Taking into account the dual aspect of Heraclitean fire, one can see that the eternal and unchanging *logos* occupies a place in his system corresponding to that occupied by What Is in Parmenides', and likewise that Parmenides' material principles, light and night, have their analogues in Heraclitus' elemental fire. Once one recognizes these correspondences, one can abandon for good the inaccurate and outmoded cliché of the opposition between the philosopher of flux and the philosopher of changelessness." Abandoning the opposition between Heraclitus and Parmenides is the annihilation of Platonism and thus Guthrie, *History of Greek Philosophy* IV, 33-34 is preferable on this point.

Chapter Two

Challenges

Section 6. Cephalus and the Meaning of Life

It is sometimes said that there's no atheist in a foxhole; Cephalus is the *locus classicus* for the sentiment. Confronted with the imminence of his own death, the wealthy old arms contractor has been having nightmares. But the unjust (and no doubt lucrative) actions of Cephalus are the precondition for the conversation narrated in Plato's *Republic* in a double sense: it is in his large and comfortable home—presumably staffed with slaves enough to insure that Socrates and the others are unobtrusively provided with drinks and snacks (including salsa)—that the conversation takes place, and it is Cephalus who supplies them with the subject that will lead them to justice.

> "'For let me tell you, Socrates,' he said, "that when a man begins to realize that he is going to die, he is filled with apprehensions and concern about matters that before did not occur to him. The tales that are told of the world below and how *the men who have done wrong here must pay the penalty there,* though he may have laughed them down hitherto, then begin to torture his soul with the doubt that there may be some truth in them.'" (330d4-e2; emphasis mine)

In short, Cephalus finds himself in a foxhole. The first mention of justice is found in the emphasized phrase: ὡς τὸν ἐνθάδε ἀδικήσαντα δεῖ ἐκεῖ διδόναι δίκην. These words are therefore worthy of careful consideration.

But as chapter 1 should have made clear, a discussion of Plato's every word would swell this book to ridiculous dimensions. And so it is that in this chapter, it will become necessary to bid farewell to the luxury of explicating Plato's every word. The charming Cephalus is a perfect example of the foreshortening required from this point on. It simply is not possible to dwell on the three charming stories he tells: (1) the aged Sophocles freed at last from the tyranny of lust,[1] (2) the brilliant reply of Themistocles—as it were, the founding father of the

1. The presentation by Sophocles of lust as tyrant (329c4) is picked up and amplified in Book IX (beginning at 573b6-7).

Piraeus[2]—to the Seriphian,[3] and (3) the sweet words of Pindar, lost forever had Plato's Cephalus not quoted them.[4] All of these are worthy of extended comment. I will content myself with pointing out that *charm* is the key to Cephalus: he can tell charming stories to the sons of men and he is now off to charm the immortal gods. Seeking an insurance policy for the misdeeds of his youth, he is betaking himself to the sacrifice in order to sleep more soundly. Plato suggests the inanity of this approach by creating the original "Charlie of the M. T. A.": Cephalus is the first "man who never returned." Socrates keeps the sons of Cephalus talking to the wee hours, but Cephalus himself stays out even longer. Either there was another entrance to his mansion or he had someplace else to go after the sacrifices were over. Or perhaps we need to take "Polemarchus' house" (328b4) literally and imagine Cephalus as merely visiting his son and returning to his own home later.

Cephalus is of the older generation and has not yet rid "the city in his soul"—through censorship—of tales concerning the world below. The younger generation has excluded such tales: Socrates will be expressly forbidden to bring up the rewards of justice (or the punishment meted out to the unjust) in the hereafter.[5] The City that Socrates will construct is notorious for its censorship:[6] it is noteworthy that the first instance of censorship is not introduced by Socrates but rather *imposed on him*, and, moreover, that all of us censor everything we read, watch, and hear as a matter of course in any case. In other words: "don't waste my time with tales of life-after-death" is censorship no less than the strictures Socrates proposes for keeping his Guardians from using their weapons against those they are guarding. One need not wonder whether Thrasymachus has re-

2. Aristophanes jokes that Themistocles "found our city half empty and left it full to overflowing, who one day gave us the Piraeus for dinner, and added fresh fish to all our usual meals" (*Knights* 814-16; O'Neill translation).

3. The relationship between City and Man is prefigured in this wonderful anecdote: while Themistocles wouldn't have achieved greatness had he been born on Seriphos, the Seriphian would still be a nobody had he been born in Athens (329e6-330a2). The basis of the anecdote is further explained in Book VI (496b3-5) but given the context (see section §14), it's probably fair to say that the *Republic* teaches that only a philosopher from a great city can practice Justice, i.e. a city in which the rewards of injustice are great and where the consequences of the philosopher leaving others to rule the city are most disastrous. It is not for everyone, then, that the *Republic* takes place "yesterday." On the other hand, my readers are scarcely from Seriphos.

4. It is, of course, not only poetic fragments that Plato preserves. The format of a compendium like *Fragmente der Vorsokratiker* by Hermann Diels tends to obscure how impoverished our knowledge of Plato's predecessors would be without Plato. On another subject, the implicit identification of justice and piety (331a4) that Cephalus illustrates by quoting Pindar prefigures the importance of the otherwise missing fifth virtue, indicated by Plato's decision to grapple with piety only in *Euthyphro*; i.e., at a most dramatic moment in the reading order of the Platonic dialogues.

5. Implicit in Glaucon, this restriction is made more explicit (see section §10) by Adeimantus (367d7-e1).

6. The process begins at 377b4.

cently been reading the tales to which Cephalus here refers. It is the older generation that still takes such stories seriously: the younger men have denied them access to the citadels of their souls (560b6-7). Hence the magnitude of the challenge to Socrates (and Plato) that explains this chapter's title.

The statement of Cephalus in which the word "justice" is first found is predicated on a dualistic vision: the one committing injustices here (ἐνθάδε) will paid the penalty there (ἐκεῖ). To this limited extent, Cephalus is a Platonist: he is an unreflective dualist rather than a monistic materialist or Heraclitean. But there is only the faintest resemblance between Plato's position and that of Cephalus while there are important differences between them: (1) Cephalus is by no means sure that the second realm beyond the visible even exists (let alone that only it actually does so): he has rejected this possibility his whole life and is by no means sure that it is probable even today. (2) Cephalus regards life here as preferable to this second realm even if it does exist: his loyalty is to the earth and he is merely scared that the fun he has had here could cause him difficulties there. (3) For Cephalus, justice is something to be feared. (4) Cephalus regards the next world—if there is one—to be the place where the claims of justice must be paid. And finally, (5) Cephalus has no appetite for philosophy and dialectic: he leaves and never returns.

But differences, especially when they take the form of polar opposition, are remarkably similar to that with which they differ. Socrates (5) clearly does have a most voracious appetite for philosophy and dialectic, as proved not only by talking through the night but also by repeating the entire conversation—to Cleitophon, perhaps—the following day. In addition, (4) he regards this world to be the arena of Justice: it is *here* we deliberately remain when we say "κατέβην," (3) Socratic Justice is necessarily something to be freely chosen, and while the Socratic response to (2) must await *Phaedo* or rather Book X, it is (1) only in the context of having seen the Idea of the Good (and therefore being certain that "the second" realm beyond the visible is actually the realm that is truly real and therefore primary) that going back down into the Cave (i.e. Justice) has any meaning. In other words, Cephalus is completely in the dark about Justice. But it is noteworthy that Socratic Justice, like the hellish night vision of the dreaming Cephalus, will also be found in the dark. The only justice in which Cephalus (only intermittently) believes (and which he now merely plans to subvert through charm) is far more like Justice than the many justices that Thrasymachus can prove are as real or unreal as anything else. As for the crucial phrase "διδόναι δίκην," it works equally well in the traditional world conjured by Cephalic poets and the new world created in Plato's *Republic*. Going back down into the Cave is the practice of Justice. The philosopher who "goes down" ipso facto "gives [back] justice."

Cephalus continues to lay bare the lineaments of his tortured soul: most striking of all is that he cannot be sure whether he is seeing things (for the first time) more clearly, or is simply turning into a senile old fool.

> "'And apart from that the man himself either from the weakness of old age or possibly as being now nearer to the things beyond has a somewhat clearer view of them.'" (330e2-4)

Not the least of justice's rewards in this life is that the soul is well-prepared by experience for just this kind of anxiety (*Phd.* 63e8-64a2): the description given here by Cephalus is similar to what happens when one of the denizens of the Cave catches sight of the fire burning there for the first time and then turns back to the accustomed shadows (515c6-d7). Is the prisoner closer to the truth? Then how does it happen that she can now see nothing? The one who returns to the Cave expects this kind of thing and knows that the shadows are unreliable no matter how clearly they are seen. In the case of poor Cephalus, he is forced to doubt his most precious possession: himself.

> "Be that as it may, he is filled with doubt, surmises, and alarms and begins to reckon up and consider whether he has ever wronged anyone. *Now he to whom the ledger of his life shows an account of many evil deeds* starts up even from his dreams like children again and again in affright and his days are haunted by anticipations of worse to come." (330e4-331a1; emphasis mine)

Although the Pindar-quoting Cephalus will soon enough perorate his way into a cozy self-presentation as one who enjoys the sweetness of old age, he has revealed the truth all too clearly here: he is absolutely terrified. Plato would save us from these night terrors. It is hardly to the credit of Cephalus that he looks at life as a balance-book: this is a real deficit in his conception. Although it is obviously anachronistic to consider Cephalus a Christian, it is not only anachronistic: any parallel indicates a complete misunderstanding of the Christian message. Christianity is not an effective way to balance the books: it is the realization that "the ledger of life"—Paul Shorey does well to preserve the bookkeeping imagery implicit in "ἀναλογίζεται" by taking this liberty—tells decisively against us. No succession of midnight masses can balance the sinner's account. In short: Cephalus would not be a Christian even if he were alive today, even if a whole nave were named for him, as doubtless it would be. Plato suggests that it is too late for Cephalus to learn what Justice is, let alone practice it. In fact, with the necessary changes having been changed, Plato too would tell us, and perhaps more emphatically than the preacher (*Ecclesiastes* 12:1): "Remember your Creator in the days of your youth."

There is thus a very real sense in which Socrates is the successor of Cephalus: Platonism is not so much a repudiation of the shadowy Cephalic afterworld and its quasi-existent and potentially implacable gods as it is their ontological radicalization. Cephalus temporalizes the relationship between self and afterworld through an ever-foreshortening procrastination: his "there" is not now until it becomes far too late. The Socratic "there" certainly exists apart in spatial terms: it is unquestionably not here. But its demands are to be met both here and now. There is no hiding from it in space and no time when it is "not yet." A Just response to the truly eternal cannot be postponed: it is here and now that the insistent intrusion of Plato's ontological radicalization of the tradition can be seen. The same quality of timelessness that gives *Republic* its classic status is related to precisely this radical abandonment of diachronicity where the other world is concerned. In Platonism, the Idea of the Good breaks through—even into so dark a place as the Piraeus—in that instantaneous moment of translucent realization that the Greeks called a "καιρός"; not so much a moment but the right moment—not one instant of time only to be succeeded, like all the rest, by another—but as a life-changing *crisis* of insight.[7]

Misguided though he is, Cephalus is serious about the perennial problem of "the meaning of life." To be sure his solutions are dodges and his defenses are straw. But Plato deliberately chooses to replace him with Socrates: after his departure, Socrates will stand *in loco parentis*. It is useful to consider these words in an academic context: it is paradigmatically the schoolteacher who temporarily stands in the place of the parent and the school that becomes *alma mater*. Aristocratic sensibilities and inherited wealth no doubt precluded Plato the Teacher from charging his students tuition but he was nevertheless their tutor. If Plato's Socrates knows how to handle the parents of prospective pupils (*Laches* and *Theages*), Plato—who actually presided over the Academy—knew how to do so too. No matter how revolutionary the teacher, the teaching style, or the lesson plan, an effective teacher must live in the world of both pupil and parent. Plato is no parricide: Socrates is a better parent than Cephalus. He knew what he was about when he placed the *Euthyphro*—in which the protagonist prosecutes his father for murder—before and in the immediate context of the *Apology*: there is a sense in which the Athenians are on the verge of committing parricide against Socrates, the only pious man among them.[8] Through the radical ontology of Platonism, Socrates preserves whatever was good about the Cephalic tradition and allows it to continue whispering its salutary word of warning to "the salad days of youth." Terrified for himself, Cephalus leaves because he has nothing to teach, not even to his own sons. It is Plato's Socrates who will show, in Shakespeare's phrase, "a tender, fatherly regard."

---

7. 580b1-c2; note the five uses of the word in this passage and the ambiguity of "the son of Ariston." Of course the decision for Justice (as opposed to justice) at 520e1 is unheralded.

8. Given Euthyphro's prosecution of his father for murder (*Euthphr.* 4a6), it is odd that even astute readers (e.g., Blondell, *Play of Character*, 347-57) have assumed that the Eleatic Stranger has Plato's sympathy for committing parricide against Parmenides in *Sophist* (*Sph.* 241d3), the dialogue that follows *Euthyphro* in dramatic sequence; if Euthyphro is a fool, so is the Stranger; if Euthyphro is justified, so is the avenger of Parmenides (cf. *Tht.* 183e6).

Section 7: Polemarchus Meets Appearance and Reality

Polemarchus, son of Cephalus, reminds us even more forcefully of Plato's abiding interest in the youth: it must never be forgotten that there is enough in Plato's Πολιτεία to hold the interest of this fine young man. We will better appreciate Plato's artistry in the *Republic* when we consider that he was trying to win over the kind of readers who would love a book like Xenophon's *Cyropaedia*: i.e., youngsters who yearned for the robust, challenging, and thrilling adventures of a soldier's life, of an officer in command of men.[9] The greater wisdom of Glaucon, the proven war-hero, makes this all the more poignant.

Given that the heart of the Πολιτεία is so obviously Books VI and VII, one is tempted to forget that its numerical center is really between Books V and VI (see section §24). The importance of Glaucon's interruption at 471c3 has already been discussed in section §4 but it is the revolt instigated by Polemarchus at the beginning of Book V (449b1-6) that creates the condition for the possibility of Glaucon's determination to see the City realized in the first place.[10] Polemarchus is intrigued by what Socrates has to say about "women and children" (449c4-5; cf. 423e5-424a3) as well as about training the Guardians for war. It is also because of Polemarchus that Glaucon compels Socrates to stay in the Piraeus: he instigates the primordial revolt against Socrates' departure (327b4-5).

---

9. This is not the place to explore the relationship between Xenophon's *Cyropaedia* and the *Republic* and thus to revise the interpretation offered by Aulus Gellius *Noctes Atticae* 14.3. But I will make an observation: it hardly seems reasonable that Xenophon was both an inferior writer to Plato (who isn't?) and yet entered into direct competition with him. In another place, I hope to show that it was Plato who built on Xenophon's foundation. See Holger Thesleff, "The Interrelation and Date of the *Symposia* of Plato and Xenophon." *Bulletin of the Institute of Classical Studies* 25 (1978), 157-170 and Gabriel Danzig, "Intra-Socratic Polemics: The *Symposia* of Plato and Xenophon." *Greek, Roman and Byzantine Studies* 45 (2005), 331-357.

10. Lampert, *How Philosophy Became Socratic* argues that Socrates compels the interruption of Polemarchus so that he can then compel Glaucon's. Determined to find in Socrates' "easy-to-ignore" (242) response to the interruption originating with Polemarchus ("I salute Nemesis" or Ἀδράστεια at 451a4) "the most breathtaking image in the whole *Republic*" (310), Lampert wants to show that Socrates is determined to supplant Zeus by means of equally non-existent Ideas (310-11 and 353); the proof that it is already his intent to do so is "what led him to prostrate himself before Adrasteia" (315). His best evidence for this reading is a tenuous link between Socrates and Prometheus (Aeschylus' chorus cites the proverb against Prometheus in *Prometheus Bound*) and despite Lampert's familiarity with "old Paul Shorey" (314n80), he ignores the proverb's other uses (including one by Demosthenes) cited at Shorey, *Republic*, 1.430-31n"d"; cf. Adam, *Republic of Plato*, 1.278. The payoff comes at 415 (emphasis mine): "a Nietzschean history of philosophy [this is what Lampert is offering the reader; see 13] can trace the future that Adrasteia fated for a teaching that elevated to the highest ideal *lies of otherworldly permanence for God and man.*"

Plato goes out of his way to show that Polemarchus is an important person in his own right, and one about whom he is genuinely solicitous.

Not every student is a Glaucon. As for Adeimantus, he may not have the raw intelligence of his brother, but he's extremely well read. On the other hand, a good teacher doesn't judge by superficialities or family connections: Polemarchus might not be as smart as Adeimantus but his heart's in the right place and he was killed by the Tyrants. It must be kept in mind that weak students—particularly when they are smart—never allow themselves to reach their ἀπορία as Polemarchus does, most charmingly ("I no longer know what I myself was saying"), at 334b7.[11] As a teacher, Plato knows that students like Polemarchus are by far the most numerous: they are every teacher's "bread and butter" even when that teacher is rich enough to collect no fees. They are not so much our livelihood as our lives: we must keep them interested and involved. The by no means insignificant role of Polemarchus in the *Republic* reveals Plato the Teacher once again: above all, a teacher of boys, young boys who were interested in war and sex.

The way Socrates treats Polemarchus is perfectly easy to understand and runs along a well-established pattern familiar to those who have read any of the shorter dialogues and it is easy to see why some scholars have conjectured that "Book I" was originally an independent little dialogue and that it only gradually grew—as it were by an afterthought—into the *Republic*. It would be better to see the *Republic* as bridging a gap between the shorter and easier dialogues—to which the conversation with Polemarchus forms a crystal clear link—and the longer and more difficult dialogues of which the *Republic* itself is doubtless one (see Introduction). In other words, the active presence of Polemarchus in the first Book of the *Republic* illustrates the pedagogy of Plato the Teacher in a double sense: he helps the average reader find a footing right from the start of this long and complicated dialogue, and the existence of other dialogues by Plato—analogous to the dialogue in Book I with Polemarchus—indicates that Plato intended his students to have read these others before reading—one is tempted to say (in the spirit of young boys) "tackling"—the *Republic*. After all, there were only two kinds of students in Plato's Academy: those that had tried to master the *Republic* and those who had not yet earned the right to try. It is difficult to imagine that any of Plato's actual students were unaware of the importance their teacher attached to his masterpiece. The presence of Polemarchus gave even average students a point of entry from which to make their bid. In short: Polemarchus' important place in the dialogue suggests that Plato was writing for a younger and less sophisticated audience than reads the *Republic* today.

This becomes perfectly obvious to the student of reading order: *Alcibiades Major* is easily accessible to any youngster who has not entirely forgotten how it feels to be ten (cf. 541a1-7). It is not accidental that so many of the earliest dia-

11. "οὐ μὰ τὸν Δί', ἔφη, ἀλλ' οὐκέτι οἶδα ἔγωγε ὅτι ἔλεγον" (translation mine).

logues—i.e., "earliest" in a pedagogical sense, based on their comparative simplicity—have been rejected by modern scholars as spurious: the *Alcibiades* pair, the mediating *Erastai*, and even the larger of the two *Hippias* dialogues have fallen under the ban; if Aristotle had not mentioned *Lesser Hippias*, it too would have been excised long ago.[12] All of these dialogues are easy to read and that has jeopardized their survival for a reason that deserves careful and dispassionate consideration: professors, not high school teachers, have dominated the modern world of Platonic scholarship. Even now, when a growing number of scholars are beginning to play with dramatic orderings based on "fictive chronology,"[13] no *teacher* could imagine that Plato intended *Parmenides*[14] or *Laws*[15] to be the first dialogue any given student would read;[16] any sensible student would skip class if they were.[17] Fortunately, even in *Republic*—i.e., even when

---

12. Guthrie, *History of Greek Philosophy* IV, 191.

13. Charles L. Griswold Jr., "*E Pluribus Unum*? On the Platonic 'Corpus.'" *Ancient Philosophy* 19 (1999), 361-97 at 386-90 and Zuckert, *Plato's Philosophers.*

14. Nails, *People of Plato*, 307-329 and Press, *Plato.*

15. Zuckert, *Plato's Philosophers*, chapter 1.

16. It looks like the "dramatic order" of Gerald A. Press, "Principles of Dramatic and Non-dogmatic Plato Interpretation" and "Introduction" to Press (as ed.), *Plato's Dialogues: New Studies and Interpretations* (Lanham, MD: Rowman & Littlefield, 1993), 122 will be used to attack the Theory of Ideas: since Socrates knew from the start (i.e., in *Parmenides*, in which Socrates is very young) that the Ideas were open to crushing objections, he never actually subscribed to them despite appearances to the contrary: e.g. *Symposium*, *Republic*, and *Phaedo*. See Victorino Tejera, "The Hellenistic Obliteration of Plato's Dialogism." In Gerald A. Press (ed.), *Plato's Dialogues: New Studies and Interpretations* (Lanham, MD: Rowman & Littlefield, 1993), 141 and "The Dialogism of Plato's *Parmenides*" in Francisco J. Gonzalez (ed.), *The Third Way: New Directions in Platonic Studies*, 211-221 (Lanham, MD: Rowman & Littlefield, 1995). It also seems that this approach involves another of the worst excesses of "the bad old days," i.e., the athetizing of any dialogue that does not fit some prior conception of the scholar. Consider Press at 122: "Plato has provided some careful indications of the dramatic order of the dialogues; and given that, with the exception of the *Laws* (which may be spurious) [here Press cites an earlier version of Tejera's *Plato's Dialogues One by One; A Dialogical Interpretation* (Lanham, MD: University Press of America, 1999), 291-308] Socrates is a character in all the genuine dialogues, it is worth looking at the set as having that order. The *Euthyphro*, *Apology*, *Crito*, and *Phaedo* will, of course, be the last in dramatic order, but interestingly, the first will be *Parmenides*." In addition to Press, *Plato: A Guide for the Perplexed* (London: Continuum, 2007), 57 and 69, see Nails, *People of Plato*, 328: "This is not the place to argue that *Laws* contains little genuine Platonic material"

17. Although *Laws* is authentic (see previous note), a telling indication that the Athenian Stranger does not speak for Plato the Teacher is found at *Laws* 808d4-7 (Taylor): "Now of all wild young things a boy is the most difficult to handle. Just because he more than any other has a fount of intelligence in him which has not yet 'run clear,' he is the craftiest, most mischievous, and unruliest of brutes. So the creature must be held in check, as we may say, by more than one bridle—in the first place, when he is out of the mother's or nurse's hand, by attendants to care for his childish helplessness, and then, further, by all the masters that teach him anything, and, as befits a freeborn man, by the

considered, albeit artificially, in isolation—the principles of Platonic pedagogy are crystal clear: Book I is a simpler introduction to the books that follow and the conversations with Cephalus, Polemarchus, and Thrasymachus are arranged in accordance with degree of difficulty.

It is Polemarchus who defines justice as benefiting friends and harming enemies (332d4-334b9). This is the point of intersection between Xenophon's pedagogical masterpiece and Plato's: Cyrus acts throughout the *Cyropaedia* in accordance with this definition of justice, and his noble and effective actions—vividly described—make it a far more attractive definition than Polemarchus, as a mere debater, is able to do here. But Plato knows full well the attractions of this definition (cf. *Clit.* 410a7-b1): he structures much of his *Republic* in relation to it.[18] He knows that his readers—especially those who can identify with Polemarchus—will find the subject of friends and foes attractive and he counts on its attractiveness. The nodal point between the dialogue with Polemarchus and the *Republic* as a whole is the education of the Guardians.[19] Taking the lead from the definition of Polemarchus, the Guardians must be taught to be both good to their friends and fierce to their foes. To this extent, the *Republic* is a war story: just the sort of tale that would appeal to a lad named "Polemarchus" ("leader in war"). But since these Guardians must be both fierce and mild—a combination made glaringly problematic by the fact that their only job will be to fight—they must receive a special kind of education. Because of this, the *Republic* becomes an educational tale in a double sense: it is an educational tale about education. What makes this tale particularly educational for Polemarchus is that it is the tale of how excellent soldiers are educated.

All of this tells us a great deal about Plato the Teacher and the students Plato taught; indeed the two are inseparable. To begin with, there is the fact that Plato is educating his students by telling them how an elite band of capable soldiers are to be educated. Just as a good playwright uses a play within a play, so

---

teaching he gets. But further chastisement, as befits a slave, shall be inflicted on the boy and his attendant and teacher as well, by any free person in whose presence he commits any of these faults."

18. Only the definition of Polemarchus is missing from the brilliant observation made at Terence Irwin, *Plato's Ethics* (Oxford: Oxford University Press, 1995), 314 about the way in which the definitions of Cephalus and Thrasymachus allow Plato "to satisfy the moral demands of justice, as they were described at the beginning of the *Republic*. . . The argument has followed an 'upward' path from Cephalus' first thoughts about justice to the form of the Good, and now it follows a 'downward' path (511b3-c2; cf. Ar. *EN* 1095a30-b4) back to the initial beliefs about justice." For further justification for extending this insight to include Polemarchus' "friends and enemies," see section §19.

19. The City of Pigs provides no luxuries (372d7-e1) and if we want them, we must go to war (373e3). By the one man for one job principle (369e3-370a4; reapplied at 374b6-d6), the soldiers will only be soldiers. The need for a special form of education (the topic is broached at 376e1) arises from the definition of justice advanced by Polemarchus: the Guardians must be both gentle to the friends and terrible to their foes (375c1-2).

too does Plato the Teacher tell the story of how a group of people with whom the student can easily identify acquire an education. Reading a *Bildungsroman* is itself a wonderful way to become educated. This is the principal pedagogical technique used by Plato in the Πολιτεία. Through readers like Polemarchus, the education of the Guardians that Socrates describes in such great detail jumps right out of the text and into the audience. Every ambitious reader inevitably finds herself asking the question: "Am I Guardian material?" and, I might add, finding precious little reason to say: "No."[20] Certainly this is the kind of question that Polemarchus is asking himself throughout the conversation. And Socrates gives readers who are like Polemarchus much food for thought in his *Republic*, with a variety of tasty condiments on the side.

The most important dish that is served up in the conversation between Socrates and Polemarchus is the difference between what seems to be the case and that which truly is. Not surprisingly, this primordially philosophical distinction—it is indeed the heart of the philosophical enterprise, enshrined in the poem of Parmenides—is inextricably connected, for pedagogical purposes, with the question of friends and foes. "May I ask whether by friends you mean those who seem to a man to be worthy or those who really are so, even if they do not seem, and similarly of enemies?" This innocuous little question (334c1-3) will be rung through its changes throughout the dialogue: Glaucon will demand that Socrates prove that a just person who seems unjust has a preferable life to an unjust person who appears to be just (361a6-d3). The Allegory of the Cave is the immortal image of the radical inadequacy of what seems to be as opposed to what really and eternally is. Indeed the distinction between Being and Becoming—upon which the Socratic definition of philosophy in Book V depends—is rooted in the contrast between knowledge of what always is what it is and opinions about what merely appears to be something which it *is* no more than it is not.[21] Having been overthrown by this distinction, Polemarchus must have been relieved to see it turned effectively against the formidable Thrasymachus—a full-grown man and very famous—who quickly succeeds him as Socrates' sparring partner. But "sparring partner" is not strong enough: the prize pupil of Ariston the Argive offers his eager young puppies[22]—both male and female

20. The most comprehensive checklist of qualifications is found at 484b4-487a5.

21. Socrates defines philosophy in relation to the one thing that is beautiful (476b6-7) as opposed to the many things that are considered beautiful (476c1): one can have knowledge of the first, mere opinions about the second (476d4-5). Being (479c7) and Becoming (at first called "the opinable" (478e3 and 479d6) arise from a three-fold—and Parmenidean (see section §5)—distinction between (1) knowledge, which can only be of that which necessarily is what it is (478c3), (2) ignorance, of that which is not (478b5-c3), and (3) opinion, of that which both is and is not in alternation (478c12-d3). Socrates uses the example of the Beautiful because both *Hp. Ma.* 286d8 and *Smp.* 210b2 and 211b1-2 have prepared the reader for this rather than for the culminating Idea of the Good introduced in the central *Republic*, although it too has been prepared by *Ly.* 219d1.

22. The first mention of philosophy arises in connection with dogs (376b9). The similarity between 'guardian' and 'hunting pup' is first employed at 375a2-3.

alike[23]—something more exciting than the Isthmian Games. Polemarchus and Socrates merely talked about friends and foes. In *Republic* I, Plato presents the encounter between Thrasymachus and Socrates as what it is: an actual war. After all, little boys love war stories and every boyish battle needs a bad guy.

Section 8. Thrasymachus and the City of Good Men Only

The use of the word "boyish" should not be taken to deny that Thrasymachus really is a bad guy: some childish notions should be retained. It goes particularly easy on one's literary conscience to give short shrift to Thrasymachus because so many others are hell-bent on eulogizing him beyond all reasonable proportions: our universities are now filled with those who devote more attention to Book I than to Book VII, some, indeed who devote more attention to Thrasymachus than anything else in the entire book. But this is not the time to analyze the causes underlying the crisis of our own republic while Thrasymachus of Chalcedon has perfectly able defenders among the students of the students of Nietzsche.

Thrasymachus merely appears to give a definition of justice: in fact, he gives an admirable, irrefutable, and indeed perfectly true definition of the infinitely many different things that are called "justice."

> "And each form of government enacts the laws with a view to its own advantage, a democracy democratic laws and tyranny autocratic and the others likewise, and by so legislating they proclaim that the just for their subjects is that which is for their—the rulers'—advantage and the man who deviates from this law they chastise as a law-breaker and a wrongdoer. This, then, my good sir, is what I understand as the identical principle of justice that obtains in all states—the advantage of the established government. This I presume you will admit holds power and is strong, so that, if one reasons rightly, it works out that the just is the same thing everywhere, the advantage of the stronger." (338e1-339a4)

His is a definition of "justices," not justice. In short, Thrasymachus is a sophist. Obviously there were philosophers before there were sophists. But the sophists were the precondition for the possibility of philosophy as practiced by Socrates and as pictured by the great artist Plato.[24] They constitute the great "from

23. The argument for the Equality of the Sexes in Book V (see section §27) arises from hunting dogs (451d4-9); the σκύλαξ and φύλαξ parallel (see previous note) is made there as well.

24. This priority is exemplified in the reading order by the initial *Protagoras* (see Preface and section §11) as well as the early placement of the *Hippias* dialogues. For echoes of the *Hippias* dialogues in the *Republic*, compare *Hp. Ma.* 283b3-e2 with 398a1-b4 and *Hp. Mi.* 372d3-7 with 382b1-4.

whence?"[25] Since the likes of Plato and Socrates are and always have been in very short supply, it is hardly on the continued existence of them that it is possible to claim that Socrates went down to the Piraeus only yesterday. It is quite a different matter with the sophists, however. They are alive and certainly appear to be well both yesterday, today, and the day after tomorrow. The most quotable in recent memory was Vince Lombardi. A post-Christian sophist, he beautifully turned scripture on its head: "Do unto others *before* they do unto you." A great competitor, he is said to have said: "Winning isn't everything, it's the only thing." It's as if Lombardi knew Greek: what an ambitious Athenian might have called the "εὐήθης" (cf. 348c12), he summed up in the immortal phrase: "Nice guys finish last." Despite his modernity, he's already almost a pre-Socratic: he is destined to survive in fragments.

But the most widely known piece of modern sophistry is properly proverbial and therefore anonymous: "Beauty is in the eye of the beholder." It contains the deadly *bacillus* of Sophistry in all its purity but veiled in a most benign—indeed beautiful—appearance. We get closer to its real ugliness when we say instead: "justice" or "what's right and wrong is in the eye of the beholder." But we only graduate into the morally bankrupt school of Thrasymachus when we say: "Justice is in the eye of the strongest beholder in the room" or "What's right and wrong is in the hands of the man with the machine-gun." In other words, Thrasymachus defines the many different things called "justice" (i.e., justices) as whatever those who hold power say that it is. And what "they will say that justice is" is not "what is in any universal sense just" but simply that which is in their own interest. Ugly as it is, it is a beautiful definition: it appears to be universal because it is true everywhere. It appears to be one because it is stated in the singular. It appears to be the one thing that justice actually is. It is actually a definition of what justice merely appears to be.

Socrates goes after this definition the exact same way he went to work on the one offered by Polemarchus: do the strongest call "justice" only that which actually is in their best interest or also, when they blunder, what merely appears

---

25. The first word of *Protagoras* (*Prt.* 309a1); although Platonic pedagogy has received little independent attention, it is noteworthy that *Protagoras* is the first dialogue discussed in Samuel Scolnicov, *Plato's Metaphysics of Education* (London: Routledge, 1988) while Gary Allan Scott, *Plato's Socrates as Educator* (Albany: State University of New York Press, 2000) devotes a chapter to *Alcibiades Major*. For the relationship between the two, see Denyer, *Alcibiades*, 122. Lampert, *How Philosophy Became Socratic*, 9-10 places *Protagoras* first, followed closely by the *Alcibiades* dialogues, exclusively on chronological-historical grounds. The pedagogical advantages of an initial *Protagoras* are suggested by Guthrie, *History of Greek Philosophy* IV, 235: "If we look to the *Protagoras* for philosophical lessons, it may seem an irritating patchwork of niggling argument, irrelevant digressions, false starts and downright fallacy. Read as a play in which the most outstanding and individual minds of a brilliant period engage in a battle of wits, it will give a different impression. This is how it should be read." A more accurate last word would be "heard."

to be so (339c1-2).[26] It is this question that prompts Thrasymachus to create the artist, or better, the technician of injustice (340d6-e7). In short, Thrasymachus presents us with a technically brilliant defense of the basis of injustice, a solid commitment to "look out for number one." But in order to dodge the Socratic bullet of appearance *versus* reality, Thrasymachus must make his boorish "number one"—for indeed it takes no brains to be selfish—a craftsman: both unerring and technical.[27]

The center of the dialogue with Thrasymachus—and by far the most significant passage in Book I—arises from the problems associated with this craftsman of injustice. Socrates cleverly reverses the "justice is to the advantage of the stronger" definition along the analogy of the technical arts to show that the craftsman, for example a doctor—clearly stronger by virtue of her medical knowledge (cf. 456e7-457a1)—applies her skill to the advantage of those she guides or, more generally, those over whom her art presides.

> "Then, Thrasymachus, is not this immediately apparent, that no art or office provides what is beneficial for itself—but as we said long ago it provides and enjoins what is beneficial to its subject, considering the advantage of that, the weaker, and not the advantage the stronger?" (342e7-11)

This reversal arises from a distinction between the doctor as technician and the doctor as self-interested moneymaker (341c5-8). It is not *qua* doctor that the enriched, incorporated, and utterly corrupt Wellbeck inspires the righteous rage of George C. Scott in *Hospital*.[28] Conversely, a good doctor—one who derives no personal benefit from practicing her art—must be given other incentives to benefit others. Moreover, this applies to politics as well.

> "That is the reason, it seems, why pay must be provided for those who are to consent to rule, either in form of money or honor or a penalty if they refuse." (347a3-5)

It is this statement that provokes Glaucon's first interruption in the *Republic* (347a6). The explanation that Socrates offers him proves that Book I never had an independent existence as *Thrasymachus*: Plato gives us here a premonition of what is to come and reveals (by concealing) what Justice is for the first time.

---

26. The clearest formula for the merely apparent advantage is placed in the mouth of "Cleitophon" (340b6-7; see Introduction). Note that only if justice is the stronger man's (possibly erroneous) opinion of what is to his advantage are the Cavemen truly looking at the shadows of *artifacts* (515c2).

27. ὥστε κατὰ τὸν ἀκριβῆ λόγον, ἐπειδὴ καὶ σὺ ἀκριβολογῇ, οὐδεὶς τῶν δημιουργῶν ἁμαρτάνει (340e1-3). Thrasymachus uses the doctor, the accountant, the grammarian, and the craftsman as examples of unerring technical proficiency.

28. Screenplay by Paddy Chayevsky (1971). Tempted first by suicide and then by the beautiful Diana Rigg, Scott's gallant doctor returns instead to the Cave; see section §25. I regard this as the finest acting performance of my time.

Thrasymachus will eventually blush (350d3) because of the discomfiture that Socrates will cause him by exploring the problems that arise in a perfectly unjust city.[29] If everyone is trying to get the better of each other, they can't work together to take advantage of others (351e4-352a4). It is apparently the exact opposite of this city that Socrates now uses to explain the penalty about which Glaucon wants to know. Socrates explains the penalty that compels good men (defined as those who are motivated neither by desire for money or honor)[30] to practice the craft of ruling over others (346e3-7). The best incentive to rule—to bring about that which is to the advantage of the weaker, i.e., those over whom your technical skill presides—is the fear of being ruled by someone worse. True it is that it would be a crushing penalty to be ruled by Thrasymachus or one of his students.[31] To illustrate the importance of this penalty, Socrates creates the first city in his Πολιτεία: the City of Good Men Only. In a single sentence, Plato (1) prefigures the whole *Republic*, (2) illustrates, in microcosm, the three elements central to my reconstruction of the Reading Order of the Platonic dialogues, and (3) points toward the Idea of Justice.

In his "Proleptic Composition in the *Republic*, or Why Book 1 was never a Separate Dialogue," Charles Kahn called this passage "the most unmistakable anticipation of things to come" among thirteen instances of "proleptic composition" in Book I.[32] Citing both Adam and the formidable Wilamowitz, he connects the passage with Glaucon's interruptions in Books II and VII as well as "the necessity of the philosopher-king to redescend into the cave."[33] Going beyond the analogy noticed by Wincenty Lutoslavski (1897) and Hans Henning Raeder (1905), Kahn also proletically connects the City of Good Men Only to Book IV *via* the tripartite Soul: "Even the moral psychology of Book 4 is delicately prefigured here in the three motives adduced as incentives to rule: moral superiority, love of honour, love of money (347a5-d2)."[34] In other words, Kahn

29. The key admission is at 349c6. The perfectly unjust city appears at 351b1.

30. 347b1-c3: "'Don't you know that to be covetous of honor and covetous of money is said to be and is a reproach?' 'I do,' he said. 'Well, then,' said I, 'that is why the good are not willing to rule either for the sake of money or of honor. They do not wish to collect pay openly for their service of rule and be styled hirelings nor to take it by stealth from their office and be called thieves, nor yet for the sake of honor, for they are not covetous of honor. So there must be imposed some compulsion and penalty to constrain them to rule if they are to consent to hold office. That is perhaps why to seek office oneself and not await compulsion is thought disgraceful.'"

31. 347c3-d2: "'But the chief penalty is to be governed by someone worse if a man will not himself hold office and rule. It is from fear of this, as it appears to me, that the better sort hold office when they do, and then they go to it not in the expectation of enjoyment nor as to a good thing, but as to a necessary evil and because they are unable to turn it over to better men than themselves or to their like.'"

32. Charles H. Kahn, "Proleptic Composition in the *Republic*, or Why Book 1 Was Never a Separate Dialogue." *Classical Quarterly* (n.s.) 43 no. 1 (1993), 131-142 at 138.

33. Kahn, "Proleptic Composition," 138.

34. Kahn, "Proleptic Composition," 138.

has discovered (or at least elucidated) what I have called "(1)." And it is well to remember that the boundless pretensions of chronological developmentalism were not confined, in the case of the *Republic*, to inter-textual but embraced even *intra*-textual development.[35] Although Kahn is undoubtedly correct, he does not explain why the conclusion Socrates reaches in the City of Good Men Only prefigures only "the undesirability of ruling" but not, as in Book VII, the necessity that the philosopher do so. This is because, in addition to the "proleptic" element discovered by Kahn, there is also what I am calling "the basanistic element" in Plato's pedagogy: having prepared his readers to catch sight of the Idea through proleptic composition, Plato repeatedly *tests* them to determine how much they have seen.

To begin with, most Platonic words for "test" are derived from the "βασάνος."[36] E. R. Dodds explains the term in his commentary on the *Gorgias*: it is "the touchstone (Λυδία λίθος), a kind of black quartz jasper . . . used for assaying samples of gold by rubbing them against the touchstone and comparing the streaks they left on it."[37] The passage from which my use of "basanistic" is derived is *Grg*. 486d2-7, partly because what Socrates says to Callicles afterwards is exactly what I conceive Plato to be saying implicitly to his students throughout: "I know well that should *you* agree with me concerning the things this soul of mine [ἡ ἐμὴ ψυχὴ] considers right, that these same things are ipso facto [ἤδη] true."[38]

> If my soul were wrought of gold, Callicles, do you not think I should be delighted to find one of those stones wherewith which they test [βασανίζουσιν] gold—the best of them—and the best one; which I could apply to it, and it established that my soul had been well nurtured, I should be assured that I was in good condition and in need of no further test [βασάνου]?[39]

It is therefore not only a question of a teacher proving a student worthy but of finding and together confirming the truth through dialectic (523a7-8).

Evidence of basanistic composition can be found in the fact that the conclusion reached in Book I is the opposite of that upon which Socrates will insist in Book VII:

> "For we may venture to say that, if there should be a city of good men only, immunity from office-holding would be as eagerly contended for as office is

35. Kahn, "Proleptic Composition," 131-32 offers a useful historical survey of the "separatists" beginning with Karl Friedrich Hermann.

36. Plato repeatedly uses both the verb βασανίζω (34 instances) and the noun βασάνος (19) throughout the *corpus*. See in particular VII 537b7-540a2 and *Grg*. 486d3-487e2.

37. Dodds, *Plato's* Gorgias, 280.

38. *Grg*. 486e5-6 (translation mine). "εὖ οἶδ' ὅτι, ἄν μοι σὺ ὁμολογήσῃς περὶ ὧν ἡ ἐμὴ ψυχὴ δοξάζει, ταῦτ' ἤδη ἐστὶν αὐτὰ τἀληθῆ."

39. *Grg*. 486d2-5 (translated by W. D. Woodhead).

> now, and there it would be made plain that in very truth the true ruler does not naturally seek his own advantage but that of the ruled; so that every man of understanding [πᾶς ὁ γιγνώσκων] would rather choose to be benefited by another than to be bothered with benefiting him." (347d2-8)

The political message of *Republic* is that unless those ruling our cities would rather be philosophizing—until philosophers go back down into the Cave and participate in politics only because it is Just to do so—our cities will be badly ruled.[40] For philosophers, "not to rule" is prized because it leaves the philosopher free to consider that thing alone which is truly good (the Idea of the Good): good rulers, on the other hand, must necessarily attend to the indefinite plurality of things that are badly managed in order to govern well. Only philosophers could become the kind of rulers whose only goal is to see things well managed and to benefit those they rule. In short, only a philosopher, having no interest in making money, being honored, or exercising power is, "in reality, the true ruler." It is because the City of Good Men Only consists *only* of the good that none of them covets money or honor. The crucial point, however, is that *the penalty of being ruled by worse men would not exist in such a city*. It follows, therefore (claims Socrates provocatively) that no one would rule in a City of Good Men: no one would be willing to do so because the penalty that persuades good men to rule does not exist there. In fact, the purpose of the City of Good Men Only is to make Justice conspicuous by its absence.

Nor is it simply absent: at the end of the sentence, Justice is carefully and specifically denied; this will give the lazy an excuse for their laziness and the virtuous the opportunity to demonstrate their virtue. When Socrates says: "every one in the know would choose rather to be benefited by someone else than be bothered with benefiting another," he is describing a moral universe where no parent would take care of an infant, no child would nurse their dying parent, and certainly no independently wealthy genius would take the time to teach students young or slow witted enough to require the crystal clarity of *Alcibiades Major*. More importantly, it flatly contradicts what Socrates himself has just said: "the true ruler hasn't the nature to watch out for his own advantage." Platonic pedagogy originally revolved around the possibility that a freeborn Greek could be brought round (518c8) to recognize that the self-interested position of πᾶς ὁ γιγνώσκων is a *slavish* point of view.[41] In any context, ancient or modern,[42]

40. 520e4-521a2: "'For the fact is, dear friend,' said I, 'if you can discover a better way of life than office holding for your future rulers, a well-governed city becomes a possibility.'"

41. Thrasymachus (344c5-6) claims that "'injustice on a sufficiently large scale is a stronger, freer [ἐλευθεριώτερον], and more masterful thing than justice.'" Socrates aims to reverse this judgment. Cf. Aristotle *Nicomachean Ethics* 4.1 (1120a21-23): "And of all virtuous people the liberal [οἱ ἐλευθέριοι] are perhaps the most beloved, because they are beneficial [ὠφέλιμοι] to others; and they are so in that they give [ἐν τῇ δόσει]."

42. Rupert Clendon Lodge, "Private and Public Spirit in Platonism." *Philosophical Review* 34 no. 1 (January 1925), 1-27 at 22 and 24: "In politics, then, public spirit makes

denying the most important of all ethical truths—i.e., that altruism is noble and good while selfishness is both bad and base—forces students to discover it for themselves.[43] The alternative to reading this passage as basanistic is a slavish literalism in defense of an even more illiberal selfishness. This is, moreover, only the first of three times in *Republic* that altruism (i.e., a willingness to promote ἀλλοτριόν ἀγαθόν; "another's good" at 343c3) is denied by Socrates.[44] It is therefore the first moment that the basanistic element appears in it. Recognizing this first statement as basanistic is, moreover, far easier for the student who has read or recently heard *Gorgias*.[45]

It is comparatively easy to see that Book I is proleptic in relation to the remainder of the *Republic*: not even Momus (487a6) could cavil with the notion that Book I must be read before Book VII. But just as an adequate understanding of Books II-VII depends on having read Book I, so too must Plato's student have read a number of dialogues before reading the *Republic*. The basanistic portion of the City of Good Men Only—where the willingness of a good man to rule is explicitly denied—is a perfect example. To begin with, the contradiction—based on the difference between active and passive verb forms—is clearer in the original:

> τῷ ὄντι ἀληθινὸς ἄρχων οὐ πέφυκε τὸ αὑτῷ συμφέρον σκοπεῖσθαι ἀλλὰ τὸ τῷ ἀρχομένῳ: ὥστε πᾶς ἂν ὁ γιγνώσκων τὸ ὠφελεῖσθαι μᾶλλον ἕλοιτο ὑπ' ἄλλου ἢ ἄλλον ὠφελῶν πράγματα ἔχειν. (347d4-8)

The true ruler (ἄρχων) considers the advantage of the ruled (τῷ ἀρχομένῳ) when ruling but every man of understanding prefers to be benefited (ὠφελεῖσθαι) rather than to benefit (ὠφελῶν)[46] when deciding not to rule. The true ruler is therefore the opposite of the man of understanding. Unlike the true ruler (τῷ ὄντι ἀληθινὸς ἄρχων), every man of understanding (πᾶς ὁ γιγνώσκων) is guided by his own advantage (τὸ αὑτῷ συμφέρον). On the

---

for the salvation of States and the progressive development of all their powers in accordance with the Divine Plan, whereas the private, self-regarding spirit contradicts itself and disrupts the community and squanders its resources, and thus tends, not towards God's Reality, but towards the bottomless abyss of not-being." It is noteworthy that Lodge is writing two years before Heidegger published *Sein und Zeit* (1927).

43. Cf. Cicero *De Finibus* 2.118 and Altman, "Tullia's Secret."

44. In addition to 347d6-8, see 489b5-c3, and 599b5-7. The other two will receive attention in sections §15 and §34 respectively.

45. Beginning with the reference to Attic pastries at 404d8, there are many echoes of *Gorgias* in the passage in Book III from 404e3 to 405c6. Among these, consider the analogy at 404e3-5, the link between courts and doctors at 405a2-3, the repetition of the important word αἴσχιον at 405b5 and 405c6, the etymology of καλλωπίζεσθαι at 405b8, the gorgeous rhetoric and its purpose at 405c1-3, and the "nodding juryman" of 405c5. This last parallel is noted by Shorey, *Plato's Republic*, 1.271n"f".

46. Having introduced the Good (τὸ ἀγαθόν) at 379b11, Socrates first asks if it is beneficial (ὠφέλιμον).

other hand, it is the nature (πέφυκε) of the true ruler not to be so guided. While the contradiction involved here is scarcely invisible, the student who turns to the *Republic* in the context of the Reading Order of Plato's Dialogues is particularly well prepared to question and reject the decision of the knowing man who would rather be benefited than to benefit others. To be more specific, it is a passage in *Gorgias* that Plato the Teacher now counts on the student remembering; indeed the passage is an unforgettable one. Socrates presents there an even more controversial variant of the ethical abyss dividing the active and passive verb forms: "τὸ ἀδικεῖν αἴσχιον εἶναι τοῦ ἀδικεῖσθαι," (i.e., "committing an injustice it is more disgraceful than suffering it").[47] Anyone selfish enough to uniformly prefer ὠφελεῖσθαι to ὠφελῶν (i.e., the man who is guided exclusively by τὸ αὑτῷ συμφέρον) is most unlikely to consider τὸ ἀδικεῖν to be αἴσχιον than ἀδικεῖσθαι. But strictly as a matter of logical argumentation, the argument in the *Gorgias* doesn't entail the opposite of what Socrates says here in the *Republic*.

The relationship between the two active/passive pairs is therefore extremely interesting:[48] although it is more difficult in practice to undergo τὸ ἀδικεῖσθαι in order to avoid the greater evil of τὸ ἀδικεῖν, it is more difficult in theory to show why it is αἴσχιον ("more shameful") to prefer ὠφελεῖσθαι to ὠφελῶν. In other words, there are many generous people who are willing to benefit others without a return who would think twice about suffering an injustice rather than avoiding it altogether by doing something unethical to someone else. In practice, then, the willingness to undergo injustice in preference to performing it is much less common than being willing to benefit others. But in theory, it is another matter. Socrates can show, as he does in the *Gorgias*, that τὸ ἀδικεῖν is bad for the soul (i.e., it is not, in fact, τὸ αὑτῷ συμφέρον) but he simply can't do this in the case of τὸ ὠφελεῖσθαι: it is hardly contrary to one's own advantage to be benefited. In other words (and strictly in the context of reading order), it makes sense that the active/passive paradox in the *Gorgias* is easier (albeit only theoretically) and therefore earlier than its counterpart in the *Republic* even if it is more striking, paradoxical, and far more difficult in practice. But any student who has truly been persuaded by Socrates in the *Gorgias* will object to what she now hears in the *Republic*: indeed the story of Socrates from first to last concerns the benefactor (ὁ ὠφελῶν) par excellence who willingly endures being wronged (τὸ ἀδικεῖσθαι), likewise par excellence. Therefore the intra-textual and fictional interruption of Glaucon at 347a6, deserves another from the extra-textual student who remembers the *Gorgias*: exactly as Glaucon interrupted the written dialogue just a moment before, so now Plato is challenging the student to reject not so much the logic as the slavish self-interest of πᾶς ὁ γιγνώσκων (cf. 339a2-3) who is guided exclusively by τὸ αὑτῷ συμφέρον. And this would

47. *Grg.* 482d8 (translation mine).

48. The subject arises at 342e7-11; cf. 344c2, 345d6-e1, and 345e6-346a1.

constitute—at the same time—a rejection of the slavish literalism appropriate to a merely mute and unresponsive text.

At *Republic* 344c5-6, Thrasymachus claims that "injustice on a sufficiently large scale is a stronger, freer [ἐλευθεριώτερον], and more masterful thing than justice." The fact of slavery has repeatedly been used to vitiate Greek Culture *in toto*; its influence is certainly visible in this claim by Thrasymachus: injustice befits a free man, justice a slave. Socrates aims to completely reverse this judgment and he depends on his audience's abhorrence of acting the part of a slave in order to do so. In contrast to the views of Thrasymachus, it is justice that is not only τὸ ἐλευθεριώτερον but even τὸ ἐλευθεριώτατον (i.e., "the freest of all"). Platonic Justice is best understood—as befits the man who was both Plato the Teacher *and* Aristocles son of Ariston—as *noblesse oblige*: it is the free choice of a free man to act nobly: to do well is also to fare well (X 621d2-3). It is a true and indwelling nobility of nature that enables true rulers to look beyond their own advantage (οὐ πέφυκε τὸ αὑτῷ συμφέρον σκοπεῖσθαι) that leads the philosopher to return to the Cave as benefactor (ὠφελῶν) to the ruled (τῷ ἀρχομένῳ). It is therefore Justice that is the "stronger, freer, and more masterful thing" *par excellence*. But it is no accident that Plato (1) puts the famous formula of the *Gorgias* first into the mouth of Callicles who (2) makes use of the comparative "αἴσχιον" as opposed to "worse" or "less desirable:" it is (3) only from the perspective of a man like Callicles—a man acutely attuned to the pressures of shame (as what decent person is not?)[49]—that Socrates can make his point about being benefited. It is both less free and more shameful—weaker and less masterful as well—to passively await τὸ ὠφελεῖσθαι than to be actively be ὁ ὠφελῶν. In other words, it is *slavish* to await the action of another instead of acting on one's own accord, even if the action in question is in another's interest.[50]

In the context of all the horrors it has engendered on the planet, slavery has but this single compensation: it shames freemen away from τὸ δουλοπρεπές ("that which befits a slave"). It would be easy to interpret the *Gorgias* as a battle between Socrates and Callicles about the meaning of "τὸ δουλοπρεπές";[51] the dangers of an ethical slavishness also leave an indelible mark on *Alcibiades Major*.[52] There is a reason for this: it is far easier to show that the self-interest (τὸ

49. See Christina H. Tarnopolsky, *Prudes, Perverts, and Tyrants: Plato's* Gorgias *and the Politics of Shame* (Princeton, NJ: Princeton University Press, 2010).

50. Aristotle *Nicomachean Ethics* 4.1 (1120a13-15): "manifestly doing good and acting nobly go with giving [τῇ μὲν δόσει], while having good done to one and avoiding base actions [μὴ αἰσχροπραγεῖν] go with getting [τῇ δὲ λήψει]."

51. Callicles uses the word at *Grg.* 485b7 but his conception of the freeman and the slave is indicated by comparing *Grg.* 485e1 and *Grg.* 486c3: the man one can beat with impunity is a slave, the man who can talk his way out of any harm is free. This formula is reversed by Socrates beginning at *Grg.* 518a2 although it is implied by *Grg.* 482d8.

52. *Alc. 1* 134c4-6: wickedness is δουλοπρεπές while virtue is ἐλευθεροπρεπές. Alcibiades is in a slavish position (*Alc. 1* 134c10-11).

αὐτῷ συμφέρον) of πᾶς ὁ γιγνώσκων is αἴσχιον, ἀνελευθέρον and δουλοπρεπές than to show it is illogical, irrational, or senseless. In other words, it is far more difficult to demonstrate that altruism is logical than it is to see that it is noble.[53] In this context, it is easy to see why Plato the Teacher found it not only useful but necessary to temporarily present the soul as tripartite: until the soaring soul drawn to the Good manifests itself in the student, Plato cannot entirely depend on τὸ λογιστικὸν but must appeal to θυμός as well.[54] This is part of the reason why the Shorter Way is necessary: only on the Longer can Plato hope to show that ὁ ὠφελῶν (as opposed to the Harmonious Man of 443c9-444a2) is acting in accordance with τὸ αὐτῷ συμφέρον. And his defense of altruism—insofar as that defense doesn't depend on the rewards of the afterlife—will decisively depend on a *good will* pre-existing in his students: he needs only to remind them of their in-dwelling desire to do the beautiful despite its difficulty having once seen themselves in relation to the Idea of the Good.[55] It is indeed the basanistic element that constitutes Plato's means for enlivening in the student—through his dialectical pedagogy—precisely that good will. To put it another way: while only an altruist will recognize that Plato is without doubt one as well—and will therefore be confirmed in her altruism if not re-made in it—even the more skeptical ὁ γιγνώσκων (guided merely by τὸ λογιστικὸν) will be led part of the way to the same conclusion by pondering the implications of Plato *qua* Teacher, i.e., ὁ ὠφελῶν.

It is now time—in accordance with "(2)"—to elucidate "the City of Good Men Only" as a microcosm of proleptic, basanistic, and finally, what I will call "visionary" elements. There are, to begin with, (I) proleptic dialogues (or, in the present case, proleptic portions of a dialogue) that are designed to whet the appetite, or, somewhat less metaphorically, to soften up areas of resistance within the student to the philosophical doctrines to come later. To put it more accurately: the goal of the Platonic prolepsis is to confuse the reader in a salutary way through paradox concerning matters about which it is pedagogically necessary for the student to be confused if they are to be prepared for what's to come. In the case of the *Republic*, the proleptic element is particularly evident in Book I. Not only is (a) Book I of the *Republic* proleptic in this sense (as Kahn has shown), but so, more specifically, is (b) the City of Good Men Only: it prepares the reader to receive Plato's Book VII teaching about Justice. Moreover, (c) the first of the three clauses in the single sentence that describes this City is perfectly proleptic. Consider the passage again, this time divided into three sections:

---

53. Aristotle *Nicomachean Ethics* 4.1 (1120a23-25): "Acts of virtue are noble, and are performed for the sake of their nobility [τοῦ καλοῦ ἕνεκα]; the liberal man therefore will give for the nobility of giving [καὶ ὁ ἐλευθέριος οὖν δώσει τοῦ καλοῦ ἕνεκα]."

54. This line of thought is embodied in Kant's *Critique of Practical Reason*.

55. Dorter, "Philosopher-Rulers," 345n13: "A recognition that we are acting altruistically rather than out of self-interest does not automatically imply that we are acting reluctantly."

"[I] Were it to happen that a city of good men came into being, not to rule would be as prized as ruling is today, [II] and there it would become crystal clear that, in reality, the true ruler hasn't the nature to watch out for his own advantage but that of the ruled; [III] for every one in the know would choose rather to be benefited by someone else than be bothered with benefiting another." (347d2-8)

Given where Plato eventually wants to take the reader—to persuade us to freely choose the life of Justice—section [I] is paradoxical on two levels: it explicitly contradicts what most of us think is true, guided as we are by what is "prized . . . today" and it is written from the philosopher's perspective—unique for prizing the chance *not* to rule—a perspective that Plato will eventually want us to choose for ourselves but that he here tells us nothing about, not even that it is the perspective of a philosopher. Plato uses prolepsis and paradox to awaken the student's curiosity about the view from the mountaintop upon which he will someday help us to take our stand (at least for the moment before going back down) and that view is presented in section [II]:

"[II] and there it would become crystal clear [καταφανὲς] that, in reality, the true ruler [τῷ ὄντι ἀληθινὸς ἄρχων] hasn't the nature to watch out for his own advantage but that of the ruled" (347d4-6)

This clause is a microcosm of the visionary[56] element embodied particularly in *Symposium*, *Republic*, and *Phaedo*.[57] Everything here is pure Platonism: here, there is neither paradox nor test. The True Ruler possesses the noble nature inseparable from *noblesse oblige*. Plato knows (has seen) that the possibility of τῷ ὄντι ἀληθινὸς ἄρχων has been realized in both Socrates and in himself. Just as Socrates enlivened this possibility in Aristocles son of Ariston, so too will the re-made Plato now do the same for us: Plato the Teacher's purpose is to actualize this natural possibility in his students. "[II]" is, in short, a crystal clear statement of altruism and, at the same time, the essence of Platonic Justice. At the risk of repetition, the purpose of the *Republic* is to exhort us to choose Justice for ourselves: to freely choose τὸ ἐλευθεριώτατον. Plato does this for our benefit, which is not to say that it is not beneficial for him to do so as well. It has been well and truly said that teaching is the least highly paid but most rewarding profession. Of course it is not only the educator who knows as a matter of fact that to be ὁ ὠφελῶν is simultaneously to experience τὸ ὠφελεῖσθαι; most every mother has proved this as well.

But Plato the Teacher was not content with expressing beautiful thoughts beautifully and that is why he also wrote (III) dialogues of test, or, to use the

56. See Andrea Wilson Nightingale, *Spectacles of Truth in Classical Greek Philosophy* (Cambridge, UK: Cambridge University Press, 2004), 108-13 for a compelling discussion of Platonic "vision" that justifies using the term.

57. Charles H. Kahn, *Plato and the Socratic Dialogue: The Philosophical Use of Literary Form* (Cambridge, UK: Cambridge University Press, 1996), 59-60.

Greek word, the basanistic dialogues (or, as in the case of the *Republic*, the basanistic portions of the dialogue) that are intended to test whether or not the student has really chosen Justice.

> "[III] for every one in the know [πᾶς . . . ὁ γιγνώσκων] would choose rather to be benefited by someone else than be bothered with benefiting another." (347d6-8)

By contradicting what he has just said in the visionary section, Socrates here states the opposite of the truth in order to test the student. In other words, Plato challenges the reader (for it is not only "the challenges Socrates and Plato must face" that are being considered here) to raise the questions—and, on their basis, to make the kind of decisions—that lead to the truth. Plato the Teacher was not inclined, at least after he had gained some teaching experience (because no teacher learns about this except the hard way), to think that the student who enthusiastically agreed with him about everything had really or necessarily gotten the point. A student could, for example, praise the Socratic position in the *Gorgias* for its logical or even rhetorical excellences but reveal—by a failure to interrupt here—her lack of commitment to its implications. In short, as this third clause shows, Plato tests his students. He can even use Socrates (to say nothing of less attractive interlocutors) to trick the reader into accepting something that is false for a pedagogical purpose. In fact, not only is testing an essential part of Platonic pedagogy but having an authority figure present falsehoods, half-truths, or merely partial truths is the principal way Plato the teacher tests his students, i.e., leads them to firm possession of the truth. As a general principle, the dialogues in which "one in the know" takes the lead—men like Timaeus, the Eleatic Stranger, and his Athenian counterpart—are all basanistic dialogues.

But there is far more to be said about this basanistic element: it has a nobler purpose. All teachers can test their students but few can do so well. A good test, on the other hand, is one from which the student will actually learn. The ideal test teaches both student and teacher. In other words, there is a danger in taking the notion of "test" too literally. To be sure Plato the Teacher wanted to test his students, but hardly as an end in itself. By teaching as well as testing them through the basanistic element, he was able to create a truly dialectical pedagogy: his students come to know themselves in battle with the errors to which Plato carefully and deliberately exposes them. When students reject for themselves the selfishness of "the man in the know," they not only show themselves worthy but also confirm the insights toward which Plato has been leading them. Just as Socrates long ago chose Callicles to be his βασάνος, so too Plato has now chosen us.

Since the term "basanistic" is absolutely central to my entire project, it may not be out of place to offer the following restatement: along with *proleptic* and *visionary*, the *basanistic* element is best understood as one of three theoretical and hypothetical springboards (511b5) toward hermeneutic clarity. Although there is a meaningful sense in which a given dialogue can crudely be called "proleptic," "visionary," or "basanistic," it is better to think of this triad as interrelated elements that can also be deployed in a single dialogue, or even a single passage. Finally, the basanistic element is like a springboard in the same sense in which a good student actually learns from taking a well-constructed test. Plato deploys the basanistic element for a triple purpose: (a) to ensure that the student has grasped his visionary teaching, (b) to cause that teaching to leap from the text into the mind of the student (435a3-4 and *Ep.* 341d1-2), and (c) to point the student to something even greater than what the teacher has already taught. It is, in short, Plato's method for making his written texts dialectical.[58]

The City of Good Men Only has now been shown (1) to prefigure the whole *Republic*, and (2) to illustrate the *proleptic*, *visionary* and *basanistic* elements. Taking us (3) beyond the *Republic* is, for example, the following question: "What, if anything, would force or persuade (and specify which it would be) a good man to rule in a city of good men only?" The answers I have received to this question over the years from my students have been very revealing, indeed a kind of philosophical Rorschach. Most, to be sure, (a) ignore what Socrates has already said about good men—i.e., that they don't care about reputation any more than money—or else somehow subvert the question by saying no government would be necessary if all the citizens were good. But the student who knows how to read and follows the text will say (b) "nothing." That's what Soc-

58. A crucial instance of the basanistic is Socrates' insistence at *Phdr.* 275d4-e5 on the mute incapacity of a written text to create dialectic with the student/reader; readers of *Republic* VII who recognize themselves as the "you" Plato has addressed at 520b5-6 know this to be untrue. Cf. Kenneth M. Sayre, *Plato's Literary Garden* (Notre Dame, IN: University of Notre Dame Press, 1995), xvi. The Tübingen School takes the *Phaedrus* passage literally. In another place, I will offer a critique of this position based on Thomas Szlezák, "Unsterblichkeit und Trichotomie der Seele im zehnten Buch der Politeia." *Phronesis* 21 no. 1 (1976), 31-58. For the present, my emphasis on the basanistic is nevertheless analogous to "the unwritten doctrines" of the Tübingen School; the former could easily take the place of the latter in the diagram at Konrad Gaiser, *Platons ungeschriebene Lehre: Studien zur systematschen und geschichtlichen Begründung der Wissenschaften in der Platonischen Schule* (Stuttgart: E. Klett, 1963), 6. In opposition to Tübingen, my claim is that Plato's teaching is to be sought by the student/reader *within* the dialogues, *Republic* in particular (cf. *Ep.* VII 341c4-d2 with 434e4-435a4; see chapter 5) although the moment of unwritten illumination takes place only within the *student.* I therefore reject in advance a reductive classification of my approach as a "text-immanent" esotericism (85) as per Thomas Szlezák, "Notes sur le débat autour de la philosophie orale de Platon." *Les Études philosophiques* no. 1 (January-March 1998), 69-90 although it is doubtless far closer to that position than it is to Szlezák's. Of course his approach is also ultimately text-immanent although the texts in question—i.e., those that reveal Plato's esoteric teaching—are not Plato's. For a summary of the texts involved, see Konrad Gaiser, "Quellenkritische Probleme der indirekten Platonüberlieferung" in *Idee und Zahl: Studien zur platonishen Philosophie*, 31-84 (Heidelberg: Carl Winter, 1968) and for some of the problems involved in interpreting them, see Gregory Vlastos, "Review of Hans Joachim Krämer, *Arete bei Platon und Aristoteles*," *Gnomon* 35 no. 7 (November 1963), 641-655, especially 644-48.

rates literally says in the basanistic clause: this is the answer of what will later be called "auxiliaries." But these "helpers" are fewer than those who (c) point to some kind of altruism to explain why a good man would willingly rule in a City of Good Men Only. And these, of course, are the true Guardians. Thus far—i.e., as far as the answers I have described are concerned—we remain within the orbit of the *Republic*: we have taken "a step beyond it" only to the extent that we have raised an extra-textual question.

But there is an answer—and I regard it as the correct answer—that "indicates the possibility of taking a step beyond" the teaching contained in the *Republic* and that answer is Justice, the maxim of "Going back down into the Cave." It is Socrates' answer to Cleitophon's "τί τοὐντεῦθεν;" (*Clit.* 408e1-2; see Introduction). And this is the definition of Justice whose existence (as "Plato's definition of Justice along the Longer Way") I intend to demonstrate in *Plato the Teacher.* My claim is that a good man's decision to take in hand the troubles of her fellow citizens—the myriad of civic responsibilities that devolve upon any polity's leadership to say nothing of preventing the rule of Thrasymachus—is simply Just: freely choosing to do so is Justice. And if Socrates basanistically attempts to persuade us that "nothing" would persuade a good man to rule in a city were there no Thrasymachean penalty for not ruling, what is it that persuades some of us that Socrates is wrong? Whether it is best understood as the liberal spirit of a freeman, the altruism native to humanity, or as the new law celebrated on Maundy Thursday, Justice is unquestionably a thing—a motivating factor—that leads to the choice of an action rather than the action itself. In the *Republic*, Socrates answers Cleitophon's Question: he literally tells us what to do next and thereby points to "the Idea of Justice." Thanks to basanistic pedagogy, we are dealing with an author who attempted to make the written conversation jump out of the text and into the minds of his readers and grow outwards from there (see chapter 5). My further claim is that he succeeded.

Poor Thrasymachus: his section has been stolen from him and such sublime reflections are utterly foreign to his slavish nature! Let's give him the last word: he deserves it. It is, after all, against Thrasymachus that Socrates returns to the Cave in order to fight: there's no Justice in the *Republic* without the many justices of the Thracian sophist. As a philosopher, Socrates doubtless yearns to draw nearer to the Idea of the Good. But the practice of Justice requires a return, and down below, one must use the tricks young Aristocles learned from Ariston the Argive, or rather their mental analogues. Immediately after the sentence under discussion, Socrates adds:

> "For this reason, to be sure [μὲν], I myself therefore in no way agree with Thrasymachus, that the just is the advantage of the stronger." (347d8-e2)

This statement completes the reversal of Thrasymachus' definition and sends his antagonist to mat. But Socrates needed a trick to score this verbal reverse, and one trick now leads to another. In order to throw Thrasymachus, Socrates needed to show that whenever the stronger rule (the stronger now understood as "those who rule by art or technical skill"), this only benefits those they rule but is personally disadvantageous (i.e., causes trouble) for them. It was, as we have seen, precisely from narrow, slavish, or un-Socratic calculations of self-interest that "the one in the know" would never take the trouble to benefit others. The magnanimous among his listeners may realize that Socrates is lying and wonder "why?" while educators may sense a profound pedagogical purpose in play. But the presence of two lies in a row shows how dangerous wrestling with Thrasymachus—i.e., going back down into the Cave—actually is.

If Socrates had here told the truth about the good man being willing to benefit others, he would not only have lost a chance to throw his opponent but would have granted Thrasymachus the chance to throw him. Socrates knows full well that benefiting others is not to the stronger man's disadvantage; his unanswered "μεν" proves that he realizes that there is more that needs to be said about the matter. By the end, of course, he will say it: it will become obvious that "one in the know" will benefit others even at the expense of trouble (even when it comes in the form of hemlock) and that trouble notwithstanding, Justice really is to the advantage of the stronger man, which is not to deny that it is also to the advantage of the ruled! One is therefore tempted to say that Socratic Justice creates a "win-win" situation, but that too would be a lie: thanks to young Polemarchus, Thrasymachus will be the loser even when Justice proves to be exactly what Thrasymachus said it was: ἀλλοτριόν ἀγαθόν ("another's good" at 343c3).

Section 9. Glaucon's Challenge to Socrates

Book I ends with a sentiment that would be familiar to anyone who had only recently read the *Gorgias* (or, for that matter the *Laches* or *Meno*): "For if I don't know what the just is, I shall hardly know whether it is a virtue or not, and whether its possessor is or is not happy."[59] Naturally it is impossible to claim that the life of Justice is preferable to the way of life recommended by Thrasymachus (surely Socrates never denies that Thrasymachus has given a perfectly adequate account of Injustice!) without knowing "whether its possessor is or is not happy": it is choice-worthy to the extent that it promotes happiness. Three times in Book I has Socrates insisted on the importance of the subject under discussion: "Do you think it is a small matter that you are attempting to determine and not the entire conduct of life that for each of us would make living most worth while?"[60] As the opening words of Book II prove, everything in the *Republic* beyond Book I occurs because Glaucon fully understands the importance of this question and its bearing:

---

59. 354c1-3. Cf. *La.* 190b8-c2, *Grg.* 448e2-7, and, most memorably, *Men.* 71b3-4 and *Men.* 86d3-6. Along with *Cleitophon*, *Charmides*, and *Theages*, these are the dialogues that immediately precede the *Republic* in my reconstruction of the reading order.

60. 344e1-3; see also 336e7 and 352d6-7. Cf. *La.* 185a3-5 and *Grg.* 492d3-5 and *Grg.* 500c1-4.

> "When I had said this I supposed that I was done with the subject, but it all turned out to be only a prelude. For Glaucon, who is always an intrepid enterprising spirit in everything, would not on this occasion acquiesce in Thrasymachus's abandonment of his case, but said, "Socrates, is it your desire to seem to have persuaded us or really to persuade us that it is without exception better to be just than unjust?" (357a1-b2)

Since Plato only wrote two dialogues (the *Republic* and the *Laws*) that are long enough to have been divided into books, no one will carp at the assertion that this is the first time in the Platonic *corpus* that such a thing occurs.[61] Plato's use of the word "prelude" indicates that Book I has been merely proleptic: the most important things are yet to come. In the context of the whole *Republic*, (1) the gap between Books I and II is to be understood—as Plato now tells us—as marking the difference between the prelude and the main body of the work. But it is important to note that this gap depends on two other things necessarily: (2) Socrates' stated desire to end the conversation here (and, presumably, to make his farewells and head back to Athens) and (3) Glaucon's stronger determination to explore what Socrates had called "the entire conduct of life that for each of us would make living most worth while." In connection with "(2)," the attitude of Socrates recalls that of Thrasymachus, who had been minded to depart after making his most compelling speech (I 344d1); indeed it was to prevent him from doing so that Socrates most forcefully emphasized the importance of the matter in the words quoted above. They are opposites even here, or course: Thrasymachus is minded to depart with his reputation as "one in the know" intact—the speech gives him the last word—while Socrates is content to escape under the mantle of Socratic ignorance. With respect to "(3)," Glaucon likewise stands in sharp contrast to Philebus, who will "throw in the sponge" after tiring of discussing a subject no less important (*Phlb.* 11c7-8).

Glaucon invokes for the third time in the *Republic* the distinction between appearance and reality, but this time it is used against Socrates. Glaucon's question indeed skewers the son of Sophroniscus: Socrates is forced to clarify what it is that he is actually trying to accomplish. Since Glaucon forces Socrates to reveal his intentions *vis à vis* Glaucon's own inner state of mind, only Glaucon himself is in a position to know whether Socrates is doing what he (Socrates) wants to be doing. And he manifestly is not: Glaucon has not really been persuaded "that it is better in every way to be just than unjust." Socrates has been brought to bay. Like a wily old bear, Socrates has temporarily been caught out in the open (he will eventually get back to his Cave) by the leader of a pack of hounds (σκύλακες). He will stall for time (accomplishing his objective all the while!) by turning this pack of σκύλακες into φύλακες (Guardians). But that's another story. Like so much else in Plato, Glaucon's Challenge will be expressed as a set of three and the first—the nature and or origin of justice—will

61. Naturally others mean "first in order of composition" where I mean "to be read first." Here they amount to the same thing, as is probably not infrequently the case.

give Socrates the excuse to stall. But there is no question that it is the third part of the challenge (360d8-362c6) that is decisive while the two others are merely preliminary. Glaucon wants Socrates to persuade him that it is better to be just than unjust, i.e. that the life of justice is better—makes the one who lives it happier—than the life recommended, and presumably practiced, by Thrasymachus. And if Socrates can persuade him of this—if Socrates can accomplish what Glaucon wishes him to accomplish—Socrates will also be doing exactly what Socrates wants to do. It will be (except where Thrasymachus is concerned, of course) "a win-win situation." This will not be easy to achieve.

To the Greeks, χαλεπὰ τὰ καλά was proverbial (435c8; cf. *Hi. Ma.* 304e8): "beautiful deeds are difficult to do." Glaucon makes things very difficult for Socrates: he therefore makes it possible for Socrates to do something truly beautiful. But it is disingenuous to put it this way: Plato is the one creating something beautiful here. By means of Socrates and Glaucon—within the downward-spiraling dance of his brother and his hero, those who were nearest and dearest to him—Plato creates a thing of enduring beauty. "Bless me, my dear Glaucon," said I, "how strenuously you polish off each of your two men for the competition for the prize as if it were a statue." Like the older son of Ariston, Plato too can reply: "To the best of my ability" (361d7).

What makes Glaucon's challenge somewhat easier is that his speech is highly proleptic (see section §8): it contains in embryo the principal elements of the answer Socrates will provide in response. Having created two men, Glaucon insists that there be an absolute separation between them: he calls it ἡ διάστασις at 360e3. Only on the basis of "this separation" can a proper choice be made:

> "But to come now to the decision [κρίσιν] between our two kinds of life, if we separate [διαστησώμεθα] the most completely just and the most completely unjust man, we shall be able to decide rightly, but if not, not." (360d8-e2)

This choice (κρίσις; also at 361d5) will prove to be "the crisis of the *Republic*" in Book VII with the Allegory of the Cave being its context. The Cave is foreshadowed here as well: although the Just philosopher's descent is the opposite of Gyges' (359c7-360b3), Glaucon repeats the word at 359d5 for "to go down."[62] The origins of basanistic pedagogy are found here as well: the just man "has been tested with respect to justice [βεβανισμένος εἰς δικαιοσύνην]" at 361c6-7. Most importantly, albeit without making the all-important separation between them, Glaucon also introduces the vocabulary of Being and Becoming:

62. Davis, *Soul of the Greeks* attempts to re-interpret *Republic* on the basis of Gyges as presented both by Glaucon (141-43 and 154-57) and Herodotus (143-54); this leads him to understand the dialogue's loftiest image in relation to its lowliest antithesis: by his descent, Gyges renders his body invisible and thus can realize his selfish objectives through murder while the philosopher's altruistic soul is invisible to those who murder him.

"From this then is the beginning of legislation and covenants between men; and they name the commandment of the law the lawful and the just, and this indeed is the genesis and essential nature [γένεσίν τε καὶ οὐσίαν] of justice—being a compromise between [μεταξὺ οὖσαν] the actual best [τοῦ μὲν ἀρίστου ὄντος], which is to do wrong with impunity, and the worst, which is to be wronged and be impotent to get one's revenge." (359a2-7; Shorey modified)

Although apparently inextricably linked here to Becoming (γένεσις in this sense will introduced at 485b2)[63] as if the genesis of a thing were its essence, (cf. 408e4), it is Glaucon who introduces the use of οὐσία as "essential nature" (Being) as opposed to material wealth (cf. 361b5). Once the clear separation (διάστασις) between γένεσις and οὐσία has been made in Books V-VII and the student understands what really stands between them—the mathematical μεταξύ between Being and Becoming is a crucial part of the story[64]—Plato will have set the stage for Socrates' response to Glaucon's challenge.

What makes Glaucon's Challenge to Socrates so difficult are the fourth and fifth applications of the distinction between what is and what merely seems to be, between appearance and reality. In comparing the just to the unjust man, Glaucon removes all polish from the one and bestows it upon the other. Naturally there are two of them: how else can we determine which of them has the happier way of life? But Glaucon once again—twice, in fact—uses the appearance and reality distinction to make the task of Socrates that much more beautiful. The just man will be perfectly just, the unjust man is the opposite. But the unjust man—a technical craftsman of injustice—will *appear* to be just (361a5-b8): everyone in the Cave will think him so. As for the Just man, everyone will misunderstand him except herself: possessing the inner reality of Justice, she will appear to be perfectly unjust (II 361c5-6) and therefore hated with a deadly hatred. The results—beautifully described by Glaucon—will be ugly:

"We must tell it, then; and even if my language is somewhat rude and brutal, you must not suppose, Socrates, that it is I who speak thus, but those who commend injustice above justice. What they will say is this: that such being his disposition the just man will have to endure the lash, the rack, chains, the branding-iron in his eyes, and finally, after every extremity of suffering, he will be crucified, and so will learn his lesson that not to be but to seem just is what we ought to desire." (361e1-362a6)

Paul Shorey takes a liberty here: the Greek word he translates with "crucified" has nothing whatsoever to do with a cross.[65] But as anyone who has ever con-

---

63. Glaucon's use of γένεσις is maintained at 371d4, 371e12, and 373e6-8.

64. See sections §13 and §28; note Glaucon's use of διάνοια at 359c1.

65. See Shorey, *Plato's Republic*, 1.124n"c": "Or strictly 'impaled.' Cf. Cic[ero] *De Rep*. 3.27, Writers on Plato and Christianity have often compared the fate of Plato's just man with the Crucifixion." ἀνασχινδυλευθήσεται (only found here) is convertible (according to LSJ) with ἀνασκολοπίζειν: "fix on a pole or stake, impale." LSJ also records

versed with one of Jehovah's Witnesses knows, Jesus Christ was not "crucified" either: he too was "impaled on a torture stake" (cf. Matthew 27:40). Required by Glaucon to defend justice under these trying circumstances more than three hundred years before Christ, Socrates faced (as it were, "yesterday") a far more daunting challenge than any of us would confront if we were minded to step into his sandals and follow his footsteps down to the Piraeus today.

Section 10. The Challenge of Adeimantus to Plato

The Athenians of Plato's day had no Bible in a double sense: they didn't have the Bible and they had nothing that any of them regarded as (*mutatis mutandis*) "the gospel truth." Homer came the closest to this status but fell well short of it. After all, Hesiod had been Homer's rival and had gone toe-to-toe with him in dueling verses. Not the worst way to begin understanding Plato is to see him as reviving Hesiod's ethical challenge to Homer's supremacy without conceding anything to the latter on purely artistic grounds. In any case, the *Republic* simply cannot be understood by anyone who has not read (or heard) Hesiod's *Works and Days*.[66] But Hesiod aside, Plato invites us to consider him as Homer's rival in the *Republic* and it is through Adeimantus that Plato presents this challenge to himself.

To begin with, of course, Adeimantus misses the point by thinking that Glaucon has done so. With his two perfect statues, Glaucon has challenged Socrates to consider justice (and the lack of it) without regard to the afterlife: "leave out of account their rewards and consequences" (358b6-7). But this effete but well-intentioned young man—like the simple soul who wants to find God in Kafka's *Castle* or Christianity in Heidegger—has his place: one should never hesitate to restate the obvious. Adeimantus pounds home the point that all of the poets have praised justice in the wrong way: they have told us to be good for the sake of rewards. At best they contradict themselves, as even our own poets—those who would celebrate Christmas—still do today: "He knows if you've been sleeping/He knows if you're awake/He knows if you've been bad or good/So be good for goodness' sake!" It is always the same old ever-new problem: Plato aims to take "for goodness's sake" literally whereas our poets—like those quoted by Adeimantus—do not. "You'd better be good because Santa's got his eye on you."

Adeimantus is a well-read young man: he has heard many poets and he can quote them *verbatim*. As the Greeks would say, Adeimantus is interested in music. As anyone who has recently read *Ion* can tell you, "music" means something quite different today. Moreover, the reader who loved the eminently lovable *Ion* is also in a better position to see Plato as "Homer's rival."[67] But music in gen-

that "it is used convertibly with ἀνασταυρόω, as in Ph[ilo *mechanicus*; B.C.].1.237, 687, Luc[ian]. *Peregr.* 11."

66. See Altman, "Reading Order," §4 and also section §30 below.

67. Cf. 595b9-c3 with *Ion* 530b9-10.

eral—whether made by the Muses, by Plato, or by Homer—has its rival as well: gymnastics. Diogenes Laertius asserts that Plato has given us a portrait of his own elementary school teacher in the *Erastai*: in any case, that slender little dialogue contains a vivid portrait of the rivalry between music and gymnastics or "athletics and academics" (as we call them today).[68] All the youngsters in the home of Polemarchus have been taught—as Aristocles himself had been taught—both music and gymnastics: both of these are things about which everyone in the room knows important things. Adeimantus is the most musical of the lot. Plato doesn't tell us who was the most athletic; perhaps it was Polemarchus. In any case, everybody in the room could be defined—and their living counterparts, in real life as lived in fifth-century Athens, had probably been defined and were known as such by others and themselves—as belonging somewhere along the continuum between culture and sport, athletics and academics.

When we think of the word "Academy" as it is commonly used today, Americans think of a private boarding school rather than a university. As the *Republic* proves, this remains a pretty good basis for understanding Plato's. Not only was Plato himself an athlete but he was known—at least to outsiders—on the basis of his athletic prowess: he was "Plato." The *Republic* proves that his students were interested in both music and sport; Plato the Teacher was (both a fortiori and a priori) interested in these things as well. The second time the ruler of a Socratic City is mentioned (if we are willing to count the True Ruler in the City of Good Men Only as the first time), it is the teacher who decides what combination of music and gymnastics are appropriate for each individual Guardian-in-training (i.e., for each student).[69] Moreover, it is very obvious (to paraphrase the most paradoxical aspect of the Third Wave of Paradox) that there is no place here for those who do one without the other (see section §24): the

---

68. *Am.* 132d1-2. The distinction is unfamiliar to Alcibiades: Socrates teaches it to him at *Alc. 1* 108c7-d8. The fact that it is taken for granted in *Amatores* indicates that it follows *Alciabiades Major* in the Reading Order. This can hardly be called a dramatic but rather a pedagogical indication of reading order. Therefore this category should be added to the laundry list at Press, "Introduction" to *Plato's Dialogues*, 5. Kahn repeatedly shows himself sensitive to these pedagogical connections.

69. 412a4-b2: "'Then he who best blends gymnastics with music and applies them most suitably to the soul is the man whom we should most rightly pronounce to be the most perfect and harmonious musician, far rather than the one who brings the strings into unison with one another.' 'That seems likely, Socrates,' he said. 'And shall we not also need in our city, Glaucon, a permanent overseer of this kind [τοῦ τοιούτου τινὸς ἀεὶ ἐπιστάτου] if its constitution is to be preserved?' 'We most certainly shall.'" This is as close to a self-description of Plato the Teacher as he allows us. Horace became famous for popularizing Plato's position with the *mens sana in corpore sano*. Horace also studied at the Academy: *inter silvas Academiae quaerere verum.* For all of his self-confessed Epicureanism, Horace's version of going back down—i.e., embracing the comfortable tyranny of Augustus—is probably close to the origin of the Stoic deformation of Platonism celebrated in Annas, *Platonic Ethics.*

jocks[70] must listen to Beethoven and the egg-heads[71] will get ample opportunity to impress Ariston the Argive with their refined musicality.

It will be seen that the elementary education of the Guardians described in Books II through IV is a matter of particular interest to Adeimantus: this explains why Socrates discourses with him on this subject. And it is the interest of Adeimantus in what the poets have said well or badly—the central theme of his speech—that explains why Socrates devotes so much attention to the subject in Books II-IV. Like any athlete or musician, Socrates knows the vital importance of warming up. He thought he was done before breaking a sweat—it is Thrasymachus who does all the sweating in Book I—but he was wrong. When he sees that serious exertions are going to be required—and Glaucon's third demand leaves him in no doubt about that—he is, in sober truth, much relieved by the comparative obtuseness of Adeimantus, who thinks his brother has neglected "the most important thing" (362d5). But Plato ensures that the speech of Adeimantus, like his brother Glaucon's, is usefully proleptic: here is the first adumbration of the Longer Way (364d3) and the first hint that any alternative may yield only a Cave-based "shadow outline of virtue" (365c4); an ability to see through

---

70. 411c4-e2: "'if a man toils hard at gymnastics and eats right lustily and holds no truck with music and philosophy, does he not at first get very fit and full of pride and high spirit and become more brave and bold than he was?' 'He does indeed.' 'But what if he does nothing but this and has no contact with the Muse in any way, is not the result that even if there was some principle of the love of knowledge in his soul, since it tastes of no instruction nor of any inquiry and does not participate in any discussion or any other form of culture, it becomes feeble, deaf, and blind, because it is not aroused or fed nor are its perceptions purified and quickened?' 'That is so,' he said. 'And so such a man, I take it, becomes a misologist and stranger to the Muses. He no longer makes any use of persuasion by speech but achieves all his ends like a beast by violence and savagery, and in his brute ignorance and ineptitude lives a life of disharmony and gracelessness.' Academics would do well to consider that Plato penned this passage in order to shame the more athletic among his students to discard their physique-borne arrogance

71. 411a5-c3: "'Now when a man abandons himself to music to play upon him and pour into his soul as it were through the funnel of his ears those sweet, soft, and dirge-like airs of which we were just now speaking, and gives his entire time to the warblings and blandishments of song, the first result is that the principle of high spirit, if he had it, is softened like iron and is made useful instead of useless and brittle. But when he continues the practice without remission and is spellbound, the effect begins to be that he melts and liquefies till he completely dissolves away his spirit, cuts out as it were the very sinews of his soul and makes of himself a 'feeble warrior.'' 'Assuredly,' he said. 'And if,' said I, 'he has to begin with a spiritless nature he reaches this result quickly, but if high-spirited, by weakening the spirit he makes it unstable, quickly irritated by slight stimuli, and as quickly quelled. The outcome is that such men are choleric and irascible instead of high-spirited, and are peevish and discontented.' 'Precisely so.'" The fact that I have reversed Plato's order suggests that contrary to what I expect of my readers, Plato expected his to be more inclined to athletics. This probably has more to do with their respective ages than with changing societal values: Plato's auditors were younger than any readers I may have will be.

"the fraudulent" (κίβδηλος at 366b5) will likewise prove crucial (see section §18). It is in Adeimantus' speech that the "best guardian" enters (367a4; cf. 334a1 and 375c10-11) and echoing Glaucon (358d3), Adeimantus makes it even clearer that he is seeking justice itself (367b5 and 367d2), i.e., Justice.

Allan Bloom performed a valuable service by identifying the interlocutors at the head of each page of his translation of Plato's *Republic*;[72] there is no doubt that a good reading of the dialogue demands distinguishing what Socrates says to Adeimantus from what he says to Glaucon.[73] It is possible that an analytical taxonomy on my *index locorum* would reveal that the five passages where Adeimantus is Socrates' discussant are cited less often than those where Glaucon is. But this might not prove to be the case: basanistic portions of the text will not be ignored and deserve no less careful consideration from the dialectical Platonist. In any case: in addition to the speech in Book II, Adeimantus (1) joins with Socrates in the founding of the City until Glaucon's City of Pigs interruption at 372d5, (2) discusses musical education with him between 376d4 and the entrance of melody at 398c1-5, (3) interrupts the conversation for the first time at the beginning of Book IV (419a1) only to be politely pushed aside by Socrates at 427c6-d7,[74] (4) interrupts again, this time to much greater effect at 487b1, and participates in a dialogue that continues until Glaucon demands further information about the Good at 506d1, and finally (5) accompanies Socrates during the discussion of defective polities between VIII 548d8 and IX 576b9. If one were inclined to reconstruct a psychobiography of Adeimantus, "(5)" furnishes the materials for such a project; this theme will not be developed here. But given the nature of basanistic pedagogy, the comforting[75] and ultimately apolitical aspect of what Adeimantus accepts from Socrates in "(4)" make it one of the most important passages in *Republic* (see section §15). Unlike Glaucon, Adeimantus is content with the Shorter Way and is persuaded that it is no mean feat to remain aloof from politics (cf. 497a1-2). It is for this reason that the true analogue to Xenophon's Glaucon—at *Memorabilia* 3.6, Socrates, as a favor to

---

72. Bloom, *Republic of Plato*, 342: "As Glaucon was daring, Adeimantus is moderate; as Glaucon turned to nature, Adeimantus turns to opinion; as Glaucon paid attention to what he saw, Adeimantus pays attention to what he hears. He is particularly addicted to poetry."

73. Bloom, *Republic of Plato*, 346: "Glaucon, with his manly intransigence, makes the most important contribution of the two interlocutors; he gives the conversation its power and height."

74. Socrates' "O son of Ariston" (427c6-7) is addressed to Glaucon while 427d6-7 is a polite acknowledgement of Adeimantus.

75. Cf. Bloom, *Republic of Plato*, 342-43: "Thus Adeimantus, too, wishes to hear a new and adequate praise of justice, but what he asks is different from what his brother asked for. Just as the latter desired an argument for pure and earnest dedication, so Adeimantus now reveals his deepest wishes by insisting that justice be easy and pleasant."

Plato, turns *Glaucon* away from politics—is not Plato's Glaucon but Adeimantus, a literary man of oligarchic tendencies.[76]

This limitation aside, Adeimantus' interest in literature, an interest shared by the audience both in and outside the house of Polemarchus, gives Socrates a chance to get limbered up. He will therefore have come into his stride before rising to the higher level—one that requires a second wind along the Longer Way—of Glaucon's daunting challenge. Even more beautiful, especially because Adeimantus shares the credit for its beauty, most generously, with Glaucon, is the challenge of Adeimantus addressed to his brother Plato:

> "And the sole cause of all this is the fact that was the starting-point of this entire plea of my friend here and of myself to you, Socrates, pointing out how strange it is that of all you self-styled advocates of justice, from the heroes of old whose discourses survive to the men of the present day, not one has ever censured injustice or commended justice otherwise than in respect of the repute, the honors, and the gifts that accrue from each. But what each one of them is in itself, by its own inherent force, when it is within the soul of the possessor and escapes the eyes of both gods and men, no one has ever adequately set forth in poetry or prose—the proof that the one is the greatest of all evils that the soul contains within itself, while justice is the greatest good. For if you had all spoken in this way from the beginning and from our youth up had sought to convince us, we should not now be guarding against one another's injustice, but each would be his own best guardian, for fear lest by working injustice he should dwell in communion with the greatest of evils." (366d5-367a4)

As revealed by Adeimantus, Plato is about "to boldly go where no man has gone before."[77] Adeimantus may not be as smart as Glaucon, but he surely comes nobly to the aid of Socrates here. Nor is it overstating the case to claim that Plato suggests in this speech that Socrates was able to derive the whole plan of educating the guardians from what Adeimantus says in the last sentence: Books II-IV are already present there in embryo. But Plato also presents his brother as coming to Plato's aid. It is Adeimantus who articulates the difficult thing that Plato must do and is even now doing: it is Adeimantus who allows Plato to present himself as accomplishing something truly beautiful.

---

76. In addition to the structural position of Adeimantus in relation to oligarchy and Hesiod's five ages (section §30), see VI 499d8-500a8.

77. *Star Trek* is at times a very useful commentary on Plato's *Republic*, above all with respect to the tripartite soul. Mr. Spock, of course, is Reason; Dr. McCoy will serve as spokesman for the appetites, or in any case the body. This suggests (by process of elimination) that Captain Kirk is the embodiment of "High Spirit." That this is in fact the case is proved when he breaks free from "the Islands of the Blessed" in "This Side of Paradise" by being reminded of honor, i.e., of his duty to a more than simply honorable Enterprise.

Chapter Three

The Shorter Way

Section 11. Introduction to Methodology

It is one thing to make Plato's intentions more visible: to humanize both him and his audience as teacher and students, to contextualize his Πολιτεία by setting it in its specific time without neglecting its perennial place. But now it is the time to dispense with the necessary preliminaries and to cross some invisible but definite dividing line into philosophy. Plato himself has given us a clear image of this division in the Divided Line at the end of Book VI. A discussion of the Line not only (1) signals the transition from (a) making Plato more visible, to (b) making the City—so vividly described in his *Republic*—more intelligible, but it also (2) holds the key necessary for distinguishing the (a) Shorter from (b) the Longer Way. This proves to be the basis for freeing the *Republic* from the encrustation of what might be called "Plato's political theory." I will use this phrase as shorthand for the view that Plato's *Republic* contains his program for an ideal or perfect City; although the commanding influence of this view must be said to have waned markedly since the Second World War, it will always remain one interpretive pole in the way the *Republic* is read.

Plato never uses the word "methodology"—despite its Greek components, it is not found in Classical Greek—but he invented it nevertheless. This statement becomes less preposterous when we reflect that Plato coined the word "method": at least no author writing before Plato whose writings survive used it. Not only is this word not found in Hippocrates, for instance, but Plato himself applies it to Hippocrates in the *Phaedrus* (*Phdr.* 270c1-e1). Despite the fact that Hippocrates discovered the *method* appropriate to medicine or at any rate a significant medical method, but it was Plato who invented a term for it. Plato stands, therefore, in the same relation to "methodology" as Hippocrates (or whoever else helped Plato coin the term) stands to "method." Since Plato coined the term—its etymology suggests "a pursuit"—it is difficult to say what his readers thought it meant when they encountered it for the first time.[1] Liddell

1. In the reading order as I have reconstructed it, the first time the student encounters the word "method" is in *Republic* IV. Note that *Phaedrus* is dependent on the tripartite psychology of the Shorter Way and constitutes the *locus classicus* of the view that no

and Scott have distinguished two meanings used by Plato: [I] "pursuit of knowledge, investigation," and [II] "mode of prosecuting such inquiry, method, system."[2] It is this second sense[3] that is crucial for all future philosophical development and the basis for what will become "methodology." In due course, I will argue that Plato also uses it in a third sense that I will call "[III]" and will define as "one of several particular elements not themselves methodically integrated into a mode of prosecuting such inquiry, system, or merely apparent method (in sense [II])." As it happens, it is in this sense that Socrates introduces it in Book IV. But explaining that first use in sense [III] requires an introduction and it is only in the next section that it will be completed. It is necessary to begin elsewhere.

The word "method" is used eight times in the *Republic*: there are two instances of [I], three of [II], two of indeterminate meaning somewhere between [I] and [II], and one in sense [III].[4] It is crucial to [II] that any particular μέθοδος is just that: one among at least two possible methods. But mere plurality is not enough: there are a variety of mathematical *pursuits* (sense [I] at 510c5 and 528d8) but only the dialectical method (sense [II] at 533c8 and possibly 510b8) can bring out their common features (531c10, 533b2, and 596a6). In sense [II], μέθοδος is not a "search or investigation" of something (528d8) but a type of investigation: above all ἡ διαλεκτικὴ μέθοδος (533c8). It should be emphasized that Plato's discovery of method in sense [II] is a highly significant breakthrough; it is parallel to the distinction he introduces (at least no writer whose writings survive used it before him) between form and content, i.e., be-

---

written work can do what the *Republic* does. With respect to the visionary *Republic*, the *Phaedrus* may conveniently be considered as the basanistic counterpart to the proleptic *Gorgias*. They are, at any rate, equidistant from the central *Republic* in my reconstruction of the reading order.

2. Although its etymology shows that the baseline concept involved is a "following after, pursuit" (LSJ), this literal sense is found in only later authors.

3. LSJ identifies *Phdr.* 270c for [2]. An investigation of the way the word is used in the later dialogues—*Phaedrus* (3 times), *Theaetetus* (1), *Sophist* (6), *Statesman* (3), *Laws* (2), and *Phaedo* (2)—is revealing and the list is intended to shed some light on the post-*Republic* reading order. The failure of the Eleatic Stranger to use the word in sense "[II]" is revealing; see George Kimball Plochmann, "Socrates, the Stranger from Elea, and Some Others." *Classical Philology* 49 no. 4 (October 1954), 223-241 at 227. With the eight times it is found in *Republic* and once in the *Letters*, there are 26 uses in the *corpus Platonicum*. Burnet, *Plato's Phaedo*, brings his characteristic light touch to the two meanings of μέθοδος discernible in the two times (first at *Phd.* 79e3) that it is used there: Plato saves the best for last (*Phd.* 97b6).

4. It is found in Books IV (once), VI (2), VII (4), and X (1). Of these, the first (IV 435d1) deserves its own treatment and will receive it in due course. But of the two uses in Book VI (510b8 and 510c5)—both in the Divided Line—the second is clearly in accordance with [I] while the first seems to fall somewhere between [I] and [II]. The first use in Book VII (528d8) is an example of [I] and the second (531c10) falls into the same category as VI 510c5. The other three (VII 533b2, 533c8, and X 596a6) are used in sense [II].

tween content ("what should be said") and form ("how it should be said") at 392c7-9. In this Section, I intend to show why the difference between the Longer and Shorter Ways is best understood in terms of methodology: the Longer Way is based on "the dialectical method" while the Shorter Way is not.

I have already called attention (in section §1) to the fact that Socrates greets the discovery of justice in the City along the Shorter Way with: "'Why, all the time, bless your heart, the thing was tumbling about our feet from the start and yet we couldn't see it'" (432d8-9), and I have applied these words to the initial κατέβην. Such an interpretation required a poetic mixture of the Shorter and Longer Ways that puts the cart before the horse. Within the universe of the Shorter Way alone (and that is the context of the Book IV discovery) the significance of the words "from the start" (ἐξ ἀρχῆς) have long been recognized; these words refer back to 369e3-370b7 and the introduction of the "one man one job" principle (ἕνα ἕκαστον ἓν at 369e3) when Socrates begins to construct the City after being confronted with the speeches of Glaucon and Adeimantus in Book II. This is spelled out clearly in the text:

> "For what we laid down in the beginning [ὃ γὰρ ἐξ ἀρχῆς ἐθέμεθα] as a universal requirement when we were founding the city, this I think, or some form of this, is justice. And what we did lay down, and often said, if you recall, was that each one man must perform one social service for which his nature was best adapted." (433a1-6)

The inquiry has ended in Book IV just where it began in Book II; "what we laid down in the beginning" has turned out to be the thing for which we sought. The circularity of this process—the absolute necessity of its circularity—is explained on a theoretical level in the simile of the Divided Line.

In describing the Second Part of the Line, third in order of presentation but second with respect to intelligibility (511d8-e1), Socrates emphasizes the fact that the practitioners of this "form of inquiry"—Socrates does not use the word "method" (cf. 369c9)—rely on hypotheses (ὑποθέσεις).

> "taking their start from these, and then proceeding through the rest, they conclude agreeably to that from which they set out to investigate [ὁμολογουμένως ἐπὶ τοῦτο οὗ ἂν ἐπὶ σκέψιν ὁρμήσωσι]." (510d1-3)

He makes the same point again at 511a5-7: this form of inquiry does not proceed "to a first principle because of its inability to extricate itself from and rise above its hypotheses [ἐξ ὑποθέσεων]." The anticlimactic discovery of justice in the city in Book IV is therefore a graphic example (he will call such things "Images") of this failure to rise above the assumptions or Hypotheses made at the outset of an investigation.[5] This is hardly coincidental and the key to my reading

5. John A Brentlinger, "The Divided Line and Plato's 'Theory of Intermediates.'" *Phronesis* 8 no. 2 (1963), 144-166 at 151n1: "Indeed the defect which Socrates finds in

of Plato's *Republic* is the discovery that the "form of inquiry" described in the Second Part of the Line depends on to the methods Socrates uses for the investigation of justice along the Shorter Way. It is therefore primarily for methodological reasons that it is justice but not Justice that is discovered in Book IV.

The discussion of the intelligible portion of the line begins at 510b4, where Socrates attempts to explain both of its segments in a single μεν/δε sentence:

> "By the [μὲν] distinction that there is one section of it which the soul is compelled to investigate by treating as images the things imitated in the former division, and by means of assumptions from which it proceeds not up to a first principle but down to a conclusion, while [δ'] there is another section in which it advances from its assumption to a beginning or principle that transcends assumption, and in which it makes no use of the images employed by the other section, relying on ideas only and progressing systematically through ideas."[6]

It is of great importance that Glaucon does not grasp Socrates' meaning as expressed in this first attempt (510b9). There are many occasions in the dialogues where Socrates needs to clarify himself by explaining something more clearly that his interlocutor has failed to understand the first time. These passages offer Plato the Teacher the opportunity to teach his readers how to teach: the student admits incomprehension while preparing to grasp the proper meaning the second time. But this is not their only purpose, as we shall see. Although Socrates will offer Glaucon increased clarity in the form of mathematical examples, he will continue to follow the logical and linguistic patterns laid down in this introductory statement in each of his next four speeches. In other words, mathematics is only the clearest example of a far more general—but nonetheless defective—form of inquiry.[7] The most important of these patterns is that the distinction between the two sections is based on two *differentiae*: the use of (1) Hypotheses[8]

---

the discussion of the four virtues, in Book IV, is that it fails to establish itself in the light of the Good; it is thus presumably on the level of hypotheses."

6. 510b4-510b8. It is the second part of the sentence—beginning with "while there is another"—that contains the second use of μέθοδος in the *Republic*: τὸ δ᾽ αὖ ἕτερον—τὸ ἐπ᾽ ἀρχὴν ἀνυπόθετον—ἐξ ὑποθέσεως ἰοῦσα καὶ ἄνευ τῶν περὶ ἐκεῖνο εἰκόνων, αὐτοῖς εἴδεσι δι᾽ αὐτῶν τὴν μέθοδον ποιουμένη (510b6-8). Note that this use is perfectly consistent with [I]: it is simply "an investigation." It becomes something more (i.e. [II]) only by contrast with the method that *does* use Images and Hypotheses. Plato's refusal to use the word μέθοδος for both of these μέθοδων is probably connected with his refusal to ever name "the Shorter Way:" it bears emphasis that he refers only to "a longer and fuller way" (435d2-3; translation mine). See also 504b2.

7. Henry Jackson, "On Plato's *Republic* VI 509 D sqq." *Journal of Philology* 10 (1882), 132-150 at 144: "this method, though here described with special reference to arithmetic and geometry, should be applicable whenever an idea is studied in its reflection." Unfortunately, Jackson means "a Platonic Idea."

8. Plato has introduced the word "hypothesis" to the student at *Meno* 86e3. Charles H. Kahn, "Did Plato Write Socratic Dialogues?" *Classical Quarterly* (n.s.) 31 no. 2 (1981), 305-320 at 318 contains a brilliant analysis of Platonic pedagogy in relation to the

and (2) Images. A paraphrase of the passage (510b4-511c2) with some important words in parenthesis will be useful.

In this segment of the Line, the soul is compelled to investigate (ζητεῖν) beginning with a Hypothesis (ἐξ ὑποθέσεως) using as Images the things that were imitated (by shadows etc.) in the visible segment. In the second part of the sentence (the clause about the higher section of the intelligible) he says that it too begins from an Hypothesis (ἐξ ὑποθέσεως) but it proceeds to an unhypothetical beginning (rather than a conclusion, as does the lower segment of the intelligible section) and further constitutes a search (τὴν μέθοδον) that uses forms, but proceeds without Images or indeed any objects of sense.[9] It should be carefully noted that it is the existence of two distinct forms of inquiry that will allow Plato to create here the enduring meaning of τὴν μέθοδον as "the method" or manner of search.

In none of the four speeches that follow does Socrates again attempt to discuss both segments of the intelligible portion of the Line in one continuous passage (much less in a single sentence) as he did at the start. He devotes three speeches (beginning at 510c1, 510d5, and 511a4 respectively) to the lower portion of the intelligible segment that is closest to the visible and only one (beginning at 511b2) to the infinitely more important First Part. Of the three speeches about the Second Part, the third (511a4-a9) is a general summary, based on the previous two speeches, but also harkening back to the language of the first single-sentence attempt. Each of the two intermediate speeches focuses on one of the two distinguishing characteristics of the lower segment of the intelligible emphasized in the preliminary attempt just quoted: (1) its dependence on Hypotheses and (2) its use of Images. The first of these (510c1-d3) introduces mathematical examples for the sake of pedagogical clarity and establishes a linguistic link to the circularity attending the discovery of justice in Book IV.

---

use of hypotheses. Kahn also alerts us to the role of *Charmides* (where only the verb is found) in this development; as remarked before, the *Charmides* and the *Meno* (along with *Gorgias*, *Theages*, and *Cleitophon*) are both prior and proximate to the *Republic* in my reconstruction of the Reading Order. Especially noteworthy is Kahn's discussion (318-19) of the proleptic introduction of the concept of Hypothesis in the *Protagoras*: "(Note that the conclusion in the *Protagoras* becomes the *hypothesis* in the *Meno*.)" The student who *returns* to *Protagoras* (as teacher) recognizes both Socratic hedonism and the *methods* upon which it is defended for what they are. See Roslyn Weiss, "The Hedonic Calculus in the *Protagoras* and the *Phaedo*." *Journal of the History of Philosophy* 27 no. 4 (October 1989), 511-529.

9. In other words, μέθοδος is here used to describe simply a *search*; it might mean "method" in sense [II] but then again it might not. Part of what confuses Glaucon is perhaps this neologism: Socrates is giving Glaucon—and Plato is giving everyone—a first lesson in methodology. At the risk of repetition, it seems that it was Plato's discovery of a new dialectical method that allowed him to see that the various mathematical investigations shared (by contrast with dialectic) a common method, although he refuses to call it this out of deference to the only method that is truly singular and methodical, i.e., the dialectical method.

Socrates is sure that Glaucon knows that those who busy themselves about geometry, calculation and similar subjects (τὰ τοιαῦτα) hypothesize (ὑποθέμενοι): (1) the even and odd, (2) the (geometrical) figures, (3) the three forms of angles (γωνιῶν τριττὰ εἴδη), and (4) a variety of kindred things other related according to the particular investigation or search involved (καθ' ἑκάστην μέθοδον);[10] these things they treat as known, making them Hypotheses (ὑποθέσεις) neither seeking nor offering any explanation of these, as if they were clear to all, but beginning from these, they run through the remaining things, "concluding conformably to that from which they set off to explore" (translation mine of τελευτῶσιν ὁμολογουμένως ἐπὶ τοῦτο οὗ ἂν ἐπὶ σκέψιν ὁρμήσωσι). This, then, is the phrase that establishes the circularity of the process, translated in context by Shorey as follows:

> "I don't fully understand what you mean by this," he said. "Well, I will try again, said I, for you will better understand after this preamble. For I think you are aware that students of geometry and reckoning and such subjects [καὶ τὰ τοιαῦτα] *first* postulate [ὑποθέμενοι] the odd and the even and the various figures and three kinds of angles and other things akin to these in each branch of science, regard them as known, and treating them as absolute assumptions, do not deign to render any further account of them to themselves or others, taking it for granted that they are obvious to everybody. They take their start from these, and pursuing the inquiry from this point on consistently, conclude [his "consistently" should be here] with that for the investigation of which they set out."[11]

---

10. This use is clearly and exclusively in sense [I]. Each branch of mathematics is a mere *pursuit*; Plato is attempting to define what all such pursuits have in common: i.e., to identify a method in sense [II]. But the crucial thing to grasp is that the Second Part of the Line does *not* describe a single method in the strict sense of [II]: it employs both Images and Hypotheses but there is no justification for doing so that is derivable from the (merely apparent) "method." By contrast with the dialectical method—the only one worthy of the name in sense [II]—mathematical pursuits (and other pursuits that use the same *methods*) are based on a method in sense [II], i.e. an alternate mode, manner, or procedure of investigation. But it is so *only* by contrast with a real method and even then not in the strict sense. My use of the phrase "the same methods" will suggest why I maintain we need to supplement LSJ with a third meaning: [III] "one of several particular elements not themselves methodically integrated into a mode of prosecuting such inquiry, system, or merely apparent method (in sense [II])." These elements are (1) Hypotheses, and (2) the use of Images. Of the 26 times that Plato uses the word μέθοδος, he employs it in the plural only once. This is at 435d1: the first time he uses it in the *Republic* and the only time he uses it to describe, by contrast with the Longer, an *unnamed* "Shorter Way."

11. 510b9-d3 (emphasis mine). Shorey's translation is obviously not based on the emendation introduced by Slings, who gives the words "but once again" (my translation) to Glaucon. See his *Platonis Rempublicam*, 256 on 510b9-c1 for a perfectly reasonable solution to what seems almost entirely unproblematic to me. More importantly, Shorey's use of the word "first" is unwarranted and would in any case have been false had Plato written it (which he didn't): there is neither even nor odd without the logically prior hypothesis of the mathematical One.

While establishing the circularity of the process, this crystal-clear description of "geometry and reckoning" must be read in context. It is important to remember that this is Socrates' *second* attempt to explain his meaning to Glaucon: the first time, he made no reference to arithmetic or geometry. Geometry and arithmetic are merely the examples Socrates now uses to explain a form of inquiry that is dependent on Hypotheses and which makes use of Images. When he adds the words "and such subjects" (καὶ τὰ τοιαῦτα) to his "geometry and reckoning" examples, those words should be taken to mean: "and such other subjects as are characterized by methods (as opposed to a content) similar to those employed in geometry and reckoning." The fact that the examples he has used are drawn from arithmetic and geometry should therefore be understood as part of Socrates' attempt to make his meaning clearer in the face of Glaucon's evident confusion following the first, more general, attempt. In other words: in his first attempt to contrast the First and Second Parts of the Divided Line (510b4-8), Socrates emphasizes only the *methodological* contrast between the two as regards (1) Hypotheses and (2) Images. This suggests another reason—other than teaching us how to teach—for the fact that Plato employed the device of an uncomprehending Glaucon: "geometry and reckoning" are only the clearest examples of methods, defined by dependence on Images and Hypotheses, that inevitably yield circular results. We must discover for ourselves that these methods have already been applied along the Shorter Way.

Section 12. Methodology II: Hypotheses

The only previous occasion that Plato uses either of the two words related to "hypothesis" (i.e., the participle and the noun) is in Book IV. Socrates has been discussing the principle of non-contradiction introduced at 436b9.[12] After a refutation of various objections to this principle, he says at 437a3:

> "All the same," said I, "that we may not be forced to examine at tedious length the entire list of such contentions and convince ourselves that they are false, *let us proceed on the hypothesis that this is so*, with the understanding that, if it ever appear otherwise, everything that results from the assumption shall be invalidated." (437a3-8; emphasis mine)

The italicized passage translates the Greek "ὑποθέμενοι ὡς τούτου οὕτως ἔχοντος." Just as the geometers and mathematicians hypothesize (literally: "are the hypothesizers— ὑποθέμενοι—of") the odd and the even etc., Socrates here proposes that they should hypothesize the principle of non-contradiction. Socrates in Book IV is therefore explicitly employing one of the distinguishing features that will characterize the methods described in the Second Part of the Di-

12. 436b9-10: "'It is obvious that the same thing will never do or suffer opposites in the same respect in relation to the same thing and at the same time.'" Cf. 602e8-9. Plato is the first author to record the law of non-contradiction.

vided Line. This example conclusively proves that at least the use of Hypotheses is characteristic of investigations that could hardly be called mathematical in respect of their content. In fact, mathematical examples (like the Divided Line itself) are not intended to be exhaustive of the methods that characterize the Second Part of the Line; it is the methods themselves that Socrates is attempting to illustrate using convenient (because comprehensible) mathematical examples. It is now time to turn to the first use of "methods" in this sense at 435d1.

> "Goodness gracious," said I, "here is another trifling inquiry into which we have plunged, the question whether the soul really contains these three forms in itself or not." "It does not seem to me at all trifling," he said, "for perhaps, Socrates, the saying is true that 'fine things are difficult.'" "Apparently," said I, "and let me tell you, Glaucon, that in my opinion we shall never apprehend this matter accurately from such methods [ἐκ τοιούτων μεθόδων] as we are now employing in discussion. For there is another longer and harder way that conducts to this. Yet we may perhaps discuss it on the level of previous statements and inquiries." (435c4-d4)

In addition to being (1) the first time the word ἡ μέθοδος is used in the *Republic*, this is (2) the only time it is used in the plural, and (3) it is used in sense [II].[13]

This crucial sentence—none more important for unlocking the structure of the *Republic*—not only introduces the word "method," but includes the first reference to the Longer Way ("μακροτέρα καὶ πλείων ὁδὸς") and by extension "the Shorter Way" as well. This conjunction suggests to the sensitive reader that there may be some kind of deeper connection between "the methods we are presently using" (whatever that neologism "methods" may eventually turn out to mean) and the fact that we are not taking the high road (whatever that may turn out to be). The sentence is therefore highly *proleptic*: it is teeming with meaning

---

13. In fact it is used in sense [III], as I will show. But for now, it is important to point out why it is being used in sense [II] (on which [III] entirely depends) and not [I]. The sentence at 435c9-d4 reads (Shorey divides it in two): "φαίνεται, ἦν δ' ἐγώ. καὶ εὖ γ' ἴσθι, ὦ Γλαύκων, ὡς ἡ ἐμὴ δόξα, ἀκριβῶς μὲν τοῦτο ἐκ τοιούτων μεθόδων, οἵαις νῦν ἐν τοῖς λόγοις χρώμεθα, οὐ μή ποτε λάβωμεν— ἄλλη γὰρ μακροτέρα καὶ πλείων ὁδὸς ἡ ἐπὶ τοῦτο ἄγουσα—ἴσως μέντοι τῶν γε προειρημένων τε καὶ προεσκεμμένων ἀξίως." The context is the transition between the search for justice in the City and justice in the Man. Poised between *two searches*, Plato could have easily used ἡ μέθοδος in the more literal sense of [I] "pursuit of knowledge, investigation" between two of which Socrates now stands. *But Plato deliberately does not do this*. The verb that Plato first associates with "method" is χρῆσθαι with the dative: 'ἐκ τοιούτων μεθόδων, οἵαις . . . χρώμεθα': it is "from such methods *as we are using*" as opposed to "in accordance with the kinds of investigations we are pursuing, making, or following." It will be seen that the use of ἐκ also indicates sense [II] (cf. 596a5) just as κατά at 510c5 indicates sense [I].

and mystery.[14] In fact, the use of the plural at 435d1 suggests a variation on [II] taking us in a very modern direction (as in our "I don't like his methods") where it becomes the plural word "methods" that means [II]: "mode of prosecuting such inquiry, method, system." In this context, then, the singular comes to mean: [III] "single aspect, or particular element in an inadequate or unsystematic mode of prosecuting such inquiry, system, or merely apparent system (in sense [II])." In relation to the Divided Line, either the use of Images or Hypotheses *individually* constitutes a μέθοδος in sense [III]; together, they add up to something less than a μέθοδος in sense [II]. Let's investigate more closely the kind of methods that Socrates is actually using when he utters these crucial words in order to see why this is a fair (and highly revealing) description of the Shorter Way.

The best clue about what Socrates means by the phrase "from such methods as we are now employing in discussion" will (not surprisingly) be found in this passage's immediate context: the logical basis for viewing the soul as having three parts. The first mention of the three parts of the soul is at 435c4 (at the beginning of the passage just quoted) where Socrates says:

> "Goodness gracious," said I, "here is another trifling inquiry into which we have plunged, the question whether the soul really contains these three forms in itself or not." (435c4-6)

This important psychological question arises because of a four-part chain of reasoning that begins immediately preceding at 435a6: (1) whether "larger" or "small," that which is called by the same name is the same (435a6-8), (2) in respect to the "the form [εἶδος] of justice," the just Man will not differ from the just City (435b1-2),[15] and (3) the City seemed to be just when each of the three types within it each did their own job. Moreover, it was temperate, wise and brave also in relation to various characteristics of these same three types (435b4-7). We will therefore expect (4) these same forms to exist in the soul (.e., the Man) and accordingly to earn the same names as the things in the city which have the same characteristics (435b9-c2). Note that each of these four points is contained in its own Socratic statement punctuated by Glaucon's replies:

> "Then," said I, "if you call a thing by the same name whether it is big or little, is it unlike in the way in which it is called the same or like?" "Like," he said. "Then a just man will not differ at all from a just city in respect of the very form of justice, but will be like it." "Yes, like." [3] "But now the city was

14. It is noteworthy that (i) the word "method" and the phrase Socrates uses for (ii) "the Longer Way," both contain (iii) the Greek word for "road." This use of cognates conjoins (i) and (ii) in the reader's mind. In other words, there exists among μεθ-όδων (as among ὅδων) a μακροτέρα καὶ πλείων μέθ-οδος; for now, we are merely making use of inadequate μέθοδοι; i.e., using shortcuts.

15. Cf. 576c5-d1, 580c1-5, and 580d2-4. Consider also the explicit use of Hypothesis at 577d1.

> thought to be just because three natural kinds existing in it performed each its own function, and again it was sober, brave, and wise because of certain other affections and habits of these three kinds." "True," he said. "Then," my friend, we shall thus expect the individual also to have these same forms in his soul, and by reason of identical affections of these with those in the city to receive properly the same appellations." "Inevitable," he said. (435a5-c2)

In other words, Socrates expects that the soul will have these (three) forms (τὰ αὐτὰ ταῦτα εἴδη) because the definitions of the virtues we came up with in the case of the City depended upon certain characteristics of the three kinds of natures (τριττὰ γένη φύσεων) found in it. It is therefore the analogy to the City that leads us to expect that:[16] *even as there were* three classes in the city, so also should there be three forms in the soul. Therefore, it will now be necessary to show that the soul has three parts. A proof of this proposition can be found only by hypothesizing the principle of non-contradiction (which will be introduced immediately following at 436b9-10).

To return for a moment to the Divided Line: note that the third example used by Socrates of what geometers and arithmeticians hypothesize is the *three* forms of angles (γωνιῶν τριττὰ εἴδη at 510c4-5). This is reminiscent of the words just used about the three classes in the city and the three forms in the soul, especially the phrase τὰ τρία εἴδη (of the soul) at 435c5. More important than this verbal parallelism[17] is the fundamental point that the view that soul has three parts not only requires a Hypothesis for its validation (i.e., the law of non-contradiction) but that its own entry into the conversation is itself dependent on a Hypothesis, or rather, on a series of Hypotheses; the points numbered (1) through (4) in the preceding summary of the passage that begins at 435a5. Though Plato does not explicitly name them "hypotheses" as he does in the case of the principle of non-contradiction, this is exactly what they are.[18] Let's exam-

---

16. Beginning with F. M. Cornford, "Psychology and Social Structure in the *Republic* of Plato." *Classical Quarterly* 6 no. 4 (October 1912), 246-265 attempts have been made—e.g. Jerome Neu, "Plato's Analogy of State and Individual: *The Republic* and the Organic Theory of the State." *Philosophy* 46 no. 177 (July 1971), 238-254 and Bernard Williams, "The Analogy of City and Soul in Plato's *Republic*" in E. N. Lee, A. P. D. Mourelatos, and R. M. Rorty (eds.). *Exegesis and Argument*, 196-206 (Assen/Maastricht: Van Gorcum, 1973)—to determine the direction of influence, i.e., whether Plato begins with psychological or political preconceptions.

17. The clearest linguistic parallel between the types of angle and the part of the soul is at 504a4.

18. In addition to Gould, *Development of Plato's Ethics*, 178-181 (see Introduction), see See Gregory Vlastos, "Justice and Psychic Harmony in the *Republic*." *Journal of Philosophy* 66 no. 16 (August 21, 1969), 505-521 at 516 and especially Cornford, "Psychology and Social Structure," 265—where he calls "(2)" an "assumption"—and 248, where he writes: "Every reader of the *Republic* is startled by the assumption, explicitly laid down at p. 427 E [and embodied in "(3)"] that these four virtues—Wisdom, Courage, Temperance, and Justice—cover the whole field of virtue, so that, if we can discover and identify the first three, we may be sure that the one left over will be Justice. This is said

ine the four one by one, starting with the last and working our way back to the primordial Hypothesis.

Hypothesis "(4)" is dependent on all three of the other Hypotheses. It is a general application of "(1)" because whatever names we used to denominate, e.g., the various virtues in the city, will be the same for the similar things we discover in the soul regardless of the fact that the city is large and the soul is small while "(2)" is the Hypothesis that this general principle is, in fact, specifically applicable to justice. Hypotheses "(1)" and "(2)" allow us to extend or transfer the results of "(3)" i.e., definitions of the four virtues based on the existence of the three classes we found the city to the corresponding (like-named) virtues in the man.

Hypothesis "(3)," on the other hand, enjoys a high degree of independence from the previous two. Like "(2)," it depends on the Hypothesis that Socrates knows what virtue actually is but this is a very distant connection in comparison to the relationship between "(4)" and each of "(1)," "(2)," and "(3)." But given Plato's evident affection for *triads*, it will probably come as no surprise that closer scrutiny of "(3)" opens up the proverbial can of worms. Let's consider it schematically: "But now the city was thought to be just because [a] three natural kinds existing in it [b] performed each its own function, and [c] again it was sober, brave, and wise because of certain other affections and habits of these three kinds."

It will be seen that Hypothesis "(3)" itself depends on three other Hypotheses: [i] that the city has exactly three classes, [ii] that justice in the city can be found by process of elimination (perhaps the most ridiculous Hypothesis of all),[19] and [iii] that there are exactly four virtues, each one of which is different from the other three. Adequate consideration of "[iii]" demands some further consideration of the Reading Order of Plato's Dialogues and will be postponed until the end of this section. For now it is enough to point out that Socrates is *assuming* both that virtue has parts and that there are four of them. As for "[ii]," a reader of the *Charmides* is amazed to find justice here what temperance was there (*Chrm.* 161b6):[20] the fault—if such it can be called—must rest with the

---

to be [Cornford cites Adam] 'the earliest passage in Greek literature where the doctrine of the four cardinal virtues (if by cardinal virtues we mean those which make up the sum of perfect goodness) is expressly enunciated' [but see *Alc. 1* 121e6-122a; note the combination of piety and wisdom at *Alc. 1* 122a2; naturally Adam regards this as a later work as indeed it may be, but not with respect to reading order]. *Plato gives no proof whatsoever that this list of virtues is really exhaustive*" (emphasis mine). Gonzalez, *Dialectic and Dialogue,* 236 confirms this point of view: "Socrates' inquiry in this dialogue [sc. the *Republic*] is therefore as 'hypothetical' as mathematics with the important difference that Socrates is not blind to the limitations of this method." See also Hartmut Erbse, "Platons *Politeia* und die modernen Antiplatoniker." *Gymnasium* 83 no. 3 (1976), 169-191 at 177.

19. Cf. Neu, "Plato's Analogy," 242: "the crude argument from elimination at 432b"

20. For the proper explanation of the curious passage at 430c8-el (cf. 441c11-d2) where Socrates attempts to skip over temperance (note Glaucon's astute refusal to allow

unexamined Hypothesis that a process of elimination will be effective in bringing justice to light once we discover the three other virtues we hypothesized with "[iii]." Finally, Socrates' use of Hesiod's *four* metals to initiate his discussion of classes (415a1-7) can only render his utterly mysterious decision to speak of only *three* somewhat later seem arbitrary, i.e., as strictly Hypothetical.[21]

Hypothesis "(2)," vitiated as it is by a *petitio principii* (i.e., it rests on the Hypothesis that we know something about the very thing we are trying to discover in the first place) seems both problematic and arbitrary. But following as it does from "(1)," we should perhaps be prepared to overlook these problems. As to "(1)" itself, it is the Hypothesis on which the construction of the City as a whole depends. Better than anything else, this shows the applicability of the methodology described in the Second Part of the Divided Line to the Shorter Way: "(1)" constitutes the nodal point connecting the use of Hypothesis and Image. In other words, "(1)" is the Hypothesis that a blown-up Image will help us discover something that is only hypothetically the same in a big thing and a small one. Having established the hypothetical character of "(1)," "(2)," "(3)," and "(4)," let's see how Socrates uses them along the Shorter Way.

Hypotheses "(1)" and "(2)" are laid down at the very beginning of the search for justice in Book II. In that sense, they constitute, when taken together, the Hypothesis upon which the whole argument of the *Republic* depends (at least up until the methodological limitations of this argument are made clear in the Divided Line). Although the City is larger than the individual Man, the justice found in the City will not differ *qua* justice from the justice in the Man.[22] Consider the words Socrates used in introducing the City:

> "The inquiry [τὸ ζήτημα] we are undertaking is no easy one but calls for keen vision, as it seems to me. So, since we are not clever persons, I think we should employ the method of search [ζήτησιν] that we should use if we, with not very keen vision, were bidden to read small letters [γράμματα] from a distance, and then someone had observed that these same letters exist elsewhere larger and on a larger surface. We should have accounted it a godsend, I fancy, to be allowed to read those letters [γράμματα] first, and then examine the smaller, if they are the same." "Quite so," said Adimantus, "but what analogy to this do you detect in the inquiry [ζητήσει] about justice?" "I will tell you," I said. "There is a justice of one man, we say, and, I suppose, also of an entire city?" "Assuredly," said he. "Is not the city larger than the man?" "It is larger,"

him to do so at 430d3-4), see Roslyn Weiss, *Philosophers in the Republic: Plato's Two Paradigms* (forthcoming from Cornell University Press).

21. At 415a6-7, it appears that the farmers are iron while the craftsmen bronze. This constitutes a strange twist on Hesiod's evident affection for agriculture and his hostile portrait of the Iron Age. But these two are apparently combined at 434b8 as one of three classes (compare 434a9-10 where the possibility of two distinct groups remains).

22. Neu, "Plato's Analogy," 241: "For Plato, the analogy thesis is an unquestioned assumption made easier by the theory of meaning embodied in the Theory of Forms."

> he said. "Then, perhaps, there would be more justice in the larger object and more easy to apprehend. If it please you, then, let us first look [ζητήσωμεν] for its quality in states, and then only examine it also in the individual, looking for the likeness of the greater in the form of the less." "I think that is a good suggestion," he said. (368c7-369a5)

Although Shorey's use of the word "method" proves nothing (μέθοδος is not found in this passage), there are other linguistic parallels with both the transitional passage in Bk. IV (435c9-d4) and the Divided Line.[23] The most important connection to the Line is the verb "ζητεῖν" and its cognates: it is found in "the inquiry we are undertaking" (τὸ ζήτημα), the phrase Shorey translates as "the method of search" (ζήτησιν)[24]and finally "let us first look for (ζητήσωμεν) its quality in states." It is this word that Plato uses when Socrates introduces the subdivision of the intelligible in the single long sentence (at 510b5) with which we began the discussion of the Divided Line: "by the distinction that there is one section of it which the soul is compelled *to investigate* [ζητεῖν]."

The search for justice that begins in Book II is an investigation or inquiry (cf. 420b8-c1); in the Divided Line, Socrates presents a typology of two types of investigations or inquiries. It is my contention that the methods that characterize the investigation of justice (in both City and Man) beginning with the passage from Book II just quoted (and continuing through Book IV) are not only identical to the methods described in the Second Part of the Divided Line but are also the methods to which Socrates refers when he says at 435d1 that "we shall never apprehend this matter accurately from such methods [ἐκ τοιούτων μεθόδων] as we are now employing in discussion." And I would argue that a narrow reading of the words "we are now employing [χρώμεθα]" (cf. 510b4, 510d5, 510e3, 511a5, 511a7, and 511c1), which would confine them to their immediate context in Book IV is impossible simply because the passage preceding this statement (435a5-c2) is in fact a summary that echoes the very start of the entire inquiry into justice which began in Book II (368c8-369a4). By repeating the words "larger" and "smaller" (among others), Plato adds a linguistic element to the obvious similarity of content between the two passages (cf. 435a5-6 with 368d6-8).

Moreover, what Socrates says at IV 435c9-d4 refers not only to the methods of investigation he has used up to this point; he fully intends (despite their inadequacy) to continue using them. Let's consider the crucial sentence more closely, this time in a more literal translation:

---

23. Of these, one will require further discussion at a later time: the repeated use of the word γράμματα (as in the phrases "small letters" and "these same letters") will suggest a connection to the importance of images, specifically drawn images (Plato will twice use the verb "γράφειν") in the definition of the method employed in the Second Part of the Divided Line (VI 510d5-511a2).

24. Adeimantus picks this up in his response: ἐν τῇ περὶ τὸ δίκαιον ζητήσει (368e1).

> "So it appears," was what I said. "And note well, Glaucon, how it seems to me: let's never receive *this* as definitively settled from the kinds of methods that in these speeches we are using now—for another greater and fuller road leads to *that*—though equally worthy of the things both said and seen already. (435c9-d4; translation mine)

The words "we are using now" mean "those we have been using and are continuing to use": that is why what we are doing now is "equally worthy of the things both said and seen already." A continuing reliance on these methods is confirmed when Socrates refers *back* to this important passage in Book VI:

> "We were saying, I believe, that for the most perfect discernment of these things another longer way was requisite which would make them plain to one who took it, but that it was possible to add proofs on a par with the preceding discussion." (504b1-4)

I am laying particular emphasis on this point because it is only in the passage that follows the first mention of the inadequacy of his present methods—for the first time in the *Republic*—that Socrates uses the crucial word "hypothesis"; this he does at 437a5 ("hypothesizing") when he concludes his discussion of the law of non-contradiction. If we assume that the law of non-contradiction is true, then we can prove that the soul has three parts; this, in turn, will allow us not only to make an analogy with the City (*via* its three classes) but also to define justice as each part of the soul doing the one job for which it is by nature suited (the point he reaches at 443b1-2). Starting then at 437a5, Socrates is explicitly speaking in terms of using assumptions without a complete investigation of their validity. But as soon as he does so, he points out that the arguments that rest on unproven Hypotheses are only as good as the assumptions on which they rest:

> "All the same," said I, "that we may not be forced to examine at tedious length the entire list of such contentions and convince ourselves that they are false, let us proceed on the hypothesis [ὑποθέμενοι] that this is so, with the understanding that, if it ever appear otherwise, everything that results from the assumption shall be invalidated." (437a5-8)

The crucial point for which I am arguing is that although this is the first time that Socrates explicitly names the assumption on which his subsequent argument rests an "hypothesis," this is by no means the first time that he has used arguments that rest on unproven assumptions which function in exactly the same way. Just as the discovery of justice in the Man depends on the Hypothesis that the law of non-contradiction is true (since only thus can it be shown that the soul has different parts), so also does the discovery of justice in the City depend on the Hypothesis made at 427e9-428a1 that there are exactly four virtues and that "if we find any of these qualities in it, the remainder will be that which we have not found."

Indeed Plato has given an implicit numbering system to the assumptions on which the investigation of justice (in both City and Individual) rests as far as Book IV: there are four virtues and they are each distinct, there are exactly three parts of the soul (and classes in the city) despite the fact that the law of non-contradiction implies only an indefinite plurality (to say nothing of the sleight of hand Socrates practices when he collapses the four metals in the soul into only three classes in Book IV), the number two is the foundation of the whole investigation starting in Book II: we are to divide our inquiry into the City and the Man and consider each separately. Finally, the concept of unity is represented by the Hypothesis that each (whether man, class, or part of the soul) will have only the one job for which it is by nature suited.[25] Nor is this the only assumption based on unity: there is also the ongoing presumption that the justice of the larger City will be identical to the justice of the smaller Man.[26]

The fact that each and every one of these propositions is at least as debatable as the law of non-contradiction adds further evidence of their essentially but not explicitly hypothetical character. If any Hypothesis is acceptable without discussion, it is the law of non-contradiction. The fact that Plato chooses to emphasize that this principle alone is: (1) hypothetical, (2) subject to objections which have not been addressed, and (3) if shown to be false, invalidates all that rests upon it (all three points made at 437a3-8), should remind us that we are dealing with Plato the Teacher. Plato is challenging the reader to question the assumptions that Socrates lays down without proof as it were twice: the first time at the moment that Socrates makes each assumption, the second time in the Divided Line when the method he has pursued in Books II through IV is described in general terms. Even before this, he has anatomized the implications of depending on Hypotheses in his discussion of the law of non-contradiction. If the reader can't recognize the methods[27] employed in the Second Part of the

---

25. These four assumptions are summarized in a revealingly compressed form at 441c4-e1. The claim that the one man-one job principle is primordial is repeated soon thereafter at 443c5-7.

26. Lack of argument for this assumption becomes the basis for a critique of Plato at Julia Annas, "Politics in Plato's *Republic*: His and Ours." *Apeiron* 33 no. 4 (December 2000), 303-326 at 308n9: "since without any argument that the structure of the 'ideal state' is a virtuous one, the moral argument [sc. 'the argument that the would-be moral person must internalize and live by this structure'] has not acquired real support from the importation of a political ideal."

27. Plato uses the plural at 435d1 because the Shorter Way (like the Second Part of the Line) is not one single method: up to 435d and then beyond it, Socrates is literally *using* (the verb χρῆσθαι with dative) two methods, and these are indicated in the Divided Line where he uses the same verb twice. This becomes clear at 511a4-9: "This then is the class that I described as intelligible, it is true, but with the reservation first that the soul is compelled to employ assumptions [ὑποθέσεσι δ' ἀναγκαζομένην ψυχὴν χρῆσθαι] in the investigation of it, not proceeding to a first principle because of its inability to extricate itself from and rise above its assumptions, and second, that it uses as images or likenesses [εἰκόσι δὲ χρωμένην] the very objects that are themselves copied and adum-

Divided Line for what they are[28] wherever they are used no matter by whom, that reader is surely never going to master the method—the only true method[29]—appropriate to the First and highest Part of the Line, which is defined strictly in contrast to the methods used in the Second. And just as the methods used in Books II-IV correspond to the Second Part of the Divided Line, so also does the method appropriate to the First correspond to the one employed along the "longer and harder way" mentioned at 435d2-3 and 504c9 (see section §17).

Recognizing the fact that Socrates bases the Shorter Way on unproven assumptions is significantly easier for the student who encounters *Republic* in the context of reading order and the obvious difficulty of discussing "the dialogues as a whole" needs to be balanced by an awareness of the danger of ignoring that each dialogue also has a context within the Platonic *corpus*. Plato offers an analogy of this danger in Book VI. To begin with, there is a perfectly

---

brated by the class below them, and that in comparison with these latter are esteemed as clear and held in honor." In other words, the Shorter Way *uses* both Hypotheses and Images. Now that the Hypotheses have been considered, section §13 will deal with the use of Images on the Shorter Way.

28. The dialectical method (533c8) will bring out the common features in (mathematical) studies. "'And what is more,' I said, 'I take it that if the investigation of all these studies [ἡ τούτων πάντων ὧν διεληλύθαμεν μέθοδος] goes far enough to bring out their community and kinship with one another, and to infer their affinities, then to busy ourselves with them contributes to our desired end, and the labor taken is not lost; but otherwise it is vain'" (531c9-d3). The πάντων is broad enough to embrace the entire *Republic* although a more literal reading can rest content with confining it to the five sciences of Book VII. Note that I classified this use of μέθοδος between [I] and [II] on the grounds that the genitives (τούτων πάντων ὧν) could be taken objectively as "the investigation of all these [things] we have gone through," i.e., in sense [I]. In any case, this is hardly the highest purpose of "the dialectical method." Bringing out kinship is, with respect to the ascension to the un-hypothetical Idea of the Good, merely "the prelude to the song itself" (531d8).

29. Only the dialectical method is truly a method. But even after "the dialectical method" (533c8 and 510b8) has illuminated the common features (531d1, 533b3, and 596a6) involved in this plurality of mathematical (and all other similar) investigations (510c5 and 528d8), what results is mere "methods" (435d1) without a single guiding method. Note that all eight instances of the word μέθοδος in the Πολιτεία are used in this sentence. Note also that there is *no intrinsic connection* between the use of Hypotheses and Images in the Second Part of the Divided Line: there is therefore no *coherent* method to join these two otherwise unrelated *methods* [III]. Images suggest the visible; Hypotheses (i.e., an axiomatic system) suggests the purely intelligible. Indeed, they may be incompatible. See Albert Einstein, *Sidelights on Relativity* (London: Methuen, 1922), 28-29: "As far as the laws of mathematics refer to reality, they are not certain; and as far as they are certain, they do not refer to reality. It seems to me that complete clearness as to this state of things first became common property through that new departure in mathematics which is known by the name of mathematical logic or 'Axiomatics.' The progress achieved by axiomatics consists in its having neatly separated the logical-formal from its objective or intuitive content" This quotation is from "Geometry and Experience" (1921).

natural desire among educators to expose the student to Books VI and VII and therefore to extract these books from the *Republic* as a whole. The analogy in question derives from the fact that just as the sun in the Allegory of the Cave stands for something infinitely higher than the sun, so also is the *Republic* itself analogous to something even greater than it: the dialogues as a whole of which it is but part, even if it should be the central and most important part. There is a meaningful sense in which the Sun, the Line, and the Cave are the central and most important part of this central and most important part.

The dangers of forgetting the whole are illuminated when Socrates tells us in Book VI how Adeimantus, when asked whether he remembers how—after having distinguishing the three parts of the soul—definitions of justice, temperance, bravery, and wisdom had been established: "'Not thus remembering,' he said, 'the rest I would be just not to hear.'"[30] It is difficult to deny that Plato knew exactly what he was doing: these words of Adeimantus are found immediately prior to the great central images that every educated person needs to read. In other words, Plato placed these words at precisely the place where they would explicitly inculpate the potential excerpting editor of perpetrating an egregious (although hardly inexplicable) literary and pedagogical crime. Plato tacitly admits thereby that the temptation to excerpt the passage leading up to the Cave will be strong. He also self-consciously defends the literary integrity of the *Republic*. And by analogy, an argument can be made for the literary or pedagogical integrity of the Platonic dialogues as a whole, considered as a Reading Order.

Socrates continues: "Do you also remember what was said before this?" Adeimantus duly says: "What?"

> "We were saying, I believe, that for the most perfect discernment of these things another longer way was requisite which would make them plain to one who took it, but that it was possible to add proofs on a par with the preceding discussion." (504b1-b4)

It is remarkable that directly on the verge of treading this Longer Way—the path that involves the Idea of the Good as illustrated by the Sun, the Line, and the Cave—Plato precludes any shortcut: if Adeimantus did not remember the Shorter Way, he would not deserve to hear the rest. Plato is scarcely denying that the Longer Way is better that the Shorter: he is merely insisting that his auditors (and therefore also his readers) remember it before treading the Longer. In other words, the reader must remember how, after distinguishing the three parts of the soul, definitions of justice, temperance, bravery, and wisdom (the four virtues as distinguished from the five mentioned in *Protagoras*),[31] had been

30. 504a7-8 (translation mine); Shorey translates: "If I did not remember, he said, I should not deserve to hear the rest." But the use of δίκαιος here can hardly be insignificant.

31. Note that the introduction of the four virtues at 427e9-10 is preceded by the claim (at 427e1-2) that "it would be impious for you not to come to the aid of justice by

established along the Shorter Way. Socrates had duly warned us that there was a Longer Way in the midst of treading the Shorter but this warning hardly prevented us from proceeding:

> "And you said that that was sufficient, and it was on this understanding that what we then said was said, falling short of ultimate precision as it appeared to me, but if it contented you it is for you to say." "Well," he said, "it was measurably satisfactory to me, and apparently to the rest of the company." "Nay, my friend," said I, "a measure of such things that in the least degree falls short of reality proves no measure at all. For nothing that is imperfect is the measure of anything, though some people sometimes thing that they have already done enough and that there is no need of further study." (504b4-c4)

Once again Protagoras comes to the reader's attention, this time the actual Protagoras who famously said: "man is the measure of all things"[32] rather than the *Protagoras* of Plato in which Socrates names the five virtues (including piety) as well as expresses a doubt whether virtue has any parts at all (*Prt.* 349b2-3), let alone four of them. It is in the context of *Protagoras* that "[iii]" must be considered: i.e., the assumption that "there are exactly four virtues, each one of which is different from the other three." In *Republic* VI, Socrates not only reminds us that the definitions of wisdom, courage, temperance and justice were established on the Shorter Way, but also that this Shorter way—like "man" in the famous maxim of Protagoras—is by no manner of means an even measurably satisfactory measure: an imperfect measure is no measure at all. Most importantly, both Protagoras and *Protagoras* have both been implicated in this inadequacy. Protagoras himself is implicated because he takes a shortcut to the most readily available measure, i.e., we ourselves as opposed to the Longer Way's sovereign Idea of the Good. But the Platonic *Protagoras* is also involved because among the few things that this vivid but difficult dialogue makes crystal clear is that it is not only doubtful whether virtue has parts—without which assumption, definitions of wisdom, courage, temperance, and justice could scarcely be established—but also whether it has four such parts and not five.[33] Especially since making man the measure of *all* things seems particularly impious, both the elimination of piety and the assumption of the divisibility of virtue into parts in the *Republic* would seem almost Protagorean had not Socrates forcibly drawn our attention to the relationship—indeed the philosophical antipathy—between himself and both Protagoras and *Protagoras* here at 504c2-3. In fact, only a reader who has already read the *Protagoras* has a negative sense—the soon to be mentioned Idea of the Good can alone provide the positive alternative—of what makes the Shorter Way not even measurably satisfactory; the rest must simply take Socrates at his word about that.

---

every means in your power" ("ὡς οὐχ ὅσιόν σοι ὂν μὴ οὐ βοηθεῖν δικαιοσύνῃ εἰς δύναμιν παντὶ τρόπῳ").

32. See Guthrie, *History of Greek Philosophy* III, 262-69.

33. The absence of piety is noted at Neu, "Plato's Analogy," 250n9(a).

Section 13. Methodology III: Images

It remains to discuss the second aspect of the methodology used in the Second Part of the Divided Line in relation to the method pursued in Books II through IV. This, of course, is the dependence of that "form of inquiry" on Images. The basis of this dependence has not been properly understood and will therefore require more detailed comment and critical dialogue with the scholarly literature. Beginning at the end of the nineteenth-century,[34] the Divided Line—and in particular the kinds of objects considered in the First and Second Parts of it—has received considerable attention;[35] given the centrality of this question for understanding Platonism, this attention is well placed. Despite encouraging signs,[36] the general Anglophone consensus seems to be that even if Aristotle was correct to claim that Plato considered mathematical objects to constitute an in-

---

34. The influence of Jackson, "On Plato's *Republic* VI 509 D" proved remarkably enduring; cf. John Ferguson, "Sun, Line, and Cave Again." *Classical Quarterly* (n.s.) 13 no. 2 (November 1963), 188-193 at 188. The most enduring legacy, predicated on blurring the distinction between mathematical objects and the Idea of the Good, was the dream of reinstituting mathematics on a dialectical basis; consider Jackson, 144: "Similarly, I conceive, every λόγος is a ὑπόθεσις so long as it has not been shown to be a correct and complete account of the appropriate idea. Whenever a λόγος can be shown to be a correct and complete account of the appropriate idea, it will no longer be an ὑπόθεσις, it will become an ἀρχή." This view runs from J. Cook Wilson, "On the Platonist Doctrine of the ἀσύμβλητοι ἀριθμοί." *Classical Review* 18 no. 5 (June 1904), 247-260 at 259 through Richard Robinson, *Plato's Earlier Dialectic* (Oxford: Oxford University Press, 1953), 155-56 and 176 to W. W. Tait, "Noesis: Plato on Exact Science" in D. B. Malament (ed.), *Reading Natural Philosophy: Essays in the History and Philosophy of Science and Mathematics*, 11-30 (Chicago and LaSalle, IL: Open Court, 2002). R. M. Hare, *The Language of Morals* (Oxford: Clarendon Press, 1952), 35-37 offers an Aristotelian critique of a "Platonic" solution to a problem Socrates never contemplates. Better is Gerasimos Santas, "The Form of the Good in Plato's *Republic*" in John P. Anton and Anthony Preus (eds.), *Essays in Ancient Greek Philosophy*, vol. 2, 232-263. (Albany: State University of New York Press, 1983) at 252-56.

35. Brentlinger, "The Divided Line," 148: "one group holds that the subject matter of the mathematical ('dianoetic') sciences is the intermediates as referred to by Aristotle, which I shall call the 'old interpretation' [in a note, he cites Adam]; another group, which I shall call 'modern' [in a note, he cites Jackson, "On Plato's *Republic* VI 509 D," F. M. Cornford, "Mathematics and Dialectic in the *Republic* VI.-VII. (II.)." *Mind* n.s. 41 no. 162 (April 1932), 173-190, W. D. Ross, *Plato's Theory of Ideas* (Oxford: Clarendon Press, 1951), and Robinson, *Plato's Earlier Dialectic*], holds that the 'dianoetic' sciences, in the *Republic* at least, have ideas as their subject matter." The most thorough accounting of opinion is at Nicholas D. Smith, "Plato's Divided Line." *Ancient Philosophy* 16 (1996), 25-46 at 32.

36. Burnyeat, "Plato on Why Mathematics is Good for the Soul," Michael J. White, "Plato and Mathematics" in Hugh H. Benson (ed.), *A Companion to Plato*, 228-243 (Malden, MA: Blackwell, 2006), and Nicholas Denyer, "Sun and Line: The Role of the Good" in G. R. F. Ferrari (ed.), *The Cambridge Companion to Plato's* Republic, 284-309 (Cambridge, UK: Cambridge University Press, 2007).

termediate class between Forms and sensible things (*Metaphysics* 987b14-18),[37] he was not correct about the Plato who wrote *Republic*.[38]

As befits an old, important, and ongoing debate, it is useful to return to its classic formulations. To begin with, then, there is Aristotle:

> Further, besides the sensible things and Forms he [sc. Plato] says there are objects of mathematics [τὰ μαθηματικὰ], which occupy an intermediate position [μεταξύ], differing from sensible things in being eternal and unchangeable and from Forms in that there are many alike [τὰ μὲν πόλλ' ἄττα ὅμοια εἶναι], while the Form itself is in each case unique [τὸ δὲ εἶδος αὐτὸ ἓν ἕκαστον μόνον].

The claim that Plato placed τὰ μαθηματικά between (μεταξύ) the Ideas and sensible objects receives powerful support from the Divided Line, where Socrates places the διάνοια of the Second Part *between* the νοῆσις ("reason") that discloses the un-hypothetical in the First Part and the πίστις that takes the existence of sensible or visible things on "faith" in the Third (511d8-e1). No less important is what Socrates says later in Book VII while describing the mathematical unit, fundamental basis of arithmetic and thus the first principle of the first of τὰ μαθηματικά:

> "Suppose now, Glaucon, someone were to ask them, 'My good friends, what numbers are these you are talking about, in which the one is such as you postulate, each unity equal to every other without the slightest difference [ἴσον τε ἕκαστον πᾶν παντὶ καὶ οὐδὲ σμικρὸν διαφέρον] and admitting no division into parts [μόριόν τε ἔχον ἐν ἑαυτῷ οὐδέν]?' What do you think would be their answer?" (526a1-5)

Every number can be divided into a finite number of units, each of which is identical to every other and none of which can be split. All of these "ones" share the same form but unlike the things Aristotle calls "Forms," there are infinitely many of them. The fact that Socrates' description of the "one" is echoed in Aristotle's explanation of the intermediate status of the so-called "mathematicals" led to the following comment from James Adam in 1902:

> Mathematical units are in every case (ἕκαστον) equal each to each (πᾶν παντί), and destitute of parts; whereas sensible units (e.g. one horse, one cow etc.) are not equal to each other, and are divisible. In πᾶν παντί Plato copies the formal language of mathematics: cf. ἑκατέραν ἑκατέρᾳ and the like in

---

37. Ross, *Plato's Theory of Ideas*, 59-67 decides against intermediates in *Republic* while arguing that Aristotle was correct about a later Plato at 176-77.

38. Vassilis Karasmanis, "Plato's *Republic*: the Line and the Cave." *Apeiron* 21 no. 3 (1988), 147-171 at 155: "However, nowadays very few scholars admit that we can find intermediates in the *Republic*. The fact is that nowhere in the *Republic* does Plato speak explicitly about mathematical intermediates."

> Euclid *passim*. For the sense see *Phil.* 56 C ff., where these two kinds of number are made the basis of a distinction between philosophical or scientific and popular or unscientific ἀριθμητική. It should be carefully noted that a plurality of mathematical units is expressly recognized both here (ἴσον τε ἕκαστον πᾶν παντί κτλ.) and in *Phil.* l. c. (μονάδα μονάδος ἑκάστης τῶν μυρίων μηδεμίαν ἄλλην ἄλλης διαφέρουσαν). This entirely confirms what Aristotle tells us, viz. that Plato placed μαθηματικά between αἰσθητά and εἴδη, τῷ τὰ μὲν πόλλ' ἄττα ὅμοια εἶναι, τὸ δὲ εἶδος αὐτὸ ἓν ἕκαστον μόνον (*Met.* A 6. 987b14 ff.).[39]

This passage has been quoted at length because it perfectly expresses my own views.

But it is no less instructive to attend to the views of one of Adam's harshest critics,[40] Paul Shorey. While commenting on the same passage, he wrote shortly before his death: "This is one of the chief sources of the fancy that numbers are intermediate entities between ideas and things. . . . Cf. on 525 D."[41] And the reader who turns back to the comment on the words "pure numbers" at 525d6 finds that Shorey's opposition to "intermediates" in Plato was longstanding:

> Lit. "numbers (in) themselves," i.e., ideal numbers or the ideas of numbers. For this and the following as one of the sources of the silly notion that mathematical numbers are intermediate between ideal and concrete numbers, cf. my *De Platonis Idearum Doctrina* [1884], p. 33, *Unity of Plato's Thought* [1903], pp. 83-84, *Class. Phil.* xxii. (1927) pp. 213-218.[42]

Although Shorey is particularly vituperative in Latin,[43] his most significant comment appears in his 1903 classic: "The theory of ideas, the hypostatization of all concepts, once granted, numbers do not differ from other ideas."[44] This

39. Adam, *Republic of Plato*, 2.115. I do not, however, agree with what Adam says in the very next sentence (2.115-16): "There are therefore three kinds of μονάδες in Plato's scheme—the Ideal μονάς, of which only one exists, the Mathematical and the Sensible, of each of which there are many." In section §28, I will return to the so-called "Ideal Numbers," the existence of which—and more importantly, the Platonic embrace of which—I reject. But despite this difference with Adam, I am even farther removed from the position of Shorey (see below) who holds that "Ideal Numbers" are being described in *Republic* VI and VII.

40. Paul Shorey, "Ideas and Numbers Again." *Classical Philology* 22 no. 2 (April 1927), 213-218.

41. The deleted words are: "Cf. Alexander, *Space, Time, and Deity*, i. p. 219: 'Mathematical particulars are therefore not as Plato thought intermediate between sensible figures and universals. Sensible figures are only less simple mathematical ones.'"

42. Shorey, *Plato's Republic*, 2.165n"d"(on 526a1).

43. Paul Shorey, *De Platonis idearum doctrina atque mentis humanae notionibus commentatio* (München: Theodor Ackermann, 1884), 33: "futilissima illa hariolatio."

44. Paul Shorey, *The Unity of Plato's Thought* (Chicago, IL: University of Chicago Press, 1903), 83.

statement succinctly describes a version of "the theory of ideas" that I reject: the Ideas are *not* the hypostatization of concepts like "man" or "horse" or "magnitude" or "three." While both the objects of διάνοια and νοῆσις are intelligible, only the latter—*locus* of the Ideas—do not depend on Images because they are radically distinct from everything sensible. For Shorey, "ideas" are indivisible unities that can be imitated by a plurality of sensibles because they themselves are merely the hypostatized concepts of the features that every member of that plurality shares. What is at stake here is therefore not only the Platonic conception of numbers but of every intelligible image of any class of sensible things. But numbers are particularly important because the assumption on which mathematics depends—the existence of the part-less or atomic monad by virtue of which any hypostatized concept becomes a unity—is so obviously a merely hypothetical Image of each "individual" thing and therefore depends as much on our access to sensible objects as on our capacity to abstract an intelligible concept from them.[45] Against Shorey,[46] my solution to the old problem of whether the methodological distinctions described in the First and Second Parts of the Divided Line have any objective correlates is that the objects of mathematics are inseparable from the method that can investigate them *only because it creates them in the first place*. In other words: the One is the Hypothesis on which every mathematical science—and, for that matter, the abstracting hypostatization of any generalized physical kind into an intelligible unit—depends.

In common, then, with the objects of *any* Hypothesis-bound inquiry that is compelled to employ sensible objects as Images,[47] the objects of mathematics are necessarily *between* the sensible objects of the Third and the *exclusively* in-

45. An unusually thoughtful and thorough discussion of the Line is the section "Mathematics and Philosophy" in R. C. Cross and A. D. Woozley, *Plato's* Republic*: A Philosophical Commentary* (New York: St. Martin's Press, 1964), 231-61. See in particular 239: "Against any view of such a kind [sc. 'Russell maintains that geometry is a deductive system proceeding by reasoning alone from a set of postulates and definitions, *and that no intuition of space or spatial construction is necessary*' (emphasis mine).] Plato appears to be maintaining that space as we experience it in sense perception cannot be dispensed with in geometry—that geometry, though it is concerned with the intelligible world, is nevertheless rooted in the space that we experience." Nor could there be numbers were there no apparently individual objects to count.

46. Paul Shorey, "The Idea of the Good in Plato's *Republic*; A Study in the Logic of Speculative Ethics." *The University of Chicago Studies in Classical Philology* (1895), 188-239 at 234: "All abstract general notions are alike 'ideas' in Plato, and there is no ground for assigning mathematical abstractions an intermediate place between ideas and the concretes of sense except a misapprehension of the passages in which the mathematical habit of mind is spoken of as intermediate between mere opinion concerning things of sense, and the highest forms of intelligence. Νοῦς and διανοία are equally conversant with ideas. The difference is one of method." In these crucial claims, Shorey has had many followers.

47. See Ian Mueller, "Mathematical method and philosophical truth" in Richard Kraut (ed.), *The Cambridge Companion to Plato*, 170-199 (Cambridge, UK: Cambridge University Press), 185.

telligible objects of the First. While it is true that the objects of the Second Part of the Line are intelligible objects, their dependence on both Hypotheses and Images inevitably leads to the same kind of circularity to which the Shorter Way likewise falls prey. As described above, this circularity is illustrated by the deliberate anticlimax of Book IV where justice proves to be identical with the Hypothesis that formed the basis of our City. The best solution to the old debate about "intermediates" in Plato grasps the objects of mathematics as *intelligible imitations of visible objects.*[48] It is this formula for the objects of the Second Part of the Line that explains why it is necessarily equal in length to the Third:[49] it is the intelligible Image of the former whereby the indefinite pluralities of the sensible world become the hypostatized and strictly hypothetical unities of διάνοια.[50] As such, it is a useful pedagogical step in the direction of the Ideas in that it emancipates our souls from the objects of sense but its objects—whether

---

48. Allan Silverman, *The Dialectic of Essence: A Study of Plato's Metaphysics* (Princeton NJ: Princeton University Press, 2002), 75: "It seems to me to be impossible to determine what Plato ultimately thinks is the metaphysical status of these objects of *dianoia*. They remain relational beings, both in origin and in their dependence on 'hypotheses.' It is easy to see them as just the physical objects considered in a special way, but that conflicts with the criterion of faculty differentiation. They are, therefore, better regarded as dematerialized images of those objects."

49. It has been customary to assume (cf. Adam, *Plato's Republic*, 2.64 through Denyer, "Sun and Line," 295-96), without any explicit statement to that effect in the text, that the degree of their clarity or lack thereof (509d9 and 511e2-4) is directly proportional to the *length* of the various Parts of the Line *as opposed to their relative place*. This assumption has forced commentators to treat the equality in length between the Second and Third Part in a wide variety of ways: as an "unavoidable defect" (Adam), "devoid of positive significance" at 77 in J. L. Stocks, "The Divided Line of *Plato Rep. VI.*" *Classical Quarterly* 5 no. 2 (April 1911), 73-88, as "unintended, and perhaps by Plato unnoticed" at Ross, *Plato's Theory of Ideas*, 45, or, more plausibly, as deliberately ambiguous (Denyer, "Sun and Line," 296). J. S. Morrison, "Two Unresolved Difficulties in the Line and Cave." *Phronesis* 22 no. 3 (1977), 212-231 recognizes that it is both deliberate and unambiguously meaningful; cf. Nicholas D. Smith, "The Objects of *Dianoia* in Plato's Divided Line." *Apeiron* 15 no. 2 (1981), 129-137 at 133. Smith, "Plato's Divided Line," 40-42 upholds an imagistic isomorphism while reversing its direction at 43: "A significant feature of Plato's philosophy, which has its place in the representations of the line, is that the originals of the visible world are, in reality, nothing but images of the intelligible originals, the Forms. Accordingly, the divided line features these objects as both the originals of the visible world and as the images of the intelligible world." Here "Platonism" is used against the transcendence of the Idea; by ignoring the sharp division between the First and Second Parts of the Divided Line, one could likewise be a "platonist" with respect to the objects of mathematics and yet not be a Platonist; cf. Julia Annas, "On the 'Intermediates,'" *Archiv für Geschichte der Philosophie* 57 no. 2 (1975), 146-166 at 152n18.

50. Cf. Brann, *Music of the Republic*, 179-80: "However, any common name is in fact a dianoetic hypothesis as well; moreover any sentence is a dianoetic structure and as much the object of dianoetic inquiry as the mathematicals to which Socrates specifically assigns the dianoetic power." See also 322-23.

mathematical objects or hypostatized "Forms"—are not Ideas because they are not *fully* emancipated.[51] The paradigmatic example of a partially emancipated intelligible is the One: it is the intelligible image of each and every sensible thing *qua* singular but not *qua* sensible.

With respect to its intelligibility, then, the One (and all that depends on it) is merely a shadow of the truly transcendent objects only accessible through a moment of vision. The monad, by contrast, is tied to the sensible world not only because we use conventionally use, for example, apples to illustrate congeries of it but even more so because it is, as it were, nothing more than a completely purified Image of an apple: the one thing ("appleness") that makes each apple an apple (cf. 596a5-8). Trivially true of an abstract non-entity like "the form of apple," it is importantly true of the mathematical One: if monads, points, numbers, and triangles were not thing-like, we could not use—let alone be *compelled* to use—visible things to represent them. This is the real reason why Plato makes us think out the geometrical equality of the Second and Third Parts of the Divided Line for ourselves: as indicated by his decision to separate the First and Second Parts, he intends to lead the student up to the Idea of the Good by means of mathematics but knows that we must ultimately transcend our mathematical crutch if we are to behold the un-hypothetical Good for the kind of being that it is. Even though the One—perfect, part-less, and atomic—is undoubtedly more abstract than "apple-ness," it is not *fully emancipated* from the objects of sense,[52] i.e., from those objects (like apples) that, though esteemed as existents by us,[53] do not actually or unqualifiedly exist in Plato's austere universe.[54]

---

51. For an early indication of the incapacity of διάνοια to reach the un-hypothetical Ideas, see 476a10-b7: "'This, then,' said I, 'is my division. I set apart and distinguish those of whom you were just speaking, the lovers of spectacles and the arts, and men of action, and separate from them again those with whom our argument is concerned and who alone deserve the appellation of philosophers or lovers of wisdom.' 'What do you mean?' he said. 'The lovers of sounds and sights," I said, "delight in beautiful tones and colors and shapes [καὶ σχήματα] and in everything that art fashions out of these [καὶ πάντα τὰ ἐκ τῶν τοιούτων δημιουργούμενα], but their thought [αὐτῶν ἡ διάνοια] is incapable of apprehending and taking delight in the nature of the beautiful in itself [αὐτοῦ δὲ τοῦ καλοῦ].'" Thanks to our natural interest in shapes (σχήματα; cf. 510c4) and artifacts (τὰ δημιουργούμενα; cf. *Ti.* 31a3-5), the Divided Line confirms the hint that it is not only the διάνοια of the non-philosophers (αὐτῶν ἡ διάνοια) but ἡ διάνοια itself that fails to apprehend the transcendent Ideas.

52. Except for the implicit assumption that concrete particulars exist, the description of Aristotle's conception of mathematical objects at Julia Annas, "Die Gegenstände der Mathematik bei Aristoteles" in Andreas Graeser (ed.), *Mathematics and Metaphysics in Aristotle/Mathematik und Metaphysik bei Aristoteles*, 131-147 (Stuttgart and Bern: Paul Haupt, 1984), 144-46 can usefully be compared with the view I am attributing to Plato.

53. Cf. 511a8-9 and the views of Stallbaum discussed at Adam, *Republic of Plato*, 2.85-6.

54. I regard all "Forms" that cannot be *fully emancipated* in this sense to be the objects of διάνοια not νοῆσις. In addition to the first and perfectly general description of

In this universe, objects like units and points—elementary mathematical objects without which the even or odd, geometrical figures, and the three types of angles cannot exist or even be defined—have a lower existential status than the objects considered in the highest or dialectical part of the Line. Moreover, the basis for this inferior status is their continued and ineluctable connection with the sensible world. The One's continuing involvement with the merely sensible—an involvement that is characteristic of all the lush and therefore easily refutable versions of Platonism that implicate the existence of even less abstract unities like "the form of apple"—is illustrated by the Divided Line in three ways: (1) the investigation of the objects of διάνοια *inevitably* depends on visual diagrams (*Republic* 510b4, 510d5-511a2, and 511a7-8), (2) in contrast with the objects of διάνοια, the objects of νοῆσις are explicitly emancipated from the objects of sense, making *no use of them whatsoever* (511e1; cf. 532a6), and (3) the length of the line segment representing διάνοια is made equal in length to the segment representing the objects of sense. This crucial and reader-discovered equality makes perfect sense only if we recognize that the atomic monad is an intelligible but strictly hypothetical representation of the unity, integrity, and individuality of each and every sensible object that, nevertheless, not a single one of them can meaningfully be said to actually possess.

In a 2008 paper, Richard Foley offers a well-researched summary and a useful typology of scholarly opinion on the subject of this equality;[55] the last section ("Method") of this fascinating piece is both thought provoking and brilliant on Platonic pedagogy.[56] But it is a 1984 paper by Kent Moors that must be quoted at length:

> The equality need not, and probably does not, indicate a precise equivalence in the domains of the two sub-segments. Rather, by placing physical things and mathematical things at parity, Socrates heightens the disparity perceived between the world of appearance and the world of what truly is. *Pistis* and *dianoia* both relate to things. *Pistis* encompasses physical objects, that which is, in other words, accepted as "real" in the world of the senses. *Dianoia*, on the other hand, is an abstraction from the world of the senses, since mathematical objects are the portrayal of a purified awareness of figure and relation. While abstractions, mathematical things still relate to what is perceived by the senses. As Socrates makes clear later in Book 7, an understanding of mathematics, though necessary as a prolegomenon to philosophy, is not itself sufficient for

---

διάνοια at 510b4-8, consider 476b6-7 and the use of διανοηθῆναι (*Phd.* 65e3) in the context of *Phd.* 65c5-e5. For "austere," see 398a8.

55. Richard Foley, "Plato's Undividable Line: Contradiction and Method in *Republic* VI," *Journal of the History of Philosophy* 46 no. 1 (2008), 1-24 at 1-8.

56. Foley, "Plato's Undividable Line," 23 (final sentence): "The equality of the middle two subsegments is a mathematical puzzle, a genuinely Socratic goad impelling one to independent philosophical thought from humbler mathematical origins."

> the acquisition of knowledge. *Dianoia* serves to remove from concern the exigencies of the sensual world but is not a complete break with it.[57]

The basis of the properly Platonic transcendence of mathematics to which Moors points is only accessible to the mathematically inclined; indeed Foley's purpose is to tease out just this paradoxical and self-transcending aspect of the Divided Line.[58] If it is only from the perspective of the First Part of the Line that the basis of this equality becomes evident to dialecticians who have entirely emancipated their own thoughts from the sensible world, it is nevertheless only from the perspective of its Second Part of the Line that the mathematician can discover this revealing geometrical equality in the first place. Both methods are necessary. And since recognizing the methodological link between the Second Part of the Divided Line and the Shorter Way is the key to my reading of Plato's *Republic*, the same dialectical relationship applies here as well: both the Longer Way and the Shorter are necessary to the revelation of Justice.

Beginning with the dream of Pythagoras,[59] applied to an element-based cosmology in *Timaeus*, placed on as firm a foundation as possible by Descartes (for the un-hypothetical self, see section §32), rendered applicable to curves by the initial hypothesis—false but useful—of the Infinitesimal Calculus,[60] Modern Science depends on our capacity to create mathematical images of the visible world and to explain what happens in it in rational terms.[61] The Line expresses Plato's rather more complex attitude toward mathematics: it is a necessary but insufficient means to reality. His Socrates does not state that the objects of

---

57. Kent Moors, "Equality and Cognition in Plato's Divided Line." *Quaderni Urbinati di Cultura Classica* (n.s.) 16 no. 1 (1984), 147-157 at 153-54.

58. Foley, "Plato's Undividable Line," 23: "With the divided line, we find that mathematical curiosity regarding the relation between B and C ends in philosophical reflection about the true relations between the four kinds of mental states and their relations to ontological classifications."

59. Philip J. Davis and Reuben Hersh. *Descartes' Dream: The World According to Mathematics* (Boston: Houghton Mifflin, 1987).

60. In his repeated remarks about τὰς ἀτόμους γραμμάς ("atomic lines"), Plato may be said to have discovered the infinitesimal; see following note. Although A. T. Nicol, "Indivisible Lines." *Classical Quarterly* 30 no. 2 (April 1936), 120-126 takes Aristotle's Plato at his word (121-22), he fails to consider that this particular "word" is a deliberate self-contradiction: an atomic line would be a point (122), points are geometrical fictions, therefore an atomic line is a deliberately self-contradictory fiction, i.e., it is a description of a fiction that makes its fictionality explicit by means of self-contradiction (see section §28). Both Xenocrates and Aristotle took the joke equally seriously despite the fact that the latter rejected the notion while the former embraced it; see Guthrie, *History of Greek Philosophy* IV, 476-78.

61. Brann, *Music of the Republic*, 185: "We can conclude nothing except that the two middle segments can be proved to be equal, which means that *pístis* and *diánoia* are in some way coextensive. This is indeed necessary, since the realm of *diánoia* is particularly closely related to the realm of *natural objects*; I would go so far as to say that the dianoetic realm is the place of a future mathematical physics."

mathematics are simply fictions:[62] he merely points out that they rest on unproven existential Hypotheses. Nor does he state that they are merely intelligible abstractions drawn from visible things:[63] he merely emphasizes repeatedly the mathematician's dependence on visible Images.[64] In *Republic* VII, Socrates will even offer something like a phenomenology of the intelligible One—the primordial Hypothesis of mathematics and the intelligible Image by virtue of which we call each of the things in the visible world "one" (see section §28)—beginning with the contradictory testimony of the senses. The Line is therefore best understood as pedagogical: it illustrates the crucial but *intermediate* place of mathematics in Platonic pedagogy and already made conspicuous in *Meno*. Without it, the student cannot easily be taught to think about intelligibles (and Recollection) and therefore its strictly hypothetical basis can only be safely revealed to those who know that not all recollected intelligibles are fictional.[65]

But this assertion of pedagogical value does not apply only to mathematics simply because it is not the objects of mathematics alone that are considered in the Second Part of the Divided Line. The strictly fictional basis of the justice discovered along the Shorter Way—dependent as it is on the methods of the Second Part of the Line—will be safely revealed only to those who have recognized Justice for themselves by following the Longer Way described in the First. Just as geometers are compelled by the nature of the objects of their science to use visible Images in order to abstract from them and thereby reach conclusions about intelligible objects, so also Socrates along the Shorter Way finds it necessary to construct an idealized version of visible things in order to reach a necessary but not sufficient conclusion about the strictly intelligible object of his own inquiry.

---

62. As Aristotle tells us that Plato did in the case of the point at *Metaphysics* 992a20-23; "Further, how will it be possible for figures to contain points? Plato steadily rejected this class of objects as a geometrical fiction [ὡς ὄντι γεωμετρικῷ δόγματι], but he recognized 'the beginning of a line,' and he frequently assumed this latter class, i.e., the 'indivisible lines' [τὰς ἀτόμους γραμμάς]. But these must have some limit; and so by the same argument which proves the existence of the line, the point also exists [ὥστ' ἐξ οὗ λόγου γραμμὴ ἔστι, καὶ στιγμὴ ἔστιν]." See David Ross, *Aristotle's Metaphysics* (Oxford: Clarendon Press, 1924) at 1.203-7 and Nicol, "Indivisible Lines."

63. This process is described at Anders Wedberg, *Plato's Philosophy of Mathematics* (Stockholm: Almqvist & Wiksell, 1955), 72-74.

64. Smith, "Plato's Divided Line," 34: "In the short passage in which the two highest sections are discussed, Plato finds as many as seven occasions to tell his readers that one significant contrast is that the mathematician employs visibles as images in his reasoning (510b4-5, 510b7-9, 510d5-6, 510e1-511a1, 511a6-7, 511c1, 511c7-8 [references are to Burnet's edition])."

65. Cf. Owen, "Eleatic Questions,"100: "His [sc. Parmenides'] argument, to adopt an analogy from Sextus and Wittgenstein, is a ladder which must be thrown away when one has climbed it." Note that it is Glaucon, not Socrates, who states that geometry is knowledge [γνῶσις] of eternal Being at 527b6-7; cf. Hermann Cohen, *Platons Ideenlehre und die Mathematik* (Marburg: G. E. Pfeil, 1878), 19-31.

> "And do you not also know that they further make use [προσχρῶνται] of the visible forms and talk about them, though they are not thinking of them but of those things of which they are a likeness, pursuing their inquiry for the sake of the square as such and the diagonal as such, and not for the sake of the image of it which they draw [γράφουσιν]? And so in all cases. The very things which they mold and draw [πλάττουσίν τε καὶ γράφουσιν], which have shadows and images [εἰκόνες] of themselves in water, these things they treat [χρώμενοι] in their turn as only images [ὡς εἰκόσιν], but what they really seek [ζητοῦντες] is to get sight of those realities which can be seen only by the mind [διανοίᾳ]."[66]

I am claiming, then, that the City that Socrates constructs in the *Republic* functions like the diagrams (i.e., τὰ γράμματα ἃ γράφουσιν)[67] used by the mathematicians. It is merely an intelligible Image of a visible thing. I therefore reject the traditional reading of *Republic*, according to which it presents Plato's political theory and portrays the City he regards as ideal. The actual subject of *Republic* is Glaucon's—and by extension the reader's—decision for Justice.

Socrates introduces the City with a discussion (368d3-5) of larger and smaller letters (γράμματα). When he says, for example, that "these same letters [τὰ αὐτὰ γράμματα] exist elsewhere larger and on a larger surface" and that we should "read those letters first, and then examine the smaller," he is claiming that we should search for Justice first in the larger "writing" of the City and then in the smaller Man, who is the real object of our inquiry. When he writes that geometers (and those who practice a method similar to theirs) pursue "their inquiry for the sake of the square as such . . . and not for the sake of the image of it which they draw (ἣν γράφουσιν)" he is describing the attitude that I believe a careful reader should take toward the City in Plato's *Republic*: it is not the center of Socrates' (or Plato's) attention: it is similar to a diagram (a γράμμα) that will help us to understand Justice in the Man and thereby help to persuade Glaucon and the rest (including, of course, ourselves) to practice Justice.

Another linguistic connection can be seen in the phrase at 510e2: "the very things that they mold and draw [ταῦτα ἃ πλάττουσίν τε καὶ γράφουσιν]." Here the analogue is found at 374a5, where Socrates refers to the Guardians for the first time. When Glaucon asks if the citizens themselves are not sufficient for the defense of the City, Socrates replies:

> "Not if you," said I, "and we all were right in the admission that we made when we were molding our city [ἡνίκα ἐπλάττομεν τὴν πόλιν]. We surely agreed, if you remember, that it is impossible for one man to do the work of many arts well." (374a4-6.)

66. 510d5-511a2; with "the square as such" and "the diagonal as such," cf. "drink itself" and "thirst itself" at 439a6-7.

67. "The diagrams that they draw." See LSJ on γράμμα and *Cra.* 431c4-d2 where Socrates shifts from using the plural noun to mean first "pictures" and then (only gradually; see *Cra.* 431c10-11) "letters."

In this one passage, indeed, we see an adumbration of both aspects that will later be said to characterize the method appropriate to the Second Part of the Line: its dependence on Hypotheses and its use of Images.[68] For the latter, the phrase "ἡνίκα ἐπλάττομεν τὴν πόλιν" contains the same word used in the Image passage just quoted from 510e2 ("ταῦτα ἃ πλάττουσίν τε καὶ γράφουσιν").[69]

More importantly, Socrates here calls attention to the fact that the argument (in this case, the argument that the City will require specially trained Guardians) rests entirely on an earlier assumption; indeed, on the Hypothesis that "we laid down . . . from the start" (432d8 and 433a1). Glaucon's suggestion that the regular citizens will also be soldiers is false "*if* you and I were right" (italics mine) in laying down "the one man one job" principle ("not if you . . . and all the rest of us agreed correctly" would be a more literal translation): the point is that the verb "agreed" here means exactly the same as "assumed," "set down," or "hypothesized." This becomes clearer by attending to the word that is the basis of "to hypothesize."

> "For what we laid down in the beginning as a universal requirement when we were founding the city, this I think, or some form of this, is justice. And what we did lay down, and often said, if you recall, was that each one man must perform one social service for which his nature was best adapted." (433a1-6)

The verb used in the phrases "what we lay down in the beginning" and "what we did lay down, and often said" (Socrates is, of course, referring to the one man one job principle both times) is ἐθέμεθα; literally, "we placed." The point is that the word "hypothesize" is cognate: the addition of the prefix "ὑπ-" would create "ὑπεθέμεθα;"[70] i.e., "we assumed" or "we hypothesized."[71] And once the student is aware of the linguistic markers that Plato uses to draw attention to the

---

68. Inadvertently indicated by a reference to "the project of founding a hypothetical, imaginary city" at Stephen Halliwell, "Antidotes and Incantations: is there a Cure for Poetry in Plato's *Republic*" in Pierre Destrée and Fritz-Gregor Herrmann (eds.), *Plato and the Poets*, 241-266 (Leiden: Brill, 2011) at 248.

69. For another related expression, see 504d6 where Socrates says that the definition of justice given in Bk. IV is only a "ὑπογραφὴν;" i.e., an "outline, sketch, general description" (LSJ) as opposed to the "most exact elaboration" (Shorey) of "the longer way.'70. Charles H. Kahn, "Did Plato Write Socratic Dialogues?" *Classical Quarterly* (n.s.) 31 no. 2 (1981), 305-20 at 318 points to *Chrm.* 160d1-2.

71. A perhaps equally important set of cognate words for the argument here advanced is that connected with the Greek word "-οδος" meaning "road" or "way." This word is used in the important phrase "longer and harder way" ("μακροτέρα καὶ πλείων ὁδὸς;" 435d3). At 504b2, this is replaced by the cognate (the result of simply adding a prefix) περί–οδος. The third cognate is the key word μέθ-οδος used twice in the Divided Line (510b8 and 510c5). This linguistic link strengthens the connection between the "way" (be it longer or shorter) and the "method" employed along that "way." Note also Glaucon's reply to the Firesticks passage (see chapter 5): ἀλλ', ἔφη, καθ' ὁδόν τε λέγεις καὶ ποιεῖν χρὴ οὕτως.

methodology in play, it becomes easier to understand the details of the Shorter Way.

Consider the curious comparison between Guardians and puppies (375a2-3). To begin with, the Law of Non-Contradiction makes a proleptic appearance:

> "Where shall we discover a disposition that is at once gentle and great-spirited? For there appears to be an opposition [ἐναντία] between the spirited type and the gentle nature." "There does." "But yet if one lacks either of these qualities, a good guardian he never can be. But these requirements resemble impossibilities, and so the result is that a good guardian is impossible." (375c10-d1)

Confronted by the impossibility of one thing having two opposite qualities, Socrates, so often wont to create it in others, justly experiences an *aporia* of his own in the pursuit of Justice:

> And I was at a standstill [ἀπορήσας], and after reconsidering what we had been saying, I said, "Justly indeed [δικαίως γε] are we at a loss [ἀποροῦμεν], my friend, for we have lost sight of the comparison [εἰκόνος] that we set before [προυθέμεθα] ourselves." (375d3-5)

Although it will only prove to be the εἰκών of the puppies—an image that reappears at 416a2-6—and not the imaginary City of which their analogues are the Hypothesis-engendered Guardians, Socrates is clearly using the vocabulary of the Shorter Way:[72] his further progress depends on the use of an Image that we had put forward earlier (προυθέμεθα) and, once again, the root of ὑπ-εθέμεθα ("we hypothesized") can be found in προ-εθέμεθα (cf. 460d9); this linguistic connection is then hammered home (376b12-c3). This Image will temporarily disable the crippling application of the explicit Hypothesis of 436b9-10: the Law of Non-Contradiction. But with the puppy Image in place, Socrates can salvage good Guardians who already combine a warlike spirit with the love of wisdom, much as Just philosophers will combine the ability to soar outside of the Cave with the courageous spirit that allows them to return to it on the Longer Way:

> "And does it seem to you that our guardian-to-be will also need, in addition to the being high-spirited, the further quality of having the love of wisdom in his nature?" (375e8-10)

It is, of course, the principal purpose of the *Republic* to produce philosophers who will choose Justice and therefore will be both of these: the Hypothesis of an Imaginable City is the means Plato uses to make this possible.

---

72. In addition to the example in the text, consider the hypothetical statement of the one man/one job principle at 400e5-6; this statement is placed between the word διάνοια at 400e3 and the word γραφική at 401a1. The word for Image then appears three times (401b2-8).

> "It becomes our task, then, it seems, if we are able, to select which and what kind of natures are suited for the guardianship of a state." (374c7-10)

The Imaginary City is therefore the "some kind of advance-work for us [τι προὔργου ἡμῖν]" Socrates mentions at 376c9 (translation mine) and Adeimantus, who takes over the conversation at 376d4-5, is quite right to see it in this light. In any case, the interlude with Glaucon (372c3-376d3) has not only adumbrated the methods of the Shorter Way (375d4-5) but has suggested the true relationship between Plato the Teacher and his readers (374e7-9).

It would require a great intellectual historian of our own times (and that's a tall order in any age) to explain why contemporary Plato scholars are more likely to dismiss this treatment of the City—i.e., to reject the traditional "Plato's political theory" reading of the *Republic*—than the harmonious tripartite man of Book IV. One could point to a number of scholars who show that while the winds of change are blowing against the authoritarian City, there is little evidence that the same applies to "the Harmonious Man." This bifurcation indicates that it is hardly because the City is merely an Image based on mere Hypotheses that it is being soft-pedaled by contemporary scholars:[73] the same methodological objections that have been lodged against the City apply no less to the Man. In other words, there is a perfectly good reason for the plural εἰκόνες at 510e3: two Images have been constructed in accordance with the "methods" of the Shorter Way. Although the Harmonious Man will receive separate treatment in the next section, the evidence already presented in the last three sections indicates that in neither the Man nor the City is Justice itself to be found.

To summarize: I have tried to show that the methods used by Socrates in Books II-IV, methods which he himself admits will never allow us to "apprehend this matter accurately" (435d1-2), instantiate the use of Images and Hypotheses as described in the Second Part of the Divided Line. In addition to Hypotheses, that method involves the use of diagrams or Images, valuable not in themselves but for the sake of something else. I am therefore suggesting that the City is a kind of geometrized Athens; an Image made even more like a mathematical diagram by its four, threes, two and ones. This City itself, like the decision to "mold and draw" it in the first place, is built on Hypotheses that are not questioned but simply assumed to be true. The dependence of this method on these Hypotheses determines that we must of necessity "conclude with that for the investigation of which" (510d2-3) we "set out." It is thus no accident that justice along the Shorter Way ends up with the astounding and deliberately disappointing anticlimax of Book IV: justice is nothing more than the principle we laid down "when we were molding our city." It is only in the Divided Line that we are provided with the tools we need in order to discover that, given the methods we were using, there could have been no other result.

---

73. An exception is Gonzalez, *Dialectic and Dialogue*, 374n69: "The *Republic* as a whole is like one of those visible diagrams used by geometers to illustrate something invisible."

Section 14. Looking Out for Number One

The elegant mathematical isomorphism[74] between City and soul not only allows Socrates to transfer the results gained in the imaged City into the individual Man (Book IV) but it will allow him (when he applies this isomorphism to other cities beginning in Book VIII; cf. 550c6) to eventually complete the three-falls victory over injustice (Book IX).[75] Once cracked open by the law of non-contradiction (436b9-10), the soul becomes—and the story is beautifully told—the arena for several (in fact, there are exactly five) healthy or diseased political arrangements. The City in which each of three classes does the one job for which it is by nature suited is not only arithmetically equal to the tripartite soul but congruent with it geometrically: both are triangles. It is on this basis that Socrates is able to define the justice he has been asked to seek in the internal political arrangements of the individual soul: each of the three parts doing the job for which it is by nature suited. The principle of (1) one job for each individual (369e3-370a4) becomes, thanks to (2) the parallel postulated between the paired City and Man (368e2-369a4), the basis for (3) a triangular congruence of three classes (434b8) with the three parts of the soul (440e8-441a4) allowing us (4) to define all four virtues (completed at 429a5-432b6), in such a way as makes crystal clear that of the (5) five forms of political arrangements (445d2 and 544c1-7), the first (and here the mathematics becomes much more complicated) is exactly seven hundred and twenty-nine times happier than the fifth (587c5-588a5). By such methods as these is victory achieved on the Shorter Way.

Considering the various multiplicities required for his creation, the Harmonious Man of Book IV is, at least apparently, a unity. In fact, his justice may be said to be simply his harmonious unity. The three parts of his soul are integrated by a musical metaphor in which the whole is greater than the sum of its parts: his justice consists of each of the three parts doing its own job but it can also be embellished as the "soul as harmony." The importance of this particular Image is indicated by the fact that Socrates will return to it—for the purpose of proving it wrong—in the prison house. But this discrepancy between *Republic* IV and the *Phaedo* constitutes no change in Plato's conception of the soul: the "soul as harmony" is—once we realize the inadequacy of the methods used along the Shorter Way—already being rejected in the *Republic*. To make matters even more striking: the Harmonious Man is by no means the sort of fellow who is

74. Cf. Vlastos, "Justice and Psychic Harmony," 515. Annas, "Politics in Plato's *Republic*," 308n9 praises Vlastos for questioning the moral ramifications of this isomorphism. Cf. 441c5-6 and 440e8-441a4.

75. Used in *Euthydemus*, the three-falls approach—borrowed from the days when "Plato" was being "fashioned" (πλαττόμενος) by Ariston the Argive—(re)appears in the *Republic* at 583b2-3. Cf. *Ep.* 334d7 (as well as *Ep.* 336c1 and *Ep.* 340a3-4; see section §24) and 544b4.

inclined to go back down into the Cave or, indeed, to do very much of anything.[76]

This does not mean that the Shorter Way is simply a joke, although it is certainly funny. The serious point is that dialogue—i.e., dialectic—requires at least two speakers. In other words, there can be no better or Longer Way without a Shorter one (although Plato insists that it is really the other way around). In addition, the number three is constitutive of dialectic: two speakers plus one topic of their conversation. Although this is not the chapter in which to explain it, Justice itself (as opposed to this merely mathematical Image of it, depending likewise on a variety of unexamined Hypotheses) will only be discovered through dialectic along the Longer Way. But the methodological unmasking of Shorter Way (the topic of the present chapter) must not be taken to imply that this Way, simply because it is defective, is therefore unnecessary: it furnishes the necessary basis for the dialectic that eventually brings us—those who travel the Longer Way—home to Justice itself. But it can do this only if we go beyond what it appears to be (i.e., "Plato's political theory" or "Plato's psychology") by interrogating it. By means of dialectic, we must unmask and reveal it for what it actually is.

If we ask no questions—if we allow the dialogue to politely remain silently and eternally equal to itself within the pages of the Plato's Πολιτεία[77]—we will, to begin with, accept Socrates' word for the fact that he created the City *only* in order to find justice first in something larger, and therefore easier to see, before discovering what it is in e.g. Glaucon's soul. As I have already suggested, this stated project must be said to work. In other words, it will allows Socrates, elegantly and beautifully, to do what he was required to do: the Harmonious Man is proved to be seven hundred and twenty-nine times happier than the tyrant. But every dialectician must wonder if this is the only reason that a City plays so large a role in Plato's dialogue about justice. It is not only because justice in the City is easier to see, it is also that we all intuitively sense that any "justice" worthy of the name is somehow political, civic, and inapplicable to the likes of Robinson Crusoe.[78] One must have, as it were, someone else to whom one can

76. If *Republic* contained no Longer Way, David Sachs, "A Fallacy in Plato's *Republic*." *Philosophical Review* 72 no. 2 (April 1963), 141-158 would be right on target; for a contextualized consideration of Sachs, see section §19.

77. *Phdr.* 275d4-9: "Writing, Phaedrus, has this strange quality, and is very like painting; for the creatures of painting stand like living beings, but if one asks them a question, they preserve a most majestic silence [σεμνῶς πάνυ σιγᾷ]. And so it is with written words; you might think they spoke as if they had intelligence, but if you question them, wishing to know about their sayings, they always say only one and the same thing." The persistence of the tripartite soul in *Phaedrus* will provide the basis for deconstructing this basanistic claim in the second volume of *Plato the Teacher*.

78. Cf. Raphael Demos, "A Fallacy in Plato's Republic?" *Philosophical Review* 73 no. 3 (July 1964), 395-398 at 396: "What is odd about Plato's 'Platonic' justice is its seemingly striking departure from common usage. Customarily, justice indicates the relation of a given person to other persons; it is a virtue which operates in social contexts.

return that which has been received. Although Platonic Justice—in its idealism no less than its altruism—is admittedly far removed from the strictures of common sense, it does not invalidate the essential dyad of the popular view (justice involves both city and man) but rather ontologically radicalizes it as a triad. One can only practice Justice in the context of others, on this point there is agreement with the popular view, but like dialectic, Justice is an interaction between [1] the philosopher and [2] others [3] in the context of the Idea of the Good. In the Cave, for example, the philosopher returns to instruct the prisoners about—and therefore points them in the direction of—the Good. Justice is that which connects these three: only by virtue of the Good's ontological transcendence with respect to Becoming can the philosopher find herself in a position to go back down into the Cave. But even before we break the code in which Plato has imbedded the true meaning of Justice beginning with the dialogue's very first word, we all intuitively know—until proleptically confused, perhaps, by the purely internal justice described in Book IV—that it is only in the interplay between an individual and her fellow-citizens (i.e., only in a city) that a person can meaningfully be said to be just. As Aristotle asks of the gods (*Nicomachean Ethics* 1178b8-17): "To whom will they give?" In other words, the Shorter Way conceals—on both a popular and a more esoteric level—the real reason that Socrates spends so much time discussing the "ideal city" in the *Republic*. Discussion of the City is necessary because only in relation to it is the common sense view that justice exists in the context of others validated and only in a city can the philosopher return to the Cave.

The psychological politics of Book IV—made possible by transferring the City into the Man—constitutes the middle (or negative) moment in a dialectical triad that connects the popular view with its ontological radicalization. There is a good reason why this phraseology echoes Hegel: especially when a reconstruction of the Reading Order of the Dialogues begins to illuminate "Plato's system," the parallels between Hegel and Plato become striking. They are opposites, of course:[79] Plato is a committed dualist while Hegel's great innovation was to sublate dualism by means of a dialectical synthesis that preserves opposition as mere moment. In other words, Hegel (unlike Plato) ends with a synthetic unity that both negates and preserves the dualistic opposition it resolves. In Plato, by contrast, the *conclusion* is dualistic: the synthesis of Justice—the philosopher returns from the sun-bright world of Being to the shadows of Becoming—is predicated on the dualism that is the meaning and ontological basis of the Cave. Nor does the philosopher return in order to abolish that dualism. But the Longer Way to this disjunction is both triadic and dialectical: these features are the common ground between Plato and Hegel.

But Platonic justice is a personal virtue, defined purely in terms of agent. One wonders why Plato should have introduced this unusual meaning" See also 604a5-7.

79. Hence the role of Ideal Numbers in the attempt to synthesize them; see Vittoriano Hösle, "On Plato's Philosophy of Numbers and Its Mathematical and Philosophical Significance." *Graduate Faculty Philosophy Journal* 13 no. 1 (1988), 21-63.

In Plato, it is the second moment that constitutes a fraudulent synthetic unity—the kind of "unity" Plato decisively rejects—that is more than a little reminiscent of Hegel's third and culminating Synthesis. Along the Shorter Way, then, the three-class City is absorbed into a self-contained tripartite Man for whom external political action of any kind will be (as will shortly be shown) unnecessary. This politically quiescent Harmonious Man is the necessary (and basanistic) counterpart to the returning philosopher that Plato's Socrates will soon enough be inviting us to be. Only in relation to a rejection of the methods that lead to the form of politics practiced internally by the Harmonious Man of Book IV can Justice become visible. In the process, the common sense necessity of interaction between the individual and others is both negated and preserved in the philosopher who practices Justice, i.e., who returns to our own city and its distinctive shadows. In summary, the critical point of difference between Plato and Hegel—both of them are equally dialectical and triadic—is that Plato is a dualist (and therefore leaves dualism intact at the end of the process) while Hegel preserves dualism (as the negative moment of opposition) only in order to create a deeper synthetic unity that both preserves it as necessary moment and negates it. This explains the fact that the second moment in Plato's Dialectic—as will be demonstrated toward the end of this section—resembles the final synthesis of Hegel's.

The inadequacies of the Shorter Way's Harmonious Man are in fact played out on three different levels: (1) methodological, (2) ethical or political, and (3) mathematical or metaphysical. The first has already been explored by analyzing the methods by which the Harmonious Man has been created in the first place (sections §11-§13). The second involves the *inaction* of the Harmonious Man, most importantly the fact that he is not the sort of person to go back down into the Cave. The *Republic* is a defense of Justice from first (327a1) to last (621d2-3) but not in the middle: Justice itself is not only absent on the Shorter Way, it is basanistically negated.[80] In other words, Justice is made conspicuous by its absence along the Shorter Way. A purely internal definition of justice—a virtue that Socrates will admit is engendered by just acts (444c11)[81]—can never be Justice. The guiding question in dealing with "(2)" is: what exactly does the Harmonious Man do (if anything) in an external sense? In other words, what outward actions (like returning to the Cave) does he actually perform? In short, my contention is that the Harmonious Man's determination to "look out for number one" reveals both his ethical (or political) and metaphysical (or mathematical) inadequacy. The latter arises from the fact that "the Number One" for

---

80. Nicholas P. White, "The Ruler's Choice." *Archiv für Geschichte der Philosophie* 68 (1986), 22-46 at 33: "I would agree that *if* all we had of *Republic* were Books I-IV, then if we attempted to pin Plato down on what considerations operate within the reason, we should have no evidence for anything but some kind of self-interest, and so would not know about any rational consideration weighing against self-interest."

81. Plato prepares the reader for making this connection early: see 352a9-353e12, especially 353b2-3.

whom he looks out is counterfeit. But the ethical or political inadequacy is far easier to describe, and must therefore come first.

There are two passages that describe the Harmonious Man on a political or ethical level: the first (442e4-443a10) may be said to tell us what he won't do in an external sense and the second (443c9-444a2) what he will do internally. It will be noticed that neither of them tells us what he will do externally. This point is crucial and therefore bears emphasis: two *differentiae* yield four possibilities: (1) what the Harmonious Man will do internally, (2) what the Harmonious Man won't do internally, (3) what the Harmonious Man won't do externally, and (4) what the Harmonious Man will do externally. The first of these is treated in IV 442e4-443a10. The second is illustrated in Books VIII and IX where four defective internal arrangements are described from the evils of which the Harmonious Man is far removed. The third is treated in IV 443c9-444a2. The fourth is not treated at all. This is Plato the Teacher's way of saying that it is not "the Harmonious Man of Book IV" who goes back down into the Cave: his intent is that it shall rather be *you* who will do so.

To begin with, then: what will the Harmonious Man not do in the way of external action? Certainly he can do nothing unjust:

> "For example, if an answer were demanded to the question concerning that city and the man whose birth and breeding was in harmony with it, whether we believe that such a man, entrusted [δεξάμενος] with a deposit of gold or silver, would withhold it and embezzle it, who do you suppose would think [τίν' ἂν οἴει οἰηθῆναι] that he would be more likely so to act [δρᾶσαι] than [μᾶλλον ἢ] men of a different kind?" "No one would," he said. (442e4-443a2)

One of the striking things about the Socratic proof that the Harmonious Man is just is that he is presented in the passage that begins here in a passive way on a strictly grammatical level. In other words, his active agency is (deliberately) suppressed by Plato's grammar. As passive as the participle δεξάμενος ("having received") undoubtedly is, it is the only participle in the passage—nominative or otherwise—that will be applied to the Harmonious Man and he will, moreover, be the subject (as we will see at 443a4) of only a single verb (an optative or merely potential form of the verb "to be"). In this passage, the active agent is not the Man but rather we who are considering him. Actually, it is we who are considering somebody else considering him: "Do you think that anybody could think?" (τίν' ἂν οἴει οἰηθῆναι). The most this passage asserts is that (1) Glaucon cannot think that (2) anyone would think that (3) the Harmonious Man—having received a deposit—would be any more likely to steal it than other kinds of men. He is thus no more likely to do (δρᾶσαι) something unjust than anybody else. This could be because he is not inclined to actually do anything: the closest this man comes to actively doing (Socrates doesn't use the word πράττειν in the passage) is that we cannot conceive of anyone conceiving him to have done (δρᾶσαι) the kind of unjust actions that Cephalus himself—he of the guilty conscience and nightmares—avoids performing. This is faint praise indeed.

> "And would not he be [ἂν οὗτος εἴη] far removed [ἐκτὸς] from sacrilege and theft and betrayal of comrades in private life or of the state in public?" "He would [ἐκτός]." (443a3-4)

Here then is the only time the Harmonious Man is the subject of a verb: "he would be" (ἂν . . . εἴη). Would be what? As Glaucon's one word reply indicates, he would be ἐκτὸς ("external," i.e., "it would be foreign to him," or "he would be outside of"). This word is striking because the second passage—the one that describes what he *will* do—emphasizes that his actions are the opposite of ἐκτός: they are not "without," "external" or "far removed from" (as Shorey felicitously translates) but rather involve what is "within" (the opposite of ἐκτός, i.e., ἐντός, is used at 443d1). The most externally that the Harmonious Man can be said to act (of course he is not actually said to act at all) is that he is external to theft, sacrilege, and the betrayal of others: all of these are external to the way he would be (εἴη). Even Thrasymachus disdains the first two of these (344b3-4). As for the third, the internal passage that follows strongly suggests that the Harmonious Man may well do nothing whatsoever in public life. In other words, it is unclear whether the Harmonious Man will have any relationship whatsoever with "the state in public." He will, however, of necessity have at least a private life. In fact, the best thing that has thus far been said of him—apart from the fact that he will be similar to Cephalus in not embezzling funds and like Thrasymachus in avoiding theft and temple-robbing—is that he will not betray his personal friends.

> "And, moreover, he would not be in any way faithless [ἄπιστος] either in the keeping of his oaths or in other agreements [κατὰ ὅρκους ἢ κατὰ τὰς ἄλλας ὁμολογίας]." "How could he?" "Adultery, surely, and neglect of parents [γονέων ἀμέλειαι] and of the due service of the gods [θεῶν ἀθεραπευσίαι] would pertain [προσήκουσι] to anyone rather than to such a man." (443a6-10)

From Shorey's translation, one would imagine that there is a verb in the first statement of Socrates, but such is not the case. The agency of the Harmonious Man has been confined to (1) a single passive participle (δεξάμενος), (2) the denial that (Glaucon would imagine that someone would imagine) he has done (δρᾶσαι) something unjust, and (3) the statement that he would be removed (ἐκτός) from (committing) a series of unjust actions. *He has not been said to do anything*. The Harmonious Man (is) not faithless, i.e., he is not without faith when it comes to oaths and agreements. He does not perjure himself. This would appear to begin a process in which a series of alpha-privatives (the negative prefix in e.g. "a-theist") are attached to him: we are going to be told what he (is) not in strictly negative terms. Is there a difference between saying that someone faithfully performs their sworn oaths and agreements (on the one hand) and stating that someone (is) not faithless with respect to them on the other?[82] If there is not, it seems a rather awkward way for Plato to put it. But I am claiming that this awkwardness—in the context of the Longer Way no less than in the grammatical consistency of the passage as a whole—is intentional. Moreover, all sense of the Harmonious Man's active *agency* becomes even farther removed when a series of unsavory actions are made the grammatical subject that pertain to "anyone rather than to such a man." Adulteries do not pertain to him and neither do lack of care (for parents) and lack of service (for gods). The closest Socrates comes to asserting that he *does* anything—because clearly he is being said, although indirectly, to care for his parents and to serve his gods—is at the greatest grammatical distance from being said to do anything. We are told what he will not do and only at the end are we obliged to say that he cares for his parents and serves the gods. How wicked would he be if he didn't do the first? To be sure he must be praised for avoiding neglect of parents, adultery, oath and agreement breaking, betraying his friends, theft, temple robbery, and embezzlement. But the one thing that he is said to do, albeit circuitously, that isn't perfectly commonplace for any non-criminal, is something that his modern defenders (and the Harmonious Man does indeed have defenders, as we will see in section §19) never seem much inclined to defend: he serves the gods: i.e., he possesses the one virtue—piety—about which the Shorter Way is silent.

The reason that the Harmonious Man has modern defenders is simply because if the *Republic* isn't about the Justice that impels the philosopher into the Cave, then the Harmonious Man must be taken as Plato's definitive account of the just person. This wouldn't be so bad—he's hardly wicked—if his modern defenders didn't also need to explain why he will also obey the founders at 520c1 and go back down into the Cave. Even when this Return is not regarded as Justice—even when it is the Guardians of the City and not you the reader who is being told by Plato the Teacher to go back down—it can't be denied that Socrates or rather Glaucon regards that return as just. The problem that the defenders of the Harmonious Man must necessarily face is: by what standard of justice is justice itself just? For those who don't realize the methodological inadequacy of the Shorter Way, its definitions are the sole standard by which the Harmonious Man can be considered just. The question then becomes: how can we show that the Harmonious Man—the just man par excellence (if it isn't the philosopher who freely chooses to go back down)—would go back down? In section §19, attempts to show just this will be analyzed. But there can be no doubt—in the context of the passage that follows next—that those attempts will necessarily be ingenious, complicated, and deeply flawed: Socrates' description of the Harmonious Man *deliberately* gives no evidence that this man would return to the

82. Aristotle *Nicomachean Ethics* 4.1 (1120a11-13): "Virtue is displayed in doing good [τὸ εὖ ποιεῖν] rather than in having good done to one [τὸ εὖ πάσχειν], and in performing noble acts [τὰ καλὰ πράττειν] rather than in avoiding base ones [τὰ αἰσχρὰ μὴ πράττειν]."

Cave, practice politics, or stop Thrasymachus from ruling by ruling instead. It is for many reasons, then, that we must regard ourselves as being tested by Plato when Socrates describes "justice in the Man" along the Shorter Way.

Socrates describes what the Harmonious Man will do internally in a single long sentence (443c9-444a2) to be analyzed piecemeal. Socrates first reminds Glaucon that the basis for his account of the internal political arrangements of the individual Soul depends on the principle "we chanced to hit upon" at "the very beginning of our foundation of the state" transferred now to a new arena:

> "But the truth of the matter was, as it seems, that justice is indeed something of this kind, yet not in regard to the doing of one's own business externally" (443c9-10)

Socrates is intent on applying the traditional "minding one's own business"[83]—a purely "idiotic"[84] notion of justice—to the microcosm of the man. This application is vividly described:

> "but with regard to that which is within and in the true sense concerns one's self, and the things of one's self—it means that a man must not suffer the principles in his soul to do each the work of some other and interfere and meddle with one another" (443c11-d3)

Here then is the geometrical (and therefore triangular) congruity between City and Man based on the parallel between the three classes and the tripartite soul: the basis (although itself based on a variety of other Hypotheses) for the entire political and psychological geometry of the Shorter Way.

---

83. Emphasized at 433a8-b4 and restated as the choice of Odysseus at 620d1 (see section §35). In connection with the latter, note that the traditional view—i.e., that justice in the City is what Plato means by justice—means that Homer has not been banished from the City after all. But since taking the *Republic* as "Plato's political theory" requires us to believe that we are encountering "Plato's ideal city"—and since that City banishes Homer—we are left at a loss to explain the contradiction of 620d1.

84. One of the most important applications of etymology—another equally important application concerns "school"—is to the word "idiot." The adjective ἴδιος means "private." In other words, an etymological (or true) idiot is *not* a fool but rather a selfish person whose only concern is their own private business: one who takes no part in public life (cf. 620c6). In other words, an idiot ipso facto does not practice Justice. (Note that an idiom is characteristic, peculiar to, and the private property of one language while an idiosyncrasy is a private peculiarity belonging to someone). The Greek word for the opposite of "idiotic" is "demotic" (cf. 443a4). A particularly valuable parallel is found by blending (in accordance with Isocrates) the 1960s slang expression "to do your own thing" with Latin. The Roman idiot attends only to *res privatae* (personal affairs). The Just man does the public thing: *res publica.* The word "school," of course, lovingly shaped and made our own by that doubled vowel, comes from the Greek σχολή: "leisure" or "free-time." The playful Plato makes this unlikely etymology plausible.

> "but that he should dispose well of what in the true sense of the word is properly his own, and having first attained to self-mastery and beautiful order within himself" (443d3-5)

Shorey takes a number of liberties here but the most important is that the word "first" is not found in the Greek. On the other hand, Socrates is in fact describing "justice in the man" as a two-part process: first comes the establishment of harmony within and only then arises the question of external step to take next. It is this first part that justifies calling him "the Harmonious Man." The importance of music in both the elementary education of the Guardians (Book III) and in the so-called "Higher Education" described in Book VII is justified by the metaphors Socrates now uses to describe this internal step:

> "and having harmonized these three principles, the notes or intervals of three terms quite literally the lowest, the highest, and the mean, and all others there may be between them, and having linked and bound all three together and made of himself a unit, one man instead of many, self-controlled and in unison" (443d5-e2)

The Harmonious Man is here revealed. By making each part of her soul do the one job for which it is by nature suited, the Harmonious Man manages to restore something quite similar to the unitary soul broken apart by the Hypothesis of non-contradiction. It is not a true unit, of course: it is a "one out of many."

But before explicating this Hegelian aspect of the Harmonious Man—the synthesis of plurality within unity—let's proceed to the next step, or rather to the lack of any inner necessity for her taking one. It is (1) in the lack of a "what follows next," (2) the abandonment of any πρακτέον ("that which must be done"), and thus (3) the absence of an answer to the burning question "where do we go from here?" (τί τοὐντεῦθεν;), that reveals the crucial importance of reading the mighty *Republic* in the context of the tiny *Cleitophon* (see Introduction).

> "he should then and then only turn to practice [πράττειν] if he find aught to do [πράττῃ]" (443e2-3)

The next step—i.e., the practical matter—is, to begin with, strictly optional. And the strictly optional nature of actually doing something with this beautiful soul is then emphasized a second way:

> "either in the getting of wealth or the tendance of the body or it may be in political action or private business" (443e3-4)

The infinite and incongruous variety of this four-fold list of options serves to emphasize the comparative inconsequence of what it is that the just individual actually does. Given what will turn out to be the teaching of the Longer Way, it is noteworthy that Plato inserts, rather incongruously, "political action" in this otherwise perfectly Californian list of activities. A wealthy consultant who goes regularly to the health club but never reads the newspaper—an apolitical solipsist who is "the best craftsman of his own work" (421c1)—has become the embodiment of the Socratic ideal of justice: both have "gotten it together" and are intent on "doing their own thing."[85]

> "in all such doings believing and naming the just and honorable action to be that which preserves and helps to produce this condition of soul" (443e4-7)

For such a one as this—whether he be called "the Harmonious Man" or "the California Consultant"—it is only the internal balance that is crucial: this kind of justice is strictly a question of "looking out for number one." Without doubt, the only criterion of "the just and honorable action" is the self-interest of the California Consultant even if this selfishness is here made musical (and therefore attractive) as the internal harmony of the Harmonious Man. Given the strength of mind (and perhaps body)—i.e., the internal discipline required from this past-master of aerobic exercise—it is probably safe to suggest that this kind of justice is truly "the advantage of the stronger": it surely advantages few others. To be sure this fellow is no criminal: he will not embezzle the company funds (although he probably prefers to work for himself) or commit adulteries (although it is by no means clear he will marry or raise children) and will doubtless find a good nursing home for his aging parent while finding time for an occasional weekend retreat to the ashram. This then is the Consultant's justice. Nor are the other virtues exempted: the Harmonious Man will call

> "wisdom the science that presides over such conduct; and believing and naming the unjust action to be that which ever tends to overthrow this spiritual constitution, and brutish ignorance, to be the opinion that in turn presides over this." (443e7-444a2)

Let's leave this excellent fellow to enjoy his post-run endorphin high over a Café Latte, lightly sprinkled with cinnamon, while mulling over his next carefully considered acquisition.

Perhaps no great intellectual historian is needed after all: there should be no question why we twenty-first century Americans like the Harmonious Man and yet reject the authoritarian City in whose congruent image he is made. As citizens of the most powerful state on the planet, we seem quite content to "tune out" the implications of the unjust actions being taken in our name on a daily basis. The irony of our presently diseased body politic is that the bodies of our most thoughtful citizens have never been healthier. The amazing thing about this irony is that Plato the Athenian was evidently so fully aware of it more than two-and-a-half thousand years ago. Truly is the *Republic* spoken by Socrates

---

85. I will hereafter refer to this Man interchangeably as the Harmonious Man and "the California Consultant." A full-time job is unnecessary: the Consultant works from the home and only on his or her own schedule.

only yesterday: its relevance to our times is remarkable if not stunning. But the less crucial point to realize is that the Harmonious Man is *our* ideal, not that of either Socrates or Plato. In fact, it is because our own attachment to a harmonious internal politics is so strong, that it is necessary to consider the inadequacy of the California Consultant not only in (1) a methodological, (2) an ethical or political sense but (3) in the context of metaphysics and arithmetic as well. This involves revisiting the passage with fresh eyes for what Plato actually wrote:

> "and having harmonized these three principles [καὶ συναρμόσαντα τρία ὄντα], the notes or intervals of three terms quite literally the lowest, the highest, and the mean, and all others there may be between them, and having linked [συνδήσαντα] and bound [καὶ παντάπασιν] all three together [πάντα ταῦτα], and made of himself a unit [ἕνα γενόμενον], one man instead of many [ἕνα . . . ἐκ πολλῶν], self-controlled and in unison [ἡρμοσμένον]" (443d5-e2)

Before examining this important and complex passage in detail, it is important to realize that the Greeks didn't regard "one" as a number (see section §28). Unity is the *origin* of number but is not itself a number. As Socrates will tell us in Book VII, real mathematicians will admit no multiplicity into the One: when someone tries to divide it, they multiply.[86] In other words, it is no accident that our symbol for "one third" (1/3) is written in just this way: we are considering one unit out of three and it is therefore *three* that is being divided into parts, not One. Unity isn't divisible, only—as in this case—"triplicity" is so. Socrates is going to teach us later in the *Republic* that (1) One does not and cannot consist of Many, (2) unity (as sharply opposed to plurality) is characteristic of Being rather than Becoming, and therefore (3) that it is completely false—negating both metaphysics and mathematics—to assert that "unity comes into being from many" [ἕνα γενόμενον ἐκ πολλῶν] as Socrates does here (cf. 443e1-2 and 524d9-526c7). One is tempted to say that there could be no clearer proof that we are presently walking the Shorter Way but Plato has already made it even clearer by means of non-mathematical, non-metaphysical—in short, by methodological and ethical—expressions. But having crossed "the dividing line" into philosophy (section §11), it is appropriate to consider not only what is first for us, but first by nature.

---

86. 525c8-e3: "'And, further,' I said, 'it occurs to me, now that the study of reckoning has been mentioned, that there is something fine in it, and that it is useful for our purpose in many ways, provided it is pursued for the sake of knowledge and not for huckstering.' 'In what respect?' he said. 'Why, in respect of the very point of which we were speaking, that it strongly directs the soul upward and compels it to discourse about pure numbers, never acquiescing if anyone proffers to it in the discussion numbers attached to visible and tangible bodies. For you are doubtless aware that experts in this study, if anyone attempts to cut up the 'one' in argument, laugh at him and refuse to allow it; but if you mince it up, they multiply, always on guard lest the one should appear to be not one but a multiplicity of parts.'"

As an indication of the capital importance of the Problem of the One and the Many,[87] it will be noted that both Being and Becoming are proleptically introduced in this passage: this is indicated by the use of the words ὄντα and γενόμενον. In other words: the seeds from which Becoming and Being will grow—themselves the basis of Platonic dualism—are embedded in the mathematical soil of "the One and the Many" from the start. In short: a sharp distinction between One and Many is a necessary first step for grasping the sharp, and infinitely more important, distinction between Being and Becoming. Just as Justice itself will depend entirely on this distinction—the dark shadows of the "Cave," after all, are simply Becoming as beheld from the sunlit heights of Being—the version of justice being presented on the Shorter Way depends on its annihilation: the "one" becomes many and many become "one." This "one" is perfectly fraudulent. But it is precisely this fraud that here receives the striking expression: ἕνα γενόμενον ἐκ πολλῶν. The "one" that comes into being from many is a playful metaphor for Becoming itself, and inextricably and inevitably involves it. The annihilation of the gaping chasm between the One and the Many is even more playful: πάντα ταῦτα συνδήσαντα καὶ παντάπασιν ἕνα γενόμενον ἐκ πολλῶν. The "one" that becomes from many is not merely the result of binding three together (συνδήσαντα) but rather all the infinite plurality (πάντα is plural) between them in all kinds of ways (παντάπασιν). The problem is that there is no way whatsoever in which the *truly* One is Many. Plato is careful to emphasize that "one" only *becomes* [γενόμενον] many in the realm of Becoming.

It is revealing that Shorey has some trouble translating this passage. His "linked and bound" replaces one Platonic word containing "all" (παντάπασιν) and "all three together" misses the point that what Plato actually writes is πάντα ταῦτα. "All these things" are undoubtedly bound (or linked completely) but they are not only three: they are both three and everything in-between the three. If there are not enough "alls" in Shorey's translation, there are too many "ones": Shorey translates Plato's single ἕνα with both "unit" and "one." Shorey knows perfectly well that a Platonic Monad is unitary and, moreover, that it is Heraclitus rather than Plato who, giving authoritative voice to mankind's *Drang nach Einheit* (see section §5) thinks that πάντα are ἕν (i.e., "that all things are one").[88] Made uncomfortable by what he apparently takes to be a rare lapse in

---

87. Introduced in the context of the City's founding hypothesis at 394e3-4 and 394e8-9, the Problem makes a proleptic appearance in the contrast between 397d9-e3 and 410e5-9.

88. It is because Parmenides is a critic of Heraclitus (Guthrie, *A History of Greek Philosophy* II, 23-26) that I do not take διά παντός at Parmenides B1.32 to be exclusively adverbial (cf. Mourelatos, *Route of Parmenides*, 205) but rather in deliberate contradiction to πάντα; what Heraclitus does unconsciously, Parmenides does as a deliberate critique through parody, as at Mourelatos, 240: "Parmenides claims he can show that the mortals' own view is unstable, and can easily lapse into Heracliteanism. And so through the goddess he makes the mortals speak the very language which they find ab-

Plato's logic, he plays up the "one" and suppresses the "all things" that are said to constitute it. This attempt to save "the unity of Plato's thought" is responsible for the worst mistake Shorey makes here: "one *instead* of many" is simply wrong.[89] Shorey is trying to derive a genuine unit from the three parts of the soul because only such a move makes his Plato consistent. The problems that arise in considering "the unity of Plato's thought" are not solved by claiming that Plato changed his views or had no doctrines whatsoever—or by rejecting as spurious any dialogue that isn't consistent with this unity—but by realizing that he wrote *basanistic* and *proleptic* dialogues as well as *visionary* ones. And in the *Republic*, we see him combining all three of these elements in a single work. The basanistic "arithmetic" of Book IV—where "a one comes into being from (or out of) many things" is the antithesis of the first thing he will teach in Book VII's Higher Education (section §28): the absolute, multiplicity-excluding unity of the true Monad (525d9-e3). In the clearest possible way, Plato has already explained (435c9-d4) the cause of this "inconsistency": we are walking the Shorter Way.

Given the paramount importance I attach to the claim that the Shorter Way is best understood in connection with the Second Part of the Divided Line, it must be emphasized that this connection is *methodological*: both rest on an initial Hypothesis and betray their merely partial emancipation from the objects of sense by their ineradicable dependence on Images. *Despite this methodological isomorphism, the relationship between the two is not one of identity.* Their difference rests not only on the obvious contrast between mathematics on the one hand and the psychological and political objects considered along the Shorter Way on the other: the infinitely more important difference is that the founding Hypothesis of mathematics, the atomic and Many-excluding One, is *antithetical* to the "One out of Many" upon which the Shorter Way's conclusions depend. Starting with a hypothetical unity—"one man does one job"—the Shorter Way discovers justice both in that principle of unity itself and, more importantly, in the "one out of many" that arises from combining many of those unities into a whole, either in the City or the Man. To put it another way: the One of mathematics, itself merely a Hypothesis from the perspective of the Longer Way, is the basis upon which the multiplex "one" of the Shorter Way must be *deconstructed*. And this deconstruction turns out to be an ongoing project: the Harmo-

---

surd and mystifying when it comes from Heraclitus." B.1.32 would then be another example of what Mourelatos calls Parmenides' use of "oxymoron" (235-240). A Platonic use of oxymoron is the notion of "an indivisible line," a deliberate self-contradiction rather than an alternative definition of an admittedly fictional geometrical point (Nicol, "Indivisible Lines"). While considering the post-*Republic* dialogues, I will argue that Plato follows Parmenides as both educator and metaphysician and that the "Way of Opinion" is the archetype of basanistic pedagogy. See section §25.

89. Cf. the translation of *Laws* 965c2—a key text for Strauss; see *Argument and Action*, 182—in Pangle, *Laws*, 370: "the capacity to look to one idea from the many and dissimilar things." This translation is unacceptable; better would be: "the capacity to look to the one idea out of [ἐκ] the many and dissimilar things." The Athenian Stranger's "Idea" is a one-out-of-many.

nious Man of *Republic* IV is not the only but merely the first instance in the Platonic *corpus* of the arithmetically inexcusable "one out of many."

To take a revealing example: the phrase "one out of many" occurs, as Shorey is well aware, at *Epinomis* 992b6-7.[90] There the Athenian Stranger claims that the man who can grasp "the single ordered scheme of all celestial revolutions" will also have "reduced the manifold within himself to unity [ἐκ πολλῶν ἕνα γεγονότα]." In fact, this is the exact same expression Socrates uses in Book IV: "having *become* one out of many." In the *Epinomis*, it is the Athenian Stranger, not Shorey, who multiplies his units: the words that precede the egregious violation of *Republic* VII's arithmetic are: "μιᾶς τε μοίρας μετειληφότα μόνον καὶ" ("both having partaken of a single allotment as one and having become one out of many"). Despite the charming alliteration and the three-fold repetition of words involving unity (μιᾶς, μόνον, and ἕνα), the true One is subverted by being constituted out of Many. And of course the Athenian Stranger doesn't only subvert the arithmetic of *Republic* VII: it is, above all, the astronomy presented there that is annihilated.[91] The Athenian Stranger is discussing the visible heavens and deriving harmony from them: he speaks beautifully of "ἁρμονίας σύστασιν ἅπασαν τῆς τε τῶν ἄστρων περιφορᾶς τὴν ὁμολογίαν οὖσαν μίαν ἁπάντων" ("a total synthesis of harmony being the unitary agreement of the motion of all the stars"; translation mine). Socrates, of course, had flatly rejected astronomy in its visible form in the *Republic*: "'For I, for my part, am unable to suppose that any other study turns the soul's gaze upwards than that which deals with being and the invisible'" (529b3-5). But the crime against the One is more basic: when the Stranger claims that his astronomical statesmen are "looking at one [εἰς ἓν βλέπων]" (*Epin.* 991e5), he means the exact opposite of what Socrates in *Republic* VII called "the study of unity [ἡ περὶ τὸ ἓν μάθησις]."[92]

It will be noted that it is the existence of the *basanistic* element in Plato's dialogues that is in question here. In the *Republic*, the inadequacy of the Shorter Way is patent and it need not disturb us that the conception of Unity used by Socrates in Book IV is inadequate given the standards of Book VII (although it does seem to disturb Shorey to some extent). Despite the fact that the Shorter Way's "one out of many" is prior to the introduction of the mathematical monad

---

90. Cf. Paul Shorey, *What Plato Said* (Chicago, IL: University of Chicago Press, 1933), 304.

91. Cf. Joan Kung, "Mathematics and Virtue in Plato's *Timaeus*" in John P. Anton and Anthony Preus (eds.), *Essays in Ancient Greek Philosophy*, Vol. 3, 309-339 (Albany: State University of New York Press, 1989) at 322: "Perhaps the most infamous line in the Platonic corpus is his admonition in this section on 'real astronomy' in *Rep.* VII to 'let be the things in the heavens' (530b7), and he speaks of concentration on the visible patterns of the heavens as 'absurd' (529e)." What divides the Athenian Stranger (along with Kung herself) from Socrates is Platonism.

92. 525a2-3; note that this study promotes "the vision of Being [ἐπὶ τὴν τοῦ ὄντος θέαν]" (translation mine). Shorey translates: "the contemplation of true being."

of Book VII, Plato may conceivably said to be testing the reader with the justice of the Harmonious Man and the false sense of unity in play there: if we don't understand the inadequacy of the methods that have constituted this man, we are certainly going to miss Justice. But the *Epinomis* is quite a different matter. I'm suggesting that it follows well after the *Republic* in the Reading Order of Plato's Dialogues and is—given its poetically pleasing but patent perversion of Platonism (as expressed in *Republic* VII)—the *basanistic* dialogue par excellence. Indeed it has failed the authenticity test—even in antiquity, there were doubts about it—precisely because it is not only a basanistic dialogue *but also the easiest one to see through*. It is easy to see that the Athenian Stranger of the *Epinomis* isn't Socrates and scarcely speaks for Plato: if we remember what Socrates said in *Republic* VII, we will hardly be inclined to follow the Athenian Stranger of the *Epinomis* even if we were attracted by him repeatedly in the *Laws*. Although it is perfectly easy when understood as a test, it is inexplicable as anything else: hence we have tended to reject it as spurious.[93] And it should surprise no one—given Shorey's misleading "one *instead* of many" translation of IV 443e1-2 no less than his well-known determination to assert "the unity of Plato's thought"—that he too rejected it. The irony here is that both Shorey and I are in perfect agreement that Plato's purpose remains unitary throughout the *corpus*. But because we disagree about the pedagogical techniques Plato used to achieve that purpose, the unity I am proposing is more dialectical, inclusive, and comprehensive, a unity that is neither the One of mathematics nor the One that Tübingen identifies with the Idea of the Good. As a dialectical Platonist, I am not obligated to reject the *Epinomis* and I don't.[94] As is very obvious, it is elegantly written: it is the doctrines it contains that have led to its rejection, not its literary inadequacy.[95] Be that as it may, it is naturally far easier to discover a unity in Plato's dialogues when, like Shorey or Schleiermacher,[96] you license yourself to exclude from consideration all data that don't confirm your own par-

---

93. See Nightingale, *Spectacles of Truth*, Chapter 4 ("Theorizing the beautiful body: from Plato to Philip of Opus") for recent consideration and bibliography on *Epinomis*.

94. See my "Why Plato wrote *Epinomis*; Leonardo Tarán and the Thirteenth Book of the *Laws*," forthcoming in *Polis* 28 no. 2 (2011).

95. Shorey, *What Plato Said*, 1933, 408 denies this: "The chief reason for doubting Plato's authorship the obscurity and abstract prolixity of style." Guthrie, *History of Greek Philosophy* V, 386 indicates that his rejection (apart from the testimony of Diogenes Laertius) relates to the fact that (Guthrie is quoting and endorsing Raeder's words): "The same significance is attached to knowledge of number as previously to dialectic."

96. See Julia Lamm, "Schleiermacher as Plato Scholar." *Journal of Religion* 80 no. 2 (April 2000), 206-39 at 236-37 for the continuity between Schleiermacher and Shorey. As mentioned earlier, the Press-Tejera School seems determined to reject *Laws* because it doesn't fit into a "dramatic order" revolving around the biography of Socrates. Nor is Zuckert's admittedly ingenious pre-Socratic solution adequate; see Catherine Zuckert, "Plato's *Laws*: Postlude or Prelude to Socratic Political Philosophy?" *Journal of Politics* 66 (2004), 374-395. For my solution, see "A Tale of Two Drinking Parties."

ticular vision of it. The path I am pursuing, by contrast, never simply negates the basanistic.

There is more to be said about the arithmetical or metaphysical problems to which the portrait of the Harmonious Man gives rise. It is not only Becoming that is given unity: Being is given plurality. The Harmonious Man is said to have "harmonized these three principles [καὶ συναρμόσαντα τρία ὄντα]." These words deserve some comment. Observe that συναρμόσαντα is an active participle: this man "has harmonized" or (actively) "joined together" the three parts of his soul.[97] But he himself is not any one of them: the Harmonious Man is nothing if not the harmonious arrangement of these three parts. Since συναρμόσαντα is an active participle, we might be tempted to take τρία ὄντα as a plural neuter accusative: he has harmonized these three existents. But who is the singular harmonizer who has accomplished this? Nor do the "three beings" seem very natural in Greek: it would have been easier to call them τὰ τρία.[98] The only natural alternative is to take ὄντα as masculine singular, nor is this too without problems: "being (singular) three (plural)." Accustomed to the Trinity, we may be inclined to accept this but it is hardly natural even in the later case. But this is what Plato is saying, as the words immediately preceding make clear: "he has become a friend to himself [φίλον γενόμενον ἑαυτῷ]." Before the man is said to be "being three" he has first become two: both the friend and the befriended in one. Having first become bisected, he is now three. Here again is the Problem of the One and the Many: how can the singular harmonizer meaningfully (or even grammatically) be said to *be* three? Joannes Stobaeus saw the problem and simply omitted the words τρία ὄντα;[99] was it because they were too Christian or simply too ungrammatical for his taste? For re-readers of the *Republic*—and given not only the dialogue's importance but also the methods Plato uses in constructing it,[100] *Republic* demands such readers—these words,

97. The passive form (ἡρμοσμένον) is used 443e2: it would have avoided the complex of metaphysical/mathematical problems if Plato had written that "being three" he "had been harmonized." The problem is that he (singular) is (actively) harmonizing (something) while *being three.*

98. The grammar of 443d3-6 is interesting: "τὰ οἰκεῖα εὖ θέμενον [the participle here takes an accusative object] καὶ ἄρξαντα αὐτὸν αὑτοῦ [here it's genitive] καὶ κοσμήσαντα [here, for the first time, an object for the participle is missing entirely] καὶ φίλον γενόμενον ἑαυτῷ [the object is now dative] καὶ συναρμόσαντα τρία ὄντα" Note that τὰ οἰκεῖα are/is in fact himself, as of course are αὑτοῦ and ἑαυτῷ. But it is the final statement that contains the metaphysical meltdown: there is no object (κοσμήσαντα has prepared us for that) and the word associated with Being (ὄντα) is used to state the thing that cannot be: that the One is Many.

99. Burnet (ed.), *Platonis Opera* IV on 443d5; 443d6 in Slings.

100. See Dominic Scott, "Metaphysics and the Defense of Justice in the *Republic*." *Proceedings of the Boston Area Colloquia in Ancient Philosophy* 16 (2000), 1-20 for a very valuable contribution at 9, emphasizing the use of περίοδος at 504b2: the second time it is mentioned, the Longer Way is described as "a round trip." Introduced at IV 435d3 as a mere ὁδός, the reader must follow the Longer Way to the Line and Cave be-

like the *Epinomis*, are basanistic. But in the context of the *Republic* (and the Reading Order in which Plato has embedded it), they are merely proleptic: the reader is invited to wonder about an entity whose three is one and whose unity becomes out of plurality (see section §25). In a positive sense, then, the Harmonious Man constitutes the proleptic introduction to the mathematical expression of Becoming and Being; in a negative sense, the less than politically active Harmonious Man basanistically prepares the reader for Justice. As the following section will begin to suggest, inadequate ontology is inextricably linked in Platonic pedagogy with bad politics: every *Sophist* deserves its *Statesman* and only the missing *Philosopher* will know why.

Section 15. Making Friends with Thrasymachus

Although the philosopher is defined, thanks to Glaucon's burning desire to see the City realized (section §4), at the end of Book V, the philosopher who returns to the Cave will only emerge from the shadows—paradoxically in the act of returning to them—in Book VII. This occurs in the third of three great Longer Way images:[101] the Sun (508a4-508d3), the Divided Line, and the Cave. But throughout Book VI, the just Man of Book IV is not properly distinguished from the philosopher described in Book V. This is extremely important because the first part Book VI—in the portion of it before the Sun and the Line are introduced—is concerned with the relationship of the philosopher with the City, or better, with our cities: the cities in which we find, or (as it were), found ourselves but yesterday. And the philosophers Socrates describes to Adeimantus do not practice Justice: they do not go back down into the Cave.

It is precisely because of this fact that Socrates will tell Adeimantus at 498d1-2 that he and Thrasymachus have just now (ἄρτι) become friends; this basanistic claim indicates no change in Socrates' position (cf. 545b1-2). It bears repeating that Thrasymachus loses only because Socrates (and, following in his footsteps, Glaucon) prevents him from ruling:[102] the philosopher must prove herself to be "the stronger" with respect to Thrasymachus[103] and thereby do that which is to the advantage of the weaker (without, of course, denying that Justice

fore returning by what now becomes a περίοδος to the important methodological passages of Book IV; see section §21.

101. It will be noted that unlike the City (or a geometrical diagram), these three are not intelligible Images of visible things: they employ visible images of things that are visible (like the sun) merely for the sake of analogous intelligible things that are fully emancipated from the objects of sense; hence they are not "Images."

102. Preventing enemies from ruling does not harm them: those who are harmed are made worse (335b6, 335e5-6, and 379b3-7).

103. The only effective way to refute an elitist is to demonstrate that you are yourself superior to the elitist in every respect valued by the elitist and then to explain yourself as an egalitarian by raising the demonstrably inferior elitist to your own level. The fact that few egalitarians are willing or able to administer such refutation accounts for the extraordinarily large number of elitists one encounters these days.

is also advantageous to the stronger). In other words, Justice creates "a win-win situation" for everyone except Thrasymachus. It is therefore important to determine exactly what has "just now" happened to make Socrates describe himself as the friend of his enemy Thrasymachus (sections §8 and §25). Nor is the moment in question hard to find: it is the radical separation of the philosopher from politics, i.e., the exact opposite of what will come to light (in the shadows of the Cave) as Justice. Consider what Socrates says about philosophers at 496d5 in connection with "making friends with Thrasymachus" at 498d1-2:

> "for all these reasons I say the philosopher remains quiet, minds his own affair, and, as it were, standing aside under shelter of a wall in a storm and blast of dust and sleet and seeing others filled full of lawlessness, is content if in any way he may keep himself free from iniquity and unholy deeds through this life and take his departure with fair hope, serene and well content when the end comes." (496d5-e3)

In this portrait of the serene Philosopher is to be seen the Shorter Way's Harmonious Man as described in the previous section, the philosopher who does not Go Back Down into the Cave, and thus the victory of Thrasymachus.

Adeimantus doesn't perceive any problem with this kind of philosopher (497a1-2): "Well," he said, "that is no very slight thing to have achieved before taking his departure." But Socrates demurs: "He would not have accomplished any very great thing either," he replies, before continuing:

> "if it were not his fortune to live in a state adapted to his nature. In such a state only will he himself rather attain his full stature and together with his own preserve the common weal [τὰ κοινὰ]."[104]

This is an important way-station on the road toward the Longer Way: Socrates states that only in a city in which the philosopher does not stand aloof from politics—what he calls here "a state adapted to his nature"—will he "attain his full stature" (i.e., achieve "the advantage of the stronger") and "together with his own preserve the common weal" (i.e., achieve "the advantage of the weaker"). Political quietism, on the other hand, secures the victory of Thrasymachus: "it is enough for evil to triumph that good men do nothing." Whether Socrates uses the temporary truce with Thrasymachus (cf. 590d1-3) to test Adeimantus, to reveal his shortcomings, or to dissuade him from entering politics (cf. Xenophon, *Memorabilia* 3.6), Plato uses it to test his reader's loyalty to the Harmonious Man or something even worse. And as of yesterday, it continues to do so.

The unwillingness of Socrates to negate himself—surrendering the city to Thrasymachus constitutes nothing less—is illustrated in the middle portion of the speech just quoted. First, Socrates offers the reader a beautiful self-portrait:

---

104. 497a3-5; with τὰ κοινά, cf. *Ep.* 324b9, *Ep.* 325b1, and section §24.

> "there is nothing, if I may say so, sound or right in any present politics, and that there is no ally with whose aid the champion of justice could escape destruction, but that he would be as a man who has fallen among wild beasts, unwilling to share their misdeeds and unable to hold out singly against the savagery of all" (496c7-d3)

As everyone knows,[105] Socrates ("the champion of justice") did not "escape destruction." This passage alludes to the trial of Socrates but, more specifically, the opposition of Socrates to the illegal trial of the generals after Arginusae.[106] In addition, one can see a vivid portrait of what would happen to any philosopher in any city who chose to go back down into the Cave. Difficult though it unquestionably is to do so (χαλεπὰ τὰ καλά), it is not as useless as Socrates now says that it is, as Socrates himself proved with deeds, and not (as here) with deliberately deceptive words:

> "and that he would thus, before he could in any way benefit his friends or the state come to an untimely end without doing any good to himself or others" (496d4-5)

Applied to Socrates himself, this Socratic description is strictly basanistic: it is far too modest an account of what Socrates actually accomplished. Even without Plato—even if Plato had never written a single one of his immortal dialogues—Socrates would still have been of immense benefit to him. Nor was Plato the only one to be benefited by Socrates despite his "untimely end." Through Plato (to say nothing of Xenophon), Socrates is posthumously enabled to continue "doing good" to many others. Moreover, Socrates never claims that his trial and death were evils for him. In short, the only claim made here that we cannot be sure Plato regarded as a lie is that Socrates failed to benefit Athens. It is probably not overstating the case to assert that by trying to win the sons of Ariston from the influence of Thrasymachus—to say nothing of the sons of Cephalus and Nicias[107]—Socrates is, at the very least, attempting to benefit the ivy-crowned city. There is also Cleitophon to be considered.[108]

---

105. The trial and death of Socrates has been introduced in *Meno, Theages*, and *Gorgias* as well as intimated in the last words of *Alc. 1* (135e6-8).

106. See John Burnet, *Plato's* Euthyphro, Apology, *and* Crito (Oxford: Clarendon Press, 1924) on the *Apology*: 131-33. Did Plato—to recur to the external reading list proposal—count on his readers having already read Xenophon's *Hellenica*? See Altman, "Reading Order," §4. It will eventually become necessary to distinguish what Plato could reasonably expect his contemporaries to know from what he can be shown to have demanded from any reader at any time.

107. The central place of Nicias during the War is familiar to everyone who cares from Thucydides. Niceratus son of Nicias is present at the home of Polemarchus (327c2). In fact, he is the first mentioned after Glaucon, Polemarchus, and Adeimantus. He never speaks and was killed by the Thirty.

108. For Cleitophon's subsequent political career as an ally of Theramenes, see Nails *People of Plato*, 102-3, Kurt A. Raaflaub, "Politisches Denken und Krise der Polis:

If Plato allows Socrates to give a self-portrait that both reveals and conceals the truth about himself with respect to the consequences of going back down into the Cave at 496a11-496e3, he has already just allowed himself the same opportunity beginning at 494c4. Socrates is describing how those who are naturally suited to be philosophers are corrupted:

> "How, then, do you think such a youth will behave in such conditions, especially if it happen that he belongs to a great city and is rich and well-born therein, and thereto handsome and tall?" (494c4-6)

This general description of an Athenian youth applies perfectly well to the son of Ariston (cf. 365a7). Of course it also applies to many others, in particular, to Alcibiades:

> "Will his soul not be filled with unbounded ambitious hopes, and will he not think himself capable of managing the affairs of both Greeks and barbarians, and thereupon exalt himself, haughty of mien and stuffed with empty pride and void of sense." (494c7-d3)

All who have already read the *Alcibiades Major* will immediately recognize the "Greeks and barbarians" allusion:[109] it seems that Plato is not describing himself after all. But he is unquestionably describing Socrates, who enters the picture at this point:

> "And if to a man in this state of mind someone gently comes and tells him what is the truth, that he has no sense and sorely needs it, and that the only way to get it is to work like a slave to win it, do you think it will be easy for him to lend an ear to the quiet voice in the midst of and in spite of these evil surroundings?" (494d5-8)

The need "to work like a slave" proves once again that this is the world of the *Alcibiades Major*.[110] But Plato next veers sharply away from Alcibiades (cf. 615b1-2) and reveals himself for the second time:

Athen im Verfassungskonflikt des späten 5. Jahrhunderts v. Chr." *Historische Zeitschrift* 255 (1992), 1-60 at 37-38n105, and Aristotle, *Constitution of Athens*, 29.2-3 and 34.3. Theramenes is little less controversial than Cicero as a politician due to his ongoing attempt to strike a reasonable and moderate balance between the Few and the Many; cf. Thucydides 8.97.2. On the second passage from Aristotle, Cleitophon's claim that the constitution of Cleisthenes (τὴν Κλεισθένους πολιτείαν) was not really δημοτική was an astute attempt to reign in the extreme oligarchs whose watch-cry was "the ancestral constitution," something rather more extreme than today's "original intent."

109. *Alc. 1* 105b5-c6; note that this text adds strength to my suggestion that Plato's intended audience had already thrilled to Xenophon's *Cyropaedia*.

110. *Alc. 1* 135c2-d1; note that these two allusions to the *Alcibiades Major* span that wonderful dialogue from beginning to end.

> "And even supposing," said I, "that owing to a fortunate disposition and his affinity for the words of admonition one such youth apprehends something and is moved and drawn towards philosophy" (494d10-e1)

This is the moment when Aristocles became "Plato" for reasons that neither of the two Aristons (neither his father nor the Argive wrestler) would have understood or appreciated. And now Plato indicates what may have been an important family secret:

> "what do we suppose will be the conduct of those who think that they are losing his service and fellowship? Is there any word or deed that they will stick at to keep him from being persuaded and to incapacitate anyone who attempts it, both by private intrigue and public prosecution in the court?" "That is inevitable," he said. (494e1-495a1)

Even if Plato isn't talking about himself in this passage—i.e., if his family had no impact on the prosecution and trial of Socrates—he himself undoubtedly continued to philosophize after the death of Socrates. And for that reason, his own existence as the philosopher we know him to be proves that what his Socrates says next is not simply a lie but rather deliberately self-refuting:

> "Is there any possibility of such a one continuing to philosophize?" "None at all," he said. (495a2-3)

Neither Plato nor Socrates exists along the Shorter Way: in the run-up to making friends with Thrasymachus, both have defined themselves out of existence. In other words, the non-existent "Plato" who gives up philosophy in the aftermath of Socrates' death—a counter-factual illusion created by the real Plato who must nevertheless be considered factual in order for an equally illusory "Socrates" to have benefited none of his friends—expresses perfectly the self-contradictory essence of the Shorter Way. It is on the Shorter Way that the philosopher *qua* the metaphysically and mathematically oxymoronic Harmonious Man does not go back down into the Cave but remains aloof from the dirty dealings of her city. The significance of the paired dialogues featuring the Eleatic and Athenian Strangers is to be found in the proximity of these failings; bastard ontology is paired with tyrannical politics beginning with the *Timaeus-Critias* dyad. But for the present, the important point is that Plato has prepared his students to meet these challenges in his *Republic*. To put it another way: the reason *Republic* poses so many challenges to the reader is because even more arduous challenges lie ahead.

Understood as a multiplex text, then, there is a good reason why Plato's *Republic* not only contains a sublime image of Justice in the Allegory of the Cave but also the basanistic negation of Justice in the remarkable Ship. If we exclude the City of Good Men Only (in any case described without any effort at vivacity) and the City itself (including its origin in the City of Pigs), the tale of Ship and her simple-minded owner, the sailors who would steer, and the steersman who alone knows how to do so, is the very first Image created by Socrates, carefully and deliberately distinguished as such. In this respect, it resembles the principle of non-contradiction: although the latter is hardly the first Hypothesis used by Socrates in the Πολιτεία, it is the first one to be carefully and deliberately distinguished as such. It is significant that this Image represents a city, as does the City. Together with the two passages I have just discussed, it is one of three times in Book VI that Socrates denies the view that Justice means going back down into the Cave. Because I have been working backwards, it is worth taking a moment to carefully delineate the correct sequence of these passages before returning to the Ship.[111]

At VI 487b1, Adeimantus interrupts Socrates' conversation about philosophy with Glaucon: he wants to know more about the relationship between the philosopher and the city. Specifically, he wants Socrates to explain why "the most capable [τοὺς δ' ἐπιεικεστάτους]"—i.e., the philosophers—become useless to their cities ("ἀχρήστους ταῖς πόλεσι γιγνομένους") by practicing the very activity that Socrates is praising: philosophy (487d3-5). This leads Socrates to (1) construct the image of the Ship and then to explain it (487e4-489d9), and next, in the process of showing how these most capable ones are drawn away from philosophy, he describes first (2) the rich, well-born, tall and handsome fellow' I'm calling "Plato" (494c4-495a1) and then (3) "the champion of justice" who is without question Socrates (496a10-e2), before (4) making the statement that Socrates and Thrasymachus "have just become friends and were not enemies before" (498d1-2). Of these passages, it is the Ship that is most important for making Justice conspicuous by its absence.

In the construction of the Ship, Plato admits the influence of Aristophanes: it is his shameless willingness to steal the plot structure of the comedian's *Knights* that probably accounts for the fact that Socrates speaks of "how greedy" he is for images (488a2). In addition, he uses one of the great coinages of Aristophanes (τραγέλαφος) to hammer home the point, this time stealing from *Frogs*.[112] As Athenian democracy's greatest and most dangerous critic—no one ever seems to pay much attention to the fact that Aristophanes vigorously attacks both democracy and Socrates—the comedian was naturally describing Athenian democracy in *Knights*. Socrates is therefore describing a democracy as well: the individual that Aristophanes called "Demos of the Pnyx"[113] is the rightful owner of the Ship. As used by Plato, however, the plot structure invented by Aristophanes is not applicable only to Athens: Socrates asks his listeners to imagine that his story takes place "on a ship or on many ships" (488a7-8). The ship-owner is both big and strong, both hard of hearing and shortsighted, and

111. Plato has prepared the reader for the nautical metaphor at 389c4-d5.

112. 488a6. See Aristophanes *Frogs* 937. Cf. section §2 of Nietzsche's "Schopenhauer as Educator," third among the *Untimely Meditations*.

113. Aristophanes *Knights* 40: "We have a very brutal master, a perfect glutton for beans, and most bad-tempered; it's Demos of the Pnyx, an intolerable old man and half deaf."

without knowledge of navigation. Socrates does not say, with Aristophanes, that he is "greedy for beans."

But Socrates does say that the ship-owner is "γενναῖος" (488c4). It is an interesting word for him to use: one suspects that Socrates is being ironic. But "γενναῖος" is also the adjective he used to describe the Noble Lie.[114] There is no basis—except our own prejudices—for insisting that the word is ironic on the Ship but not in the Lie. Moreover, the political implications of the Noble Lie and "the noble ship-owner" are exactly the opposite: one justifies class-conscious elitism and the other popular sovereignty. In other cities—and what polity lacks its Noble Lies?—most citizens are taught to believe that the land belongs to the king, nobles, or "its rightful owners": all such stories are, in any case, about the hereditary basis of our political arrangements.[115] By juxtaposing the two passages by means of the same word, Plato is asking us to ponder who really owns the Ship. As for γενναῖος, it is either ironic in both places or it is used not to illustrate what we mean by "nobility" (in any morally positive sense) but rather the hereditary or *genetic* (a better choice because it preserves the generative aspect at the root of γενναῖος)[116] origins of the city's most basic political question: to whom does our "city" actually belong by birth?

In order to get control of the Ship, the quarreling sailors—these represent the politicians—cluster around the ship-owner and importune him for the tiller (488c1-2). These sailors must (1) compete—violently when necessary—with each other, (2) they will cooperate forcefully to eliminate any rival who pretends to know how to steer the Ship, and either (3) beg—i.e., persuade—the ship-owner to entrust the Ship to them, or (4) use other means to accomplish this result (488c2-5). Aristophanes emphasizes "(1)" but not "(2)": his "Sausage Seller" is no "true steersman." Aristophanes also emphasizes "(3)" but not "(4)": the rival politicians (none of whom know statecraft) must flatter Demos. The politicians of the Ship described by Socrates use what appear to be even uglier means to this end: while the Sausage Seller employed merely a tasty relish,[117] the sailors on Plato's Ship stupefy the ship-owner with "drugs, wine, or in some other way" (488c5). In other words, Socrates describes the politicians as being even worse than Aristophanes does and clearly states that there is a good ("win-win") solution: there is on board an individual who could prevent the ship-owner from being duped (cf. 565b9-c1) by the drug-dealers.

The question is: will "the true steersman" do what is required: enter the competition with a dangerous throng of rivals in order to persuade the ship-

114. See section §26 for Plato's use of γενναῖος in the *Republic* as well as "the Genetic Fiction."

115. Woody Guthrie's Depression-era "This Land is Your Land" was hardly intended to endear him to wealthy landholders.

116. This question will also receive attention in section §26.

117. Aristophanes *Knights* 214-15 (anonymous translator). "Continue your trade. Mix and knead together all the state business as you do for your sausages. To win the people, always cook them some savory that pleases them."

owner to ignore the illusory goods they offer in order to save the Ship? If Plato had written the *Republic* two thousand years after he actually did, he would have placed his navigational philosopher aloft—on the topmast, perhaps—in order to make the analogy more obvious. But the attention that the True Steersman pays to the starry heavens (488d4-8) makes the point perfectly plain notwithstanding the fact that there may have been no physical aloft on the ship of Plato's day. It will be seen that the first image in Book VI deals with exactly the same question as the first image in Book VII: will the philosopher go back down into the Cave of political life? The most important thing to realize about this juxtaposition is that the two different Images give and were deliberately (and basanistically)[118] intended to give two *opposite* answers: such is the difference between the Shorter and the Longer Way. In other words, Justice itself is not to be found on the former although its basanistic antithesis will be.

Having constructed his Ship, Socrates next explains the applicability of the image to Adeimantus (489a4-e2). Note that the point he is trying to prove to Adeimantus—that "the most capable" (τοὺς ἐπιεικεστάτους) are useless to the city (487d3-5)—is exactly the opposite of what he will prove to Glaucon with the Cave.

> "You are right in affirming that the finest spirits among the philosophers are of no service to the multitude [ὡς ἄχρηστοι τοῖς πολλοῖς οἱ ἐπιεικέστατοι τῶν ἐν φιλοσοφίᾳ]. But bid him blame for this uselessness, not the finer spirits, but those who do not know how to make use of them." (489b3-5)

The point of the Ship is, in other words, that it is not the fault of the True Steersmen ("the finest spirits among the philosophers") that they do not take the tiller despite the fact that they are the only ones on board who know how to navigate: it is presumably the fault of the ship-owner who does not solicit their services and lets the ignorant sailors guide the Ship's destiny instead.

> "For it is not the natural course of things that the pilot should beg the sailors to be ruled by him or that wise men should go to the doors of the rich. The author of that epigram was a liar" (489b5-8)

This is an interesting passage for three reasons: the image of the Ship makes it plain that (1) it is hardly a question of the True Steersman begging the sailors to turn over the tiller: (a) it is the ship-owner that must be besought to do this whereas (b) the sailors are the rivals of the True Steersman. And for just this reason, (c) the sailors do not need to be begged *but bested* by the True Steersman. (2) It is also not a question of the philosopher soliciting "the rich"; the

---

118. The word "dialectically" could be easily substituted. Cf. Owen, "Eleatic Questions," 85 on Parmenides: "So, on this construing of the lines [sc. B8.61], no ontological claims have been made and the cosmology [sc. of 'The Way of Opinion'] need be no more than a dialectical device." For Owen's "dialectical," "pedagogical" could easily be substituted if by "pedagogical" we mean "basanistic."

ship-owner in question is the Many. When Socrates negates the applicability of "(2)" by saying: "The author of that epigram was a liar," he (3) doesn't even begin to address the validity of "(1)" or consider the possibility that "(2)" has no application whatsoever to this democratic image in which the Many are the poor. An indication that Socrates is aware of this problem follows:

> "But the true nature of things is that whether the sick man be rich or poor he must needs go to the door of the physician, and everyone who needs to be governed [τὸν ἄρχεσθαι δεόμενον] to the door of the man who knows how to govern, not that the ruler should implore his natural subjects to let themselves be ruled [τὸν ἄρχοντα δεῖσθαι τῶν ἀρχομένων ἄρχεσθαι], if he is really good for anything [οὐ ἂν τῇ ἀληθείᾳ τι ὄφελος ᾖ]." (489b8-c3)

The point of the simile, Socrates now explains, is that it is unnatural for "the natural ruler to beg the ruled to be ruled [τὸν ἄρχοντα δεῖσθαι τῶν ἀρχομένων ἄρχεσθαι]". The natural course is that "the one begging to be ruled [τὸν ἄρχεσθαι δεόμενον]"—in this case, the people as represented by the shipmaster—must first "go to the door of the physician." Would it be humorless to point out that those who are most in need of a doctor are too sick to betake themselves thither? Although Socrates may have a point about what is natural in general, it is difficult to conceive of anything besides a lively sense of personal honor preventing any particular True Steersman from offering help—without first being begged, that is—to one as desperately in need as the befuddled ship-owner, surrounded by scoundrels. Indeed it may well make sense for the beneficial philosopher to await the begging of the *rich* (see section §24)—only thus will such as these show that they recognize their spiritual poverty—but in the case of the Many, this aloofness is out of place. In any case, Socrates maintains that since the True Steersman—"if he is really good for anything [οὐ ἂν τῇ ἀληθείᾳ τι ὄφελος ᾖ]"—is evidently beneficial (ὄφελος) to those who need guidance, the very least they can do (such is presumably the thought process of the True Steersman) is to acknowledge their need for that guidance and show the proper deference by begging for it. In short, the "natural ruler" is a spoiled brat.[119]

At this point, it is necessary to recall the City of Good Men Only from Book I (section §8). Both images, to begin with, are about a natural reluctance to rule

---

119. Cf. δυσσύμβολός ("hard to please, driving a hard bargain;" LSJ). Socrates excludes this characteristic (and links it with both injustice and slavishness) at VI 486b6-8: "'What then? Could a man of orderly spirit, not a lover of money, not illiberal [μηδ' ἀνελεύθερος], nor a braggart nor a coward, ever prove unjust, or a driver of hard bargains [δυσσύμβολος ἢ ἄδικος]?' 'Impossible.'" The "stingy brat" is linked to the active/passive construction at Xenophon *Memorabilia* 2.6.3: "Again, what about the skilful man of business who is eager to make money, and consequently drives a hard bargain [δυσσύμβολός ἐστι], who likes to receive [λαμβάνων] but is disinclined to repay [ἀποδιδόναι]?" Cf. Aristotle, *Nichomachean Ethics* 1120a13-15. Bargains enter the conversation at I 333a13-14.

on the part of those who would do so well: the connection between them is established by the fact that these are called "the most capable" in both passages.[120] In the City of Good Men Only (347d6-8), Socrates suggested that it was unnatural for "the man in the know" to be benefiting (ὠφελῶν) others because it is better to be benefited (ὠφελεῖσθαι). The second image implicitly turns on a similar (if more complicated) active/passive construction: it isn't natural that τὸν ἄρχοντα δεῖσθαι τῶν ἀρχομένων ἄρχεσθαι ("the ruler beg from the ruled to be ruled") but that τὸν ἄρχεσθαι δεόμενον [δεῖσθαι τῶν ἀρχόντων ἄρχειν] ("the one needing to be ruled beg the rulers to rule"). The same active/passive contrast is, however, explicitly present in the visionary clause in the City of Good Men Only: the (active) ἄρχων seeks advantage for the (passive) ἀρχομένῳ (347d5-6) and not for herself: she does not look for her own advantage (τὸ αὐτῷ συμφέρον).[121] In the Ship, by contrast, it is evidently better for ὁ ἄρχων to be begged than to do the begging because it is unnatural for the one providing the benefit (the word ὄφελος at VI 489c3 recalls the ὠφελῶν at I 347d7) to do the begging. The morality of the two reluctant rulers is similar: they both prefer to be benefited by others (one by being begged and the other by being benefited) and must either be begged in order to benefit others or—when no penalty compels them to do so (as is the case in the City of Good Men Only)—will not bestow this benefit even, presumably, if they are begged.

"The penalty" proves to be the crucial point of contrast between the two images: it is this difference that makes the decision of "the most capable" not to willingly compete with the throng of rivals in the Ship—i.e., to go back down into the Cave—the antithesis of Just. Socrates conjured up the City of Good Men Only in order to illustrate the proposition that good men—those who care nothing for being either honored or paid—only rule when they do so in order to avoid being ruled by others who are worse. Once he has created this city, we discover that the good man in question is just as selfish as everybody else: it is natural to prefer being benefited to benefiting others. In other words, the basanistic portion of this city repudiates altruism in the context of illustrating the only binding motive for good men to rule: to avoid being ruled by worse men.

---

120. See 347a6-b4: "'What do you mean by that, Socrates?' said Glaucon. 'The two wages I recognize, but the penalty you speak of and described as a form of wage I don't understand.' 'Then,' said I, 'you don't understand the wages of the best men for the sake of which the finest spirits [οἱ ἐπιεικέστατοι] hold office and rule when they consent to do so. Don't you know that to be covetous of honor and covetous of money is said to be and is a reproach?'"

121. Aristotle *Nicomachean Ethics* 4.1 (1120b4-6): "But the liberal man [ἐλευθερίου] is certainly prone to go to excess in giving, so as to leave himself the smaller share; for it is a mark of a liberal nature [ἐλευθερίου] to be regardless of self [τὸ μὴ βλέπειν ἐφ' ἑαυτὸν]." Incidentally, the fact that Aristotle has been repeatedly quoted to illustrate the excellence of liberality and altruism does not prove that he is more just than Plato; Platonic pedagogy required his students to learn such things for themselves or rather to recollect them.

The Ship constitutes the second time in the *Republic* that altruism is repudiated: only if begged to do so will the True Steersman consent to benefit others because it is natural to prefer to be begged rather than to beg others for the opportunity to benefit them.[122] But the Ship goes well beyond a *basanistic* repudiation of altruism—this is why we can *know* that Plato was testing us in Book I just as he is testing us once again in Book VI—by tacitly abandoning even the purely selfish motive left standing in the wake of the City of Good Men Only. The Ship is the opposite of the City of Good Men Only: it is filled with ignorant and wicked politicians clamoring for power and therefore the penalty is very much alive in it. The sailors who crowd about "the noble ship-owner" know nothing of navigation and will waste the resources of the Ship if not wreck it entirely (488c5-7). In other words, the True Steersman should (in conformity with the doctrine illustrated by the City of Good Men Only) willingly rule in the Ship, without being begged to do so or otherwise benefited in any way, simply to avoid being ruled by the ignorant sailors.

As befits its position between them, the Ship of Book VI is *proleptic* with respect to the Cave of Book VII and *basanistic* with respect to the City of Good Men Only. The absence of the philosopher's free decision to take an active part in the politics of the Cave is made conspicuous in the Ship and the reader is simultaneously tested with respect to the Book I penalty that is itself a mere springboard to Justice. Above all, the Ship constitutes a political reductio ad absurdum (or ad injusticiam) on the Harmonious Man, already convicted on methodological, practical, and metaphysical grounds. If the True Steersman (the Harmonious Man *qua* philosopher on the Ship) is truly a good man as defined in Book I, she (1) cares nothing for money, (2) cares nothing for being honored and (3) will rule rather than pay the penalty of being ruled by those who are worse (347b6-c2). In the Ship, all of the potential rulers—the sailors thronging about the dazed ship-owner who insist that navigation cannot be taught—are far worse men than the True Steersman. But in Book VI, it seems not only that—to treat the foregoing list in reverse order—(3) the penalty is insufficient motive to compel the True Steersman to take the situation in hand by begging the ship-owner to turn the tiller over to the only qualified person, i.e., to run for office, (2) that some form of honor (in the form of being begged) must be added as an incentive if she is to do so (one could wait a lifetime for this even in the most endangered city) and perhaps even (1) that by treating the Many as one would logically treat the rich—awaiting an acknowledgement of their spiritual poverty—the philosopher seems to care more for money's influence than she should. Certainly both "(2)" and "(3)" indicate that the True Steersman of the Ship is not the good man of Book I to say nothing of the true Guardian of Book VII who voluntarily returns to the Cave, i.e., Plato's chosen reader. It is there-

122. Any decent human being and certainly every born teacher is perfectly familiar with being in this apparently thankless but infinitely rewarding position; the mere fact that Plato was a teacher is ipso facto educational. Cf. "Babette's Feast" on "the lonely cry of the artist."

fore no wonder that Socrates is about to claim that he has made friends with Thrasymachus (498d1-2): the Harmonious Man, unmoved by either altruism or a civic refusal to be ruled by Thrasymachus, requires to be benefited—i.e., to be begged—by those she would not otherwise benefit. Petulant selfishness on the part of this "philosopher" can therefore only benefit Thrasymachus and his modern epigones, of which he has, alas, all too many.

At this point, then, with the "True Steersman" diffidently scanning the heavens and Thrasymachus—mandragora in hand—standing at the side of the noble but befuddled ship-owner, let's leave the Shorter Way behind.

Chapter Four

The Longer Way

Section 16. The Speech to the Guardians

The great importance Plato attaches to dialectic probably made it inevitable that he would attempt to bring the reader into the dialogue: the amazing thing is that he was actually able to do so. But there are both risks and rewards involved; let's consider the risks first and save the best for last. The risk is: that without the reader's active involvement, the true teaching of the Πολιτεία remains hidden. In other words, Plato risks being misunderstood because he depends on the reader to supply the missing link that reveals his true purpose. In this section, then, I will analyze the passage that proves Justice to be the philosopher's free choice to go back down into the Cave. But the only proof I can offer—and this limitation is the risk that Plato willingly ran in writing *Republic* as he did—depends entirely on the reader. Unlike other critics who offer their readers what they themselves regard as the true reading of a text, I will admit at the outset that my reading depends entirely on them: the reader must inevitably supply the proof that my reading is the Platonic one.

This does not mean that "the true reading of the text" is a purely arbitrary matter and that Plato's masterpiece means whatever any one of its readers takes it to mean. The *Republic* has a meaning—indeed a most beautiful, soul-stirring, and univocal meaning—but that meaning nonetheless depends on the reader: there's simply no other way to put it.[1] Perhaps it would be clearer if two different situations beyond the words "the reader" were distinguished. The relativist's understanding of the phrase "the true meaning of Plato's *Republic* depends entirely on the reader" considers the reader as absolutely free to take Plato to mean whatever they themselves see fit to believe him to mean, whereas the alternative

1. A parallel can be cited in Stanley Fish, *Surprised by Sin: The Reader in* Paradise Lost, second edition (Cambridge, MA: Harvard University Press, 1997), 49: "To summarize: *Paradise Lost* is a dialectical experience which has the advantage traditionally claimed for dialectic of involving the respondent in his own edification." Although Fish's account of Platonic dialectic (49-50) remains strictly intra-textual ("text imminent"), Fish's Milton directly implicates the reader (38) in much the same way that I claim Plato does.

presented here leaves the reader free to either apply or not to apply to her- or himself a specific directive that Socrates, speaking as the overseer of the Guardians, addresses to those same Guardians, but also (if the reader permits it), to the reader herself. In other words, Plato's intent is to direct the reader but he is fully aware that the reader must not only be open to, but must also somehow seek out, that direction. Like a patient genie, Plato knows how to be ignored.

I am, of course, prepared to show (and have all along been showing) why that Socratic directive—"καταβατέον" ("it is necessary to go back down" at 520c1)—expresses the true meaning of the *Republic* and thus the definitive answer to Cleitophon's "τί τοὐντεῦθεν." But the only reader who will be persuaded that this is the case is the one who allows this directive to be addressed to her- or himself directly. In the self-contained universe of the *Republic*, Justice (as distinguished from the justice that is clearly defined on the Shorter Way) exists on a practical but not a theoretical level: it is never explicitly defined there at all. This omission is deliberate on Plato's part. From the very beginning, Plato and Socrates are practicing what readers will instantly recognize as Justice once they have allowed themselves to see Justice on the theoretical level. But this they can only do by putting themselves not only in the sandals of Glaucon but more importantly where Socrates wishes Glaucon to put himself: in the even more unlikely place of the imaginary Guardians of Socrates' hypothesized City. It is very easy for them to refuse to do this: hence the risk. But the rewards are even greater: Plato has written a book that is truly alive and overcomes, in the process, the limitations of the written form of which he was so keenly aware and to which he gives so persuasive an expression in his beautiful but basanistic *Phaedrus*.

The crucial passage occurs when Socrates is explaining the Cave to Glaucon, a process that begins at 517a8. Since Glaucon is the interlocutor, he can't literally be said to interrupt Socrates at 519d8-9 when he pointedly asks: "Do you mean to say that we must do them this wrong, and compel them to live an inferior life when the better is in their power? [ἀδικήσομεν αὐτούς, καὶ ποιήσομεν χεῖρον ζῆν, δυνατὸν αὐτοῖς ὂν ἄμεινον;]." This question is "Glaucon's Defense of the Guardians." Given that Socrates is "one of the self-styled advocates of justice" (the choice phrase of Shorey's Adeimantus at 366d7-e1), Glaucon's question is almost rhetorical: Glaucon is subjecting the suggestion of Socrates—who has himself said nothing whatsoever in the Cave about justice—to a reductio ad injusticiam. Socrates is being unjust to the Guardians. A more literal translation might be: "Shall we commit this injustice upon them?" but it is difficult to capture the tone along with the words: "Is *this* what you're saying, Socrates?" Translation aside, this question is important because Glaucon's first reaction to compelling the Guardians to go back down into the Cave is not that this is Justice but that it is exactly the opposite: it is unjust. Glaucon's Defense compels Socrates to *Justify* sending the Guardians back down into the Cave. In other words, if sending the Guardians back down into the Cave is Justice, Glaucon's Defense must be said to give Socrates the perfect pedagogical opportunity to Justify Justice. And this is what "he" does although naturally all of this is really Plato's doing.

Before examining the two responses of Socrates to this Defense—it is the second that is decisive—let's back up a little and attend to what provokes it. Of the three images in Book VI (the Ship, the Sun, and the Divided Line), the last two, along with the Cave, involve the ascent to the vision of the Good. The analogue of the verb καταβαίνειν ("to go down")—itself the basis for both the opening κατέβην and the prescriptive καταβατέον—is the verb (derived from the same root) ἀναβαίνειν ("to go up" or "to ascend"). In fact, there is no verb meaning: "to go [back] down"; the element expressed by "back" depends entirely on the fact that καταβαίνειν follows ἀναβαίνειν. Socrates emphasizes the importance of the latter (without which the Platonic significance of καταβαίνειν simply doesn't exist) when he describes the first thing we (as the City's founders) must compel our Guardians to do:

> "It is the duty of us, the founders, then," said I, "to compel the best natures to attain the knowledge which we pronounced the greatest, and to win to the vision of the good, to scale that ascent, and when they have reached the heights and taken an adequate view, we must not allow what is now permitted." (519c8-d2)

Socrates glosses the words "to win the vision of the good [ἰδεῖν τε τὸ ἀγαθὸν]" by stating the same thing in terms of ἀναβαίνειν: "καὶ ἀναβῆναι [to ascend] ἐκείνην τὴν ἀνάβασιν [this ascent], καὶ ἐπειδὰν ἀναβάντες [having ascended] ἱκανῶς ἴδωσι, μὴ ἐπιτρέπειν αὐτοῖς ὃ νῦν ἐπιτρέπεται." In other words, the element of "going up" is hammered into the reader's mind by these repetitions. And Socrates provokes Glaucon's question by leaving, as it were "up in the air," exactly what it is that we will *not* "turn over to them" (μὴ ἐπιτρέπειν αὐτοῖς) that is *now* turned over to them, i.e., made subject to their sovereign choice.[2]

In reply to Glaucon's enforced question ("What is that?" at 519d3), Socrates replies:

> "That they should linger there," I said, "and refuse *to go down again* [πάλιν καταβαίνειν] among those bondsmen and share their labors and honors, whether they are of less or of greater worth." (519d4-7; emphasis mine)

This is the second of three times in the *Republic* that Plato uses the crucial formula πάλιν καταβαίνειν and it is useful to examine it in the context of the two

2. It is noteworthy that wherever there exists this ἐπιτρέπειν (i.e., everywhere except in the fictional world of the City), all that Socrates or Plato can hope to do is προτρέπειν ('exhort or persuade'). In other words, the *Republic* can only be *protreptic*. See *Clit.* 408d4-e2, with respect to which, Cleitophon's objection is both preserved and negated.

others, particularly with respect to verb tense (the relevant translations will be mine). The first (at VII 516e3-4) occurs in the Allegory of the Cave itself and refers to going back down as something that has already occurred: "εἰ πάλιν ὁ τοιοῦτος καταβὰς" means: "if such a person *having gone* back down." The second, in the passage under consideration, refers not to the past but to the present: "μὴ ἐθέλειν πάλιν καταβαίνειν" (519d4-5) means that we cannot *now* be allowing the Guardians "not to wish *to be going* back down." To complete the triptych of tenses, the third and final instance (VII 539e3-4) refers to the *future*. "καταβιβαστέοι ἔσονταί σοι εἰς τὸ σπήλαιον πάλιν ἐκεῖνο" means: "it is required by you that *they will be going* back down into that cave." In addition to this temporal element, there is also a modal component that is even more important. In the Allegory itself, Socrates makes it clear that although "going back down" is unpleasant in itself (516d4-7) and offers no substantial rewards (516c8-d4); "such a one" has nevertheless "gone back down." This "having gone back down" is not explained (i.e., the motive that "such a one" might have to already have done so is not discussed). In other words, it could have been either an enforced or a voluntary decision, i.e., it may or may not have been Just. In the third instance, by contrast, the compulsion to go back down is built into the verb-form itself (καταβιβαστέοι). But even though the thirty-five year old Guardians (539e2-3) will be compelled to go back down, they may, for all the words tell us, do so either willingly or unwillingly. They may be being compelled, but this compulsion may be freely embraced.[3]

In the crucial second instance, by contrast, the Guardians are not to be allowed even "to be *wishing* not to go back down" (519d4-5):

> "we must not allow [ἐπιτρέπειν αὐτοῖς] what is now permitted." "What is that?" "That they should linger there [καταμένειν]," I said, "and not wish to go back down [μὴ ἐθέλειν πάλιν καταβαίνειν] among those bondsmen and share their labors and honors, whether they are of less or of greater worth."[4]

This states a compulsion to go back down in a strong and completely negative sense: we are not only *not* turning over to them (ἐπιτρέπειν αὐτοῖς) the freedom to "to remain" (καταμένειν) outside the Cave but we are also withholding from them the choice "not to wish to go back down." At the cost of a split infinitive: we cannot turn over to them the power even "to not wish to go back down."[5] By being prevented from *not wishing to do so*, they are also ipso facto

3. Indeed they are also compelled (once more through a verbal adjective) to behold the Good (540a6-b1; cf. 519c9), a clear indication that we, not the imaginary Guardians, are the philosophers about whom Plato cares. Cf. the discussion of "singularism" in section §19.

4. 519d2-7; I have modified Shorey's translation.

5. The element of "wishing" to practice Justice reoccurs at IX 592a5-8. See section §31. A fourth (metaphorical) instance of πάλιν καταβαίνειν will be discussed in section §17.

prevented from voluntarily wishing so to do: they will do so as a matter of course, without question, volition, or even the lack of it. In other words, the second instance—occurring immediately before the hidden revelation of Justice,[6] states the formula in its most slavish form and therefore challenges the freedom-loving reader (562c2) to revolt. And it is Glaucon whom Plato uses to initiate or prompt this revolt: Glaucon shows the reader the way by taking the reader's first step. But Glaucon does not explore the ramifications of this lack of freedom at 519d8-9—he focuses only on the more obvious contrast between the better life above in comparison with the worse one below—and therefore, in accordance with Plato's purpose, leaves it to the reader to make a crucial discovery: there really is an important sense in which we will be being unjust (ἀδικήσομεν) to the Guardians. Denying them the freedom to *freely* decide to go back down makes it impossible for them to be Just. What greater wrong can you do to a person than deprive them of their natural right to fulfill their highest human potential? In short, it is this speech that inspires Glaucon's Defense:

> "Do you mean to say that we must do them this wrong [ἀδικήσομεν], and compel them to live an inferior life when the better is in their power?" (519d8-9)

Socrates' response to the question is the most important passage in Plato. The first part of that response is that the City wasn't created for the happiness of the Guardians and that it is "the common good" that is our object as founders.[7] This response does not address Glaucon's point that we are perpetrating an injustice on our Guardians. In fact, since Socrates has spent a good deal of time trying to get Glaucon and the others to identify with the Guardians, this invocation of "the common good" is hardly compelling to them. When Glaucon has heard this statement of orthodoxy, he is nonplussed and momentarily confessed to having done something unworthy of a Guardian: "'True,' he said, 'I did forget it.'"[8] In fact, it is his statement of founding orthodoxy that is insufficient and

---

6. Cf. the use of "δυσδιερεύνητος" ("hard to search out") at IV 432c9.

7. 519e1-520a4: "'You have again forgotten, my friend,' said I, 'that the law is not concerned with the special happiness of any class in the state, but is trying to produce this condition in the city as a whole, harmonizing and adapting the citizens to one another by persuasion and compulsion, and requiring them to impart to one another any benefit which they are severally able to bestow upon the community, and that it itself creates such men in the state, not that it may allow each to take what course pleases him, but with a view to using them for the binding together of the commonwealth.' 'True,' he said, 'I did forget it.'" Note that the harmonizing motif recalls the California Consultant of section §14.

8. Since the Guardians must possess a good memory (486c7-8), Glaucon is hereby distancing himself from them. He had emphasized his memory at 504a7-8: the words that Shorey translates colloquially as "'If I did not remember,' he said, 'I should not deserve to hear the rest'" are really much more significant in their literal form: μὴ γὰρ μνημονεύων, ἔφη, τὰ λοιπὰ ἂν εἴην δίκαιος μὴ ἀκούειν (roughly: "As one not re-

that is why Socrates must give a second justification for sending the Guardians back down into the Cave. To push this point a bit further, it is probably not too much to say (although it is awkward to write it) that his first response is a justification and the second a Justification. Certainly "the common good" response is expressed in harmonic terms familiar to those who remember the California Consultant of the Shorter Way.

We have now reached "the crisis of the *Republic*." Socrates announces that he next intends to address explicitly (something he did not do in his first response) the Defense offered by Glaucon that we are wronging (i.e., perpetrating an injustice upon) our Guardians:

> "Observe, then, Glaucon," said I, "that we shall not be wronging, either, the philosophers who arise among us, but that we can justify our action when we constrain them to take charge of the other citizens and be their guardians." (520a6-b1)

From the opening words, a crucial ambiguity is visible. If the words "the philosophers who arise among us" mean only the Guardians who now are to be imagined by us as demanding an explanation from the City's founders (i.e., Socrates) as Glaucon has just now done—a thing that they could never really do since we didn't concede to them even the chance "to not wish to go back down"—then why does he call them "philosophers" first and "guardians" last? This Socratic speech is manifestly persuading *philosophers* to become Guardians on behalf of their fellow citizens. Socrates has just given us some reason to think that the Guardians of the City do not need to be persuaded to do so and also has, for some time now (since Book II) been speaking as if these fictional folks are Guardians first and philosophers second. The crucial point is: from the beginning of the second response to Glaucon's Defense, the possibility arises that the words "the philosophers who arise among us" may refer to *us* (and, of course, Glaucon and the rest). This "Critical Ambiguity" is therefore detectable from the start.

As if to support this outlandish proposition—i.e., that it is we ourselves to whom Socrates has just referred with the words "the philosophers who arise among us"—Socrates next precedes to mention precisely *us*:

> "For we will say to them that it is natural that men of similar quality who spring up in other cities should not share in the labors there." (520b1-3)

Here we are, then. Philosophers like ourselves—"men of similar quality who spring up in other cities"—have no obligation whatsoever to go back down into

---

membering I would be just not to hear." Since "justice" is conflated with remembering in Book VI, it is probably important that *not* remembering becomes somehow conflated with Justice in Book VII. In any case, Glaucon's admission that he lacks an important qualification prepares us to do what Plato requires: distance ourselves from the imaginary Guardians of the Hypothesis-based City.

the Cave. Just as "the man in the know" (in the City of Good Men Only) preferred not to benefit others when he could be benefited by them (and just as it would be unnatural for the True Steersman to beg others to let themselves be ruled by him in the Ship when it is they who should be begging), so also it would be unnatural for us to go back down into the Cave. Socrates has deftly sucked us into his argument and we raise no protest at this point because he is letting us off the hook. Next he praises us (and who hates to be praised?):

> "For they grow up spontaneously from no volition of the government in the several states, and it is justice that the self-grown, indebted to none for its breeding, should not be zealous either to pay to anyone the price of its nurture." (520b3-5)

No philosophical founders took *our* education in hand, no City nurtured us in useful studies in order that we own ourselves bound to devote some of our efforts in later life to the common good. No! We are "self-grown," we owe nobody anything. Preferring to be benefited rather than to benefit (just like everybody else is "in the know"), we in fact are too autonomous for either. Not having been benefited, we are under no obligation to benefit our fellow-citizens. And true enough it certainly is that we became philosophers "from no volition of the government in the several states."

But it is not some representative of our own government who speaks to us next; it is Plato:

> "'But you [ὑμᾶς] we [ἡμεῖς] have engendered for yourselves [ὑμῖν τε αὐτοῖς] and the rest of the city [τῇ τε ἄλλῃ πόλει] to be, as it were, king-bees and leaders in the hive. You have received a better and more complete [ἄμεινόν τε καὶ τελεώτερον] education than the others, and you are more capable of sharing both ways of life. Down you must go [καταβατέον] then, each in his turn, to the habitation of the others and accustom yourselves to the observation of the obscure things there.'"[9]

Although Plato is perfectly well aware that we can take these words at face value—the speech of a fictional founder addressed to the fictional Guardians who, perhaps uncharacteristically, need to be persuaded to take part in politics in the fictional City Socrates created when he went down to the Piraeus more than two thousand years ago—he opens up a second possibility by means of the Critical Ambiguity. The question that provokes "the crisis of the *Republic*" is: "Who is this 'you' (ὑμᾶς)?" If we are willing to find first Socrates and then Plato behind this "we" (ἡμεῖς), then honesty will compel us to admit that Plato the Teacher—who has just taught us what philosophy is (Books V and VI) and

---

9. 520b5-c3. Slings, *Platonis* Rempublicam, 267 has astutely added quotation marks to this crucial "Speech to the Guardians" (520b5-d5) and I have modified Shorey's translation accordingly. The bee-imagery reappears in Book VIII where bees are used to explain the origins of tyranny (beginning at 552c2-3) and the antidote to it (564c1-5).

therefore made it possible for us to become Platonic philosophers, and who has, moreover, created his Πολιτεία for us—has taught us all of this for exactly the purpose the speaker now owns: he wrote the *Republic* to persuade philosophers in other cities ("in the other city") to Go Back Down into the Cave. The proper pride of the man born as Aristocles son of Ariston (a pride more than justified by the immortal dialogues of Plato) makes it possible for him to say that, thanks to him, we "have received a better and more complete education than the others." To be sure it is natural for the self-grown, "indebted to none for its breeding," to be under no obligation "to anyone the price of its nurture." But here comes this apparently dead—but actually immortal—Athenian asking us to weigh up the extent of our obligation *to him*.[10] And those obligations are considerable.

Platonists naturally revere Plato as their teacher. But he hasn't only benefited the Platonists who own his teaching as their guide. Plato has kept philosophy alive and deserves no small measure of gratitude from everyone. Both skeptics and mystics have seen themselves reflected in his dialogues. Dead in the middle between the dogmatic and dialogic readings—no closer to one than to the other—Plato himself will continue to playfully teach all philosophers to discover philosophy as reflected in his twinkling eyes. Plato wrote for us in a double sense: it was for our own personal benefit—for all of us (ὑμῖν αὐτοῖς), mystics, skeptics, and philosophers alike—that he gave this perfectly equipoised pedagogical treasure. But he also wrote for us in a far more specific sense: it is now these United States that are that Other City (τῇ τε ἄλλῃ πόλει)[11] for whose sake this noble son of famous Athens gave us the best and most complete education available, he who invented academics in the Academy.

The education he has given us is both better and more complete (ἄμεινόν τε καὶ τελεώτερον). On what basis can Plato claim such a thing in our case, i.e., if we are prepared to allow ourselves to be being addressed through the Critical Ambiguity? To begin with, the statement would probably be true if only on the basis of having read Plato's *Republic* through VII 520c1: the reason that the Cave is so frequently excerpted is because many teachers feel that it is a necessary component of any well-educated person's training, as indeed it is. But the first six books of the *Republic* are not all of Plato that the young academi-

10. Robert Browning captures this kind of thing beautifully in his "A Toccata of Galuppi's" where the long-dead composer enters into a dialogue with the poet's persona only after having been asked a question (stanza VIII). Although Plato is not the skeptic on immortality that Galuppi evidently is, there is mutatis mutandis considerable connection between Athens and Venice: "Yes, you, like a ghostly cricket [the poet's persona addresses Galuppi], creaking where a house was burned: / 'Dust and ashes, dead and done with, Venice spent what Venice earned, / The soul, doubtless, is immortal—where a soul can be discerned" (stanza XII). Thanks to Plato—and many others—Athens did not spend all she earned. Nevertheless, what she saved for us was unquestionably written "where a house was burned," i.e., in what Mary Renault calls "the last of the wine."

11. "How many ages hence shall this our lofty scene be acted over? In States unborn, in accents yet unknown?" Cf. 499c7-d6.

cians had completed by the time they reached their teacher's central καταβατέον. And if we are encountering the dialogues in anything like their proper reading order, the Socratic statement about Platonic pedagogy becomes even more defensible. Having been initiated into the Academy with the proleptic puzzles of the *Protagoras*, the student has long since progressed through the *Alcibiades* and the *Hippias* twins (between which stands the mediating *Erastai*)[12] to the *Ion*, *Menexenus*, *Symposium* and *Lysis*. By the end of this sequence, the student has been proleptically prepared for the visionary Diotima and then been tested for the spiritual assimilation of her Idea of Beauty. Nor are these ten dialogues sufficient preparation for the *Republic*. A more difficult series awaits the student who has followed Socrates from Agathon's house to the Lyceum in the second course, semester or year: the *Euthydemus*, *Laches* and *Charmides* prepare the way for the *Gorgias*, *Meno*, and *Cleitophon* (to say nothing of the *Theages*).[13] How long students remained at the Academy remains, of course, a matter of speculation but for one proposition I will argue: the *Republic* stands in the middle of any adequately Platonic course of studies. In the absence of any other evidence, *five* years during which the student would work or play through *thirty-five* dialogues might be harmlessly proposed (539e2-540a5; see section §29). In any case, at the end of that course, a man like Aristotle who received an appointment from King Philip—even if he needed to be begged to take it—proved himself less of a Platonist than Demosthenes, who repeatedly begged the Many to permit him to benefit them by upholding Democracy against the Tyrant.[14]

It should be carefully noted that Plato isn't trying to persuade anybody who doesn't acknowledge that we were all born in the Cave and who hasn't made the ascent to the sunlight of the Idea of the Good,[15] to go back down into the Cave.

---

12. The word "ἀντεραστής" is found three times in Plato: at 521b5, *Am.* 132c5, and *Am.* 133b3. Cf. 521b1-5 with *Erastai* and Alcibiades.

13. A glance at the variety of meanings (see LSJ) that the word "τέλειος" can have in Greek (the qualifying "more" of "τελεώ-τερον" must be supplied throughout)—a list including "perfect," "fully constituted," "full grown," "married," "accomplished," "perfect in [its] kind," "complete," "fulfilled," "accomplished," "perfect" (as in the numbers six, twenty-eight, and nine), and even "*third*"; the first number with a beginning, middle, and end (ἀρχή, μέσον, and τέλος)—suggest a variety of ways in which we can begin to imagine Platonic Pedagogy.

14. The assertion that Demosthenes was Plato's auditor appears in Cicero at *Brutus* 121, *de Oratore* 1.89 and *Orator* 15. See Andrea Wörle, *Die politische Tätigkeit der Schuler Platons* (Darmstadt: Kümmerle, 1981), 47-52.

15. This ascent need not be defined out of existence *per impossibile*: a willingness to orient one's life by a transcendent and otherworldly standard of ethical excellence is within the reach of most every human being. For a particularly strong statement of the alternative easily available in English, see Norbert Blössner, "The City-Soul Analogy" (translated by G. R. F. Ferrari) in Ferrari (ed.) *The Cambridge Companion to Plato's* Republic, 345-385 (Cambridge, UK: Cambridge University Press, 2007) at 381: "As long as Socrates does not claim to have certain *knowledge* of the Form of the Good, he is not

In short, it is only the Platonists whom Plato is trying to persuade and the definition of philosophy given on the Longer Way applies only to Platonic philosophers. It simply doesn't apply to Aristotelians and Hegelians, to empiricists, materialists, monists, nihilists, pantheists, and a thousand others. The goal of the *Republic* is to persuade those whom Plato regards as philosophers to practice Justice. And those whom Plato regards as philosophers are ipso facto Platonic philosophers: those whom Plato has taught to philosophize. To be sure most of those who call themselves "philosophers" do not consider themselves—despite the Academy, the Ideas, and anything said by A. N. Whitehead—to be Platonic philosophers. But those who do—those who have learned everything they know in what Cicero called "the open spaces of the Academy" (see Introduction)—find ourselves with an obligation to pay Plato back for what he has so freely, delightfully, and generously given.[16] He craves no temple, no statue of gold. He asks us for something far more precious: the dedication of our earthly existence (and he never says that there is no other kind!) to preventing Thrasymachus from taking control in any other "Athens" there might come to be someday. Nor should this last statement be left in the subjunctive mood: the fact that our own republic is in crisis makes the present-day United States no less ideal a venue to discover "the crisis of the *Republic*" than the Piraeus of Athens was but yesterday.

Plato marks the crucial importance of this passage in three ways once it is finished. To begin with, (1) Socrates asks Glaucon a question that is anything but leading and which, in any case—given the Critical Ambiguity of Socrates' second response—is addressed to Glaucon in a double sense: "'Will our alumni, then, disobey us when we tell them this, and will they refuse to share in the labors of state each in his turn while permitted to dwell the most of the time with one another in that purer world?'" (520d7-9). This is Plato's burning question and upon the reader's response to it depends the passing of the torch. The reader's choice is sovereign. Plato has given us as many "outs" as anyone could possibly need; he has also contrived, with utmost skill and care, to create a crisis for any reader willing and able to undergo a spiritual revolution (521c6) at the unlikely hands of an apparently long-dead Greek. Playful as ever, he likewise depends on the reader to recognize eternity in Socrates' "most of the time."

In the meantime, Plato's brother Glaucon (2) takes his crack at answering it. Glaucon's answer (a) makes crystal clear that Plato has now revealed to us what Justice is[17] and (b) that the precious young man has chosen the life of Justice for

---

able to (and, in fact, does not) claim that such knowledge about whether it is really good to be just—despite the fact that he is deeply convinced of it. (But to be convinced of something is not to know it.) That is the deeper reason for the fact that the Socratic argument is (and can only be) provisional." In fact it is readers like Blössner himself—and the Tübingen School in general—who constitute "the deeper reason."

16. See Irwin, *Plato's Ethics*, 314 on Cephalus.

17. On the Shorter Way, Socrates warned us that justice was about to be discovered and we felt disappointed when we finally discovered it after such a dramatic build-up. On

himself: "'Impossible,' he said: 'for we shall be imposing just commands on men who are just [δίκαια γὰρ δὴ δικαίοις ἐπιτάξομεν]'" (520e1). This is the sweetest moment in *Republic*, the moment of Socrates' victory, and the dead center of Platonic pedagogy. Having accomplished his appointed task, (3) Socrates rewards the reader by giving the *Republic* its most succinct summary: "'For the fact is, dear friend,' said I, 'if you can discover a better way of life than office-holding for your future rulers, a well-governed city becomes a possibility'" (520e4-521a2). Socrates has now shown what Justice is, persuaded Glaucon to choose it as his way of life, and revealed his formula for good government at any time and place: the philosopher's altruistic decision to forego freely a better life for the sake of benefiting others, i.e., to Go Back Down into the Cave.

Section 17. Justice and the Good on the Divided Line

Plato's *Republic* therefore contains no definition of Justice. What it does offer readers is: (1) a portrait of Socrates practicing Justice, (2) a dialogue that is itself a product of Plato's own practice of Justice, and (3) the opportunity to discover Justice for themselves thanks to the numerous clues Plato has woven into his story beginning with its opening word. Although it doesn't provide a theoretical account of the practice of Justice (but see section §30), it does provide a theoretical account of what makes Justice intelligible. This distinction is important but difficult to explain. Justice is both an action and a choice: it is, in fact, an action freely chosen. So freely is it chosen, in fact, that only the reader who freely chooses to do so will see it for what it is. But Justice also has a theoretical basis in Plato's ontology. The Allegory of the Cave is an attempt to bring these two things together: it illustrates both the theoretical foundations of going back down—i.e., the distinction between intelligible Being and visible Becoming[18]—and the actual practice of Justice: the returning philosopher whom the shadow-loving Cavemen would kill if only they could get hold of her (517a4-6). The

---

the Longer Way, Socrates tells us what has happened only *after* it has happened. The reader who didn't notice it is, of course, none the wiser. But the reader Plato wanted—the reader who dared to wonder whether Plato was speaking directly to her or him—finds now a comforting confirmation along with an awesome responsibility. On the structural parallels between the Two Ways, notice that (1) Plato names the Longer Way and calls it a Method but [1] refuses to do either for the Shorter Way. [2] The *much-trumpeted* discovery of justice in accordance with [3] the *concealed* methods of the Shorter Way (concealed because neither is ever named as such) stands in direct opposition to (2) the *concealed* discovery of Justice in accordance with (3) the *much-trumpeted* Dialectical Method of the explicitly named "Longer Way." Dialectic must be applied three times: (a) to the Shorter Way (i.e., the Divided Line must be applied to it and its common methodology discovered by the reader), (b) the reader must enter into a dialogue with the text at 520c1, and finally (c) must struggle with the message received. "(c)" will be considered in chapter 5.

18. 525b3 and 526e7-8; the vocabulary of Being and Becoming will be discussed with more precision in section §28.

Cave is therefore a nodal point between the portrait of Socrates practicing Justice—as we now realize that he has been doing from the opening word—and the ontological foundations of Justice as presented outside the Allegory of the Cave. Politics and ontology are inseparable in Plato.

Just as the Second Part of the Divided Line explains why the definition of justice discovered on the Shorter Way will be something like "one man" (and, by yet another hypothetical extension—or rather a teeming host of them—"one part of the soul") "doing the one job for which it is by nature suited," so also does the First Part of the Divided Line explain why Justice is Going Back Down into the Cave on the Longer Way. No investigation based on the methodology of the Second Part can transcend the Hypotheses on which it is based. This perfectly general limitation applies both to the mathematical examples Socrates uses to explain the Line and to the search for justice on the Shorter Way. The methodology dictates that the object of investigation—in this case justice—will be whatever it is with which we began, in this case, the principle of the division of labor. No more than the Second Part of the Divided Line tells the reader what justice is does the First do so for Justice. The descriptions of both segments clearly indicate, however, what each of the two will be like. To be more specific: what Socrates says about the First Part of the Line offers a theoretical explanation of why Justice turns out to be Going Back Down into the Cave.

Although the First Part is of infinitely greater value than the Second, Socrates devotes only a single sentence to it (511b2-c2) rather than three for its counterpart. This circumstance, it should be added, reflects the relationship between the Shorter and Longer Ways: Socrates can bring to light the latter only because he has already labored to elucidate the former.[19] The dependence of dialectic on the earlier *methods* is obvious from the start:

> "Understand then," said I, "that by the other section of the intelligible I mean that which the reason itself lays hold of by the power of dialectics, treating its assumptions not as absolute beginnings but literally as hypotheses, underpinnings, footings, and springboards so to speak" (511b2-5)

This then is the *via negativa*: unlike the Second Part of the Line, the First treats its Hypotheses as mere hypotheses. This explains why, for example, Justice (as opposed to justice) is not "one man doing the one job for which he is by nature suited" upon which Hypothesis, the entire Image of the City was unquestioningly based. The passage continues:

> "to enable it to rise to that which requires no assumption and is the starting-point of all [ἐπὶ τὴν τοῦ παντὸς ἀρχὴν ἰών], and after attaining to that again

19. But *qua* method in sense [I]—see Section §11 above—the exact reverse is true: Dialectic eschews the methods [III] of the third part but it is only in contrast to "the dialectical method" [II] that the various pursuits [I] described in third part of the Divided Line can be said (somewhat misleadingly) to share a common *method* (or perhaps *methods*).

> taking hold of the first dependencies from it [πάλιν αὖ ἐχόμενος τῶν ἐκείνης ἐχομένων]" (511b5-7)

Shorey has made two interesting translation choices here. First of all, there is no hint of his "rise" in Plato's text: Socrates' words (ἐπὶ τὴν τοῦ παντὸς ἀρχὴν ἰών) have no directional element whatsoever. Shorey takes a revealing liberty: arriving at (i.e., ἐπὶ . . . ἰών) the Idea of the Good is—in properly Platonic terms—"rising" to it or "going up." But if Shorey imports a fully warranted trace of "going up" into the passage, he fails to notice the element of "going back down" that Plato actually includes here. And the first clue to this failure is the word "πάλιν." Two things should be noted: in combination with καταβαίνειν, πάλιν is the phrase Socrates used for "to go *back* down" (section §16) and Shorey leaves this word untranslated here. Without πάλιν, the phrase 'αὖ ἐχόμενος τῶν ἐκείνης ἐχομένων' already means "again taking hold of the first dependencies from it."[20] And Shorey's omission of πάλιν becomes of crucial importance when we push a little farther into the passage:

> "again taking hold of the first dependencies from it, so to proceed downward to the conclusion, [πάλιν αὖ ἐχόμενος τῶν ἐκείνης ἐχομένων, οὕτως ἐπὶ τελευτὴν καταβαίνῃ]" (511b6-c1)

Here there can be no question of importing a directional element into the text: Socrates explicitly says that the method "descends" or "goes down" (καταβαίνῃ).[21] But it clearly does even more than that. It will be noted that—although separated by quite some distance—both πάλιν and καταβαίνῃ are found at either end of the phrase I have quoted. Grammatically, they are even more closely related: the nominative ἐχόμενος (which *is* in close proximity to πάλιν) is the subject of the verb καταβαίνῃ. Shorey decides not to translate πάλιν because doing so is very difficult. The first step toward doing so is to remove the comma that Burnet followed by Slings have (perfectly understandably) inserted between ἐχομένων and οὕτως and replace it with a close parenthesis as in: πάλιν (αὖ ἐχόμενος τῶν ἐκείνης ἐχομένων) οὕτως ἐπὶ τελευτὴν καταβαίνῃ. Even here the temptation remains to absorb πάλιν into αὖ: it is too difficult to translate the distant words together. But what now emerges is that "again taking hold of things taking hold of it" (a literal translation that better captures "τῶν . . . ἐχομένων") is a parenthetical comment for what the method

20. It will be noticed that the two discrepancies numbered (1) and (2b) balance each other and therefore each justifies the other. Since there is no "going back down" without first "going up," Shorey "translates" the directional element present in πάλιν when he adds the word "rises."

21. This receives some much-needed attention at Claudia Baracchi, *Of Myth, Life and War in Plato's* Republic (Bloomington, IN: University of Indiana Press, 2001), 96 and 128n8.

"is holding" (the οὕτως refers back to the parenthesis) when it "goes down" or rather "goes *back* (πάλιν) down to the conclusion."

This becomes clearer in context. The words immediately before the phrase contain another nominative participle: ἀψάμενος αὐτῆς. Two things should be noted: this participle refers to the only other verb besides καταβαίνῃ in the passage (ἅπτεται at 511b3) that describes what the method in question actually *does*, and it is an aorist participle unlike, for example, ἐχόμενος. This yields (in proper word order): "having attained that, back (still holding onto the things that are holding onto it) thusly to a conclusion it goes down." But the actual meaning is that "having done all of these things on the way up to the Idea of the Good," the method reaches its conclusion precisely by *going back down*.[22] It is here that metaphysics and ethics, politics and methodology, become one: going back down from the Good is exactly what the philosopher must do. And this crucial sentence ends with words that have already been cited repeatedly in section §13 because they differentiate the "fully emancipated" First from the Second Part of the Line:

> "making no use whatever of any object of sense but only of pure ideas moving on through ideas to ideas and ending with ideas." (510c1-2)

Unlike the abstractions of mathematics (to say nothing of the "forms" of physical things), the Good and its offspring are fully emancipated from sensible things. Among those offspring, Justice is primary because it is meaningless without the Idea of the Good while the dualism of Being and Becoming is the condition of its possibility. In his one-sentence description of the First Part of the Divided Line at the end of Book VI, Socrates has shown, or rather proleptically intimated, exactly how Justice will be reached in Book VII. Having constructed an image that demotes the physical world to shadows while pointing beyond it to the unspeakable excellence of the Idea, Plato situates Justice between the two: it depends on the sun-like Good but requires a return to the Cave. Insofar as Going Back Down is or represents an *idea*, it completely depends on the Idea par excellence (i.e., the Idea of the Good). In other words, if it is the "Idea of Justice" that motivates the philosopher's free decision to return to the Cave, that idea is perfectly meaningless without both the Idea of the Good and the Cave, itself merely the intelligible demotion of Becoming as the realm where no one—except the Just philosopher—has seen the Idea. Without the Idea of the Good, there is no awareness that there is a Cave and, without the Cave, there can be no Justice. But without an act of Justice on the part of the philosopher, there is no one to teach that there is either an Idea of the Good or a Cave. Without Plato's practice of Justice, there would have been no Academy and *a fortiori* no *Republic* to teach in it and here as well. And without the Idea of Justice—

---

22. There is therefore something to be said for including 511b7-8 as a *fourth* instance (along with 516e3, 519d4-5, and 539e3) of καταβαίνειν and πάλιν being used together (see section §16).

without that which motivated Plato the Teacher to write the *Republic* for us, his students—an awareness of the Cave is unthinkable. In other words, anything like a popular or pre-experiential awareness of the intelligible realm of Being depends entirely on a Plato's Justice. We therefore owe it to Plato to return the favor he freely did for us and those who know the world of sense is not the final reality have pressing obligations to fulfill while here below.

Section 18. The Idea of the Good and Plato's Theory of Forms

Although the words "the Good" are used repeatedly, the specific formula "the Idea of the Good" is used only five times in the *Republic* and then only in Books VI (2 uses) and VII (3). A consideration of these instances (and of the sixteen other times in the *Republic* where "idea" is used without the Good) is perhaps long overdue.[23] In section §5, for example, I wrote: "The heart of Plato's philosophy is the Idea of the Good." This statement must now be anchored in the text.

To begin with, then, the word "heart" is obviously a mere metaphor. But it captures well the desirable analogy to a statement like: "Books VI and VII are the heart of the *Republic*." Other more accurate synonyms for "heart" would be: "core," "center," "high-point," and "most important part"; I'll use "central core" as a compromise between them. In other words, a statement like: "the Idea of the Good is the central core of Plato's philosophy" rests on the assumptions that (1) there is a central core of Plato's philosophy, (2) *Republic* contains it, and (3) Books VI and VII contain the central core of Plato's *Republic*. I take "(3)" for granted: this is widely acknowledged to be the case. "(2)" is commonly believed as well although the rival claims of *Timaeus* will eventually need to be addressed. But he centrality of "the Idea of the Good" in the *Republic* with respect to "(3)" can be demonstrated by attending carefully to each of the twenty-one times that Plato uses the word "idea."

To begin with, it is useful to distribute these uses by Books:

Book II	4
Book V	1
Book VI	6
Book VII	3
Book VIII	1
Book IX	3
Book X	3

23. See Fritz-Gregor Herrmann, *Words and Ideas; The Roots of Plato's Philosophy* (Swansea: Classical Press of Wales, 2007) for a thorough treatment treatment of ἰδέα and related words in Plato. Particularly significant is his "The Idea of the Good and the Other Forms in Plato's *Republic*" in David Keyt and Fred D. Miller (eds.), *Freedom, Reason, and the Polis: Essays in Ancient Greek Political Philosophy*, 202-230 (Cambridge, UK: Cambridge University Press, 2007) at 224-25.

The first use of ἰδέα in the *Republic* proleptically announces its singular importance with a single use (we will see that Plato tends to use the word 'ἰδέα' in sets of three):

> "Then, perhaps, there would be more justice in the larger object and more easy to apprehend. If it please you, then, let us first look for [ζητήσωμεν] its quality in states, and then only examine it also in the individual, looking for the likeness of the greater in the form of the less [ἐν τῇ τοῦ ἐλάττονος ἰδέᾳ]." (368e7-369a4)

This passage is crucial for the structure of the *Republic*, i.e. the hypothesized parallel between City and Man. Socrates is, in fact, inaugurating "the Shorter Way" investigation (cf. the use of ζητήσωμεν here with the Divided Line; see section §12) by laying down the principal Hypothesis: the justice we find in the City will be the same as that for which we are seeking in the Man. This first use—by locating the ἰδέα specifically in the smaller Man instead of being the common element that joins the two—may be said to be a perfect example of Platonic prolepsis: Justice will guide the man, not the city while precluding the possibility that the Idea of Justice will be the quality shared by City and Man.[24] An important term has thus been introduced in a way that provokes questions (cf. the first use of μέθοδος in the plural at IV 435d1) and it would be impossible to derive either a Theory of Ideas or the Idea of the Good from it.

The other three times the word appears in Book II are concentrated in a single passage. Here the word is used to mean something like "the form of a god" or perhaps more accurately "the form of God." The context is Socrates' legislation concerning poetic theologizing in the Primary Education of the Guardians. He reviews the first of two such laws:

> "This, then," said I, "will be one of the laws and patterns concerning the gods [εἷς ἂν εἴη τῶν περὶ θεοὺς νόμων τε καὶ τύπων] to which speakers and poets will be required to conform, that God [τὸν θεὸν] is not the cause of all things, but only of the good." (380c7-10)

The abrupt transition from plural to singular in this passage is very striking and really quite funny. It is particularly striking when one keeps in mind that the soon to be revealed *second* law respecting the gods is that God will not appear in a variety of forms. The comical part is that if there are many gods, then, by definition, the divine must necessarily appear in a variety of forms. It should be carefully noted that there is no *third* law about poetic theologizing laid down by Socrates and the reader will hardly be surprised when I say that Plato intends us to discover it for ourselves.

---

24. Cf. Richard Kraut, "The Defense of Justice on Plato's Republic" in Richard Kraut (ed.), *Plato's Republic; Critical Essays* (Lanham, MD: Rowman & Littlefield, 1997), 203.

> "And an entirely satisfactory one," he said. "And what of this, the second [ὁ δεύτερος]. Do you think that God [τὸν θεὸν] is a wizard and capable of manifesting himself by design, now in one aspect, now in another [ἐν ἄλλαις ἰδέαις], at one time himself changing [γιγνόμενον] and altering his shape [τὸ αὐτοῦ εἶδος] in many transformations and at another deceiving us and causing us to believe such things about him; or that he is simple and less likely than anything else to depart from [ἐκβαίνειν] his own form [τῆς ἑαυτοῦ ἰδέας]?" "I cannot say offhand," he replied. "But what of this: If anything went out from its own form [τῆς αὐτοῦ ἰδέας], would it not be displaced and changed, either by itself or by something else?" "Necessarily." (380d1-e2)

If theology were not so unpopular among us these days, this passage would warrant its own chapter, not a single paragraph. The logical (as opposed to the theological) point is, however, that the word ἰδέα will come to mean that which is by no means part of τὸ γιγνόμενον (this passage constitutes a prolepsis of Becoming): i.e., Plato uses ἰδέα here to introduce proleptically "the unchanging" Being. But the fact that he does so in the context of God is noteworthy and can't simply be passed over in conformity to the atheism of our own age. Plato's decision to use both ἰδέα and εἶδος in this context suggests that theology and "the Idea of the Good' are not quite as separated as many might wish.[25] Perhaps we could all agree that by conflating ἰδέα and εἶδος (concepts that Plato is on the verge of giving an entirely new meaning as something like "the unchangeable *look* of the invisible") are used here proleptically by linking them to what Plato's audience already believes to be mysterious and somehow or other beyond our ken. And that, of course, is the only point I need to make here.[26]

---

25. Paradoxically, the identification of the two becomes easier for those who reject both God and the Platonic Ideas; see Lampert, *How Philosophy Became Socratic*, 283-86 and 351-54. While undertaking "the introduction of a new kind of god" by "his new doctrine of ideas" (336), Socrates "is, so to speak, the only non-Platonist, the only one to doubt the adequacy of his concepts of the beautiful, just, and good."

26. But for the more theologically inclined, I will not only flesh out my earlier statement about the invisible presence of a Third Law regarding poetic theologizing but will call attention to the use of ἐκβαίνειν. I submit, to begin with (and proleptically as well) that the need to search for "the missing third" will hereafter rear its head enough times (the two Noble Lies, the two acceptable musical modes, and the two Ways are but three examples) for us to wonder about its presence here. I would argue that monotheism is not anything that we need to superimpose (or project) onto this passage: *it is already present as the unspoken logical basis of Socrates' other two laws*. In fact, monotheism exists here in much the same way that justice exists in relation to the other three virtues in Book IV: it is its basis, and indeed it is its very *basicality* (as it were) that makes it, like the one man/one job Principle in Book IV, difficult to find. I suggest that Socrates has no desire to give his enemies proof positive that "he does not believe in the gods of the city." He is brave enough to reject the concept of "quarreling gods" (377e6-378a6): making explicit the fact that the (many) gods are (a single) God—already implicit in the transition from θεοὺς to τὸν θεὸν at 380c7-9—is unnecessary for the dialectical reader. As for ἐκβαίνειν, Socrates may leave open the possibility that τὸν θεὸν, without changing τὸ

Having considered the four uses in Book II—although it would be more accurate to think of those four uses as constituting a singleton and a triad rather than a set of four—it is now time to consider the heart of the matter: Books V through VII (ten uses). Far more important is the fact that half of these refer specifically to "the Idea of the Good." To begin with, then: opponents of the proposition that "the Idea of the Good is the central core of Plato's philosophy," fall into two categories: (a) those who acknowledge the centrality of "Plato's Theory of Ideas" and (b) those who do not. I have already dealt with "(b)" in section §5: only those in "(a)" will be addressed now. The alternative to the proposition that "the Idea of the Good is the heart of Plato's philosophy" is that the Idea of the Good is (i) not the only Idea or (ii) not the most important of the Ideas. Nothing need be said about "(ii)" except that it simply can't be sustained on the basis of the *Republic* nor is there any evidence for it elsewhere in Plato. But even if the Eleatic Stranger is an exception, there could be no *better* Idea than the Good and not even a plurality of ideas that include the Good could be better than the singular Good. Nevertheless, the contrary of "(i)" (i.e., that the Idea of the Good is the only Idea) would be universally or at least generally considered too strong a position for a reasonable Plato scholar to take. My view is that if "the Idea of the Good" is not the only Idea in Plato's philosophy, it is by so way and away the most important—not only higher than any other but also the cause by which any other is known—that it might just as well be; i.e., its absolute primacy is, at the very least, the *sine qua non* of any adequate version of "Plato's Theory of Ideas." Emphasis on the primacy of the Idea of the Good on the one hand and a rigorous exclusion all "forms" that prove, on inspection, to be nothing more than intelligible images of visible things (cf. 511c1), is the basis of what I would describe as a properly austere Platonism.[27]

The first time the Idea of the Good is mentioned is at 505a2:

> "For you have often heard that the greatest thing to learn is the idea of good [ἡ τοῦ ἀγαθοῦ ἰδέα] by reference to which just things [δίκαια] and all the rest become [γίγνεται] useful and beneficial. And now I am almost sure you know that this is what I am going to speak of and to say further that we have no adequate knowledge of it. And if we do not know it, then, even if without the knowledge of this we should know all other things never so well, you are aware that it would avail us nothing, just as no possession either is of any avail without the possession of the good [τοῦ ἀγαθοῦ]. Or do you think there is any profit in possessing everything except that which is good, or in understanding

αὐτοῦ εἶδος and without any alteration of τῆς ἑαυτοῦ ἰδέας (since both ἰδέα and εἶδος are not *visible* but merely *intelligible*) is able—without any intent to deceive but with only the Idea of Justice to guide or fulfill Him—to κατα-βαίνειν; a move that requires no significant departure or alteration of His nature.

27. Consider also David Lachterman, "What Is 'The Good' of Plato's *Republic*." *St. Johns Review* 39 (1989-1990), 139-171 at 169n22: "nowhere in *The Republic* is the canonical idiom of participation, μετέχειν, used." Cf. 476c7-d2 and 585c9-d3.

> all things else apart from the good [τοῦ ἀγαθοῦ] while understanding and knowing nothing that is fair and good [καλὸν δὲ καὶ ἀγαθὸν]?" (505a2-b3)

This momentous introduction to the Idea of the Good—crystalline in its visionary clarity—has been preceded by two other uses of the word ἰδέα, one of which (following *Symposium*) uses it of τὸ καλὸν (V 479a1), a use that reminds us of the old visionary moment but does not quite rise to the level of the new one made luminous in ἡ τοῦ ἀγαθοῦ ἰδέα.[28] The second of them offers an adumbration of "the Theory of Ideas" (by which I mean the theory that Plato regards the existence of many Ideas as the central core of his Philosophy) that overshoots the Idea of the Good by referring to "the Idea of each thing that is" (VI 486d10).[29] But the passage at VI 505a2 that introduces the Idea of the Good shows the inadequacy of both of these. The following points are noteworthy: (1) the supremacy of the singular Idea of the Good (ἡ τοῦ ἀγαθοῦ ἰδέα), (2) the notion that just things, specifically identified as occurring within the realm of Becoming (γίγνεται), derive their goodness from it, and (3) that even τὸ καλόν of the *Symposium* (note Glaucon's presence at *Smp.* 172c3) is presented as secondary to ἡ τοῦ ἀγαθοῦ ἰδέα. While one often hears that neither Socrates or Plato knows anything about the Idea of the Good, these three points make it obvious that Socrates actually knows a considerable amount about "the greatest thing to learn."

But whatever else Socrates may know about the Idea of the Good, he flatly refuses to gratify Glaucon's demand for more information about it:

> "Nay, in heaven's name, Socrates," said Glaucon, "do not draw back, as it were, at the very goal. For it will content us if you explain the good [τοῦ ἀγαθοῦ] even as you set forth the nature of justice, sobriety, and the other virtues." "It will right well content me, my dear fellow," I said, "but I fear that my powers may fail and that in my eagerness I may cut a sorry figure and become a laughing-stock. Nay, my beloved, let us dismiss for the time being the nature of the good [τἀγαθὸν] in itself; for to attain to my present surmise of that seems a pitch above the impulse that wings my flight today."[30]

---

28. Cf. the conscious imprecision (indicated by the absence of the definite article, the double formula, and the indefinite τινά) of "αὐτὸ μὲν καλὸν καὶ ἰδέαν τινὰ αὐτοῦ κάλλους" ("a self-beautiful and a kind of idea of beauty itself;" translation mine of 479a1-2) with ἡ τοῦ ἀγαθοῦ ἰδέα.

29. 486d7-487a2: "'And do you think that truth is akin to measure and proportion or to disproportion?' 'To proportion.' 'Then in addition to our other requirements we look for a mind [διάνοιαν] endowed with measure and grace, whose native disposition will make it easily guided to the aspect of the ideal reality [τὴν τοῦ ὄντος ἰδέαν] in all things.' 'Assuredly.' 'Tell me, then, is there any flaw in the argument?'" As indicated by its explicit dependence on διάνοια, there may well be.

30. 506d1-e1; the invocation of Glaucon as "O blessed one" will be shown to be significant in section §30. The actual words for "the impulse that wings my flight" (κατὰ τὴν παροῦσαν ὁρμὴν ἐφικέσθαι) perhaps contain a playful suggestion of Justice if

As the Divided Line will show, he certainly cannot discuss the un-hypothetical Good as he did "justice, sobriety, and the other virtues." But despite being unwilling—as distinguished from unable—to discuss "the nature of the good in itself" at the present time, Socrates is willing to discuss something derived from it:

> "But of what seems to be the offspring of the good [ἔκγονός τε τοῦ ἀγαθοῦ] and most nearly made in its likeness [ὁμοιότατος] I am willing to speak if you too wish it, and otherwise to let the matter drop." "Well, speak on," he said, "for you will duly pay me the tale of the parent another time." "I could wish," I said, "that I were able to make and you to receive the payment and not merely as now the interest. But at any rate receive this interest and the offspring of the good [τὸν τόκον τε καὶ ἔκγονον αὐτοῦ τοῦ ἀγαθοῦ]." (506e2-507a4)

What Socrates says next introduces a passage that bears on two crucial and closely related questions in Platonic metaphysics: (1) the true relationship between "the offspring of the Good" and the visible sun, and (2) the distinction between the Idea of the Good and "Plato's Theory of Ideas."

> Have a care [εὐλαβεῖσθε], however, lest I deceive you unintentionally with a false reckoning [κίβδηλον . . . τὸν λόγον] of the interest." "We will do our best [κατὰ δύναμιν]," he said, "to be on our guard [εὐλαβησόμεθα]. Only speak on." (507a4-6)

The boys (εὐλαβεῖσθε is imperative plural) are commanded to be careful and Glaucon answers for all of us to the effect that we will be (εὐλαβησόμεθα). But all of us can be so only to an extent commensurate with our abilities (κατὰ δύναμιν). We have just been given a clear indication of a *genuine* account: it will be an offspring of the Good (the ἔκγονός τε τοῦ ἀγαθοῦ at 506e2). But we have now been expressly warned that we are about to be tested with a *spurious* account [κίβδηλον . . . τὸν λόγον]. This proves to be the case. And what makes the accounts of both the ideas and the offspring of the Good that follow this warning spurious is that they fail to preserve the transcendence of the Good and thereby the important truth that the truest offspring of the Good, is, like its generator, intelligible. In short: the warning is followed by a triad of passages that promulgate "the Theory of Ideas" without reference to "the idea of the Good" followed by a passage that has confirmed scholars in the view that the visible sun is the single and exclusive "offspring of the Good"

The importance of distinguishing "the offspring of the Good" from the physical sun has been emphasized from the start (see Introduction) and my reasons for making this distinction are inseparable from the post-warning context in which the following passage is found:

κατὰ be allowed to retain just a hint of its literal "down" alongside its obvious meaning here of "along."

> "This, then, you must understand that I meant [φάναι με λέγειν] by the offspring of the good [τὸν τοῦ ἀγαθοῦ ἔκγονον] which the good begot [ὃν τἀγαθὸν ἐγέννησεν] to stand in a proportion [ἀνάλογον] with itself: as the good is in the intelligible region [ἐν τῷ νοητῷ τόπῳ] to reason and the objects of reason [πρός τε νοῦν καὶ τὰ νοούμενα], so is this in the visible world [ἐν τῷ ὁρατῷ] to vision and the objects of vision [τὰ ὁρώμενα]." (507b12-c2)

It is here, then, that Socrates makes the strongest theological claim in Plato's *Republic*:[31] the Good literally begot (ἐγέννησεν) the sun and thus the sun is the literal "offspring [ἔκγονος] of the good." Without being entirely sure that Plato is leaving no room whatsoever for the Good's creative agency, I believe that only a λόγος ("an account") that is truly ἀνάλογος ("analogical") rather than exclusively literal avoids being κίβδηλος ("false" or "fraudulent"). The condition for the possibility of the sun's "standing in proportion" to the Good is the sharp distinction between the visible (ἐν τῷ ὁρατῷ) and the intelligible region (ἐν τῷ νοητῷ τόπῳ): the sun is to the visibles (τὰ ὁρώμενα) what the Good is to the intelligibles (τὰ νοούμενα). Literalism threatens to replace the distinction that makes this disjunctive analogy possible with a genetic account that either suggests that the sun is more Good-like or the Good is more sun-like than is the case. The important claim I am making is: any λόγος about the ἔκγονος is κίβδηλος that minimizes the fact that the condition for the possibility of its being ἀνάλογος is the gap between τὰ νοούμενα and τὰ ὁρώμενα.

The words "offspring of the Good" appear three times in the passage following the warning: the passage just quoted is the third and the other two were quoted earlier (see 506e2-507a4). But it is not only an account of the ἔκγονος that follows Socrates' warning to Glaucon; more important in the context of this section is that three more instances of the crucial word ἰδέα follow it as well, all three of them appearing before the λόγος about the ἔκγονος that, if taken too literally, proves to be κίβδηλος. In short: the introduction of "the Idea of the Good" at VI 505a2 is followed by a warning and then by three uses of ἰδέα that would seem to anchor a more general "Theory of Ideas" firmly in the text of Plato's *Republic* despite the crystal clarity of 505a1-b3. The first of the three at

31. Cf. the note on "the offspring of the good" at Shorey, *Plato's Republic*, 2.102n"a": "i.e. creation was the work of benevolent design. This is one of the few passages in the *Republic* where the idea of good is considered in relation to the universe, a thesis reserved for poetical or mythical development in the *Timaeus*." Shorey then adds: "It is idle to construct a systematic metaphysical theology for Plato by identification of τἀγαθόν here either with God or with the ideas as a whole." Certainly with the latter: note the singular "God" at 379b1. Beginning with "'Neither, then, could God,' said I, 'since he is good,'" 379c2-7 suggests that it is not *entirely* idle to consider the identification, especially given the God/good switch at 379b5-c4 that makes it possible for Socrates to develop what at least resembles "a systematic metaphysical theology" in which God *qua* good is blameless (ἀναίτιος at 379c4) for evil. Shorey, attempting to salvage τὸ ἀγαθον (introduced at 379b11) from, as it were, contamination from God, wrestles with this at 1.183n"d".

507b5 suggests that the Good, the Beautiful, and an indefinite plurality of other things are all ideas:

> "We predicate 'to be' of many beautiful things and many good things [πολλὰ καλά . . . καὶ πολλὰ ἀγαθὰ], saying of them severally that they are, and so define them in our speech." "We do." "And again, we speak of a self-beautiful and of a good [αὐτὸ δὴ καλὸν καὶ αὐτὸ ἀγαθόν] that is only and merely good, and so, in the case of all the things that we then posited as many [ὡς πολλὰ ἐτίθεμεν], we turn about and posit each as a single idea or aspect [κατ' ἰδέαν μίαν], assuming it to be a unity [ὡς μιᾶς οὔσης τιθέντες] and call it that which each really is."[32]

By using Beauty and the Good as examples, this passage does not cross the line into a "Theory of Ideas" in which the common or essential feature of any multiplicity of visible things is hypostatized into an intelligible "form." But it does indicate the process by which this dianoetic process (see section §13) can occur: a hypothetical *unity* is posited in place of a physical *plurality*. Having introduced plurality in the context of many things united by a single ἰδέα, the second use of the word that follows the warning (at 507b19) pluralizes the ἰδέαι ("ideas"):

> "And the one class of things we say can be seen but not thought, while the ideas can be thought but not seen [καὶ τὰ μὲν δὴ ὁρᾶσθαί φαμεν, νοεῖσθαι δ' οὔ, τὰς δ' αὖ ἰδέας νοεῖσθαι μέν, ὁρᾶσθαι δ' οὔ]." "By all means."[33]

While upholding and indeed asserting the gap between the visible and intelligible that makes the relationship between the sun and the Idea of the Good merely ἀνάλογος, the assertion of an indefinite plurality of ἰδέαι (τὰς . . . ἰδέας) opens the door to the κίβδηλος version of the Idea as a hypostatized intelligible unity that captures the essential being of a visible plurality and, by so doing, threatens to making every visible thing the ἔκγονος of an intelligible one. Finally, the third use of ἰδέα at 507e5 uses the word to describe what links "the sense of sight" (and one would think this might make a reader suspicious) to "the power to be seen."

---

32. 507b1-6. Cf. V 476c2-4: "'He, then, who believes in beautiful things [καλὰ μὲν πράγματα], but neither believes in beauty itself [αὐτὸ δὲ κάλλος] nor is able to follow when someone tries to guide him to the knowledge of it [ἐπὶ τὴν γνῶσιν αὐτοῦ]—do you think that his life is a dream or a waking?'"

33. 507b8-11; in Book V, it was pluralities that were "seen but not thought" and unities that were "thought but not seen." Cf. 476b4-7: "'The lovers of sounds and sights,' I said, 'delight in beautiful tones and colors and shapes [τάς τε καλὰς φωνὰς . . . καὶ χρόας καὶ σχήματα] and in everything [πάντα τὰ] that art fashions out of these, but their thought is incapable of apprehending and taking delight in the nature of the beautiful in itself [αὐτοῦ δὲ τοῦ καλοῦ].'"

> "The bond, then, that yokes together visibility and the faculty of sight is more precious by no slight form [οὐ σμικρᾷ ἄρα ἰδέᾳ] that which unites the other pairs, if light is not without honor." (507e5-508a2)

Although not inconsistent with the Idea of the Good as Idea—indeed this passage proleptically prepares for the "the third thing" (507d1) in the realm of the intelligible—the potential immanence of the ἰδέα *qua* light likewise prepares for the potentially κίβδηλος λόγος that identifies the sun as the (as it were) only-begotten ἔκγονος of the Good immediately thereafter at 508b12-13.

By bringing the ideas ever closer to the visible, these three passages prepare the reader to accept at face value the genetic literalism of the Idea of the Good begetting the sun. But because these three passages are sandwiched between the warning and the second mention of "the Idea of the Good," the reader is also being tested. As an indication that the foregoing account has been κίβδηλος, consider the next time the Idea of the Good is mentioned at 508e1-2, a passage that quickly follows the third post-warning use of idea (507e5) and the third and final mention of "the offspring of the Good" (508b12-13):

> "Apply this comparison to the soul also in this way. When it is firmly fixed on the domain where truth and reality shine resplendent it apprehends and knows them and appears to possess reason; but when it inclines to that region which is mingled with darkness, the world of becoming and passing away, it opines only and its edge is blunted, and it shifts its opinions hither and thither, and again seems as if it lacked reason." "Yes, it does," "This reality, then, that gives their truth to the objects of knowledge and the power of knowing to the knower, you must say is the idea of good, and you must conceive it as being the cause of knowledge, and of truth in so far as known." (508d10-509a5)

In other words, Plato places what I will call "the Theory of Ideas" (a triad at 507b4-508a2) along with the claim that the Good has begotten the sun between a warning that what follows may be deceptive and a restatement of *the absolute centrality of the Idea of the Good* (already announced at its introduction at 505a2) while reasserting the gap between the darkness implicit even in the brightest of τὰ ὁρώμενα as contrasted with the truth and reality of τὰ νοούμενα. This placement anchors my contention that it is the Idea of the Good and not the Theory of Ideas that is the central core of Plato's philosophy and that it is the *analogy* between the visible sun and the Good, not the genetic link between them, that points us to Plato's true concern in *Republic*: Justice as intelligible ἔκγονος of the Idea of the Good. It also offers further support to my contention that Plato employs basanistic pedagogy. The condition for the possibility of a basanistic test is a discourse or even dialogue (likewise a λόγος) that is κίβδηλος. After warning his auditors to be on their guard, Plato has now embedded one such κίβδηλος λόγος within his *Republic*. Other fraudulent discourses will follow *Republic* and their literary independence will make them in some ways more difficult to spot unless, that is, we realize that in the Reading Order of Plato's Dialogues, these dialogues follow *Republic*. And it is in *Repub-*

lic that we are warned—as we just have been—and must therefore hold ourselves in a state of guarded readiness.

But all of this is in the future: for now, we are standing in the center of the central visionary dialogue, itself the dead center of the Platonic dialogues as a whole. The first use of "the Idea of the Good" in Book VII will be located in the context of the Cave:

> "This image then, dear Glaucon, we must apply as a whole to all that has been said, likening the region revealed through sight to the habitation of the prison, and the light of the fire in it to the power of the sun. And if you assume that the ascent [τὴν δὲ ἄνω ἀνάβασιν] and the contemplation of the things above [τῶν ἄνω] is the soul's ascension [ἄνοδον] to the intelligible region, you will not miss my surmise, since that is what you desire to hear. But God [θεὸς δέ που] knows whether it is true." (517a8-b7)

This passage puts the physical sun in its proper place: inside the Cave. As for the "sun" outside, it is of an entirely different order of being. A vision of the Good requires leaving visible sunlight behind before returning to its shadows in accordance with Justice, true ἔκγονος of the Idea of the Good. There is no going back down without first going up and it would have been difficult for Plato to add a fourth expression for "up" into this passage. It is difficult to imagine why Plato chose to use the pleonastic "upwards ascent" (ἄνω ἀνάβασιν): is there any other kind? Perhaps there is: imagine, for example, a downwards ascent that would (although speaking the language of the ideas) pluralize the Good and distribute it among a variety of forms, some of them embodied in visible goods. Conversely, imagine that in addition to an equally pleonastic "downwards descent" there were an upwards version—the "upwards descent" of Justice—that soared on its way back down.

It is remarkable that Socrates invokes no well-known Olympian deity as the arbiter of his account's veracity: his is an unknown God (θεὸς δέ που). It is therefore the second time that the word "Idea" has been linked by Plato with the singular divine. If one of us—wayward children of Judaism and Christianity—were to speak this way, it would be a slap in the face of the Judeo-Christian-Muslim God: divine revelation has no need of που ("of some indefinite kind in some wholly indefinite place") where God is concerned. Although presumably neither Plato nor Socrates has heard of this God, the θεὸς δέ που makes room for Him. And despite all my best Cave-based efforts to "absolve" the Idea of the Good from being diminished as begetter of the physical sun, it is in the light of Israel's simultaneously transcendent and creative God (cf. "Let there be light!"; cf. 616b4-c2) that I fear the following passage must be read:

> "But, at any rate, my dream as it appears to me is that in the region of the known the last thing to be seen and hardly seen is the idea of good [ἡ τοῦ ἀγαθοῦ ἰδέα], and that when seen [ὀφθεῖσα δὲ] it must needs point [συλλογιστέα] us to the conclusion that this [αὕτη] is indeed the cause [αἰτία] for all things [πᾶσι] of all [πάντων] that is right and beautiful [καλῶν], giving

> birth in the visible world to light, and the author [κύριον] of light and itself in the intelligible world being the authentic source of truth and reason" (517b7-c4)

If there was pleonasm on "up" before, it is now "all" that is hammered into our ears. The "Idea of the Good" is just as *up* as it could possibly be: if it is beyond Being, it is unquestionably *above* Being; i.e., even farther over our heads. But once it has been seen in the visionary moment, it also compels us to bind all things together—every single one of them—with it as their utterly transcendent cause. Recognized as universal causal agent, the Idea of the Good has doubtless given birth to the literal sun, thus even to the light in the Cave and thus the things seen there: this perhaps explains why the escapee, having seen the Good, is reminded of those whose vision is circumscribed by the literal sun. But to view it as immanent in any way would be to completely and willfully forget the transcendental anodyne of the ἄνοδος among τὰ ἄνω and, above all, ἡ ἄνω ἀνάβασις. If we can't hear an echo of the Κύριε in Plato's light-dispensing κύριος, it's simply because we don't want to listen. In any case: although the things of which the Idea of the Good is cause (αἰτία) are plural (πᾶσι, πάντων, καλῶν, etc.), it itself (αὕτη) is repeatedly and emphatically singular: συλλογιστέα, ὀφθεῖσα, and ἡ τοῦ ἀγαθοῦ ἰδέα.

Above all, the Idea of the Good is identified as the more than efficient cause of things *that are even more like unto it*: intelligible things like "truth and reason," indeed "all that is right and beautiful." And foremost among these intelligible things is Justice, best understood in this context as the realm-connecting synthesis of sight in the intelligible realm and action in the visible. Unlike the literal sun, Justice is not merely the visible analogue to the Idea of the Good but is itself intelligible. It also proves to be strangely sun-like:[34] Justice is instantiated when the philosopher, inspired by the obligation to synthesize the infinite causal reach of the intelligible Good—analogous to Shakespeare's "largesse universal, like the sun"—remembers, pities, and finally brings aid by going back down to the Cavemen (see section §1). If the literal sun is the offspring of the Good in the visible region, it is Justice *qua* offspring that binds the two suns together in the Allegory of the Cave: the one who has seen the intelligible light practices Justice amidst the shadows of the merely visible sun. It is on this basis that Justice proves to be "the offspring of the Good" of which Socrates is most willing to speak in Plato's *Republic*.

The second time that "the Idea of the Good" is found in Book VII, it is related to the fundamental dualism of Platonism: the distinction—divided by the

---

34. Following *Republic* and preceding Socrates' trial in the reconstructed Reading Order, *Cratylus* makes this point at *Cra*. 412c6-b5, climaxing with the identification of justice with the sun. The extended and emphasized discussion of the etymology of τὸ δίκαιον—see Sedley, *Plato's* Cratylus, 114-19—should be considered in the context of *Cra*. 428a3-5: the only passage in Plato that makes a direct connection between being δίκαιος and acting altruistically, thereby recalling Justice.

plateau that is Plato, or rather by Aristocles *qua* "plateau"—between Being and Becoming:

> "But still," I said, "for such purposes a slight modicum of geometry and calculation would suffice. What we have to consider is whether the greater and more advanced part of it tends to facilitate the apprehension of the idea of good [τὴν τοῦ ἀγαθοῦ ἰδέαν]. That tendency, we affirm, is to be found in all studies that force the soul to turn its vision round to the region where dwells the most blessed part of reality [τὸ εὐδαιμονέστατον τοῦ ὄντος], which it is imperative that it should behold." "You are right," he said. "Then if it compels the soul to contemplate essence [οὐσίαν], it is suitable; if genesis [γένεσιν], it is not." "So we affirm." (526d7-e9)

Within the realm of Being, the Idea of the Good holds not only the uppermost (517b4) but also the happiest place: happiness is orientation to the Good and is therefore a synonym for Justice. And on the basis of what Plato has already told us about the Idea of the Good, one might well ask: "How could anyone who has caught sight of (and therefore believes in) the highest good not own themselves to be down below it as a matter of principle?" Is Justice fundamentally different from the explicit recognition of Plato's dualistic ontology? (See section §32). The distinction between οὐσία and γένεσις—an abyss bridged only by Justice (or Divine Love)—is the central idea of Platonism: it is, in fact, Plato's Idea. In other words, while Plato's Idea (and also what we would call "the central core of Plato's thought") is what he called "the Idea of the Good," it is also the *condition for the possibility* of that Idea: Plato's "big idea" is the radical distinction—the *Kluft*, χωρισμὸς, or "plateau"—between Being and Becoming that makes the Idea of the Good highest, non-Caved, anti-immanent, otherworldly, and utterly transcendent. This distinction is the *sine qua non* of Platonism.[35]

We can embrace Platonic dualism or reject it, as Aristotle did. It matters little to show that Aristotle rejected it less than is traditionally thought: he rejected it to the best of his ability. What we cannot do is to claim that Plato did not sharply distinguish Being from Becoming. Hans-Georg Gadamer's *The Idea of the Good in Platonic-Aristotelian Philosophy* (even more than the Neoplatonism that preceded it) should stand as the perfect symbol of a radical misunderstanding of Plato's ontology (the more political Heideggerians simply ignore the Idea of the Good completely,[36] and therefore cannot be said to misunderstand it) than which no greater can be conceived or even imagined. This is hardly to say that Plato himself did not conceive of this radical misunderstanding: as the teacher of the Idea, he knew full well that his less than geometrical students (in the pure sense of "geometry" celebrated in the passage above) showed a marked

35. Erich Frank, "The Fundamental Opposition of Plato and Aristotle." *American Journal of Philology* 61 nos. 1 and 2 (1940), 34-53 and 166-185 at 34-35.

36. Cf. Catherine H. Zuckert, *Postmodern Platos: Nietzsche, Heidegger, Gadamer, Strauss, Derrida* (Chicago, IL: University of Chicago Press, 1996), 154-55.

proclivity to bind the Idea to the sensible world of γένεσις, i.e., to the only world they knew. Plato the Teacher's formula is: geometry on the way up and e.g. the *Philebus* on the way down. The *Philebus* figures prominently in Gadamer's book: indeed he makes the *Philebus* the central *locus* of Plato's teaching about the Good rather than the *Republic*. It is no different from what Joseph Cropsey does to the *Statesman*:[37] he attacks a visionary dialogue (in Cropsey's case the *Phaedo*) on the basis of a basanistic one. In contrast to a crude chronological developmentalism that argues that the *Philebus* represents a later and therefore higher stage of Plato's thought, even the radical isolationist hermeneutic, antithetical to the reading order hypothesis, is infinitely preferable: at least *it* allows us to (momentarily) take the truth-claims of the mighty *Republic* seriously. But there is a third way to read Plato. Once we recognize that the *Philebus* and the *Statesman* are basanistic dialogues, we can see that Hans-Georg Gadamer and Seth Benardete failed these tests by reading *Republic* in their dark light (cf. 585a3-4) rather than reading them in the light of the Idea of the Good.[38]

In short: we can embrace the Platonic *Kluft* or we can reject it. What we cannot legitimately do is read Plato as if he—like ourselves, perhaps—were an

---

37. Joseph Cropsey, *Plato's World: Man's Place in the Cosmos* (Chicago, IL: University of Chicago Press, 1995).

38. Although this is not the place to sort out all the implications, particularly for interpreting *Philebus*, the simple fact is that Gadamer was Heidegger's student, not Plato's; cf. Hans-Georg Gadamer, *Plato's Dialectical Ethics: Phenomenological Interpretations Relating to the* Philebus, translated by Robert M. Wallace (New Haven, CT: Yale University Press, 1991), 21n4, P. Christopher Smith at 86n4 of Hans-Georg Gadamer, *Dialogue and Dialectic: Eight Hermeneutical Studies of Plato*, translated by P. Christopher Smith (New Haven, CT: Yale University Press, 1980), and Andrew Fuyarchuk, *Gadamer's Path to Plato: A Response to Heidegger and a Rejoinder by Stanley Rosen* (Eugene, OR: Wipf and Stock, 2010). Although he appropriated the word "Being" and repeatedly sought to make it his own, Heidegger was no more Platonic than Nietzsche had been. For a thoughtful and thorough differentiation, see Francisco J. Gonzalez, *Plato and Heidegger: A Question of Dialogue* (University Park: Pennsylvania State University Press, 2009). I would argue that Heidegger's "Being" is Plato's Becoming with the sole exception—and this exception gives the later Heidegger not only the *opportunity* but also the *necessity* of being poetic, fateful, and obscure—that Heidegger's version treats Becoming (now masquerading as "Being") as if there were no alternative to it except an inauthentic forgetfulness that lacks the courage to look the abyss in the face, or (after the defeat of the Third Reich) the "forgetfulness of Being" at the root of "the Question concerning Technology." In any case, Heidegger's thought—not unlike Aristotle's, Hegel's or Nietzsche's thought in this fundamental respect—is radically anti-dualist. But at least Aristotle, Hegel, and Nietzsche build dualism into their Systems if only as the body-hating enemy, a mere Moment, or "separability in thought." Heidegger, on the other hand, must "jump over his own shadow" and some of us remember with crystal clarity where this "leap of faithlessness" landed *him*. See Martin Heidegger, *An Introduction to Metaphysics*, translated by Ralph Manheim (New Haven, CT: Yale University Press, 1959), 199.

anti-dualist. The uses to which the real anti-dualists—whether of the Continental or Anglo-American school hardly matters—put, e.g., the *Philebus*, is the proof that it is a basanistic dialogue. The fact that Plato wrote the *Philebus* does not, therefore, demonstrate that Plato was an anti-dualist or that a German-Platonic-Aristotelian synthesis is anything but neo-Neoplatonism. In short: Plato is not an anti-dualist because he knew that Aristotle was coming along with the legions that would follow him like so many other footnotes, or because he was determined to spot them among his students *in ovo* and flush them out from their coverts, or because, having once vouchsafed his readers the vision of *Republic* VII, he then repeatedly tested them in his "later dialogues" (as well as in Books VIII, IX, and X). These things merely prove that Plato is "Plato the Teacher."

> "And is not this true of the good likewise—that the man who is unable to define in his discourse and distinguish and abstract from all other things the idea of the good, and who cannot, as it were in battle, running the gauntlet of all tests, and striving to examine everything by essential reality and not by opinion, hold on his way through all this without tripping in his reasoning—the man who lacks this power, you will say, does not really know the good itself or any particular good; but if he apprehends any adumbration of it, his contact with it is by opinion, not by knowledge; and dreaming and dozing through his present life, before he awakens here he will arrive at the house of Hades and fall asleep for ever? " "Yes, by Zeus," said he, "all this I will stoutly affirm." (534b8-d2; Shorey modified)

This, then, is "the Battle Hymn of the *Republic*." And with Plato's own war cry ringing in the reader's ears, it is appropriate to jettison any other polemical tones. In section §29, this crucial passage will be considered in the context of reading order. For now, it is enough to hammer home the central point: Plato's philosophical loyalty is to the Idea of the Good and not to "the Theory of Ideas." *It's just that simple.*

To summarize, then: taken together, the ten uses of the word "Idea" that are found in Books V (1 instance), VI (6) and VII (3) serve well to indicate the *locus* of the visionary portion of the *Republic*. In fact, the central core of that visionary part is clearly indicated as Book VII: all three uses of the word "Idea" in Book VII (517b8, 526e2, and 534b9-c1) explicitly involve "the Idea of the Good." Following four uses of the word in Book II—three of them clustered around the gods or rather God—the first reference to "the Theory of Ideas" is sandwiched between a recollection of Beauty from the *Symposium* and first mention of "the Idea of the Good." All of these, then, I would consider to be proleptic: (1) the Book II singleton introduces the Hypothesis on which the Image of the Shorter Way depends without making clear what Plato means by "idea," (2) the Book II triad implicates the Ideas with the Divine and proleptically indicates that the relationship between gods and God is unclear, (3) after the first use in Book V (479a1) treats "beauty" as an Idea (in conformity with the *Symposium*), while the second (486d10), introduces the theory of (plural) ideas and is expressly linked to διάνοια. Then comes the opening moment of

Plato's visionary teaching (VI 505a2): the Idea of the Good is introduced and its absolute priority to any other things—including just things and beauty—is emphasized. In other words, a series of six passages leads up to a moment of vision and proleptically prepare for it.

Socrates then warns the reader to be on guard (507a4-5): this indicates the beginning of a basanistic passage: another triad. The three uses of "idea" ("ideas" at 507b9) between 507b5 and 507e5 are intended to test whether the reader can distinguish the Idea of the Good from a more general account of the Theory of Ideas which has the tendency—very marked by 507e5-508a2—to drag the ideas down into the realm of the visible and to make the visible sun the sole "offspring of the Good" (508b12-c2). The visionary element of the separated intelligible is then reasserted at 508e1-2 and carried through the triad of uses in Book VII, climaxing with the Battle Hymn of the *Republic*. Once the vision of Book VII is past, the remaining seven uses in Books VIII-X are all basanistic. I have now considered the ten uses connected with the visionary element as well as the four proleptic uses in Book II.

The seven remaining uses of ἰδέα are distributed as follows: Book VIII (once), IX (3), and X (3). It will be noted that the triads in IX and X constitute the fourth and fifth such triads among the twenty-one uses of the word: the first was the theological triad in Book II, the second was the basanistic "Theory of Ideas" triad in Book VI, and the third the "Idea of the Good" triad in Book VII. So striking is the repetition of the triadic formula that it seems to be the rule, rather than the exception. This impression is strengthened by viewing the two uses (one in V, the other in VI) along with the first mention of "the Idea of the Good" they precede as another triad. It would, indeed, be an anomalous triad because (1) the three, although continuous, are much more widely scattered than the other five, and (2) they are heterogeneous with respect to the proleptic, visionary, basanistic typology. There is, however, a certain pedagogical elegance to sandwiching the first "Theory of Ideas" passage between a passage that recalls the vision of the *Symposium* and another that points to the Idea of the Good. Moreover, if it is admitted that the three spanning Books V and VI are a sixth triad, then the three remaining singletons together form an even more widely scattered seventh.[39]

In any case, the use of ἰδέα in Book VIII complements its first proleptic use at II 369a4: there it was applied only to the Man, here it is applied only to the City: "Can you mention any other type of government [τινα ἄλλην ἔχεις ἰδέαν πολιτείας], I mean any other that constitutes a distinct species [ἐν εἴδει διαφανεῖ τινι κεῖται]?" (VIII 544c7-d1). In context, Socrates is simply asking

39. Arranged in the order of each triad's completion, however, the Book VII triad is central: (1) the Idea of the gods or God (Book II), (2) the introduction of the Idea of the Good (V 479a1 and VI 486d10, and VI 505a2), (3) the Theory of Ideas (Book VI, beginning at 507e5), (4) the Idea of the Good (Book VII), (5) the Structural Singletons (II 369a4, VI 508e1-2, and VIII 544c8), (6) the Beast-Lion-Man Image (Book IX), and (7) the Idea of Bed (Book X).

whether the four defective cities constitute an exhaustive list. But the combination of both ἰδέα and εἶδος suggests the passage's importance. In addition to testing the reader's commitment to the Idea of the Good (this is obviously the first time that the word has been used since Book VII), it has a proleptic purpose as well: it prepares for what I will call "the CITY." This is the CITY "ἐν λόγοις κειμένῃ" ("the one constituted in speeches") at IX 592a10 (see section §31). The whole purpose of the adjacent nuptial number passage (the number is first mentioned at VIII 546b5) is to explain how the (Shorter Way, i.e. Image) City degenerates; there is, of course, no such City. The most important—and missing—CITY (to distinguish it from the City of the Shorter Way where the Guardians are compelled to go back down) is the one on the north side of the plateau in which the philosopher enjoys, as it were, "Dual Citizenship." "'There is a pattern of it laid up in heaven for him who wishes to contemplate it and so beholding to constitute himself its citizen'" (IX 592b1-2). It is in this CITY that the philosopher *will* practice politics ('τά γε πολιτικὰ . . . πράττειν') when she goes Back Down into the Cave in the city of her birth. In other words, there is—in answer to the question that Socrates poses at VIII 544c8) no "other idea of a polity" (ἄλλη ἰδέα πολιτείας) in the *worldly* sense: the philosopher goes back down in response to eternal Justice regardless of native constitution (but see section §30) and in her own city.

But *qua* idea—or better, in relation to the Idea of the Good—the essence of polity (and political things) does in fact exist elsewhere: in Plato's *Republic* (ἐν λόγοις). His Πολιτεία is itself the missing ἰδέα πολιτείας because that CITY alone is defined in relationship to the Idea of the Good, the philosopher, and Justice. The potentially missing ἰδέα πολιτείας of VIII 544c8 is the CITY in which the philosopher willingly practices Justice. The fact that this is the only use of the word ἰδέα that occurs in a question, indicates its dual nature: if we answer the question "no, there is no other kind of city" (as Socrates expects us to do) it is purely basanistic: this is a fraudulent use of the word "idea." But if we treat it as the open question that it is, then it can only be proleptic: it points away from the City toward the philosopher who enjoys dual citizenship in both her native city—for example Cicero's Rome—and the CITY (see section §31). Despite its proleptic potential, however, the Book VIII passage obscures the meaning of ἰδέα that Socrates has been teaching throughout Book VII and must therefore be regarded as primarily basanistic, especially since it invites us to think of the City (as distinct from the CITY) as an ἰδέα rather than retaining ἰδέα as the un-hypothetical Idea of the Good that can only be reached by the dialectical method of the First Part of the Line rather than as the Hypothesis-based Image that the City really is. There is certainly something to be said for the view that, along with II 369a4 and VI 508e1-2, VIII 544c8 completes a triad of structural singletons in which both the Shorter and the Longer Way are made to pivot around the word "idea." Be that as it may, the remaining six uses of ἰδέα can only to be understood in relation to the Shorter Way. The fact that they follow Book VII proves the existence of Plato's basanistic pedagogy.

The three uses in Book IX involve the image of man, the lion, and the multi-headed beast, itself one of the most perfect poetical constructions in the *Republic*. For purposes of explication, a single continuous passage containing all three uses of the word will be punctuated by commentary:

> "Let us, then, reason with its proponent now that we have agreed on the essential nature of injustice and just conduct [τὸ δίκαια πράττειν]." (588b6-8)

Note that Justice is described perfectly here: τὸ δίκαια πράττειν ("to do the just things;" translation mine) is halfway between the "τά γε πολιτικὰ . . . πράττειν" ("to do *the* political things;" translation mine) of IX 592a5 and the final εὖ πράττωμεν ("let us both do and fare well;" translation mine) of X 621d2-3.

> "How?" he said. "By fashioning [πλάσαντες] in our discourse [λόγῳ] a symbolic image of the soul [εἰκόνα . . . τῆς ψυχῆς], that the maintainer of that proposition may see [εἰδῇ] precisely what it is that he was saying." (588b9-11)

In this sentence, Socrates is using the vocabulary of the Divided Line's Image-methodology—note the use of πλάττουσίν, εἰκόνες, and the two forms of the verb ἰδεῖν at VI 510e2-511a1—in order to describe the tripartite soul. In fact, given the City/soul isomorphism, this passage constitutes the most explicit textual link in the *Republic* between the Shorter Way and the Second Part of the Divided Line.

> "What sort of an image?" he said. "One of those natures that the ancient fables tell of," said I, "as that of the Chimaera or Scylla or Cerberus, and the numerous other examples that are told of many forms [ἰδέαι πολλαὶ] grown together in one [εἰς ἓν γενέσθαι]." "Yes, they do tell of them." (588c1-6)

The first use of ἰδέα in the plural will be picked up in the Bed of Book X: this will *become* "the Theory of Ideas." As already discussed in section §14, the true ἓν (i.e., the One) does not become (γενέσθαι) nor is it a "one out of many" (πολλαὶ). But even "the true one" is a mere Hypothesis in comparison with the Idea of the Good (see section §28). In other words, the use of the word "idea" in the beast-lion-man passage—here in its plural form—is at *two* removes from Platonic reality: it is neither the plurality-excluding Monad of mathematics nor the Idea of the Good. As the vocabulary indicates, Socrates is applying ἰδέα to the indefinite plurality that is Becoming.

> "Mould, then, a single shape [ἰδέαν] of a manifold and many-headed beast that has a ring of heads of tame and wild beasts and can change them and cause to spring forth from itself all such growths." "It is the task of a cunning artist [πλάστου]," he said, "but nevertheless, since speech is more plastic [εὐπλαστότερον] than wax and other such media, assume that it has been so fashioned [πεπλάσθω]." (588c7-d2)

The repetition of various forms of the verb πλάττειν remind us that we remain squarely in the Second Part of the Divided Line: these ἰδέαι are merely intelligible images of a visible thing. While the ἰδέαι here are at least partly *by nature* (as opposed to the Bed of Book X which is "by art") they are not the true ἰδέα that is found only in the First Part of the Line through dialectic.

> "Then fashion one other form [ἰδέαν] of a lion and one of a man and let the first be far the largest and the second second in size." "That is easier," he said, "and is done [πέπλασται]." "Join the three in one, then, so as in some sort to grow together." "They are so united," he said. "Then mould [περίπλασον] about them outside the likeness [εἰκόνα] of one, that of the man, so that to anyone who is unable to look within but who can see only the external sheath it appears to be one living creature, the man." "The sheath is made fast about [περιπέπλασται] him," he said. (588d2-e3)

In conclusion, the vivid Image of the tripartite soul (itself the explicit result of the Hypothesis of 'non-contradiction') is sub-ἰδέα and this point is hammered into our heads by the repetition of vocabulary from the Second Part of the Divided Line (VI 510e2-3).

Perhaps it is not entirely surprising that the last three uses of ἰδέα in Book X remind the reader of the dependence of the Shorter Way's methodology on Hypotheses explicitly. This is clear from the beginning of the Bed.

> "Shall we, then, start the inquiry at this point by our customary procedure [ἐκ τῆς εἰωθυίας μεθόδου]? We are in the habit, I take it, of positing [τίθεσθαι] a single idea or form [εἶδος γάρ πού τι ἓν] in the case of the various multiplicities to which we give the same name. Do you not understand?" "I do." (596a5-9)

It would appear that Socrates is finally calling the Shorter Way's methodology "a method" after all. But "the accustomed method" is even less methodical than such a usage would suggest. It is, to be sure, a method that posits (τίθεσθαι either implies or suggests ὑπο-τίθεσθαι) a kind of unity as the origin of its pursuits (of course μέθοδος is here used in sense [II]; see section §11). But there is a good reason that Socrates must employ a circumlocution (i.e. εἶδος γάρ πού τι ἓν) for the "unity" involved with the ἰδέαι he is now about to introduce: these "unities" are even farther removed from reality than the strictly Hypothetical Monads of arithmetic; i.e., they are once again two steps removed from Platonic reality. The mathematical Monad—I call it "mathematical" because it will be preserved as the logical basis of the other four Higher Education μαθήματα as well (see section §28)—is a Hypothetical intelligible Image of the singularized integrity of each and every individual visible object (see section §13). With the so-called "ideas of sofas and tables," by contrast, Socrates is about to introduce another class of Hypothetical intelligible Images, to be sure, but rather than create an image of (as it were) the *singularity* of an individual thing (i.e., the Monad), these embrace a *plurality* of differentiated things in a mathematically spurious "one out of many" (see sections §14 and §28). Every mathematician knows that no true unity contains plurality (VII 525d8-526a4). Not only does "the accustomed method" remain subject to the same methodological limitations as the Second Part of the Divided Line (i.e., a reliance on both Images and Hypotheses), but it is even less methodical. Its unities are a sham.[40]

> "In the present case, then, let us take [θῶμεν] any multiplicity you please; for example, there are many couches [κλῖναι] and tables." "How could it be otherwise? [πῶς δ' οὔ]" (596a10-b2; Shorey modified)

The words "any multiplicity you please," are comical as is Glaucon's response: Glaucon had desiderated these very "beds" at II 372d8 and now he has one more of them than he thought he needed. The "Third Man" argument waits in the wings and the ἰδέαι are about to *become* exactly what the ἰδέα eternally *is* not: an Hypothesized (note the use of θῶμεν) Image of visible things.

> "But these utensils imply, I suppose, only two ideas or forms [ἰδέαι], one of a couch and one of a table." "Yes." "And are we not also in the habit of saying that the craftsman [ὁ δημιουργὸς] who produces either of them fixes his eyes on the idea or form [πρὸς τὴν ἰδέαν βλέπων], and so makes in the one case the couches and in the other the tables that we use, and similarly of other things? For surely no craftsman [οὐδεὶς τῶν δημιουργῶν] makes [δημιουργεῖ] the idea itself [τήν γε ἰδέαν αὐτὴν]. How could he?" "By no means." (596b1-9)

This passage gives a clear indication of where Plato the Teacher will be testing us next: we have already entered the basanistic world of the *Timaeus* (see section §29). Whether as human or divine, the demiurge (ὁ δημιουργὸς) needs this kind of ἰδέαι. But do we? Not if we are philosophers. At 540a8, Socrates uses the verb ἀποβλέψαι for what the philosophical Guardians do to τὸ πᾶσι φῶς παρέχον ("the light-provider to all things"); i.e., to τὸ ἀγαθὸν αὐτό (VII 540a8-9). But unlike us—Plato's real philosophers—these Guardians must be *compelled* to behold the Idea of the Good.

---

40. This is why the Theory of Ideas (in this form) is habitually taken to be Plato's: it is a theory that can easily be refuted by anyone who has been taught to think by Plato the Teacher. Of course its critics rarely bring up the *Platonic* argument against the Theory of Ideas (nor am I now referring to the *Parmenides*) and are therefore forced to follow Aristotle and make up their own, if this is possible. On the other hand, Alexander Nehamas, "Self-Predication and Plato's Theory of Forms." *American Philosophical Quarterly* 16 no. 2 (April 1979), 93-103 is to be consulted by those who prefer the question as posed in the literature.

Section 19. An Intellectual History of the Return

Arguably the best-known contemporary treatment of what I am calling "Justice" is Richard Kraut's "Return to the Cave: *Republic* 519-521";[41] in any case, it is a decent place to begin a review of scholarly opinion on the subject. Kraut must demonstrate that Going Back Down into the Cave is consistent with justice (and here I must revert to the small case 'j') as elucidated on the Shorter Way. In other words, Kraut must show that the return to the Cave is just,[42] as of course it is. The problem that Kraut faces is showing that the action Plato uses to reveal Justice—and without which action, Justice doesn't exist in the *Republic*—is itself just. This attempt opens up a can of worms: even if Going Back Down were consistent with the tripartite soul of the Harmonious Man, it must necessarily become difficult to prove that the paradigmatically Just action is itself just. On the present account, Going Back Down into the Cave isn't just: Justice is the maxim of this action. Kraut—and he is hardly alone in this, as will shortly appear—must necessarily identify some other definition of justice, and then show why the action that reveals Platonic Justice is consistent with it. The problem is: if the maxim of the Just action were explicitly present elsewhere in the *Republic*, its literary expression as Going Back Down into the Cave would be superfluous. In other words: Kraut must show that Justice—which isn't the center of the dialogue's solar system only because the Idea of the Good is—is merely derivative from, consistent with, and is indeed orbiting some other center of philosophical or ethical gravity within the text. Which it isn't.

It is worthwhile to belabor this planetary metaphor. Naturally the Idea of the Good is the sun of Plato's *Republic*. And Justice—as opposed to the Shorter Way's justice—is fully dependent upon and indeed orbits around that sun. The sun itself, of course, cannot find full expression in *Republic*: its principal concern is *down* from the Good, i.e., its principal concern from beginning to end is Justice. Darkly intimated from the first word, playfully indicated immediately before the discovery of justice in the City, the nature of Justice is finally revealed in the reader's free choice to return to the Cave by heeding the command issued by the (non-existent) Founders to the (equally non-existent) Guardians as if it came directly from Plato himself to each and every reader, as indeed it does.

---

41. "Return to the Cave: *Republic* 519-521" in Gail Fine (ed.), *Plato 2: Ethics, Politics, Religion, and the Soul*, 235-254 (Oxford: Oxford University Press, 1999).

42. In point of fact this use of "just" is inappropriate since the small case has heretofore denoted (and will, apart from this footnote, hereafter denote) the Book IV account; here the word is being used in the everyday sense of the term. It is important to note that Justice bears more resemblance to "everyday justice" than justice. In other words, Kraut's task is easy in the sense that the return is unquestionably just. But his task is impossible because he must derive its justice from some standard external to it: in the universe of the *Republic*—as distinct from life itself (where every ethical person knows that "Going Back Down" is just)—there is no other such standard, least of all one that is at two metaphysical removes from the unitary Idea of the Good like the soul of the Harmonious Man.

Going Back Down into the Cave is Justice and—in the absence of the blindingly light "white hole" of the Good—this is the central teaching around which everything in the *Republic* as well as *everything in the Platonic dialogues as a whole* revolves. If the Good isn't, it is "the Return" that is the center of gravity in Plato's *Republic*. Since that Return *is* Justice, it will scarcely be possible to show that it is unjust although it may well appear to be inconsistent with the Shorter Way's justice. But to show that it is *just* will require making the center a mere satellite.[43] In other words, the Longer Way—by deriving Justice from the central Idea of the Good—is "Copernican" while all attempts to justify the Return by deriving it from the spiritual constitution of the Shorter Way's Harmonious Man will require the equivalent of Ptolemaic epicycles in order to redeem the error implicit in its earth-bound and strictly hypothetical starting point.

Kraut illustrates the most important of these epicycles: ignoring the unitary Idea of the Good, he must begin by pluralizing *the Forms* in order to build a bridge between the tripartite soul of the Harmonious Man and that Man's political activity (!) inside the Cave. Since the Shorter Way's justice is the harmony of either the three classes in the City, the three parts of the soul, or both, the only way that this kind of justice can replace the Good—a replacement required by trying to prove that the Return is just—is for the Good to lose its unity and become a plurality. Somehow or other the plurality of the California Consultant's harmonious soul must become the standard by virtue of which the Return is just. Since the Good cannot be ignored, it must be modified: it cannot be One, it must be—like the Consultant's soul—Many. So this is therefore what Kraut must inevitably make of it:

> This external harmony, in which each person does his own job and receives his due, is structurally similar to the inner justice by which each part of the soul does its own job. And both of these structures—civic and individual justice—reflect the harmonious relationships that exist externally among the forms.[44]

There is an inner necessity that compels Kraut to replace the Idea of the Good with "the harmonious relationships that exist externally among the forms" despite the fact that there has been little warrant for this replacement in the text. The main burden of Kraut's claim must therefore come from the basanistic dialogues that follow the *Republic*:

> For the forms are objects that constitute a pattern; each has relationships to the others, and therefore none can be understood in isolation. In Plato's later dialogues, particularly in the *Sophist*, *Statesman*, and *Philebus*, he explores these

43. Since the only thing in Plato's universe that Justice does orbit is the Good, and since the only Good-centered account of justice in the *Republic* is Justice, whatever justice in relationship to which Justice can be shown to be just must necessarily take the place of the Idea of the Good.

44. Kraut, "Return to the Cave," 246.

> relationships and develops the conceptual equipment needed to understand them.[45]

The absolute centrality of the Idea of the Good is here made conspicuous by its absence[46] and Kraut unwittingly foreshadows my own reading of the dialogues in question. But Kraut knows that he can't let it go at that: he must find textual support for his plurality of forms in *Republic*. Naturally he can only find it in a passage prior to the introduction of the Good at 505a2. And it happens that Plato has given him the rope with which he can hang himself: between the "making friends with Thrasymachus" passage at 498c9-d1 and the second Longer Way passage at 504b2 is to be found the following:

> "For surely, Adeimantus, the man whose mind [τὴν διάνοιαν] is truly fixed on eternal realities has no leisure to turn his eyes downward [κάτω βλέπειν] upon the petty affairs of men, and so engaging in strife with them to be filled with envy and hate, but he fixes his gaze upon the things of the eternal and unchanging order [τεταγμένα ἄττα καὶ κατὰ ταὐτὰ ἀεὶ ἔχοντα], and seeing that they neither wrong nor are wronged by one another, but all abide in harmony as reason bids, he will endeavor to imitate them, and, as far as may be, to fashion himself in their likeness and assimilate himself to them."[47]

As indicated by the explicit reference to διάνοια in the context of this eloquent the justification of stargazing True Steersman who disdains even to look, let alone *go* down, this speech to Adeimantus expresses the essence of the Shorter Way. As the post-*Republic* dialogues will repeatedly prove, friendship with Thrasymachus is linked with cosmology. And it is in this profoundly apolitical passage—especially in the "one out of many" that Timaeus and the Athenian Strangers will soon enough be finding in the heavens[48]—that Kraut finds the best available bridge between the contemplations of the tripartite soul and its just return to politics: "a harmonious soul is more akin to the forms than an unjust soul."[49] This kinship, through the elegant isomorphism, thus becomes political: "just patterns in human relationships are better imitations of the relationships between the forms than are unjust civic institutions."[50] In fact, Kraut's

45. Kraut, "Return to the Cave," 245. See also Richard Kraut (ed.), *The Cambridge Companion to Plato* (Cambridge, UK: Cambridge University Press, 1992) at 42n34.

46. Kraut, *Cambridge Companion to Plato*, 9 mentions a more accurate perspective.

47. 500b8-c7. Naturally I take this passage to exhibit the same relationship to Justice as the Ship: Justice is here being proleptically denied in relation to the stargazing True Steersman.

48. Zuckert, *Plato's Philosophers*, 419: "In contrast to Timaeus and the Athenian Stranger, Socrates never suggests that human beings can discover what is good for them by contemplating the intelligible movements of the heavens."

49. Kraut, "Return to the Cave," 246n17.

50. Kraut, "Return to the Cave," 246n17.

defense of the Return—his argument that it is just—depends primarily on this passage:

> These further points [i.e., the two just quoted in the text] are most fully expressed at 500c-d, where we are told that the philosopher becomes orderly by studying the order among the forms, and is able to mould human institutions so they reflect the divine order.[51]

The Return offers the just person the chance to imitate the forms externally as she has already imitated them—by constructing a harmonious soul in imitation of "the order among the forms"[52]—internally. "Imitating the forms" becomes the *Leitmotiv* of Kraut's article[53] and it is the institution of harmony among plurality—already constitutive of the Consultant's soul—that Kraut takes to be the ethical essence of the Return, and which therefore constitutes and proves the justice thereof.

The passage Kraut cites (VI 500b8-c7) admonishes us not to engage even with Thrasymachus, let alone Kraut, in a spirit "filled with envy and hate." His argument is certainly ingenious. But it is also vitiated by the passage on which it depends. It is not only that Socrates is talking to Adeimantus rather than Glaucon (see section §10) or that the passage justifies the philosopher's rejection of politics rather than participation in it (section §15), or even the fact that there's no actual mention of "forms" here: the real problem is far deeper and is related to Kraut's decision to ignore—and he is hardly unique in doing so—not only the great chasm dividing the Longer from the Shorter Way but the more important *Kluft* or χωρισμός that divides Being from Becoming:

> "Then the lover of wisdom associating with the divine order [θείῳ δὴ καὶ κοσμίῳ] will himself become orderly and divine [κόσμιός τε καὶ θεῖος] in the measure permitted to man. But calumny is plentiful everywhere [διαβολὴ δ' ἐν πᾶσι πολλή]."[54]

---

51. Kraut, "Return to the Cave," 246n17.

52. G. R. F. Ferrari, *City and Soul in Plato's* Republic (Chicago, IL: University of Chicago Press, 2005) at 105: "The model in the heavens that is Callipolis is not astronomical, but like the heavenly bodies is to be imagined as a picture or diagram drawn by a master draughtsman—not Daedalus, however, but Plato." For plural forms in Ferrari, cf. 101-02: "But here is the crucial point: it is not to their own souls that the rulers of Callipolis look when they regulate their city. They look to the forms directly, and regulate the city after that pattern, just as they look to the pattern to regulate their own souls (484c, 500d, 501b)."

53. Starting at Kraut, "Return to the Cave," 247 (four instances), and following through 258 (one instance), 250 (two), and 251 (one). See also Kraut, *Cambridge Companion to Plato*, 328.

54. 500d1-3; the remarkable coda to this uplifting passage warns against the very διαβολή of the divine that Socrates has just cautiously expressed; his "everywhere" includes this passage itself.

This basanistic passage is the battleground of Platonism. Socrates does not lie—a Platonist will rightly emphasize how limited "the measure permitted to man" really is in relation to the Good—but he leaves the door open to the mystic's attempt to become one with God. Born from our *Drang nach Einheit* (see section §5), this ongoing temptation lures the non-Platonist to bridge the unbridgeable and it is in order to simultaneously whet and expose this temptation that Socrates refers here not to the Idea of the Good or even "the forms" but rather to the planets of the visible cosmos.[55] Adam's commentary confirms this: although he is willing to overlook the double meaning of κοσμίῳ at 500d1,[56] the echo of Euripides[57] at 500b8-c5 leaves no doubt that this passage is perfectly consistent with the basanistic *Epinomis*: the "philosopher" Socrates describes here derives a divine order from the visible heavens.[58] The harmony between the tripartite

55. Consider Shorey, *Plato's Republic*, 2.68n"b" (emphasis mine): "This passage is often supposed to refer to the ideas, and ἐκεῖ in 500 D shows that Plato is in fact there thinking of them, though in *Rep.* 529 A-B ff. *he protests against this identification.* And strictly speaking κατὰ ταὐτὰ ἀεὶ ἔχοντα in C would on Platonic principles be true only of the ideas. Nevertheless poets and imitators have rightly felt that the dominating thought of the passage is the effect on the philosopher's mind of the contemplation of the heavens. This confusion or assimilation is, of course, still more natural to Aristotle, who thought the stars unchanging." Platonism means never having to say you're confused by this kind of assimilation.

56. Adam, *Republic of Plato*, 2.40: "It has been thought that there is a play on κόσμος in the sense of the Universe or Heavens. But the philosopher's gaze outsoars the Heavens, and is fixed on the ὑπερουράνιος τόπος, where the Ideas dwell (*Phaedr.* 247 C)." Because he is unaware of the basanistic element in Platonic pedagogy, Adam's amiable loyalty to Platonism causes him to explain away this deliberate deviation from it.

57. Adam, *Republic of Plato*, cites Euripides Fr. 902 in Greek at 2.40 (translation mine): "'Blessed is he who makes the learning of his study not the calamity of citizens nor striving to understand their unjust deeds but rather contemplating the ageless cosmos of deathless nature—to what end, wherefore, and how it comes together—and never to these kinds of vicious acts his practiced care directs.' Euripides' lines are conceived in the spirit of Plato [it would be more accurate to say that Plato alludes to Euripides while describing philosophy as the physicists and Euripides understand it; cf. 486a4-10] and exactly illustrate his meaning, especially if, as is usually supposed, they refer to the philosopher Anaxagoras." Cicero carefully and accurately distinguishes Socrates and Anaxagoras in his *Tusculan Disputations*: see Altman, "Womanly Humanism," section §3.

58. Kraut, *Cambridge Companion to Plato*, 322-23 suggests that he is not entirely unaware of this. Cf. Annas, *Platonic Ethics*, 108: "If one accepts the idea that the Form of the Good, which is mysteriously 'beyond being,' is not itself a Form, or a mega-Form, but is better conceived of as the ordered structure of the realm of Forms, then the *Republic* contains a parallel to the idea of the *Gorgias* and *Philebus* that we should by the exercise of rational thought in some way emulate the larger-scale rationality in the cosmos which philosophical thinking reveals. This is, I think, the best way to understand the role of the Form of the Good—as rational structure on a cosmic scale which our own reason is to be moved to emulate." Annas's Plato is perhaps best understood as a Stoic.

soul and this kind of cosmos—not one based on the Idea of the Good[59]—initiates us into the tempting half-truths of *Timaeus*. In the conversation with Adeimantus in *Republic* VI, Plato is already indicating the connection between the Shorter Way and the basanistic dialogues that will follow, dialogues that will elide both Justice and the condition of its possibility: the transcendent Idea of the Good. In Book VII, the words κάτω βλέπειν ("to look downward") are the basis for Socrates' rejection of astronomy (529a7); on the Shorter Way, these same words reject concern with the affairs of men in accordance with Euripides' ode to cosmology (500c1). Given this radical opposition—as radical as the Platonic distinction between Being and Becoming—it is no wonder that the passage Kraut needs is not adequate for his purpose. But without recognizing the Shorter Way for what it is, the Return can only be shown to be just if justice is a harmonious cosmos of forms, i.e., if it is not recognized as Justice and oriented exclusively to the Idea of the Good.

With this discussion of Kraut's approach as a kind of introduction, it is now time to provide a more systematic and comprehensive account of the broader scope of the questions involved as they have emerged in the relevant scholarly literature. In an effort to situate my reading in this broader context, the remainder of this section will therefore be devoted to various controversies intimately connected with the Return. Attention will be confined to the English-speaking world during the last eighty years,[60] a period of time roughly commensurate with Plato's own life.

Although he had already published his most important claim about Plato's *Republic* in 1912,[61] H. A. Prichard's 1928 lecture "Duty and Interest" may usefully be taken to mark the beginning of this intellectual history.

> There is no escaping the conclusion that when Plato sets himself to consider not what *should*, but which *actually does* as a matter of fact, lead a man to act,

59. Harold Cherniss, "The Philosophical Economy of the Theory of Ideas." *American Journal of Philology* 57 no. 4 (1936), 445-56 illuminates the correct relationship between the Theory of Forms and Astronomy.

60. Justifying this parochialism is G. R. F. Ferrari (ed.), *The Cambridge Companion to Plato's* Republic (Cambridge UK: Cambridge University Press, 2007), 498 (emphasis mine): "The question whether the philosopher sacrifices personal happiness by returning to the cave is a topic also addressed by many of the comprehensive treatments of the *Republic* in section III.A [sc. of Ferrari's valuable Bibliography], *particularly those in English.*"

61. H. A. Prichard, "Does Moral Philosophy Rest on a Mistake?" *Mind* (n.s.) 21 no. 81 (January 1912), 21-37 at 22-23: "To show that Plato really justifies morality by its profitableness, it is only necessary to point out (1) that the very formulation of the thesis to be met, *viz.*, that justice is ἀλλότριον ἀγαθόν [another's good], implies that any refutation must consist in showing that justice is οἴκειον ἀγαθόν, *i.e.* really, as the context shows, one's own advantage, and (2) that the term λυσιτελεῖν [to be profitable to] supplies the keynote not only to the problem but to its solution."

> when he is acting deliberately and not merely in consequence of an impulse, he answers 'The desire for some good to himself and that only.'[62]

A Kant scholar,[63] Prichard aimed at a more than Kantian standard of ethical purity that derived moral obligation from a direct awareness[64] of the intrinsic truth of the moral principle that obliges us to perform some particular action.[65] It is ironic that Prichard's own position, often called "intuitionism,"[66] is anticipated by the Socratic καταβατέον[67] but Prichard ignores the importance of verbal

---

62. H. A. Prichard, "Duty and Interest" (1928), reprinted in H. A. Prichard, *Moral Writings*, 21-49. Edited by Jim MacAdam (Oxford: Clarendon Press, 2002), 33.

63. H. A. Prichard, *Kant's Theory of Knowledge* (Oxford: Clarendon Press, 1909); for criticism and praise for Kant, see Prichard, "Duty and Interest," 28-29 and 48-49.

64. Prichard, "Duty and Interest," 4: "We should not ask the reason for the principle, nor, if we did, could we find one. And we should be—inclined to say—truly I think—that anyone must either recognize the truth of the principle directly, i.e., as self-evident, or fail to see it altogether."

65. Prichard, "Duty and Interest," 4: "Obligations are always obligations to do particular things." With good reason Prichard's editor Jim McAdam calls the previously unpublished manuscript "What is the Basis of Moral Obligation" (Prichard, *Moral Writings*, 1-6) "among the most interesting and helpful of Prichard's essays." Prichard's proclivity in his published work to refute the views of others rather than explicate his own—regretted by W. G. de Burgh, "Review of 'Duty and Interest. An Inaugural Lecture delivered before the University of Oxford, on October 29, 1928. By H. A. Prichard.'" *Journal of Philosophical Studies* 4 no. 14 (April 1929), 259-261 at 260—is probably attributable to the influence of his teacher John Cook Wilson (see section §28). See Prichard, *Moral Writings*, xv and 26-27; also H. A. Prichard, "John Cook Wilson." *Mind* (n.s.) 28 no. 111 (July 1919), 297-318 at 318.

66. Jonathan Dancy, "Harold Arthur Prichard." *Stanford Encyclopedia of Philosophy* (January 30, 2009) at plato.stanford.edu/entries/prichard/ (accessed August 5, 2011); see Prichard, *Kant's Theory of Knowledge*, 24: "An 'ought,' if it is to be derived at all, can only be derived from another 'ought'." Although far more applicable to Justice than justice, Norman O. Dahl, "Plato's Defense of Justice" in Gail Fine (ed.), *Plato 2:Ethics, Politics, Religion, and the Soul*, 207-234 (Oxford: Oxford University Press, 1999), 229-34 notes the connection between Plato's justification for just actions from "intuitionism." Cf. John Mackie, *Ethics: Inventing Right and Wrong* (New York: Penguin, 1977), 40: "The Form of the Good is such that knowledge of it provides the knower with both a direction and an overriding motive; something's being good both tells the person who knows this to pursue it and makes him pursue it." Cf. Dahl, "Plato's Defense of Justice," 230n38; Prichard is discussed Hare, *Language of Morals*, 30 and 160-61.

67. Cf. the following synopsis of Prichard's own position in "Duty and Interest" in de Burgh's "Review," 259: "The moral rightness of an action—and it is actions only that are right—is intrinsic to the action and entirely independent of its conduciveness to our own or anyone else's happiness or good. The idea of duty cannot be resolved into terms of anything but itself; no rational, *i.e.* inferential explanation of it is possible." This beautiful analysis is purely Platonic: "like a flame kindled from a leaping spark," the "crisis of the *Republic*" clearly implicates Prichard's intuitionism, i.e., the Kant scholar failed to grasp that Plato was, as it were, a Kantian.

adjectives in Plato[68] and also passes over the moral implications of the Idea of the Good.[69] Nor does he ever discuss the philosopher's Return to the Cave.[70]

This omission was rectified by J. D. Mabbott's 1937 response ("Is Plato's *Republic* Utilitarian?") to M. B. Foster's "A Mistake of Plato's in the *Republic*" (1937).[71] Replying to both Foster and Prichard,[72] Mabbott cites the Return in order to show that "the ultimate reason for a just act does not lie in its consequences":

> Why do the philosophers leave their thinking and descend into the cave? Because some one must rule the city. But why should they do it and no one else? Because only so will the city be well ruled. But why should such considerations

---

68. Prichard, *Moral Writings*, 172: "There is no obvious word in Plato for 'ought' in the moral sense, duty or obligation." Consider also Prichard, *Kant's Theory of Knowledge*, 24: "The word 'ought' refers to actions and to actions alone."

69. Recognized early by C. R. Morris, "Plato's Theory of the Good Man's Motive." *Proceedings of the Aristotelian Society* (n.s.) 34 (1933-1934), 129-142 at 138; cf. Prichard, *Moral Writings*, 33: "It might be objected that these statements [sc. in Book VI] do not bear out that view that is attributed to Plato [sc. by Prichard in "Duty and Interest"], since Plato certainly did not mean by an ἀγαθόν a source of satisfaction or happiness to oneself. But to this the answer is that whenever Plato uses the term ἀγαθά (goods) elsewhere in the *Republic* and in the other dialogues, such as the *Philebus*, the context always shows that he means by a good a good to oneself, and, this being so, he must really be meaning by an ἀγαθόν, a source of satisfaction, or perhaps, more generally, a source of happiness." The Idea of the Good as "advantage" has recently been pressed by Terry Penner, "The Good, Advantage, Happiness and the Form of the Good: How Continuous with Socratic Ethics are Platonic Ethics" in Douglas Cairns, Fritz-Gregor Herrmann, and Terry Penner (eds.). *Pursuing the Good; Ethics and Metaphysics in Plato's* Republic, 93-123 (Edinburgh: University of Edinburgh Press, 2007).

70. Neither does Morris, "Plato's Theory of the Good Man's Motive," although a far more Kantian Plato (139) emerges from his critique of Prichard's "Duty and Obligation" (129n); he derives moral obligation directly from the Good at 142: "The philosopher is moved by the knowledge of the Idea of the Good, not by the desire for his own good." Plato's καταβατέον would have justified the remark at 139: "Yet for all this, the truth is, I think, that Plato came nearer to the Kantian view—that is, the view that reason in its practical employment can command, and that good action is action done in obedience to such a command." This, of course, is Prichard's own position, or very close to it; he simply failed to see that it was Plato's.

71. M. B. Foster, "A Mistake of Plato's in the *Republic*." *Mind* (n.s.) 46 no. 183 (July 1937), 386-393 at 386-7: "Socrates' defense of justice, which culminates in the ninth book, consists in the demonstration that happiness is the natural consequence of justice; he nowhere argues that justice would be good if it were not attended by this consequence." According to Foster, Plato's mistake is for Socrates to have claimed that justice was "that which we love both for its own sake and for the sake of its consequences" (386); he does only the latter.

72. J. D. Mabbott, "Is Plato's *Republic* Utilitarian?" *Mind* (n.s.) 46 no. 184 (October 1937), 468-474 at 469n1 and 469n3.

> weigh with them when they are so happy in the outer world? Because they are just men. δίκαια δικαίοις ἐπιτάξομεν.[73]

Foster's noteworthy response to this compelling argument is found in his "Rejoinder to Mr. Mabbott" (1938):

> In the whole course of his article he cites only one passage which supports it [sc. that justice "would still be worthwhile even if it did not make its possessor happy"]; that is the passage of the *Republic* in which the duty is imposed upon the philosophers of "returning to the cave" on the ground that justice demands it, in spite of the fact that this will entail a diminution of their happiness. I admit this single passage, but as I have already devoted an article [n. 2] to the attempt to show that its implications are inconsistent with all the rest of the moral philosophy of the *Republic*, I may perhaps be excused from dealing further with it now.[74]

In the 1936 article cited in note 2 ("Some Implications of a Passage in Plato's *Republic*"), Foster shows that the Return is "an exception to Professor Prichard's dictum (*Duty and Interest*, p. 10 [cf.] that Plato implies 'that it is impossible for any action to be really just, i.e., a duty, unless it is to the advantage of the agent.'"[75] By calling for "the self-sacrifice of the guardians,"[76] Plato may well be thought to have transcended the limits of Platonism[77] while anticipating

73. Mabbott, "Is Plato's *Republic* Utilitarian?" 474; regrettably, this passage was not included in the well-known reprinted version found in Gregory Vlastos (ed.) *Plato*, volume 2 (New York: Anchor Books, 1971), 57-65. For the importance of these words, see section §16.

74. M. B. Foster "A Mistake of Plato's in the *Republic*: A Rejoinder to Mr. Mabbott." *Mind* (n.s.) 47 (April 1938), 226-232 at 230. 230n2 cites M. B. Foster, "Some Implications of a Passage in the *Republic*." *Philosophy* 11 no. 43 (July 1936), 301-308.

75. Foster, "Some Implications," 302n2; the note continues: "Granted his [sc. Prichard's] assumption [sc. that δίκαιος when applied to actions means 'morally obligatory'; cf. Prichard, *Moral Writings*, 26], I think his conclusion [sc. that 'such actions are necessarily conducive to the agent's good'] would follow, provided only that he would except the passage now under consideration; but I would reject his assumption, and prefer to express the facts by saying that δίκαιος has not the meaning of 'morally obligatory' in any passage of the *Republic* except this." Cf. Strauss, *Persecution and the Art of Writing*, 30: "The real opinion of an author is not necessarily identical with that which he expresses in the largest number of passages." For the contrast between Straussian and Platonic exotericism, see my "Altruism and the Art of Writing."

76. Foster, "Some Implications," 303; Foster recognizes the role of both duty (304) and choice (305).

77. Foster, "Some Implications," 301: "It has often been recognized that the injunction to the philosophers to return to the cave is the point above all others in which Plato transcends the limits of Platonism." In fact, this injunction—and the dualistic ontology on which it entirely depends—*is* Platonism.

Christianity,[78] Kant,[79] and "contradicting the fundamental principle of classical Greek political philosophy."[80] It is only by insisting on Plato's inconsistency[81] and elitism[82] that Foster can vindicate "the historical importance of Christianity"[83] and, without invalidating the conclusions Mabbott drew from the Return, he provides considerable evidence for Nietzsche's famous claim that Christianity is Platonism for the masses.

Albeit in misleading forms, Kant, Prichard, and Nietzsche all reappear in *Merit and Responsibility* by A. W. H. Adkins (1960), the next significant landmark in the intellectual history of Anglophone debate on the Return. Posing as a Kantian,[84] Adkins extends (without mentioning) Prichard's critique of Plato

---

78. Foster, "Some Implications," 304: "The point to which I wish to draw attention is the following: what this doctrine of Plato presupposes, Christianity revealed."

79. Foster, "Some Implications," 304: "Thus of the Kantian ethics, for example, it would not be untrue to say that it assigns to all acts of all men the character which Plato assigns (if only by implication) to a single act of a single class." This is why Kant is best understood as a secret Platonist.

80. Foster, "Some Implications," 305; i.e., "that man is by nature a member of the state." By freely choosing the worse, i.e., the political life (305), the philosopher accepts a duty higher than the city's law (304): "The act by which a man subjects himself to the Nomos of a city cannot be prescribed by that Nomos. If, therefore, it is nevertheless a duty, it is a duty prescribed by a law prior to, and independent of the state." This correctly identifies Platonic dualism as the philosophical origin of the separation of Church and State.

81. Foster, "Some Implications," 303 (emphasis mine): "If 'his own work' is defined by reference to the agent's soul, and means the work in which his nature finds the fullest realization of which it is capable, the proposition that justice conduces to his highest good is analytic, because the full realization of his nature is the highest good. But if 'his work' is defined by reference to his place in the city, and means the work which the well-being of the whole society requires from him, then the proposition in question is synthetic. I do not myself believe that either interpretation can claim to exhaust Plato's meaning, because I think both meanings are present *in confusion* together in the *Republic*." An awareness of Plato's basanistic pedagogy removes this confusion.

82. Foster, "Some Implications," 305: "The 'better life than the political,' the voluntary membership of the state, the subjection to a moral obligation—the farthest to which Plato's thought reaches, or can be made to stretch, is (so it appears) to the attribution of these things to the guardian class."

83. Foster, "Some Implications," 308; cf. 307: "It is mere historical anachronism to suppose that Plato, lacking the revelation of the doctrine, nevertheless drew the full consequences of it." The article's last sentence is (308): "It is not lightly to be assumed of any pre-Christian philosopher, however great, that he was in secure possession of an enlightenment which became after Christianity the common birthright of educated men." This apparently "Christian" argument will be revisited in section §25.

84. The pose, always vitiated by his ironic use of "we"—Arthur W. H. Adkins, *Merit and Responsibility* (Oxford: Oxford University Press, 1960), 2-3—was formally repudiated at Arthur W. H. Adkins, "Gagarin and the 'Morality' of Homer." *Classical Philology* 82 no. 4 (April 1987), 311-322 at 313n9: "I can see no sense in which *Merit and Responsibility* is a Kantian study of Greek values." But the claim to moderation in

while casting the central insight of Nietzsche's *Genealogy of Morals* (1887) in "acceptable scholarly form."[85] The notion that ethics involves "duty and responsibility" is merely a modern prejudice:[86] given the limitations of Greek ethics,[87] Platonic justice can and could only be advantageous for the one who practices it.[88] Hence his account of the Return:

> The philosophers would be more *eudaimon* if they remained aloof from politics: accordingly Plato can offer no real reason why they should go back. Admittedly the city would be better governed, and hence more *eudaimon*, if they went back; but Plato cannot explain why, if one's own *eudaimonia* is the end of life, one should prefer the city's—or anyone else's—*eudaimonia* to one's own.[89]

---

the same note is hardly less misleading. More revealing is a comparison between Adkins, "Gagarin," 311n1 and his description of Protagoras at Arthur W. H. Adkins, "ἀρέτη, τέχνη, and Sophists: *Protagoras* 316b-328d." *Journal of Hellenic Studies* 93 (1973), 3-12 at 12.

85. Mihai Spariosu, *The Wreath of Wild Olive: Play, Liminality, and the Study of Literature* (Albany: State University of New York Press, 1997), 303n3: "Many of his [sc. Nietzsche's] insights about the agonistic nature of archaic values, for example in ancient Greece, have been cast into acceptable scholarly form by such well-respected classicists as E. R. Dodds, Arthur W. Adkins, Eric Havelock, and Walter Burkert." Despite the important Appendix in Dodds, *Plato,* Gorgias, there is, surprisingly, only a single reference to Nietzsche (68) in E. R. Dodds, *The Greeks and the Irrational* (Berkeley: University of California Press, 1951). Arthur W. H. Adkins, *From the Many to the One: A Study of Personality and Views of Human Nature in the Context of Ancient Greek Society, Values and Beliefs* (Ithaca, NY: Cornell University Press, 1970) is dedicated to Dodds; see also Adkins, *Merit and Responsibility*, 279n2.

86. Adkins, *Merit and Responsibility*, 2: "For any man brought up in a western democratic society the related concepts of duty and responsibility are the central concepts of ethics; and we are inclined to take it as an unquestionable truth, though there is abundant evidence to the contrary, that the same must be true of all societies. In this respect, at least, we are all Kantians now." Adkins was not the first University of Chicago professor to employ such tactics as these.

87. Adkins, *Merit and Responsibility*, 2-3: "That there should exist a society so different from our own as to render it impossible to translate 'duty' in the Kantian sense into its ethical terminology at all—impossible, that is to say, to translate 'duty' by a word not only of equivalent connotation but also equivalent status and emotive power—is, despite the evidence, a very difficult idea to accept. Even if we do accept it, we are only too inclined to interpret it as an indication of the moral deficiency of those who are so fortunate as not to be Kantians; and we are most unlikely to see the full implications of the system of which this 'deficiency' is a symptom." Naturally this last "we" does not include either Adkins or Nietzsche. Cf. Strauss, *City and Man*, 128n49 and Altman, *German Stranger*, 469-72.

88. Although "the moral philosophy of Plato and Aristotle" is his subject from the start (Adkins, *Merit and Responsibility*, 1), a more specific focus is finally disclosed at 260: "Plato's solution, or solutions, is of the utmost importance to the question of moral responsibility."

89. Adkins, *Merit and Responsibility*, 291.

In no way can the Return be disinterested or benevolent—the success of *Merit and Responsibility* indeed hinges on this—and Adkins claims that it is inconsistent[90] and even dangerous[91] to imagine it as such. Repeatedly dispensing good advice to Thrasymachus,[92] Adkins is misleading on the Idea of the Good.[93]

Nor does the Idea of the Good have any significant role to play in Leo Strauss's *The City and Man* (1964).[94] No less influenced by Nietzsche than Adkins,[95] Strauss also shares a willingness to distinguish our sensibilities (*qua* Moderns) from those of the Greeks. No less sympathetic to Thrasymachus,[96] Strauss advances beyond Adkins (and, more importantly, Nietzsche) by posing as a defender, not a critic, of Plato. Most importantly, because Strauss regards the City as a deliberately contrived impossibility, his rejection of the Return applies not only to the Guardians but also to every philosopher; indeed Strauss deduces the impossibility of the City from *any* philosopher's unwillingness to Go Back Down.[97] The result is a self-regard exempt from the chronological limits suggested by Adkins:

---

90. Adkins, *Merit and Responsibility*, 290: "They [sc. the philosophers] will treat the time which they spend in governing the city not as something *kalon* but as something 'necessary'. This, by the principles with which Plato set out, is scandalous."

91. Adkins, *Merit and Responsibility*, 292-93: "It is, however . . . one must abide by the conclusion."

92. Adkins, *Merit and Responsibility*, 287-92 and 274-81.

93. Adkins, *Merit and Responsibility*, 283 and 291: "To philosophize is an absolute good." This point is important because if Adkins is right, no philosopher would make the Return. Cf. Bloom, *Republic of Plato*, 402: "Philosophy, which was introduced as a means to actualize the city's good and is being used to discover *the* good, turns out to be the end, the human good." This ignores or repudiates Platonic "Copernicanism."

94. Strauss, *City and Man*, 119-20: "The doctrine of ideas which Socrates expounds to his interlocutors is very hard to understand. . . . However this may be, Glaucon and Adeimantus accept the doctrine with relative ease."

95. Strauss to Karl Löwith, Cambridge (U.K.), June 23, 1935 in Strauss, *Gesammelte Schriften* 3 648 (translation mine): "I can only say that Nietzsche so dominated and bewitched me between my 22nd and 30th years, that I literally believed everything that I understood of him." See Altman, *German Stranger*, 154-55, 163, and 425-444.

96. Strauss, *City and Man*, 73-74.

97. Strauss, *City and Man*, 124: "Strange as it may sound, in this part of the conversation it appears easier to persuade the multitude to accept the rule of the philosophers than to persuade the philosophers to rule the multitude: the philosophers cannot be persuaded, they can only be compelled to rule the cities (499b-c, 500d4-5, 520a-d, 521b7, 539e2-3). Only the non-philosophers could compel the philosophers to take care of the city. But given the prejudice against the philosophers, this compulsion will not be forthcoming if the philosophers do not in the first place persuade the non-philosophers to compel the philosophers to rule over them, and this persuasion will not be forthcoming, given the philosophers' unwillingness to rule. We arrive at the conclusion that the just city is not possible because of the philosophers' unwillingness to rule." The Return is specifically denied at Leo Strauss, "On a New Interpretation of Plato's Political Philosophy." *Social Research* 13 no. 3 (September 1946), 326-367 at 361, in a review of John Wild, *Plato's Theory of Man* (Cambridge, MA: Harvard University Press, 1946).

> In other words, the philosopher is the only individual who is just in the sense in which the city can be just: he is self-sufficient, truly free, or his life is as little devoted to the service of other individuals as the life of the city is devoted to the service of other cities.[98]

Naturally it is always difficult to determine when the author of "Persecution and the Art of Writing" is himself "writing between the lines";[99] it is for this reason that Strauss's letters to his best friend Jacob Klein are so important.

> The *Republic* is *beginning* to become clear to me. My conjecture from the previous year, that its actual theme is the question of the relationship between the political and theoretical life, and that it is dedicated to a radical critique and condemnation of the political life, has proved completely right. It has therefore defined itself with utmost precision: the *Republic* is indeed an ironic justification [*Rechtfertigung*] of injustice [ἀδικία], for Philosophy *is* injustice—that comes out with wondrous clarity in the dialogue with Thrasymachus.[100]

Revealing his awareness that the radical selfishness of his "philosopher" is actually unjust, Strauss falls victim to an involuntary self-contradiction while explicating his version of Plato: even in two different languages, injustice cannot be justified.[101] But the radical separation of philosophy from "the political life" would bear important fruit: although Allan Bloom would generally follow his teacher in the "Interpretive Essay" attached to his translation of the *Republic*,[102] he made an important discovery in support of Strauss's separation:

---

98. Strauss, *City and Man*, 127; cf. Strauss, *Classical Political Rationalism*, 161 (from an 1958 lecture): "Socrates speaks less of doing one's job well than simply of doing one's job, which has a common meaning of minding one's own business, not to be a busybody, or to lead the retired life. To lead the just life means to lead the retired life, the retired life *par excellence*, the life of the philosopher. This is the manifest secret of the *Republic*. The justice of the individual is said to be written in small letters, but the justice of the city in large letters. Justice is said to consist in minding one's business, that is to say, in not serving others. Obviously the best city does not serve other cities. It is self-sufficient." Cf. Thrasymachus at 351b4-5.

99. Strauss, *Persecution and the Art of Writing*, 36: "Exoteric literature presupposes that there are basic truths which would not be pronounced in public by any decent man, because they would do harm to many people, who having been hurt, would naturally be inclined to hurt in turn him who pronounces the unpleasant truths."

100. See Strauss to Jacob Klein, New York City, February 16, 1939 at *Gesammelte Schriften* 3, 567-68. It would be more accurate to say that on the Shorter Way, injustice—i.e., the self-concern of the Harmonious Man—*appears* to be justified.

101. Cf. Bloom, *Republic of Plato*, 411: "The *Republic* finally teaches that justice as total dedication to the city cannot be simply good for the philosopher, and hence it is somewhat questionable for other men as well."

102. Bloom, *Republic of Plato*, 407: "The people must be persuaded to accept the philosophers; but the philosophers must be compelled to persuade the people to compel them to rule. And who would do that?"

> Glaucon objects to the injustice of forcing the philosophers to return to the cave. This is injustice in the fullest sense of the word: it would be contrary to their good to return. Or to put it into the formula for justice: the city would force one man to do two jobs, to be both philosopher and king.[103]

The inadequacy of justice as discovered on the Shorter Way—clearly articulated in Bloom's brilliant observation—was given its most fertile formulation by David Sachs in his "A Fallacy in Plato's *Republic*" (1963). Ignoring the Justice implicit in and motivating the Return (which he never mentions) Sachs drives a wedge between two other varieties of justice: the Platonic justice of the Harmonious Man and what he famously calls "the vulgar conception of justice."[104] The former is a minimal concept—it lacks any other-regarding[105] let alone self-sacrificing element—but Sachs shows that even a baseline unwillingness to commit unjust acts cannot be deduced from Plato's strictly internal definition of justice in Book IV.[106] Following Prichard,[107] Foster,[108] and Adkins,[109] Sachs

---

103. Bloom, *Republic of Plato*, 407; see section §22.

104. Sachs, "A Fallacy," 142: "I will call the first the vulgar conception of justice, the second the Platonic conception." The Harmonious Man is described at 152. For the enduring influence of Sachs, see Dominic Scott, "The *Republic*" in Gail Fine (ed.). *Oxford Handbook to Plato*, 360-382 (Oxford: Oxford University Press, 2008), 366.

105. First noted at Raphael Demos, "A Fallacy in Plato's Republic?" *Philosophical Review* 73 no. 3 (July 1964), 395-398 at 396; see G. K. Singpurwalla, "Plato's Defense of Justice in the *Republic*" in Gerasimos Santas (ed.), *The Blackwell Guide to Plato's* Republic, 263-282 (Malden, MA: Blackwell, 2006) at 264: "The problem for Plato's defense of justice, however, is that his account of justice appears to have nothing to do with justice in the ordinary sense of the term, which at the least implies acting with some regard for the good of others. . . . Plato cannot assuage our worries about justice by giving an account of it that ignores this essential other-regarding aspect of justice." She mentions Sachs at 281n8; cf. 268-69.

106. Sachs, "A Fallacy," 154: "It [sc. the missing 'demonstration that the vulgarly just man is Platonically just'] would, however, leave open the possibility of there being men who were Platonically just, and consequently as happy as anyone else, yet capable of vulgar injustices and crimes." More revealing is 155: "In this regard it is tempting to assert that the most that can be said on behalf of Plato's argument is that crimes and evils could not be done by a Platonically just man in a foolish, unintelligent, cowardly, or uncontrolled way." This seems unduly harsh to the California Consultant. Demos, "A Fallacy" is "useful in curbing such Sachsian exuberance" at Jerome Schiller, "Just Men and Just Acts in Plato's *Republic*." *Journal of the History of Philosophy* 6 no. 1 (January 1968), 1-14 at 4; this is a plausible position.

107. Sachs, "A Fallacy," 141n2.

108. Sachs, "A Fallacy," 145n9: "Foster continued to maintain, in my belief rightly, that Plato did not try to prove justice a good in itself, or good for its own sake—in the sense in which those qualifying phrases usually bear at present." Sachs never mentions Foster, "Some Implications" and deletes the "crucified" of Shorey, *Plato's Republic* (see section §9) at 149; Glaucon's description of the Just man receives too little attention in debates about the Return (see section §25).

109. Sachs, "A Fallacy," 149n17.

shows "that Plato consistently viewed his defense of justice as one made solely in terms of justice's effects."[110] But more important and original is Sachs's claim that "the lack of connection between two conceptions of justice that Plato employs . . . wrecks the *Republic's* main argument."[111] Naturally Plato did not find himself without defenders and Sachs immediately came under attack.[112]

But before considering the most distinguished of those who sought to defend Plato by attacking Sachs, it is important to situate my own approach in relation to the critics already discussed. Equally determined to refute an analysis that leaves Plato confused and his *Republic* in wreckage, my approach is nevertheless far closer to Sachs than to his opponents despite the fact that the latter have far better intentions. The problem to which Sachs points the way is real; he principally fails to realize that Plato has created this problem *deliberately*. Plato's critics were right: the justice brought to light on the Shorter Way is only praised with regard to happiness (Prichard), it is to the advantage of only the one who practices it (Adkins), it barely guarantees fulfillment of the universally recognized demands of "vulgar justice" (Sachs), and it certainly does not adequately motivate the philosopher's Return. Foster is perfectly correct that the self-sacrificing duty of the Return is the great exception in Plato's *Republic*; he fails to realize that Plato intended it to be nothing less.[113] Christianity is endowed with something greater than "historical importance" and Christ is not diminished by any resemblance to the prior example of Socrates. Of course there is no proof that the Harmonious Man would endure being impaled on a torture stake (362a2); only a selfless response to the generosity of Good embodied in self-imposed obligation to freely perform an action of surpassing beauty[114] justifies the ethical purity that Prichard fails to realize was Plato's long before it was

110. Sachs, "A Fallacy," 141; see also 145. The fallacy that Socrates inconsistently regards happiness as "the consequence" of justice is challenged by Christopher Kirwan, "Glaucon's Challenge." *Phronesis* 10 no. 2 (1965), 162-173 and refuted by Nicholas P. White, "The Classification of Goods in Plato's *Republic*." *Journal of the History of Philosophy* 22 no. 4 (October 1984), 393-421; in the context of Glaucon's statue (who enjoys no worldly consequences), only the rewards of the afterlife are to be excluded as the consequences of Justice.

111. Sachs, "A Fallacy," 141: "The fallacy of irrelevance that wrecks the *Republic's* main argument, in my judgment, is due to the lack of connection between two conceptions of justice that Plato employs."

112. Included in Vlastos, *Plato* 2 as a riposte to Sachs, "A Fallacy," Demos, "A Fallacy?" anticipates the approach of Irwin, *Plato's Ethics* (first published in 1977) with respect to *Symposium* (398) and invokes the Idea of the Good as the ultimate object of reason; this is also the approach taken by Rudolph H. Weingartner, "Vulgar Justice and Platonic Justice." *Philosophy and Phenomenological Research* 25 no. 2 (December 1964), 248-252 beginning at 250.

113. Spoken immediately after the καταβατέον, the words of Glaucon emphasized by Mabbott (δίκαια δικαίοις ἐπιτάξομεν) are the only textual evidence of Justice as opposed to justice: "We will be enjoining Just actions upon the Just" (520e1).

114. Adkins, *Merit and Responsibility*, 291: "He might believe that it is *kalon* to act in this manner; but Plato says expressly that the philosopher-king will not believe this."

his or Kant's. The Straussians also perform a valuable service: Plato's *Republic* is unquestionably an exoteric text once the Shorter Way is recognized as merely its surface. But the deliberate concealment of altruism and self-sacrifice isn't simply a furtive attempt to avoid "persecution";[115] Plato's pedagogy requires his students to earn for themselves the crown of Socrates.

Although his polemical purpose was not immediately obvious,[116] Gregory Vlastos responded so forcefully to Sachs in "The Argument in the *Republic* that 'Justice Pays'" (1968) that he was forced to later deplore his own "unforgivably strong-armed methods"[117] in "Justice and Psychic Harmony in the *Republic*" (1969). He had, in fact, made an egregious error:[118] he derived a proof that the Harmonious Man would perform the "vulgarly"[119] just actions of Sachs from the one man-one job definition of justice of the City.[120] But little of substance has changed in the second piece:[121] Vlastos maintains the question-begging with which he had begun,[122] and evinces an ongoing willingness to identify and cor-

---

115. On altruism in the ancient context, see David Konstan, "Altruism." *Transactions of the American Philological Association* 130 (2000), 1-17. For discussion of the post-Straussian possibility that Plato conceals his altruism in order to avoid persecution, see Altman, "Altruism and the Art of Writing," 79.

116. Sachs, "A Fallacy" is the only modern work cited in Gregory Vlastos, "The Argument in the *Republic* that 'Justice Pays."' *Journal of Philosophy* 65 no. 21 (November 7, 1968), 665-674 at 672n1.

117. Vlastos, "Justice and Psychic Harmony," 515n33; this is a far more scholarly production than Vlastos, "Justice Pays" and cites it along with Sachs, "A Fallacy," Demos, "A Fallacy?", Weingartner, "Vulgar Justice and Platonic Justice," and Schiller, "Just Men and Just Acts," in the first note (505n1). He owns a debt to Bloom (with respect to translation) at 513n27.

118. Vlastos, "Justice and Psychic Harmony," 511: "'doing one's own' was not meant to constitute a definition of the justice of an ordinary person" a statement to which is attached the following note (511n21): "As I erroneously maintained in JP [sc. Vlastos, "Justice Pays"]"

119. The courtly Vlastos prefers to call them "commonly just" at Vlastos, "Justice Pays," 672.

120. Vlastos, "Justice Pays," 669: "In their primary signification 'just' and 'justice' are relational predicates: they refer to the way in which a person, or group of persons, acts or is disposed to act, *toward* persons or groups of persons. This would be true not only on the popular conceptions of justice but also on the conception that Plato's social definition has in view: 'doing one's own work' is an obligation one has to one's community and imposes inner constraints on what one may do" These inner constraints turn out to be "psychic justice." In Vlastos, "Justice Pays," "psychological" is derived from "social" justice.

121. It is tempting to read the last sentence of Vlastos, "Justice and Psychic Harmony," 521 as self-referential.

122. Vlastos, "Justice Pays," 665 (last sentence in first paragraph): "Now performing a single just act or some odd assortment of just acts is by no means equivalent to being a just man, or, in Plato's phrase, 'having justice in the soul.' So in 'justice pays' *justice* is a property not of actions as such, but of agents; it stands for the active disposition to behave justly towards one's fellows." The last twelve words are true of Justice, not

rect Plato's errors in order to prove that Plato "was trying to say" what Vlastos wants him to say:

> On my interpretation Plato offers in 443C-E [i.e., the description of the Harmonious Man] a definite argumentative bridge between $justice_2$ [sc. justice as "psychological"] and $justice_1$ [sc. justice as "social"]; if this bridge had been sound, he would have proved that $justice_1$ pays iff $justice_2$ pays and would thus have met Glaucon's challenge.[123]

The unsound "bridge" in this "contrary-to-fact conditional sentence"[124] is Plato's erroneous,[125] characteristic,[126] but (in the generous if patronizing style of the school) reparable[127] insistence on the perfect isomorphism[128] between justice in the City and justice in the Man. Vlastos discovers a sounder bridge in Aristotle;[129] this permits him to correct an error in Plato's that he regards as uninten-

---

justice. Also 669 ("In their primary signification 'just' and 'justice' are relational predicates") and Vlastos, "Justice and Psychic Harmony," 517 ("In its primary signification 'just' is a relational predicate")

123. Vlastos, "Justice and Psychic Harmony," 521.

124. It is because this conditional is contrary to fact that Sachs has not been refuted; cf. Vlastos, "Justice and Psychic Harmony," 521: "If the interpretation of the argument of Book IV of the *Republic* offered here and in JP is correct, Plato is completely exonerated of the charge leveled against him in recent years"

125. Vlastos, "Justice Pays," 670: "Now that we have spotted the error [sc. equivocation on 'justice'], we can see a simple way to patch things up: allow Plato, as a tacit premise, (H) The soul is $just_1$ iff it is $just_2$." Cf. Vlastos, "Justice and Psychic Harmony," 517: "The simplest way to spot the error in this argument is to notice the equivocation to which I called attention in JP [sc. "Justice Pays"]."

126. Vlastos, "Justice and Psychic Harmony," 519-20; when considering the first of these errors—what Vlastos calls "P(II)" at 519, discusses in 516n35-6, and defines at 516 ("If the same predicate is predicable of any two things, then, however they may differ in other ways, they must be exactly alike in the respect in which it is predicable of each")—it is remarkable that he must ultimately invoke the Ideas against Sachs at 521 (see following note): "$justice_2$ represents that condition of the soul in which all the diverse components function harmoniously because, and only because, they are all controlled by allegiance to the Ideas of Justice and Goodness in which the norms of decent conduct towards our fellows (the norms of justice1) are comprehended." It is easy to see why the Idea of the Good itself must eventually become "some kind of harmony" at Richard Kraut, "The Defense of Justice on Plato's *Republic*" in Richard Kraut (ed.), *Plato's Republic; Critical Essays* (Lanham, MD: Rowman & Littlefield, 1997), 208 (first published in 1992).

127. Consider Vlastos, "Justice and Psychic Harmony," 520-21: "And the mistake is *not irreparable* . . . are comprehended."

128. Vlastos, "Justice and Psychic Harmony," 515-17 beginning with "2. First the isomorphic structure of state and soul" Vlastos never mentions the all-important passage (434e4-435a3) where Socrates calls the isomorphism into question; the passage will be considered in section §21.

129. Vlastos, "Justice and Psychic Harmony," 519n47.

tional.[130] Socrates' equivocation on "justice" is thereby avoided, "social" justice is derived from "psychic harmony,"[131] while Sachs is refuted not on the basis of what Plato says but what he should and could have said, and indeed "what Plato is trying to say."

Neither Vlastos nor Sachs had mentioned the philosopher's Return to the Cave but their supporters and followers would do so: Simon H. Aronson in "The Happy Philosopher—A Counterexample to Plato's Proof" (1972) reaches "the same conclusion as did Sachs"[132] while Richard Kraut, a student of Vlastos, published both "Reason and Justice in Plato's *Republic*" and "Egoism, Love, and Political Office in Plato" in 1973. Kraut responds to Sachs[133] in the first of these and to Prichard, Adkins, and Bloom[134] in the second. The first article could be ignored were it not for a Vlastos-inspired remark Kraut makes in a footnote:

> I believe, however, that Plato was wrong in thinking that an unjust action would always weaken or subvert the normative rule of reason. Consider a philosopher who refuses to help rule the polis. This act would be unjust (520A-D), but I do not see how such a philosopher would be bringing it about that spirit or appetite dominates his reason.[135]

Although the admission that the Harmonious Man may sometimes act unjustly weakens the case against Sachs, it supports the thesis of the second article—where this same admission is made in the conclusion[136]—that Plato "is not an ethical egoist."[137] Kraut appears to maintain loyalty to this thesis in the 1999

---

130. This, of course, is the key word: Vlastos regards the "error" as unintentional and he therefore sets out "to patch things up"; for me, the construction of a definition of justice that is disconnected from action toward others is a deliberate provocation to discover the Justice that is not: Plato's students close the gap by voluntarily Going Back Down into the Cave in their native city, not by supplying "a tacit premise."

131. Vlastos, "Justice and Psychic Harmony," is an attempt to deduce $justice_1$ from $justice_2$; $justice_2$ derives from "allegiance to the Ideas" in which $justice_1$ is "comprehended" (521). In Vlastos, "Justice Pays," the Ideas are not mentioned at 672 where he responds to Sachs.

132. Simon H. Aronson, "The Unhappy Philosopher—A Counterexample to Plato's Proof." *Journal of the History of Philosophy* 10 no. 4 (October 1972), 383-398 at 383.

133. Richard Kraut, "Reason and Justice in Plato's *Republic*" in E. N. Lee, A. P. D. Mourelatos, and R. M. Rorty (eds.). *Exegesis and Argument*, 207-224 (Assen/Maastricht: Van Gorcum, 1973), 207 (first sentence): "My aim in this paper is to solve a problem posed by David Sachs several years ago."

134. Richard Kraut, "Egoism, Love, and Political Office in Plato." *Philosophical Review* 82 no. 3 (July 1973), 330-344 at 330n3: "H. A. Prichard, in *Moral Obligation* (Oxford, 1949), p. 108, says that Plato contradicts himself in this passage [sc. 519D-521B]. So too Arthur Adkins in *Merit and Responsibility* (Oxford 1960), pp. 290-291, and Allan Bloom in *The Republic of Plato* (New York, 1968), pp. 407-408."

135. Kraut, "Reason and Justice," 216n12.

136. Kraut, "Egoism, Love, and Political Office," 343-44.

137. Kraut, "Egoism, Love, and Political Office," 330.

article with which this section began but he has by that time changed his mind on the point made in the 1973: for Plato, "justice and self-interest (as normally construed) always coincide."[138] By the end,[139] it will be in the self-interest of the philosopher to Return and a failure to do so would be both unjust and self-destructive.[140] A far different conclusion is reached by Aronson: "there is a real conflict between two senses of justice, both of them Platonic."[141]

> Moreover, unless Thasymachus' challenge can be met, it would seem that what Plato is saying is that the development of a social conscience in the best of men, while necessary if mankind as a whole is to be benefited, may be at the expense of some happiness on the part of those who are wisest.[142]

The first clause in this otherwise admirable conclusion unfortunately cannot be ignored: Aronson believes his discovery will "undermine Plato's own argument and strengthen Thrasymachus' position."[143] In short: Kraut will ground the Return in the enlightened self-interest of the Harmonious Man while Aronson will recognize the benevolent self-sacrifice involved as undermining Plato's position; both miss the essence of Platonism.

In considering the first great explosion of interest in the Return during the 1970s, it is useful to consider a three-fold classification recently introduced by George Rudebusch: in his discussion of *Republic* I, he distinguishes between what he calls "Egoism, Altruism, and Neutralism."[144] Perhaps the most stunning

---

138. Kraut, "Return to the Cave," 253n23.

139. Kraut, "Return to the Cave," 254: "Both of these concerns—self-interest and the good of others—animate Plato's attempt to show that justice and one's own well being necessarily coincide."

140. Kraut, "Return to the Cave," 254: "If we do not investigate where one's own good lies but simply accept prevailing and unreflective views of human happiness, we are likely to do great harm not only to ourselves but to others as well."

141. Aronson, "Unhappy Philosopher," 397-98; this is, of course, Kraut's 1973 position as well: if it is in the self-interest of the Harmonious Man to avoid the Return by preserving justice in the soul and yet also just to Return by surrendering delightful contemplation, then the same act is both just and unjust and justice both is and is not in the just person's self-interest. Once again it is Plato's *deliberate* self-contradiction that neither recognizes (see Aronson, 389n15). But Aronson is strangely closer to the truth (he cites 434e at 389) even if it is Kraut who reaches the correct conclusion: the Just philosopher does Go Back Down into the Cave. This peculiar dialectic is the *Leitmotiv* of the present section.

142. Aronson, "Unhappy Philosopher," 398.

143. Aronson, "Unhappy Philosopher," 384.

144. George Rudebusch, "Neutralism in Book I of the *Republic*" in Douglas Cairns, Fritz-Gregor Herrmann, and Terry Penner (eds.), *Pursuing the Good; Ethics and Metaphysics in Plato's* Republic, 76-92 (Edinburgh: University of Edinburgh Press, 2007), 76. Not surprisingly, it is the "egoist" category that generates controversy; Rudebusch includes a useful discussion of Terry Penner's oral attempts to finesse the label at 77n2. The best discussion of egoist and altruist readings is C. D. C. Reeve, *Philosopher-Kings*.

feature of the ongoing debate about the Return has been the comparative rarity of altruistic readings in the scholarly literature in English;[145] one is far more likely to encounter words like "sacrifice" and "duty"[146] in older books that mention the Return only in passing.[147] An exception is *A Companion to Plato's* Republic by Nicholas P. White (1979); he breaks ground by arguing that the Return is not in the self-interest of the philosopher but is motivated by the Idea of the Good.[148] Although there is at times some murkiness of expression,[149] White is willing to challenge boldly the analysis of Prichard and Adkins:[150] ruling is not in the best interest of the rulers, they sacrifice their own happiness by doing so, *and* Plato does not vitiate his overall purpose.[151] White's emphasis on "exempli-

---

(Princeton, NJ: Princeton University Press, 1988), 269-73. Since Darwinian apologetics—e.g. the popular Richard Dawkins, *The Selfish Gene* (Oxford: Oxford University Press, 1976)—requires that altruism be ultimately reducible to self-interest, any sharp distinction between them, no matter how logical, cannot at present be called "popular."

145. A welcome willingness to grapple with the problem ("is there room in Plato for a more universal altruism?" at 147) is Andrew S. Morgan, *Plato* (Durham: Acumen, 2010); he is answering the right question in a thoughtful way at 149: "However, while it seems clear that Plato is committed to the thought that it is rational, and therefore just, to pursue the good of others, it does not become clear exactly why this should be. Given that some—such as Callicles in the *Gorgias* and Thrasymachus in Book 1 of the *Republic*—did challenge that view, this is a gap in Plato's arguments."

146. A distinguished holdout is W. K. C. Guthrie, *The Greeks and their Gods* (Boston: Beacon Press, 1950), 347: "Lest, therefore, what has been said should suggest a picture of him [sc. Plato] sitting with his eyes ever fixed on another world, let us remind ourselves of the sense of duty which he inculcates, for example, in the allegory of the Cave." Due to the tremendous influence of Great Britain during the nineteenth-century, a study of the revolt against Benjamin Jowett's Plato at Oxford would make a useful contribution to the political significance of intellectual history.

147. A useful review of this literature is found at Joseph Beatty, "Plato's Happy Philosopher and Politics." *Review of Politics* 38 no. 4 (October 1976), 545-575 at 548n11; Arnold Toynbee is another example. One gets the sense that the altruist reading was simply taken for granted before the First World War.

148. Nicholas P. White, *A Companion to Plato's* Republic (Indianapolis, IN: Hackett, 1979), 195: "A ruler, then, is someone who not only has a firm grasp of the knowledge of the Good, but who is moved to pursue it and the exemplification of it in the world, rather than to follow any particular interest of his own which may conflict with it."

149. White, *Companion to Plato's* Republic, 192 (emphasis mine): "Therefore, when he says they [sc. the Guardians] are forced, he does not mean that they do not in any sense choose to do so *but* are compelled against their wills. *Rather*, he means that they consent to rule in spite of the realization that they could otherwise be better off." Only in the light of "rather" does the "but" lose its more natural adversative force; "and" would have been clearer.

150. White, *Companion to Plato's* Republic, 196-97; also his "The Ruler's Choice." *Archiv für Geschichte der Philosophie* 68 (1986), 22-46 at 43-45.

151. White, *Companion to Plato's* Republic, 195: "In fact, however, it is perfectly consistent for Plato to hold that the rulers sacrifice their own interests in choosing to rule as well as to philosophize, and at the same time to argue, as he indeed does, that if one is

fication"[152] of the Good lacks metaphysical clarity and more importantly causes him to miss the fact that a new conception of justice (i.e., Justice) is the exemplification of the Good that is really operative here. But the central problem with White's admittedly refreshing account is his insistence that the obligation to Go Back Down applies to no one other than the City's Guardians:

> This case arises, I believe, for nobody that you or I will ever meet or need to persuade to be just, but only for the rulers of Plato's ideal city, who are philosophers, when they arrive at the end of their education.[153]

This view, generally embraced without comment as a matter of course in discussions of the Return, I will call "singularism."[154] Even though I consider singularism to be a profound mistake,[155] the fact that White makes his commitment to it explicit must be reckoned as another excellent feature of his discussion of the Return.

But it is ironically critics of Plato like Aronson[156] and Foster—who see the Return as altruistic and therefore inconsistent with the remainder of *Republic* as read by Prichard—who are closer to an altruist reading than those who attempt to derive it from the justice of Book IV. Even those who deny altruism's possibility (Adkins) or desirability (Strauss and Bloom) actually create a healthier debate than either those who attempted to refute Sachs (Demos, Weingartner, and Vlastos) or who anticipate the trajectory of Kraut and begin with egoism. Neutralism, the position of Rudebusch, made its entrance in the 1970s with Sarah Waterlow's "The Good of Others in Plato's *Republic*" (1972-1973) and it is also the tendency of John M. Cooper's "The Psychology of Justice in Plato" (1977), identified by White in 1979 as the recent reading "closest to the

---

just one will be happy and, in particular, that the completely just man is far better off than the completely unjust man."

152. White, *Companion to Plato's* Republic, 195: "A ruler, then, is someone who not only has a firm grasp of the notion of the Good, but who is also moved to pursue it and the exemplification of it in the world."

153. White, "Ruler's Choice," 23; cf. 41: "For remember that according to the present interpretation, the exception is the only one that Plato admits to the general rule that one benefits by being just, and moreover it can apply only to those people who are philosopher-rulers in an ideal city, at the stage of having comprehended the good at the end of their training."

154. For a recent and ingenious example—the *reluctant* Guardians are not yet fully trained—see Nicholas D. Smith, "Return to the cave," in Mark L. McPherran (ed.), *Plato's* Republic: *A Critical Guide*, 83-102 (Cambridge, UK: Cambridge University Press, 2010).

155. An egregious example is Joseph Beatty, "Why Should Plato's Philosopher be Moral and Hence, *Rule*?" *Personalist* 57, 132-144 at 144n11. This is not to say that a rejection of singularism always achieves good results; see Nightingale, *Spectacles of Truth*, 100 and 106.

156. Aronson, "Unhappy Philosophers," 396.

truth."[157] By aiming at an end (i.e., the Good) that is neither altruistic nor self-interested, the Guardians illuminate aspects of Plato's thought that are misguided (Cooper)[158] or potentially dangerous (Waterlow);[159] this latter claim apparently influenced Kraut in seeking to incorporate self-interest from the start.[160] There is, of course, considerable neutralism in the early Kraut and he continues to resist the name if not the substance of an egoist justification.[161] But the great majority of those who have considered the question are not so squeamish and considerable skill and ingenuity have been expended in showing that the Return is in the Guardian's—if not any given philosopher's—self-interest and a common feature of all of these attempts is a determination to deny Aronson's claim:

> One must take seriously this reluctance to return, for it cannot be argued that these philosophers do not yet know what is in their interest.[162]

The dialogue between Joseph Beatty and Thomas Brickhouse, for example, revolved around the compulsion applied to the Guardians: the former, following Aronson, claims that Plato made "a slip"[163] by emphasizing their unwillingness

---

157. White, *Companion to Plato's* Republic, 196.

158. John M. Cooper, "The Psychology of Justice in Plato." *American Philosophical Quarterly* 14 no. 2 (April 1977), 151-157 at 157: "This means that though the just man in Plato is no egoist, and no altruist either, but a sort of high-minded fanatic" Aristotle's approach is endorsed instead: "Aristotle was right, I think, to insist most emphatically that there is no such thing as a good-itself and that even if there were, one ought not to direct one's practical thinking to it as ultimate end."

159. Sarah Waterlow, "The Good of Others on Plato's Republic." *Proceedings of the Aristotelian Society* (n.s.) 73 (1972-1973), 19-36 at 36: "Thus when we, and Plato, speak of agents and their actions, of morality, self and others, according to the theory we have been considering [sc. the absolute primacy in Plato of reason over both 'one's own and other souls' (33) and the consequent elision of 'the person' (33-4)] we use concepts valid only on a certain [i.e. non-Platonic] level, and if on this level we affirm that a man's goodness must find expression in his actions, we cannot not while remaining on it give the Platonic reasons for the truth of what we affirm." Neutralist readings tend to be critical of Plato on these grounds, cf. Julia Annas, *An Introduction to Plato's* Republic (Oxford: Oxford University Press, 1981), 267-69.

160. The quotation from Waterlow, "Good of Others," 1972 at Kraut, "Return to the Cave," 254n24 is poorly chosen to illustrate the valid point he makes in the text.

161. Kraut, "Return to the Cave," 252: "Finally, I believe that the interpretation I have proposed indicates that in an important way Plato is not an egoist. Admittedly, he does believe that one can never go wrong if one consults self-interest, properly understood, and does whatever is best for oneself. If that is egoism, then he is an egoist."

162. Aronson, "Unhappy Philosophers," 394.

163. Beatty, "Why Should Plato's Philosopher be Moral," 143: "Thus, my contention is that Plato's description of the philosopher's unwillingness to rule is misleading and does not square with the *Republic*'s defense of justice. It is indeed as 'slip,' as Aronson says, and while unfortunate it is not, I think, necessitated by the argument and, hence, not fatal." These last two words echo Vlastos, "Psychic Justice," 520: "And the mistake

to Return while the latter weakens the kind of "constraint"[164] that overcomes that unwillingness: it is a "moral constraint"[165] to which they willingly submit. Brickhouse's position would be frequently echoed in the second phase of interest in the Return.[166] But the most influential attempt to show that no self-sacrifice is involved in the Return was made by Terence Irwin in *Plato's Moral Theory* (1977):

> Plato's theory of the virtuous man's motives is tested in VII when he tries to explain why the philosopher who knows the Forms can fairly be expected to return to the cave and take part in ruling. But he does not make the best of his theory, because he is influenced by the contemplative view of the philosopher, and describes him in terms excluded by the practical view. He mistakenly suggests that the philosopher will want to stay contemplating the Forms and will not voluntarily undertake public service (519c4-6).[167]

Having already introduced a philosopher who is by definition both contemplative and active,[168] Irwin has carefully prepared for this climactic moment with his insistence that the "psychic justice"[169] of the scarcely active Harmonious

---

is *not irreparable.*" Rather than patching up Socrates' arguments to make his text consistent, I argue that Plato employs deliberate self-contradiction for a pedagogical purpose.

164. Thomas C. Brickhouse, "More on the Paradox of the Philosopher's Rule." *Personalist* 59 (1978), 304-306 at 305.

165. Brickhouse, "More on the Paradox," 306: "and with the disappearance of the philosopher's reluctance to rule upon the recognition of the moral constraint he is under, the paradox itself likewise vanishes."

166. Cf. Peter Vernezze, "The Philosopher's Interest." *Ancient Philosophy* 12 (1992), 331-349 at 334 with Thomas A. Mahoney, "Do Plato's philosopher-rulers sacrifice self-interest to justice?" *Phronesis* 37 no. 3 (1992), 265-282 at 271. The fullest treatment of the question is Christopher Shields, "Forcing Goodness in Plato's *Republic*" in David Keyt and Fred D. Miller (eds.), *Freedom, Reason, and the Polis: Essays in Ancient Greek Political Philosophy*, 21-39 (Cambridge UK: Cambridge University Press, 2007) at 29-33. Weakening the sense of "compulsion" is the defining characteristic of what are aptly called "deflationary readings" in Eric Brown, "Minding the Gap in Plato's *Republic*." *Philosophical Studies: An International Journal for Philosophy in the Analytic Tradition* 117 nos. 1-2 (2003), 275-302 at 281.

167. Terence Irwin, *Plato's Moral Theory* (Oxford: Oxford University Press, 1977), 242.

168. The distinction between the "contemplative" and "active" aspects of the philosopher is introduced at Irwin, *Plato's Moral Theory*, 236-37 and Diotima is particularly important for proving the existence of the latter (emphasis mine): "The *Symposium* suggested the practical view, when it explained the work of teachers and legislators by the desire to *propagate* virtue" (237). Along with "express" ("Throughout Plato assumes that the philosopher's knowledge of the forms will create the desire to express his knowledge in his actions") "propagate" can be used to create a seamless and consistent connection between contemplative and active aspects.

169. Irwin, *Plato's Moral Theory*, 205: "Plato needs to find a psychic virtue corresponding to the state's justice, and can call this 'psychic justice' (p-justice)" The continu-

Man[170] necessarily "propagates" or "expresses" itself it in accordance with the discourse Socrates attributes to Diotima in *Symposium*;[171] in accordance with singularism, the grateful Guardian voluntarily makes the Return.[172] Given that the Return is merely an expression of that Guardian's "p-justice," Irwin's Plato is inconsistent in emphasizing the need for compulsion because no self-sacrifice is required.[173]

In turning to Julia Annas, who is far more critical of Plato than Irwin,[174] the same peculiar dialectic mentioned earlier remains operative: Irwin reaches all the right conclusions but Annas, a neutralist,[175] is somehow closer to the mark even in the process of missing it completely.[176] Irwin is correct: the true philosopher, having been stirred by the first great vision of Platonism in *Symposium*, chooses the active life, rejects the self-absorption of the Harmonious Man,

---

ing dialogue with Sachs, "A Fallacy" (cf. 333n33) modified by the influence of Vlastos (ix) explains Irwin's decision to contrast p-justice with "the common conception of justice ('c-justice')" (208).

170. Given that Socrates is perfectly evasive about what, if any, actions the Harmonious Man will perform except that they will preserve his inner harmony (443e2-6), considerable care must be expended in section "10.3. *Psychic justice and just actions*" (Irwin, *Plato's Moral Theory*, 210) which concludes (emphasis mine): "It seems much more promising to claim that the just man's action *expresses* his p-justice than to insist that it must always produce and maintain it."

171. Irwin, *Plato's Moral Theory*, 241: "Now the p-just man values for itself his own p-justice; and so he will want to produce p-justice in other people's lives too. As *Republic* IV said, he will regard as just those actions which produce p-justice; but Plato's theory of desire supplies what Book IV did not supply, a reason for the p-just man to aim at other people's p-justice, as well as his own. He acts on the same motives as the Platonic lover, whose ascent to Beauty and desire to give birth in beauty moves him to create justice and temperance in his beloved or in households and states (*Symp*. 208e5-209a8)."

172. Irwin, *Plato's Moral Theory*, 243: "He will value the society in which he acquires and expresses his conception of the good, the relations with the state and with other citizens from which these demands arise: and he will want to express his conception of p-justice in the state. The practical conception of the philosopher justifies Plato's appeal to gratitude; but a pure contemplative has no reason to be moved by such an appeal."

173. Irwin, *Plato's Moral Theory*, 243: "Plato cannot consistently claim that both the philosopher will be a pure contemplative who will not rule voluntarily, and that he has good reason to accept the state's demand for just action. The second view is much more likely to answer the questions about justice in the *Republic*."

174. She follows Irwin in making the distinction between active and contemplative conceptions of the philosopher at Annas, *An Introduction to Plato's* Republic, 260-61. Cf. "the two views are destined for conflict" (264) with Irwin, *Plato's Moral Theory*, 237: "These two views need not be inconsistent."

175. Annas, *An Introduction to Plato's* Republic, 267: "They are not seeking their own happiness. Nor are they seeking that of others." In general, see 266-67 and 268-69.

176. Annas, *An Introduction to Plato's* Republic, 270-71: "We have seen that the most obvious source of Plato's difficulties is his shift from the practical to the theoretical conception of the philosopher . . . Plato does not see that such a notion of reason is bound to split, and to threaten the coherence of his argument for the worthwhileness of justice."

and voluntarily descends into the Cave. But as a committed singularist,[177] he is wrong to argue that Socrates' imaginary Guardian will do so. He fails to realize that it is the Guardians who are inconsistent, not Plato. With his elaborate attempt to paper over the gap between Diotima and the Harmonious Man, Irwin makes it impossible to recognize that this gap is not only deliberate on Plato's part but a necessary moment in the reader's recognition of Justice. Just as Hegel famously claimed that the resolution of the irreconcilable conflicts enacted in Attic Tragedy occurred only in the audience,[178] a dialectical reading of Plato's *Republic* requires a preliminary recognition of the text's inconsistency before resolution is reached in the student's mind. Irwin is intent on purging the text of inconsistency: he prefers to locate a problem in Plato rather than finding its solution in the reader. Although Annas incorrectly leaves Plato in the grip of an ugly dilemma,[179] her recognition of his self-contradictory text[180] is a necessary if not sufficient moment in a dialectical process: only a non-singularist reading that passes through the negativity of Annas *en route* to Irwin's sunny conclusions reaches Platonic Justice.

---

177. Irwin, *Plato's Ethics*, 315: "Plato argues that the philosopher, and therefore the just person, does not have exactly the same obligation to a city that lacks a just constitution and does not train philosopher-rulers to embody their psychic justice in the city as a whole (520a9-c1)."

178. T. M. Knox, (trans. and ed.). *Hegel's* Philosophy of Right (Oxford: Clarendon Press, 1942), 102n: "The tragic destruction of figures whose ethical life is on the higher plane can interest and elevate us and reconcile us to its occurrence only in so far as they come on the scene in opposition to one another together with equally justified but different ethical powers which have come into collision through misfortune, because the result is that these figures acquire guilt through their opposition to an ethical law. Out of this situation there arises the right and wrong of both parties and therefore the true ethical Idea, which, purified and in triumph over this one-sidedness, is therefore reconciled in *us*."

179. Annas, *An Introduction to Plato's* Republic, 269: "The Guardian' return to the Cave has always been recognized as a major problem in the *Republic*. For the results are very ugly whether the Guardians suffer real loss by doing it or not. If they suffer real loss, because their own prospects of happiness are sacrificed, then justice is not in their interests—and yet they are the paradigms of justice in a just society [this passage clearly indicates the importance of recognizing the Return not as just but as Justice], and Plato set out to show that justice was in the agent's best interests. But if they do not suffer real loss, because they view their own happiness as rationally and impersonally as they do everybody else's, then justice seems to demand an ideal, impersonal viewpoint which is not in the interests of any actual people to adopt." Her discontent with singularism is also noteworthy.

180. An awareness of a reversal in the "one man, one job" account of justice—necessary for discovering the humorous side of the deliberate inadequacy of the Shorter Way (see section §22)—is suggested at Annas, *An Introduction to Plato's* Republic, 271: "There is a grandeur in the way that Plato makes the wise ruler be an intellectual genius *as well*, refusing to allow that the detached study of eternal truths is not an extension of the same thing as the just person's powers of practical judgment, but is something entirely different."

It was the Straussians, who reject the City, who began calling singularism into question: for them, it was not a question of compelling unwilling Guardians to return to the Cave but rather their Plato's implicit claim that no philosopher would do so. In 1977, J. C. Davies published "The Philosopher and the Cave," an egoist reading noteworthy for its vigorous singularism[181] and an eloquent statement of the altruism its author nevertheless rejects.[182] Building on Davies,[183] Dale Hall took an important step by responding to "Professors Strauss and Bloom."[184] This in turn provoked Allan Bloom's "Response to Hall" (1977). Without making it obvious that he was following Strauss in reading the *Republic* as "an ironic justification of injustice,"[185] Bloom's response flouts the Ideas,[186] banishes "moral virtues" (including justice)[187] from the center of Plato's serious

181. J. C. Davies, "The Philosopher and the Cave." *Greece & Rome* 24 no. 1 (April 1977), 23-28 at 27-28.

182. Davies, "Philosopher and the Cave," 24: "Such an argument [sc. compelling the Return] might be developed with the claim that if Plato considered it justifiable to make such a demand on the philosopher, he was evoking as a criterion for duty something other than the real long-term interest of the individual, and it might even be suggested that this is an instance of the gross inconsistency of Plato's moral theory and represents, rather, an implicit recognition that men have a duty to help one another—a presentiment of the Christian ideal—and that duty and interest, so far from being identical, are sometimes opposed to one another [the attached note refers to N. R. Murphy, "The 'Simile of Light' in Plato's *Republic*." *Classical Quarterly* 26 no. 2 (April 1932), 93-102; actually Foster, "Some Implications" is the antecedent]. The present writer believes, however, that it is not necessary to hold such a view" N. R. Murphy, *The Interpretation of Plato's* Republic (Oxford: Clarendon Press, 1951) exerted a considerable influence on Irwin, *Plato's Moral Theory*, 337-39.

183. Dale Hall, "The Philosopher and the Cave." *Greece & Rome* (2nd series) 25 no. 2 (October 1978), 169-173 at 168.

184. Hall, "Philosopher and the Cave," 169: "According to them the *Republic* does not offer the *kallipolis* as a paragon, but ironically reveals the 'limits of politics' by demonstrating how misconceived is the search for a perfect community in which the individual fulfills himself through serving the common good. Apparently, by showing the superiority of the private life of contemplation, and emphasizing that the philosophers must be compelled to rule, the *Republic* actually defends the philosophers from the claims of the polis. Contrary to the usual view, Plato repudiates the *kallipolis* because he prefers happiness to duty."

185. Allan Bloom, "Response to Hall." *Political Theory* 5 no. 3 (August 1977), 315-330 at 321: "The *Republic*, while demonstrating Socrates' concern for justice, culminates in providing a foundation not for justice but for moderation." In other words, moderation demands that the popular understanding of justice must not be rejected too openly.

186. Introduced ambiguously at 316, the Ideas vanish, along with Plato, at Bloom, "Response to Hall," 319: "In fine, what is needed is an openness to things as they appear unaided by the abstractions which so impoverish things that they can no longer cause surprise or wonder and a freedom from a moralism which forbids us to see what in nature defies convention and refuses to console us in our hopes and fears."

187. Leo Strauss, *What is Political Philosophy?* (Glencoe, NY: The Free Press, 1959), 94: "The attempt to answer this question [sc. 'What is virtue?'] leads to a critical

concerns,[188] cloaks nihilism in Socratic garb,[189] and rejects Justice in the strongest possible terms: "There is, on the evidence of the *Republic*, no enlightened, nonillusionary love of the common good."[190] Most importantly, it is not as a singularist that Bloom addresses the following challenge to Hall:

> I challenge him to find a single statement in the *Republic* that indicates that the philosophic life requires ruling or that the activity of ruling in any way contributes to philosophizing.[191]

Sufficient evidence has now been presented that reveals the Straussian approach, like that of Plato's other critics, to be of considerable dialectical value. Both John D. Harman[192] and Edward Andrew[193] have proved this by writing interest-

---

distinction between the generally praised attitudes which are rightly praised, and those which are not; and it leads to the recognition of a certain hierarchy, unknown in the pre-philosophic life, of the different virtues." See also Strauss, *Classical Political Rationalism*, 163: "Virtue in the strict sense is nothing but knowledge or understanding, and vice in the strict sense is nothing but ignorance—knowledge or ignorance of the *akra physeos*, of the peaks of being." Cf. Bloom's "what in nature defies convention" in previous note; also Strauss, *Natural Right and History*, 105-7.

188. Bloom, "Response to Hall," 319: "The only authentic virtue is that of the mind contemplating its proper objects [for these, see previous note]. It is not I who Aristotelianize. The *Republic* is not the *Ethics*; there are no moral virtues in it." This is less an interpretation of Plato than an attack on Platonism.

189. Bloom, "Response to Hall," 328: "The real questions will only come to light by looking at the texts in full consciousness that we do not know what the real questions are, let alone the answers to them."

190. Bloom, "Response to Hall," 319; the use of "enlightened" is elucidated by Bloom, *Republic of Plato*, 403.

191. Bloom, "Response to Hall," 317; Strauss's 1934 equation of philosophy and injustice in the letter to Klein quoted above explains the substitution of "the philosophic life" and "philosophizing" for "the just life" and "practicing justice."

192. John D. Harman, "The Unhappy Philosopher: Plato's *Republic* as Tragedy." *Polity* 18 no. 4 (Summer 1986), 577-594 at 593: "Thus, the lesson a tragic interpretation teaches to the philosopher is one of noble dedication to the task of ruling, a task that can never be finally accomplished, but that must nonetheless be undertaken. In contrast to the comic interpretation [cf. Bloom, "Response to Hall"], the philosopher's task requires heroic dedication to realizing justice in the city and a willingness to make the personal sacrifices this involves."

193. Edward Andrew, "Descent to the Cave." *Review of Politics* 45 no. 4 (October 1983), 510-535 at 513: "What I wish to argue is that the compulsion in the descent to the cave, as in the ascent, is an expression of philosophic *eros*. The ascent from, and the descent to, the cave are the two sides of education—being taught and teaching. Descending to teach in this interpretation is no more antithetical to philosophic *eros* than being taught. I want to argue against Strauss that the philosopher is not self-sufficient insofar as he is a teacher." This may be too generous; cf. Leo Strauss, *Thoughts on Machiavelli* (Chicago, IL: University of Chicago Press, 1958), 168 and Altman, *German Stranger*, 375-80.

ing, perceptive,[194] and powerful refutations of Bloom's claims while the Straussian position on the Return has been defended in a refreshingly unorthodox manner by Mary P. Nichols.[195] Among others,[196] Stanley Rosen has recently upheld a chastened version of the Straussian approach to the Return.[197]

Perhaps because he was in dialogue with both the Straussian and mainline critics of Plato,[198] Mitchell Miller broke new ground with his magisterial "Platonic Provocations: Reflections on the Soul and the Good in the *Republic*" (1985). On the basis of what Socrates actually does in *Republic*—i.e., descends into the shadows of the Piraeus[199]—Miller deplores and rejects singularism.[200]

---

194. It is a staple of the Straussian position that Odysseus is "the archetype of the wise man . . . a prudent man who minds his own business" (e.g. Bloom, *Republic of Plato*, 321). I am much indebted (see section §35) to Andrew, "Descent to the Cave," 525 for indicating the true Platonic position: "In contrast to Orpheus, lovers such as Alcestis, Achilles or Codrus who, like Socrates, were willing to lay down their lives for their beloved, displayed, in the face of death, the extent of their love in order to win eternal fame from posterity (*Symposium* 208d)." Reminiscent of Irwin's position, Andrew's pedagogical solution (and the inclusion of Socrates) points toward the overcoming of singularism.

195. Mary P. Nichols, "The *Republic*'s Two Alternatives: Philosopher Kings and Socrates." *Political Theory* 12 no. 2 (May 1984), 252-274 attempts to connect mathematics (260) with *thumos* (267) but she intuits the link between the Second Part of the Divided Line and the City at 259. Cf. Gerald M. Mara, "Politics and Action in Plato's *Republic*." *Western Political Quarterly* 36 no. 4 (December 1983), 596-618.

196. E.g., Jacob Howland, "The *Republic*'s Third Wave and the Paradox of Political Philosophy." *Review of Metaphysics* 51 no. 3 (March 1998), 633-657 at 656: "But the philosopher is not initially willing to rule, and can be compelled to do so only by an argument that adverts to his debt to the city that has given him a philosophical education—a debt that is not incurred by any philosopher in any actual regime (520a-b). Hence the only argument that can persuade the philosopher to try to convince the citizens that philosophers should rule presupposes that a city ruled by philosophers already exists."

197. See Stanley Rosen, *Plato's* Republic*: A Study* (New Haven, CT: Yale University Press, 2005) at 282-84; with Rosen's characteristic insistence on the compulsion exerted on Socrates from the start, cf. Strauss, *City and Man*, 63-64 and Bloom, *Republic of Plato*, 1968, 310-12. Zuckert, *Plato's Philosophers*, 363n153 is illuminating; frightening is "a descent with images" at Lampert, *How Philosophy Became Socratic*, 371-73.

198. See Miller, "Platonic Provocations," 168n9 (on Bloom, *Republic of Plato*) and 172n12 (on Sachs, "A Fallacy"); the influence of the Reagan Administration may also have played its part.

199. Miller, "Platonic Provocations," 185: "As we observed earlier, Socrates seems to contradict what he *says* by what he *does*. The philosopher *par excellence*, he has spent his life going down into the cave—whether this be the marketplace, a Callias' or an Agathon's house, or the Piraeus—and seeking out his 'likes' by relentless provocative elenchus."

200. Miller, "Platonic Provocations," 185n26: "Discussions of the philosopher's motivation in the face of the task of ruling generally focus on the express argument of the *Republic* (what Socrates says), ignoring its dramatic dimension and the portrait of Socrates as the exemplary philosopher that this contains." Cf. Bloom, "Response to Hall," 320: "My difference with Hall can be summarized by saying that he does not take the form of

Although his position must be classified as neutralist,[201] he asks exactly the right question:

> If the philosopher does not want to take up the responsibility of "caring for and guarding" others, and if he does take it up only in an act of self-sacrifice, has Socrates really presented an alternative to the selfishness that Thrasymachus proclaimed as universal at the outset (especially 338d ff.)?[202]

But the principal excellence of this important article is not so much its emphasis on the Idea of the Good as containing the solution to this dilemma but the concept of "Platonic provocation" emphasized in the title:

> There is, however, a second level of provocation and initiation as well: precisely by Socrates' exchange with his interlocutors, *Plato* challenges *us*, the listeners outside the dialogue.[203]

Combined with a rejection of singularism, his willingness to present Plato as "breaking the frame" (for such it will be called hereafter)[204]—i.e., by allowing the argument of Plato's *Republic* to jump off the written page and into the life of the reader—puts Miller in the vanguard of all those who have considered the Return: he needed only to have integrated these two elements to have realized

---

the dialogue seriously, that he does not begin where it fairly cries out for us to begin, with the story or the drama"

201. Miller, "Platonic Provocations," 192n34: "On this reading, therefore, we do not do justice to the philosopher's motivation to rule by characterizing it as egoistic or unselfish, or, indeed, as a coincidence of interest and duty." An emphasis on the impersonal Good also leads to neutralism in Waterlow, "Good of Others," Cooper, "Psychology of Justice," and Annas, *An Introduction to Plato's* Republic. Miller's own approach is dependent on Diotima in *Symposium* (186n28); he mentions Demos, "A Fallacy?" (186n29) but not Irwin, *Plato's Moral Theory*, with whom he has a great deal in common.

202. Miller, "Platonic Provocations," 167; in the sentence that follows, Miller explains the problem besetting both Straussian and altruist readings: "However distinct in their actions, *at the level of inclination* the philosopher would seem convergent with the tyrant [sc. in a Straussian reading where 'the philosopher does not want to take up the responsibility of 'caring for and guarding' others'], and justice, as he embodies it [sc. by an altruistic Return], would seem to come only at the cost of his happiness."

203. Miller, "Platonic Provocations," 165.

204. Mahoney, "Do Plato's philosopher-rulers sacrifice?" 271: "I submit that the speech [sc. 520a9-d4] is directed at Glaucon and Plato's readers, not at the philosopher of the model *polis*." For another example that nearly breaks the frame while adding a welcome addition to the repudiation of singularism, see D. C. Schindler, *Plato's Critique of Impure Reason; On Goodness and Truth in the* Republic (Washington D.C.: Catholic University of America Press, 2008), 335: "Once we recognize philosophy's intrinsic need for writing, the *Republic* yields one last secret to us. This need prompts us to read the first word of the dialogue as spoken not just by Socrates, but also, through him, by Plato to himself: to take up his pen a fabricate a poetic image intended to say more than it says, and thereby to make truth public, is to 'go down' into the cave of appearances."

that it is the reader who is being provoked by Plato to follow the example of Socrates and Go Back Down into the Cave.[205]

Beginning in the 1990s there followed a second great explosion of scholarly interest in the Return. Although this interest shows no signs of abating,[206] Eric Brown's "Minding the Gap in Plato's *Republic*" (2004) probably deserves to be the *terminus ad quem* of this outburst in a theoretical sense:[207] he breaks new ground as a historian of the problem with the concept of "the gap" that so many readings have attempted to close between psychic and common justice.[208] Depending on a resolute singularism to explain the compulsory Return,[209] Brown makes his own attempt "to exorcise from the *Republic* the ghost of a gap."[210] Far more useful is his discussion of "gap-filling strategy,"[211] particularly the terms "deflationary" (referring to readings that weaken the force of compulsion applied to the Guardians),[212] "expressivist" (that he aptly applies to Irwin's explication of the Return on the basis of *Symposium*),[213] and "imitationionist" (applied paradigmatically to Kraut's use of 500b-d in the reading with which this

---

205. Miller, "Platonic Provocations," 165-66: "In this sense, even as we witness Socrates' examination of his partners and, as witnesses, take their measure, the dialogue is examining us and taking our measure; its deepest function, if I am right, is to provoke us, to move us beneath and beyond its own explicit content into philosophical insight of our own." Had he added "and just action" after "insight," Miller's anticipation of my position would be complete.

206. The reappearance of a Christian element is noteworthy; even though Simon Blackburn, *Plato's* Republic*; A Biography* (London: Atlantic Books, 2006), 119-29 may be said to privilege "the mathematical scientific model" of the Return (128), in his discussion of "the religious interpretation" (111) and "the poetic interpretation" (116-17)—neither of which is simply dismissed (129)—the Christian aspect is emphasized; although in a more polemical vein, the same is true of the conclusions reached by Roger Huard, *Plato's Political Philosophy: The Cave* (New York: Algora, 2007).

207. Eric Brown, "Justice and Compulsion for Plato's Philosopher Rulers." *Ancient Philosophy* 20 (2000), 1-17 is at least equally important for grasping Brown's theoretical innovations.

208. Brown, "Minding the Gap," 275: "In other words, Glaucon and Adeimantus ask whether it is better to be practically just than practically unjust [sc. 'c-just' for Irwin and 'vulgarly' just for Sachs; see 293n2], and Socrates answers that it is better to be psychologically just than psychologically unjust. The past generation of scholarship on the Republic has been haunted by the worry that there is a gap between this question and its answer."

209. Brown, "Justice and Compulsion," 13 and 15.

210. With the use of education at Brown, "Minding the Gap," 288 and 290 should be compared the use of *techne* in Dorter, "Philosopher-Rulers," 340-46 and Kenneth Dorter, *The Transformation of Plato's* Republic (Lanham, MD: Rowman & Littlefield, 2006), 222-35.

211. Brown, "Minding the Gap," 277.

212. Brown, "Minding the Gap," 280-83.

213. Brown, "Justice and Compulsion," 4-5; both Vernezze, "The Philosopher's Interest" and Mahoney, "Do Plato's Rulers sacrifice?" are subsumed under this category; see 5n13.

section began).[214] In the process, Brown not only discusses most of his predecessors but also creates a useful way of classifying those he does not.[215] Even a reading that celebrates rather than attempting to close or eliminate the gap can be usefully classified in Brown's terms.[216]

I have already explained why a *celebration* of Brown's gap—rather than his own attempt to exorcise it along with expressivist or imitationist approaches to closing it—is a necessary but not sufficient moment in reaching a dialectical reading that does justice to Platonic pedagogy. For this reason, a resolute restatement of the case against Platonic consistency by Robert Heinaman is very welcome despite its anti-Platonic conclusion.[217] But even though there is a dialectical necessity for this kind of reading and little justification for avoiding or eliding the moment of negativity that characterizes it, there is no doubt that the better angels of our nature have committed themselves to upholding Platonic consistency. Darrell Dobbs has no doubt learned from experience the unsought benefits of a selfless return to the Cave; his writings deserve careful attention.[218]

---

214. Brown, "Justice and Compulsion," 5; Annas, *An Introduction to Plato's* Republic and Ferrari, *City and Soul* also belong here.

215. The use of "nomic necessitation" at Shields, "Forcing Goodness" is a fresh addition to deflationary readings and tends toward imitationism while Alan Silverman, "Ascent and Descent: The Philosopher's Regret" in David Keyt and Fred D. Miller (eds.), *Freedom, Reason, and the Polis: Essays in Ancient Greek Political Philosophy*, 40-69 (Cambridge, UK: Cambridge University Press, 2007) takes a Neoplatonic approach to expressivism (see 52n27) that makes use of *Timaeus*; cf. Mahoney, "Do Plato's Rulers sacrifice?" 279n22 and J. C. B. Gosling, *Plato* (London: Routledge and Kegan Paul, 1973), 70-71.

216. Jiyuan Yu, "Justice in the *Republic*: An Evolving Paradox." *History of Philosophy Quarterly* 17 no. 2 (April 2000), 121-141 at 136: "Seen in this way, the whole argument is aimed at establishing the [philosopher-king] paradox. This is why I claim that the central theme of the *Republic* is precisely to bring about and explicate the inevitability of this paradox." Dorter, "Philosopher-Rulers," 335 supplies useful bibliography for the proposition "that the concept of philosopher-ruler violates the just city's founding principle of 'one person one job' (370c) . . . (Bloom 1968, 407; Annas, 1981, 262, and 1986, 17-18; cf. Nichols 1984, 256)" to which Beatty, "Plato's Happy Philosophers" should be added (570). Acknowledging the gap but making it merely temporary is the contribution of Donald R. Morrison, "The Happiness of the City and the Happiness of the Individual in Plato's *Republic*." *Ancient Philosophy* 21 (2001), 1-24.

217. Robert Heinaman, "Why Justice Does Not Pay in Plato's Republic." *Classical Quarterly* (n.s.) 54 no. 2 (2004), 379-393 at 379: "So it is fundamental to the *Republic*'s political philosophy that those who rule regard ruling as something that is not in their self-interest, as something that is evil rather than good for themselves. The present paper will argue that this essential requirement for the government of the ideal city is clearly present in the *Republic*: the philosopher-kings rightly regard ruling as an intrinsic evil. But then in this case, a very important case, Plato's argument that justice is in one's self-interest breaks down."

218. Darrell Dobbs, "The Justice of Socrates' Philosopher Kings." *American Journal of Political Science* 29 no. 4 (November 1985), 809-826, "Choosing Justice: Socrates' Model City and the Practice of Dialectic." *American Political Science Review* 88 no.

And Richard Parry's application of Platonism to an admittedly premature resolution of the problem in *Plato's Craft of Justice* (1996)—obviously the product of many years devoted to inspiring students to treasure Plato's *Republic*—is a good place to terminate this intellectual history. On the face of it, Parry's reading is a synthesis of expressivist and imitationist approaches while deriving the philosopher's activity from the Idea of the Good in much the same way that Miller does.[219] But even without giving the negative moment its proper due or breaking the frame, Parry nevertheless manages to transcend singularism by his eloquent embrace of the Idea of the Good in all its generous grandeur.[220] More importantly, what Parry writes about the Good applies quite perfectly to its offspring.[221]

It may be useful to conclude this section with a summary of my own approach situated in relation to the literature just reviewed: mine is an altruist reading that celebrates the unbridgeable gap between other-regarding justice (i.e., Justice) and the one-sided psychological justice that depends on the deliberate methodological inadequacies of the Shorter Way. The *deliberate* gap in Plato's text is intended to serve his pedagogical purpose while the rejection of any deflationary approach to the compulsion applied to the Guardians identifies the Speech to the Guardians in Book VII as the Platonic provocation that forces the reader to abandon singularism, allows Plato to break the frame, and thereby both

---

2 (June 1994), 263-277, and "Plato's Paragon of Human Excellence: Socratic Philosopher and Civic Guardian." *Journal of Politics* 65 no. 4 (November 2003), 1062-1082.

219. See Richard D. Parry, *Plato's Craft of Justice* (Albany: State University of New York Press, 1996), chapter 4 ("Imitation and Inspiration in the *Republic* and the *Symposium*").

220. Parry, *Plato's Craft of Justice*, 207: "The good itself is the cause of the goodness of the activity of imitation for the imitator. We can explain the causal role by casting it in terms of final causality—by saying that the Form of goodness is the final cause of imitation."

221. Parry, *Plato's Craft of Justice*, 205 will be quoted continuously with interspersed commentary: "The philosopher admires the good itself because it is unconditionally good." It might be more accurate to say that the philosopher admires Justice because, being the offspring of the Good, it is *conditionally* good, i.e., the human good; this question will be revisited in section §25. "Of course, this aspect is the root of the problem of the reluctant philosopher." The philosopher's admiration for the Good is unconditional but his knowledge of the human condition precludes "instantiating the Form of goodness" (211) because Justice is the human, i.e., conditional, expression of the Good and only it can be instantiated by the philosopher. "However, the account being given here is that this admiration gives rise to, even expresses itself, as the desire to disseminate goodness." It would be more accurate to say that the philosopher's unconditional admiration for the Good expresses itself as the desire to practice Justice. "This desire arises because the good itself shows the necessity to propagate goodness." This is correct with the understanding that *Justice* is the philosopher's obligatory choice to propagate goodness. "If one understands the good itself, one understands the necessity to disseminate goodness; and thus, one desires to disseminate goodness." In fact, if one understands the Good, one understands Justice and thus desires to practice it.

permits and compels the personal crisis of the *Republic*.[222] Plato's readers catch sight of Justice as the maxim of their own contemplated action, i.e., as a moral obligation derived from a verbal adjective enjoining upon them their own personal duty to make the Return. Its own intrinsic excellence and moral grandeur compels philosophers to imitate Justice but they—in accordance with what they know or rather recollect to be right—nevertheless express it voluntarily by going back down into the Cave. Whether or not altruism ultimately proves to be in their self-interest becomes a matter of complete indifference.[223] Born from the Good and conceived in Beauty, Justice is revealed in a vision: an intuitionist moment of recollection intersecting with the reader's hermeneutic triumph over the exoteric surface of this miraculous text. Eager to repay Plato the Teacher for directly administering this life-altering counsel, determined to give both friends and enemies their due,[224] content to make Justice the advantage of the weaker in this life without ruling out the possibility that its ultimate consequences will be the advantage of the stronger elsewhere, the philosopher's choice consummates and redeems the whole of the *Republic* and thus Plato's purpose in writing it. And when Justice ends up being another's good (ἀλλότριον ἀγαθόν), the altruistic philosopher who goes back down into the Cave in order to defeat the avatars of Thrasymachus annihilates his victory at the same instant the Thracian sophist achieves it.[225]

Section 20. Whistling a Tune on the Way Down

If Justice is what Socrates preaches, it is hardly obvious that he practices it himself.[226] Just as Ion makes the apparently ludicrous boast that he could be a general (*Ion* 540d1-6), Socrates may well claim in *Gorgias* that he (alone) has what it takes to be an excellent politician:

> I think that I am one of the few Athenians, not to say the only one, engaged in the true political art, and that of the men today, I alone practice statesmanship [πράττειν τὰ πολιτικὰ]. (*Grg.*521d6-8; Woodhead)

---

222. White, *Companion to Plato's* Republic and his "Ruler's Choice" illustrate the intimate connection between a deflationary approach to compulsion and singularism.

223. A complete indifference to securing for oneself the rewards of altruism may safely be regarded as the necessary and sufficient condition for the possibility of receiving them.

224. This is the only Book I definition of justice passed over in the brilliant passage at Irwin, *Plato's Ethics*, 314.

225. Although not entirely without humor, Platonists will not admit to *harming* Thrasymachus (335d11) by preventing him and his kind from ruling the city although it is understandable why the friends of Thrasymachus will not see things in this light.

226. James S. Hans, *Socrates and the Irrational* (Charlottesville: University of Virginia Press, 2006), 69.

But if *Republic* answers Cleitophon's Question (see Introduction) in the eminently practical manner sketched above, the question inevitably becomes a burning one: "Why didn't Socrates practice politics himself?" It is in relation to this question that the significance and place of *Theages* in the Reading Order of Plato's Dialogues becomes visible.

Socrates addresses this question twice, the first time in *Apology* (*Ap.* 31c7-d6).[227] Here he tells us that: (1) the Sign is purely negative and only prevents him from doing something he intended to do (31d3-4) and (2) the Sign prevented him from entering politics (31d5). In other words, by combining "(1)" and "(2)," we learn for ourselves an important truth that is not made fully explicit in either of them: (3) that Socrates wished to enter, and was indeed on the verge of entering politics—no doubt for compelling reasons—but was prevented from doing so by the Sign.[228] This is therefore a crucial point for the interpretation of *Republic* that emerges in the context of *Cleitophon*: only if Socrates himself, having exited from the Cave, willingly chose to practice politics (πράττειν τὰ πολιτικὰ) can he *consistently* exhort us—i.e., those who have themselves exited from the Cave (*Republic* 520c1-5)—to do so. But *Apology* is not the only or (in the light of the reading order hypothesis) the *first* time that Plato's readers have been told about this blocked attempt in the dialogues.

The other time Plato tells us these same things is through a reader-made synthesis, not unlike "(3)" in this respect, of two passages from two different dialogues: *Republic* and *Theages*. Theages is mentioned only twice in Platonic dialogues other than *Theages*: in *Apology* it is implied that he is dead (*Ap.* 33e7) and in *Republic* that he is sick (496c2). In *Republic*, Socrates is discussing the corruption of the philosophical nature and explaining that "the most capable" are prematurely—i.e., before having exited the Cave—diverted from philosophy into political life (496a11-b7). Socrates tells Adeimantus that Theages is one of the very few who withstood this corrupting diversion.[229] This, then, is the noteworthy passage where Socrates describes not only "the bridle of our

227. By which I mean: "first for us." It is worth noting that even those who don't believe that there is any such thing as a Platonic Reading Order have already read whatever dialogues they have read in "a reading order"; i.e. there already exist as many de facto "reading orders" as there are readers of Plato. The *Euthyphro*, *Apology*, *Crito*, and *Phaedo* are among those dialogues that nearly everyone who has read Plato has read: i.e., they are very near the beginning of a de facto "reading order," implicitly defended at Rowe, *Plato and the Art*.

228. Thomas C. Brickhouse and Nicholas D. Smith, "Socrates' Gods and the *Daimonion*" in Nicholas D. Smith and Paul B. Woodruff (eds.), *Reason and Religion in Socratic Philosophy*, 74-88 (Oxford: Oxford University Press, 2000), 83-84.

229. This allusion is briefly discussed at Jacques Bailly, *The Socratic* Theages*; Introduction, English Translation, Greek Text and Commentary* (Hildesheim: Georg Olms, 2004), 48, Mark Joyal, *The Platonic* Theages (Stuttgart: Franz Steiner, 2000), 59, and, most suggestively perhaps, Joseph Souilhé, *Platon; Oeuvres Complètes*, volume 13.1 (Paris: Budé, 1949), 138 (translation mine): "It is not impossible that reading this passage [sc. 496a11-b7] and the connection [*rapprochement*] between the example of Theages and the example of the *daimonion* has furnished our dialogue-writer with a theme to de-

worthy passage where Socrates describes not only "the bridle of our comrade Theages [ὁ τοῦ ἡμετέρου ἑταίρου Θεάγους χαλινὸς]" but a little divine something about himself:

> "For in the case of Theages all other conditions were at hand for his backsliding from philosophy, but his sickly habit of body keeping him out of politics holds him back [ἀπείργουσα αὐτὸν τῶν πολιτικῶν κατέχει]. My own case, the divine sign [τὸ δαιμόνιον σημεῖον], is hardly worth mentioning—for I suppose it has happened to few or none before me." (496b7-c5)

Given that only in *Theages* could a reader who has not yet read *Apology* learn of "(1)," the fact that Plato here mentions Theages (which would necessarily remind the reader who has read it of *Theages*)[230] immediately before asserting "(2)," this passage—causing a mindful reader to derive "(3)" from the synthesis of "(1)" and "(2)"—should be considered as the kind of playful puzzle about serious subjects that great writers love to create. Here is the relevant passage:

> There is something spiritual [δαιμόνιον] which, by a divine dispensation, has accompanied me from my childhood up. It is a voice that, when it occurs, always indicates to me a prohibition of something I may be about to do [ὃ ἂν μέλλω πράττειν, τούτου ἀποτρεπήν] but never urges me on to anything [προτρέπει δὲ οὐδέποτε]; and if one of my friends consults me and the voice occurs, the same thing happens: it prohibits, and does not allow him to act.[231]

It will be noticed that *Theages* contains a clear statement of "(1)" but no hint of "(2)." It should also be emphasized that there is no indication in *Theages* of what we learn only in *Republic*: that Theages is sickly with respect to body. In fact, it is quite entertaining to return to *Theages* with this passage in mind: imagining a very bright Theages afflicted with e.g. muscular dystrophy (496c2 refers to ἡ δὲ τοῦ σώματος νοσοτροφία) sheds new light on the apparent reluctance

---

velop." This seems considerably less likely that the solution proposed here but at least addresses the curious *rapprochement*.

230. Clay, "Gaps in the 'Universe,'" 145: "No Platonic dialogue can ever explicitly hearken back to an earlier Platonic dialogue." This statement depends on giving full force to the word "explicitly"; otherwise it is false. But it is essential to Clay's overall argument: in addition to this passage, the claim appears at 136 and is then repeated at 152-53. He thus must explain away at 154 "one of the rare internal references in the Platonic dialogues" (the direct references to *Parmenides* in *Theaetetus* and *Sophist*) by distinguishing historical fact—presumably the "real" conversation between Socrates and Parmenides (154n36)—from the fiction presented in the dialogue. When adding a fourth iteration of the claim immediately following this inconvenient passage, he asserts that Plato avoids "any *overt* reference from one dialogue back to another" (154, emphasis mine). But consider the fifth and final iteration at 156: "No Platonic dialogue ever repeats or refers to any incident related in another." My claim is that the reference to Theages at 496c1 does not refer to "any incident"; it refers to *Theages*.

231. *Thg.* 128d2-5; translations from *Theages* will be those of Nicholas Smith.

of Socrates to undertake his political education. It is certainly difficult to imagine that a forger would repress the only genuine (i.e., *Republic*-based) fact about the living Theages while constructing a fraud that results in such a cleverly interwoven allusion about so crucial a subject. More importantly, without having read *Theages*, the juxtaposition of the Sign with Theages' physical disability in *Republic* VI is a *non sequitur* for the reader who is not aware of "(1)" and therefore cannot deduce "(3)." Only if we assume that Theages is mentioned in order to remind us of *Theages* does the passage in *Republic* VI become perfectly clear for the reader who hasn't read *Apology*. Not only does the apparent non sequitur vanish but the juxtaposition of two passages from two dialogues forces the reader to discover for herself—through *recollection*, as it were—something she has actually known from the very beginning of *Republic*: that Socrates could meaningfully say "κατέβην" ("I went down"). In short, the merely protreptic mission—of whose infinite regress Cleitophon (justly) complains—was not, it turns out, the first choice of Socrates, blocked as it was by the Sign: πράττειν τὰ πολιτικὰ is the course of action he intended for himself and likewise intends for those of us who intend to prove ourselves Just.

In relation to the reading order hypothesis, the pertinent question here is whether Plato intended the reader of *Republic* VI to have read (a) both *Apology* and *Theages*, (b) neither *Theages* nor *Apology*, (c) *Apology* but not *Theages*, or (d) *Theages* but not *Apology*. An exploration of these alternatives is intended to simultaneously prove the existence of the Reading Order of Plato's Dialogues and strengthen the argument for the authenticity of *Theages*.

Any reader who admits the importance of "(3)" will see that "(b)" can be safely excluded because—given the absence of "(1)" in *Republic*—the reader could not derive "(3)" from it alone. If this line of argument is admitted, the reading order hypothesis may be said to have been thereby confirmed: Plato wanted the reader of *Republic* to know that Socrates intended to go back down into the Cave in a unequivocally political sense, even if Socrates will call this "going up to the majority" at *Apology* 31c6. If the *Theages* is spurious, therefore, our only remaining choice is "(c)." But if the *Theages* is genuine, there are two more possibilities: "(a)" and "(d)." Of these, "(a)" seems uneconomical because it is only by combining old information from *Theages* with new information from *Republic* VI that *Theages* is germane for generating "(3)" in the first place. And if the reader has already read *Apology*, there is a double redundancy: the reader *already knows* that there is no need to discover the synthesis upon encountering "(2)" in *Republic* while remembering "(1)" from *Theages* because they have already encountered both of them together in *Apology*.[232] If *Theages* is

232. It is perhaps for this reason that Friedrich Schlegel—who initiated the translation project that led to Schleiermacher's momentous *Platons Werke* (see Demetriou, "Reconsidering the Platonic *Cleitophon*," 133n2)—rejected the *Apology* as spurious but pronounced the *Theages* genuine. Lamm, "Schleiermacher as Plato Scholar," 213: "A second turning point [sc. in the troubled relations between Schleiermacher and Fr. Schlegel] occurred in December 1800, when Schlegel finally came through with his "Complexus of

genuine, "(d)" is preferable to "(a)" because "(a)" is uneconomical and renders nugatory the synthetic thought-process demanded by "(d)." That leaves only "(c)" and "(d):" the old dilemma. But now there is a new twist: if the Reading Order exists, the best answer will be "(d)." To put it another way: if *Theages* is genuine, the reading order hypothesis has been confirmed.[233]

A proof of the authenticity of *Theages* based on reading order therefore requires that it precedes—and *Apology* follows—*Republic* in the reconstructed Reading Order of Plato's Dialogues. A backwards pointing allusion to *Theages* at 496b6-7 (in order to remind the reader about the apotreptic Sign) coupled with a prophetic prediction of the fate of Socrates both explains the mention of Theages and also justifies the order in which Plato has actually constructed the speech of Socrates at 496a11-e3. The self-portrait with which the speech in Book VI concludes prophetically describes the dangers that would befall "the champion of justice" who did enter politics:

> "there is nothing, if I may say so, sound or right in any present politics, and that there is no ally with whose aid the champion of justice could escape destruction, but that he would be as a man who has fallen among wild beasts, unwilling to share their misdeeds and unable to hold out singly against the savagery of all" (496c7-d3)

In the context of reading order, the speech at *Republic* 496a11-e3 looks forwards and back: backwards to *Theages* while foreshadowing *Apology*. Socrates intended to enter the Cave of active political life but was prevented by the Sign.

In the light of how political the life of Socrates was notwithstanding the Sign, all of those who would follow his teaching must ask themselves: "What's warding *me* off from an active part in τὰ πολιτικά?" For a contemporary citizen of the United States who is also a Platonic philosopher, the textually defensible answers can only be (1) exile (itself almost certainly the result of political activity), (2) physical disability, (3) the Sign, or (4) Injustice. Such is the stern message of Plato's *Republic*.[234] It is a message addressed to the vigorous and coura-

---

Hypotheses," in which he offered a brief chronology of Plato's dialogues (divided according to the three periods of Plato's career) and an even briefer explanation of his fundamental principles. Taking the concept of irony as his guiding principle, he arrived at the unusual conclusion that the *Theages* is authentic and the *Apology* inauthentic."

233. See my forthcoming "Reading Order and Authenticity" for discussion of the circularity involved here; i.e., if *Theages* is genuine, there is a reading order while the most compelling argument for the authenticity of *Theages* depends on the reading order hypothesis.

234. 496a11-b7. "'There is a very small remnant, then, Adeimantus,' I said, 'of those who consort worthily with philosophy, some well-born and well-bred nature, it may be, held in check by exile, and so in the absence of corrupters remaining true to philosophy, as its quality bids [an exemption that applies to an Athenian, or one who lives in a polity similar to her], or it may happen that a great soul born in a little town scorns and disregards its parochial affairs [an exemption that does not]; and a small group perhaps

geous, not the faint of heart. It appeals to manliness and virtue (neither understood as being a special preserve of the male; see 540c5-9) and there's no point to be served in concealing this fact. As most any high school teacher or coach will confirm for you, Plato probably thought that the sternness of the message would make it more, not less attractive to those to whom he addressed it. "Do the difficult!"[235] is an injunction that appeals to those for whom beauty is not *only* in the eye of the beholder and χαλεπὰ τὰ καλά is proverbial, to say nothing of those who can imagine themselves in Alcibiades' place at the start (cf. *Thg.* 125e8-126a4).

Although those who insist that he has no discernible intentions will necessarily demur, Plato intended the reader to take Socrates as the model of what it means to go back down into the Cave. But the only time Plato actually uses those exact words, Socrates is speaking of the Guardians who have now attained the age of thirty-five after completing a five year program of Higher Education:

> "For after that you will have to send them down into the cave again [καταβιβαστέοι ἔσονταί σοι εἰς τὸ σπήλαιον πάλιν ἐκεῖνο], and compel them to hold commands in war and the other offices suitable to youth [καὶ ἀναγκαστέοι ἄρχειν τά τε περὶ τὸν πόλεμον καὶ ὅσαι νέων ἀρχαί], so that they may not fall short of the other type in experience either." (539e3-6)

It is difficult to say whether this passage does or does not contain the Critical Ambiguity but the evidence inclines toward the negative. The word "καταβιβαστέοι"—found nowhere else in Greek literature—is also far removed from Plato's reality: it is only the *fictional* Guardians who will be "required to have been sent down" into that Cave once again. But for those who freely choose to do so, there may be some clues as to what Plato expected: both "to lead in battle" and perform "whatsoever are commands of youth." While this probably means "the type of commands appropriate to youth" (that's the sense in which Shorey translates it), I am less than sure. Plato may have intended his readers to consider "ruling the youth"—i.e., being a teacher—a sufficient instantiation or fulfillment of "going back down into the Cave." Certainly the founders—i.e., the ones who will compel the thirty-five-year-olds to go back down into the Cave—sound a great deal like teachers (cf. 412a4-b1):

> "And in these offices, too, they are to be tested [βασανιστέοι] to see whether they will remain steadfast under diverse solicitations or whether they will flinch and swerve." (539e6-540a2)

---

might by natural affinity be drawn to it from other arts which they justly disdain [Plato shows himself to be a man of experience: have *you* never met a craftsman who seemed more philosophical than any professional educator?] and the bridle of our companion Theages also might operate as a restraint.'"

235. In the words of Karl Tunberg, author of the towering screenplay for *Ben-Hur* (1959), for which it was worth—at least in the eyes of posterity—to have been blackballed for taking credit.

Although it is not certain, I would argue that Plato regarded his own life—the life of "Plato the Teacher"—as a Just one.[236] But he never says so, and the only strong evidence points to the conclusion that he wanted Socrates to be our model rather than the son of Ariston. Moreover, he probably didn't expect many of us to have our own Sign. In other words, he probably expected us to do nothing less than participate actively in politics. Certainly no other conclusion has any textual support. But for what my own somewhat less stern opinion is worth, I would suggest that Socrates as described by Plato is the mean between two extremes and that any of the three constitute what Plato means by Justice. In other words, there are (1) the active political life (the first choice of Socrates), (2) the actual life of Socrates (political enough to get him killed), and (3) the life of Plato the Teacher. Another list of three that probably leads to the same conclusion is given by Socrates when he describes what "the defender of justice" (it's his own self-portrait at VI 496d1) would nowadays be unable to do: (1) benefit the City, (2) benefit his friends, and (3) benefit herself. Given the easy path of the California Consultant, "(1)" must be considered the *sine qua non* of the three. An annual contribution to the Sierra Club doesn't cut the mustard.

For many years now, I've been offering my students an optional and extra-credit "final examination" question about Plato's *Republic* that puts each one of them exactly where their teacher intends that they should be: in the place of the Just Man or returning philosopher. As is probably the case with the most effective of such questions, I remain open to persuasion as to the best answer and have not yet found myself compelled to make a final judgment. I have, moreover, received many excellent responses on both sides of the question: "If Socrates were whistling a tune on the Way Down to the Piraeus, would it be in the Dorian or Phrygian Mode?" This question forces the student who has caught sight of Justice to confront the question: does the philosopher go back down into the Cave voluntarily or not. The specific context of the question is Socrates' description of the Dorian and Lydian modes in Book III:

> "I don't know the musical modes [τὰς ἁρμονίας]," I said, "but leave us that mode that would fittingly imitate the utterances and the accents of a brave man who is engaged in warfare [ἔν τε πολεμικῇ πράξει] or in any enforced business, and who, when he has failed, either meeting wounds or death or having

---

236. 539e5; cf. William Chase Greene, "The Paradoxes of the *Republic*." *Harvard Studies in Classical Philology* 63 (1958), 199-216 at 211: "And though Athenians of the closing years of the fifth-century and the opening years of the fourth were disillusioned by war and by political and moral decay, and indulged in the escapism of a retreat from Athens and reality, as in some of the tragic-comedies of Euripides and the *Birds* of Aristophanes, and though Plato had his private despair at the death of Socrates, reflected in his *Gorgias* and the *Seventh Epistle*, nevertheless his retreat was merely from practical politics to the career of the teacher and writer, and in the end a more influential career than that of an Alcibiades. One thinks of several curious parallels in the life of John Milton, likewise in despair, and likewise turning to writing, though Milton also did battle for the Commonwealth, albeit with the pen and not the sword."

> fallen into some other mishap, in all these conditions confronts fortune with steadfast endurance and repels her strokes. And another for such a man engaged in works of peace, not enforced but voluntary [ἐν ἑκουσίᾳ πράξει], either trying to persuade somebody of something and imploring [δεομένου] him—whether it be a god, through prayer, or a man, by teaching and admonition—or contrariwise yielding himself to another who petitioning [δεομένῳ] or teaching him or trying to change his opinions, and in consequence faring according to his wish, and not bearing himself arrogantly, but in all this acting modestly and moderately and acquiescing in the outcome. Leave us these two modes—the forced and the voluntary [βίαιον, ἑκούσιον]—that will best imitate the utterances of men failing or succeeding, the temperate, the brave [σωφρόνων, ἀνδρείων]: leave us these." (399a5-c4)

Does the Philosopher go back down into the Cave on a forced or voluntary basis? Throughout the first four chapters, I have emphasized that it is the latter. I have denominated Justice as "an action freely chosen" and "a next step freely taken." It is certainly noteworthy that Socrates twice uses the word translated as "to beg" (δείσθαι) on the Ship for what the Phrygian harmony permits the Guardians to do here: it is not beneath the dignity of Phrygian philosophers to beg the people for their votes before they themselves are begged.

But if would be silly to deny that going back down is a no less dangerous business than war (ἔν τε πολεμικῇ πράξει), and that Plato clearly intended the Critical Ambiguity to compel his readers to do their duty. If "no man does evil willingly," then a fortiori a decent person, having caught sight of the right thing to do (no matter how unlikely the source), is compelled to do it. On balance then, I think Plato either believed that *both* modes are required, i.e., that the philosopher is both forced *and* self-persuaded to practice Justice, or that there is some missing third harmony—a music not heard with the ears, perhaps—in which the true song of Justice is most properly whistled or sung.[237]

One indication that Plato conceives the possibility that neither the involuntary or voluntary mode is sufficient—or even both in alternation—is the chiastic order at the end: it would have been much more logical to write "ἀνδρείων, σωφρόνων" than "σωφρόνων, ἀνδρείων." After all, it is the soldier who is doing the dirty business and therefore needs to be brave. Perhaps Plato was saying that it is the steadfast soldier at her post who must preserve "safe-mindedness" and that it requires no little courage to go door to door petitioning folks for their votes. In any case, we can be perfectly sure that here, as everywhere else, Plato the Teacher, however playfully, was doing his duty by trying to educate us: to first lead us out and then send us back down into the Cave.

---

237. Rather a nice little tune can be constructed out of a Tone, its Octave, the Fifth and the Fourth. Since all modes possess these intervals, they may be said to be "a Third Thing" that forms the basis of the other two. Perhaps Cicero got it right in his *Republic*: the Music of the Spheres (see Introduction) is composed in the unheard *third* Mode and the philosopher returns to the earth with that heavenly music—*quis est qui complet aures meas, tantus et tam dulcis sonus*? (*de Republica* 6.22)—ringing in her ears.

Chapter Five

The Firesticks

Section 21. 434d1-435a4

If the Divided Line shows us how the Shorter and Longer Ways are to be divided and how each of them actually works, then it is what I will call "the Key Passage" beginning at 434d1 that shows how the boys ended up seeing a torchlight race after all: it is here that we are taught to bring the Shorter and Longer Ways together in order to create a third thing from their opposing intersection and reciprocal friction: the Idea of Justice.

The problem that arises when one tries to explain the *Republic* as "Justice is the philosopher's free decision to go back down into the Cave" is that it provokes the perfectly appropriate question: "Then what the hell's all that other stuff doing there?" Less colorfully expressed, the question remains: "If the Shorter Way does not elucidate what you call 'Justice,' then why did Plato go to all that trouble in describing a City that you claim is not what we've always thought it is (i.e., a description of the just City or 'Plato's Political Theory') and waste our time by applying a methodology that Plato knows from the outset won't get us where we want to go?" That's a perfectly good question and the answer to it is found in the passage beginning at 434d1.

Socrates has only just revealed justice in the City at IV 433b1-2 having first caught sight of it at 432d2-4. But it is not until 434c7-10 that he makes his meaning crystal clear (by contrast with the inter-meddling in each other's business by the three classes described at 434b8-c2): "'The proper functioning of the money-making class, the helpers and the guardians, each doing its own work in the state, being the reverse of that just described, would be justice and would render the city just.'" It is this definition that will make it possible for Socrates, after having brought to light the three corresponding parts of the soul—to complete the elegant isomorphism between the City and the Man. Adeimantus is perfectly satisfied with this account of justice. But Socrates is not so sure:

> "Let us not yet affirm it quite fixedly, " I said, "but if this form [τὸ εἶδος τοῦτο] when applied to the individual man, accepted there also as a definition of justice, we will then concede the point—for what else will there be to say?

But if not, then we will look for something else [εἰ δὲ μή, τότε ἄλλο τι σκεψόμεθα] (434d1-4)

Three points are worthy of note: (1) we are explicitly looking here for the Form of Justice, and (2) Socrates is raising for the first time the possibility that we are in fact following the path he will soon enough contrast (at 435c9-d4) with "another longer and harder road." There he will blame "the methods" being used. Here, however, he puts it differently: if justice in the Man proves to be something different from the justice we've now discovered in the City, we will need to revisit the question of justice in the City: we will need to look for something else (ἄλλο τι). These, then, (3) are the opening words of a crucial page (434d1-435d4) that, along with the Divided Line and the Allegory of the Cave, likewise deserves recognition as a "Key Passage" in Plato's *Republic*, extending as it does through the first mention of the Longer Way.[1]

"But now let us work out the inquiry in which we supposed that, if we found some larger thing that contained justice and viewed it there, we should more easily discover its nature in the individual man. And we agreed that this larger thing is the city, and so we constructed the best city in our power, well knowing that in the good city it would of course be found. What, then, we thought we saw there we must refer back to the individual [ἐπαναφέρωμεν εἰς τὸν ἕνα] and, if it is confirmed, all will be well." (434d5-e4)

This is a succinct summary of the central Hypothesis on which the Shorter Way rests: the identity of justice in both Man and City. Although one could quibble with the phrase "the best city in our power" out of loyalty to the City of Pigs, Socrates seems to have confidence in what they have now discovered. The problem, he suggests once again, will arise if what we found in the City is not confirmed in the Man. Given the central importance of directional words (like κατα-βαίνειν) it is important that the approach he is now describing does not involve the Man going down to the City but applying (by bringing up) what we have found in the City to the man (the verb "ἐπ-ανα-φέρωμεν" means that "we'd carry up [ἀνα-] and apply to [ἐπι-]." Next comes the important part:

"But if something different manifests itself in the individual, we will return again to the state and test it there [πάλιν ἐπανιόντες ἐπὶ τὴν πόλιν βασανιοῦμεν]" (434e4-435a1).

---

1. It bears repeating—in the light of the crucial importance of this Key Passage for elucidating the methodology of the Shorter Way (see Chapter 3)—that Plato does the exact opposite thing here that he will do in Books VI and VII later. In Book VII, Justice is discovered in the Cave without fanfare; in Book IV (432b8-d4), the discovery of justice is over-dramatized. But the Divided Line—clearly referenced in the discussion of the Cave (517a8-b6)—is a very clearly marked statement of methodology. In other words, the *methodology* of the Longer Way is emphasized but *the object* for which we are searching (i.e., Justice) is hidden. In Book IV, it is the reverse.

To begin with, Socrates once again raises the possibility that justice in the Man will differ from we have found in the City. This is, in fact, the third time he has mentioned the relationship between them: (1) the first time (at 434d3-4) is positive: "all would be well" so long as the two were the same, while (2) raised the negative possibility (434d4) and Socrates then said we would need to find "something else," and finally (3) this passage. If justice in the Man proves to be different, we will come back [πάλιν] to the City we have now completed. It is important to bear in mind that πάλιν, when combined with the verb "to go" (βαίνειν) and a *downward* directional preposition (κατα-) will mean: "to go back down." *Here it means exactly the opposite*: "coming back up to" (πάλιν ἐπ-αν-ιόντες). Since Justice in the Man will be revealed as a philosopher Going Back Down to an actual city like Athens or Rome, the philosopher who has done this must be (somehow) brought back up and (somehow) applied to the Book IV City so that we may subject this "something else" to a (basanistic) test. Socrates now clarifies what each "somehow" might mean:

> "and it may be that, by examining them side by side and rubbing them against one another [παρ' ἄλληλα σκοποῦντες καὶ τρίβοντες]" (435a1-435a2)

We are now told that the "bringing back up" is for the purpose of (1) testing this "something else," (2) examining the City and the Man side-by-side, and then (3) "rubbing them against each other." To help us make sense of "(3)," Socrates employs one of the most stunning images in the *Republic*:

> "as it were from the fire sticks we may cause the spark of justice to flash forth [ὥσπερ ἐκ πυρείων ἐκλάμψαι ποιήσαιμεν τὴν δικαιοσύνην], and when it is thus revealed confirm it in our own minds." (435a2-4)

In Book VII, Glaucon indicates that Justice in the Man has truly been found by defending the Socratic καταβατέον: "we will be enjoining just actions on the just" (VII 520e1). But the "Firesticks Passage"[2] indicates the only way that Justice (τὴν δικαιοσύνην) can be found as a Form or Idea (what he called in the first sentence "τὸ εἶδος τοῦτο") is on the Longer Way. The Justice we will eventually discover in the Man (i.e., going back down into the Cave) is only one of two Firesticks necessary to bring the Idea of Justice to blazing light. This is

---

2. 434d1-435a4 has received very little scholarly attention. It is cited at Neu, "Plato's Analogy of State and Individual, 251n15 and Blössner, "The City-Soul Analogy," 347 as evidence of Plato's ironclad commitment to the City/Man isomorphism or what Bernard Williams (who also cites it) calls "the analogy of meaning" in "The Analogy of City and Soul in Plato's *Republic*" in E. N. Lee, A. P. D. Mourelatos, and R. M. Rorty (eds.), *Exegesis and Argument*, 196-206 (Assen/Maastricht: Van Gorcum, 1973), at 196. Because he has no interest in upholding Socratic consistency, Aronson, "The Unhappy Philosopher," 389 cites it to better effect and accurately identifies it as "a rather clear warning." Miller, "Platonic Provocations," 169 cites it to illustrate Glaucon's failure "to respond to Socrates' ironic indication of problems."

the problem that first arose in connection with the City of Good Men Only (see section §8): what is it that would motivate a good man to rule in a city in which there was no penalty for good men refusing to rule? This was the first proleptic anticipation of Justice *qua* Form. This Key Passage (its comparative neglect should justify the nomenclature) beginning at 434d1 is highly proleptic as well: only in response to the Sun—and in the shadows of the Cave—can it bring forth its blazing light. Only by "bringing it back up" so it can be examined side-by-side with the Book IV City and (as it were) rubbed against it, can Justice (as action) become Justice as εἶδος.

Socrates is doing nothing less than adding a hidden third method to those employed on the Shorter and Longer Ways. Given the importance of triads in Plato (e.g., 397b7), this is not terribly surprising. Socrates tells us explicitly that he went down to the Piraeus "to pay my devotions to the goddess, and also because I wished to see how they would conduct the festival" (327a2-3; cf. 327b1); he never says that he went down in accordance with Justice. This will not be the only time that Plato uses the difference between an obvious two to illuminate a hidden and synthetic third. But there is a sobering grandeur of conception about all of this that must not pass unnoticed. It is a commonplace that Plato wrote dialogues and that the reader is somehow invited to participate in the discussion. But the rigor with which Plato implements this commonplace in his *Republic* is stunning. The practice of dialectic begins in the text with the two Ways: it is only through the dialectical method that we can identify the methods being used along the unnamed Shorter Way, unnamed because we must discover them for ourselves. Once discovered, the result of these methods becomes one of two necessary Firesticks, the other is the path that leads back down into the Cave. It will be by comparing these two paths that Justice will be brought to light; this is the unnamed "third method" of the Firesticks.

The Key Passage in Book IV therefore explains how to implement the Divided Line: it teaches us how to use hypotheses correctly as mere springboards and approach ramps (VI 511b5) en route to the un-hypothetical Idea and its dependencies. If the limitations of the Shorter Way are invisible without dialectic, the existence of the Firesticks presupposes not only dialectic but also the Shorter Way. It is *friction* that sets the torch of Justice ablaze and friction requires two opposed things. That friction is dialectic: the middle term between the Shorter Way and that torch. Dialectic is therefore Janus-like. It looks back at the Shorter Way and sees its methods for what they are: it then raises the heterogenous "Shorter Way" to become its temporarily univocal sparring-partner in the frictional encounter that leads the process forward to the torch's flame. But it is the flame itself—not some third method—that is the real third thing: the Idea of Justice. In other words, the Idea or εἶδος of Justice is a third thing between the Idea of the Good and the Cave. And that third stands outside of the doubling, dialogic, radically and intentionally incomplete text of Plato's *Republic*.[3] In

3. It will be noticed that Hegel remains a ghostly presence: (1) the double-nature—both positive and negative—of the second moment of "the speculative method" (see *En-*

short: Justice as Idea can only blaze in the reader because the text contains two Ways and therefore the friction that results from their contradictory results.[4]

It is tempting to claim that the reader must always supply the missing third in Plato. Certainly we must supply the third thing that motivated Socrates to go down to the Piraeus with Glaucon in the first place. But the two stated motivations—curiosity and piety—are scarcely unnecessary: both knowledge (arising only because we are curious about the truth) and divine inspiration both have their parts to play in Platonic pedagogy. The same phenomenon of the missing third appears in the two theological laws of Book II, the Phrygian and Dorian modes of Book III, the Shorter and Longer Ways of Books IV-VI, and, as will become clear in chapter 6, there is also a third Noble Lie. For the present, it is enough to realize that both Shorter and Longer Ways are necessary in the *Republic*: both of them are needed to light the torch of Justice as Idea because the conclusions of both become our Firesticks. The precondition of Plato's passing Justice on to the reader is that it must be an actual something that can be seen—blazing—with the eyes of the soul as εἶδος: this it can only be by virtue of this third method. Given that the concept of testing is crucial to understanding Plato the Teacher, it is hardly inconsequential that Socrates tells us that "we will test" (βασανιοῦμεν) what we find in the man by "coming back up to and applying it to the city" (πάλιν ἐπανιόντες ἐπὶ τὴν πόλιν). I suspect that Plato is indicating here his final exam on the *Republic*:[5] having read the Πολιτεία, the student will be asked to explain this passage and must (1) identify Justice in the philosopher who responds to the καταβατέον, (2) realize the doubled points of friction between it and the Book IV City (i.e., that the Just philosopher must do two jobs; see section §22) as well as the Book IV Man (i.e., that the Harmonious Man minds his own affair; see section §14), and (3) can therefore see, as a result of this friction, the εἶδος of Justice. As further indication of Plato's intentions,

---

cyclopaedia §239-242) and (2) the analysis of tragedy in the *Philosophy of Right* (where the resolution of the staged conflict is in the audience) are unquestionably most useful here. But (3) Hegel's text, unlike Plato's, cannot rest content with being "radically incomplete": its highest good must be contained within it as *Absolute Wissen* while Plato qua dualist leaves the Idea of the Good outside of his "system" and makes room there for the student as well.

4. Greene, "The Paradoxes of the *Republic*," 201-2: "So the *Republic* begins by demolishing popular notions and half-truths, and steps forward to build an hypothesis; this, in turn, is subjected to new criticism and amplification, and faith is verified by experience. Dialectic, the Socratic clash of minds, elicits the spark of truth. Now Socrates, or shall we say Plato, becomes more dogmatic, and hypothesis is for a dazzling moment lifted into paradox; but even as it flashes before us it is sadly withdrawn. We have experienced an anagnorisis. We have seen a pattern, an idea; who knows whether we can ever translate it into solid fact? But in the process there has been a peripeteia, and nothing in the world about us will ever be or seem the same that it was before."

5. On the theoretical level, of course: the practical examination is the conduct of the student's life from this point forward outside of the Academy, the kind of test that Demosthenes may be said to have passed and that Alexander's tutor failed.

consider the close proximity of (a) two backwards pointing references to the Firesticks at 442d8-9 and 443b4 (the first of three is at 441a5-6), (b) the description of the "one man, one job" version of justice in the City as "a sort of adumbration [εἴδωλόν τι] of justice" at 443c4-5, and (c) the Harmonious Man passage beginning at 443c9.

It will be seen that the Key Passage between IV 434d1 and 435d4 is just that: it unlocks the door to Justice as Idea and brings to light the methodological distinctions that—in tandem with the Divided Line—disclose that Justice as action is to be found inside the Cave. At the end of the stunning speech with which the Key Passage begins, Adeimantus is perfectly content; one wonders what he had made of what he'd just heard.

> "Well," he said, "that seems a sound method [καθ' ὁδόν] and that is what we must do." (435a5)

Of course Shorey is taking another liberty here although this great scholar's mistakes are consistently illuminating: it really is a third *method.* Given that Socrates is about to introduce the word "μέθοδος" (albeit in the plural) just a few lines later at 435d1, it is interesting that Plato allows Adeimantus to take this first step toward its discovery. One can only wonder if καθ' ὁδόν (literally "a way down" although colloquially "along the road") is another one of Plato's many serious jokes.

Section 22. Two Jobs for One Man: Beyond the Tripartite Soul

The best joke in Plato's *Republic* is the friction that makes those Firesticks blaze: the stark contradiction between the one man/one job principle (i.e., justice) and Justice: it is only when the philosopher does *two jobs* that Justice in either City or Man is possible. This joke is extremely funny in itself: it becomes even more so in the twilight of how few readers have gotten it.[6] Plato must have expected this. He must have known that many readers would never see through the Shorter Way and would remain on the surface of his text. Why would he allow such a thing to happen? Why would he make it so difficult to see his meaning? Because he knew that the tests and difficulties to which a Just philosopher would return as politician would make his own literary puzzles seem

---

6. In addition to Bloom, *The* Republic *of Plato*, 407; Annas, *An Introduction to Plato's* Republic, 262, and Nichols, "The *Republic*'s Two Alternatives," 256, see Beatty, "Plato's Happy Philosophers," at 550 and 570: "The question for Plato the social engineer was: educate individuals so that they would—contrary to the one-man/one-job principle—be qualified for two jobs but love only one." More recently, see Nightingale, *Spectacles of Truth*, 134: "In the *Republic*, then, a tension arises not because the philosophers must engage in different *activities*—contemplative and practical—within a single, philosophical life, but because they are asked to engage in two different *lives* which, by definition, are opposed."

like child's play: he was not, after all, preparing his students to get right answers in the classroom but to effectively combat Thrasymachus (and others far more clever) among the shadows of the Cave. Inevitably, the most difficult tests must remain outside of the dialogues. As for the mighty *Republic*, even those who dug deeper than the typical reader—into the Cave, as it were—might only get the κατέβην, the joke of the first word. But this third level, buried beneath the surface and the Cave—this sublime text-deconstructing joke—is truly amazing. There's nothing else like it in literature.[7]

Even without Justice (i.e., Justice in the philosopher), one man doing two jobs is explicitly made the precondition for the just City in Book V: either the kings become philosophers or the philosophers become kings. This Third Wave of Paradox—irrefragable textual proof of the joke if any readers still need it—will be discussed later in section §23. But for the reader who has grasped the meaning of καταβατέον, Plato's insistence (at 435a1) that "we will test it by going back up to apply it to the City" (πάλιν ἐπανιόντες ἐπὶ τὴν πόλιν βασανιοῦμεν) raises the question of "nature" in an extraordinary way. The question of nature (i.e., the one job for which he is "by nature" suited) is of particular interest to any educator. No great teacher—at least none I've ever met—is content with "letting nature take its course" where students are concerned. While good teachers cooperate with nature, they are in the business of improving natural capacity by art.

The formula "the one job for which he is by nature suited," when examined side by side with the philosopher-king, raises inevitably the question of which of the two jobs is natural for the philosopher. There are three possibilities: (1) they are not actually two jobs but only one—i.e., a synthetic philosophical-statesman or even simply the statesman[8]—and consistency is therefore preserved, (2) ruling is the natural job of those who are most capable, and the most capable are called "philosophers" only when they do not rule, or (3) the philosopher by nature goes back down and assumes a job for which her nature qualifies her to perform *better than any others* but which is not the job for which she herself is suited by nature. If there is a logical fourth possibility, it can safely be excluded.

As for "(1)": the attempt to short-circuit the joke seems the inevitable popular favorite. In order to save the traditional Plato—especially because he's made a fool of so many on the alternate reading—we will exert our ingenuity to demonstrate that he is not contradicting himself even if the view that he is doing so *intentionally* makes him twice the genius that our attempt to preserve his consistency allows him to be (see section §19): we'll defend him at his own expense (*Euthydemus* 297d1-2). In short, "(1)" restores 434d to oblivion in order to pre-

---

7. The Preface to *Don Quixote* and Ovid *Tristia* 5.12 might be cited in rebuttal of this claim.

8. Mitchell Miller, *The Philosopher in Plato's* Statesman *together with "Dialectical Education and Unwritten Teachings in Plato's* Statesman" (Las Vegas, NV: Parmenides, 2004).

serve the *Republic* as Plato's political theory or his defense of the Harmonious Man. As for "(2)," I'm not sure it's really different from "(1)." There's no real conflict between nature and job in either "(1)" or "(2)": the True Steersman ipso facto possesses the highest, i.e., the philosophical nature. As we have seen, this hardly guarantees his Justice. It is therefore only "(3)" that preserves Platonism.

If the essence of what is truly Plato's political theory could be reduced to a sound-bite, it would be the following: "εἰ μὲν βίον ἐξευρήσεις ἀμείνω τοῦ ἄρχειν τοῖς μέλλουσιν ἄρξειν, ἔστι σοι δυνατὴ γενέσθαι πόλις εὖ οἰκουμένη" ("'For the fact is, dear friend,' said I, 'if you can discover a better way of life than office-holding for your future rulers, a well-governed city becomes a possibility;'" 520e4-521a2). In other words: only if those who are to lead us would rather be philosophizing—i.e., blissed out (and blessed) in the meditative pursuit of and attempted proximity to the heaven-bright Idea of the Good than which not even Beauty is more beautiful—we will always be led by ambitious disciples of Thrasymachus. This doesn't mean that ambitious young men or women who believe (and are taught) that it is their nature to rule over the herd will simply acquire a tincture of philosophy so as to do so more effectively. It means that only if our rulers are and would rather remain philosophers will we have decent cities. Socrates makes the same point immediately after he utters his fateful καταβατέον; the Critical Ambiguity of the word "you" (see section §16) remains in full play here.

> "So our city will be governed by us and you with waking minds, and not, as most cities now which are inhabited and ruled darkly as in a dream by men who fight one another for shadows and wrangle for office as if that were a great good, when the truth is that the city in which those who are to rule [οἱ μέλλοντες ἄρξειν] are least eager to hold office [ἥκιστα πρόθυμοι ἄρχειν] must needs be best administered and most free from dissension, and the state that gets the contrary type of ruler will be the opposite of this." (520c6-d5)

The Firesticks blaze out most brightly only for those who are ἥκιστα πρόθυμοι ἄρχειν ("least of all eager to rule"): indeed the true philosophers hate and loathe the very thought of doing so. Drawn to the Good like a moth to light, loathing the lies and pettiness inevitably involved in politics from the very soul (no part of which says anything in its defense) they fight their stern and Dorian teacher and yearn to make music much more beautiful than this. But their teacher is no mean musician in his own right, and he—with tears of compassion in his eyes, perhaps—calmly proves that this music too is beautiful: this manly call to Justice. Nor is the philosophical nature selfish enough to trample on the stern and inevitable logic of political things. It is perfectly obvious to the upwards-soaring philosophers that they *will* rule better than those who desire to do so. The job of Plato the Teacher was and is to develop and encourage to its utmost reach the philosophical nature—to nurture it with utmost care among things of great beauty—and then to persuade it, through his *Republic*, that it must learn the political art. In fact, the Πολιτεία aims to do nothing less than both of these at the same time: to confirm the philosophical nature while teaching it the art of politics. The conflict between these two projects is the Firesticks: the blazing torch of Justice *qua* Idea lights the way of those philosophers who despite nature, strongest inclination, and the entire fabric of their being, become what they are not: οἱ μέλλοντες ἄρξειν ("those who are intending to rule"). These are the only students that Plato seeks and their journey is a hard one.

The stated precondition for the Firesticks of 434e1 is that what we have found in the City may not be found in the Man and the dazzling sentence that points to the Idea of Justice is itself conditional: "But if something different manifests itself in the one" is its protasis. Is this condition really met? "By no means!" comes the response. The triangular congruence of three classes in the city with three parts of the soul makes possible the elegant isomorphism of "the City in the Man" (see section §14) and thanks to the tripartite division of the soul, (1) the second half of Book IV combined with (2) the stunning portraits of defective cities and men in Books VIII and IX, leads triumphantly to (3) the three-fall victory of the just over the unjust man. The Firesticks passage deserves its oblivion because something different did *not* manifest itself in the individual man. Such is the traditional view.

But Plato doesn't defeat Thrasymachus in either Book I or Book IX but only in Book VII; in fact, only the reader secures the victory over Thrasymachus and does so outside of the text. Only the altruistic philosopher who returns to the Cave overthrows Thrasymachus in both theory (i.e., Justice is the mutual advantage of both the weaker and the stronger) and practice. (1) The merely verbal victory in Book I unquestionably has its value as does (2) the more extensive (and educational) Shorter Way triumph celebrated in Book IX; but Plato's argument (the quarrel with Thrasymachus) does not depend decisively on either: it is only (3) what happens in between Book IV and VII—only "the crisis of the *Republic*"—that is decisive. In other words, the claim that "something different manifests itself in the individual" by no means jeopardizes Glaucon's decision to choose the life of Justice over that advocated by Thrasymachus because that choice does not depend on the Shorter Way. A rejection of the traditional view is therefore no victory for Plato's enemies. The construction of the two Ways is the price Plato must pay for allowing Thrasymachus to speak the truth: Justice is another's good (343c3 and 367c3). The man of sense who lacks sufficient idealism to embrace altruism still has seven hundred and twenty-nine reasons to reject the example of Thrasymachus.

It must be remembered that Glaucon was not the only young man in the room: there were others there that Socrates was trying to persuade.[9] They will regard the three-fold victory of Book IX as definitive and it is, after all, perfectly true that a just man (to say nothing of a just woman) is happier than the tyrant. Socrates is not lying on the Shorter Way. He is bringing Adeimantus and the rest of them along for the all-night ride, allowing Plato to teach his students (and everybody else who has ever used the word) the meaning of "method," and cre-

---

9. See Scott, "Metaphysics and the Defense of Justice in the *Republic*," 18-20.

ating, for those who can learn how to use them, the Firesticks whose friction will bring to light the Form of Justice. What triggers the need for them—what causes the friction between the City and Man on a textual level—is the fact that, according to Socrates, the soul doesn't have three parts (although it can clearly be seen or appear to have them) as he finally makes clear in Book X.

The process by which the unitary soul comes to appear as the sea god Glaucus (611c7) deserves a lengthy commentary on its own. The problems arise not only because the passage is difficult to separate from its context but also because it looks forward to *Laws* and *Phaedo*. But I will dive right into the ocean of argument ignoring for the present its immediate antecedents as well as its more distant consequents.

> "But," said I, "we must not suppose this, for reason will not suffer it nor yet must we think that in its truest nature [τῇ ἀληθεστάτῃ φύσει] the soul is the kind of thing that teems with infinite diversity and unlikeness and contradiction in and with itself [διαφορᾶς γέμειν αὐτὸ πρὸς αὐτό]." "How am I to understand that?" he said. (611a10-b4)

We have not been seeing the soul in its truest nature, Socrates now tells us: the fact that it engenders self-contradiction (i.e., that it becomes subject to division by means the principle of non-contradiction) does not prove that it has three parts.

> "It is not easy," said I, "for a thing to be immortal that is composed of many elements not put together in the best way, as now appeared to us to be the case with the soul [ὡς νῦν ἡμῖν ἐφάνη ἡ ψυχή]." "It is not likely." (611b5-8)

Leaving behind the question of immortality, then, the text is stating clearly that the analysis of the tripartite soul is adequate only for appearances, not for seeing the soul "in its truest nature." The tripartite soul is, therefore, merely "how the soul seemed to us just now."

> "Well, then, that the soul is immortal our recent argument and our other proofs would constrain us to admit. But to know its true nature we must view it not marred by communion with the body and other miseries as we now contemplate it, but consider adequately in the light of reason what it is when it is purified, and then you will find it to be a far more beautiful thing and will more clearly distinguish justice and injustice and all the matters that we have now discussed." (611b9-c4)

As he did in the Key Passage in Book IV (434d1-435d4), Socrates is indicating that "justice and injustice and all the matters that we have now discussed" are being inadequately presented along the Shorter Way.[10] But here he is clearly

10. This is particularly true of Book V where the erstwhile tripartition of Book IV temporarily gives way to the community of soul and body (462c10-11), united by plea-

connecting that inadequacy to the tripartite soul. "In its truest nature," the soul has no (physical) appetites: it appears to have them only because it is "marred by communion with the body and other miseries." Beautiful though the arrangement of high, middle, and low undoubtedly is in the psychic harmony of the California Consultant, there yet remains something far more beautiful. Only by contemplating "in the light of reason what it is when it is purified" will the Soul permit us to "more clearly distinguish" Justice.

> "But though we have stated the truth of its present appearance, its condition as we have now contemplated it resembles that of the sea-god Glaucus whose first nature can hardly be made out by those who catch glimpses of him, because the original members of his body are broken off and mutilated and crushed and in every way marred by the waves, and other parts have attached themselves to him, accretions of shells and sea-weed and rocks, so that he is more like any wild creature than what he was by nature—even such, I say, is our vision of the soul marred by countless evils." (611c4-d6)

Plato is properly proud of his previous account of the tripartite soul: "we have stated the truth of its present appearance." But he now uses a visible Image of an intelligible thing of which he was evidently even prouder. In the Cave, Socrates gave an account of the things we observe—the things that are objects to us—as prisoners of the human condition in which we are born. The vivid Image of Glaucus captures the most invisible aspect of the Cave: a self-portrait of what a Caveman is *as observing subject*. It is as if Socrates were (in Shakespeare's phrase) to "hold the mirror up to nature."[11] In the aqueous distortions of the ocean's impenetrable depths, aided primarily by our own imaginations, Socrates helps us to see ourselves not for what we are but for what we have become and are only just now—thanks to his reminders—ceasing to be. Plato insists that we are not Cavemen by nature: we are merely born there into time and physicality. There is only one mirror in which the soul can see itself for what it is: philosophy.

> "But we must look elsewhere, Glaucon." "Where?" said he. "To its love of wisdom [εἲς τὴ̀ν φιλοσοφίαν αὒτῆ̃ς]. " (611d6-8)

Only by looking to the soul's "love of wisdom" (as an object) can we see it as it actually is. But this is self-knowledge (see *Alc. 1* at 132c7-133c16.): it is also the

---

sure and pain (462d1-5, 462b4, 462e2, 464a1-b4, and 464d2-4; cf. 584c3-5). The self-contradiction involved emerges at 464d7-8 where only the body is one's own (cf. 485d10-e1). For the generation of a related problem, see 460d1 (to\ au9th=j) with the principle that each does his own.

11.Glaucus is named at 611c7 ("τὸ̀ν θαλάττιον Γλαῦ̃κον") and Glaucon's name is only 'a big O' away ("ὦ̃Γλαύ́κων" at 611d6). On the other hand, that's a pretty big difference when it comes to Greek: see Altman, *German Stranger*, 450n23.

observing subject itself that is "the love of wisdom." Here then, is the upwards-soaring soul, drawn to the Good like a moth to the light.

> "And we must note the things of which it has apprehensions, and the associations for which it yearns, as being itself akin to the divine and the immortal and to eternal being, and so consider what it might be if it followed the gleam unreservedly [ὑπὸ ταύτης τῆς ὁρμῆς ἐκκομισθεῖσα] and were raised by this impulse out of the depths of this sea in which it is now sunk [ἐκ τοῦ πόντου ἐν ᾧ νῦν ἐστίν], and were cleansed and scraped free of the rocks and barnacles which, because it now feasts on earth, cling to it in wild profusion of earthy and stony accretion by reason of these feastings that are accounted happy." (611d8-612a3)

Philosophy brings us out of the Cave, now imaged by Socrates as the sea. Were we to allow the soul to follow its own natural impulse toward the Good, we would see it as it is. And in the moment just before the Firesticks blaze, this is what happens to the student: "by this impulse it had been borne up and out" only to encounter on its flight Plato—himself no stranger to these ethereal heights—the persuasive philosopher of the Phrygian Mode. The purified and unitary soul meets there the requirement that it perform a job for which it is not by nature suited. And in the ensuing flames—"like a refiner's fire"—the last disfiguring encrustations of the deep seabed are melted to nothingness away.

> "And then one might see whether in its real nature [τὴν ἀληθῆ φύσιν] it is manifold or single in its simplicity [εἴτε πολυειδὴς εἴτε μονοειδής], or what is the truth about it and how. But for the present we have, I think, fairly well [ἐπιεικῶς] described its sufferings and the forms it assumes in this human life of ours." "We certainly have," he said. (612a3-7)

Yes, then we will see. But the true philosophers have long since seen ἡ ἀληθής φύσις of the soul: that is what—thanks to the *Greater Alcibiades*—being a Platonic philosopher has meant practically from the beginning. It is the reality of the soul as μονοειδής—undermining as it does the elegant isomorphisms of the Shorter Way—that triggers the need to "go back up to the City" and test the just individual there, i.e., to rub the Firesticks together.

Speaking of "going up," the playful Plato has already warned us in his own characteristic way not to take the three parts of the soul too seriously back in Book IV, where he first introduces it. Leontius son of Aglaion, the young fellow who screams at his own eyes for trampling on his reason in order to sate their appetite for horror by staring at the piled up corpses (439e7)—the incident Socrates uses to illustrate the tripartite soul—is specifically said to be walking *up* from the Piraeus (ἀνιὼν ἐκ Πειραιῶς).

Section 23. The Third Wave of Paradox

Socrates makes it crystal clear that he regards the Third as: "the greatest wave of paradox" (473c6-7) in Book V. But the most paradoxical part of that Third Wave of Paradox requires more attention than it has received. The paradox is really a set of four separate paradoxes organized into two pairs. It is the first pair that has become notorious:

> "Unless," said I, "[1] either [1.a] philosophers become kings in our states or [1.b] those whom we now call our kings and rulers take to the pursuit of philosophy seriously and adequately, and there is a conjunction of these two things, political power and philosophic intelligence" (473c11-d3; brackets mine).

Between [1.a] and [1.b], the two possible ways for there to be "a conjunction of these two things, political power and philosophic intelligence" are exhausted. Together, [1] states the Third Wave paradox in its positive form: the two things must be combined and there are two ways to combine them.

The less famous (but far more paradoxical) part of the paradox is stated in a negative form:

> "while [2] the motley horde of the natures who at present pursue [2.a] either [2.b] apart from the other are compulsorily excluded, there can be no cessation of troubles, dear Glaucon, for our states, nor, I fancy, for the human race either." (473d3-6; brackets mine)

This second point requires the reader to elucidate what Socrates has just said. And what he has just said in [2] is that [2.a] all rulers who are not philosophers and [2.b] all philosophers who are not rulers must be "compulsorily excluded."

To begin with, my distinction between positive and negative does not go far enough: there are also the differences between three logical connectives (AND, OR, and IFF) and what logicians call the "existential" and "the universal quantifiers" to be considered here as well. To state it in a somewhat more technical way: There can exist a "cessation of trouble" IFF [1.b] all rulers become philosophers OR [1.a] if philosophers fill any openings for rulers that may exist AND [2.a] all rulers who aren't philosophers disappear AND [2.b] all philosophers who aren't rulers disappear. It will be noted that [2.a] adds nothing to the two parts of [1]: if all positions of power are filled by philosophical rulers OR ruling philosophers, there will *ipso facto* be no rulers who are not philosophers. [1.b] is therefore the most economical approach if we ignore [2]; even [1.a] merely suggested that as long as there exist sufficient philosophers to become rulers, there can be a cessation of troubles. Taken together, the two parts of [1] suggest that the paradox is a question of who rules. But [2.b] breaks new ground by raising a much wider question: "what must philosophers do?"

IFF everyone acknowledged that Justice for Plato requires the free choice of philosophers to Go Back Down into the Cave, [2.b] wouldn't be the most paradoxical part of the Third Wave of paradox: it would simply be stating that principle in a highly proleptic fashion. But those who do not acknowledge the free choice of philosophers to go back down into the Cave to be Platonic Justice, must either (i) find [2.b] problematic, paradoxical, and eminently worthy of fuller discussion, or (ii) ignore it completely. Naturally "(ii)" has been the popular alternative. But it is nevertheless a completely unacceptable one for any serious student of Plato. At the very least, there should be further discussion in accordance with "(i)." And in that discussion, the view that [2.b] is simply the first playful presentation of Justice in the *Republic* deserves a place. No sooner is philosophy mentioned than Justice itself appears, albeit in the literary shadows.

There are, to begin with, philosophers and philosophers. Of course Socrates has low regard for "the bald-headed tinkers" (495e5) who delight in applying distinctions worthy of Prodicus (*Protagoras* 337a-c3) to questions far removed from the all-important issue of the right conduct of life (VI 487b7-c3). He probably wouldn't have regarded those who would someday be called "Epicureans" or "logical positivists" to be philosophers at all. It is unclear what Plato would have called those who deny the ideas and assert that he himself (secretly) denied them, or later repudiated them, or some variation on this theme. But the real point of the [2.b] paradox is to express his rejection of those who stay outside the Cave in order to receive a spiritual suntan from the Idea of the Good. These are the illiberal or Unjust philosophers. It is these he would banish: they are far more dangerous and unjust than any poet. Indeed the mountain-dwelling sage—the world-denying Neo-Platonist, for example—is the most Unjust of men. Plato is far more famous for banishing the poets and yet who was a greater poet than Plato? The Third Wave banishment of selfish philosophers is less well known but infinitely more characteristic and important. But self-contradiction is not enough to spark flame from the Firesticks and light the Torch: if it were, the Third Wave of Paradox would be sufficient. After all, what makes the just City possible—the philosopher-king is Socrates' response to Glaucon's interruption (471c3)—contradicts the one man-one job principle. The student who realizes this is ready to make a bonfire blaze out of the wreck of the Shorter Way's City.

Plato places the Firesticks before the Cave: the student must *return* to the Key Passage. This hermeneutic return is best understood as a response to the crisis provoked by the Critical Ambiguity in the Speech to the Guardians. Having confronted in Book VII the possibility that Plato may be speaking directly to the reader, the reader at first is naturally skeptical. More importantly, Plato's chosen reader has ample cause to reject such an obligation quite apart from the fact that it emanates from such an improbable source: it is only in times of grave political crisis—when Democracy teeters on the brink of Tyranny—that the philosopher both must *and can* return to the Cave of political life. This prospect is terrifying and is, moreover, terrifying in direct proportion to its necessity. A dodge is sought and easily found in Book IV's Harmonious Man. "Isn't it enough to keep my own soul in order?" Having been brought up in what Socrates aptly calls "a pasturage of poisonous herbs" (401b9), is it not enough to free oneself from the appetites of the moneymakers and consecrate oneself to philosophy? It is to *escape* the Return that the reluctant philosopher returns to the Firesticks. Neither the justice of the City nor that of the Man in Book IV requires from the reader anything like the kind of sacrifice that Plato merely *may* have enjoined upon us in Book VII. And this hermeneutic uncertainty becomes the friction: will the student follow the easy way that Plato has written in his mute and long-suffering text or choose the harder path that Socrates chose and is still choosing to tread and—this thought, once conceived, is not so easy to shake—that Plato is actually demanding, even now, from *you*? How easy is it to escape the net of truth once one knows what Justice demands? Escaping that net becomes all the more difficult for anyone who considers the Third Wave of Paradox with care. Since Plato has constructed the dilemma for just this contingency, he knows that no worthy student, having progressed this far, will ever escape it. But he also knows that the more they struggle against it—the more friction there is between what they hope but doubt and what they know but fear—the more adamantine will be their commitment to Justice once having made it.

Section 24. Plato's *Letters*

The best external evidence for the decisive importance of 434d1-435a4 is not found in the secondary literature but rather in the Seventh Letter;[12] two passages there emphasize the importance of the Firesticks. In the first, Plato is explaining to "the Friends of Dion" why there will never be "a treatise of mine" about "the things to which I devote myself":

> For it does not at all admit of verbal expression like other studies, but, as a result of continued application to the subject itself and communion therewith, it is brought to birth in the soul on a sudden, as light that is kindled by a leaping spark [ἐξαίφνης, οἷον ἀπὸ πυρὸς πηδήσαντος ἐξαφθὲν φῶς], and thereafter it nourishes itself.[13]

This is a remarkable text: the deepest matters cannot be communicated in words and, using words to illustrate this very proposition, Plato deploys the very same image that appears in the deepest of his written works. A few paragraphs later, there is a second and somewhat longer passage that begins with a clear statement of something every teacher has experienced: that a student's good intentions aren't always enough but they constitute the *sine qua non* of genuine edu-

---

12. For example, Guthrie does not mention the Firesticks while discussing *Republic* in volume IV but the relevant passage appears in *History of Greek Philosophy* V, 410-11 in the context of the Seventh Letter.

13. *Ep.* 341c4-d2; (Harward translation). Note that philosophy has already been likened to fire: cf. πυρός at *Ep.* 340b3.

cation nevertheless.[14] Next, emerging from the seemingly innocuous pairing of "virtue and vice," comes a clue to the importance of true/false testing for Plato the Teacher:

> For both must be learnt together; and together also must be learnt, by complete and long continued study [μετὰ τριβῆς πάσης], as I said at the beginning, the true and the false about all that has real being.[15]

The reference to "rubbing" (τριβῆς) is particularly noteworthy since it also appears in the Firesticks (τρίβοντες at 435a2). And if Plato didn't write the Seventh Letter, he certainly put this pedagogical principle into practice: this is the justification for the basanistic dialogues that follow the *Republic*.[16] In any case, the Firesticks are once again clearly visible in what follows:

> After much effort, as names, definitions, sights, and other data of sense, are brought into contact and friction one with another [τριβόμενα πρὸς ἄλληλα αὐτῶν ἕκαστα], in the course of scrutiny and kindly testing by men who proceed by question and answer without ill will, with a sudden flash there shines forth understanding [ἐξέλαμψε φρόνησις] about every problem, and an intelligence whose efforts reach the furthest limits of human powers.[17]

Whether written by Plato or someone else, these passages from the Seventh Letter makes it rather difficult to believe that the Firesticks have played such an insignificant role in the interpretation of Plato's *Republic* to date.

Nor is this the only reference to *Republic* in the Seventh Letter: Plato refers three times to the Third Wave of Paradox. In the first (*Ep.* 326a7-b4), Plato introduces the Paradox in the context of the personal circumstances that made him aware of it: his own thwarted "desire [ἡ ἐπιθυμία] to take part in public life and in politics [τὸ πράττειν τὰ κοινὰ καὶ πολιτικά]."[18] The wording of this passage is particularly noteworthy because it makes no reference to philosophers becoming kings; achieving a leadership position in the city is sufficient:

---

14. *Ep.* 344a2-b1 (Harward): "In one word, the man who has no natural kinship with this matter cannot be made akin to it by quickness of learning or memory; for it cannot be engendered at all in natures which are foreign to it. Therefore, if men are not by natural kinship allied to justice and all other things that are honorable, though they may be good at learning and remembering other knowledge of various kinds—or if they have the kinship but are slow learners and have no memory—none of all these will ever learn to the full the truth about virtue and vice."

15. *Ep.* 344b1-3 (Harward).

16. Without *Timaeus* and the *Statesman*, our vision of the Good—no less than of the philosopher who died in its service—remains incomplete. We too must fight for the Idea of the Good and only our own commitment to Justice decisively acquits Socrates.

17. *Ep.* 344b3-c1 (Harward).

18. *Ep.* 325a7-b1 (L. A. Post translation). Plato hammers home this point a few lines later by referring to himself as "at first . . . full of eagerness for a public career" at *Ep.* 325e1-2; see also *Ep.* 324b9, *Ep.* 325c6, and *Ep.* 327a3-4.

> the human race will not see better days until either the stock of those who rightly and genuinely follow philosophy acquire political authority [εἰς ἀρχὰς ἔλθῃ τὰς πολιτκὰς], or else the class who have political control be led by some dispensation of providence [ἔκ τινος μοίρας θείας] to become real philosophers.[19]

Albeit with no reference to divine providence (θεία μοίρα), Plato's second reference to the Third Wave of Paradox justifies his attempt to convert Dionysius to philosophy and thereby to confirm "the doctrine and the way of life that I always preach."[20] Finally, the unwillingness of Dionysius "to put justice into practice" had far reaching consequences for that doctrine:

> He possessed great power, and if in his empire philosophy and political power had really been united in the same man, its glory would have shown forth among all men, Greek and barbarian, and would in itself have brought home to them the true belief, namely, that neither city nor individual can attain happiness except through a life wisely conducted under the rule of justice, whether a man be guided by his own sense of justice or be brought up and trained in righteous habits under the control of holy men. In preventing this, Dionysius inflicted an injury in comparison with which I count the others as slight indeed.[21]

In fact, the connection between the Seventh Letter and the Third Wave of Paradox goes well beyond the three explicit references I have now documented because these references, in turn, depend on the intimate connection between Plato's Sicilian expeditions in general and the *Republic* as a whole. Consider, for example, the juxtaposition of Dionysius and Dion that immediately precedes the passage just quoted:

> Now I persuaded [ἔπειθον] Dion when I explained to him these doctrines and others of the sort [ταῦτά τε καὶ ἄλλα τοιαῦτα], so that I have every reason to be angry [δικαιότατ' ἂν ὀργιζοίμην ἐγὼ] with his slayers in a certain way exactly as with Dionysius. In both cases I and all the rest of mankind, you may say, received the greatest injury. For the slayers of Dion made away with the man who intended to make justice effective [τὸν βουλόμενον δικαιοσύνῃ χρῆσθαι], while Dionysius would not consent to put justice into practice [οὐδὲν ἐθελήσας χρήσασθαι δικαιοσύνῃ] throughout his empire.[22]

To begin with, there is the repeated emphasis on justice. Secondly, the contrast between Dion and Dionysius with respect to justice instantiates the choice of lives initiated by Glaucon by raising the question: who is happier, the reigning tyrant or the dead Dion? Finally, there is Plato's emphasis—an emphasis that

---

19. *Ep.* 326a7-b4 (Post); the increased practicality with respect to [1.a] combined with the dependence of [1.b] on divine assistance is noteworthy.

20. *Ep.* 328a4-b1 (Post).

21. *Ep.* 335d1-e2 (Post).

22. *Ep.* 335c2-d1 (Post; I have replaced "convinced" with "persuaded").

my reading of the *Republic* as a whole has attempted to explain and justify—that justice is something to be practiced: the difference between Dionysius and Dion is anatomized by the fact that one of them wishes *to act* in accordance with justice (χρήσασθαι δικαιοσύνῃ) while the other does not. And as the words ταῦτά τε καὶ ἄλλα τοιαῦτα suggest, Plato has already told us about the doctrines he persuaded Dion to embrace, the same ones that he failed to persuade Dionysius to embrace and that he is now attempting to persuade the friends of Dion to embrace.[23]

These doctrines lead to the practical conclusion that Sicily should not be enslaved by human tyrants but by laws (*Ep.* 334c6-7). Slavery proves injurious to both the enslaved and their enslavers, along with their descendents (*Ep.* 334c8-d1) while those who enslave others render their souls small and un-free (*Ep.* 335d1-3) and know nothing of the things that are good or just, whether divine or human, here or hereafter (*Ep.* 335d3-5). He then goes farther, to the theoretical basis of what it means to χρήσασθαι δικαιοσύνῃ, a basis that depends on the choice of lives as instantiated by Dionysius and Dion:

> Be guided also by the example of Dionysius and Dion, for of those two the one who would not be convinced is now leading an ignoble life [ὁ μὲν μὴ πειθόμενος ζῇ τὰ νῦν οὐ καλῶς], while he that was convinced has met a noble death [ὁ δὲ πειθόμενος τέθνηκεν καλῶς].[24]

This μεν/δε contrast is considerably stronger in Greek: the one who was not persuaded is still alive now, the other is dead and therefore the οὐ καλῶς/καλῶς contrast must be taken to offset the difference between life and death. Dion has not simply chosen "the best life"; he has chosen an honorable death in preference to life that is οὐ καλῶς. This passage recalls the epitaph for the soldiers who saved Hellas at Plataea ("If to die nobly [τὸ καλῶς θνήσκειν] is the greatest part of virtue, then to us, beyond all others, chance has allotted this")[25] and Plato follows it with his own epitaph for Dion:[26]

> Thus the striving for the noblest things, both for himself and for his city, suffering [πάσχειν] whatever he may suffer, is completely right and noble [τὸ γὰρ

23. *Ep.* 334d5-6 (Post): "Of this truth I attempted first to convince Dion, secondly Dionysius, and now the third time you. Be then convinced of it for the sake of Zeus who saves the third time." Note that Plato here gives a theological basis to his ongoing fascination with triads.

24. *Ep.* 334d7-e1 (Post).

25. Translation mine from Gilbert Murray, Cyril Bailey, E. A. Barber, T. F. Higham, and C. M. Bowra (eds.), *The Oxford Book of Greek Verse* (Oxford: Clarendon Press, 1930).

26. J. Harward, "The Seventh and Eighth Platonic Epistles." *Classical Quarterly* 22 nos. 3-4 (July-October 1928), 143-154 at 143: "Certainly one of Plato's objects in writing it [sc. the Seventh Letter] was to raise a worthy memorial to his friend."

> τῶν καλλίστων ἐφιέμενον, αὐτῷ τε καὶ πόλει, πάσχειν ὅτι ἂν πάσχῃ, πᾶν ὀρθὸν καὶ καλόν].[27]

Like most epitaphs, this is really an exhortation in disguise and Plato follows it with a soldier's stern warning that, in any case, all of us must die (*Ep.* 334e3-5).

In Plato's celebration of the austere dignity of Dion's self-sacrifice for the common good, the reader will recognize Justice. Whether embodied or not, it is only our souls that experience what is truly good or base (*Ep.* 334e5-335a2) and with this having been premised, he attempts to persuade Dion's friends to embrace the same doctrines he had persuaded Dion to embrace:

> But it is necessary always truly to be persuaded [πείθεσθαι δὲ ὄντως ἀεὶ χρὴ] by the ancient and holy doctrines which declare to us that the soul is immortal and that it has judges and pays the greatest penalties, whensoever a man is released from his body; wherefore also one should account it a lesser evil to suffer [πάσχειν] than to perform the great iniquities and injustices.[28]

Given that the intervening passage (*Ep.* 335a7-c1) contains a detailed description the man who has not been persuaded,[29] we can be sure that we have now heard the things "I persuaded Dion when I explained to him ταῦτά τε καὶ ἄλλα τοιαῦτα (*Ep.* 335c2)" We can also recognize that the most important of these is the famous claim about justice and injustice from *Gorgias* because Plato repeats it: having introduced πάσχειν in what I have called "Dion's epitaph," he mentions two more times that it is better to suffer (πάσχειν) an injustice than to do one (*Ep.* 346a1-4 and *Ep.* 351c6-7). The presence of Justice in the Seventh Letter is likewise indicated by Plato's repeated claim that peace is only made possible by the self-sacrifice of the winners (*Ep.* 336e3-337a3 and *Ep.* 337c4-d2) and by their voluntary slavery to the law (*Ep.* 337a6-8), a theme that reappears in the Eighth (*Ep.* 354c5-6).

It is important not to miss the forest for the trees: the Seventh Letter in particular and the Platonic *Epistles* in general are very obviously connected with the short-cut option of the Third Wave of Paradox. As already indicated, "[1.b]" (see section §23)—i.e., the conversion of kings to philosophy—is the most economical approach: there are a finite number of rulers and perhaps all (or at least some, or one) can be converted to philosophy. Thanks to the thirteen letters that have come down to us as Plato's, the name of Plato is inextricably linked with

27. *Ep.* 334e1-3 (translation mine; the commas in the Greek text are likewise mine). It is no less moving than the elegiacs attributed to Plato at *Greek Anthology* 7.99 on which see C. M. Bowra, "Plato's Epigram on Dion's Death." *American Journal of Philology* 59 no. 4 (1938), 394-404. For an illuminating discussion of Dion, see Alexei J. Zadorojnyi, "The Ethico-Politics of Writing in Plutarch's *Life of Dion*." *Journal of Hellenic Studies* 131 (2011), 147-163.

28. *Ep.* 335a2-7 (Harward modified).

29. Although Dionysius should certainly be recognized here, there is also a reference to *Republic* 330e1. cf. Cephalus' καταγελώμενοι with καταγελῶν at *Ep.* 335b1-2.

exactly this economical approach: the failed attempt to convert Dionysius of Syracuse to philosophy. No one seems willing to deny that Plato made this attempt although every one of the Platonic letters (including the central Seventh, which is currently enjoying a reputation for authenticity) has been rejected as inauthentic over the years.[30] In fact the game of unmasking the spurious literature of antiquity seems to have its *fons et origo* in epistolary fraud; it is on this basis, for example, that the teacher-student relationship between Plato and Demosthenes has been rejected.

Whoever arranged this collection of Plato's letters made some very interesting choices about the order in which to present them. There are three points about the arrangement that strike me: (1) there is no attempt to place the thirteen in chronological order and indeed what is called "order of composition" is flagrantly ignored, (2) the letter that must be considered the orphan among the thirteen—the one that has found no modern defenders or at any rate fewer than any other[31]—is placed first, and (3) the longest, most important, and most widely conceded to be authentic, is placed in the center of the collection. Since my project not only involves putting things in order but doing so without consideration for the order of composition, the arrangement of the Plato's letters interests me a great deal. While I find it unlikely that a clever forger would place the most obvious fake at the start of the collection, I find it even more interesting that whoever arranged this collection placed the Seventh Letter in the middle: this decision offers at least some support for my view that the *Republic* stands in the same relation to the dialogues.

If the letters, or any number of them, are genuine and were intended by Plato to be read in the Academy along with the dialogues, then any investigation

---

30. While Luc Brisson, *Platon: Lettres. Traduction, introduction, notices et notes* (Paris: Flammarion, 1987) accepts the Seventh and Eighth as genuine, more skeptical winds are currently blowing: see for example Malcolm Schofield, "Plato and Practical Politics" in Christopher Rowe and Malcolm Schofield (eds.) in association with Simon Hornblower and Melissa Lane, *The Cambridge History of Greek and Roman Political Thought*, 299-302 (Cambridge, UK: Cambridge University Press, 2000). The classic products of the glory days of the authenticity debate remain interesting and valuable: prepared by R. Hackforth, *The Authorship of the Platonic Epistles* (Manchester: at the University Press, 1913), the highpoint occurred between the World Wars: L. A. Post, *Thirteen Epistles of Plato, Introduction, Translation and Notes* (Oxford: Clarendon Press, 1925). Franciscus Novotný, *Platonis Epistulae commentariis illustratae* (Brünn: Opera Facultatis Philosophicae Universitatis Masarykianae Brunensis, 1930), and J. Harward, *The Platonic Epistles, Translated with Introduction and Notes* (Cambridge, UK: Cambridge University Press, 1932). A comparatively recent treatment that bridges the great divide between Tübingen and the English speakers is Mauro Tulli, *Dialettica e scrittura nella* VII Lettera *di Platone*, preface by Graziano Arrighetti (Pisa: Giardini, 1989). But the most valuable treatment of the *Letters* in English is Glenn R. Morrow, *Plato's Epistles. A Translation with Critical Essays and Notes* (Indianapolis, IN: Bobbs-Merrill, 1962). A reception history of the Platonic epistles would be illuminating and well worth reading.

31. The table in Guthrie, *History of Greek Philosophy* V, 401 is very interesting.

of the reading order of Plato's dialogues is incomplete without considering when these letters should be read. I will therefore hazard a guess on this admittedly tangential issue: if Plato intended a work called "*Letters*" to be read (if, that is, they are both genuine and were intended by Plato to be read at all) he intended them to be read in tandem with the *Republic*. The evidence for this claim has already been presented but should be restated: (1) the Seventh Letter repeatedly emphasizes the Third Wave of Paradox while the *Letters* generally reveal the practical limitations of implementing its short-cut (cf. *Ep.* 328c2-3), (2) in its austere praise for Dion and the virtue of self-sacrifice for the common good he embodies, the Seventh Letter offers support for Justice as I have presented it in *Republic*, and (3) by twice echoing the Firesticks, the Seventh Letter confirms the importance of a passage crucial to the reading of *Republic* that brings Justice to light. Although the central Seventh Letter is by far the most important, the collection as a whole has persuaded me that it is a genuine work of Plato and that he intended it to be read between Books V and VI of his *Republic*.[32] This placement has the advantage of giving the ten-book dialogue a center (the *Letters*) that itself has a center (the Seventh Letter). It also explains why Plato's *Letters* are particularly relevant to the Firesticks (Book IV) and the Third Wave of Paradox (Book V) while preparing the reader for the Divided Line (Book VI)[33] and Justice (Book VII). Most importantly: if the reader who has finished *Republic* V has not yet given the Firesticks their due, Plato's *Letters* provides a second chance.

The first step toward rehabilitating the *Letters* is to recognize it as an integrated work of art, no different from any Platonic dialogue in that respect. The fact that Plato's *Letters* deals with historical events and personages does not require that it consists of accurate and unaltered historical documents whose purpose is to preserve the facts of Plato's three journeys to Sicily. To put this

32. Without evidence that anyone other than Plato divided his *Republic* into books, a dogmatic assertion that he didn't based on probabilities is out of place; we simply don't know whether or not he was responsible. But I do feel sure that whoever divided them made the decision to have Socrates address Glaucon by name at the end of Book III (417b9); this prepares for the interruption of Adeimantus at the beginning of IV (419a1).

33. At *Ep.* 342a7-344c1, Plato uses a geometrical example to illustrate the five steps involved in trying—but necessarily failing—to express in words a reality like the circle itself (*Ep.* 342c2-3); it needs to be reconsidered in the context of the Divided Line, not *vice versa*. Consider also that the passage from the Seventh Letter (*Ep.* 342d3-8) that follows the five-fold classification, also based on the number five (Harward translation; brackets mine): "The same doctrine holds good [1] in regard to shapes and surfaces, both straight and curved, [2] in regard to the good and the beautiful and the just, [3] in regard to all bodies artificial and natural, in regard to fire and water and the like, and in regard to every animal, [4] and in regard to every quality of character, and [5] in respect to all states active and passive." Since '[1]' corresponds to the Second and '[3]' and '[5]' to the Third Part of the Divided Line, it is only '[2]' and '[4]' that involve the First or highest: those investigated by a dialectician "making no use whatever of any object of sense" (511c1).

point in an exaggerated way: the fact that in the Seventh Letter Plato three times explains the importance of "the third time for the savior" (*Ep.* 334d7, 336c1, and 340a3-4; cf. 583b2-3) may be—given the crucial role of triads in his *Republic*—closer to the collection's purpose than any matters of chronology or causality. If the *Letters* are by Plato, they are ipso facto by Plato the Teacher and therefore must be understood to have a pedagogical purpose. The fact that so much of the debate surrounding the authenticity of the *Letters* has revolved around issues of historical accuracy therefore makes most of that debate irrelevant to my purpose.

On the other hand, my approach is not without precedent. Its foundations were laid in 1934, when Franz Dornseiff wrote a brief but brilliant piece called "Platons Buch 'Briefe.'" Here he wrote: "The thirteen Letters not only do not contradict themselves but play off against each other; there is a distinct motive that will be deliberately developed there."[34] In particular, it was Dornseiff who first recognized the significance of the Seventh Letter being seventh of thirteen and on that basis challenged the interested student to reread the entire collection, in order, as a literary work.[35] His defense of the First Letter is worth quoting:

> The fact that he shows some nervousness in the First Letter that alienates today's reader—who has constructed his image of Plato in accordance with the rejuvenated Socrates of the dialogues—demonstrates its personal authenticity. And the fulsome taste in literary citations demonstrates forcefully that this is a fictionalized letter. . . . Even the fact that Plato in this First Letter has so strongly emphasized the political importance of his own person in Sicily creates a serious difficulty only when one accepts the letter as real and chronologically earliest. About that, no one can make a definitive decision and the difficulty disappears if the First Letter is the somewhat self-advertising opening of a book of letters.[36]

But Dornseiff goes off the rails in the sentence he writes next: "We stand face to face with the surprising fact that Plato published a series of letters with himself as hero."[37] In fact, the thirteen letters don't present Plato in a very favorable light: it bears emphasis that it was the Thirteenth Letter and not the First that was the first to fall under suspicion.[38] Plato not only fails in the *Letters*, he comes off as cowardly;[39] to take a particularly damning example, he abandons

34. Franz Dornseiff, "Platons Buch 'Briefe.'" *Hermes* 69 no. 2 (1934), 223-226 at 223; translations from this article are mine.

35. Dornseiff, "Platons Buch," 224.

36. Dornseiff, "Platons Buch," 225-26.

37. Dornseiff, "Platons Buch," 226.

38. Morrow, *Plato*, Epistles, 100-9 must refute the claim that the Thirteenth Letter casts Plato's character in a negative life in order to defend the Letter's authenticity. The opposite but equally one-sided approach is found in Konrad Gaiser, "Platone come 'kolax' in una lettera apocrifa (13a Epist.)," *Sandalion* 4 (1981), 71-94: the letter is a forgery because it slanders Plato.

39. In his review of Ludwig Edelstein, *Plato's Seventh Letter* (Leiden: Brill, 1966), T. M. Robinson writes in *Phoenix* 21 no. 2 (Summer 1967), 141-143: "Edelstein [who

his resolve to act in accordance with Dion's heroism the second time he cites the *Gorgias* preference in the Seventh Letter. But it is precisely Plato's failure that confirms my sense that the *Letters* should be read in tandem with the *Republic*. The fact that Plato himself tried the easy way (i.e., [1.b]) in Syracuse—and *failed*—further emphasizes the importance of both [1.a] and [2.b]. If the *Republic* is any guide, then the final cause of the Academy and the instruction offered there was [1.a], a view that finds some support in the Seventh Letter (*Ep.* 325d4-5). By performing a reductio ad absurdum on [1.b], the *Letters* supplement *Republic* in a most instructive manner. By presenting himself in the First Letter as having been αὐτοκράτωρ,[40] Plato may also have hoped to increase the confidence his students had in him as having experienced first-hand the reality of political power whereas by the end of the Thirteenth, they would have come to see him as human, all too human. Great teachers need to do this because they intend their best students to surpass them. Plato the Teacher needed no worshippers and self-criticism is a crucial part of effective pedagogy. In addition to being an invitation to surpass him, Plato's critical self-presentation has an equalizing effect: none of his students need be any more perfect than he was.

No account of the Platonic *Letters* can ignore the passage on which the Tübingen School so heavily depends: the same passage that anticipates the Firesticks has repeatedly been taken to prove that Plato never communicated his serious views to writing. In fact, the interesting circumstance that the Seventh Letter uses the language of the Firesticks in order to show why Plato never wrote about "the subjects which I seriously study" refutes the basanistic claim that Plato himself is making in the Seventh Letter. The "leaping spark" passage is prefaced with these words:

> And I am even told that later on he himself wrote a treatise on the subjects in which I then instructed him, composing it as though it were something of his own invention and quite different from what he had heard; but of all this I know nothing. I know indeed that certain others have written about these same subjects; but what manner of men they are not even themselves know. But thus much I can certainly declare concerning all these writers, or prospective writers, who claim to know the subjects which I seriously study, whether as hearers of mine or of other teachers, or from their own discoveries; it is impossible, in my judgment at least, that these men should understand anything about this

---

rejects all the *Letters* as spurious] is firmly in the Shorey tradition of Plato the saint." Robinson does not add that the author of "Platonic Anonymity" could hardly be expected to accept the possibility that Plato does in fact speak for himself (cf. 393c10-d1).

40. *Ep.* 309b2-3. This single word seems to be central argument against the authenticity of the First Letter; see Hackforth, *Authorship of the Platonic Epistles*, 36-39. Isn't it at least possible that the word was a title (cf. *Ep.* 353b3) that had become by this time far less grand than it sounded? Perhaps it entitled Plato (and others) to enjoy the privilege Herodotus tells us was accorded to Otanes (3.83) or that signal honor, reserved for Plato, that Plutarch describes in his *Life of Dion* 19.3; cf. 13, 16.1. The reader should also consider the way Plato treats Dionysius in the Thirteenth Letter, particularly at *Ep.* 362d1-e1.

> subject. There does not exist, nor will there ever exist, any treatise of mine dealing therewith. (*Ep.* 341b3-c5)

Because knowledge can only be passed "as light that is kindled by a leaping spark" (341c7-d1), the fact that Plato has recorded in writing—and only once, only in the *Republic*—this exact same conception, negates the claim being made here: the *Republic* is explicitly harnessing the only form of communication sanctioned for a serious purposes by the Seventh Letter. In other words, if Plato intended *Letters* to be read, then reading it in tandem with the *Republic* would—in addition to diverting the student from the Syracusan short-cut—create a powerful symbiotic relationship between the Seventh Letter and the *Republic* similar to the Firesticks themselves. The Seventh Letter would emphasize the importance of the Firesticks passage and—by pointing back to *Republic* IV—at the same time contradict their intersection with respect to the claim that "there does not exist, nor will there ever exist, any treatise of mine dealing therewith." It is important to bear in mind that once Plato's *Letters* is recognized as a literary work as opposed to a set of historical or quasi-historical documents, it too must be read dialectically. And the fact that there are intimations of Justice in the *Letters* can be shown to contradict both the Tübingen School *and itself.*

A good example is the way Plato treats Archytas in *Letters*. To begin with, Archytas is a link between Plato and Pythagoreanism;[41] his influence has been detected in *Timaeus* and beyond.[42] Meanwhile, the Tübingen School is particularly keen to find traces of the One and Indefinite Dyad—what they call Plato's "protology" or *Prinzipienlehre*—in both *Timaeus* and the Seventh Letter. But aside from the problematic assumption that what Plato refuses to write in the Seventh Letter is identical to what they require him to have taught orally in the Academy, the best evidence of the protology there is a reference to "the first and highest principles of nature" (*Ep.* 344d4-5).[43] Plato's use of this phrase is revealing:

> One who has followed my tale and its meanderings [τῷ μύθῳ τε καὶ πλάνῳ] will be assured of the fact that, whether Dionysius has written anything on the first and highest principles of nature [τῶν περὶ φύσεως ἄκρων καὶ πρώτων],

41. Guthrie, *History of Greek Philosophy* I, 333: "Archytas of Tarentum brings Pythagoreanism down to the time of Plato and the Academy. More than that, with him Pythagoreanism makes a direct and personal impact on Plato himself, for the two men formed a lasting friendship."

42. See in particular Erich Frank, *Plato und die sogenannten Pythagorer; ein Kapitel aus der Geschichte des griechischen Geistes* (Halle: M. Niemeyer, 1923). More modest claims are made in Charles H. Kahn, *Pythagoras and the Pythagoreans: A Brief History* (Indianapolis, IN: Hackett, 2001).

43. Reale, *New Interpretation*, 67n46, 67, 67n55, and especially 279: "[*Ep.* 344d4-5] which was our basis for coining the term 'protology' to indicate as suggestively as possible the Unwritten Doctrines."

> or anyone else great or small, that man in my opinion has neither received any sound instruction nor profited by it in the subjects of which he wrote.[44]

Plato is not stating or even implying that his own highest concerns are with τά περὶ φύσεως ἄκρα καὶ πρῶτα ("the first and highest Principles of reality" is Reale's translation)[45] but rather indicating *and perhaps even naming* the topic of Dionysius' treatise and, in any case, the concerns of those who, unlike Plato, taught him to philosophize.[46] In an ingenious attempt to cast doubt on the authenticity of the Seventh Letter, G. E. R. Lloyd has shown that Plato's critical attitude toward Archytas—who had certified the progress of Dionysius in philosophy (*Ep.* 339b2-4 and d1-3)—is at odds with the Pythagoreanism found in *Timaeus* and *Philebus*.[47] But if we are willing to read the *Letters* as preceding these dialogues in the Reading Order, then it makes perfect sense that Plato reminds Archytas in the Ninth Letter "that each of us has not been born for himself alone" (a beautiful phrase admired by Cicero)[48] even though "the pleasantest thing in life is to do one's own thing [τὸ τὰ αὑτοῦ πράττειν]."[49] Even before encountering the Divided Line, then, the Ninth Letter has given the student good reason to question the justice Socrates discovers along the Shorter Way.

---

44. *Ep.* 344d3-7 (Post's translation modified); I take the words τῷ μύθῳ τε καὶ πλάνῳ to refer to Plato's story (*Ep.* 342a7-344d2) about the circle itself and the incapacity of name, definition, image, and knowledge to express it without distortion.

45. Reale, *New Interpretation*, 67; I take the doubled use of αὐτὰ (instead of ταῦτα) in the next sentence to mean "such things" rather than "these things." Cf. Strauss, *Rebirth of Classical Political Rationalism*, 163: "Virtue [according to "the Platonic as well as the Xenophontic Socrates"] in the strict sense is nothing but knowledge or understanding, and vice in the strict sense is nothing but ignorance—knowledge or ignorance of the ἄκρα φύσεως, of the peaks of being." A comparative study of Strauss and the Tübingen School is needed.

46. G. E. R. Lloyd, "Plato and Archytas in the Seventh Letter." *Phronesis* 35 no. 2 (1990), 159-174 argues persuasively that Plato intends us to recognize Archytas behind the words "anyone great or small" at *Ep.* 344d5.

47. Lloyd, "Plato and Archtyas," 169: "But whoever the author is, it [sc. the 'philosophical digression' in the Seventh Letter] does very nicely the job of work of establishing that Plato was . . . [sic] no Pythagorean. Indeed compared with the *Timaeus* and the *Philebus*, *this* version of Plato's fundamental doctrines is notable for being a good deal *less* Pythagorean than they." See 169n18 for Archytas' impact on *Timaeus*. It further deserves mention that the astute Lloyd draws attention to the Firesticks passage at 161n7.

48. *De Finibus* 2.45 (Raphael Woolf translation): "As Plato wrote to Archytas, we bear in mind that we are born not just for ourselves [*non sibi se soli natum*] but for our country and our people, so much so that only a small fraction of us remains for ourselves."

49. *Ep.* 357e6-358a3 (translations mine). In context, the definition of justice from *Republic* 433b4 applies to the philosophical activities of Archytas from which politics (τὰ κοινά at *Ep.* 358a7; cf. *Ep.* 324b9) deflects him. For Plato's ironic distance from Archytas in the Tenth Letter, see Dornseiff, "Platon's Buch," 224.

Victoria Wohl has made a very promising start in reading "the thirteen letters as a corpus"[50] and more work of this kind is likely to follow. For the present, it may be useful to give some sense of its structure and symmetries when read as an integrated text, point out its ongoing thematic connections with *Plato the Teacher*, and finally to offer explanations for several passages that have troubled scholars. In terms of structure, the salient fact is the centrality of the Seventh Letter. Almost certainly unaware of Dornseiff, Leo Strauss cited this centrality in 1939 to argue excitedly for the artistic integrity and thus the authenticity of the work.[51] With the Seventh recognized as pivot, the following symmetries may be significant:[52] the First and Thirteenth are opposites and contrast Plato at his angriest (*Ep.* 309b6-8) with the friendliest phase of his relationship with Dionysius. The Second and Twelfth, which both refer to Plato's other writings (cf. *Ep.* 314c3-4 and *Ep.* 359d6-e1), are the only letters that state or imply that they should be burned (cf. *Ep.* 314c4-6 and *Ep.* 359e1-2), and the Sixth and Eighth both call for triple ententes. Dion's character is emphasized in both the Fourth and Tenth (as well as the Seventh) and even though Plato excuses himself from direct political involvement in both the Fifth and the Eleventh (not the Ninth, as ring-composition would dictate), there may be a self-deprecatory contrast between Plato's criticism of Archytas in the Ninth and his own elegiac or peev-ish resignation in the Fifth.[53] Finally, both the Third and the Eleventh emphasize, along with the central Seventh, that without the prior philosophical education of the reformer, political reform is impossible. For the present, I find these symmetries a better indication of artistic integrity of the work than any interconnections within the ordinal series itself. It is also suggestive that the fifty-four Stephanus pages of the *Letters* make it comparable in length with *Protagoras* (53), *Symposium* (51), *Philebus* (56), *Phaedrus* (52), *Cratylus* (57), *Sophist* (52), and *Statesman* (54).

The author of the *Letters* leaves no doubt that he is an experienced educator. To begin with, the lesson plan is simple and, once learned, it is never forgotten (*Ep.* 344d9-e2). Although the student must discover the truth for herself, the teacher is always aware of the goal to be reached and knows how to exploit "teachable moments" (*Ep.* 352e1-2). While careful to observe and assess the motivations of his students (*Ep.* 331a5-b4), the author knows that even the most sensitive teacher cannot be sure of a happy result (*Ep.* 344a1-2). Students are

50. Victoria Wohl, "Plato avant la Lettre: Authenticity in Plato's Epistles." *Ramus* 27 no. 1 (Spring 1998), 60-93 at 60.

51. Leo Strauss to Jacob Klein, Schenectady (Union College), November 28, 1939 at Strauss, *Gesammelte Schriften* 3, 586.

52. Cf. Rachel Barney, "Platonic ring-composition and *Republic* X," in Mark L. McPherran (ed.), *Plato's* Republic: *A Critical Guide* (Oxford: Oxford University Press, 2010), 32-51.

53. *Ep.* 322a8 (Post translation modified): "Plato has been born late for his fatherland, and the people, when he came to them, were already rather well on in years and had acquired from his predecessors the habit of doing many things at variance with his advice." Cf. Plutarch, *Life of Dion*, 32.5 and 37.7.

different and only a combination of intelligence and character is requisite for academic success (*Ep.* 344a2-b1). Although he knows a good student when he sees one (*Ep.* 327b1), he is aware of youth's limitations (*Ep.* 328b3-5). His pride in his profession is evident (*Ep.* 329b1-2) and he recommends teaching to others (*Ep.* 360d6-e3). His advice to Dionysius is noteworthy: "Be stalwart and philosophize and guide others, the younger ones" (*Ep.* 363c9-d1).

The *Letters* also allow Plato the Teacher to reveal himself as the author of dialogues; he specifically refers to himself as having written *Phaedo* in a passage where he leaves no doubt that he calls his dialogues his λόγοι (*Ep.* 363a5-7; cf. *Ep.* 327a7). Among these, he distinguishes the Socratic (cf. *Ep.* 314c3-4).[54] He considers "any dialogue or letter from me" (τις παρ' ἐμοῦ λόγος ἢ ἐπιστολή) as a teaching aid (*Ep.* 363d2-5) and his word-choices in this passage suggest that he may also have called his dialogues ὑπομνήματα (*Ep.* 359c6 and *Ep.* 359d6-e1; cf. *Tht.* 143a1). When he tells Dionysius that he is sending him "some Pythagorean treatises and some classifications [τῶν τε Πυθαγορείων πέμπω σοι καὶ τῶν διαιρέσεων at 360b7-8]," there is some reason to think that he may be referring to dialogues like *Timaeus*, *Philebus*, *Sophist*, and *Statesman*. And although it may well mean nothing in the context of the Eighth Letter, Plato emphasizes the number thirty-five there (*Ep.* 356d5-7); it will reappear in a more significant context at *Republic* 537d3 and 539e3 (see section §29).

It is clear that Plato regards a proper philosophical education as a long and difficult affair and I take the words πᾶν τὸ πρᾶγμα ("the whole thing" at *Ep.* 340b8) to designate the entire Reading Order of Plato's Dialogues. In a remarkable passage (*Ep.* 340b1-341b3), Plato describes how he tested Dionysius by revealing to him at the start the difficulty of the πρᾶγμα (*Ep.* 340c2-3, 340e1-2, and 341a7) or "road" (ὁδός at *Ep.* 340c3, 340c5, and 340d8) and the large number of πράγματα (*Ep.* 340c1 and 341a3) or "studies" (μαθήματά at *Ep.* 340d8) it contains as a whole (τὸ ὅλον at *Ep.* 341a2). While describing the path of his successful students, Plato clearly speaks from experience and with that paradoxical combination of sternness and sympathy, of humility and perfect self-assurance, that distinguishes great teachers:

> To such persons one must point out what the subject is as a whole [πᾶν τὸ πρᾶγμα], and what its character, and how many subjects [δι' ὅσων πραγμάτων] and how much labor [ὅσον πόνον] it involves. For on hearing this, if the pupil be truly philosophic, in sympathy with the subject and worthy of it [ἄξιος τοῦ πράγματος], being divinely gifted [θεῖος ὤν], he believes that there is yes, even now [τε εἶναι νῦν] a marvelous pathway [ὁδόν . . . θαυμαστὴν] that one must strive earnestly to have heard [ἀκηκοέναι συντατέον], and moreover that life will not be worth living if he does otherwise. After this he braces both himself and him who is guiding him on the path [τὸν ἡγούμενον τὴν ὁδόν], nor does he desist until either he has reached the

54. It deserves notice that Plato does not refer to his dialogues at συγγράμματα at *Ep.* 314c1-4 because this contradicts the case made at Reale, *New Interpretation*, 68.

> goal of all his studies [τέλος . . . πᾶσιν], or else has gained such power as to be capable of directing his own steps without the aid of the instructor.[55]

And a curriculum based on reading order—aptly described here as ἡ θαυμαστὴ ὁδός ("the wonderful path")—is also consistent with Plato's description of the unsuccessful student:

> Those, on the other hand, who are in reality not philosophic, but superficially tinged by opinions—like men whose bodies are sunburned on the surface—when they see how many studies are required and how great labor, and how the orderly mode of daily life is that which befits the subject [κοσμία τῷ πράγματι], they deem it difficult or impossible for themselves, and thus they become in fact incapable of pursuing it; while some of them persuade themselves that they have sufficiently heard the whole [τὸ ὅλον] and in no way require certain subjects [τινων πραγμάτων].[56]

One might therefore think of Plato's curriculum (πᾶν τὸ πρᾶγμα) as a πρᾶγμα πραγμάτων (*Ep.* 340b8-c1).

It is important to bear in mind that the context of the foregoing passage is the test (πεῖρα at *Ep.* 340b5 and 341b3) that Plato administered to Dionysius: the importance of testing is emphasized throughout the *Letters*. The basic principle of basanistic pedagogy—that if the test is true (ἡ βάσανος at *Ep.* 313d2; see also 312c8 and 314b1), "these principles will grow to be a part of you, and you will be their friend as well as mine"[57]—appears in the Second Letter along with the image of the purified gold (*Ep.* 314a6) that can pass the touchstone's test (cf. *Grg.* 486d2-7). Although Plato may be able to turn his students upside down when it comes to ontology (*Ep.* 314a1-b5) and ethics (*Grg.* 481c3), he is remarkably down to earth as an educator: he is an empiricist not only with respect to testing his students (cf. *Ep.* 316c7-d1 and 323a1-2) but he exhorts them to test his own teachings in both the Second (*Ep.* 313c7-d3) and the Eighth Letter:

> That these words of exhortation from me are true you will know by experience [ἔργῳ γνώσεσθε] if you sample by tasting [γεύσησθε] what I have just said about laws. Experience seems to be the surest touchstone [βάσανος ἀληθεστάτη] for everything.[58]

The role of testing is particularly interesting in the Thirteenth Letter: along with "the Pythagorean treatises and some classifications" mentioned earlier, Plato

55. *Ep.* 340b7-d1 (Harward translation modified).

56. *Ep.* 340d6-341a3 (Harward translation modified).

57. *Ep.* 313d1-3 (Post); the ultimately derivative importance of staying the course and preserving what you have already learned is the subject of the Tenth Letter (*Ep.* 358c7-8).

58. *Ep.* 355c5-8 (Post translation modified).

sends Dionysius a young man named Helicon. The paradoxical mixture of fulsome praise and persistent suspicion that permeates Plato's detailed description of this young man (*Ep.* 360b8-e3) makes this a remarkable passage and a useful analogue to the way readers should entertain Timaeus and the Eleatic Stranger.

The principal thematic connections between the *Letters* and the *Republic* have already been mentioned; to these must be added a reference to the penalty that compels good men to rule (*Ep.* 358a6-b3). Given Plato's emphasis throughout on the central and indeed sacred importance of the rule of law (*Ep.* 334c6-7, 350c1-6, and 354b8-c7), it is difficult to believe that the Eleatic Stranger speaks for Plato in *Statesman*.[59] Although plainly aware of the errors (*Ep.* 325b5-d1) and excesses of democracy (*Ep.* 354d1-e3), Plato's treatment of democracy even in these passages is remarkably balanced: the restored democracy that killed Socrates behaved decently to its enemies (*Ep.* 325b1-5) while the worst result of the excess of freedom is the rise of tyranny (*Ep.* 354e3-5). Although implicitly criticizing several of her famous statesmen (*Ep.* 351a5-c1), Plato twice defends the reputation of Athens (*Ep.* 334b1-4 and 336d6-7) and his nostalgic remark about the Thirty Tyrants is noteworthy: "these men in a short time proved [ἀποδείξαντας] the earlier constitution [πολιτείαν] gold."[60] The word πολιτεία appears repeatedly in Plato's *Letters* and despite the Tübingen School's heavy reliance on the Seventh, it is remarkable how much politics its adherents must ignore in order to valorize it.

Having correctly identified the "philosophical digression" of the Seventh Letter as one of the most important texts in Plato's writings, the proponents of "the unwritten doctrines" cannot explain why this crucial passage is found in a letter describing Plato's political activity in Syracuse.[61] But by reading Plato's *Letters* as a literary whole constructed for a pedagogical purpose and locating it between *Republic* V and VI in the Reading Order of Plato's Dialogues, I have accounted for this fact. By way of summary, the principal justification for locating the *Letters* after Book V that is that its subject matter is repeatedly framed in the context of, and made intelligible by, the Third Wave of Paradox. And the principal justification for considering the *Letters* as Plato's deliberate construction is that the most important passage in the *Letters* is located in the center of a text that Plato has placed in the center of his *Republic* and without which his masterpiece has no center. More importantly, the most important text in the central Seventh Letter illuminates the easily overlooked Firesticks, without which the only justice in Plato's *Republic* is found along the Shorter Way. Just as

59. The Eighth Letter recalls or anticipates the Athenian Stranger—and tends to valorize him—at *Ep.* 354e5-355a1 and generally by Plato's use of the dead Dion as mouthpiece (*Ep.* 355a8-357d2). For anticipation of *Laws* in *Republic*, consider 425d3-c4.

60. *Ep.* 324d7-8 (translation mine); cf. Strauss, *What Is Political Philosophy*, 55: "He [sc. Nietzsche] thus prepared a regime [sc. The Third Reich] which as long as it lasted, made discredited democracy look again like a golden age."

61. See Reale, *New Interpretation*, 450; the only letter he cites is the Seventh and those citations are confined to *Ep.* 340b4-345b7.

Plato's *Republic* cannot be understood without the Firesticks, the significance of the Firesticks cannot be fully grasped without the Seventh Letter. But once having used the Firesticks to cause the Idea of Justice to shine forth, the reader will realize in a flash—and never thereafter forget— that Plato's "Unwritten Doctrine" was written in the λόγος that begins κατέβην.

As was the case with Socrates' statement that the Good is "beyond being" in the *Republic*, Plato's claims about writing in the Seventh Letter should not constitute the textual basis of one's conception of Platonism but rather one's interpretation of these deliberately enigmatic passages (cf. *Ep.* 332d6-e1) should follow from and serve to confirm a coherent conception of Platonism. Primarily but not exclusively on the basis of the Firesticks, I have argued that Justice is "the unwritten doctrine" of the Seventh Letter toward which the *Letters* as a whole repeatedly point the reader. In the Seventh (*Ep.* 332c7-d2), book-ended by the Third (*Ep.* 319c1-2) and Eleventh (*Ep.* 359b1-3), Plato makes it evident that philosophical education must precede political action; the ethical presuppositions of this self-evident proposition will be obvious to any philosopher who, having beheld the transcendent Idea of the Good, has chosen to return to the dangerous Cave of political action.[62] Finally, this interpretation can be used to clear up two problematic passages in the *Letters*: it is not Plato but Dionysius who has framed his philosophy around "protology" and it is not Plato but the Idea of the Good that Dionysius has dishonored by making it at most (cf. *Ep.* 312d7) one of τά περὶ φύσεως ἄκρα καὶ πρῶτα instead of having honored it as "the guide and lord of these things" (*Ep.* 345c1-2; cf. *Ep.* 323d3 and 312e1-3). And when Plato allows that a serious man's most serious thoughts "are lying somewhere in the most beautiful place [ἐν χώρᾳ τῇ καλλίστῃ] among his things" (*Ep.* 344c7-8; cf. 516b6), he is referring to the sun-lit realm outside of the Cave, illuminated by the transcendent Good.

As is also the case with the strictures against writing in the lovely *Phaedrus*, we are in far too great a hurry to doubt that the *Republic* contains—albeit in a wondrous new and dialectical sense of "containment"—Plato's account of what he called "the subjects which I seriously study" (*Ep.* 341c1-2). What is true of Shakespeare's Berowne ("How well he's read to reason against reading") is certainly true mutatis mutandis of Plato: "How perfectly has he written against writing." Between Socrates' speech against rhetoric in the *Gorgias*[63] and the attack on writing we can still read in the *Phaedrus*,[64] stands the immortal *Repub-*

62. See Frank, "Wages of War," 461: "That the *Republic* does its philosophizing from 'the cave' argues against those who use Books VI-VII to separate politics and philosophy, to make politics safe for philosophy, or to subordinate politics to philosophy."

63. See David L. Roochnik, "Socrates' Rhetorical Attack on Rhetoric" in Francisco J. Gonzalez (ed.), *The Third Way: New Directions in Platonic Studies*, 81-94 (Lanham MD: Rowman & Littlefield, 1995). The discovery of this deliberate paradox was made by Cicero: see *de Oratore* 1.47.

64. Charles L. Griswold Jr., "Irony in the Platonic Dialogues." *Philosophy and Literature* 26 no. 1 (April 2002), 84-106 at 95: "In writing these criticisms of writing, Plato

lic (see Preface, figure 1). Could there be any subject more important than the one addressed there? Following Socrates, Plato considered no subject more serious than "the right conduct of life" (344e1-2) and he was right to do so. Unfortunately, most of us may be more comfortable with a Plato who practiced politics to no effect in Syracuse—and who returned to the Academy in order to discuss with aging academicians a cosmological protology far too sublime to be written down—than with a battle-tested teacher who demands, much like our own Uncle Sam, that we abandon our selfishness, altruistically embrace suffering injustice in preference to doing it, and voluntarily return to the Cave in order to arrest the slide of our own beleaguered republic into tyranny.[65]

Section 25. Untimely Meditations on the Idea of Justice

Verity Harte proved worthy of her name by clearly stating an oft-neglected truth: "I suspect that few Plato scholars are card-carrying believers in the Forms."[66] As one of these few, I would suggest that "the Forms" are misunderstood because one imagines too many of them: the greater the number of Platonic Ideas, the easier it becomes to refute "Platonism." It is an error to conceive of Forms as intelligible images of physical objects as if each class of material thing was, simply by being a class, ipso facto entitled to its own "Form." An indefinite plurality of Forms makes it less and less clear that it is visible Becoming that imitates intelligible Being as opposed to Aristotle's view that Plato's spurious intelligibles needlessly duplicate the actual world.[67] At the opposite

creates a tension between the surface meaning of the text (what is said in the text) and the form of the text itself (and by extension all of Plato's dialogues). In so doing Plato as it were silently points to his own position about writing, a position partly at odds with that which he puts in Socrates' mouth. That is, by the deed of writing, Plato denies that Socrates' criticisms of writing are decisive. By writing dialogues, he partially accepts those criticisms."

65. It is worth noting that Plutarch's decision to pair Dion with Brutus suggests, given the roles Plato and Cicero played in educating them, that he shared Quintilian's judgment that Cicero was *Platonis aemulus* (see Introduction) and that opposition to tyranny was an important part of the Platonic lesson plan. See Hermann Strasburger, *Ciceros philosophische Spätwerk als Auruf gegen die Herrschaft Caesars* (Hildesheim: Georg Olms, 1990). John Dillon, "Dion and Brutus: Philosopher Kings Adrift in a Hostile World" in Noreen Humble (ed.), *Plutarch's Lives: Parallelism and Purpose,* 87-102 (Swansea, UK: Classical Press of Wales, 2010) never mentions the books Cicero dedicated to Brutus analyzed by Strasburger and is probably too quick to assume that the man who paired Demosthenes with Cicero and Dion with Brutus (but not Alexander with Augustus or Philip of Macedon with Julius Caesar) actually regards the Roman Empire as "the end of history" (89).

66. Verity Harte, "Review of P. Pritchard, *Plato's Philosophy of Mathematics.*" *Journal of Hellenic Studies* 118 (1998), 227.

67. *Metaphysics* 990b2-4; cf. G. E. L. Owen, "A Proof in ΠΕΡΙ ΙΔΕΩΝ." *Journal of Hellenic Studies* 77 part 1 (1957), 103-111 at 108-10 and R. E. Allen, "Participation and Predication in Plato's Middle Dialogues." *Philosophical Review* 69 no. 2 (April 1960),

extreme from a "second world" of Forms, a single transcendent Good is more difficult to refute; few would claim, for example, that belief in the monotheistic God of Judeo-Christian-Muslim revelation has been or even can be *refuted.*

Despite the speciously "God"-made "Bed" of *Republic* X (see section §18), what makes Plato a Platonist is that in *Republic* V-VII, his Socrates asserts the real and eternal existence of what he calls "Being"; i.e., he makes the claim that whatever "is what it is" is not of this visible world. As if this weren't unacceptable enough to those for whom every true proposition must "make sense," he also makes the rather more provocative claim that our world of Becoming, radically distinct from Being, cannot be said to truly exist.[68] In other words, the absolute division, χωρισμός, or *Kluft* between the visible world of Becoming and the realm of Being over which the Idea of the Good presides is the basis of Platonic ontology: the *Kluft* is the primordial "crisis" in Plato's thought and hence it is precisely "the separation of the Forms" that Aristotle rejects.[69] Conceived in section §5 as a two-dimensional plane or plateau, "Plato" is synonymous with this metaphysical *Kluft* and I agree with Aristotle that it is this χωρισμός that makes Plato a Platonist. To say that Plato is a dualist actually gives the physical world too much credit: there are "two worlds" in Platonism only to the extent that his readers cling, as they always have and will continue to cling, to the reality of what we call "the real world." But in Plato's world—an inverted world that Nietzsche was still Platonic enough to hate Plato for "inventing"—our visible world of Becoming is merely lent a specious existence by comparison with Being, i.e., with that alone which truly is and alone must necessarily be.

Considered as either an indefinite plurality or the collective sum of all things, Becoming cannot be described without the primordial assumption of mathematics and the same holds true of the unique or central Idea of the Good. Along with conceiving of the *Kluft* as a two-dimensional Platonic plateau dividing a three-dimensional metaphysical space, any rational account of Being, Becoming, and the distinction between them, necessarily presupposes the merely hypothetical monad of mathematics and its arithmetical and geometrical avatars like "two," "three," "plane," and "solid." It is this logical dependence

---

147-164 at 156-7 and 164: "The fundamental difficulty underlying the Third Man is ontological, not linguistic. Not only the regress arguments but all the objections to participation in the *Parmenides* posit an identity of character between Forms and particulars; the Many and the One are to be unified. These arguments demonstrate conclusively that this supposition is absurd." A beautiful use of Aristotle in defense of Platonism can be found at 162-63n24.

68. Gregory Vlastos, "Degrees of Reality in Plato" in Renford Bambrough (ed.), *New Essays on Plato and Aristotle*, 1-19 (London: Routledge & Kegan Paul, 1965) seeks to exculpate Plato from this embarrassing view.

69. *Metaphysics* 1086b5-12; cf. Christopher Shields, "Plato and Aristotle in the Academy" in Gail Fine (ed.), *Oxford Handbook to Plato*, 504-525 (Oxford: Oxford University Press, 2008), 507 (#5) and 523: "Indeed, although Aristotle's writings contain many important and perfectly appropriate criticisms of Plato's theory of Forms, no one of them needs to be accepted by a Platonist as unanswerable."

that confirms Aristotle's claim that Plato located the objects of mathematics in an intermediate position between Ideas and sensibles.[70] But Aristotle was wrong in thinking that it is the fact that there is an infinite plurality of identical mathematical objects that distinguish them from the necessarily unique Ideas of Plato in which he, of course, did not believe. I am claiming that mathematical intermediates are not Ideas for the same reason that Socrates' "Bed" and Aristotle's "Man" are not Ideas while, on the other hand, the Idea of the Good undoubtedly is. The first step toward taking "the Forms" seriously is recognizing that Plato's Ideas are not intelligible imitations of sensible things. Although it may well be humanity's native intuition of a higher reality that makes our capacity for mathematical or linguistic abstraction possible (*Phdr.* 249b6-c1), those mathematical or linguistic objects are no more the basis of that higher reality than is our capacity for abstraction the origin of our capacity to intuit it. It is only the unhypothetical Good that actually exists, not the physical world nor we who inhabit it. Holding fast to this paradoxical truth, Plato the Teacher discovered that the best available route to the Good (and its offspring) moves from the Second to the First Part of the Divided Line by first using and only then transcending the abstractions—mathematical or otherwise—that both bestow a rational structure on the strictly hypothetical "world" of Becoming at the same time that they demarcate its relation to Being. In his *Republic*, it is for the sake of Justice that Plato uses the Divided Line to explain both the usefulness and inadequacy of the intelligible objects that stand between Ideas and the sensible world.

In the all-important case of Justice, a Platonic Idea comes to light in complete accordance—this distinguishes it from both the objects of mathematics and, e.g., "the intelligible world" *qua* paradigm in *Timaeus*—with the *Kluft*-based method ("making no use whatever of any object of sense" at 511c1) peculiar to the highest part of the Divided Line. The Idea of Justice depends for its existence only on the Good, to which it is the paradigm of the philosopher's Just response. And Justice is not alone in being closely connected to the Good: primary from a pedagogical perspective, it is the Idea of Beauty that not only makes an early appearance in *Symposium* but constitutes the basis for the definition of philosophy in *Republic* V. Immediately after the introduction of the Idea of the Good in Book VI (505a2), the Good and Beautiful are linked (505b3). At 505d5, good things are contrasted with things that are beautiful and just but this

70. *Metaphysics* 987b14-18; cf. the forceful statement in Burnyeat, "Why Mathematics is Good," 34-35 and 42: "That is the main result of the Divided Line passage: the introduction of a new intermediate epistemic state, which turns out to have an intermediate degree of clarity when it is compared with the ordinary person's opinion about sensibles, and on the other side with the dialectician's understanding of Forms. Socrates can then correlate this intermediate degree of cognitive clarity with the intermediate degree of truth or reality which belongs to the non-sensible objects that mathematicians talk about (511de). Its intermediate placing in the larger epistemological and ontological scheme of the *Republic* will enable it to play a pivotal, and highly positive, role in the education of the future rules."

pair, still linked, is quickly rehabilitated in connection with what makes good things good at 506a4-5. This process culminates in Socrates' reply to Glaucon—temporary spokesman for the Guardians in Book VII—when he refers to the philosopher's "having seen the truth about beautiful, just, and good things" (520c5; translation mine). Having been introduced in *Gorgias* (*Grg.* 459d1-2 and 461b6), this "Platonic trinity" of the Good, the Just, and the Beautiful will reappear three more places in the *corpus*: in the Seventh Letter (*Ep.* 342d4-5), *Parmenides* (*Prm.* 130b7-8) and *Phaedo* (*Phd.* 65d4-7).[71] Having asserted the primacy of the Idea of the Good in the central books of the *Republic*, Plato privileges the Just and the Beautiful by linking them to it repeatedly there (451a6-7, 484d1, 520c5, and 538d7-e4). In contrast with a "Theory of Forms" in which next to no one believes, these three Platonic Ideas deserve serious attention.

Marked by Burnyeat's Question (section §1), the literary apparition of the Idea of Justice in the *Republic* is remarkably subtle and its complexity prepares the reader to meet the further hermeneutic challenges that lie ahead. The Firesticks passage sets an enormously important literary precedent: Plato has revealed that a single Key Passage (434e3-435a3) unlocks his vast but secret treasury. Armed with that precious key, the reader is emboldened to suspect, reject, and finally to reverse the text's surface teaching about justice: Justice is exactly the opposite of "one man doing the one job for which he is by nature suited." Plato's technique can usefully be compared to Beethoven's: a remarkably complex structure can be pressed into the service of a single chord; perfect peace and enlightenment are only revealed amidst environing darkness and despair while the most perfect harmony is predicated on deliberate discord. Beethoven's contemporary Hegel is another analogue: the implicit promise of κατέβην can be fulfilled by the καταβατέον only because of the dialectical antithesis implicit in the mediating Firesticks. Paired with the equally proleptic introduction of the Longer Way, Plato's Firesticks therefore both predict and constitute the moment of extreme negativity through which the conflict between surface meaning and secret teaching will be resolved or ignited into a moment of synthetic epiphany.

The decisive importance of the Firesticks is confirmed by means of the very same dialectical antithesis that it describes. As shown in section §24, Plato uses the imagery of the Firesticks in the Seventh Letter (*Ep.* 341c4-d2) to explain why there will never be a composition (σύγγραμμα) "about those things that I take seriously" (*Ep.* 341c1-2). By employing the same imagery in the *Republic* itself, Plato reveals that his *Republic* actually is the apparently nonexistent σύγγραμμα.[72] Of course it will not appear to be so: the long-overlooked Fire-

71. On *Phaedo* 65d4-e5, see Verity Harte, "Plato's Metaphysics" in Gail Fine (ed.), *Oxford Handbook to Plato*, 191-216 (Oxford: Oxford University Press, 2008), 197: "Here, we have a list of examples of Forms: Just, Beautiful, Good, Largeness, Health, and Strength. This list, in itself, is a rather odd assortment of items, including values, a size property, and physical characteristics. It is completed by a generalization—'all the rest'—whose scope is utterly opaque."

72. Cf. Guthrie, *History of Greek Philosophy* V, 410-11.

sticks can be safely ignored for the sake of the text's surface while the Seventh Letter can either be taken literally or rejected as inauthentic. But the reader who takes the Firesticks seriously will ipso facto know how to use them in connection with the similar passage in the Seventh Letter while the reader who attends to the Seventh Letter will quickly grasp that it is by examining Man and City side by side and rubbing them together that Justice would shine forth (435a1). By doing so, the dialectical reader will not only recognize that *Republic* already is the σύγγραμμα that Plato claims he would never write but also that it has brought to light those matters that Plato evidently takes most seriously. And it is the implications of this second recognition that are so far-reaching: thanks to the Firesticks, the Idea of Justice now joins the Good and Diotima's Beauty at the dead center of Platonic philosophy, the primary concern of which is the right conduct of life (336e3-9, 344e1-3, and 352d5-6). This concern explains why Plato would place *Euthyphro*, *Apology of Socrates*, *Crito*, and *Phaedo* after *Republic*: the trial and death of Socrates is not only the culmination of a vivid and dramatic story but also a visible instantiation of the Idea of Justice. It is no accident that aside from the Firesticks passage, the best evidence for the Idea of Justice in Plato's *Republic* is the proleptic reference in the Allegory of the Cave to the philosopher's "being compelled in courtrooms" (517d7-8) to contend "about the shadows of the just" (517d8-9), the passage to which Burnyeat's Question refers.

Although Socrates justly claims priority for the Idea of the Good in Plato's *Republic*, it is not clear that this priority makes it greater than either Beauty or Justice in degree: surely it is no more just than Justice nor more beautiful than Beauty. Nor would it be good, right, or beautiful to say that Beauty and Justice are completely distinct from the Good or that the Good would continue to be what it is if it were not both just (cf. 491c1-4) and beautiful. In other words, there is some reason to think that the "Platonic Trinity" transcends the assumptions of mathematics in much the same way its Christian analogue does: its "three" is compatible with its "one" and vice versa (cf. 588d5). Diotima's Beauty is the first of the Ideas to which the reader is introduced: it is our principal reminder of Being, i.e., of what truly and eternally is what it is. The Idea of Beauty draws the soul, even while complicated by the downward drifting of the body, away from the world of Becoming and upwards toward what truly and eternally is. Without being less or lower than uplifting Beauty, the Idea of Justice then sends the soaring soul back down into the Cave.[73] Both ascent and descent instantiate or participate in the Good. By being the condition for the possibility of Justice, the Beauty that summons us upward is just while it would be difficult to point to anything more beautiful than Justice; both Ideas are con-

---

73. For a valuable discussion of eights points of comparison between *Symposium* and *Republic*, see Moors, "Argument Against a Dramatic Date," including 14-15: "(2) the *Republic* begins with a descent (κατεβήν) into Piraeus, while the *Symposium* begins with an ascent (ἀνιὼν) from Phalerum (located a few miles due east of Piraeus, Phalerus was also connected to Athens by the "Long Walls");"

summately good. And a strange interchange occurs with respect to "one" and "three" as the philosopher orients herself toward Being: on the way up, one's soul appears to be three while unity appears to abide on the other side of the *Kluft* with the unitary Good. On the way back down, by contrast, the philosopher's soul is simplified by its love of wisdom (611d8) while the Good has joined with Justice and Beauty.

Platonism's history is a long one and the concerns of modern Plato scholars will probably seem just as out of date in the future as those of Christian Platonists who found evidence of Plato's pre-discovery of the Holy Trinity in the Second Letter,[74] do today. In defense of these untimely meditations, it is particularly inappropriate for Plato scholars to ignore the powerful influence of their own time's prejudices. Ours is an historical age but we have learned nothing from history unless we recognize ourselves as nothing more than the latest chapter in the long and multi-faceted history of Plato scholarship Alas, it is not so easy: the self-evident claim that "Plato doesn't change even if the concerns of Plato scholars do" is in practice belied by the fate of the Second Letter, without which the speculations of Ficino on the adumbration of the Trinity in Plato would have been impossible.[75] But even though it is a matter of fact that Christians like Ficino accomplished the revival of Plato studies during the Renaissance and that, far earlier, Platonists had laid the foundations of Christian theology, it is interesting that discussion of the philosopher's return to the Cave in Plato's *Republic* is entirely absent from the historical records of this long and fruitful intersection.

And this absence is remarkable, considerably more remarkable than the almost complete absence of any reference to Glaucon's vivid description in *Republic* II of the perfectly Just Man (who appears to be perfectly unjust) in the voluminous literature devoted to the Guardian's happiness with respect to the Return surveyed in section §19.[76] Despite the fact that the fate of Glaucon's just man is what any philosopher who returns to the Cave can expect, modern scholars have not considered whether Plato proves or even attempts to prove that such a man is happy while being misunderstood, tortured, and killed even though this is exactly what his Socrates is being challenged to do. This can be easily explained: despite Paul Shorey's willingness to use the word "crucified" in trans-

---

74. *Ep.* 312e1-4 (Post): "It is in relation to the king of all and on his account that everything exists, and that fact is the cause of all that is beautiful. In relation to a second, the second class of things exists, and in relation to a third, the third class." I take this passage to refer to Being (with the Idea of the Good being "king of all" and therefore "beyond Being"), the mathematical Intermediates (in relation to the monad), and the indefinite plurality which characterizes the sensible world of Becoming.

75. See Michael J. B. Allen, "Marsilio Ficino on Plato, the Neoplatonists and the Christian Doctrine of the Trinity." *Renaissance Quarterly* 37 no. 4 (Winter 1984), 555-584.

76. The exception, not surprisingly, is Sachs, "A Fallacy in Plato's *Republic*," 149 although, as noted above, he cannot bring himself to quote Shorey accurately, choosing instead "impaled."

lating this important passage,[77] Plato is no longer being considered in a Christian context.[78] But if, as all of us can admit today, it is possible for Judeo-Christian prejudice to have blinded Renaissance Platonists about Plato's intentions, it is equally possible for us to be misled about those intentions by our own anti-theological prejudices. If we are willing to admit that Plato met Glaucon's Challenge in *Republic*, that Socrates did so in *Phaedo*, and that Cicero met it by offering his neck to the assassins dispatched by the Triumvirate (Plutarch *Life of Cicero* 48.3; cf. *Tusculan Disputations* 2.41), what legitimate cause do we have for ignoring that Jesus met it as well? Whether as philosopher or as the incarnated Son of God, Jesus Christ unquestionably descended into a perfectly recognizable Cave and paradigmatically suffered Glaucon's canonical consequences for doing so.[79] It is therefore far less remarkable that a modern agnostic or atheist would ignore the Judeo-Christian aspect of the return to the Cave than that the early Platonic Christians failed to mention it.[80]

I suggest that the early Christian Platonists did not dare to do so.[81] To begin with, "the opponents of Christianity forced the Church Fathers to answer charges that a number of Christian tenets were borrowed from Greek philosophers, especially Socrates and Plato."[82] It would therefore give comfort to the enemy to suggest any anticipation of the crucifixion of Jesus in Plato. Justin

77. 361e4-362a1; see William Christian, "Waiting for Grace: Philosophy and Politics in Plato's *Republic*." *Canadian Journal of Political Science / Revue canadienne de science politique* 21 no. 1 (March 1988), 57-82 at 61n12: "This is of course the passage which many subsequent writers have seen as prefiguring Christ's crucifixion. The word strictly means 'impaled' but the word itself, *anaskinduleuthesetai*, is obscure and one of its synonyms was used in the New Testament to describe Christ's fate." Cf. Paul W. Gooch, "Socrates: Devious or Divine?" *Greece & Rome* (2nd series) 32 no. 1 (April 1985), 32-41 at 34-35.

78. Cf. E. K. Rand, *The Founders of the Middle Ages* (Cambridge MA: Harvard University Press, 1928), 65: "If we call Plato and Cicero the first Christian humanists, we should not be altogether wrong. The paradox of Christian humanism was present in their natures, which were large enough to solve it."

79. Cf. Adam, *Republic of Plato*, 2.94-95 on 517a4-5 (καὶ τὸν ἐπιχειροῦντα κτλ.): "a manifest and touching allusion to the death of Socrates, whose fate was the most conspicuous example in Greek history of the principle here laid down. [some citations follow]. Read in the light of another and even more momentous sacrifice, the sentence assumes a kind of prophetical import, like the famous passage about the λόγος θεῖος in the *Phaedo* (85 C, D)."

80. The same is naturally true of the secondary literature; e.g. C. J. De Vogel, "Platonism and Christianity: A Mere Antagonism or a Profound Common Ground?" *Vigiliae Christianae* 39 no. 1 (March 1985), 1-62, a thorough study devoted to the "profound common ground" between Platonism and Christianity, does not mention the Cave.

81. Cf. Allen, "Marsilio Ficino on Plato," 582-83.

82. See Paul Ciholas, "Plato: The Attic Moses? Some Patristic Reactions to Platonic Philosophy." *Classical World* 72 no. 4 (December 1978-January 1979), 217-225 at 217.

Martyr is bold to suggest that Christ was "partially known" by Socrates;[83] he more safely turns the tables on Christianity's critics by proving Plato's dependence on the Old Testament.[84] This became a popular dodge. But in the context of Tertullian's famous challenge[85]—and even of Clement's humane alternative[86]—one begins to sense that it was other Christians, not pagans, who ensured that no Christian Platonist could assert or even discuss Plato's possible influence on Christ.[87] Ambrose wrote a book on this subject but it is lost.[88] Augustine is the most revealing case: in his *Against the Academicians*—in the context of an extended discussion of how the New Academy adopted a merely exoteric skepticism while secretly remaining otherworldly Platonists[89]—he writes the following enigmatic sentence immediately after suggesting that the "one system of really true philosophy" is a synthesis of Plato and Aristotle:[90]

> This philosophy is not of this world—the philosophy that our Holy Writ rightly abhors—but of the other world, the intelligible world. Yet the most subtle chain of reasoning would never call back to this intelligible world souls that had been blinded by the manifold shadows of error and rendered forgetful by the deepest filth from the body had not God the Highest, moved by a certain compassion

83. *Second Apology of Justin* 10 in Alexander Roberts and James Donaldson (eds.). *The Ante-Nicene Fathers; Translations of the Writings of the Fathers down to A.D. 325*, reprint of the 1885 edition (Edinburgh: T&T Clark, 1989), vol. 1, 191: "For no one trusted in Socrates so as to die for this doctrine [sc. 'to become acquainted with God who was to them unknown, by means of the investigation of reason'], but in Christ, who was partially known even by Socrates"

84. Ciholas, "Plato: The Attic Moses," 223: "In his *Hortatory Address to the Greeks* he [sc. Justin] endeavors to demonstrate almost *ad nauseam* that Plato structured all his ideas on a pattern which he copied from Mosaic traditions while in Egypt."

85. *De praescriptione haereticorum* 7 (Henenson): "What is there in common between Athens and Jerusalem? What between the Academy and the Church?"

86. *Stromata* 1.5 in Roberts and Donaldson, *Ante-Nicene Fathers*, vol. 2, 305: "Perchance, too, philosophy was given to the Greeks directly and primarily, till the Lord should call the Greeks. For this was a schoolmaster to bring 'the Hellenic mind,' as the law, the Hebrews 'to Christ.'"

87. Ciholas "Plato: The Attic Moses," 225: "To make Plato agree with Christian theology was the only way open to those apologists who could not conceive of a universal monotheism which would not take into account the powerful religious tenets of Platonic philosophy. The idea, however, that Jesus himself might have been instructed by the writings of Plato was categorically denied."

88. Ciholas, "Plato: The Attic Moses," 225n37.

89. Augustine, *Contra Academicos* 3.17.37-41; see Peter King (trans. and ed.), *Augustine,* Against the Academicians *and* The Teacher (Indianapolis, IN: Hackett, 1995), 87-90.

90. Cf. King, *Augustine,* Against the Academicians, 91n182 with *Contra Academicos* 3.18.41.21-3.

for the multitude, humbled and submitted the authority of the Divine Intellect even to the human body itself.[91]

Augustine is claiming that Plato could never have led his students up to the intelligible world—which he knew was not the case,[92] especially because Cicero, whom he recognized as a true lover of Plato,[93] had led him to God[94]—had Christ not gone back down into the Cave.[95] Given that Augustine is openly discussing the strictly exoteric skepticism of earlier Platonists, it is worth wondering whether we are here listening to a sincere Christian's confession of his own strictly exoteric anti-Platonism.

The purpose of these admittedly untimely meditations is not to claim or even suggest that Jesus was a Platonist but rather to prove that Plato, thanks to Socrates and truth, caught sight of the eternal and unchanging Idea of Justice. It is no accident that the last word in *Phaedo* is "most just" (*Phd.* 118a17); Plato leaves his readers in no doubt as to where the son of Ariston first saw Justice temporarily embodied, imitated, or present in some other way (cf. *Phd.* 100d5-8). In *Republic*, Plato distilled the meaning of the life he had watched Socrates live and die into a universally applicable and intelligible image of Justice: the philosopher's voluntary return to the Cave. As befits a teacher, it was Plato's intention that Socrates should not remain unique: having learned from Socrates what Justice was, Plato would now teach us what it was, is, and always will be. It may well then be the case that Plato, as a metaphysician influenced by the

---

91. *Contra Academicos* 3.19.42 in King, *Augustine,* Against the Academicians, 91. The reference to Paul probably explains Augustine's obfuscations: "Watch out lest there will be anyone who takes you captive through philosophy and empty deception in accord with the doctrine of men, in accord with the elements of the cosmos and not Christ." Naturally *Timaeus* justifies applying this verse to Plato far better than *Republic.*

92. Charles Brittain, "Plato and Platonism" in Gail Fine (ed.). *Oxford Handbook to Plato*, 526-552 (Oxford: Oxford University Press, 2008), 538n50 allocates even the cautious *Contra Academicos* to Augustine's "exuberant early Platonist phase."

93. *Contra Academicos* 3.18.41 in King, *Augustine,* Against the Academicians, 90: "After Philo's death, our Cicero buried all Antiochus's remains, for he didn't tolerate anything he loved to be weakened or undermined while he was alive."

94. *Confessions* 3.4.7 as quoted in John Hammond Taylor, "St. Augustine and the *Hortensius* of Cicero." *Studies in Philology* 60 no. 3 (July 1963), 487-498 at 493: "For I did not apply that book [sc. Cicero's lost dialogue *Hortensius*] to the sharpening of my tongue, and it was not its style but rather its matter that moved me. How did I burn, O my God, how did I burn to soar from earth to Thee; and I did not know what thou wouldst do with me."

95. Cf. Charles Norris Cochrane, *Christianity and Classical Culture: A Study of Thought and Action from Augustus to Augustine* (Oxford: Oxford University Press, 1940), 424-25n1: "So his [sc. Augustine's] criticism boils down to this: that, although he had discovered God as *principium nostrum, lumen nostrum, bonum nostrum* ('causa constitutae universitatis et lux percipiendae veritatis et fons bibendae felicitatis'), this God is strictly transcendental. Accordingly, Plato cannot display his [sc. His] immanence while, at the same time, doing justice to the *vitia* of the material world."

great Parmenides, discovered that every thing that really exists is a timeless Idea.[96] But ascending to Being with the goddess was not enough for Plato the Teacher.[97] No less significant than his ethical ontology were the ramifications of his discovery that learning is recollection.[98] He would not be communicating his own discoveries but rather reminding us of what we all know and feel to be true simply because it is true.[99] This is why the life of Jesus becomes an even greater testimonial to Plato's Idea of Justice if there was absolutely no worldly connection between them. The essence of righteousness,[100] intelligibly imaged in the Cave as visibly instantiated or imitated by Socrates, might well be called "Plato's discovery." But that essence had existed from the beginning and will continue to exist forever.[101] A willingness to share what one has with others, to benefit others without regard for whether one will be benefited by them in return, and to sacrifice life itself for the good of one's friends; these are universally recognized by simple people everywhere to be the essence of moral excel-

---

96. A. H. Coxon, *The Fragments of Parmenides; A Critical Text with Introduction, Translation, the Ancient testimonia and a Commentary (*Assen/Maastricht: Van Gorcum, 1986), 27: "it is clear that the 'being' which Socrates attributes to the Forms [sc. in *Parmenides*] is Eleatic in the sense that each is regarded as having all the characters which Parmenides had argued to belong to τὸ ἐόν." See also Guthrie, *History of Greek Philosophy* V, 34.

97. Svetla Slaveva-Griffin, "Of Gods, Philosophers, and Charioteers: Content and Form in Parmenides' Proem and Plato's *Phaedrus*." *Transactions of the American Philological Association* 133 no. 2 (Autumn 2003), 227-253, at 250: "The journey of the charioteer in Parmenides and Plato [sc. in *Phaedrus*] represents a new kind of heroic quest: the quest of the philosopher's mind to separate itself from the popular beliefs of sensible reality and through contemplative introspection, to enter into the realm of metaphysical existence."

98. Cf. Gonzalez, *Dialectic and Dialogue*, 274-75 and Michael Ferejohn, "Knowledge, Recollection, and the Forms in *Republic* VII" in Gerasimos Santas (ed.), *The Blackwell Guide to Plato's* Republic, 214-233 (Malden: Blackwell, 2006), 221-24.

99. Kenneth M. Sayre, "A Maieutic View of Five Late Dialogues" in James C. Klagge and Nicholas D. Smith (eds.), *Methods of Interpreting Plato and his Dialogues*, 221-243 in *Oxford Studies in Ancient Philosophy*; Supplementary Volume, 1992 at 234-35 is a summary of a position that Sayre himself modifies but which comes very close to my own: "If this theory of innate knowledge can be taken literally, then one intelligible account of why Plato wrote dialogues is that he hoped thereby to stimulate in the reader the same effect that might be achieved by direct conversation with Socrates himself." See also J. A. Stewart, Stewart, *Plato's Doctrine of Ideas* (Oxford: Clarendon Press, 1909), 192-97.

100. See John Wild, "Plato and Christianity: A Philosophical Comparison." *Journal of Bible and Religion* 17 no. 1 (January 1949), 3-16 at 6. Robin Waterfield (trans.), *Plato,* Republic (Oxford: Oxford University Press, 1993) translates δικαιοσύνη as "morality."

101. *pace* Sachs, "A Fallacy in Plato's *Republic*," 157: "Partly on this basis [sc. 331c4-5], partly because of similar passages in other dialogues, I believe it is likely that Plato held that there are allowable exceptions to every moral rule, or virtually every moral rule, of conduct." Note that "there is an exception to every rule" is a self-contradiction.

lence.[102] This willingness, imaged in the parable of the Cave, is activity in accordance with the Idea of Justice.

If it was safer for Christian Platonists to link Socrates with Moses rather than Jesus, they neglected the most crucial connection between them. Having killed a man in Egypt (*Ex.* 2:12), Moses has fled (*Ex.* 2:15) from "the house of bondage" (*Ex.* 20:2) and finds himself shoeless (*Ex.* 3:5; cf. *Symposium* 220b6) upon a mountain in conversation with the only Being that can say "I am that I am" (*Ex.* 3:14). On Mount Horeb, a hallowed καταβατέον (*Ex.* 3:8) is enjoined upon Moses (*Ex.* 4:19) and back down into Egypt he therefore goes. Those to whom he repeatedly descends (*Ex.* 19:20-21) prefer a visible image of a false God to the lively Word of the unseen Lord (*Ex.* 32:1-7). He dares death (*Ex.* 4:18-9), accepts suffering (*Ex.* 32:32), and willingly embraces being misunderstood (*Ex.* 4:1) by those whose freedom and salvation he selflessly ensures (*Ex.* 32:10-12). Did Plato derive "Going Back Down into the Cave" from Moses? Is there some unrecorded moment of transition, in fecund Egypt perhaps, where Plato learned the lesson of the Mosaic descent from some Greek-speaking Jew? This is no more likely and no less superfluous than the notion that Jesus was influenced by Greco-Roman Platonism in Alexandria before returning to face crucifixion in Judaea. In both Moses and Jesus, any modern philosopher capable of moving beyond the virulent anti-theological animus that has dominated Western civilization since the First World War need find nothing more than additional external evidence that Plato had seen the Idea of Justice. Justice is not only encoded in the text from its opening word but its manner of transmission presupposes Plato's awareness that it is also written in the souls of his readers, i.e., in the human heart.

And it is. In a vivid and visible image of a Just Man's willing descent into the Cave, Plato created an adumbration of the timeless, unchanging, and universal Idea of Justice. Confirmed by obvious examples in the Judeo-Christian West, its clearest instantiations in the East are Arjuna's return to battle in the *Bhaghavad Gita* and Buddhism's Bodhisattva. Shall we therefore hunt for some historical connection that would derive Plato from the Buddha or Mahayana Buddhism from the *Republic*? The sage who foregoes Enlightenment, who returns to the agonizing cycle of rebirth willingly, who once again takes on the illusions of Maya when Nirvana is in reach is the instantiation of all that is just, beautiful, and good in human action. There have been Platonists in the East and Boddhisattvas in the West: the Idea of Justice knows no nation.

---

102. *pace* M. F. Burnyeat, "Platonism and Mathematics. A Prelude to Discussion" in Andreas Graeser (ed.), *Mathematics and Metaphysics in Aristotle/Mathematik und Metaphysik bei Aristoteles*. Akten des X. Symposium Aristotelicum (Bern and Stuttgart: Paul Haupt, 1984), at 233: "The *Republic* is first and foremost a work of political persuasion, and one of the tasks of persuasion which Socrates (Plato) undertakes to get Glaucon (the reader) to accept that the most important kind of knowledge is out of his reach. True ethical insight presupposes an intense mathematical training, which he (the reader) has not had." Note that Burnyeat is "breaking the frame."

Nor does it know any gender. The primary instantiation of Justice is our mother, condition for the possibility of that amazing animal we call "man." In inventing our current image of human nature, our teachers have operated on the ridiculous principle that the egg came before the chicken: what else can it mean for them to have repeated *ad nauseam* that human nature is fundamentally selfish? Children lisp the oft-repeated lesson that man is an animal but who will remind us that man is also a mammal, a being made possible and defined by the mammalian mother's generous application of her breast to the greedy lips of the only temporarily self-centered newborn *homo sapiens*? The generously generative mammalian mother, from whose belly we emerge and in the light of whose love we are nourished, undertakes countless sufferings in order that as "students of human nature" we may ignore her, see ourselves as selfish by nature, and teach our children that everyone else is too. Her willingness to give us birth, to send her sensitive and generous consciousness back down into the Cave from whence we emerge at the cost of her agony, is mankind's primordial and natural righteousness. To put it another way: when the conception to which an ambitious and capable young man gives birth is altruism, the pedagogy that accomplishes this sublime result is maieutic par excellence (cf. *Tht.* 150b7-8): there is no nobler offspring than a passion for Justice. And even Platonists who never ask why it is true know from experience that it is easier to teach women the Allegory of the Cave.[103]

The movie theater has likewise made teaching the Cave easier and we have certainly been exposed thereby to "the shadows of justice." But the subject of *It's a Wonderful Life*, arguably America's best-loved film, is the Idea of Justice and this is one more piece of evidence that Plato was right about the essence of righteousness. No one can think that the one job for which George Bailey is by nature suited is running the Building & Loan. Despite the fact that he so clearly yearns "to kick the dust of this measly little town off my feet," George returns to the Cave of Bedford Falls when his father's death leaves no alternative to the tyrannical Potter, when he gives up his honeymoon to save the Building & Loan from the panic-stricken doubters, and when he prays at the bridge: "Dear God, let me live again!" At that moment, George doesn't realize that he's not going to be arrested and sent to prison; he isn't thinking of Sam Wainwright and his brother Harry any more than about his own comfort: "I don't care what happens to me." He simply can't stand the idea of leaving Mary in the otherwise empty world his altruism has spared her, a world where Tommy, Susie, Janie, Pete, and

---

103. Cf. Anne-Marie Bowery, "Plato's Theory of Forms" in William A. Welton (ed). *Plato's Forms; Varieties of Interpretation*, 111-136 (Lanham, MD: Lexington Books, 2002) at 125: "From the beginning, I was taught to see Plato the dramatist and through those masterful eyes, I saw philosophy as that beautiful soul-infused practice which asks the largest questions in aesthetically compelling ways. It was the drama of Plato that captured me, not the nuances of the Third Man Argument or the paradoxes of universal and particular, or the one and the many. It was the pathos, the drama, the aesthetic nuance of Plato's philosophy that grabbed my soul and has never let go."

Zuzu don't even exist. The democratic hero—"playing nursemaid to a lot of garlic eaters," as the erstwhile oligarch Potter puts it—proves to be the last ditch against what would have otherwise become a tyrannical Pottersville, just as in *Republic* VIII. And the angel Clarence who descends from heaven to save George is Capra's Socrates, apparently simple but in fact every bit as clever as the job that he must perform requires him to be.

There have been so many famous instances of Justice that one might well think that Plato could have arrived—if he were alive today and thought as we do—at the Idea of Justice through mere induction: given men like Moses, Socrates, Jesus, Gandhi, and Martin Luther King Jr., all he would have needed to do was distill their ethical essence, the common maxim of their actions, and reify it into the universal image of a generalization, like the philosopher's voluntary return to the Cave. If something similar actually happened in Plato's case,[104] it was certainly Socrates who provided the essential empirical basis from which the Cave or the Idea of Justice could then be abstracted. Unlike the mathematician, however, the dialectician proceeds back down from the un-hypothetical while deriving or deducing all other Ideas from it. So even if those Ideas—beginning with Justice—are necessarily imitated or even instantiated by human beings on the south side of the *Kluft* and thereby can furnish latter-day empiricists with observable instances of their existence *in fact* (and therefore of the existence of something like the Idea of Justice in theory), in Plato's world, they necessarily exist on the north side of the plateau and must be deduced from the Good rather than generalized by induction from particulars.

It is this difference in direction that divides the First from the Second Part of the Divided Line: like Beauty, mathematics pulls the soul upwards while Justice does exactly the reverse. And it is because the other Ideas are derived from the Good by proceeding downwards from it (section §17) that Justice is at once the offspring of the Good and the matrix of other Ideas. In other words, the Idea of Justice is not simply a thing to be imitated by human beings as, e.g., the essence of ethical excellence but rather as a metaphysical principle constitutive of the creative agency of the Good.[105] It is certainly not difficult to see how Courage, Wisdom, and Temperance might be derived from the Good through the mediation of Justice.

Operating in accordance with the First Part of the Divided Line, such a procedure—"making no use whatever of any object of sense but only of pure ideas moving on through ideas to ideas and ending with ideas" (511c1-2)—might be called "a transcendental deduction of the virtues."[106] Since any Idea other than

104. Mark Gifford, "Aristotle on Platonic Recollection and the Paradox of knowing Universals: Prior Analytics B.21 67a8-30." *Phronesis* 44 no. 1 (February 1999), 1-29 at 22-24.

105. Miller, "Platonic Provocations," 190-91 and Parry, *Plato's Craft of Justice.*

106. Cf. Gerasimos Santas, "The Form of the Good in Plato's *Republic*" in John P. Anton and Anthony Preus (eds.), *Essays in Ancient Greek Philosophy* Vol. 2, 232-263 (Albany: State University of New York Press, 1983) at 253-54 where he perceptively

the Idea of the Good requires proceeding downwards from the Good, the Idea of Justice would then be the metaphysical and epistemological prerequisite for the existence and intelligibility of the Ideas of all the other virtues and would also thereby confer upon them a derivation from the Good. As the philosopher's imitation of the Idea of Justice, Justice is therefore the characteristically human instantiation (335c4; cf. 609d4-7) of a divine principle that is at the same time ethical, epistemological, and metaphysical. Having risen to knowledge of the sovereign existence of that alone which is what it is, the philosopher's downward path leads to a dangerous way of life lived south of the *Kluft*. Courage would then be that which a philosopher needs in order to brave Going Back Down into the Cave. Temperance and Wisdom could then be derived from Justice in a similar way. If Courage makes the philosopher willing to sacrifice for others, Temperance might be conceived as a corrective that prevents the philosopher from doing so in a self-destructive or foolish manner. George Rudebusch has found a useful example of enlightened self-interest in an airliner's oxygen mask; in the broader context of Justice and the Good, perhaps this is Temperance.[107] Recognizing the right balance between altruism and prudence for the sake of the Good (*Ep.* 351c6-7) might then be the role of Wisdom although the simple recognition of the Platonic "plateau" may bring us closer to the truth. Naturally these are only suggestions; it is difficult to determine what kinds of Ideas and how many of them Plato might have envisioned the Academy's dialecticians deducing from the Good. But if the Idea of the Good is to be joined to other Ideas in accordance with the method described in the First Part of the Divided Line, the Idea of Justice would constitute the point of intersection between the Platonic Trinity and the Virtues (*Ep.* 342d4-7). The privileged place of Justice in this deduction would explain why Plato embedded the Divided Line in his *Republic*.

Piety, of course, is not one of the four virtues famously considered in *Republic* in accordance with the methods of the Second Part of the Line. There is a good reason for this: there is no room for Piety on the Shorter Way.[108] But for

---

rejects the notion of a Platonic "deduction" of mathematical objects from the Good; see section §13.

107. Rudebusch, "Neutralism in Book I of the *Republic*," 81: "The familiar rule for managing a loss of pressure in an airplane is to put the oxygen mask on oneself before putting masks on those needing assistance. The aim of this self-first rule is to maximize health in general, not to maximize one's own health. One risks failure to safeguard anybody's health if one ignores the health of the body of the expert." On the other hand, consider the simple soul/body temperance of 431a3-b2.

108. But see 383c1-5 (Shorey modified): "'When anyone says that sort of thing about the gods, we shall be wroth with him, we will refuse him a chorus, neither will we allow teachers to use him for the education of the young if our guardians are to be god-fearing men [θεοσεβεῖς] and become god-like [θεῖοι γίγνεσθαι] in so far as that is possible for humanity [καθ᾽ ὅσον ἀνθρώπῳ]." To be θεοσεβεῖς, human beings must know the very limited extent to which they can "become god-like"; piety leads Socrates to add καθ᾽ ὅσον ἀνθρώπῳ (cf. 500d2, 501c2-3, and 613a7-b1). The proverb at 492e5-6 is

the philosopher who travels the Longer Way, there is an austere Platonic beauty that joins Justice to Piety: both are practiced south of the *Kluft* by human beings who know the truth about human things (517d4-5). Having rejected the dictum of Protagoras, Plato's philosophers refuse to locate themselves at the center of things. In this sense, Justice is necessarily pious and Piety is the condition for the possibility of reaching the heights from which alone a philosopher can practice Justice: one cannot leave the Cave without acknowledging in advance that there is something out there.[109] Even for the philosopher who has emerged from the shadows, it is the clear-eyed knowledge of the Good's infinite majesty that makes it easy to recognize that practicing Justice, the distinctively human virtue (335c4), restores humanity to its proper place. Thus when Socrates points Glaucon to a Good "beyond Being," he does so in accordance with the clear-eyed knowledge that is Platonic Piety.

---

applicable while Socrates' defense of Justice is connected to his piety at 368b7-c8 and 427d8-e1, see also 331a4, 458e1-2, 461a4, 463d5, 479a7, and 615b6.

109. See Darrell Dobbs, "The Piety of Thought of Thought in Plato's *Republic*, Book I." *American Political Science Review* 88 no. 3 (September 1994), 668-683 at 674: "The acknowledgment of the dearness of the unknown good, I shall suggest, constitutes genuine piety or reverence."

Chapter Six

Democracy and Education

Section 26. Genetic Fictions

Yet another reason for thinking Plato intended the Seventh Letter to be read in tandem with the *Republic* is that keeping in mind the following passage might have prevented one of *three* common misunderstandings about the well-known Noble Lie of Book III:

> For both must be learnt together; and together also must be learnt, by complete and long continued study, as I said at the beginning, the true and the false about all that has real being. (*Ep.* 344b1-3; translation Harward)

Yes, the true and the false must always be considered together. But it is hardly necessary to have read these words to ask oneself the perfectly obvious but all too infrequently posed question: "What does Socrates regard as true if these 'noble lies' are what all lies must inevitably be: false?" This is a particularly pertinent question because Socrates is perfectly explicit: both nationalism[1] and class distinctions[2] are based on lies. It is therefore with the truth, denied by the Noble Lie, that any adequate account of Plato's relationship to "democracy and

---

1. 414d1-e5 (emphasis mine): "'And yet I hardly know how to find the audacity or the words to speak and undertake to persuade first the rulers themselves and the soldiers and then the rest of the city, that in good sooth all our training and educating of them were things that they imagined and that happened to them as it were in a dream; but that in reality at that time they were down within the earth being molded and fostered themselves while their weapons and the rest of their equipment were being fashioned. And when they were quite finished the earth as being their mother delivered them, and now *as if their land were their mother and their nurse they ought to take thought for her and defend her against any attack and regard the other citizens as their brothers and children of the self-same earth.*'"

2. 415a2-7 (emphases mine): "'*While all of you in the city are brothers,* we will say in our tale, *yet* God in fashioning those of you who are fitted to hold rule mingled gold in their generation, for which reason they are the most precious—but in the helpers silver, and iron and brass in the farmers and other craftsmen.'" Note that they are not only lies but also inconsistent with each other, as the italicized words indicate.

education" must begin. If Socrates had called egalitarianism generally and the equality of the sexes in particular "noble lies," it would be much easier to misunderstand Plato as anti-democratic and use his *Republic* against "the open society." But he didn't.

As another example of the importance of triads in the *Republic*, consider: (1) the fact that there are only two noble lies, (2) the parallels between *them* and the first two waves of paradox, and (3) that these parallels suggest there may be a *third but hidden* noble lie floating about somewhere in the textual shadows. The parallel between the Second Wave of Paradox (i.e., communism) and the first Noble Lie is obvious: "the earth as being their mother delivered them, and now as if their land were their mother and their nurse they ought to take thought for her and defend her against any attack and regard the other citizens as their brothers and children of the self-same earth." In other words: "all of you in the city are brothers." Consider also the following: (a) the entire breeding apparatus upon which the Second Wave of Paradox is based depends on lies, (b) the net result of the Book V communism is expressed in terms of universal brotherhood,[3] and (c) the word we translate as "noble" (γενναίος) is used there three times in its true sense:[4]

> "Tell me this, Glaucon. I see that you have in your house hunting-dogs and a number of pedigree cocks [τῶν γενναίων ὀρνίθων]. Have you ever considered something about their unions and procreations?" "What?" he said. "In the

---

3. 461d5-e1: "'And, similarly, he will call their offspring his grandchildren and they will call his group grandfathers and grandmothers. And all children born in the period in which their fathers and mothers were procreating will regard one another as brothers and sisters'"

4. The word γενναῖος is used twenty times in the *Republic*. These uses fall into the following main groups: (1) "well-bred" at II 375a2, II 375d11, V 459a3, and V 459a6, (2) simply "noble" at II 363a8, III 409c1, IV 440c1, and IV 440d1 (the also the superlative at 409c1), and (3) ironic usages: I 348c12 (applied by Thrasymachus to the just man), VI 488c4 (applied to the Ship-owner), VIII 544c6 (applied to Tyranny), and VIII 558b8 (applied to Democracy's contempt for the rules governing the City). There is another class of intermediary usages, classified according to which of the main groups they fall between: (1/2): VI 494c6 (applied to the tall and handsome "Plato"), VI 496b2 (applied to exiles like Xenophon and Thucydides in the "bridle of Theages" passage), VII 527b8 (applied to Glaucon by Socrates), and VII 535b1 (applied to the tested academicians: see section §29), (2/3): II 361b7 (applied by Glaucon to the just man), II 372b3 (applied to barley-cakes in the City of Pigs), and (1/3): III 414b8 (the Noble Lie). This exhausts nineteen of the twenty uses. The remaining one—in fact the eleventh in order of presentation—is at V 454a1: "What a grand thing [γενναία], Glaucon, said I, is the power of the art of contradiction!" "Why so?" "Because, said I, many appear to me to fall into it even against their wills, and to suppose that they are not wrangling but arguing, owing to their inability *to apply the proper divisions and distinctions to the subject under consideration.* They pursue purely verbal oppositions, practicing eristic, not dialectic on one another" (V 454a1-8; emphasis mine). The dialectical reader must therefore apply distinctions to the use of the word "γενναῖος" in accordance with an art that is itself γενναία.

first place," I said, "among these themselves, although they are a select breed [ὄντων γενναίων], do not some prove [γίγνονται] better than the rest?" "They do." "Do you then breed [γεννᾷς] from all indiscriminately, or are you careful to breed from the best?" (459a1-10)

To begin with, the root of the matter is the stem (γεν-) of the eminently flexible and important verb γίγνεσθαι: "to come into being, to become" translated here, with excessive liberty, as "to prove, by coming into being." It is obviously the basis of important words like "genesis" and "genetic." It is also the basis of Plato's word for Becoming as opposed to Being. Genetics (a modern coinage) might be etymologized as "the science by which things come into being." But that which breeders do (i.e., those among the ancients who originally discovered what we now call "genetics") is something like "to bring animals into being according to scientific principles." They actively produce, engender, and breed. The verb γεννᾶν (obviously the basis of γενναίος) is simply the *causal* form of γίγνεσθαι; hence Glaucon's birds and dogs are "born and bred" (according to scientific principles) to do certain things well.

In short (and this begins to address the *second* misunderstanding) the Noble Lie isn't noble in any honorable or moral sense: combined with the first misunderstanding, then, it is no more *noble* than it is true. It is best understood as "a Genetic Fiction." This is why Socrates calls it "a Phoenician Tale," like the story of Cadmus and the warriors sprung from the giant's teeth cited by Adam. Note also the frequency of words derived from γίγνεσθαι as the Genetic Fiction is first brought into being:

> "How, then," said I, "might we contrive [μηχανὴ γένοιτο] one of those opportune falsehoods [τῶν ψευδῶν τῶν ἐν δέοντι γιγνομένων] of which we were just now speaking, so as by one noble [γενναῖόν] lie to persuade if possible the rulers themselves, but failing that the rest of the city?" "What kind of a fiction do you mean?" said he. "Nothing unprecedented," said I, "but a sort of Phoenician tale, something that has happened [γεγονός] ere now in many parts of the world, as the poets aver and have induced men to believe, but that has not happened [γεγονὸς] and perhaps would not be likely to happen [γενόμενον] in our day and demanding no little persuasion to make it believable." (414b7-c7)

Due to the fact that too few bother to ask themselves what Plato regards as true given that these Lies are false, the defenders of a comprehensive and absolute Platonic elitism are forced into saying that Socrates calls them lies only because the specific details they contain are false. This allows them to claim that he still regards elitism (i.e., the thing that they themselves either treasure or abhor) as being in substance true. And calling these lies "noble" is also highly misleading: I have now given my reasons for preferring "Genetic Fiction." This leaves only the third common misunderstanding. Discussion of it must be delayed because the pivotal role of Hesiod in the *Republic*[5]—the poet who might well be called "Homer's first rival" and is the source of the four metals that form the basis for the second and most anti-democratic of Plato's Genetic Fictions—is so rich a topic that it really deserves its own monograph and will, in any case, be treated in a separate section (§30). But I have also suggested a connection between the three waves of paradox and *three* genetic fictions; one of these has now been supplied. The second—the parallel between the metallic caste system (the second Noble Lie) and the equality of women (the First Wave of Paradox)—will be treated in the following section (§27). That leaves only the third: a Genetic Fiction analogous to the Third Wave of Paradox.

The crux of the Third Wave is the relationship between the philosophy and politics: it is therefore in the Cave that its analogue must be found. More specifically, it is to be found in Socrates' response to Glaucon's defense of the fictional Guardians against whom it would be, as Glaucon claims at the outset, an act of injustice to compel them to go back down into the Cave. As already shown in section §16, the power of the passage depends on the Critical Ambiguity: readers must decide in a moment of crisis to reject the only reading of the passage warranted by the text *qua* text—i.e., that it is only these fictional Guardians who are being addressed—or whether to conceive of Plato as addressing each one of them directly. It is a paradoxical situation: the reader can escape the Plato's point only by insisting that the *fictional* Guardians are something they manifestly are not: *real*. And Plato makes clear that they are not real with what I am calling "the Third Noble Lie" (520b6-7): "But you we have engendered [ἐγεννήσαμεν] for yourselves and the rest of the city to be, as it were, king-bees and leaders in the hive." What Socrates says to the Guardians about having *bred* them to go back down may well be true in the fictional world of the City. But what he says to them is merely a Genetic Fiction when applied to us. Despite Plato's intention to engender readers who will respond to "the crisis of the *Republic*," it is only our own Justice that is the truth and only our own innate humanity that prepares us to both embrace and practice it.

Section 27. The Equality of the Sexes

Considering the fact that his *Republic* contains world's first argument (and for thousands of years the only one) for the proposition that boys and girls should receive the exact same education, one would think that Plato would be treated more like the world-class culture-hero he undoubtedly is. If the equality of the sexes is a basic principle of what most of our contemporaries would call "justice," it is little short of amazing that Aristocles son of Ariston was (1) the first

5. The connection between Democracy and Hesiod's Age of Heroes is derived from Strauss, *City and Man*, 130-32 and Strauss, *Liberalism Ancient and Modern*, 35; although he doesn't draw the proper conclusions from the parallel he discovered, his discovery is itself of capital importance for appreciating Plato's *Republic* and all serious students of Plato are in his debt for it.

to defend it, (2) defended it in a book about justice, and (3) clearly saw that only rulers motivated by Justice would ever engender justice of this kind. Plato is clearly aware that what he is proposing is revolutionary and will be silenced with ridicule even before it is actively opposed: what Socrates will propose is "παρὰ τὸ ἔθος γελοῖα" (V 452a7)—i.e., "present custom would make much in our proposals look ridiculous"—and "would seem ridiculous, at least [γε] as things presently stand" (γελοῖον γὰρ ἄν, ὥς γε ἐν τῷ παρεστῶτι, φανείη; 452b4-5). While Socrates admits that men are physically stronger than women, his answer to the crucial question is clear:

> "And we must throw open the debate to anyone who wishes either in jest or earnest to raise the question whether female human nature is capable of sharing with the male all tasks or none at all, or some but not others, and under which of these heads this business of war falls." (452e4-453a4)

The co-guardianship of women makes it clear that the answer is: "all."

Plato knew, of course, that he'd be misunderstood: when he announces the principle of sexual equality in its purest form, Glaucon is presented as misunderstanding what Socrates has just said. But the entire passage is important and Glaucon's misunderstanding must be considered in context. Socrates begins by reminding Glaucon what it actually means "to be by nature suited" for any particular job and only a teacher could have written the following:

> "Was this the basis of your distinction between the man naturally gifted for anything and the one not so gifted—that the one learned easily, the other with difficulty; that the one with slight instruction [καὶ ὁ μὲν ἀπὸ βραχείας μαθήσεως] could discover much for himself in the matter studied [ἐπὶ πολὺ εὑρετικὸς εἴη οὗ ἔμαθεν], but the other, after much instruction and drill [ὁ δὲ πολλῆς μαθήσεως τυχὼν καὶ μελέτης], could not even remember what he had learned [μηδ' ἃ ἔμαθε σῴζοιτο]; and that the bodily faculties of the one adequately served his mind, while, for the other, the body was a hindrance? Were there any other points than these by which you distinguish the well endowed man in every subject and the poorly endowed?" "No one," said he, "will be able to name any others." (455b4-c3)

Here then is a proof-text for Plato the Teacher: an educator who has experienced both the frustration of seeing well-taught and even well-drilled lessons (πολλῆς μαθήσεως . . . μελέτης) slip away as well as the unmixed delight of the student who begins making their own discoveries (i.e., the student who is εὑρετικὸς) from the start (ἀπὸ βραχείας). The educational context of Plato's argument for the equality of the sexes is hardly accidental: every teacher who has taught both girls and boys knows that the equality of the sexes is an indisputable fact. To state the same thing negatively, in a social context (like fifth-century Athens) in which boys and girls were not educated (1) together, (2) in the same subjects (3) by the same teacher, it would have been difficult to discover this fact. Therefore, even without the anecdote in Diogenes Laertius,[6] it is obvious from this passage that Plato taught women (albeit some may have dressed as males) in the Academy.

> "Do you know, then, of anything practised by mankind [τι οὖν ὑπὸ ἀνθρώπων μελετώμενον] in which the masculine sex does not surpass the female on all these points?"[7]

Here then is the question—a merely rhetorical question for Plato—that Socrates poses to Glaucon. Unlike English, Greek possesses in ἀνθρώπος a perfectly generic word for "man" or "human being" that has no trace of the male in it. "What then is practiced among Men . . . ?" To speak nothing of the fact that no man has ever brought forth another human being in birth—amidst agonies only veteran soldiers have experienced, as Euripides' Medea famously said[8]—there are a great many things that women do better than men. In fact, there are even some things that it would be shameful for Glaucon, Adeimantus, Polemarchus, Cleitophon and the rest *not to be worse at doing than women.* Socrates deftly turns the confinement of women to weaving, cooking, etc. against those who have unjustly confined them to these things.

> "Must we make a long story of it by alleging weaving and the watching of pancakes and the boiling pot, whereon the sex plumes itself and wherein its defeat will expose it to most laughter?" (455c5-7)

I suspect that Socrates paused after the first (rhetorical) question and, on perceiving that it was a real question for Glaucon—that he'd never really stopped to think about it—he then added this second question just quoted. There may be skilled Egyptian weavers (such are the worthy personages who inhabit the learned commentaries on this passage) and even pastry chefs (perhaps of the same variety that arraign Socrates before a jury of children in the *Gorgias*) that

6. *Lives of Eminent Philosophers* 3.46. In the course of listing Plato's disciples, Diogenes writes: "and many others, among them two women, Lastheneia of Mantinea and Axiothea of Phlius, who is reported by Dicaearchus to have worn men's clothes" (Hicks). This suggests that Lastheneia didn't disguise her gender; Diotima was also from Mantinea and Echecrates (*Phaedo* 57a7) from Phlius, a center of Pythagoreanism. See Burnet, *Plato's* Phaedo, *ad loc.*

7. 455c4-6; cf. Julia Annas, "Plato's *Republic* and Feminism," reprinted (original 1976) in Gail Fine ed., *Plato 2: Ethics, Politics, Religion, and the Soul*, 265-269 (Oxford: Oxford University Press. 1999), 267: "Men are better equipped both mentally and physically (455b4-c6). So in every pursuit men can do better than women, though it is not true that all men do better than all women (455d3-5). Women, *he* says" (emphasis mine). Throughout the whole passage, Annas refers to Plato as "he"; she demonstrates no awareness that Glaucon and not Socrates is speaking at 455d3-5.

8. Euripides *Medea* 248-251 (Kovacs): "Men say that we live a life free from danger at home while they fight with the spear. How wrong they are! I would rather stand three times with a shield in battle than give birth once."

dance before Glaucon's dazzled eyes at this point. But we need not remember individuals like Phaenarete,[9] Diotima,[10] and Aspasia[11] to realize there are many things crucially important things that women do better than males.

> "You are right," he said, "that the one sex is far surpassed by the other in everything, one may say. Many women, it is true, are better than many men in many things, but broadly speaking, it is as you say." (455d2-5)

So Glaucon gets about half the point. He has learned enough to acknowledge that the existence of exemplary women like Aspasia, Diotima, and Phaenarete is enough for Socrates to continue on his way. But the point of Socrates was bigger and Glaucon missed it. What needs to be considered is the probability that Plato the Teacher intended that we would recognize that he had. The equality of the sexes runs counter to convention but it has nature on its side and Socrates is bold enough to say as much (456c1-3). But Plato knew he'd be misunderstood and he was unwilling to compromise his defense of Justice in order to disabuse Glaucon

---

9. Socrates mentions his mother twice (*Alc. 1* 131e4 and *Tht.* 149a1-4). In the latter, Socrates is scarcely ashamed to follow in her footsteps: "'*Socrates*: Have you then not heard, you absurd boy, that I am the son of a noble and burly midwife, Phaenarete? *Theaetetus*: Yes, I have heard that. *Socrates*: And have you also heard that I practise the same art?'" Notice that distinguishing Socratic midwifery as *superior on spiritual grounds* and allowing the female only *an inferior physical type of it* can't be sustained: Socrates goes out of his way to emphasize in the *Meno* that he has learned the doctrine of recollection—the ultimate basis for Socratic midwifery—specifically from both "men *and women* wise about divine matters" (*Men.* 81a5). He repeats this point for emphasis (*Men.* 81a10). Phaenarete corresponds to the *proleptic* element in Platonic pedagogy.

10. *Smp.* 201d1-8 (Harold N. Fowler): "And now I shall let you alone, and proceed with the discourse upon Love which I heard one day from a Mantinean woman named Diotima: in this subject she was skilled, and in many others too [ἣ ταῦτά τε σοφὴ ἦν καὶ ἄλλα πολλά]; for once, by bidding the Athenians offer sacrifices ten years before the plague, she procured them so much delay in the advent of the sickness. Well, I also had my lesson from her in love-matters [ἣ δὴ καὶ ἐμὲ τὰ ἐρωτικὰ ἐδίδαξεν]; so now I will try and follow up the points on which Agathon and I have just agreed by narrating to you all on my own account, as well as I am able, the speech she delivered to me" Fowler downplays the praise Socrates lavishes on Diotima in his 1925 translation: "she was wise [with respect to love] and many other things as well" and "she indeed also taught me erotics [i.e., the *ars amatoria*]" better capture the bracketed Greek. This last statement is important because erotics was the only matter Socrates claimed to know (*Smp.* 177d6-7, *Ly.* 204b8-c2, and *Thg.* 128b2-6). Since *Theages* doesn't get read enough, I'll quote from it (Smith): "But what I always say, you know, is that I am in the position of knowing practically nothing except one little subject, that of love-matters [των ἐρωτικων]. In this subject, however, I claim to be skilled above anybody who has ever lived or is now living in the world." Diotima represents the *visionary* element in Platonic pedagogy.

11. In Plato's *Menexenus*, it is Aspasia who composes "the Funeral Oration of Pericles" (*Mx.* 236a8-b6). This highly misleading account of Athenian politics reveals that Aspasia represents the *basanistic* element in Platonic pedagogy. See Altman, "Reading Order," section §4.

(and all the rest of us) about that thing that we now call "justice," in the fairness of which, the equality of the sexes is a necessary component. Perhaps there is something to be learned about going back down into the Cave here; perhaps he realized that philosophers committed to Justice would eventually secure the equality of the sexes.[12] In any case, the passage continues:

> "Then there is no pursuit of the administrators of a state that belongs to a woman because she is a woman or to a man because he is a man. But the natural capacities are distributed alike among both creatures [ὁμοίως διεσπαρμέναι αἱ φύσεις ἐν ἀμφοῖν τοῖν ζῴοιν], and women naturally share in all pursuits and men in all [πάντων μὲν μετέχει γυνὴ ἐπιτηδευμάτων κατὰ φύσιν]— yet for all the woman is weaker than the man [ἐπὶ πᾶσι δὲ ἀσθενέστερον γυνὴ ἀνδρός]." "Assuredly." "Shall we, then, assign them all to men and nothing to women?" "How could we?" (455d6-e4)

Here again Plato speaks as the teacher he was and is: no educator could fail to be moved by the forceful insight behind "ὁμοίως διεσπαρμέναι αἱ φύσεις ἐν ἀμφοῖν τοῖν ζῴοιν." On the other hand, there is something to be said for the view that Plato derives his insight from dogs (hence the general "ζῴοιν"). This origin in the animal kingdom would explain the insistence of Socrates on equality "by nature" (κατὰ φύσιν) as well as the words he uses here for strength and weakness, first used by Glaucon about his hounds (see V 451d10-11). Nevertheless, I suggest that this lesson was learned by Plato—in accordance with *discere docendo* ("to learn by teaching")—in the classroom. It is well to remember that the dogs are Glaucon's: Socrates chooses an example that Glaucon, who has already missed part of the point, cannot deny. And—regardless of the insight's origin—Socrates refuses to compromise the basic principle:

> "We shall rather, I take it, say that one woman has the nature of a physician [γυνὴ ἰατρική], and another not, and one is by nature musical, and another unmusical?" "Surely." (455e5-7)

It evidently requires one who has seen the timeless Idea to be as far ahead of his time as Plato proves himself to be here now. One can still trick most people today with the riddle that depends on the otherwise indeterminate doctor turning out to be a woman. Down in the Piraeus yesterday, however, Socrates is leading not only Glaucon but also all the other lads in a quick review of the primary education of the Guardians: Polemarchus wanted this and now he's getting it:

> "Can we, then, deny that one woman is naturally athletic and warlike and another unwarlike and averse to gymnastics?" "I think not." (456a1-3)

---

12. For the development of Platonic feminism, see my "Tullia's Secret Shrine" and "Womanly Humanism in Cicero's *Tusculan Disputations*." For Plato as a feminist, see Martha C. Nussbaum, *The Fragility of Goodness: Luck and Ethics in Greek Tragedy and Philosophy* (Cambridge, UK: Cambridge University Press, 1986), 4n.

Even if Plato believed that women were less inclined toward waging, e.g., the Peloponnesian War—as Aristophanes claimed they were in *Lysistrata*—he could hardly say it here. So he bites the bullet and sends his women into war, where perhaps they need to be if justice (as we understand it today) is ever to become fully realized. But the criterion for Plato is far more important and far less debatable:

> "And again, one a lover, another a hater, of wisdom [φιλόσοφός τε καὶ μισόσοφος]? And one high-spirited, and the other lacking spirit?" "That also is true." (456a4-6)

The actual arena in which Aristocles learned about the equality of the sexes was neither the classroom nor the kennel: he discovered it *on the plateau.* As Socrates will explain later in Book V, philosophy is the love of that which truly is. While there are doubtless opinions about which of any two things—men and women, for example—is better, there can be *knowledge* only of the unchanging Good. There is a perfectly good (and beautiful) reason why Diotima is Plato's (and Socrates') mouthpiece in the *Symposium*. With respect to the Good and the Beautiful—that merely intelligible Idea which has no physical body and neither waxes nor wanes—sexual differences simply do not exist: they are burned away in the refining fires of philosophy. In Plato's day, every woman was held back from politics by "the bridle of Theages"[13] but, as of "yesterday," this is no longer the case. Plato's immortal ὁμοίως διεσπαρμέναι αἱ φύσεις ἐν ἀμφοῖν τοῖν ζῴοιν considerably overstates the case: the claim that the philosophical nature is equally disseminated among men and women is a compliment to males everywhere. If the Good is equally within reach of both, women have a distinct advantage—a willingness to give life to another is responsible for it—when it comes to Justice (see section §25). It amounts to the same thing to say that the son of Ariston learned this from the son of Phaenarete.

But it would be misleading to define Platonic egalitarianism only in the context of the academic equality of women; its roots are pedagogical but even more deeply rooted in the bedrock of Platonism.[14] Even to a student who had not just read the *Meno*—the slave's only qualification is that he knows Greek (*Men.* 82b4)—it should be crystal clear that Socrates thought none incapable by nature

13. But Plato (presciently) doesn't act as if this is the way things really are: consider the following exchange at the end of Book VII (540c3-9; emphasis mine): "A most beautiful finish, Socrates, you have put upon your rulers [τοὺς ἄρχοντας], as if you were a statuary. " "And on the women too, Glaucon," said I [καὶ τὰς ἀρχούσας γε, ἦν δ᾽ ἐγώ, ὦ Γλαύκων]; "for you must not suppose [μηδὲν γάρ τι οἴου] that my words apply to the men more than to all women who arise among them endowed with the requisite qualities." "That is right," he said, "if *they are to share equally in all things with the men* [ἴσα γε πάντα τοῖς ἀνδράσι κοινωνήσουσιν] as we laid it down." Passages like this make it easier for female Plato scholars to abandon singularism (section §19).

14. A recent statement is "The Equality of Women: Plato's Blindfold" in Gerasimos Santas, *Understanding Plato's* Republic (Chichester: Wiley-Blackwell, 2010), 107-117.

of being turned "forcefully upwards"; he doesn't even make an exemption for the half-witted. Plato's classic statement of educational egalitarianism is presented—and this is hardly surprising—while describing the Cave:

> "Then, if this is true, our view of these matters must be this, that education [τὴν παιδείαν] is not in reality what some people proclaim it to be in their professions. What they aver is that they can put [ἐντιθέναι] true knowledge into a soul that does not possess it [οὐκ ἐνούσης ἐν τῇ ψυχῇ ἐπιστήμης], as if they were inserting vision into blind eyes." "They do indeed," he said. (518b7-c3)

Although well known to students of the classics, it is worth pointing out that the Greek word for "education" is in fact "παιδεία," a word that suggests the intersection of both "child" and "play." To this limited extent, Plato's remarks on education are guided by a wholesome tradition for which he himself can take no credit. But the conception of learning already explicated in *Meno*[15]—the genitive absolute Socrates uses here makes plain that it is *already* a case of "knowledge being present within the soul" (ἐνούσης ἐν τῇ ψυχῇ ἐπιστήμης)—is a completely original break with the traditional view that knowledge is something "implanted" (ἐντιθέναι) by a competent teacher.

> "But our present argument indicates," said I, "that the true analogy for this indwelling power in the soul [τὴν ἐνοῦσαν ἑκάστου δύναμιν ἐν τῇ ψυχῇ] and the instrument whereby each of us apprehends [τὸ ὄργανον ᾧ καταμανθάνει ἕκαστος] is that of an eye [ὄμμα] that could not be converted to the light from the darkness except by turning the whole body." (518c4-7)

Reminding the reader with "ἐνοῦσαν" of the *Meno*-conception of "knowledge being present within the soul," Socrates now refers to "the indwelling capacity in the soul." Plato's use of δύναμις here is explicated perfectly by Aristotle: this knowledge is merely potential and requires education to be actualized. But the most stunning aspect of this passage—although the slave in the *Meno* had already indicated the breadth of Plato's pedagogical revolution—is the word "ἕκαστος" (i.e., "each" as in "each and every one of us"). This "indwelling capacity in the soul" belongs to *each* of us regardless, for example, of sex: it is the tool "by which each one of learns." Perhaps the 'κατα-' in 'καταμανθάνει' is the other side of the 'ἀνα-' in the word for recollection used in the *Meno*. In any case, the truth behind the class-affirming lie of the Genetic Fiction has been disclosed in the classic formulation of Platonic pedagogy. The Equality of Women is its corollary.

---

15. The theory of recollection is introduced at *Men.* 81c5-d5. The *Meno* immediately precedes the *Cleitophon* in my reconstructed reading order and is itself preceded by the *Gorgias*. A familiarity with *Meno* is therefore presupposed in this passage. Charles H. Kahn, "Plato on Recollection" in Hugh H. Benson (ed.), *A Companion to Plato*, 119-132. (Malden, MA: Blackwell, 2006), 130 admits only "a close analogue to the process of recollection" after stating (127) that recollection "disappears from the *Republic* entirely."

As indicated earlier, it's impossible to refute elitism without elitism. It has often seemed to me that the Socratic revolution in ethics consisted simply in a reversal of the traditional question crucial to any society that values traditional elites: "Who's his father?" Against this, Socrates responds: "Who are his sons?"[16] Education—for what father who knew what virtue is would fail to pass it on to his sons and daughters?—supplants noble birth. *But elitism remains*. On the other hand, the intersection of "democracy and education" results in an eminently democratic elitism. Platonic pedagogy is even more beautiful: it asserts a stunning egalitarianism where the *student* is concerned. But there's still plenty of room for elitism: in no sense whatsoever are all *teachers* equal.[17] Plato the Teacher is an excellent teacher: to such a one, the claim that anyone is "a natural slave" is an insult not only to the alleged slave but also to the educator who loves a challenge. Like all teachers, Plato needs both 'A' and 'F' as well as an indeterminate spectrum between them. But no student is assumed by Plato (or any good teacher) to be uneducable by nature. Of course it often happens that the teacher arrives on the scene too late. Indeed if teachers didn't think students could be ruined by their upbringing, they wouldn't have so much confidence in their own ability to effect happier results.

Platonic pedagogy is therefore the real subject of this passage and a powerful description of the revolution on which it depends is waiting in the wings. But everything in Plato—and in particular, his distinctive conceptions of both elitism and egalitarianism—depends entirely on the plateau of Platonism. It is therefore with a succinct description of its essence that Socrates prefaces his description of the true teacher.

> "Even so this organ of knowledge must be turned around from the world of becoming [ἐκ τοῦ γιγνομένου] together with the entire soul [σὺν ὅλῃ τῇ ψυχῇ], like the scene-shifting periact [περιακτέον] in the theater, until the soul is able to endure the contemplation of essence [τὸ ὂν] and the brightest region of being [καὶ τοῦ ὄντος τὸ φανότατον]. And this, we say, is the good [τἀγαθόν], do we not?" "Yes." (518c7-d2)

---

16. *Men.* 93c7-8. The fact that Socrates is conversing with Anytus (who would later accuse him) suggests that it was this reversal that brought about his trial and death. The unfinished business with Anytus at the end of *Meno* is the dramatic or thematic connection to the *Cleitophon*, which begins and ends with an accusation that leaves the reader in some doubt as to whether Cleitophon will continue the attack in another forum. The fact that *Republic* answers Cleitophon's Question—suggests that he didn't.

17. The conclusion that Socrates draws from the failure of Themistocles, Aristides, Pericles, and Thucydides to raise sons as excellent as themselves—i.e., that virtue cannot be taught (*Men.* 94d6-8)—was not Plato's. Moreover, the fact that Protagoras, Hippias, Gorgias, and Thrasymachus can't teach it either hardly proves that it can't be taught. The teachability of virtue is at the very heart of *Plato the Teacher*: it is the question with which he begins in *Protagoras*. See Altman, "Leo Strauss and the Euthydemus."

In fact, the entire revolution is already present in this passage: the verbal adjective περιακτέον ("reoriented" or "brought round must it be"). Platonic pedagogy has two distinct moments of reorientation or change of direction: the prisoners must be turned upwards and the philosophers turned down-wards. In short: this passage to contain the truth about Platonism, i.e., *this is Platonism*. And this, in turn, is another way of saying that Plato's *Republic* is the axis around which the Reading Order of Plato's Dialogues revolves.

Just as the Idea—whether of the Good, Beauty,[18] or Justice—"neither waxes nor wanes,"[19] neither did Plato's commitment to it change: to this extent I flatly reject (and present my own researches as a corrective to) the hypothesis upon which no small amount of the search for the order of composition of Plato's dialogues and developmentalism itself depends: the hypothesis that Plato's thoughts about Being and Becoming altered over the course of his working life. It is upon the common-sense principle that Plato's conception of the eternal remains itself unchanging throughout the *corpus Platonicum* that my reconstruction of the Reading Order of Plato's Dialogues depends. This is not, of course, to deny that Plato developed this reading order gradually and may have continued to tinker with it until the end.

But the essential matter is that the categories of Platonism must be named and explained as such: Becoming, Being, and the Idea of the Good. In the present passage, he calls the latter simply "τἀγαθόν"; later in Book VII he will give it its full form as "the Idea of the Good" (see section §18). But here he makes most evident the Good's relationship to Being (τὸ ὄν): it is "the most evident [aspect] of Being" (τοῦ ὄντος τὸ φανότατον). If there are other ideas, they are in every conceivable way dependent on the Good (or rather they are inconceivable without the Good): such is the teaching of the Sun. The logical priority of the Good to any meaningful discussion of Plato's theory of ideas is clearly expressed in the present passage and I take it as canonical. Access to Being is made possible only by turning the integrated soul (ὅλῃ τῇ ψυχῇ) "away from Becoming" (ἐκ τοῦ γιγνομένου). The boundary between Being and Becoming is therefore *Plato*: i.e., what I am calling "the plateau." Non-Platonists will always demand from Platonists a detailed account of what is north of that plateau; they would do better to attend to how a true Platonist regards what is south of it. The world of Becoming is not what actually is; this awareness is the mark by which Plato's disciples are known and it depends entirely on an awareness of the dividing line between τὸ ὄν and τὸ γιγνομένον. It is only from the perspective of τὸ ὄν that τὸ γιγνομένον is one and always the same with itself; in itself it is none of those things. In itself, τὸ γιγνομένον is many—an indefinite plurality—

---

18. 531c5-7: "A superhuman task," he said. "Say, rather, useful, said I, for the investigation of the beautiful and the good [τὴν τοῦ καλοῦ τε καὶ ἀγαθοῦ], but if otherwise pursued, useless." See also VI 508d10-509a5.

19. Diotima on Beauty in the *Smp.* 211a1-2.

and even in Book VII, it is equipped with a variety of names.[20] It should be added that Plato makes it impossible to refer to Being exclusively as neither neuter, masculine, or feminine but employs all three genders at various times.[21]

After the sublime preface of 518c7-d2—in fact, it is rather "the song itself" (531d7) to which "Higher Education" is the mere prelude—Socrates gives an account of the Platonic revolution in pedagogy:

> "Of this very thing, then," I said, "there might be an art [τέχνη], an art of the speediest and most effective shifting [τῆς περιαγωγῆς] or conversion of the soul, not an art of producing vision in it [οὐ τοῦ ἐμποιῆσαι αὐτῷ τὸ ὁρᾶν], but on the assumption that it possesses vision [ἀλλ' ὡς ἔχοντι μὲν αὐτό] but does not rightly direct it [οὐκ ὀρθῶς δὲ τετραμμένῳ] and does not look where it should [οὐδὲ βλέποντι οἷ ἔδει], an art of bringing this about [τοῦτο διαμηχανήσασθαι]." (518d3-7)

Plato the Teacher is in possession of a τέχνη that might be described not so much as "pedagogy" but as "periagogy": it is a turning around of the soul.[22] It is here that Platonic elitism is undoubtedly to be found: Plato the Teacher is evidently proud of having discovered—and being in sole possession (although he is happy to pass along the secret and share it)—of what he calls the "art of the speediest and most effective shifting or conversion of the soul." In short, Plato remains an elitist. It is the same kind of thing that prevents Plato from being a relativist: he knows there is something that is absolutely Good that is by no

---

20. Although Plato repeatedly uses (e.g., 521d4-5) τὸ γιγνομένον in opposition to τὸ ὄν ("What, then, Glaucon, would be the study that would draw the soul away from the world of becoming [τοῦ γιγνομένου] to the world of being [τὸ ὄν]?") he broadens the formula for Becoming to include passing away at 527b4-5: "That it is the knowledge of that which always is [τοῦ ἀεὶ ὄντος], and not of a something which at some time comes into being and passes away [τοῦ ποτέ τι γιγνομένου καὶ ἀπολλυμένου]." These are also synthesized in yet another formula: "he must rise out of the region of generation [γενέσεως] and lay hold on essence [τῆς οὐσίας]" (525b3). Adam's comprehensive note (at 519d7) on γενέσεως suggests to my mind some word-play connecting "generation" and "earthbound."

21. τὸ ὄν can only be neuter, but τοῦ ὄντος can be either neuter or masculine. The feminine form is used at 525b3: "he must rise out of the region of generation [γενέσεως] and lay hold on essence [τῆς οὐσίας]." This may be another indication of "the Platonic Trinity" (section §25).

22. See 521c5-8: "So this, it seems, would not be the whirling of the shell in the children's game, but a conversion and turning about of the soul [ψυχῆς περιαγωγὴ] from a day whose light is darkness to the veritable day—that ascension [ἐπάνοδον] to reality [τοῦ ὄντος] of our parable which we will affirm to be true philosophy." It is worth repeating that καταβατέον is the second (and no less important) περιαγωγὴ for the Soul that has achieved the ascent ἐπάνοδος. Scott, "Metaphysics and the Defense of Justice," 9 makes a very valuable contribution by emphasizing the use of περίοδος at 504b2; the Longer Way must proceed forwards to the Cave and then back again to the Key Passage.

manner of means a matter of opinion. If there were not, there would be no one with enough intellectual vigor to prevent Thrasymachus from drugging the noble Ship-owner—relativism is indeed the mandragora of Thrasymachus; this is what makes him less formidable than the Eleatic and Athenian Strangers—and substituting his own opinion for the indefinite dyads of ours. But Plato is not the kind of elitist that the traditional view loves to criticize or that the Thrasymachean Platonists love to celebrate.[23] The master teacher assumes that every student has the natural capacity but hasn't been correctly oriented and therefore is looking for truth in all the wrong places. Plato's pedagogical art contrives to thoroughly engineer (διαμηχανήσασθαι) a much better result: i.e., a result oriented to the Idea of the Good.

In the case of educating women, Socrates doesn't back off one inch. Not everyone can be a Platonic philosopher (or a Just man) but who is and who isn't has nothing whatsoever to do with their sex: Plato hammers home the point that both have the same nature:

> "Then it is likewise true that one woman has the qualities of a guardian and another not. Were not these the natural qualities of the men also whom we selected for guardians?" "They were." "The women and the men, then, have the same nature [ἡ αὐτὴ φύσις] in respect to the guardianship of the state, save in so far as the one is weaker, the other stronger." "Apparently" ["καὶ γυναικὸς ἄρα καὶ ἀνδρὸς ἡ αὐτὴ φύσις εἰς φυλακὴν πόλεως, πλὴν ὅσα ἀσθενεστέρα, ἡ δὲ ἰσχυροτέρα ἐστίν." "φαίνεται." (456a7-12)

So it merely appears (φαίνεται) to Glaucon. But it was no matter of appearance to Plato. And thus arises the parallel with the second Noble Lie. The real point—the point of the playful Plato—is that it is not only the fictional City of Socrates that practices censorship and bases itself on otherwise baseless Genetic Fictions. Most of the people—both women and men—who have passed their lives on this planet have believed a lie where the natural differences between the sexes are concerned. The communism of Book Five is a way—based on an ever growing number of lies—to make the first Genetic Fiction, if not true (that can't be done), then at least practical. The equality of women is, however, Plato's explicit rejection of the most common form of caste system—a form in which Athenians, all Greeks, and most everybody else in his day actually believed—and therefore the essence of the second Genetic Fiction. Whether Plato the Philosopher passed this knowledge—learned on the plateau outside of the Cave—down to Plato the Teacher *or* Plato the Teacher brought the amazing tidings up to Plato the Philosopher is a matter of complete inconsequence: thanks to Justice, the two are one and the same.

---

23. In addition to ignoring Phaenarete, failing to consider Diotima's use of deliberate self-contradiction (30), and relying on the basanistic misogyny of *Laws* and *Timaeus* (28-31), Elizabeth V. Spelman, *Inessential Women: Problems of Exclusion in Feminist Thought* (Boston: Beacon Press, 1988) regards not only Plato's "somatophobic lessons" (30) but also his elitism (19 and 35) as fundamentally incompatible with his feminism.

Section 28. Higher Education: Why the Good is not the One

In the context of the Idea of the Good—the true ἀρχή ("beginning" or "guiding principle") of Platonism—it is easy to see why there is something infinitely higher than Book VII's Higher Education and why the Tübingen School is wrong to identify the Good and the One. Of course this false identification is not theirs alone: the equation of the Good and the One marks, as clearly as any other, the boundary dividing Neoplatonism from Platonism. In fact, the equation threatens to take us even farther away from Platonism: if the Good is the One, and the One is repeatedly instantiated in every concrete particular, each of the things that exist derives its being from the Good *without the Good being a separable Idea.*[24] To put it another way: in Neoplatonism, it is the "idea" that "goes back down" while in Platonism, it is only the philosopher who does so. But a *bon mot* will not do here: the stakes are too high and the problems so old that more rigorous argument is required before returning to the sublime simplicity of the Higher Education that Socrates describes in *Republic* VII.

The source of the problem is Aristotle and what makes the situation particularly difficult is that Aristotle's account of Plato's mathematics combines important truths with serious misunderstandings. The extreme case of the latter is the claim upon which the Tübingen School is based: that Plato identified the Good and the One;[25] the extreme case of the former is Aristotle's claim that Plato regarded mathematical objects as Intermediates between Ideas and sensible objects (see section §13). I will argue that these two positions are incompatible and therefore that they testify to Aristotle's confusion. To put it simply: since the Idea of the Good is the Form par excellence, and since the ἀρχή of mathematical objects is the One, the One cannot be the Good because the former is an Intermediate and the latter an Idea. The problem arises because on Aristotle's account, there would seem to be more than one One in Plato's thought.[26] There

---

24. Cf. Penner, "The Good, Advantage, Happiness and the Form of the Good," and Gerasimos Santas, "The Form of the Good in Plato's *Republic*" in John P. Anton and Anthony Preus (eds.), *Essays in Ancient Greek Philosophy* Vol. 2, 232-263 (Albany: State University of New York Press, 1983), 246-49.

25. Particularly in the lost Περὶ τἀγαθοῦ. References to the fragments will be based on David Ross (ed), *Aristotelis Fragmenta Selecta* (Oxford: Clarendon Press, 1955), 111-20. See also *Eudemian Ethics*, 1.8 (1218a20). Ian Mueller, "Review of *Aristotle's* Metaphysics, *Books M and N* by Julia Annas." *Philosophical Review* 87 (1978), 479-485 at 480-82 is a succinct summary of the relation between Harold Cherniss and the proponents of Plato's "unwritten doctrines." See also Findlay, *Plato*, 455-73.

26. It is sometimes very difficult to determine just how many kinds of numbers any given scholar thinks Plato embraced. Wedberg, *Plato's Philosophy of Mathematics* is particularly exuberant: after distinguishing "popular" and "philosophical" arithmetic (64), he then (on the authority of Aristotle) divides "two kinds of ideal arithmetical entities" (65) one of which embraces "Mathematical" and the other "Ideal Numbers." This allows Wedberg to accept Aristotle's doctrine of Intermediates while simultaneously rejecting it as definitive (66): "The Mathematical Numbers are 'Intermediates' between the Ideal

are, to begin with, the infinitely variable countable objects of everyday life: the individual apple when we are counting apples and sheep when sheep. Then comes the mathematical One that Aristotle rightly understands Plato to regard as intermediate; it is in contrast to the sensible "ones" of everyday life—units that are no more unitary than indefinitely plural—that Socrates explains the One of Book VII. None of this is problematic on Platonic terms; the monad of mathematics is clearly distinct from the sensible objects that the man on the street routinely counts. The bridge to the protology of the Unwritten Doctrines and the so-called "Ideal Numbers" is a third kind of One that Aristotle attributes, falsely, to his Pythagorean Plato.[27] The difficult problem that must be faced squarely here is: how could Aristotle have been so confused as to misunderstand his teacher on this important point?

It was a profound misunderstanding of Plato's dialectical pedagogy that allowed Aristotle to believe his teacher had identified the Idea of the Good and the One. In the context of Aristotle's accurate ascription of the Doctrine of Intermediates to his teacher,[28] his testimony about "indivisible lines" and "incomparable numbers"[29] not only offers additional evidence about Plato's dialectical

---

Numbers and sensible things, or collections of sensible things." I can find no basis for this approach: one should either claim that Numbers are Ideas and that Aristotle is wrong about Intermediates *or* that Aristotle was right about Intermediates and that therefore Numbers are not Ideas. Either alternative makes the phrase "Ideal Numbers" (Ross, *Plato's Theory of Ideas*, 176-205) less than ideal.

27. See *Metaphysics* A.6; Sextus Empiricus has preserved the Pythagorean (or perhaps only the Neo-Pythagorean) approach at *Adv. Mathematicos* 10.261 (translation mine): "Pythagoras said that the ἀρχή of things that exist is a monad from which, by virtue of participation, each of the things that exist is called one."

28. Based on consideration of the Platonic *corpus* as a whole, Harold Cherniss, *Aristotle's Criticism of Plato and the Academy* (Baltimore, MD: Johns Hopkins University Press, 1944) and the same author's *The Riddle of the Early Academy* (New York: Russell & Russell, 1945) has already made a strong case for impeaching Aristotle's authority as an expert witness on his teacher's views. But thanks to the breadth of his critique, Cherniss, *Riddle*, 75-78 did not accept as Platonic the doctrine that best explains why no equation of the One and the Good is possible: the Doctrine of Intermediates. And following John Cook Wilson (Cook Wilson, "Platonist Doctrine" is cited at 93n6 and, on Intermediates, at 102n79; a fuller discussion is found at Cherniss, *Aristotle's Criticism*, 1.303-4 and 1.513-24), Cherniss accepts another of Aristotle's claims that likewise tends to support the equation: that Plato embraced the concept of Ideal Numbers, i.e., "numbers" that cannot be combined (ἀριθμοί οὐ σύμβλητοι). While upholding Aristotle's claim that Plato *discussed* numbers that cannot be combined, I will argue that Aristotle misunderstood his teacher's dialectical motive for doing so, a motive that also explains why Aristotle's Plato discussed indivisible lines, another class of equally *self-contradictory* "entities."

29. It is worth noting that it is the Doctrine of Intermediates that tends to disappear from—and therefore it is Ideal Numbers that tend to dominate—recent accounts of Plato's philosophy of mathematics (Shorey's views have been considered in section §13): although Wedberg, Plato's *Philosophy of Mathematics*, 64-67 followed Aristotle in at-

pedagogy but also indicates the source of Aristotle's confusion. A careful reading of two related passages in *Metaphysics* A.9 and M.8 suggests that just as "indivisible lines" are an absurd consequence of denying that the point—in accordance with the dependence of the Second Part of the Divided Line on Hypotheses (section §13)—is "a geometrical fiction," so too are "incomparable numbers" an absurd consequence of affirming that the One, along with the Indefinite Dyad, is a metaphysical principle or ἀρχή. I will show that both consequences are incompatible with the view that "mathematicals" are intermediate between visible objects and Forms but are constitutive of the "Platonism" that erroneously identifies the Good with the One. It is Plato's use of *deliberate self-contradiction for a dialectical purpose* that explains why Aristotle believed that Plato identified the Good with the One, something Aristotle could not have done had he thought through the fact that Plato embraced the un-hypothetical existence of the Idea of the Good as opposed to the merely hypothetical existence of mathematical objects (510b4-511d5).

It is this distinction, famously described by Socrates in the Divided Line of *Republic* VI, which furnishes the best textual basis for Aristotle's claim that Plato regarded such objects as Intermediates, objects of which the primary example would be the geometrical point if it were not for the logically prior, pre-arithmetic monad.[30] As already indicated, this priority is central: although Socrates specifically identifies as hypothetical only several *logically posterior* objects while elucidating the Divided Line (510c2-5) and Aristotle's Plato specifically identifies only the point as "a geometrical fiction" in *Metaphysics* A.9, the traditional or Pythagorean definition of a point ("a unit having position")[31] points to the logical priority of the monad and it is this priority that accounts not only for the careful and preliminary consideration given to the indivisible unit at 524b3-526c7 but also to the priority of arithmetic among the five sciences described in the Higher Education of Book VII.[32]

---

tributing *three* kinds of numbers to Plato, vulgar, mathematical (i.e. Intermediates), and Ideal. But Paul Pritchard, *Plato's Philosophy of Mathematics* (Sankt Augustin: Academia Verlag, 1996), 156 (cf. 94-6)—by rejecting Intermediates—reduces the number of number-types to *two*, as do I. The difference is: instead of excluding Intermediates, as do Cook Wilson, Shorey, Cherniss, and Pritchard, I exclude Ideal Numbers, leaving only vulgar "numbers" consisting of *sensible* units (cf. *Phlb.* 56d9-e3) and mathematical numbers consisting of strictly intelligible but nevertheless strictly hypothetical monads, all of which are therefore identical; see 526a3-4.

30. "Pre-arithmetic" because One is not a number; see Jacob Klein, *Greek Mathematical Thought and the Origin of Algebra*, translated by Eva Brann (Cambridge, MA: M.I.T. Press, 1968), 39-42, 48-54, and 69-79; cf. Cherniss, *Aristotle's Criticism*, 1.497 and Pritchard, *Plato's Philosophy of Mathematics*, 14-18, who regard the monad as an Idea or Form respectively.

31. E.g., *De Anima* 1.4, 409a6.

32. See Burnyeat, "Why Mathematics is Good," 19. Incidentally, the passage about the number twelve at 337b2-4 suggests that Kant's use of seven and five to illustrate the

Aristotle's misunderstanding of Plato's dialectical pedagogy can be illustrated by consideration of the following passage from *Metaphysics* A.9 (translation mine):

> Further, as to points: from what are they to be derived? To this class of things, Plato was [repeatedly] objecting [διεμάχετο] as being [in fact] a geometrical fiction [ὄντι γεωμετρκῷ δόγματι] but he was calling "beginning of a line" [ἀρχὴν γραμμῆς]—and this he was often asserting [τοῦτο δὲ πολλάκις ἐτίθει]—"the indivisible lines." However it is necessary even of these [for there] to be some limit [εἶναί τι πέρας]; therefore the argument by which a line exists proves also that a point exists.[33]

Although the current definition of point was apparently not ἀρχή but πέρας γραμμῆς ("limit of a line"), it suffered from the same fatal flaw: it defined the prior by the posterior.[34] Aristotle's ultimate response will be to introduce another definition, apparently Pythagorean in origin: "a monad with position added."[35] But here Aristotle tells us—and he is the first to do so—that Plato's response was very different: instead of redefining "the point," he called *points* "indivisible lines." This "definition"—the plural indicates that it was hardly intended by Plato to be such—suffered from two fatal flaws, not one: it defined the logically prior point in terms of the logically posterior line *and* it hypothesized a self-contradiction: the possibility of lines without length. Using the old one, Aristotle easily refutes this Platonic "definition"; even an atomic line must have a πέρας. One would think, in fact, that it must have *two* of them.[36] And that is the joke: anyone who regards the line as anything like "the breadth-less length between two points" (implying as it does two distinct points and something between them)[37] must regard the concept of "indivisible lines" as self-contradictory. My claim is that Plato (who, unlike Aristotle, was alive to the humor involved) created this self-contradiction in order to emphasize the partless purity of the point *qua* One to which Socrates devotes so much attention in

---

synthetic aspect of arithmetic was not adventitious; he would have had a harder case to make with six and six, eight and four, nine and three, to say nothing of eleven and one.

33. A.9 (992a19-24); naturally my translation follows Ross on certain points. See Jonathan Barnes (ed), *The Complete Works of Aristotle*, the Revised Oxford Translation, two volumes (Princeton, NJ: Princeton University Press, 1984). The close proximity of ὄντι and δόγματι may be Platonic, suggesting as it does deliberate self-contradiction.

34. *Topics* 6.4 (141b15-22).

35. Thomas L. Heath, *The Thirteen Books of Euclid's* Elements; *translated from the text of Heiberg with Introduction and Commentary*. Three Volumes. (New York: Dover Books, 1956), 1.155-6.

36. Heath, *Euclid's* Elements, 1.156 (emphasis mine): "To which Aristotle replied that even 'indivisible lines' must have *extremities*" The joke, of course, is that if an indivisible line has two extremities, it is divisible while if it has but one—if it *is* its limit—it is not a line.

37. Cf. *Prm.* 137e3-4.

Republic VII and was therefore fully aware of "the multilayered incoherence" involved in defining points as "indivisible lines."[38] Without denying that Plato spoke of points in this way—it is central to my argument that Aristotle is correct: Plato *did* speak in this manner and did so repeatedly (πολλάκις)—I will argue that Aristotle misunderstood his dialectical motives for doing so.

My position is that when Aristotle attributes to Plato views that are unsubstantiated in the dialogues AND easily refutable, we should not—given Aristotle's evidently polemical purpose[39]—assume that they are Plato's IFF there is a plausible explanation of how Aristotle could have mistakenly believed that they were. Aristotle's claim that Plato called points "indivisible lines" is unattested in the dialogues and it is also easy to refute: "There is no difficulty in refuting the theory of indivisible lines."[40] Aristotle's polemical purpose is indicated by the fact that he cites Plato's "definition" only to refute it, despite the fact that by doing so, he must once again define a point in terms of a line, i.e., he falls back on the flawed definition. In fairness to Aristotle, this lapse was momentary: as already indicated, he either adopted or invented another definition based on the monad. But there are *plausible* grounds for thinking that Aristotle has misunderstood Plato's intentions with respect to "indivisible lines."

Aristotle tells us something else in this passage that is unattested in the dialogues: that Plato considered the point to be "a geometrical fiction."[41] Taken simply as a claim about what Plato thought, it is not as unlikely as Plato's commitment to "indivisible lines" because it is widely regarded to be true: it would be difficult to find a person—apart from a certain kind of strictly hypothetical "platonist"[42]—who believes that an Ideal Line that cannot be divided actually

38. Although I am excluding *Timaeus* from consideration at this time, it is worth noting that John J. Drummond, "Indivisible Lines and the Timaeus." *Apeiron* 16 (1982), 63-70 has imported the concept of indivisible lines into *Timaeus* in order to solve a problem (the variable sizes of the "elementary" triangles constituting the faces of the various Platonic solids) that in fact emerges from "the multilayered incoherence"—see Kenneth Sayre, "The Multilayered Incoherence of Timaeus' Receptacle" in Gretchen J. Reydams-Schils (ed.), *Plato's* Timaeus *as Cultural Icon*, 60-79 (Notre Dame, IN: University of Notre Dame Press, 2003)—of treating *as elementary* a plane geometrical figure that depends on the logically prior line and point, the last of which is nowhere to be found in the dialogue. It is tempting to regard the logically prior point as "the missing fourth."

39. For a recent discussion of Aristotle's reliability as an historian of thought generally, see Michael Frede, "Aristotle's Account of the Origins of Philosophy" in Patricia Curd and Daniel W. Graham (eds.), *The Oxford Handbook of Presocratic Philosophy*, 501-529 (Oxford: Oxford University Press, 2008).

40. *Physics* 3.6 (206a16-17).

41. For this translation, see Heath, *Euclid's* Elements, 1.156; cf. "geometrical dogma" at Ross, *Aristotle's* Metaphysics, 1.189. But Ross translates it as "a geometrical fiction" in the Revised Oxford Translation.

42. It is an exaggerated Platonism that characterizes the attempt of Pritchard, *Plato's Philosophy of Mathematics*, 94-96 to purge the Divided Line of the objects of διάνοια, i.e., of Intermediates. Not only mathematical, but also visible objects are there made images of the Forms accessible to νοῆσις; naturally Pritchard does not commit himself to

exists. Thus, when Socrates tells us in his account of the Divided Line: "that students of geometry, calculation, and the like *hypothesize* the odd and the even, the various figures, the three kinds of angle,"[43] it is obvious, given the rigorous nature of mathematical proof, that they must also hypothesize the logically prior point. According to Aristotle, however, Plato was attacking thoroughly (διε–μάχετο) "this class of things" by pointing out that they were "a geometrical fiction," i.e., that the point was hypothetical. In the passage under consideration, Aristotle connects the fact that Plato was repeatedly positing (ἐτίθει) "the indivisible lines" to his teacher's ongoing battle to show that points are "a geometrical fiction" but he says nothing more about the *prior* claim than to implicitly deny its truth as indicated by his refutation of the posterior: the point exists.

This procedure indicates that Aristotle misunderstood Plato's purpose in hypothesizing deliberately self-contradictory "atomic lines" without denying that he had a plausible reason for doing so. From the facts Aristotle presents, Plato's intentions were not entirely clear. What does seem clearer to me than to Aristotle is that Plato's intention was not to redefine the point but to support the view that points had no real existence, i.e., that they were a geometrical fiction that rested on an initial hypothesis to which dialectical objections could be, should be, and indeed actually were being brought by Plato. By attacking the point as ἀρχὴ γραμμῆς, Plato probably supplemented the obvious dialectical objection to deriving the point from the line that Aristotle remarks in *Topics* with another less commonplace dialectical objection, recorded here, to deriving a line from a point.[44] Only if points were always *already* lines—or if they moved[45]—could they give rise to lines. By bringing objections against the point and thus the logically posterior structures that rested upon it,[46] Plato was engaged in dialectic[47] as described in the First Part of Divided Line rather than asserting the actual existence of "indivisible lines."

---

the actual existence of these forms (cf. Klein, *Plato's* Meno, 119). Richard D. Mohr, "The Number Theory in Plato's *Republic* VII and *Philebus*." *Isis* 72 (1981), 620-627 is another example of exaggerated "Platonism"; note the early citation of Cook Wilson, "Platonist Doctrine," at 621n2 (cf. Klein, *Greek Mathematical Thought*, 62). Preferable is Burnyeat, "Why Mathematics is Good," 30-31.

43. 510c2-5 (G. M. A. Grube translation revised by C. D. C. Reeve); emphasis mine.

44. By attacking the point from both sides—from end to end, as it were—Plato would also be justifying Aristotle's use of δια–μάχεσθαι.

45. *De Anima* 1.4 (409a4-5); cf. Heath, *Euclid's* Elements, 1.159.

46. 437a3-8: "'All the same,' said I, 'that we may not be forced to examine at tedious length the entire list of such contentions and convince ourselves that they are false, let us proceed on the hypothesis that this is so, with the understanding that, if it ever appear otherwise, everything that results from the assumption shall be invalidated.'" The subject, of course, is the principle of non-contradiction, introduced at 436b9-10.

47. Ross, *Aristotle's Metaphysics*, 1.207 (on 992a20): "This is interesting as an instance of the procedure of dialectic τὰς ὑποθέσεις ἀναιροῦσα (*Rep.* 533c)." Shorey translates these Greek words as: "doing away with hypotheses."

Further evidence for this misunderstanding can be found by considering the passage quoted above in its polemical context. In the relevant section of *Metaphysics* A.9, Aristotle is demolishing two possible arguments in support of the position he attributes to Plato that Forms are numbers. The first argument rests on the assumption that all units are identical,[48] and Aristotle suggests that this assumption vitiates the doctrine of Intermediates instead of realizing that this constitutes its basis. Ironically, it is Plato's claim that numbers are intermediate between Forms and sensible objects that shows why Plato could not consistently have thought that Forms *are* numbers, another doctrine unsubstantiated in the dialogues that Aristotle can easily refute. The second argument, on the other hand, rests on the opposite assumption, i.e., that all units are diverse, a corollary of the claim that Plato embraced the existence of incomparable or incommensurable (οὐ σύμβλητοι) numbers. It is in the course of offering a reductio ad absurdum on this second assumption that Aristotle introduces the important claim that Plato regarded the point as a geometrical fiction. The irony here is that Aristotle uses a *true* claim about Plato, i.e., that he regarded the point—geometrical counterpart of the pre-arithmetical One—as a fiction, to attack a view he *falsely* attributes to Plato, i.e., that there is an ideal class of "Incomparable Numbers" apart from either numerable sensible objects (vulgar "numbers") and numerable instances of identical hypothesized units *whereas* if units, like points, are merely mathematical *fictions*, there is certainly no absurdity in the view, attacked in the first argument, that all units are identical. In fact, if their existence is hypothetical, the hypothesis that creates them necessarily creates their equality and makes them ipso facto indistinguishable.

In summary, it is Aristotle's failure to examine Plato's secondary or dialectical statement (points as "indivisible lines") in the context of Plato's principal statement (points as "geometrical fictions") that suggests that Aristotle has misunderstood Plato's dialectical intentions. But even if Plato linked the two statements in a more plausible manner than Aristotle imagines, they are not equally implausible. Aristotle can easily refute the second statement by considering it in isolation but it is by no means clear that Plato held this view as Aristotle presents it. But Plato's principal statement is a perfectly plausible position for someone to take and indeed it is very similar to Aristotle's own position as described in *Metaphysics* M.3.[49]

Aristotle's presentation of his own views on mathematics in M.1-3 certainly has a polemical aspect: he is denying that mathematical objects exist either *in* (1076a38) or *separate from* (1076b12) sensible substances. It will be noted that if they exist in neither of two possible ways, the presumption is *that they do not actually exist at all.* But the last sentence of M.1 (1076a36-37) makes it clear

48. A.9 (991b24-992a1).

49. See Jonathan Lear, "Aristotle's Philosophy of Mathematics." *Philosophical Review* 91 (1982), 161-192, especially 168, 170, 173, 175, 182, 188, culminating in 191: "Talk of nonphysical mathematical objects is a fiction, one that may be convenient and should be harmless if one correctly understands mathematical practice."

that Aristotle is not going to deny the existence of mathematical objects; it is only a question of the *manner* in which they do so. In the last sentence of M.2 (1077b17), he gives himself considerable latitude in this respect: "For 'exist' has many senses." In M.3 (1077b33-34), Aristotle is willing to announce: "it is true also to say, without qualification, that the objects of mathematics exist." Upon which W. D. Ross comments: "They do not exist in the unqualified or strict sense, but we can say in an unqualified or general way that they exist."[50] What Aristotle himself says at M.3 (1078a22-23) is: "Each question will be best investigated in this way—by supposing [θείη] separate what is not separate, as the arithmetician and the geometer do." As is so frequently the case, Aristotle is attacking Plato. But if Aristotle is correct that his teacher regarded the point—on which all other geometrical elements logically depend—as a geometrical fiction, then there is good reason to think that Plato, along with the arithmeticians of his day,[51] applied the same kind of reasoning to the One.[52] Reasons for thinking he did so have been presented in chapter 3.

The primary evidence of dialectic in Aristotle's description is the already mentioned self-contradiction it involves. It is, of course, a strictly polemical necessity that compels Aristotle to frame the entire argument in terms of what is both separable and inseparable instead of what is merely fictional.[53] But he can only avoid self-contradiction by claiming that mathematical objects are separable "in formula" (τῷ λόγῳ) but inseparable "in being" (τῇ οὐσίᾳ).[54] Naturally Aristotle does not emphasize the fact that to the extent that mathematical objects are separable—which they are only τῷ λόγῳ—they do not exist: "For 'exist' has many senses." But the use of the word οὐσία implies that they do not exist *qua* separable; indeed Aristotle's critique of Plato's separable Ideas is that they

---

50. Ross, *Aristotle's* Metaphysics, 2.417; presumably he contents himself with "vaguely" as a translation for Aristotle's ἁπλῶς. Cf. Lear, "Aristotle's Philosophy of Mathematics," 170: "Thus, for Aristotle, we can say truly that separable mathematical objects exist, but all this statement amounts to—when properly analyzed—is that mathematical objects are truly instantiated in physical objects and, by applying a predicate filter, we can consider these objects solely as instantiating the appropriate properties." Lear's "predicate filter" is designed to overcome Frege's objections to psychologism (184-86).

51. See Pritchard, *Plato's Philosophy of Mathematics*, 14-15.

52. *Posterior Analytics* 2.9 93b24-25 (emphasis mine): "This too is the actual procedure of the arithmetician, who assumes both the nature *and the existence* of the unit." Cf. Lloyd Gerson, *Aristotle and Other Platonists* (Ithaca, NY: Cornell University Press, 2005), 238n134 and C. C. W. Taylor, "Plato and the Mathematicians: An Examination of Professor Hare's View." *Philosophical Quarterly* 17 (1967), 193-203.

53. James G. Lennox, "Aristotle, Galileo, and 'Mixed Sciences'" in William Wallace (ed.), *Reinterpreting Galileo*, 29-51 (Washington D.C.: Catholic University of America Press. 1985), 36-37 attempts to advance beyond Lear, "Aristotle's Philosophy of Mathematics," by purging the notion of "useful fiction" at the risk of re-importing psychologism.

54. M.2 (1077a36-b2).

do not exist. It may not be entirely out of place to suggest that the easiest way to refute Platonism is to make Plato out to be more of a "Platonist" than he actually is.[55]

Perhaps the most important evidence of dialectic here is the word θείη; Aristotle's best practice is not to assert that the inseparable is separable but merely to proceed *as if it were*. "To place" is not only the etymological basis of "hypothesis" (see section §13) but is used by Plato as a synonym for "hypothesize."[56] As Plato's Socrates points out in the Divided Line, geometers simply *presuppose* the definitions of mathematical elements and do not bother to examine the truth of their Hypotheses by bringing dialectical objections against them. My claim is that Aristotle's testimony about indivisible lines not only proves that Plato offered dialectical objections of this kind but in fact records an objection that Plato himself brought against the most elementary of geometrical elements. In short: Aristotle's Plato gives us even more reason than Plato's Socrates to believe that Plato himself denied the *existence* of mathematical objects. Nor should those of us who recognize his evident commitment to the autonomy of the Idea of the Good be altogether surprised by Plato's ontological austerity in this case, as in others.

In short, if Aristotle is correct that Plato regarded the point as a δόγμα γεωμετρικόν, this illuminates the claim Plato's Socrates makes while discussing the Second Part of the Divided Line in *Republic* that mathematicians must *hypothesize* the elements on which their investigations depend. In contrast with the ultimate object of the Line's First Part, the objects of its Second never become independent of the initial Hypotheses upon which they depend. It would be equally unsafe to assert that these objects exist as to deny that we can meaningfully proceed *as if they did*.[57] But in a Platonic universe in which the objects of opinion do not actually exist, it is significant that the adjective "unhypothetical" is applied only to those objects that unquestionably do. For non-Platonists, by contrast, the verb "to hypothesize" does not entail the non-existence of its object any more than we would regard a δόγμα as ipso facto a fiction.[58] But Plato's ontology is far more austere than ours, so austere in fact that even the objects of mathematics, while doubtless intelligible,[59] are as far

55. In addition to Pritchard, *Plato's Philosophy of Mathematics*, 12 ("Platonic metaphysics"), 14, 22n37, 74, 94-95, 110, 123n17, 118n71, 124, 137, and 159-60, see Lear, "Aristotle's Philosophy of Mathematics," 188n35. For an alternative, cf. Gerson, *Aristotle and Other Platonists*, 237n133 and *Phd.* 64c6.

56. 433a1-6; cf. 510c6-d3; also cf. *Chrm.* 171d2-3 and 172c8-9.

57. Cf. Burnyeat, "Why Mathematics is Good," 22: "What are these abstract, non-sensible things that mathematics reasons about? . . . What is their exact ontological status? We shall see that the *Republic* leaves the external question tantalizingly open."

58. Cf. Gerson, *Aristotle and Other Platonists*, 237: "In particular, mathematicians are said [sc. by Plato] to 'hypothesize' (ὑποθέμενοι) their objects of study. These hypotheses would seem to be primarily, if not exclusively, existential."

59. See the conclusion of §5 at Burnyeat, "Why is Mathematics Good," 22.

removed from the un-hypothetical Good in existential terms as a visible shadow or reflection is from the physical objects esteemed as existent among us.[60]

In contrast to the un-hypothetical Idea of the Good that is the center of Plato's ontology, the merely Hypothesized does not actually exist.[61] Among Hypothesized objects, the unit or monad has logical pride of place: just as arithmetic precedes geometry and astronomy, so also does the unit precede the point to say nothing of the Platonic astronomer's highly idealized planet. Just as the dialectician must recognize why the point is logically prior to all other geometrical objects—and thus why it cannot be defined accurately as the extremity of a line—so also must that same dialectician recognize that the atomic monad is prior to the point. But this logically prior One is no less Hypothetical than the point and therefore no more existent in relation to or rather in comparison with the un-hypothetical existents discovered by νοῆσις. As already indicated in section §13, this conception justifies and complements Aristotle's claim that Plato regarded "the mathematicals" as intermediate between Ideas and sensible things. And like the statement about geometrical fictions to which I claim it is inseparably linked, regarding mathematical objects as Intermediates is a perfectly plausible position to take.[62] Aristotle's implicit argument against mathematical objects as intermediate is simply that it makes mathematical objects *separate*; I have now suggested that it is Aristotle's polemical purpose that compels him to distort Plato's position—a position that Aristotle ironically helps us to see more clearly—or rather to claim that his own position is different from Plato's; this in turn opens a way to understand the doctrine of Intermediates in a different manner from the way Aristotle understands it.

But the bulk of Aristotle's critique of Plato's Intermediates (and of Plato generally in *Metaphysics* A, M, and N) comes from another direction and involves a series of doctrines, closely related to one another. These are the incomparable or Ideal Numbers,[63] the Indefinite Dyad,[64] and the more than merely mathematical One. I want to show that Aristotle's extended attack on these doctrines also demonstrates a misunderstanding of Platonic arithmetic and the dialectical arguments he used to explicate it. This demonstration will develop by

60. Consider "AD : DC :: CE : EB" at Adam, *Republic of Plato*, 2.64.

61. To put it another way: if mathematical objects actually exist for Plato, then the Good is truly "beyond being."

62. Probably because the doctrine of mathematical Intermediates necessarily *presupposes* the existence of Ideas, insufficient attention has been given to whether the doctrine is plausible: the debate has centered on whether or not Plato embraced it. Shorey, *Unity of Plato's Thought*, 82-85 now seems quaint because he accepts the Theory of Ideas and rejects the view that mathematical objects are intermediate only because they are already Ideas and therefore Plato doesn't need them to be anything less.

63. Ross, *Plato's Theory of Ideas*, has given this term a still wider currency. For a more precise manner of speaking, see Cook Wilson, "Platonist Doctrine," especially §8 where he discusses the three times that Aristotle uses the expression.

64. The most lucid account is found in the *Metaphysics* Commentary of Alexander Aphrodisiensis (55.20) at Ross, *Aristotelis Fragmenta*, 113-15.

analogy with the relationship between the point as geometrical fiction and indivisible lines discussed above: like the doctrine of indivisible lines—a doctrine that Aristotle could easily refute—Ideal Numbers, the Indefinite Dyad, and the One as Principle are positions he attributes to Plato because he does not understand the true implications of Plato's doctrine of Intermediates, just as, in the previous and closely related case, he did not understand the implications of Plato's claim that the point was a geometrical fiction. Stated as an analogy, I intend to show that Ideal Numbers, the Indefinite Dyad, and the One as metaphysical Principle are to the Intermediates what Indivisible Lines are to the Point as Geometrical Fiction.

Aristotle's assumption that Platonism sought the causes of change in physical things (A.9 992a24-29)[65] informs his entire critique of the Forms, as the opening sentence from M.5 (1079b12-15), also found at A.9 (991a9-11), indicates:

> Above all one might discuss the question what on earth the Forms contribute to sensible things, either to those that are eternal or to those that come into being and cease to be; for they cause neither movement nor any change in them.

The claim that the Forms were introduced as the causes of physical things—"it was in seeking the causes of sensible things that they proceeded from these to the Forms" (M.4; 1079a1-2 and A.9; 990b5-6)—is in fact the only one for which Aristotle offers textual evidence: "In the *Phaedo* it is stated in this way—that the forms are causes both of being and of becoming."[66] It is important to be crystal clear about the fact that the more inextricably the Forms become entangled with physical processes in the sensible world and thereby envisioned solely as causes

65. In his classic *Aristotle; Fundamentals of the History of his Development*, translated by Richard Robinson, second edition (Oxford: Oxford University Press, 1934), Werner Jaeger has taught us that in *Metaphysics* A, Aristotle is still speaking as a Platonist while in *Metaphysics* M—similar though it is in many ways—he no longer does so (171-72). It is essential to Jaeger's argument that as late as his *Protrepticus*, Aristotle remained an orthodox Platonist (80). In order to prove this, Jaeger must emphasize the mathematical, metaphysical (82), and generally Pythagorean (97) elements in Platonism, i.e., he not only defines Platonism as a late development in Plato's own development (chapter 1)—visible only partially in *Timaeus*, *Philebus*, *Laws*, and *Epinomis* (82)—but in a manner remarkably consistent with the way Aristotle defines wisdom in the cited passage: late Platonic philosophy (cf. 97-98), abandoning the example of Socrates (82), seeks the *causes* of physical things (95). In short, Aristotle's emphasis on the primordial One (87-88), the Indefinite Dyad, and the Ideal Numbers in *Metaphysics* A and M-N reflects Aristotle's own "Platonism," not Plato's, to which—and this is the premise of *Plato the Teacher* as a whole—Plato's *Republic* is our safest guide.

66. M.5 (1080a2-3), identical to A.9 (991b3-4); Ross, *Aristotle's* Metaphysics, 1.199 cites *Phaedo* 100d, a passage about the Beautiful (*Phd.* 100d7-e3). Consider the causal agency of the "better" and "more just" at *Phd.* 98e3-5.

"of becoming,"[67] the easier it will be for Aristotle to reject that their existence as separate. Once he does so, he makes the fresh start at the beginning of M.6 (1080a12-14) that connects M.1-3 with M.6-10 and indeed *Metaphysics* N:

> Since we have discussed these points, it is well to consider again the results regarding numbers which confront those who say that numbers are separable substances and the first causes of things [αἰτίας πρώτας].

It is only at the end of N.6—i.e., of *Metaphysics*—that Aristotle asserts the conclusion of what should be recognized as a single central argument (1093b26-29):

> The fact that they have much trouble with the generation of ideal numbers and can in no way make a system of them, seems to indicate that the objects of mathematics are not separable from sensible things, as some say, and that they are not first principles [τὰς ἀρχάς].

Despite all of its twists and turns, the argument makes clear that it is, among the objects of mathematics, the One and the Indefinite Dyad that have the best claim to being "first principles" and "first causes of things."

Despite Aristotle's evident awareness that Heraclitus persuaded Plato that the physical world was unknowable in M.4 (1078b13-17) and that the Ideas were introduced by Plato to objectify *qua* separate (1078b31-32) the *ethical* definitions sought by Socrates (1078b17-19), he says remarkably little about the Good,[68] the Beautiful, and the Just (see section §25) in his account of Plato in *Metaphysics*. It is clearly not a Socratic Plato but Plato *qua* Pythagorean[69]—for whom numbers really were causes of physical things—that Aristotle is describing in both A.6 and M.9. My claim is that this description does not fit "the late

---

67. Salvaging something even remotely resembling Aristotle's account of Plato's use of Forms as causes in *Phaedo* (99, 106 n. 66) requires the subtlety of Gail Fine, "Forms as Causes: Plato and Aristotle" in Andreas Graeser (ed.), *Mathematics and Metaphysics in Aristotle/Mathematik und Metaphysik bei Aristoteles*, 69-112 (Stuttgart and Bern: Paul Haupt, 1984), 105 and 107, an advance in this respect over C. C. W. Taylor, "Forms as Causes in the *Phaedo*." *Mind* (n.s.) 78 (1969), 45-59.

68. The Good and the Beautiful appear briefly in N.4, further comments about the Good, which has vanished by the time Aristotle writes the first sentence of N.6, appear in N.5. Especially important is N.4 (1091b19-24).

69. See the valuable discussion of Aristotle's emphasis on the Pythagorean influence on Plato at Ross, *Aristotle's* Metaphysics 1.xlv-xlvii. Although he raises the problem of Aristotle's elision of Parmenides, he solves it in a most inadequate manner at xlvii. My claim, by contrast, is that Parmenides was, after Socrates, the decisive *positive* influence on Plato not only with respect to drawing a line between reality and the visibles but also with respect to dialectical pedagogy. The fact that Aristotle's version of Platonism ignored the former is related to the point I am making here: Aristotle was most likely temperamentally unsuited to recognize the latter.

Plato" but rather the early and "Platonic" Aristotle.[70] The two are not always easy to distinguish.[71] But regardless of how Aristotle conceives of the interrelationship between the Ideas, the Dyad, Ideal Number, and the self-dependent One, it is evident that there were certain thinkers who showed, as Aristotle is now showing, that arguments *for* the Forms actually destroyed the Forms. If we claim that philosophy's purpose is to explain the causes of change in physical things and that the Ideas were introduced in order to do so, and if it was only through linking the Forms with Ideal Numbers that they could—through the One and the Dyad—become the causes of sensible things,[72] then *these men* could refute the Ideas by following received *opinions* about the Ideas and opposing them to the first principles of that theory.

It should now be evident why Aristotle ignores the Idea of the Good: there is in fact nothing "for whose existence the assertors of the Forms are more anxious," nothing, that is, if by "assertors of the Forms" we mean Plato. The Idea of the Good is the cause of *intelligible* things in Plato's *Republic*;[73] with the possible exception of the sun (see section §18), it is not presented as the cause of visible things. Above all, no internal inconsistency can be found here. On the other hand, numerous inconsistencies can be found in Aristotle's account of Plato's Theory of Ideas. As previously stated, the inconsistency in which I am principally interested here is between the Ideal Numbers, Dyad, One complex (hereafter "the Complex") on the one hand and the doctrine of Intermediates on the other. I am claiming that this inconsistency is not within Plato's Theory but rather within Aristotle's account of Plato's Theory. If Aristotle had ever understood or accepted Plato's position on mathematical Intermediates, he would have discovered that this doctrine was inconsistent with "the opinions held about the Forms"

70. Consider M.4 (1079a14-19) and A.9 (990b18-22), a passage that makes the most sense if Aristotle is referring to himself as τινές: "And in general the arguments for the Forms destroy that for whose existence the assertors of the Forms are more anxious than for the existence of the Ideas; for it follows that not the dyad but number is first, and the relative is prior to that and prior to the self-dependent—and besides this there are other points on which certain people [τινές], by following out the opinions held about the Forms [ταῖς περὶ τῶν ἰδεῶν δόξαις], have come into conflict [ἠναντιώθηναι] with the principles of the theory [ταῖς ἀρχαῖς]." Ross declines to identify or even to discuss the identity of τινές.

71. Consider Philoponus at Ross, *Aristotelis Fragmenta*, 112 (translation mine): "And the unwritten colloquia of Plato Aristotle himself wrote up [ἀπεγράψετο]."

72. A.6 (987b19-22): "Since the Forms are the causes of all other things, he [sc. Plato] thought their elements were the elements of all things. As matter [ὕλην], the great and the small were principles; as substance [οὐσίαν], the One; for from the great and the small, by participation in the One, come the numbers." The reader should keep this passage in mind in what follows, particularly the identification of the Indefinite Dyad—what Aristotle calls here "the great and the small"—with ὕλη (matter).

73. 508d10-e2: "This reality, then, that gives their truth to the objects of knowledge and the power of knowing to the knower, you must say is the idea of the good." See also 517b8-c4.

that he now needed to follow in order to refute the Ideas on the basis of the easily refutable Complex.

Aristotle is unusually explicit while explaining Plato's role in the development of the Complex at M.8 (1083a34-b1):

> But if the 1 is the starting-point [εἰ δέ ἐστι τὸ ἓν ἀρχή], the truth about numbers must rather be what Plato used to say, and there must be a first 2 and 3, and the numbers must not be comparable with one another [καὶ οὐ συμβλητοὺς εἶναι τοὺς ἀριθμούς πρὸς ἀλλήλους]. But if on the other hand one supposes this, many impossible results, as we have said, follow. But either this or the other [sc. "If . . . one supposes mathematical number alone to exist, the 1 is not the starting-point;" 1083a28-30] must be the case, so that if neither is, number cannot exist separately.

Ross performed a valuable service when he called attention to the fact that this is the only passage in *Metaphysics* M-N where Plato is mentioned by name; he failed to mention that this circumstance makes it analogous to the passage in A.9 linking the point as geometrical fiction with indivisible lines, which Aristotle deletes from M-N, in effect replacing it with this one.[74] Noting the shared structure, I read both of them in the same way. Plato pointed out, for a dialectical purpose, that *if* the monad is *not* merely a mathematical fiction but an absolute ἀρχή, then numbers are not comparable with each other, i.e., they cannot be added to, subtracted from, and multiplied or divided by each other.[75] No less than lines that cannot be divided, numbers that cannot be added are *self-contradictory*. And once again, it is the *consequences* of incomparable numbers—i.e., "many impossible results"—that makes this doctrine easily refutable and therefore, guided by his polemical purpose, Aristotle prefers to take it as Plato's position *while ignoring the hypothesis of which it is a consequence*, i.e., εἰ δέ ἐστι τὸ ἓν ἀρχή ("if the one is a principle"). But in this case, Aristotle's failure to detect his teacher's dialectical pedagogy—as Intermediates, all numbers, separable *qua* intelligibles but not *qua* Ideas,[76] depend equally on the mere-

74. The reference to "indivisible magnitudes" just below at 1083b12-16 may be germane to discovering Aristotle's motives in making this replacement.

75. This accounts for the fact that Aristotle tells us at M.6 1080b9-10 that nobody believed that *only* Ideal Numbers exist. But this is not true for the Moderns: see Ross, *Aristotle's* Metaphysics, 2.427: "So far as ideal numbers are concerned, the doctrine that they are 'incomparable', i.e. incapable of being added or subtracted, multiplied or divided, is a perfectly sound one which is misunderstood by Aristotle . . .The weakness of Aristotle's position is that he believes in mathematical numbers, which do not exist, and does not believe in ideal or universal numbers, which do." According to Aristotle, then, there were no platonists (in the modern sense, i.e. relating to numbers) in the Academy *including Plato*. The view that Plato was "a platonist" in this sense is incorrect; see Julia Annas (ed. and trans.). *Aristotle's* Metaphysics, *Books M and N* (Oxford: Clarendon Press, 1976), 3.

76. This is the heart of the matter and my position is diametrically opposed to that of Cook Wilson, "On the Platonist Doctrine of the ἀσύμβλητοι ἀριθμοί." For his Plato, the

ly hypothetical monad and must therefore be comparable with each other—has a deeper explanation. Of course it would be difficult to say whether Aristotle fails to grasp that Ideal Numbers are an absurd consequence of assuming that the One is an ἀρχή because (1) he was temperamentally unsuited to appreciate Plato's dialectical humor, (2) he rejected the ontological autonomy of the Idea of the Good, true ἀρχή in the Platonic universe, or (3) he himself had once taken the Complex seriously *qua* Platonist; all three factors were probably in play.

Aristotle introduces mathematical Intermediates immediately before he introduces the Complex in *Metaphysics* A.6 (987b14-22):

> Further, besides the sensible things and Forms he says there are objects of mathematics, which occupy an intermediate position [μεταξύ], differing from sensible things in being eternal and unchangeable and from Forms in that there are many alike, while the Form itself is in each case unique. Since the Forms are the causes of all other things, he thought their elements were the elements of all things. As matter, the great and the small were principles; as substance, the One; for from the great and the small, by participation in the One, come the numbers.

Until Eduard Zeller emended the text by deleting τὰ εἴδη,[77] its last clause made the passage as a whole self-contradictory: "for from the great and the small [this

doctrine of Intermediates is *incompatible* with the Divided Line because Numbers *are* Ideas; see his §9. Both on his own and through others, John Cook Wilson (1849-1915) did considerable damage to Platonism; this development, perhaps originating with Henry Jackson, deserves further study. Cf. M. F. Burnyeat, "Platonism and Mathematics. A Prelude to Discussion" in Andreas Graeser (ed.), *Mathematics and Metaphysics in Aristotle/Mathematik und Metaphysik bei Aristoteles.* Akten des X. Symposium Aristotelicum (Bern and Stuttgart: Paul Haupt, 1984), 235: "There was one truth in Cook Wilson's much-cited paper." Cook Wilson's only obvious error (he was very smart)—and even it is concealed by ellipsis—is that he misinterprets M.6 1080a30-32 at 254: "Thus clearly the property of being ἀσύμβλητος is sufficient and necessary to constitute a kind of ἀριθμός a series with πρότερον καὶ ὕστερον." But properly read, 1080a30-32 clearly contradicts his earlier claim: "Thus if there is a serial order of the numbers they must be ἀσύμβλητοι." For Ross's acceptance of this claim, see 1.237 (my emphasis): "*Now according to the Platonists* ideal numbers had, and mathematical numbers had not, this relation of priority and posteriority (M. 1080b11)." The passage cited applies only to the conception of Ideal Number among those who claimed there are two types of numbers, i.e., the doctrine that really *is* incompatible with the Divided Line. On Cook Wilson's incompatibility claim about Intermediates in the Divided Line, Ross, *Aristotle's* Metaphysics, 1.168 says as much as can accurately be said: "Yet it seems impossible to say that the doctrine is actually stated in the passage."

77. Ross, *Aristotle's* Metaphysics, 1.172) explains the interpretive crux before Zeller made the emendation: "Nor is Zeller's interpretation, 'out of the great and small the Forms become numbers by participation in the One', a tenable one; it mistranslates εἶναι, ignores τοὺς, and attributes to Plato a doctrine of which we have absolutely no evidence." My translation (that follows) does not suffer from Ross's first two objections.

is one of Aristotle's expressions for the Dyad], by participation in the One, the Forms are the numbers [τὰ εἴδη εἶναι τοὺς ἀριθμούς]." If the Forms *are* Numbers, then Numbers cannot be *between* (μεταξύ) Forms and sensible things. But Aristotle's failure to understand Plato's mathematical μεταξύ is already evident even if we are willing to emend the text: the difference between mathematical objects and the Ideas is that while both are intelligible as opposed to sensible, the latter are the only things that truly exist while the former must be hypothesized. Once hypothesized, of course, every point—and every monad—will be identical to every other: each will be purely intelligible, unchanging, and indivisible.[78] But at the very least, the doctrine of Intermediates is that they (1) are not sensible, and (2) do not exist in the way that the Forms exist. If we are willing to see the geometrical point as mathematicians saw it—as a monad with position added[79]—and if, moreover, Plato regarded the point as "a geometrical fiction" as Aristotle tells us that he did, then mathematical objects, including "the One," do not, strictly speaking, exist. Such a claim is all the more easily made by a Platonist, who, in accordance with an austere and properly Platonic ontology based on the Idea of the Good, regards the visible things that populate Aristotle's world as even less existent—and certainly more distant from the highest class of intelligibles as per the Divided Line—than the objects of mathematics.

Aristotle's problem in M.1-3 was to exempt mathematics from his attack on Platonism's separables. Aristotle's strategy in M-N as a whole is, having first described mathematical objects in a plausible manner, to attack the Forms on the basis of an implausible conception of mathematics, i.e., by showing inconsistencies between the Forms, the principles of the Forms, and Numbers. Naturally the Numbers he needs here in order to refute Plato are not the plausible numbers of M.2-3: i.e., inseparables that are merely *posited* as separate. Nor, as will be shown below, can he get any traction against Plato on the basis of what he calls "mathematical numbers," i.e., numbers consistent with both the doctrine of Intermediates and the extended implications of the point as geometrical fiction. The reason that he refuses to distinguish mathematical objects from Forms on an

---

The fact that his third point is true hardly proves that Aristotle did not write τὰ εἴδη εἶναι τοὺς ἀριθμούς.

78. See 524b3-526c7. Plato's numbers are strictly intelligible because the things they count are indivisible, i.e., dimensionless, monads. Euclid speaks as Platonist—as Theaetetus does not at *Sph.* 238a10-11, *pace* Annas, *Aristotle's* Metaphysics, *Books M and N*, 5—when he defines "monad" (Heath, *Euclid's* Elements, 2.277): "An unit [μο-νάς] is that by virtue of which [cf. Burnyeat, "Why is Mathematics Good," 25n37] each of the things that exist [τών ὄντων] is called one." By definition, the One—and by extension Number—is not numbered among τών ὄντων. An analogous approach to the Good allows non- or rather anti-Platonists to define it out of transcendent existence on the basis of 509b8, "beyond Being."

79. Consider also M.8 (1084b27): "the unit is a point without position."

existential basis is that, Ross notwithstanding,[80] he needs Forms to be Numbers in order to refute the Forms. Ignoring the fact that Plato, *his* Plato, also considered mathematical numbers to be existentially intermediate—and that, in the light of "geometrical fiction," is probably to understate the case—Aristotle must and does create a new intermediate between Plato's "merely" mathematical numbers and his Forms: these are "the Ideal Numbers."[81] I have now suggested, on the basis of Aristotle's testimony, that Plato originally hypothesized these ἀριθμοί οὐ σύμβλητοι as a dialectical *modus tollens* on the One as a metaphysical principle (ἀρχή) but that Aristotle *qua* Platonist—no doubt in company with many others whom he calls "assertors of the Forms"—took them more seriously.[82] To put it another way: Ideal Numbers are perfectly consistent with

---

80. It is not only Aristotle's critique of Plato that is in play here: the scholarly tradition that includes Ross mounts an even more lethal attack on Plato, on the basis of Aristotle, than Aristotle does. It is instructive to compare the manner in which Ross treats the doctrine of Intermediates and the Dyad in his commentary on the passage just quoted from A.6. In the former case (Ross, *Aristotle's* Metaphysics, 1.166-68), there is extended discussion of (a) whether or not the doctrine is true (e.g. "the doctrine appears to be right with regard to the objects of geometry, and wrong with regard to those of arithmetic" at 166), and (b) whether or not Plato actually subscribed to it. Ross is inclined to doubt that he did (168): "If, instead, he were setting up the objects of διάνοια as a class of Intermediates, it would not be in his manner to introduce the new doctrine with so little indication of novelty and so little attempt to indicate his meaning." In the latter case (1.169-172), by contrast, there is *no discussion of whether or not the Dyad doctrine is true* while Ross concludes that Plato embraced, or rather came to embrace it (171): "we must suppose that the doctrine of the *Philebus* was the starting point from which Plato worked in developing the later doctrine." The reader will note the discordant analogy between the manner in which Ross uses *Philebus* and *Republic*; neither contain the doctrine in question (cf. 168 and 171) but only one of them is read as a way station toward Plato's eventual embrace of it. *This suggests that the doctrine of "Plato's development" is originally Aristotelian and thus that its original purpose was as much polemical as explanatory.* In the context of my earlier remarks about Cook Wilson, Ross's reference to "Prof. Jackson's gallant effort" (171) to find Aristotle's Dyad in *Philebus* should be juxtaposed with Jackson, "On Plato's *Republic* VI 509 D," *fons et origo* of the Anglophone assault on Intermediates in the Line, discussed in section §13.

81. Aristotle's Plato thought that some numbers are vulgar, some intermediate, and some Ideal; these are the *three* number-types described in Wedberg, *Plato's Philosophy of Mathematics*; cf. Pritchard, *Plato's Philosophy of Mathematics*, 154-57. When Aristotle identifies Forms with numbers—an identification that Cherniss emphatically rejects—he is not identifying Forms with Intermediates. Rather, he is saying that there are numbers that are not the objects of mathematics used by arithmeticians, i.e., Ideal Numbers. That Aristotle did not think Plato identified Forms with Intermediates should be clear from passages such as Z.2 1028b19-21 (emphasis mine): "Plato posited *two kinds* of substance—the Forms and the objects of mathematics—as well as a third kind, viz. the substance of sensible bodies." For passages where Aristotle says that Forms are numbers, see M.7 (1081a8-17 and 1082b23-32) and M.8 (1083a17-20, 1084a12-17, 1084a18-21, and 1084a21-25).

82. Jaeger, *Aristotle's Development*, 87.

Aristotle's account of Platonism: a doctrine based on the view "that there must be Ideas of all things that are spoken of universally."[83] This, of course, is Shorey's "hypostatized" conception of Ideas (see section §13).

There is no reason to doubt that Aristotle believed that Plato believed that there was a Form of Three no less than a Form of Man. But readers guided only by Plato's dialogues will be considerably less certain about this than Aristotle was, especially because "The Third Man" can *only* be applied to "Forms" of perceptible objects and their properties.[84] As I have read Aristotle's account of Plato, it contains information not included in the dialogues some of which is accurate and some of which is not. Discriminating between the two— precisely what is being undertaken here—is not an easy task but a very important one. I have attempted to accomplish this task by juxtaposing two such doctrines. I am claiming that Incomparable Numbers, dependent on regarding the One as unhypothetical ἀρχή rather than as Hypothesis, are analogous to Indivisible Lines in that they are not doctrines Plato actually held because, (a) they are not found in Plato, (b) they are easily refutable, indeed self-contradictory, (c) they arise in a polemical context, and yet (d) Aristotle had plausible grounds to believe that Plato believed them. But Aristotle also gives us, in (1) the doctrine of Intermediates, (2) the view that the point is a geometrical fiction, and (3) the absurd consequences of embracing the One as ἀρχή, good reason to think that Plato actually did not. The fact that Aristotle pays more attention to the merely dialectical doctrine he can easily refute than to the doctrine that, when taken seriously, is inconsistent with it, is hardly amazing: he is attempting to refute Plato.

As it happens, Indivisible Lines are more than merely analogous to the Incomparable Numbers: *they are plausibly understood as the same doctrine*. Consider pseudo-Aristotle in *On Indivisible Lines* (968a9-11):

> Again, if there is an Idea of line, and if the Idea is first of the things called by its name, then, since the parts are by nature prior to their whole, the Ideal Line must be indivisible.

It will be recalled that Aristotle introduced Plato's indivisible line in the context of the point: there is therefore some basis for the claim that Plato invented, if only for a dialectical purpose, the self-contradictory concept of the infinitesimal.[85] Pseudo-Aristotle, by contrast, is envisioning a line—a line with length—that is atomic not because it is infinitesimally small but because it is the Idea of Line: it is the "ideal Line." This indivisibility is also essential to the Ideal Numbers to which Aristotle gives so much attention in both *Metaphysics* A and M-N.

---

83. M.4 (1078b33-34); cf. the opening of A.9.

84. Cf. *Prm.* 131a1-2 and *Prm.* 132a2-b3 with *Phd.* 65d4-12 and *Phd.* 100e5-6. Consider also the limited scope of Gail Fine, *On Ideas: Aristotle's Criticism of Plato's Theory of Forms* (Oxford: Clarendon Press, 1993), 225-241.

85. See the valuable discussion in Maria Timpanaro Cardini, *Pseudo-Aristotele,* De lineis insecabilibus (Milan: Instituto Editoriale Cisalpino, 1970).

Because they are *not* composed of merely Hypothetical units—each of which is therefore identical to all the others in being purely intelligible, unchanging, and indivisible—*they themselves are indivisible.* We are thus confronted once again with the same kind of paradox: indivisible and mutually incomparable "numbers" are the inevitably self-contradictory result of the unique metaphysical monad *qua* ἀρχή just as "lines" without length are the self-contradictory alternative to considering the geometrical monad as a merely Hypothetical δόγμα. "Indivisible Lines" and "Incomparable Numbers" are therefore best understood as deliberately self-contradictory concepts exemplifying Plato's basanistic pedagogy and employed here to bring dialectical objections to any attempt to make mathematical objects un-hypothetical. And if Plato (1) regarded the Idea of the Good as prior to and indeed the ultimate cause of all other intelligibles (as he unquestionably did), and if (2) among the intelligible objects of διάνοια the primordial *hypothesis* was the indivisible unit (as it certainly is), and (3) that if all other arithmetical and indeed mathematical objects, being either derived from the point or composed of identical, combinable, and indivisible units, were therefore by definition *divisible* (which they are), then Plato would have had no reason to fear any of the consequences of "mathematical number" that Aristotle discovers in the following passage from M.7 (1081a5-16):

> If all units [μονάδες] are comparable [σύμβλητοι] and without difference, we get mathematical number and this alone, and the Ideas cannot be numbers. For what sort of number will the ideal man or animal or any other Form be? There is one Idea of each thing, e.g. one of the ideal man and another one of the ideal animal; but the similar and undifferentiated numbers are infinitely many, so that this 3 is no more ideal than any other 3. But if the Ideas are not numbers, neither can they exist at all. For from what principles will the Ideas come [ἐκ τίνων ἔσονται ἀρχῶν αἱ ἰδέαι]? Number comes from the 1 and the indefinite dyad, and the principles and the elements are said to be the principles and elements of number, and the Ideas cannot be ranked as either prior or posterior to the numbers.

It is only proper, having allowed Aristotle to speak for himself, to leave the final judgment on this passage to the reader.

Aristotle himself has considerably more to say—and it requires the rest of M.7, M.8-10, and most of N for him to say it—about what follows from the conditional that begins "if units are non-comparable," i.e., about the claim that there are Ideal Numbers. This claim creates a variety of problems on both ends: how Ideal Numbers can come to be through the agency of the Dyad and the One and how they can act as prior causes of other things. Aristotle will devote particular attention to the problems involved in the generation of ἀριθμοί ἀσύμβλητοι; when these problems prove insuperable, as they are pronounced to be in the last sentence of *Metaphysics* N—i.e., of Aristotle's *Metaphysics* as a whole—Aristotle will have refuted "those who introduced" the One, the Dyad, and the Ideal Numbers. I am claiming that we should take Aristotle's indirect mode of speech seriously albeit if not exclusively because Aristotle is intent on speaking the truth about Plato. The exhaustive attention Aristotle gives to these problems indicates to this reader that they were once real problems *for Aristotle* but there is no evidence, independent of Aristotle, that they were so for Plato. They can, however, plausibly be considered as "Platonic" problems. I would also like to suggest, if only as an incentive to further study, that they are problems to which Aristotle's eventual solution was hardly less "Platonic."[86]

When read in the context of Aristotle's testimony, the Divided Line suggests that the Idea of the Good—the true basis of Platonism to the revelation of which, the discovery of the dialectical unity of the mathematical sciences serves merely as "prelude"[87]—is in fact the logical *antithesis* of the One: the latter is the *first* unquestioned hypothesis of διάνοια while the former is the ultimate un-

86. It would be interesting to read the extended discussion of the Complex, with which *Metaphysics* concludes, as a record of Aristotle's intellectual development. In M-N, Aristotle points out "many impossible results" arising from the attempt to generate Ideal Numbers by the One and the Indefinite Dyad. But something quite different is actually being generated here: Aristotelianism. Given that Aristotle identifies the Dyad with matter, it is interesting that when he needs the distinction between potency and act at the end of *Metaphysics* M, he writes of it as follows: "For knowledge, like knowing, is spoken of in two ways—as potential and as actual. The potentiality, being, as matter, universal and indefinite, deals with the universal and indefinite; but the actuality, being definite, deals with a definite object,—being a 'this', it deals with a 'this'." The context of this remark suggests the analogy with the One and the Indefinite Dyad. This becomes more obvious in N.2: having by this point frequently recurred to potency and act—(1088b1-3, 1088b18-20, 1089a27-31—the addition of "bodies" to numbers and lengths at 1089a3, the reference to "the cause" (Ross correctly identifies τὸ αἴτιον at 1089b3 with *Aristotle*'s ὕλη at 2.476: "Aristotle means ὕλη, which is the same in all the categories, or analogically the same; i.e. in all things matter and form are in the same relation to one another"), and then the important passage from 1089b16-32 (worthy of extended commentary in its own right), allow us to see the "Platonic" origin of Aristotle's explanation of how Matter's indefinite plurality, through Form, becomes an individual substance (cf. πῶς πολλὰ τὸ τόδε τι at 1089b29). Wrestling with the Indefinite Dyad and the One, Aristotle turned them against themselves in order to generate *inseparable* substances and all that could be predicated of them. Even if the ease with which he could do so indicates that he was actually wrestling with himself from the start, all who value their "individuality" must be grateful to Aristotle for embodying the indivisible One in the concrete particular. More specifically, all Anglophone students of Greek Philosophy must be grateful for—and North Americans can be very proud—of the monumental contribution of Edward Halper to the study of Aristotle; I regret that the third volume of his study was not available before "going to press."

87. The word is used twice at 531d6-7 and a third time at 532d7. Cf. Lachterman, "What is 'The Good'?," 159: "Guided by this indication [sc. 'the dialectician is . . . the one who can see things in their togetherness'], I would have tried to show that coming to know *The Good* is not a matter of learning something new over and above the antecedent studies; instead, knowledge of *The Good* consists in coming to see how those studies are akin to one another, that is, how their order and array constitutes a complete whole [n26]." Given 531c9-d8, it is a good thing he did not try to do this but it is revealing that he cites *Epinomis* as justification at 170-71n26.

hypothetical reality disclosed by νοῆσις through dialectic, i.e., "the song itself." If Plato did lecture on the Good and identify it with the One, there is no reason to doubt the rest of Aristoxenus' testimony: Aristotle was one of the few who were not disappointed by this performance.[88] This should by no manner of means be taken as proof that Aristotle alone was capable of understanding his teacher. Since it is self-evident that Plato knew how to be entertaining when he wished to be,[89] this result probably reflected his pedagogical intent.[90] If he wished to *test* the extent of any given student's commitment to Platonism as *Plato* understood it,[91] he could easily have done so by discovering who would publicly challenge a statement that every Platonist who understood Plato's view of mathematics—and who, more importantly, shared his Socratic commitment to ethical action in accordance with the transcendent Good[92]—would find no less *deliberately* self-contradictory than the joke he repeatedly made (τοῦτο δὲ πολλάκις ἐτίθει) about "indivisible lines."

And now, with the playful Plato finally restored to sight, it is easy to see that it is the One *qua* Intermediate that constitutes the essence of the so-called "Higher Education" of Book VII: it is the hypothesis upon which everything else

---

88. Cf. Diogenes Laertius 3.37: "And according to Favorinus, when Plato read the dialogue *On the Soul*, Aristotle alone stayed to the end; the rest of the audience got up and went away." The sane Simplicius (151.8 at Ross, *Aristotelis Fragmenta*, 117) locates Speusippus, Xenocrates, "and others" along with Aristotle as audience for "On the Good." On the connection between Speusippus and the subjects under consideration here, see Ian Mueller, "On Some Academic Theories of Mathematical Objects." *Journal of Hellenic Studies* 106 (1986), 111-120.

89. Cf. Michael J. B. Allen, "Ficino's Lecture on the Good?" *Renaissance Quarterly* 30 (1977), 160-171 at 169: "Ficino's gifts as a lecturer, musician, group-psychiatrist, and mage make it inconceivable that he did not realize exactly what he was doing when he cast his first public lectures into such an intractable metaphysical mould. One has to suppose that he did not accept the malicious view that Plato had bungled but assumed that Plato chose to lose most of his audience deliberately."

90. Given the crucial role of *Philebus* in the attempt to discover the Complex in the dialogues (in addition to Ross, *Aristotle's* Metaphysics, 1.170-71 and Jaeger, *Aristotle's Development*, 87-90, see Reale, *New Interpretation*, 265-76 and 335-357), it is noteworthy that Protarchus proposes and Socrates ignores the need for a *fifth* principle of division (διάκρισις) at *Phlb.* 23d9-e1. There is an extended discussion of "the fifth element" and a "fifth life" lived in accordance with it in Book II, Chapter 4 of Ficino's *Philebus* Commentary; see also Michael J. B. Allen (ed.), *Marsilio Ficino: The* Philebus *Commentary* (Berkeley: University of California Press, 1975), 420-22.

91. Hermann Gundert, "Zum philosophischen Exkurs im 7. Brief" in Hans-Georg Gadamer and Wolfgang Schadewaldt (eds.), *Idee und Zahl; Studien zur platonischen Philosophie*, 85-105 (Heidelberg: Carl Winter, 1968), 89-90 and 104-5. Although Gundert presumably believes that Aristotle passed it, his identification of the lecture as a test (πεῖρα and G. *Probe*) is significant for Tübingen and has therefore been repudiated by Gaiser, "Plato's Enigmatic Lecture," 16-17 and 32n44.

92. M.3 (1078a31-32): "Now since the good and the beautiful are different (for the former always implies conduct as its subject"

in it depends: the merely mathematical monad, the intelligible image of each sensible thing. Once having hypothesized the existence of this infinitely repeatable abstraction, a wonderfully rigorous system of thought can then be built upon it. To call it "the number one" is, of course, illegitimate: "One" is crucially not a number but rather the other-excluding opposite of the very plurality (i.e., of the Many as distinguished from the One) that it nevertheless makes possible. Unlike a number, which is nothing but a finite number of monads, the mathematical One contains no parts and cannot be split.[93] That which *can* be split is by definition a number at least as large as two while the One is merely "the origin of number." In fact, that's the whole point—the geometrical pun is intended because the point is merely a monad with position—of Plato's "Higher Education." In short: Plato's One is by no manner of means the mystical ἀρχή ("beyond Being") that binds all things together in an emanationist monism.

But as simple as all this really is, the Indefinite Dyad, paired with the metaphysical One as the second "principle" in Aristotle's account of Plato's system, *can* be found in *Republic* VII,[94] albeit not as ἀρχή. Its appearance there is, however, archeological: Socrates uses the indefiniteness arising when something is no more one thing than its opposite to introduce the mathematical One that stands at the beginning, middle, and end—it is indeed its be-all and its end-all—of Higher Education. Starting from the mixed messages it receives from the same sensible object,[95] the soul must learn to think each of the two opposite qualities as one and therefore both as two:

> "And if it should seem to be two, each seems both different and one [ἕτερόν τε καὶ ἓν ἑκάτερον]." "Yes." "If, then, each is one [ἓν ἑκάτερον] while both are two [ἀμφότερα δὲ δύο], the soul will know [νοήσει] the two to have been separated [τά γε δύο κεχωρισμένα] for it would not be knowing [οὐ γὰρ ἂν . . . ἐνόει] an inseparable two [ἀχώριστά γε δύο] but one [ἀλλ' ἕν]." "Right."[96]

93. This is necessarily the first thing that must be taught: the principal principle, the ἀρχή (as in both "beginning" and "rule") of the Higher Education and guides it throughout. As one who would follow Plato the Teacher must always be saying: "½ is only one half *of Two*, not of One: that's why it's 'one over two' or 'one part out of two.' See 525d8-e4, especially: "'If you divide it, they multiply.'" In other words, it is always only *number* that can be split, cut, or divided; the one is literally *individual* (i.e. indivisible).

94. It makes its first appearance in Book IV, first at 438a7-c4 and then, in an anticipation of *Philebus* (where numbers occupy the middle ground between the limited and the unlimited) at 445c4-7. See also 585b9.

95. 524b1-6 (Shorey modified): "'Yes, indeed,' he said, 'these communications to the soul are strange and invite consideration [ἐπισκέψεως].' 'Naturally, then,' said I, 'it is in such cases as these that the soul, first [πρῶτον μὲν] summoning [παρακαλοῦσα] logistic and reason [λογισμόν τε καὶ νόησιν], tries to consider [ἐπισκοπεῖν] whether each of the things reported to it is one or two.' 'Of course.'"

96. 524b7-c2 (Shorey modified).

The Indefinite Dyad (ἡ δύο ἀχώριστά), implicated by contradictory impressions, therefore gives rise to a legitimate alternative: "a definite dyad" (τά δύο κεχωρισμένα) composed of two units, each being one (ἓν ἑκάτερον).

> "Sight too saw the great and the small [μέγα . . . καὶ σμικρὸν], we say, but not separated [οὐ κεχωρισμένον] but as something mixed together [ἀλλὰ συγκεχυμένον τι]. "Is not that so?" "Yes." "And for the sake of the clarification of this, the intelligence [ἡ νόησις] is compelled to contemplate the great and small [μέγα αὖ καὶ σμικρὸν], not mixed together [οὐ συγκεχυμένα] but distinguished [διωρισμένα], in the opposite way from sensation." "True."[97]

Appearing in Aristotle as a metaphysical ἀρχή from which numbers are generated,[98] "the great and the small" is actually overcome when reason (ἡ νόησις) sorts out "the indefinite dyad" of contradictory sense impressions by means of first One and then Number, the latter beginning with "the definite two." In the pedagogy or perhaps even in the phenomenology of νόησις, the Indefinite Dyad—or rather the mathematical transcendence of the Indefinite Dyad by means of the mathematical One—plays a crucial if purely negative part.

> "And is it not in some such experience as this that the question first [πρῶτον] occurs to us, what in the world, then, is the great and the small [τί οὖν ποτ' ἐστὶ τὸ μέγα αὖ καὶ τὸ σμικρόν]?" "By all means." "And this is the origin of the designation "intelligible" [τὸ μὲν νοητόν] for the one, and "visible" [τὸ δ' ὁρατὸν] for the other." (524c10-13)

Although Book VII offers evidence for the Indefinite Dyad, it is not the kind of evidence that Tübingen School is likely to emphasize: it appears there not *qua* ἀρχή but rather as what might be called "pseudo-dyadic indistinctiveness." Although the critical role of the mathematical One in overcoming this indistinctiveness is not explained until the Divided Line has prepared the student for Book VII, proleptic intimations of it have already appeared in Books I-IV.

---

97. 524c3-9 (Shorey modified). Consider Shorey's comment on this passage at *Plato's Republic* 2.159n"e": "My suggestion that this passage is the probable source of the notion which still infests the history of philosophy, that the great-and-the-small was a metaphysical entity or principle in Plato's later philosophy, to be identified with indeterminate dyad, has been disregarded. Cf. *Unity of Plato's Thought*, 84. But it is the only plausible explanation that has ever been proposed of the attribution of that 'clotted nonsense' to Plato himself. For it is fallacious to identify μᾶλλον καὶ ἧττον in *Philebus* 24 C, 25 C, 21 E, and elsewhere with the μέγα καὶ σμικρόν. But there is no limit to the misapprehension of texts by hasty or fanciful readers in any age."

98. *Metaphysics* A.6 (987b19-23): "Since the Forms are the causes of all other things, he thought their elements were the elements of all things. As matter [ὡς μὲν οὖν ὕλην], the great and the small [τὸ μέγα καὶ τὸ μικρὸν] were principles [ἀρχάς]; as substance [ὡς δ' οὐσίαν], the One [τὸ ἕν]; for from the great and the small, by participation in the One, come the numbers."

But the introduction of philosophy arising from the Third Wave of Paradox increases the stakes involved in using the One to distinguish a definite Two:

> "It would be by no means easy to explain it to another," I said, "but I think that you will grant me this." "What?" "That since beautiful is the opposite [ἐναντίον] of base, they are two." "Of course." "And since they are two, each is one [ἓν ἑκάτερον]." "That also." "And in respect of the just and the unjust, the good and the bad, and all the ideas or forms, the same statement holds, that in itself each is one, but that by virtue of their communion with actions and bodies and with one another, everywhere each [ἕκαστον] appears as many [πολλὰ] aspects." "Right," he said.[99]

Here Socrates can count on Glaucon's moral sensibilities to keep the beautiful and the base distinct without yet having introduced the mathematical One. But the need for that humble One has by this point become acute: in addition to the "one out of many" that defines the Harmonious Man in Book IV (section §14), Socrates' justification of the Second Wave of Paradox in Book V provides important evidence for this fraudulent but seductive "One."[100] In spite, then, of the considerable difference between Socrates' claim here that Beauty is one and its claim that the Idea of Good is *the One*, the Tübingen School can draw considerable comfort from the following passage:[101]

> "Is not the logical first step [ἀρχὴ] towards such an agreement: to ask ourselves what is the greatest good [τί ποτε τὸ μέγιστον ἀγαθὸν ἔχομεν] we could name for the constitution of a state and the proper aim of a lawgiver in his legislation, and what is the greatest evil [καὶ τί μέγιστον κακόν], and then to consider whether the proposals we have just set forth fit into the footprints of the good [τὸ τοῦ ἀγαθοῦ ἴχνος] and do not suit those of the evil?" "By all means," he said. "Do we know of any greater evil for a state than the thing that distracts it and makes it many instead of one [πολλὰς ἀντὶ μιᾶς], or a greater good [μεῖζον ἀγαθὸν] than that which binds it together and makes it one [συνδῇ τε καὶ ποιῇ μίαν]?" "We do not."[102]

By analogy with demoting the Indefinite Dyad from the metaphysical ἀρχή discussed by Aristotle to a pseudo-dyadic indistinctiveness that inevitably infects a sense-based epistemology that Socrates describes in *Republic* VII, the other ἀρχή of "the Unwritten Doctrines," i.e., the One that is the Good, is like-

---

99. 475e6-476a9 (Shorey modified).

100. Lachterman, "What is 'The Good,'" 160: "The means that The Good, as the ground of the integrative ordering of Forms, serves as the model for political and psychological integration." Given Lachterman's acknowledged debt to Heidegger (168-69n21), the close connection between his views and those of Tübingen is suggestive.

101. Reale, *New Interpretation*, 207-12; naturally Reale fails to cite 457d6-8 and 464b1-6 where there is no greater good than the community of women and children.

102. 462a2-b3; cf. 422e1-423c4. For the connection between the unity of the City and its grounding Hypothesis, see 423d3-6.

wise present in *Republic* but equally deserving of an analogous demotion. Both the Indefinite Dyad and the One *qua* Good are actually present in the text, the latter in the passage just quoted, and in neither case is the doctrine actually "unwritten." But they are present in a strictly negative sense: as an *alternative* to the truth that Plato uses the Divided Line to teach. Particularly in the post-*Republic* dialogues, the true relationship between the One and the Many will become the front-line of an interpretive battle and the student's awareness that the only true One is never simultaneously Many will be repeatedly tested, as in *Epinomis*. It is worth recalling that from the very beginning, philosophy *qua* physics had attempted to explain the underlying *unity* of all *things*. This confusion of singularity and plurality is the origin of the famous Problem of the One and the Many. In accordance with mankind's "*Drang nach Einheit*" (its earnest yearning for unity), an ongoing attempt to show that "all things are one" necessarily confuses the One and the Many. Plato, by contrast, solved and disposed of this ancient Problem:[103] the merely mathematical One of *Republic* VII—so useful for freeing the soul from the objects of sense—is the origin of number but not of all things and no composite substance can in any accurate sense be called "one." Plato's One is a mere Hypothesis, not a metaphysical ἀρχή: an Image, not a reality. Humble though it may be, the One that alone makes the Many *many* is the only true One; the unity that makes the Many *one* is fraudulent no matter how harmonious (cf. G. *Einklang*) it may be. Neither the one nor the other is the Idea of the Good although, as the later history of "Platonism" would prove,[104] the cosmogonical One is unquestionably seductive and—this claim will be more fully developed elsewhere—is best understood as Plato's basanistic alternative to it.

An ability to distinguish the One from the dyadic indistinctiveness of sensible things therefore proves to be the most important by-product of the child's play that is arithmetic when properly understood in the context of the Divided Line.

> "This, then, is just what I was trying to explain a little while ago when I said that some things are provocative of thought [παρακλητικὰ τῆς διανοίας] and some are not, defining as provocative things that impinge upon the senses together with their opposites, while those that do not I said do not tend to awaken reflection [οὐκ ἐγερτικὰ τῆς νοήσεως]." "Well, now I understand," he said,

103. Cf. Michael C. Stokes, *One and Many in Presocratic Philosophy* (Washington D.C.: Center for Hellenic Studies, 1971), 218: "There is no reason why late fifth-century Pythagoreans should not have presupposed innocently in their practice, like the Atomists and others, that it was possible to call a thing 'one' when it was in some senses 'many.'" By failing to grasp Plato's solution to it, Aristotle *restored* the Problem.

104. Even more than his *From Platonism to Neoplatonism* (The Hague: Martinus Nijhoff, 1953), Philip Merlan, "Greek Philosophy from Plato to Plotinus" in A. H. Armstrong (ed.), *The Cambridge History of Later Greek and Early Medieval Philosophy*, 14-192. (Cambridge, UK: Cambridge University Press, 1967) is required reading for every serious student of Plato and this brilliant scholar will be my constant companion and dialectical inspiration in the second volume of *Plato the Teacher*.

> "and agree." "To which class, then, do you think number and the one [ἀριθμός τε καὶ τὸ ἕν] belong?" "I cannot conceive [οὐ συννοῶ]," he said. "Well, reason it out [ἀναλογίζου] from what has already been said."[105]

Considered as an end in itself, the goal of the Higher Education is the emancipation of διάνοια from the pseudo-dyadic indistinctiveness of the sensible world. But in the context of the First Part of the Divided Line, it makes possible the emancipation of νοῆσις from διάνοια. Using the analogy Socrates suggests to Glaucon here, we might say that just as the Higher Education emancipates the soul from pseudo-dyadic indistinctiveness by means of διάνοια, so also νοῆσις emancipates us from the Hypothetical Image—i.e., the mathematical monad—upon which the Higher Education itself entirely depends. It is the dependence of all five mathematical sciences on the One that furnishes the theme for the prelude; the song itself begins with the dialectical questioning of this dependence, a dialectical questioning in which, if Aristotle's testimony is to be believed, "Indivisible Lines" and "Incomparable Numbers" played important parts. The highest vision of the cosmologists—the inaudible harmony of the heavenly spheres bound together in a circulating *universe*—is mere child's-play for the Platonist and its "one out of many" unity is antithetical to the One on which its structure nevertheless entirely depends. To put it another way: if Plato had been a pre-Socratic physicist, he might well have been interested in deriving sensible things from the Highest Good by means of Numbers; in such a project, the *Prinzipienlehre* would indeed prove useful.[106] But his Socrates is not interested in this kind of "reality" and moreover points out that even though the true One is necessary for freeing us from the contradictions of perception, it is neither "the dialectical One which as the Whole is the source of Being"[107] nor even an emanated way-station on the way toward it:

---

105. 524d1-d8; cf. Shorey, *Plato's Republic*, 2.160n"a": "To waive metaphysics, unity is, as modern mathematicians say, a concept of the mind which experience breaks up. The thought is familiar to Plato from the *Meno* to the *Parmenides*. But it is not true that Plato derived the very notion of the concept from the problem of the one and the many. Unity is a typical concept, but the consciousness of the concept was developed by the Socratic quest for the definition."

106. Krämer, *Arete bei Platon und Aristoteles*, 547-48 (translation mine): "The One in its nimble worldliness [*Weltzugewandheit*] is the highest standard [*Maßstab*] of existence [*Seiendheit*], value, and truth and thereby, as measure (μέτρον), is in relation to the world [*auf die Welt bezogen*]. The concept of the ἕν [one] as μέτρον [measure] indicates thereby the basis of Being [*Seinsgrund*] in its relationship to the world generally and thus represents the correlation, the point of contact between the resting-in-itself [*in sich ruhenden*], transcendent Absolute and reality [*der Realität*]." For Krämer's critique of Heidegger—Krämer's Plato is far more Heideggerian than Heidegger's—see 555n4.

107. Brann, *Music of the Republic*, 235: "we recall that the mathematical one, the atomic, least and indifferent unit (525e ff.), is the total inverse of the dialectical One which as the Whole is the source of Being in its fullness and the differentiated *eíde* under it (p. 220, 511b7 [a diagram based on Brann's conception of the Line]; on these disparate functions of the Platonic One, see *Metaphysics* 1084b13ff.)." It is revealing that she can

> "For, if unity [τὸ ἓν] is adequately seen by itself or apprehended by some other sensation, it would not be drawing [οὐκ ἂν ὁλκὸν εἴη] toward Being [ἐπὶ τὴν οὐσίαν], as we were explaining in the case of the finger."[108]

As this important but easily overlooked text makes clear, it is not the One of διάνοια that leads directly to the objects of νοῆσις; after having reached the One and working our way through the sciences that depend on it, we must begin all over again. But even if the One as unquestioned Hypothesis is not the *metaphysical* gateway to Being, it is nevertheless the *pedagogical* gateway: it offers the student emancipation from the self-contradictory (or pseudo-dyadic) indistinctiveness that characterizes Becoming.

> "But if some contradiction [ἐναντίωμα] is always seen at the same time [ἅμα] with it, so that it appears to be no more one than even its opposite [μηδὲν μᾶλλον ἓν ἢ καὶ τοὐναντίον], there would forthwith be need of something to judge between them, and it would compel the soul to be at a loss and to inquire [ἀπορεῖν καὶ ζητεῖν], by moving thought [τὴν ἔννοιαν] within it, and to ask, whatever then is the one as such [τί ποτέ ἐστιν αὐτὸ τὸ ἕν], and thus among those that guide and convert the soul to the contemplation of true being [ἐπὶ τὴν τοῦ ὄντος θέαν], there would be learning about the one [ἡ περὶ τὸ ἓν μάθησις]."[109]

Through all trials—and both the Harmonious Man of Book IV and the unified City of Book V are early indications of the many trials that will follow *Republic*—the student must never forget Plato's simple arithmetical solution to the ancient Problem of the One and the Many:[110]

---

quote Plato on the mathematical one but, following Tübingen (354-361), must rely on Aristotle for the One that she (but not I) regards as fully Platonic. We agree, however, that one is "the total inverse" of the other.

108. 524d8-e2 (Shorey modified).

109. 524e2-525a3 (Shorey modified). In response to Socrates' nuanced defense of διάνοια as re-orientation rather than revelation, Plato allows his brother to introduce "the Indefinite Dyad" at 523e1-524a3 and 525a4-6 (Shorey modified): "'But surely,' he said, "the visual perception of it does especially involve this. For we see at the same time [ἅμα] the same thing [ταὐτὸν] as both one [ὡς ἕν τε] and as an indefinite plurality [καὶ ὡς ἄπειρα τὸ πλῆθος].'" On this passage, see Shorey, *Plato's Republic*, 2.161n"d": "This is the problem of the one and the many with which Plato often plays, which he exhaustively and consciously illustrates in the *Parmenides*, and which the introduction to the *Philebus* treats as a metaphysical nuisance to be disregarded in practical logic."

110. 525d8-e4 on which Shorey (2.164n"c") comments: "Numbers are the aptest illustration of the principle of the *Philebus* and the *Parmenides* that thought has to postulate unities which sensation (sense perception) and also dialectics are constantly disintegrating into pluralities. Cf. my *Ideas of Good in Plato's Republic*, p. 222. Stenzel, *Dialektik*, p. 32, says this dismisses the problem of the one and the many 'das ihn (Plato) später so lebhaft beschäftigen sollte.' But that is refuted by *Parmen.* 159 C: οὐδὲ μὴν μόριά γε ἔχειν φαμὲν τὸ ὡς ἀληθῶς ἕν. The 'problem' was always in Plato's mind. He

> "For you are doubtless aware that experts in this study, if anyone attempts to cut up the 'one' in argument, laugh at him and refuse to allow it; but if you mince it up, they multiply, always on guard lest the one [τὸ ἓν] should appear to be not one [μὴ ἓν] but a multiplicity of parts [ἀλλὰ πολλὰ μόρια]." "Most true," he replied. (525d8-e3)

It is necessary to grasp the utterly simple point about the merely mathematical monad that Socrates makes here. As part-less thought-atom, the One of *Republic* VII is not only the perfectly simple solution to the Problem of the One and the Many but also the outer wall that protects the fortress of Platonic ontology. Hypostatizing this merely hypothetical image as a metaphysical ἀρχή, by contrast, threatens its defenses from within. Reading several of the post-*Republic* dialogues as basanistic will show that Plato anticipates this development without embracing it and thereby both tests his students and teaches them how to circumvent it. Several passages from *Republic* have now been used to illustrate how "the unwritten doctrines" can be present in a strictly negative sense while the later history of Platonism will soon enough reveal how οὐσία ("being") can be reconfigured as a whole of distinguishable but inseparable parts whereby the unity of each thing becomes its goodness.[111] Although guarded by the radical distinction between the Idea of the Good and the One, the citadel of Platonism is the alternative to the Indefinite Dyad first made accessible to νοῆσις by the mathematical One of διάνοια: the "definite dyad" of Becoming and Being described by Socrates in his defense of geometry:

> "What we have to consider is whether the greater and more advanced part of it makes it easier [ῥᾷον] to catch sight of the idea of good [τὴν τοῦ ἀγαθοῦ ἰδέαν]. That tendency, we affirm, is to be found in all studies that force the soul to turn its vision round to the region where dwells the most blessed part of reality [τοῦ ὄντος], which it is necessary to behold by any means [παντὶ τρόπῳ]." "You are right," he said. "Then if it compels the soul to contemplate Being [οὐσίαν], it is suitable; if Becoming [γένεσιν], it is not." "So we affirm."[112]

By forcing us to think abstractly, the One is the ultimate origin of the legendary message over Plato's door denying entry to the un-geometrical.[113] It is easy to see why the geometrical point is most similar to this humble but necessary One: it is "that which has no part," as Euclid will say. The geometrical

---

played with it when it suited his purpose and dismissed it when he wished to go on to something else."

111. See Klein, *Greek Mathematical Thought*, 98.

112. 526d7-e9 (Shorey modified).

113. The inscription is first mentioned by Joannes Philoponus, a Christian Neoplatonist of the sixth-century A.D. in his commentary on Aristotle's *De Anima*. Harold Cherniss, "Plato the Mathematician." *Review of Metaphysics* 4 no. 3 (March 1951), 395-425 offers a balanced approach.

point is merely this same atomic monad now imagined in an equally imaginary space. One could certainly think of a line as coming out of a moving point.[114] But the One doesn't become number by movement; it is an act of imagination that multiplies this marvelous Hypothesis into the numbers that depend on it. By the same token, the infinitely divisible line can no more be generated by the point than a plurality of monads can be generated from nothing more than unity itself. There are, of course, many other things beside the point—everything, in fact—that may be called "one" and could be said, inaccurately, to be "unities" or "individuals." But none of them is either really one or indivisible, especially not a number, which "is" necessarily a plurality and at best a strictly fraudulent "one" that *are* really "many." To be sure some geometrical objects more closely resemble the One because of their uniformity: despite its three dimensions—or better yet, its center, radius, and surface—a sphere is particularly "one-like" and the same applies, among plane figures, to the single line of the circle. But none of these—to say nothing of an equilateral triangle or four of them arranged in the perfect Platonic pyramid called a Tetrahedron—can be said to do anything more than distantly resemble the One; despite their congruencies and equalities, they are "one" only in a strictly borrowed and logically illegitimate sense. The Problem of the One and the Many arises from a failure to keep these senses separate. Already prefigured in *Republic* VII, the exercises performed in *Parmenides* and elsewhere will prove just how important Plato thought it was for the student to have solved this Problem, i.e., to cleave to Plato's solution to it.[115]

Parmenides aside, none of this is what we would call "rocket science." So here's the fun and easy program that Socrates teaches us how to administer: "I *suppose*," said the teacher to the kids, "that if the point *did* have any dimensions that it would be . . . a sphere. Do you like playing ball? I've got some of them right here!" And out they come as the playful teacher continues: "Like everything else in this world of ours (although nothing else we've got is half as fun to play with as these!) these balls have three dimensions. The things of geometry—lines and planes (a plane has two dimensions, a line only one, but a point?

114. As Proclus did (also our witness for the Pythagorean origins of Aristotle's definition). See Heath, *Euclid's* Elements, 1.155: "Proclus gives another alternative definition as "*flux of a point*" (ῥύσις σημείου), i.e., the path of a point when moved. The idea is also alluded to in Aristotle (*De anima* 409a4 above quoted): 'they say that a line by its motion produces a surface, and a point by its motion a line.'" Also 1.159: "'This definition," says Proclus (p. 97, 8-13), 'is a perfect one as showing the essence of the line: he who called it the flux of a point seems to define it from its genetic cause, and it is not every line that he sets before us, but only the immaterial line, for it is this that is produced by the point, which, though itself indivisible, is the cause of the existence of things divisible.'" See *Laws* 894a1-5 and the commentary at E. B. England, *The Laws of Plato,* two volumes (Manchester: University Press, 1921), 2.466

115. Cf. Shorey, "The Idea of the Good," 222n2: "It is from the opposition of these ['absolute'] unities to concrete unities that the paradoxes of the *Parmenides* are for the most part deduced." And it is from a failure to grasp the strictly Hypothetical existence of "absolute unity" (222) that the rest are deduced.

Our friend the point has none at all!)—are "infinitely drawn nowhere," as the poet says. But look here: I've attached some string to this sphere: look, I've looped it through. And when I spin this over our heads . . . listen! Can you hear what happens when I spin it more quickly? Fine! Now imagine that all the planets—yes, the wandering stars—are just like these balls and each of them is spinning about creating a its own individual tone, just like this (some higher, some lower) as it whirls around. And speaking of tones, let me show you something else."

In short: the "Higher Education" of Book VII—(1) arithmetic, (2) geometry, (3) stereometry, (4) astronomy,[116] and (5) music—is one and all child's play. And while it's undoubtedly true that you can—as so many followers of Plato did—turn the ἀρχή of arithmetic into a sublime metaphysical system, the fact remains that Socrates does not do so in the *Republic* and is never presented by Plato as having done so anywhere else; hence the need for extra-textual Unwritten Doctrines. As for what Socrates does do, it doubtless requires from us some musical sense (as well as a patient teacher armed with a monochord) to understand the harmonic implications (the arithmetic of tuning being much more complicated than meets the ear!) of $9 \times 9 \times 9 = 729$,[117] or the equally harmonious fact that 60 (which is divisible by 2, 3, 4, 5, and 6 *and* is also $3 \times 4 \times 5$) $\times 60 \times 60 \times 60 = 12{,}960{,}000$,[118] and finally since (1) $\sqrt{49}$ is 'the *rational* diameter of five,' (since $\sqrt{50}$ isn't rational) and (2) $49 = 50 - 1$ just as $48 = 49 - 1$ that (3) a rectangle one of whose sides is 4800 and (4) and whose other side, in turn, is 'a hundred cubes of three' (i.e. 2700) equals (5) 12,960,000 once again.[119] But what is required first and foremost is a sense of humor: all this is play.

---

116. The "astronomy" of Socrates refuses to be limited by the apparent realities of the physical heavens; see Alexander P. D. Mourelatos, "Plato's "Real Astronomy": *Republic* 527D-531D" in John P. Anton (ed.), *Science and the Sciences in Plato*, 33-73 (New York: EIDOS, 1980). Note that the use of the physical heavens as the basis for reasoning at 529d7-e3 supports my contention (section §13) that mathematical objects are intelligible Images of visible things: there could be no Socratic astronomy without the visible world which it imitates but those imitations, themselves images of the transcendent Good simply by being on the north side of the *Kluft*, are intelligible and should therefore rise above their worldly origin.

117. Since nine is a triad of triads, 729 (the tyrant's number from IX 587d3-588a5) must be regarded as the triad of triads cubed. See Ernest McClain, *The Pythagorean Plato: Prelude to the Song Itself* (Stony Brook, NY: Nicolas Hays, 1978), 33-40.

118. This is the nuptial number, ignorance of which among the Guardians causes the City to degenerate (VIII 546a1-547a5; cf. 424a5-10). One might well ask: what kind of ignorance (i.e., ignorance of what?) is causing our city's degeneration?

119. 546b4-d3; unfortunately, this passage has received far more attention from interpreters than the Key Passage of IV 434d1-435d4. I refer those interested once again to McClain's *Pythagorean Plato* although they would be better served by starting with his *The Myth of Invariance* (York Beach, ME: Nicolas-Hays, 1976): the implications of both numbers are, as he has shown, primarily musical and demonstrate a playful appreciation of the mathematical problems that arise from "just tuning." As every piano-tuner knows,

This is not to say, of course, that play is unimportant for Plato the Teacher: least of all that it isn't highly educational. The following words alone would entitle us to speak of Plato as not only "Plato the Teacher" but also as somehow the teacher par excellence:

> "Now, all this study of reckoning and geometry and all the preliminary studies that are indispensable preparation for dialectics must be presented to them while still young, not in the form of compulsory instruction." "Why so?" "Because," said I, a free soul ought not to pursue any study slavishly; for while bodily labors performed under constraint do not harm the body, nothing that is learned under compulsion stays with the mind." "True," he said. "Do not, then, my friend, keep children to their studies by compulsion but by play." (536d4-537a1)

And at the root of all this Platonic play, the source from which all the fun emanates, is simply the indivisible Monad: the indivisible thought-atom, the One, the intelligible placeholder, the Image of the unencumbered soul, and the intelligible imitation of all that is sensible, the intelligibility of which *qua* non-sensible is made possible by the χωρισμός-cleaving majesty of the Idea of the Good. The mathematical One is the most accessible of all intelligibles: without "being" in the strict sense, it makes the sciences that depend on it the first "learnables," a decent etymology for the word "mathematics." Particularly for post-Cartesian moderns like ourselves, duly (and dully) schooled by "the number line" to imagine an infinitely divisible magnitude between zero and "one," it comes as a real surprise to meet a teacher schooled in the Academy who knows why One is not a number and thus, cannot be divided: "I can't give you a number of reasons why One is not a number, I can only give you one of them and I just did." Or, as Socrates proudly puts it:

> "τοῦτό γε, ὃ νυνδὴ ἐλέγομεν, ['this arithmetic, indeed, which just now we were discussing'] ὡς σφόδρα ἄνω ποι ἄγει τὴν ψυχὴν ['how forcefully *upwards* does it lead the soul!'] καὶ περὶ αὐτῶν τῶν ἀριθμῶν ἀναγκάζει διαλέγεσθαι ['compelling us to speak of numbers in themselves'] οὐδαμῇ ἀποδεχόμενον ἐάν τις αὐτῇ ὁρατὰ ἢ ἁπτὰ σώματα ἔχοντας ἀριθμοὺς προτεινόμενος διαλέγηται ['permitting in no kind of way that anyone pretending numbers merely visible or having bodies joined, would dare to speak of them!']."[120]

Properly taught, mathematics leads children out of the Cave, a process in which the humble monad of mathematics necessarily plays the unique, primary, primordial, and principal part. But Plato's One is not an end in itself and thus the best that can be said of it is: "How forcefully upwards does it lead the Soul!" Of

---

compromises must be made in order to make "the well-tempered clavichord" possible. Plato knew this as well.

120. 525d5-8 (translation mine).

course this is hardly faint praise from a Platonist. Moreover, the strictly hypothetical One will prove to be the final solution to the Problem of the One and the Many. But for anyone who still insists that the One actually exists, the Idea of the Good is unquestionably "beyond Being."

Section 29. Reading Order Revisited

Why does Plato make it so difficult for the student to discover his meaning? This objection can be brought up repeatedly against both the interpretation of *Republic* offered here as well as against any reconstruction of the Reading Order of Plato's Dialogues based on his repeated use of the basanistic element. This objection gains force because I have also repeatedly called attention to "the playful Plato." Even if it is admitted that playfulness and humor are always present—i.e., even in the most difficult tests, traps, and puzzles Plato has given to the reader—the fact remains that the cumulative effect of all these difficulties is something quite like "the paranoid Plato": a grim and humorless austerity becomes visible, bent on ensuring that no student will do things the easy way. For all the dramatic delight of the initial *Protagoras*, for example, palpable perils lurk behind its genteel urbanities. Even the introductory *Alcibiades* reveals this aspect of Plato's character: Alcibiades appeared to have all the necessary qualifications to serve Athens and yet, more than anyone else, he was responsible for the destruction of the democracy (see section §30). Plato clearly thought that the stakes were high: for all his playfulness, there was probably never any doubt among his students about his demanding, highly critical, and perhaps even overly zealous determination to allow no counterfeit philosophers to claim the authority of his superior instruction. To put it another way: for all of his idealism, Plato is an empiricist with respect to education (cf. 467d3-5).[121]

Evidence of Plato's self-awareness on these questions can be found in Book VII. Having sounded the Battle Hymn of the *Republic* (534b8-d1), Socrates considers the qualifications necessary for those students who are to be trained in dialectic (535a3-536a8). Having considered what qualities the student will need—the list of qualities is also relevant to the question, and will be considered in due course—Socrates describes the obligations that the teachers must shoulder:

> "But we," I said, "must be on our guard [διευλαβητέον] in all such cases, since, if we bring men sound of limb and mind to so great a study and so severe a training, justice herself [ἥ τε δίκη] will have no fault to find with us, and we shall preserve the state and our polity [τήν τε πόλιν καὶ πολιτείαν σώσομεν]. But, if we introduce into it the other sort, the outcome will be just the opposite,

121. Cf. G. E. R. Lloyd, "Plato as a Natural Scientist." *Journal of Hellenic Studies* 88 (1968), 78-92.

> and we shall pour a still greater flood of ridicule [ἔτι πλείω γέλωτα] upon philosophy." "That would indeed be shameful [αἰσχρὸν]," he said. (536b1-7)

Before the first explicitly demarcated basanistic test in the *Republic*—the Theory of Ideas triad conjoined with "the offspring of the Good" at VI 507b2-508c2 (see section §18)—Socrates had commanded the boys to take care: εὐλαβεῖσθε![122] Now this same verb, in an intensified and obligatory form, is applied here to the teacher. This is the only time in literature that the word "διευλαβητέον" is found: we "must be thoroughly watchful" lest—by letting the unworthy pass—we incur the righteous rage of righteousness (ἡ δίκη) and thereby destroy τήν πολιτείαν ("the polity" or the *Republic*?). If the Critical Ambiguity can be said to make the Guardians disappear into us, so also do the plural founders of the City (the literal sense of τήν τε πόλιν καὶ πολιτείαν) by the same calculus now disappear into Plato. In order to create philosophers who will (1) preserve his *Republic* (τήν πολιτείαν σώσομεν), he can only (2) pass muster with respect to the righteous by (3) ensuring the grandeur of philosophy; hence Plato must be watchful, critical (and basanistic) to an almost paranoid degree. Socrates is made to indicate as much about his creator:

> "Most certainly," said I: "but here again I am making myself a little ridiculous [γελοῖον]." "In what way?" "I forgot," said I, "that we were jesting [ἐπαίζομεν], and I spoke with too great intensity [ἐντεινάμενος]. For, while speaking, I turned my eyes upon philosophy, and when I saw how she is undeservedly reviled, I was revolted, and, as if in anger [ὥσπερ θυμωθεὶς], spoke too earnestly [σπουδαιότερον] to those who are in fault." "No, by Zeus, not too earnestly for me as a hearer." "But too much so for me as a speaker [ῥήτορι]," I said. (536b8-c7)

In order to ensure that philosophy does not become an object of ridicule (γέλωτα), Socrates must make himself—through both his basanistic watchfulness and the intense philosophical commitments that engender it—ridiculous (γελοῖον). Although it is Glaucon who says that it would be shameful (αἰσχρὸν) for him *not* to act in this way, Socrates himself refuses to actually say more than that he spoke "as if in anger" (ὥσπερ θυμωθεὶς): the "high-spirited" (or polemical) part of the soul is not quite in play here, although he speaks as an orator. Even though the obligations imposed by the διευλαβητέον may well justify that we stretch ourselves to the utmost (ἐντεινάμενος) in our determination to discriminate the worthy from the unworthy, Plato reminds us that he is fully aware of the playful side of the oxymoronic description of his self-description: "we have been playing around very seriously" (σπουδαιότερον ἐπαίζομεν). The interpretation of the *Republic* presented here is consistent with

---

122. 507a4-6: "'Have a care [εὐλαβεῖσθε], however, lest I deceive you unintentionally with a false reckoning [κίβδηλον . . . τὸν λόγον] of the interest.' 'We will do our best [κατὰ δύναμιν],' he said, 'to be on our guard [εὐλαβησόμεθα]. Only speak on.'"

this complicated enterprise. And of course the *Republic* is only one part, albeit the most important part, of a congruently complicated oxymoron, i.e., a serious and playful One out of Many: the Reading Order of Plato's Dialogues.

Republic is the best place to broach the reading order question not only because it combines all three elements on which my reconstruction of it is based, but also because *Republic* looks both forwards and backwards to the other dialogues, both those to be read hereafter and those that have already been read. Difficult in itself, *Republic* requires from the student considerable preparation, application, and skill. But despite the proleptic exercise constituted by *Symposium-Lysis*,[123] it is only after the introduction of the Idea of the Good that Plato has given the student a doctrine that now needs to be preserved (cf. 412e5): hence the basanistic dialogues that follow the *Republic* are implicit in the *Republic* itself no less the preparatory dialogues—for example the *Symposium*, *Meno*, *Gorgias* as well as the whole series from *Protagoras* and *Alcibiades* through *Theages* and *Cleitophon*—that make the vision it contains fully accessible. In the passage between VII 535a6 and 536a7, for example, the careful reader can see both backwards and forward references to the other dialogues. The basanistic dialogues to come—from *Timaeus* and *Critias* to *Laws* and *Epinomis*—are precisely those "severe [dialectical] studies"[124] in which the student must prove her- or himself at one and the same time virile,[125] sharp,[126] and

123. Altman, "Reading Order," §3.

124. 535b6-9: "'They must have, my friend, to begin with, a certain keenness for study, and must not learn with difficulty. For souls are much more likely to flinch and faint in severe studies [ἐν ἰσχυροῖς μαθήμασιν] than in gymnastics, because the toil touches them more nearly, being peculiar to them and not shared with the body.'" It is important to bear in mind that in Greek, τὰ μαθήματα does not refer only to what we call "mathematics." The root of the word is "to learn." It is obvious from this passage that they refer generally to mental as opposed to physical disciplines. See also 591c1-4.

125. 535b1-3: "'But in addition we must now require that they not only be virile [βλοσυροὺς] and vigorous in temper, but that they possess also the gifts of nature suitable to this type of education.'" Plato uses the word βλοσυρός ("hairy, shaggy, bristling" and "virile, burly"; LSJ) twice: here and at *Theaetetus* 149a2, where it is applied (in the feminine) to Phaenarete, Socrates' mother. There is a close connection between the basanistic and the maieutic because it is by contradicting the truth that Plato prompts the student to conceive by recollection.

126. 535b5-6: "'They must have, my friend, to begin with, a certain keenness [δριμύτητα] for study [πρὸς τὰ μαθήματα], and must not learn with difficulty." The word δριμύτης is used twice in Plato: here and at *Plt.* 311a6-9 where the Eleatic Stranger remarks: "Magistrates of the moderate type are exceedingly cautious [εὐλαβῆ], fair [δίκαια], and tenacious of precedent [σωτήρια], but they lack pungency [δριμύτητος] and the drive [τινος ἰταμότητος ὀξείας] that makes for efficiency [πρακτικῆς].'" While the Stranger divides the two and says the Statesman weaves both types together externally, Plato requires the Philosopher to possess aspects of both (compare τὰ ἤθη at 535b2 with *Plt.* 311a7), albeit with a heavy emphasis on the just and cautious side. And while Plato's Socrates says that students must be δριμύτης—if only to see through the Eleatic

painstaking.[127] Only in application to these dialectical difficulties can the authentic student be discriminated from the spurious (535c6-9 and 536a4). With those prospective indications made, Socrates next makes a rapid-fire series of allusions to five dialogues that have already been read: *Meno*,[128] *Erastai* (535d1-7), *Lesser Hippias* (535d9-e5), *Charmides*, and *Laches* (536a2).

The present section, then, is devoted to persuading the reader that the Higher Education described in Book VII is, in addition to being what it appears to be—i.e., the consideration of five mathematical disciplines capped by dialectic—an adumbration of the place of reconstructing the Reading Order of Plato's Dialogues in Platonic pedagogy. Generally conceded to be a valuable—indeed our best—guide to what Plato actually taught in the Academy, the Higher Education of Book VII also contains texts that closely mesh with three important principles relating to reading order. These texts will either suggest to the reader (as they do to me) that my quest for the reading order is perfectly Platonic, i.e., that Plato intended someone like me to do just what I am doing here, or, in any case, furnish *three methodological principles* on which my own reconstruction project will be based.

These principles are derived from the following facts about the fictional world of the City's Higher Education: (a) the Guardians are required to discover the systematic order in which "the studies which they disconnectedly pursued as children" are to be arranged, (b) the Guardians will be tested in order to determine the depth of their attachment to Being as opposed to Becoming, and (c) throughout all their studies the Guardians are expected to defend the Idea of the Good—as it were in battle—from all attempts to seduce them away from it. These facts generate the following principles, applicable to Plato's readers by analogy: (1) the dialogues to be read after the *Republic* constitute a sequential series of dialogues that Plato expected us to reconstruct, (2) these basanistic dialogues test our attachment to Being as opposed to Becoming, and (3) are aimed specifically at determining the extent of our continued loyalty to a Just response to the Idea of the Good as it had been taught by "the crisis of the *Republic*."

There are two passages in Book VII that are specifically germane to the question of placing things in a sequential series and thus relevant to "(1)." But it should be noted that the structure of Books VII and VIII (the latter continuing into Book IX) is defined by a sequential series of (five) things (doubled to ten in

---

Stranger—he never says they must possess ἰταμότης, least of all a certain acute form of it.

127. In addition to the introduction of work (ὁ πόνος) at 535b8, see 535c1, 535c3, and 535d1-7. Particularly important is the use of "φιλοπονία" in the latter passage. The great value Plato attaches to hard work makes sense of the reading of *Republic* offered here (cf. *Ep*. 340c1 and 341a5).

128. *Meno* is the only other dialogue in which μεγαλοπρέπεια (536a3) is found (*Men*. 74a5 and 88a8) and likewise ζητητικός ("investigative;" 535d5) is only found again at *Men*. 81e1: it is what the doctrine of recollection makes the student. Divorced from this origin, the word "zetetic" plays an important role in Straussian apologetics.

Books VIII-IX) each of which is closely connected to that which precedes and follows it. In other words, the study of Astronomy links Stereometry and Music in Book VII no less than Democracy evolves from Oligarchy and gives rise to Tyranny in Book VIII. In fact, Plato is so determined to present the Higher Education as a logical sequence of five interconnected studies that Socrates asserts that when these studies are first taught, they will not be presented (as they are in Book VII) in sequential order. This assertion—or rather Socrates' description of the (fictional) "Higher Education of the Guardians in the City" in accordance with this assertion—is the necessary precondition for the need to arrange in sequence a series of studies *that have already been arranged in sequence.*

> "Surely it is," he said. "After this period," I said, "those who are given preference from the twenty-year class will receive greater honors than the others, and they will be required to gather [συνακτέον] the studies which they disconnectedly [τά τε χύδην μαθήματα] pursued as children in their former education into a comprehensive survey [εἰς σύνοψιν] of their affinities with one another [οἰκειότητός τε ἀλλήλων τῶν μαθημάτων] and with the nature of things [καὶ τῆς τοῦ ὄντος φύσεως]." (537b6-c3)

The importance of verbal adjectives (like καταβατέον, περιακτέον and διευλαβητέον) in Platonic pedagogy has been emphasized throughout. Here is another: the subjects that the Guardians have already studied (μαθήματα) "must be gathered together" (συνακτέον). While the word "μαθήματα" inevitably suggests mathematical studies to us (and is therefore specifically appropriate to Book VII), the Greek word is general: the verb μανθάνειν means "to learn." Plato is thereby suggesting an analogy between these fictional studies (which is not to say that he regarded them in themselves as unimportant *qua* propaedeutic to philosophy and Justice) and the Platonic dialogues. The word μαθήματα can reasonably be applied to the dialogues (see section §24) and dramatic connections between them could be described in terms of "affinity" (οἰκειότης) while their thematic connections reflect "the nature of things." In short: what Socrates calls a "σύνοψις," I am calling "the Reading Order of Plato's Dialogues": a comprehensive vision of the only surviving Platonic μαθήματα the reconstruction of which would fulfill the mandated συνακτέον in accordance with both οἰκειότης and ἡ τοῦ ὄντος φύσις.

There are therefore three possibilities: (i) the Higher Education of Book VII is only what it literally is: a proposed curriculum for the (fictional) Guardians of the (fictional) City (cf. 502c9-d3), (ii) in its literal form (i.e., from arithmetic through music to dialectic) it is somewhere between Plato's ideal curriculum for the Academy and an actual description of the Academic curriculum, and (iii) a metaphorical analogue to some other curriculum, e.g., one based on the Platonic dialogues. Since my entire interpretation of *Republic* depends on the Critical Ambiguity of the pre-curricular portion of Book VII, I reject "(i)" as too limited: Plato the Teacher wants his readers to apply the precepts of his fictional world to their own lives. This leaves "(ii)": the traditional view that in Book VII, we are learning about the Academy. This interpretation is consistent with the application of these principles to the reading order question. But if we simply assume that the Higher Education of Book VII is a more or less precise account of the curriculum in the Academy, we are left with the problems posed by the detailed chronology of what Socrates says in Book VII: what, for example, is the Academic analogue of this "twenty-year class"? And there is one specific detail that both strengthens "(iii)" and weakens "(ii)": the place of "thirty-five" in this chronological sequence of studies; however old we must imagine the Academicians, there are thirty-five dialogues that have been preserved as Plato's. In any case, it is impossible to believe that Plato's dialogues played no part in academic pedagogy.

But the present passage indicates an aspect of Platonic pedagogy that must remain forever beyond our reach: the order in which Plato, having constructed a σύνοψις of thirty-five dialogues, actually taught them in the Academy. I refer to the word "χύδην" ("indiscriminately mixed up and jumbled") in τά τε χύδην μαθήματα. If I am right about the analogical identity between τά μαθήματα and the dialogues, Plato is indicating that the dialogues (or at least some significant number of them, perhaps five) were deliberately taught in deliberately random sequence (of course they could only be taught "out of order" if there were already an order out of which to scramble them) and that the students were then asked to fulfill the συνακτέον by restoring them as the systematic σύνοψις their teacher had designed them to be. In other words, this passage suggests that the Platonic Reading Order was not necessarily identical to the order in which Plato intended the dialogues to be taught: reconstructing it was always an essential but unwritten part of Platonic pedagogy. Leaving aside the question of whether Socrates is indicating that the elementary μαθήματα (and, by analogy, the pre-*Republic* dialogues) had *already* been taught χύδην, or that Plato is only now introducing a new technique and therefore pointing forward to how the post-*Republic* dialogues will be presented, a broader view of μαθήματα suggests that students in the Academy were required to recreate an already existent σύνοψις, just as we must do today. In any case, the modern student who attempts to reconstruct the Reading Order of Plato's Dialogues resembles these twenty-year old Guardians as Socrates describes them because the dialogues have unquestionably come down to us χύδην. And there is some evidence that Plato intended us—indeed required us with the verbal adjective συνακτέον—to recreate, out of a merely apparent chaos, his own pre-existing σύνοψις.[129]

129. The return to stereometry (528a6-b3) is programmatic. Socrates illustrates "logographic necessity" at *Phdr*. 264b7-e2 with a poem whose four lines can be read in any order and therefore has no beginning, middle, or end. It is therefore difficult to understand the insistence of Kent F. Moors, "Plato's Use of Dialogue," *Classical World* 72 no. 2 (October 1978), 77-93 at 85: "Logographic necessity operates on each dialogue independently, not on the canon of Plato taken as a whole." Is it not also logographic necessity that requires us to place *Crito* between *Apology of Socrates* and *Phaedo* and likewise to place *Theaetetus* between *Euthyphro* and *Sophist*?

An earlier passage—clearly related to the one just considered although it describes only the preliminary steps to recreating a *sequential* σύνοψις—indicates that the συνακτέον (what might be called "Plato's synagogy" by analogy to periagogy) is a synthetic investigation of all those studies that employ the methods of the Shorter Way.

> "And I'm thinking also that the investigation of all these studies we've just gone through [ἡ τούτων πάντων ὧν διεληλύθαμεν μέθοδος], if it arrives at the connection between them [ἐπὶ τὴν ἀλλήλων κοινωνίαν ἀφίκηται] and their common origin [συγγένειαν] and synthesizes [συλλογισθῇ] them with respect to their affinities with each other [ᾗ ἐστὶν ἀλλήλοις οἰκεῖα], then to busy ourselves with them contributes to our desired end, and the labor taken is not lost; but otherwise it is vain."[130]

Socrates is stating that only if the connections between the five studies that comprise the Higher Education are discovered, are these studies truly useful. In other words, these studies must be guided by a synthetic investigation that connects them (συλλογισθῇ) or else they are useless. As I suggested in the "child's-play" account of the Higher Education at the end of section §18, all of these μαθήματα depend on the primal hypothesis of the Monad and therefore Plato may mean nothing more here than that the Higher Education is useful IFF we realize that the sequence from arithmetic to music depends on unexamined Hypotheses and intelligible Images of visible things. But the words here can certainly be applied to reading order. There is certainly a kinship (συγγένεια) between, for example, the *Sophist* and the *Statesman* and the student would undoubtedly ask if there is a κοινωνία between *this* pair of genetically identical dialogues and the likewise paired (also on the basis of συγγένεια) *Euthyphro* and *Apology of Socrates* to which they are explicitly linked by dramatic details. By attending to the dramatic connections between the dialogues (ᾗ ἐστὶν ἀλλήλοις οἰκεῖα), we can discover a more profound κοινωνία between them as well.

Transitional between the passages in Book VII connected with (1) the Guardians being compelled to arrange their studies sequentially and (2) being tested on their capacity to distinguish Being from Becoming, is the following, which immediately follows the σύνοψις passage of VII 537b7-c3.

> "That, at any rate, he said, is the only instruction that abides [ἡ τοιαύτη μάθησις βέβαιος] with those who receive it." "And it is also," said I, "the

130. 531c9-d3. This translation is my own modification of Shorey's who translates as follows: "And what is more," I said, I take it that if the investigation of all these studies goes far enough to bring out their community and kinship with one another, and to infer their affinities, then to busy ourselves with them contributes to our desired end, and the labor taken is not lost; but otherwise it is vain." The use of μέθοδος here I took to fall in between [I] and [II] in section §11.

chief test [μεγίστη γε . . . πεῖρα] of the dialectical nature and its opposite [διαλεκτικῆς φύσεως καὶ μή]. For he who can view things in their connection is a dialectician; he who cannot, is not [ὁ μὲν γὰρ συνοπτικὸς διαλεκτικός, ὁ δὲ μὴ οὔ]." (537c4-7)

It will be remembered that the Shorter Way depended on *methods* that are entirely different from the dialectical method used on the Longer Way. Similar to the passage just considered (531c9-d3), this one suggests the application of a synthetic investigation of the pursuits described in the Second Part of the Divided Line on the basis of the dialectical method that emerges only in the First.[131] Obviously the First Part's method is dialectical par excellence and depends entirely on reaching the Idea of the Good and then working downwards from that un-hypothetical origin (VI 511b6-c1). This passage suggests that the transitional form of dialectic is the process by which the Guardians discover the common basis of the Higher Education in the methodology of the Shorter Way (which seems trivially easy, especially in comparison with what Plato has already expected the reader to do by connecting that methodology to the Second Part of the Divided Line) but these is also reason to think that the reader will be required to grasp the dialectical connections between other, more difficult, μαθήματα, e.g. the Platonic dialogues that follow *Republic* in the Reading Order.

In addition to dramatic and thematic connections, it is therefore also necessary to search for "dialectical connections" among the dialogues. To state the matter more clearly in Socratic terms: the more obvious dramatic (οἰκεῖα) and thematic connections (συγγένεια) should never be sacrificed for more speculative dialectical connections (διαλεκτικά) *but* the κοινωνία based on both dramatic and thematic connections should never be considered in isolation from Plato's dialectical purpose in creating the σύνοψις (or Reading Order) in the first place. Only the reader who reads every dialogue *synoptically* (i.e., on the basis of reading order) has a firm knowledge (μάθησις βέβαιος) of what makes the dialogues trebly dialectical: the dialogues are dialectical (a) in the sense that they are imitations of live dialectic, (b) they create an extra-textual dialogue between the text and the student, as in "the crisis of the *Republic*," and (c) the student's discovery of the interconnections between the dialogues makes possible another dialectic that those dialogues create but do not strictly speaking contain. Against Tübingen, Plato's "unwritten doctrine" is best understood as the

---

131. 533c8-d6: "'Then,' said I, 'is not dialectics [ἡ διαλεκτικὴ μέθοδος] the only process of inquiry that advances in this manner, doing away with hypotheses, up to the first principle itself in order to find confirmation there? And it is literally true that when the eye of the soul [τὸ τῆς ψυχῆς ὄμμα] is sunk in the barbaric slough of the Orphic myth, dialectic gently draws it forth and leads it up [ἀνάγει ἄνω], employing as helpers and co-operators in this conversion [συμπεριαγωγοῖς] the studies and sciences which we enumerated, which we called sciences often from habit, though they really need some other designation, connoting more clearness than opinion and more obscurity than science.'"

reading order of his writings and it is in the context of "(c)" that the words of Socrates ring most true: ὁ μὲν γὰρ συνοπτικὸς διαλεκτικός, ὁ δὲ μὴ οὔ.

Socrates here calls this the "μεγίστη πεῖρα" of "the dialectical nature and its opposite." But the more important Platonic words for "test" is found in a passage that illustrates principle "(2)":

> "when they have passed the thirtieth year to promote them, by a second selection from those preferred in the first, to still greater honors, and to examine, testing [βασανίζοντα] by the capacity for dialectic [τῇ τοῦ διαλέγεσθαι δυνάμει], who is capable of disregarding eyes and the other senses and go on to Being itself [ἐπ' αὐτὸ τὸ ὂν] along with truth. And it's no doubt a task for careful guarding, my dear fellow."[132]

As I have been suggesting throughout, the existence of the basanistic element is essential to the reconstruction of the Reading Order of Plato's Dialogues. In this passage, Socrates regards as a πεῖρα (trial) the job of viewing the studies synoptically but states that the founders will be testing (βασανίζοντα) the thirty-year old Guardians not only on the basis of their synagogy (i.e., the fulfillment of the συνακτέον by means of ἡ τοῦ διαλέγεσθαι δύναμις) but by their ability to free themselves from the sensible world and reach Being. Plato the Teacher is always in search of a touchstone (cf. 523a7-8 and *Grg.* 487e1-3): the student who will both validate his soaring intuitions (cf. 523a8 with 538a7, 538a9, and 538b7) *and* defend αὐτὸ τὸ ὂν ("Being itself") against any basanistic challenge he will himself construct. The Eleatic Stranger is therefore not the result of Plato modifying his Theory of Ideas in old age but rather of Πλάτων βασανίζων (i.e., "the testing Plato") employing the tools he learned from Parmenides (see section §5). Plato may well have written, e.g., *Sophist* late in his career—the stylistic details point in that direction—but stylometry can never prove the principle it is often used to support: that Plato changed his ideas (to say nothing of the Idea!) and that therefore the late dialogues better reflect what Plato came to think. This entire line of inquiry in its crude and most pervasive form—always excepting the great achievements of Lewis Campbell—is clear proof that, since the nineteenth-century, no small number of otherwise brilliant Plato scholars have failed the test to which the imaginary Guardians are subjected between thirty and thirty-five years of age:[133] they have rejected unchanging Being for a

---

132. 537d3-8. My modification of Shorey's translation. His is: "'when they have passed the thirtieth year to promote them, by a second selection from those preferred in the first, to still greater honors, and to prove and test them by the power of dialectic to see which of them is able to disregard the eyes and other senses and go on to being itself in company with truth. And at this point, my friend, the greatest care is requisite.'"

133. 539e2-540a6: "'Do you mean six or four?' he said. 'Well,' I said, 'set it down as five. For after that you will have to send them down [καταβιβαστέοι] into the cave again, and compel them to hold commands in war and the other offices suitable to youth, so that they may not fall short of the other type in experience either. And in these offices, too, they are to be tested [βασανιστέοι] to see whether they will remain steadfast under

Plato who merely becomes. In terms of reading order—i.e., a question they entirely ignore—a significant number of prominent modern philosophers (to say nothing of Plato scholars) have fallen prey to the basanistic dialogues, just as Plato knew that many students would. They have forgotten the eternal lesson of the Socrates who both said and practiced the immortal κατέβην, thereby passing along the truly Platonic torch: the εἶδος of Justice.

Not surprisingly, the whole question really turns on the Idea of the Good, the third principle that I am borrowing from Book VII to apply to any attempt to reconstruct the reading order of the Platonic dialogues. To be perfectly clear about the matter: my attempt to reconstruct that order depends entirely on the proposition that Plato never wavered in his adherence to the Idea of the Good. Indeed, I have suggested (section §5) that the sharp distinction between Being and Becoming is the condition for the possibility of "Plato" *qua* philosopher.

> "What we have to consider is whether the greater and more advanced part of it tends to facilitate the apprehension of the idea of good [τὴν τοῦ ἀγαθοῦ ἰδέαν]. That tendency, we affirm, is to be found in all studies that force the soul to turn its vision round to the region where dwells the most blessed part of reality [τὸ εὐδαιμονέστατον τοῦ ὄντος], which it is imperative that it should behold." "You are right," he said. "Then if it compels the soul to contemplate essence [οὐσίαν], it is suitable; if genesis [γένεσιν], it is not." (526d7-e8)

It is this text—and the many other texts that put the same point in similar ways—that I regard as the dead center of Platonic pedagogy and, *a fortiori*, the pivot around which the Reading Order of Plato's Dialogues must be reconstructed: the student is to be led up to the Good in the *Republic* and then, before being sent back down into the Cave of political life, will be tested—while still in the Academy—as to the strength of her commitment to the Idea of the Good.[134] In the Battle Hymn of the *Republic*—a single sentence so long and filled with rich

---

diverse solicitations or whether they will flinch and swerve.' 'How much time do you allow for that?' he said. 'Fifteen years,' said I, 'and at the age of fifty those who have survived the tests and approved themselves altogether the best in every task and form of knowledge must be brought [ἀκτέον] at last to the goal.'" I suggest that Plato taught the thirty-five dialogues over a course of study divided into five units, possibly years: the central "semester" (of whatever length it may have been) was devoted to the *Republic*.

134. See Walter Watson, "Dogma, Skepticism, and Dialogue" in Francisco J. Gonzalez (ed.). *The Third Way: New Directions in Platonic Studies*, 189-210 (Lanham, MD: Rowman & Littlefield, 1995), 204: "Each dialogue and each philosophy possess a high degree of internal unity that results from the idea that determines all its parts. If the whole set of dialogues, or of philosophies, were to have this kind of unity, they would all need to be determined by a single idea such as the idea of the good." Unfortunately, Watson rejects this possibility: "But this kind of unity, as Socrates indicates in the *Phaedo*, is beyond our grasp." Not surprisingly, I claim that an interpretation of the dialogues based on reading order that acknowledges or rather emphasizes the basanistic element is the best candidate for "the third way" desiderated throughout Gonzales, *The Third Way*.

insights that I must consider it in three separate parts—Socrates proleptically describes his post-*Republic* pedagogy.[135]

The first part of the sentence—one of two distinct protases (in other words, I am warning the reader that there will be no "then" to answer the first fragment's implied "if")—Socrates describes the negative characteristics of the inadequate Guardian in such a manner as to bring, or begin to bring, the true philosopher into sight:

> "And is not this true of the good [τοῦ ἀγαθοῦ] likewise—that the man who is unable to define [διορίσασθαι] in his discourse [τῷ λόγῳ] and distinguish and abstract from all other things [ἀπὸ τῶν ἄλλων πάντων ἀφελὼν] the idea of the good [τὴν τοῦ ἀγαθοῦ ἰδέαν]" (534b8-c1; Shorey modified)

The Good is the central issue in every case and I apply these words to the dialogues as follows: (a) if the Good is present in the dialogue (τῷ λόγῳ) but hidden, the student must find it and cleave to it, (b) if the presence of the Good is merely apparent, the student must expose this appearance as fraudulent, and (c) if the Good is entirely absent, that is decisive for anything else the discourse may contain. It will be noted that, although I have for the most part retained Shorey's translation for this first section (I will be using my own translations for the next two), his rendering of τῷ λόγῳ as "*his* discourse" is unwarranted by the Greek. I am suggesting that the student, not while speaking his own speech but while reading any particular dialogue(as if it were 'τῷ [τοῦ Πλάτωνος] λόγῳ') must be able to separate (i.e., to διορίσασθαι by ἀφελὼν) the wheat (i.e., ἡ τοῦ ἀγαθοῦ ἰδέα) from the chaff (i.e., ἀπὸ τῶν ἄλλων πάντων), all explicitly named, defined, and treated as such.

> "and who cannot, as if in battle [καὶ ὥσπερ ἐν μάχῃ], through all refutations emerging [διὰ πάντων ἐλέγχων διεξιών], not eager to refute by recourse to opinion but to essence [μὴ κατὰ δόξαν ἀλλὰ κατ' οὐσίαν προθυμούμενος ἐλέγχειν], proceeding throughout its way [διαπορεύηται] in all of these [ἐν

135. The fullest treatment of this passage is Hans Joachim Krämer, "Über den Zusammenhang von Prinzipienlehre und Dialektik bei Platon; Zur Definition des Dialektikers *Politeia* 534 B-C." *Philologus* 10 (1966), 35-70; so important is this text for Krämer—the greatest intellectual force of the Tübingen School in my judgment—that he reveals Plato's secret teaching ("the arcana of Plato's unwritten teaching") at 66-67: "The origin [sc. "the aOrxh/, the e4n, and aOgaqo\n"] is the most exact, i.e., absolutely partless measure of the primary multiplicity and number." Krämer distinguishes between the two part-less Ones, only one of which I recognize as truly One, at 65; for the multiplicity implicit in the other, see 61n3. Leaving aside the question of *Weltbezug* (66 and 66n1), the root problem here (at the risk of over-simplification) is that Krämer's project requires that there can be no distinction whatsoever between the Idea of the Good, the One, and the aOrxh/ whereas the passage in question requires the student to distinguish the Good "from all other things" (534b9).

πᾶσι τούτοις] [sc. refutations] with the discourse untoppled [ἀπτῶτι τῷ λόγῳ]" (534c1-3; translation mine)

Interpreting the basanistic dialogues will be analogous to war; hence "the Battle Hymn." Wherever the Idea of the Good is ignored or attacked—as it will be in various ways by Timaeus, the Eleatic and Athenian Strangers, even by Socrates himself in *Philebus*—the student must eagerly (προθυμούμενος) defend it by refuting everyone (διὰ πάντων ἐλέγχων) who fails to give it its due. In evaluating the arguments of men like these—venerable, intelligent and impressive gentlemen—the student must judge and criticize *only on the basis of Being* (κατ᾽ οὐσίαν) and not according to what seems to be reputable (μὴ κατὰ δόξαν) even if that means refuting (ἐλέγχειν) Socrates himself. Students must prove themselves able to procede through all of these tests (ἐν πᾶσι τούτοις) with what Socrates calls "the discourse intact."[136] The stakes are high:

> "the man who lacks this power, you will say, does not really know the good itself [αὐτὸ τὸ ἀγαθὸν] or any particular good [οὔτε ἄλλο ἀγαθὸν οὐδέν] but if he joins himself in any way to some image [ἀλλ᾽ εἴ πῃ εἰδώλου τινὸς ἐφάπτεται] he does so by reputation but not knowledge [δόξῃ, οὐκ ἐπιστήμῃ ἐφάπτεσθαι]."[137]

Once again revealing the influence of Parmenides, Socrates mentions the dangers of judging only on the basis of reputation or opinion (δόξα) but it is, above all, the transcendent importance of the Idea of the Good that receives solemn emphasis: without knowledge of the Good itself, the student knows absolutely nothing about morality, excellence, or what makes one thing better than anything else. Without the Good, we are helpless: we all too prone to attach ourselves to shadows and make ourselves easy prey for a wily hunter (εἰδώλός τις) who has the skills to persuade us that e.g. the correct constitution might be one in which rich men rule without laws over unwilling subjects as long as its rulers "have expert knowledge" (*Plt.* 293c7-d1). But knowledge of what? For all the divisions he makes, the Eleatic Stranger will never distinguish unchanging Being from the flux of Becoming; for all the many things he evidently knows, he never mentions the Idea of the Good. You do the μαθ.

---

136. It is difficult to say what this means but I will suggest three possibilities: (1) τῷ λόγῳ refers to each individual dialogue, as in the previous clause, and means that the student must be able to explain how this particular dialogue is actually, if only negatively, oriented to the Good, and therefore maintains deserves its place (i.e., is ἀπτῶτι in the sense that it couldn't fall out of its place with out damaging the σύνοψις, (2) τῷ λόγῳ here means something that it did not before—Platonism as expressed in the *Republic*—and the student is expected to keep that discourse "on its feet," and (3) Shorey was correct earlier and τῷ λόγῳ in both cases refers only to the internal commitment of the student to maintain the true account intact.

137. 534c4-d6. Note that the Afterlife is perhaps the most important aspect of the "high stakes" in the text: 534d6-8.

Section 30. The Age of Heroes

The testing begins almost immediately but the arrangement of things in their natural order continues. The five interconnected μαθήματα of Book VII are succeeded in Books VIII and IX with the series of five interconnected cities, along with the kind of man that corresponds to each of them. Socrates had tried to do this before, in Book V (449a7-b1): "And I was proceeding to discuss them in an orderly fashion [τὰς ἐφεξῆς] as each of them seemed to me to develop [μεταβαίνειν] each from one another [ἕκασται ἐξ ἀλλήλων]" But it is here that Polemarchus, Adeimantus, Glaucon, and Thrasymachus (yet another set of five) prevent Socrates from arranging his five cities in the proper order (ἐφεξῆς), here as elsewhere a properly Platonic project. Instead, Socrates leads the boys to lead him onto the Longer Way: it is only after the hidden revelation of Justice in Book VII that Socrates returns to where he has already been. But things are completely different this time: Socrates has now given his Guardians fair warning that they will be tested after having imposed upon them the καταβατέον, itself dependent on the two-world ontology of the Allegory of the Cave.

The obvious test is the nuptial number that Socrates uses to explain how the City will degenerate into a timocracy. This test—requiring the reader to decipher the perfect combination of arithmetic and music involved—is, like the Higher Education it completes, merely the prelude to another, likewise involving a city's degeneration. The most important test, of course, is what the student will do after leaving the Academy: i.e., what the reader does after reading the *Republic* and the dialogues that follow it ἐφεξῆς. But Plato constructs an important political test within the text itself, a test dependent on the fact that when Democracy degenerates, Tyranny is the result. Unlike the mathematics of the number, then, this degeneration bears directly on the question of Justice: i.e., the student's willingness to participate qua philosopher in the political life. This willingness is tested by the reader's response to Socrates' description of Democracy: if this attitude is based on opinion (δόξα) rather than the Good, the student fails.

There are plenty of clues, of course: such is Plato's way. Even in Book V, there were exactly *five* of them: Socrates, Polemarchus, Adeimantus, Glaucon, and Thrasymachus and in that order (449b1-450a6). Having read about the five cities in Book VIII, it becomes, if we wish it, a matter of child's-play to make the connections: Thrasymachus corresponds to Tyranny and Socrates to the City. Two of the remaining three pairings may well surprise us: apparently Polemarchus, not entirely unlike Xenophon, is as much a Spartan warrior as an Athenian intellectual while Adeimantus is an oligarch: perhaps his wide reading, to say nothing of the fact that we find him already in the company of Thrasymachus and the son of Nicias, were clues about this all along. But we need not be surprised that Glaucon—fourth from Socrates in the Book V interruption—is paired with Democracy in the list of five cities: Glaucon's free choice for Justice is the subject, and Glaucon himself the hero, of Plato's *Republic*. And Democracy—appearances notwithstanding—is, for Plato, the Age of Heroes. As noted earlier, Leo Strauss was the first to make this connection.

Explaining this connection will finally square the debt incurred in section §26: in addition to the misunderstandings that arise when it is forgotten that the Noble Lie is first, and foremost (1) a lie, and (2) that this lie, concerning the genetic basis of an inborn nobility, is more accurately thought of as a Genetic Fiction, there yet remains (3) the fact that the second of these lies is derived from the passage in Hesiod's *Works and Days* where gold, silver, bronze and iron are used to describe not inborn differences and inequalities but four successive ages. It is only by considering Book VIII in the context of the Hesiod passage—*locus classicus* of "the golden age" and the *fons et origo* of the speculative philosophy of history[138]—that Democracy shines forth, amidst the pages of that well known elitist and famous anti-democrat Plato, as the Age of Heroes. The essential point is that Plato borrows the five-stage development described in Book VIII from Hesiod's *Works and Days* where, in addition to the four metallic ages, "the Age of Heroes" is inserted in the fourth position, intermediate between Bronze and Iron, or, to make the analogy with the *Republic* explicit, between Adeimantus and Thrasymachus or Oligarchy and Tyranny.

Hesiod is both quoted and mentioned by name several times in Book II of the *Republic*;[139] the reader has therefore been alerted to his importance several times before the Genetic Fiction is introduced.[140] Socrates does not mention Hesiod by name when he introduces it in Book III but he does so later in Book VIII (at 547a1) when he refers to "Hesiod's and our races of gold, silver, bronze, and iron." Socrates says this immediately after describing the nuptial number, i.e., immediately before presenting his own version of five ages succeeding each other in time and constituting a process from best to worst. Socrates is therefore reminding us that Hesiod has already described what Plato himself is about to describe and this reminder is crucial: only the reader who retains a lively memory of Hesiod will appreciate Plato's characteristically serious joke: despite appearances, Democracy—fourth on Plato's list as the Age of Heroes is fourth in Hesiod—is philosophy's golden age; i.e., the golden age *tout court*.

The arithmetic parallel between Democracy and the age of heroes is all the more striking because the Age of Heroes, inserted between the bronze and iron ages, arrests the pattern of successive decline within the series of four metals: the heroes are better and more just than those of the bronze age. "But when this race too had been covered by earth, Zeus, son of Cronos, made another, the fourth, upon the fruitful earth, juster and more righteous, a divine race of hero-

138. W. H. Walsh, *Philosophy of History: An Introduction* (New York: Harper & Row, 1960), 16 cites C. D. Broad's authority for the distinction between the speculative and critical philosophy of history.

139. Mentioned and quoted at 363a8-b4 and quoted at 364c8-d2. Both are quotations from *Works and Days*.

140. The playful Plato (through Adeimantus) calls Hesiod (along with Homer) "γενναῖος" at 363a8.

men who are called demi-gods—the race immediately preceding our own throughout the boundless earth."[141] By considering what Socrates says about Democracy in the context of the Good, Plato's reasons for making this parallel become plain. The essential point is found at VIII 557d2-d7 where Socrates is describing the high level of freedom (or license) in the democratic city.[142] After saying that a democracy is "the fit place . . . in which to look for a constitution," Socrates explains:

> "Because, owing to this license, it includes all kinds, and it seems likely that anyone who wishes to organize a state, as we were just now doing, must find his way to a democratic city and select the model that pleases him, as if in a bazaar of constitutions, and after making his choice, establish his own."[143]

For all its evident flaws, a democratic city is *the condition for the possibility* of precisely the search for the just City (and therefore Justice itself) that is Plato's *Republic.* If Plato represents the CITY (i.e., the dialectical form of the City; see section §18) and Thrasymachus the Tyranny which *he* advocates, it is not difficult to see Polemarchus, Adimantus, Glaucon, and even the departed Cephalus as so many various internal constitutions made possible by the wondrously fecund freedom of fifth-century Athens: what Thucydides (or Pericles) called "the

---

141. *Works and Days* 156-60 (translation Hugh G. Evelyn-White).

142. Beginning with Arlene Saxonhouse, *Athenian Democracy: Modern Mythmakers and Ancient Theorists* (Notre Dame, ID: University of Notre Dame Press, 1996), particularly with "Plato and the Problematical Gentleness of Democracy" (87-114) in that collection, there has now begun a full-scale re-evaluation of Plato's position toward democracy. Picked up (167-68) by S. Sara Monoson, *Plato's Democratic Entanglements: Athenian Politics and the Practice of Philosophy* (Princeton, NJ: Princeton University Press, 2000), this trend, sparked by North American women, sets fair to carry the day. Saxonhouse in particular deserves praise; see also her "Democracy, Equality, and *Eidê*: A Radical View from Book 8 of Plato's *Republic*." *American Political Science Review* 92 no. 2 (1998), 273-284 and *Free Speech and Democracy in Ancient Athens* (Cambridge, UK: Cambridge University Press, 2006). Cf. David L. Roochnik, *Beautiful City; The Dialectical Character of Plato's Republic* (Ithaca, NY: Cornell University Press, 2003), 79 where he argues that Plato offers the reader in Book VIII "a qualified and cautious defense of democracy." It is Roochnik himself, who is being qualified and cautious.

143. 557d2-5; cf. Roochnik, *Beautiful City*, 79: "An extraordinary admission: probably only *in a democracy* is political philosophy, at least of the sort practiced in the *Republic*, possible." Along with Roochnik, consider Gerald M. Mara, *Socrates' Discursive Democracy:* Logos *and* Ergon *in Platonic Political Philosophy* (Albany: State University of New York Press, 1997), J. Peter Euben, *Corrupting Youth: Political Education, Democratic Culture, and Political Theory* (Princeton, NJ: Princeton University Press, 1997), J. R. Wallach, *The Platonic Political Art: A Study of Critical Reason and Democracy* (University Park: Pennsylvania State University Press, 2001), and Greg Recco, *Athens Victorious; Democracy on Plato's* Republic (Lanham, MD: Lexington Books, 2007), all salutary steps toward a more accurate view of Plato's relationship to democracy.

school of Hellas"[144] is also Plato's "bazaar of constitutions." Indeed all of these are "democratic men" and Democracy is the condition of the possibility that they vary as they do. To put it more strongly: since the *Republic* is about choice—about the philosopher's free choice for Justice—the freedom of choice only made possible by Democracy is a necessary condition for the possibility of Justice. No less important is the fact that those who recognize themselves as by nature free (562c2) know that this choice is humanity's birthright. Democracy is not a regulated utopia like the City: without being exposed to the doctrine of Thrasymachus and its temptations, neither Glaucon nor anyone else would be a hero for being guided by Socrates to choose Justice. This would be especially true if, like the Guardians of the just City, Glaucon had never been given either the freedom to listen to Thrasymachus or the democratic freedom to choose his own way of life.[145] Living in the well-regulated City might even prove hazardous to one's long-term spiritual health (619c6-d1).

In the parallel columns of five cities and the five men who interrupt Socrates at the beginning of Book V, Glaucon and Democracy both stand fourth. Plato's elder brother therefore constitutes an alternative and far more sympathetic portrait of "the democratic man." The playful Plato even tells us that the Democratic Man likes relish (559b6). For many reasons, many of which I discussed in section §4, Glaucon is surprisingly well cast as the hero of the *Republic*. There is no doubt that Socrates himself is given a task of heroic proportions and that he performs it heroically; in that sense, it seems silly to name anyone other than Socrates the hero of the *Republic*. On the other hand, it is Glaucon who makes that heroism possible, and that in a double sense. To begin with, it is Glaucon who imposes the heroic labor on Socrates at the beginning of Book II. Moreover, Socrates can only succeed in his assigned task if he persuades Glaucon to choose the life of Justice. Glaucon's recognition and choice of Justice (520e1) is the object of the entire Socratic discourse that is the *Republic* as well as the ultimate proof of its success.

The importance of Glaucon must not be overstated, however. He is the most important member of Socrates' *fictional* audience to be sure: the audience in the house of Cephalus that exists within the carefully designed world of Plato's *Republic*. But, as I have insisted throughout, there exists—and thanks to the Critical Ambiguity implicit in Socrates' reply to the rebellious Guardians, we can be sure that Plato was perfectly well aware of its existence—a more important audience outside of the world created by the text: the readers of the *Republic*. There can be little doubt that Plato wishes us to admire his ability, as a writer, to

144. Thucydides 2.41.1.

145. This is a central theme of the *Republic*. We have all been brought up in "a pasturage of poisonous herbs" (III 401b9)—this is our "from whence" (*Prt.* 309a1) as Plato knows—and it is only one who is tested (VII 535b1-3), not the one who has never experienced evil within (III 409a1-c1), who is truly γεννα῀ιος. In that sense, Democracy's contempt for the City *is* truly noble (VIII 558b1-8; cf. X 619c7-8). Cf. Pericles on Sparta at Thucydides 2.39.1.

create such a compelling fictional world and "boldly go where no man has gone before." On the other hand, it is the reader who ultimately becomes, through identification with the fictional Glaucon, the hero of the *Republic* and only this reader will be qualified to adjudicate the apparently rival claims of Plato and Homer (see section §35) to be the preceptor of Hellas. Plato knows that this identification is easiest for readers who are living in a democratic city. To put it another way, it is at the moment of crisis in which the reader opens her- or himself to the power of Plato—*via* the Critical Ambiguity of the Platonic καταβατέον—that the reader discover him- or herself to be living in the Age of Heroes. Plato is perfectly well aware that he is asking us—through Socrates no less than through Socrates' version of what the fictional founders of the fictional City will say to the fictional Guardians who protest against being sent back down into the Cave—to do something heroic. But only if we are living in a Democracy can we actually do it.

Of the many freedoms that the just City denies its Guardians, the most significant for the *Republic* as a whole is the right to choose whether or not to return to the shadows of the Cave. Plato deliberately contrasts the just City with the democratic one of Glaucon's day in respect of the freedom of choice to hold office or to avoid it. The just City compels its philosophers to enter politics; it therefore makes the importance of this freedom conspicuous by its absence.[146] But Socrates emphasizes this very aspect of democracy; immediately after likening democracy to a "bazaar of constitutions," he adds:

> "And the freedom from all compulsion to hold office in such a city, even if you are qualified, or again, to submit to rule, unless you please" (557e1-3)

This freedom is emphasized because Democracy not only makes philosophy as practiced in the *Republic* possible but it is also the only political context in which the reader can actually practice Justice by entering politics as a voluntary duty and not as a means to grasping power. In other words, Democracy is the necessary condition for the possibility of Justice in a three distinct ways: (1) it is the fit place to find Justice, as we have just now been doing in our search for the best constitution, (2) without the freedom *not* to hold office (and therefore not to return to the Cave by compulsion), Justice cannot exist, and (3) all of those free of "the bridle of Theages" are equally free to lead the political life for the sake of Justice *only* in a democratic city.

Those who have read the *Republic* as a defense of a totalitarian ideal and an attack on democracy have forgotten: (α) that Plato's evident—though seldom

---

146. In fact, as Hegel suggested in the Preface to *Philosophy of Right*, this could be said to be the principal feature of the City as a whole: it negates the individual's free choice. Hegel's self-revealing critique of Plato is considered in my doctoral dissertation "The Problem of Time in Hegel's Philosophy of History" (Universidade Federal de Santa Catarina; 2010), a revised version of which I hope to publish as "The End of History? Hegel and the Problem of Time."

emphasized—abandonment of "Aristocles son of Ariston" has political implications as does (β) his decision to become Plato the Teacher. Moreover, consider (γ) the fact that Socrates speaks the single most important truth about democracy in Book VIII: "anyone by nature free regards this city alone as a fit place to live,"[147] (δ) his decision to use the plebian Socrates as his mouth-piece as his central character,[148] and (ε) his decision to set all of his Socratic dialogues—making exception thereby for the appearance of the Athenian Stranger—in democratic Athens in the hey-day of Athenian democracy shows that he well understood what democracy (and only democracy) had and could make possible. Since Plato himself lived in a significantly less democratic Athens, it is surprising that no one has bothered to interpret his evident nostalgia for the good old days in political terms.[149] Nor should it be overlooked that the basis of basanistic pedagogy is the presumption that the student's free choice of the Good is only made possible by deliberate exposure to those evils that would tend to obscure it.[150]

This is not to say, of course, that Democracy values the Idea of the Good: none of the defective cities do this. But unlike the false forms of the merely apparent good sought after in Timocracy (honor), Oligarchy (wealth) and Tyranny

---

147. 561c1-2: "ἐν μόνῃ ταύτῃ ἄξιον οἰκεῖν ὅστις φύσει ἐλεύθερος" (translation mine).

148. One wonders if Xenophon ever realized the full extent to which *he was himself* the finest product of Athenian democracy; see Edith Hamilton, *The Greek Way* (New York: W. W. Norton, 1930), ch. 10. Certainly no Athenian better proves the truth of what Pericles says about democracy in the Funeral Oration than the son of Gryllus: "and I doubt if the world can produce a man who is equal to so many emergencies when he is on his own as an Athenian" (Thucydides 2.41.1; Jowett).

149. To these, the following could be added: (ζ) he was not only an Athenian but (η) a brilliant literary innovator who (θ) polished his smallest dialogues with the same loving attention as his greatest ones, (ι) took great care to hold every reader's attention, (κ) included such an unbelievable variety of theme, image, and technique, that there is literally something for everybody, (λ) expressed sublime truths in highly entertaining stories, (μ) not infrequently took the time to be simple enough for a child to understand, (ν) embodied his abstractions in a life-like context that anyone could visualize, (ξ) taught the equality of women, (ο) presented women in a teaching role on important subjects, (π) replaced the aristocratic question "who's your Daddy?" with the democratic alternative: "who's your son?," (ρ) taught Justice, (σ) endowed a permanent institution of higher learning, (τ) charged no money, as the sophists did, for attending it, (υ) loved people for their moral excellence, not their innate advantages of birth and breeding, (φ) redefined "innate advantage" in terms of Recollection, (χ) taught that no man was any more like the highest good than any other, (ψ) chose a hero with a beautiful soul but no physical beauty in a society that equated beauty with nobility, and (ω) evidently attached great value to that most democratic of all excellences: φιλοπονία (i.e., "the love of *hard work*").

150. Basanistic pedagogy makes an explicit entrance in *Republic* III; in the context of the three tests introduced at 412d9-c4, consider 413c5-414a4 and especially 413e1 and 413e6. This passage is then reprised at 503a1-7, especially 503a1-2 and 503a6.

(absolute power), Democracy's good is merely an indefinite plurality: freedom (cf. 562b10-c2). Of course Plato does not regard freedom *per se* as the Good. In fact, it is worth repeating the central Idea of Platonism as often as necessary: *Plato regards only the Idea of the Good as the Good.* But because the citizens of a democracy (unlike other cities) can agree on no one thing that is absolutely good—other than the freedom to seek after their own good—only here is the door is left open to philosophy, as "the bazaar of constitutions" passage indicates.

The vivid picture of Democracy that Socrates paints in Book VIII shows Plato to be under no illusions about his future readers and thus the potential heroes of his book. He relies on us to find philosophy appealing but is well aware that we will find other things appealing as well. Of the Democratic Man he writes:

> "And does he not," said I, "also live out his life in this fashion, day by day indulging the appetite of the day, now winebibbing and abandoning himself to the lascivious pleasing of the flute and again drinking water and dieting, and at one time exercising his body, and sometimes idling and neglecting all things, and at another time seeming to occupy himself with philosophy."[151]

How much confidence can be placed in such a person? Although guided only by the appetite for wealth, the oligarchic man at least has a sense of purpose. The Democratic Man, by contrast, does not so much fail to do the right things but fails to do them with any consistency.

> "And frequently he goes in for politics and bounces up and says and does the first thing that enters his head. And if military men excite his emulation, thither he rushes, and if moneyed men, to that he turns, and there is no order or compulsion in his existence, but he calls this life of his the life of pleasure and freedom and happiness and cleaves to it to the end." (561d3-8)

Attacking "the democratic man" as a lazy, scatter-brained, selfish, shape-shifter, incapable of any sustained and consistent dedication to fixed principle, should be recognized for what it is: effective pedagogy. Certainly no effective teacher of adolescent males is unfamiliar with Plato's technique. Through Socrates, Plato is challenging the freedom-loving reader *to prove him wrong* by overcoming the typical democrat's directionless drift, a drift that leads to Tyranny. Encouraged by neither the state nor the prevailing temper of the times, any student capable of shame may yet, under the influence of a good teacher, seek other influences—the influence of Greek philosophy, for example—and practice an internal politics quite different from what prevails. And there is always the fear of what may follow Democracy: of what may happen if no heroes arise.

Indeed the highest praise Plato has for Democracy is indirect. Why wouldn't it be? Everyone who has ever fought for Democracy with intellectual

151. 561c6-d3. Shorey borrows from *Richard III*: "the lascivious pleasing of a *lute*."

weapons knows that it is the worst form of government except for all the rest of them. Our vision of Democracy in the *Republic* is obscured if we see it simply as fourth in a list of five—as one step from the bottom of a succession of degenerated regimes. The Hesiodic context is an allusive, subtle, but unmistakable bulwark against this appearance: the fourth age—the Age of Heroes—is in fact superior both to the age that follows and that which precedes it. Above all, Democracy is the alternative to Tyranny, the worst regime of all. With Democracy lost, we find ourselves in the iron age of the tyrant. Because Plato places Democracy between two regimes that are far worse than it is, he can appear to be attacking it without really doing so. To be sure the democratic man is misguided and the democratic city carries within it the seed of its own destruction. But it is nevertheless infinitely better than the alternative that follows it while Oligarchy from which it emerges makes no room for philosophy. Moreover, it also makes possible countervailing forces: above all, the philosopher who practices Justice. The cast of characters assembled at the house of Polemarchus no less than Plato's *Republic* itself is living proof of Democracy's excellence. The fact that the alternative to Democracy is represented by one of these—i.e., Thrasymachus—reminds the reader of the penalty that drives good men to rule even when they aren't philosophers: the fear of being ruled by someone worse (347c3-d2).

Socrates provides a detailed description of the process by which Democracy is transformed into Tyranny in Book VIII. This process contains many moments when the intervention of a philosophic statesman willing to undergo the Herculean labor involved (cf. 426e3-7) would have halted or at least slowed the march to Tyranny. I would suggest that Plato intends this description to flesh out the practical implications—the actual tests to be taken and the price to be paid—of going back down into the Cave for one of his democratic readers who takes his message to heart, rejects Thrasymachus, and embraces Justice (545b1-2). The theoretical and the allegorical are here made tangible. Certainly a case can be made for the proposition that Plato's description achieved exactly this effect on Marcus Tullius Cicero. In fact, the sketch of the road to Tyranny offered by Socrates closely resembles the period of Roman History connected with the fall of the Roman Republic.[152] The demagogue who becomes tyrant closely resembles Cicero's apparent victim and apparent arch-enemy Catiline as well as Julius Caesar, Cicero's actual nemesis who eventually emerged—or rather re-emerged through Augustus—as the successful tyrant indeed. While Cicero's political career could easily be explicated in the context of *Republic* VIII, we of the twenty-first century must find the details of this transformation somewhat less compelling. In the United States, for example, it hardly seems like the oligarchic regime of the moneymakers has been replaced by the kind of democracy that Plato describes. Our modern regimes are, in any case, further to the right than the generalized portrait of fifth-century Athens found in the *Republic*. It is diffi-

152. See Bruce MacQueen, *Plato's* Republic *in the Monographs of Sallust* (Chicago, IL: Bolchazy-Carducci, 1981), ch. 3 for the influence of *Republic* VIII on Cicero's contemporary Sallust.

cult, for example, to imagine the dangerous tyrant-in-waiting as the one who "hints at the abolition of debts and the partition of lands" (566a1-2). This is reminiscent of Catiline but hardly of Hitler. As for a more positive political program, Plato probably would have opposed the aggressive divulgation of credit cards (556a9-b4) and perhaps that remains as good a place to start as any.

Although the dialogue between Book VIII and contemporary political realities existing outside the text is necessarily subject to the vicissitudes of time and the changed circumstances they inevitably bring, the dialogue between Plato and Hesiod remains timeless. In addition to the five ages parallel, Plato picks up other themes from *The Works and Days.*[153] Hesiod's description of the iron age, for example, reminds us of the enduring danger of Thrasymachus: he was Hesiod's enemy as well.[154] But it is when the Platonist returns to Hesiod's description of the life of his heroes with fresh eyes that his continuing influence on the *Republic* becomes most palpable

Of their trials, Hesiod emphasizes that the heroes will need to fight and that some of them will die:

> Grim war and dread battle destroyed a part of them, some in the land of Cadmus at seven-gated Thebes when they fought for the flocks of Oedipus, and some, when it had brought them in ships over the great sea gulf to Troy for rich-haired Helen's sake: there death's end enshrouded a part of them. (*Works and Days* 162-165; Evelyn-White translation)

I suggest that the two wars mentioned here—the wars at Thebes and Troy—correspond to two types of trials that Plato's heroes too must face. The Trojan War is between cities; the conflict between the sons of Oedipus rips a city apart. Plato preserves this bifurcation between foreign and civil strife by having Socrates describe how Democracy falls prey to Tyranny as a matter of political conflict (analogous to the Trojan War) and also the internal process by which the

---

153. For an indication of the importance and breadth of this relationship, see Mauro Tulli, "Esiodo nella memoria di Parmenide" in Graziano Arrighetti (ed.), *Litteratura e Riflessione sulla Letteratura nella Cultura classica*, 65-81; Atti del Convegno (Pisa: Giardini, 1999), especially 76.

154. Hesiod *Works and Days* 182-196 (Evelyn-White): "The father will not agree with his children, nor the children with their father, nor guest with his host, nor comrade with comrade; nor will brother be dear to brother as aforetime. Men will dishonor their parents as they grow quickly old, and will carp at them, chiding them with bitter words, hard-hearted they, not knowing the fear of the gods. They will not repay their aged parents the cost of their nurture, for might shall be their right: and one man will sack another's city. There will be no favor for the man who keeps his oath or for the just or for the good; but rather men will praise the evil-doer and his violent dealing. Strength will be right, and reverence will cease to be; and the wicked will hurt the worthy man, speaking false words against him, and will swear an oath upon them. Envy, foul-mouthed, delighting in evil, with scowling face, will go along with wretched men one and all."

democratic becomes the tyrannical man (a civil war like that of Thebes).[155] The philosopher who returns to the Cave can expect both external opposition from others and internal temptations to abandon Justice. Socrates gives examples of both that ring as true as if they had been penned but yesterday.[156]

But Socrates also preserves Hesiod's account of the rewards that await those heroes who survive the wars:

> But to them Zeus, son of Cronos, the father, gave a life and a dwelling apart from men, at the ends of the earth. And they dwell with hearts free of sorrow in the islands of the blessed by deep-eddying Ocean, happy heroes, for whom the grain-giving earth bears honeyed fruit, flourishing thrice a year.[157]

These same Islands of the Blessed appear in the *Republic* as well:[158] having reached the age of fifty, the Guardians who have gone back down are given the chance to enjoy their golden years in the sunlight.

> "We shall require them to turn upward the vision of their souls and fix their gaze on that which sheds light on all, and when they have thus beheld the good itself they shall use it as a pattern for the right ordering of the state and the citizens and themselves throughout the remainder of their lives, each in his turn, devoting the greater part of their time to the study of philosophy, but when the turn comes for each, toiling in the service of the state and holding office for the city's sake, regarding the task not as a fine thing but a necessity. And so, when each generation has educated others like themselves to take their place as guardians of the state, they shall depart to the Islands of the Blessed and there dwell." (540a6-b7)

On the external level, whether battling entrenched and powerful oligarchs over the welfare of the indebted poor or persuasive and unscrupulous demagogues for the very survival of the state, philosophers who return to the Cave can expect to have a never-ending fight on their hands (Cicero *in Catilinam* 4.22). The internal conflicts that arise—the temptations to which money, power, and adulation expose the soul—strongly suggest that it is only the most self-controlled philoso-

---

155. Socrates has already compared the internal politics of a disordered soul to a Civil War at IV 440e3-4, prepared by 351d3, 351e1, 352a2, and 352a9.

156. Plato is frightening in his emphasis on the usefulness of endless enemies to the budding tyrant at 566e8-9: "'in the first place he is always stirring up some war so that the people may be in need of a leader.'" Also 567a5-8: "'And if, I presume, he suspects that there are free spirits who will not suffer his domination, his further object is to find pretexts for destroying them by exposing them to the enemy? From all these motives a tyrant is compelled to be always provoking wars?'"

157. Hesiod *Works and Days* 167-73 (Evelyn-White).

158. There are two routes to the Islands of the Blessed in the *Republic*, one fraudulent (519c5-6) and the other well deserved (540b6-7). The word "blessed" is the one Socrates applies to the eager Glaucon who has just demanded that Socrates describe the Idea of the Good (506d7).

pher who can resist them. There are also rewards. In any case, Plato's description of Democracy constitutes the first real test contained in Plato's *Republic*: the basanistic dialogues have begun in earnest. Only the reader who realizes that Democracy is being praised in Book VIII[159] has grasped what Justice really is: the free choice of philosophers to Go Back Down into the Cave.

159. Notice that Socrates invites us to reject Democracy on the basis of misogyny at 557c4-9, 561e5 and most dramatically in the following (563b5-10): "'And the climax of popular liberty, my friend,' I said, 'is attained in such a city when the purchased slaves, male and female, are no less free than the owners who paid for them. And I almost forgot to mention the spirit of freedom and equal rights in the relation of men to women and women to men.'" Perhaps the decisive impact of female scholars on the recovery of a democratic Plato—a trend that Jill Frank will continue in her forthcoming book on *Republic*—is connected with an ability to read this passage in a more thoughtful way. It would also have been interesting for a capable teacher practicing the art in a democracy to discuss with Plato the irony of 563a5-7: "The teacher in such case fears and fawns upon the pupils, and the pupils pay no heed to the teacher or to their overseers either."

Chapter Seven

Choices

Section 31. The Sewer of Romulus

"You don't love our Cato any more than I do, but even so: by exercising his unparalleled spirit and unsurpassed loyalty, he not infrequently damages the Republic: for he speaks his opinion as if living in the *Polity* of Plato and not in the shit-hole of Romulus [*in Romuli faece*]."[1] In this sentence from a letter to Atticus written in 60 B.C.—perhaps at the very moment when Julius Caesar was helping M. Licinius Crassus to assemble what we now call "the First Triumvirate"—Cicero illuminates what it means to be a Platonist. The honest Cato is speaking as if Plato's City were a reality in Rome: this suggests that Cato is putting Platonism into practice. Clearly Cato thought he was doing so: his decision to hear *Phaedo* before committing suicide[2] is a high compliment to the son of Ariston, despite the fact that *Phaedo* contains world literature's first condemnation of suicide.[3] In fact, Cicero's sentence points to the chasm dividing two different interpretations of the Πολιτεία. Because of Plato, Cato sees the Roman Republic as the *Polity*—i.e., as the perfect or ideal City of Plato's "Political Theory"—whereas Cicero sees both himself and Cato living *in Romuli faece*. To Cicero, the active political life was not an opportunity to exercise his "unparalleled spirit and unsurpassed loyalty" at the expense of the Republic,[4] but required returning to the Cave and acting accordingly. In other words, preserving

1. Cicero *Letters to Atticus* 2.1.8 (translation mine). "*Nam Catonem nostrum non tu amas plus quam ego; sed tamen ille optimo animo utens et summa fide nocet interdum Rei Publicae; dicit enim tamquam in Platonis Politeiai, non tamquam in Romuli faece sententiam.*"

2. Plutarch, *Life of Cato* 68.2 (Perrin). "After entering his chamber and lying down, he took up Plato's dialogue 'On the Soul,' and when he had gone through the greater part of the treatise, he looked up above his head, and not seeing his sword hanging there (for his son had taken it away while Cato was still at supper), called a servant and asked him who had taken the weapon." The entire passage is fascinating.

3. *Phd.* 61e5-62c8; cf. Alexei V. Zadorojnyi, "Cato's Suicide in Plutarch." *Classical Quarterly* 57 no. 1 (May 2007), 216-230.

4. Plutarch, *Life of Cato* 30.6

Rome's Republic required considerable compromise from a philosopher who was, like everyone who practices Justice as Socrates defined it, also a citizen of Plato's CITY (see section §18).

Two points already made in the Introduction may now be decently repeated. To begin with, it is only because of Cicero that we are even speaking of "Plato's *Republic*" in the first place. Unlike *The Laws* and the *Statesman* (the *Sophist* occupies a middle ground in this respect), it would have been easy to treat *Republic* the same way the *Apology of Socrates* and *Symposium* were treated: i.e., to preserve the Greek and call it (as Cicero does here) "Plato's *Polity*." It would never have occurred to Cicero to call the Πολιτεία "*Republic*" and it was only after the fall of the Roman Republic, and therefore after Cicero's own death,[5] that Plato's *Polity* could become what it is for us. The second point is more profound: the best external evidence for the interpretation of the *Republic* offered here is the life and death of Cicero. Like any good interpretation of Plato's Πολιτεία, Cicero's was necessarily embodied in his life: the philosopher returned from Athens and repeatedly chose to go back down into the sewer of Romulus. In addition to putting Plato's *Republic* into practice, he also defended its essence on the theoretical level. Along with the facile dismissal of Cicero as a mere eclectic copyist where "serious philosophy" is concerned, the fact that critics never mention the parallel between his Dream of Scipio and the Cave speaks volumes not only about our underestimation of Cicero but about our equally great and certainly no less ruinous misunderstanding of Platonism.[6]

---

5. Plutarch, *Life of Demosthenes*, 3.3 (Perrin translation): "For in my opinion two other orators [sc. other than Cicero and Demosthenes] could not be found who, from small and obscure beginnings, became great and powerful; who came into conflict with kings and tyrants [τυράννοις]; who each lost a daughter; who were banished from their native cities and returned with honor; and who, after taking to flight again and being captured by their enemies, ended their lives as soon as their countrymen ceased to be free." For Plutarch on Cicero and Plato, see *Comparison of Demosthenes and Cicero*, 3.4; for Plutarch on Demosthenes and Plato, see *Life of Demosthenes*, 5.5. For Plato's influence on Plutarch's *Lives*, see Timothy E. Duff, *Plutarch's Lives: Exploring Virtue and Vice* (Oxford: Oxford University Press, 1999), ch. 3 ("The Soul of a Plutarchan Hero; Plutarch and Platonic Psychology").

6. Insofar as Cicero is admitted to be a Platonist, he is viewed as a follower of Antiochus; see David Sedley, "Plato's *Auctoritas* and the Rebirth of the Commentary Tradition" in Jonathan Barnes and Miriam Griffin (eds.), *Philosophia Togata II: Plato and Aristotle at Rome*, 110-29 (Oxford: Oxford University Press, 1997). But Augustine knew better; consider *Contra Academicos* 3.18.41 (King): "After Philo's death, our Cicero buried all Antiochus' remains, for he didn't tolerate anything he loved to be weakened or undermined while he was alive." Cf. Charles Brittain, "Plato and Platonism" in Gail Fine (ed.). *Oxford Handbook to Plato*, 526-552 (Oxford: Oxford University Press, 2008), 534: "Antiochus' position was an empiricist one, and accordingly substitutes an immanent Stoic god for the transcendent metaphysical principles that were central to Platonism." For Cicero's strategies for burying Antiochus while appearing to praise him, see Altman, "Tullia's Secret Shrine."

It is because Cicero was Plato's best student—"Plato's rival" is what Quintilian called him (*Platonis aemulus* at *Education of the Orator* 10.123)—that he can teach us what it means to live in two cities at once.

> "'Down you must go [καταβατέον] then, each in his turn, to the habitation of the others and you must accustom yourselves [συνεθιστέον] to the observation of the obscure things [τὰ σκοτεινὰ] there. For once habituated [συνεθιζόμενοι] you will discern them infinitely better [μυρίῳ βέλτιον] than the dwellers there, and you will know what each of the 'idols' [τὰ εἴδωλα] is and whereof it is a semblance, because you have seen the reality of the beautiful, the just and the good [διὰ τὸ τἀληθῆ ἑωρακέναι καλῶν τε καὶ δικαίων καὶ ἀγαθῶν πέρι.].'"[7]

In addition to the καταβατέον, Socrates enjoins upon the Guardians a second obligation: συνεθιστέον. Cicero's life and death bear witness to his obedience to the first of these, the content of his voluminous writings to the second: he grew so accustomed to the shadows that it is his descriptions of them that have kept alive an amazingly vivid picture of the late Republic. Cato behaves as if he were living in the City, not *in Romuli faece*: Cicero, on the other hand, illustrates the meaning of "Dual Citizenship." Never forgetting Plato, he learns to see in the dark. The Republic comes alive in his speeches, letters, treatises, and dialogues; thanks to him, we too can see. Late Republican examples of τὰ εἴδωλα are the two great rivals in Rome's Civil War: Caesar and Pompey. The actions of neither were beautiful, just, or good. But Cicero saw in 60 B.C. what Cato could not: that Pompey was the lesser of two evils and therefore needed, at all costs, to be kept clear of Crassus and Caesar,[8] whom Cicero suspected before any of the others did (Plutarch *Life of Cicero* 20.4). No doubt Cicero would have found it more congenial to consider the connections joining the Good to the Just and Beautiful than devising strategies to split Pompey from Caesar and Crassus.[9] But there were duties to consider amidst the gathering σκοτεινά of Late Republican Rome and Cicero the Platonist—"having become accustomed"—not only saw τὰ εἴδωλα ten thousand times better (μυρίῳ βέλτιον) than Cato the Stoic

---

7. 520c1-5; in addition to the additional quotation marks of Slings, I have added "you must" before "accustom yourselves" in order to capture the fact that συνεθιστέον is a verbal adjective. Note the previous use of σκοτεινός at 432c9 (see section §1).

8. Cf. Erich S. Gruen, *The Last Generation of the Roman Republic* (Berkeley: University of California Press, 1974), 70n88.

9. Inspired by M. Cary, "*Asinus Germanus*." *Classical Quarterly* 17 no. 2 (April 1923), 103-107, it is L. G. Pocock, *A Commentary on Cicero* in Vatinium; 1926 (Amsterdam: Adolf M. Hakkert, 1967), 9-28 and 146-151 who offers the most compelling vision of late Republican politics, a vision attacked in Erich S. Gruen, "P. Clodius: Instrument or Independent Agent?" *Phoenix* 20 no. 2 (Summer 1966), 120-30 under the influence of Hermann Strasburger, *Caesars Eintritt in die Geschichte*; 1938 (Darmstadt: Wissenschaftliche Buchgesellschaft, 1966); see Gruen, *Last Generation*, 75n117.

did, but preserved his observations for all of the rest of us to see so that we too may learn.[10]

On the whole, we have learned a great deal from Cicero (see Introduction) and we still have our Republic to prove it: "These republicans were for the most part young men who, nourished by the reading of Cicero in school, had become enamored of liberty." But we have also fallen a long way from the ideals of 1789.

> Caesar's dramatic triumph casts antecedents in the shade. Hence earlier events have become precursors and determinants of that denouement—a dangerous fallacy. And perspective can lead us astray in another direction. Information on the late Republic rests heavily on the pronouncements of Cicero. A figure of no small significance, he looms even larger through the survival of his voluminous writings. But Cicero's attitudes grew out of personal—and atypical—experiences. One cannot understand the history of the late Republic as an extension of Cicero's biography or as an evolving blueprint for Caesar's dictatorship.[11]

As Erich S. Gruen admits in his classic *The Last Generation of the Roman Republic*, there would be no great amount of material for him to study without Cicero's "voluminous writings";[12] one might well think that all historians of Republican Rome would therefore be more grateful to the man who provides them with their livelihoods. But so complete and vivid is Cicero's description of τὰ εἴδωλα that he gives his enemies all the information they need to dismiss its ultimate source;[13] it is on the basis of Cicero's own testimony that Gruen can

---

10. Much has been lost, however. For example, the evidence that Crassus and Caesar were complicit in the revolutionary schemes of Catiline in 65 B.C. depends on a reference to a lost work of Cicero's in a fragmentary commentary by Asconius on a lost speech of Cicero; see Thomas Stangl (ed.), *Ciceronis Orationum Scholiasticae*; 1912 (Hildesheim: G. Olms, 1964), 65.5-11); the attempted demolition of this testimony by P. A. Brunt, "Three Passages from Asconius." *Classical Review* 7 nos. 3-4 (December 1957), 193-195 is frequently cited.

11. Gruen, *Last Generation*, 2

12. Of the one hundred and eighty-five footnotes in his chapter 6 (Gruen, *Last Generation*, 260-310), only twenty-eight do not cite either Cicero or Asconius.

13. Gruen, *Last Generation*, 503: "It is hazardous to place faith in the tortured exaggerations of Cicero. Of course one may find numerous bemoanings of the Republic's fate in Cicero's correspondence: assertions that the state is about to go under, or, indeed, that it has already gone under, that the senate, courts, and institutions of the government had been wrecked, that a fatal disease has left only the trappings of former glory. Ciceronian hyperbole must be recognized for what it is. Once more, these statements belong almost exclusively to the years 59 and 54, and they reflect the orator's personal plight: the fear of Clodius' machinations in 59, the chagrin of having to defend adherents of the dynasts in 54. Cicero too readily equates his own problems with the ills of the Republic. When he was more secure and confident in his personal position, the letters brim with confidence—and the Republic is sound. The orator, it is clear, can serve as no reliable weath-

write almost six hundred pages demolishing the "dangerous fallacy" that Caesar's tyranny was a long time in preparation and that Cicero knew it.[14] In fact there are more dangerous fallacies than this one and a patriotic citizen of these United States could do far worse than "understand the history of the late Republic as an extension of Cicero's biography or as an evolving blueprint for Caesar's dictatorship." It is because Cicero practiced the συνεθιστέον and recorded his astute observations of the passing shadows that the history of the late Republic cannot really be anything else.

Having considered the test Plato administers to his readers in Book VIII (see section §30)—i.e., will we recognize Democracy as the Age of Heroes?—this section will consider the even greater test that Socrates administers to Glaucon at the end of Book IX, a passage that points to the way Platonism survived the fall of Cicero's Republic. In a passage that resembles closely the Harmonious Man of 443c9-444a2—i.e., the just Man with a City in her soul—Socrates is once again touching on what such a just individual will actually do in the city of his birth, if anything (cf. 443e3).

> "He will rather," I said, "keep his eyes fixed [ἀποβλέπων] on the constitution in his soul [τὴν ἐν αὑτῷ πολιτείαν], and taking care and watching lest he disturb anything there either by excess or deficiency of wealth [οὐσίας], will so steer his course and add to or detract from his wealth [τῆς οὐσίας] on this principle, so far as may be." (591e1-4)

Although Shorey's translation of οὐσία is unimpeachable, the repetition of this word—when Socrates had used it as a synonym for Being beginning at the end of Book V (479c7)—might suggest to a thoughtful reader that true wealth is something quite different from money.[15] This man's confusion about "where her

---

ervane for the condition of the *res publica*." Cf. *Last Generation*, 2: "Cicero's contemporaries did not know what was in store."

14. Cf. Cicero *Philippics* 2.116 along with Plutarch *Life of Caesar* 4.4 and Gruen, *Last Generation*, 2: "The era that produced Caesar, Pompey, Cato, Cicero, Catullus, Lucretius and Sallust can hardly be reckoned merely as the prelude to disaster." Presumably Gruen means that the cultural efflorescence visible in Cicero, Catullus, Lucretius and Sallust (and the political acumen shown by Caesar, Cato, and Cicero) precludes the possibility that this was an age of decline. Does the presence of Mahler, Freud, Schnitzler, von Hofmannsthal, Klimt, Musil, and Wittgenstein in pre-War Vienna demonstrate that there was no cultural decline in the city of Gruen's birth? Do Stresemann, Hitler, Thälmann, Heisenberg, Brecht, Grosz, Heartfield, Lang, Reinhardt, Gropius, and Rosenzweig prove that the Weimar Republic wasn't doomed? There is a deep pessimism about politics, morals, and general outlook in Sallust, Catullus, and Lucretius, while Cicero's lonely fight against Caesar and Cato for the soul of Pompey is not without its tragic aspect quite apart from its futile outcome. The most buoyant writings from the period were Cicero's own, designed to survive the coming wreck and prepare us for preventing our own.

15. The switch back to οὐσία as "wealth" occurs in Book VIII (551b3, 553b5, and 554d3): it had been used in this sense from the start (another triad at I 329e4, 330c3, and 330d2; note the proximity to "good" in the last of these). The properly Platonic sense of

true treasure is laid up" is reinforced by the double use of ἀποβλέπων: Socrates is here discussing the Harmonious Man who decides how much οὐσία is appropriate by contemplating his internal constitution while the Book VII philosopher, by contrast, contemplates (notice the use of ἀποβλέψαι at 540a8) the real οὐσία and it is this and this alone that determines—to use Ciceronian imagery—how much of "the shit-hole of Romulus" is now to be endured.

> "Precisely so," he said. "And in the matter of honors and office [τιμάς] too this will be his guiding principle [εἰς ταὐτὸν ἀποβλέπων]: he will gladly take part in and enjoy those which he thinks will make him a better man [ἀμείνω], but in public and private life [ἰδίᾳ καὶ δημοσίᾳ] he will shun those that may overthrow the established habit of his soul [τὴν ὑπάρχουσαν ἕξιν]." (591e5-592a4)

This passage would appear to resurrect the moral universe of the Harmonious Man: political practice is strictly optional and the decision to participate in politics is based on internal—i.e., purely self-centered rather than altruistic—considerations. Nevertheless, the application of this passage to political life specifically is appropriate for three reasons. The fact that Socrates raises the political question explicitly with δημοσίᾳ (it is well to recall that an idiot is not a fool but rather "one who takes no part in political life") is a simple connection but the far more subtle resonances with the City of Good Men Only from Book I require explication. It will be remembered that good men rule (when they rule) not for the sake of money (Socrates used much more accurate words like "silver" and "possessions" at 347a5 and 347b6-7) or honors (but he uses the same word there as here: i.e., τιμή), but because of the penalty (347a5). The penalty has everything to do with another word Socrates uses here: ἀμείνω. The good man rules because there is no one as well qualified or *better* than her: she is the better man for the job even if it should turn out the ruling is hardly the job for which he is by nature suited. In other words, Socrates gently alludes to the City of Good Men Only but is silent about the penalty. Perhaps this is because, at least for the man he is describing, it is not a question of a good man in a city but rather of a man who is good by virtue of having a good city within. In other words, although "(1)" raises the question of possible political action, "(2)" seems to negate its primordial necessity: i.e., to prevent worse men from ruling. The suggestion that *noblesse oblige* is here being negated prompts (3) Glaucon's response. It is, in fact, this response that proves this passage to be political:

> "Then, if that is his chief concern," he said, "he will not willingly take part in politics [οὐκ ἄρα, ἔφη, τά γε πολιτικὰ ἐθελήσει πράττειν, ἐάνπερ τούτου κήδηται.]." (592a5-6)

---

the word has a monopoly in Books VI-VII; note the triad at 523a3, 525b3, and 526e7 introducing the distinction between οὐσία and γένεσις at 525b3. For 359a5 and 361b5, see section §9.

Of all the tests in all the Platonic dialogues, this is the one that goes most explicitly to the heart of the matter: Glaucon raises here the question of Justice. It is crucial to realize that Glaucon does not fail the test by saying these words: quite the contrary. It is Socrates who has been slyly (i.e., basanistically) calling Justice into question by (a) mixing Shorter Way discourse with (b) a misleading word for treasure and (c) a studied indifference to the penalty Socrates knows was of considerable interest to Glaucon (347a6-8). Glaucon's response is a beautifully constructed sentence: it does not at first appear to be conditional, this "future more vivid." "He will not wish to practice politics" appears at first to be no mere apodosis and the "οὐκ ἄρα" adds to our sense that we are about to hear a definitive, not a conditional statement. The words used are of utmost clarity: I have insisted that the only meaning of Going Back Down into the Cave that is warranted by the text (see section §20)—despite Plato *qua* teacher (and any other Platonic educators there may be)—is doing as Marcus Tullius Cicero did: not only leading the political life in some vague and amorphous way but becoming a *rector* or *conservator rei publicae* even if that means dying for it, as Cicero himself did. The Greek words τά γε πολιτικὰ . . . πράττειν capture it wonderfully: not only the literal "to practice" or "do the political things" but the perfectly colloquial "to enter politics" applies. Thanks to the last words of the *Republic*, the πράττειν will become crucial: the philosopher who goes back down into the Cave both does *and* fares well. And finally, there's that wondrous monosyllable: the particle "γε" indicates that the philosopher must deal, as it were, with "*all* the shit that's to be found *in faece Romuli*."

And that is only part of the apodosis: nothing has yet been said of the word "ἐθελήσει."[16] Since Socrates is going to respond along the lines of: "O yes she will!," Plato's decision to use the infinitive of πράττειν rather than a finite form (i.e., "he will not then practice politics") makes it even more dramatic: the philosopher does not simply march down to the Piraeus to the stern measures of the Dorian mode. If the philosopher practices Justice, it is because the philosopher *wishes* to practice Justice. It may be a duty but it's a sweet one that is rewarded in the best possible way: both in itself and by its consequences (358a1-3). And Glaucon's postponement of the protasis means that he has learned enough to doubt—and here a German word is useful—the unjust *Richtung* (i.e., the tendency or direction toward which) the words of Socrates have seemed to be aiming. Finally, "ἐάνπερ" is a mighty big "if" in Greek or any other language.

16. The philosopher's *wish* to return to the Cave first emerges as an issue at 519d4-5 (as discussed in section §16): there the Guardians must not be permitted even to wish not to go back down. This complete lack of freedom in the city is contrasted in the strongest possible way with the present passage. Here Socrates will argue that the free philosopher *wishes* to do what the fictional Guardians are prevented even from being able not to wish to do. The central point bears repeating: the city makes freedom—the necessary condition of Justice—conspicuous by its absence. Too many have rejected the city as illiberal without so much as considering the duty to exercise the principal freedom it was designed to render conspicuous.

Meanwhile, "τούτου κήδηται" suggests to me the same Biblical passage that echoed in my ear before: "if that is where his treasure is."

Socrates answers this most serious business with his most seriocomic oath:

> "Yes, by the dog, " said I, "in his own city he certainly will, yet perhaps not in the city of his birth, except in some providential conjuncture [νὴ τὸν κύνα, ἦν δ' ἐγώ, ἔν γε τῇ ἑαυτοῦ πόλει καὶ μάλα, οὐ μέντοι ἴσως ἔν γε τῇ πατρίδι, ἐὰν μὴ θεία τις συμβῇ τύχη]." (592a7-8)

It will be seen that this reply of Socrates settles next to nothing: the ambiguous oath is succeeded by an equally ambiguous reply. The words "in his own city" seem to keep the door wide open for the harmonious California Consultant and therefore each of us is relieved of wishing to practice politics here at home as long as we can persuade ourselves that no "providential conjuncture" applies to us: that's none too difficult, especially if we're atheists. Yes, we have always had the choice not to apply the *Republic* to ourselves. But at least for citizens of these United States—where it is infinitely easier for a New Woman, to say nothing of a New Man (Cicero was a *novus homo*), to climb the slippery ladder to political power than it was in late-Republican Rome[17]—especially at a moment of crisis when the very *Republic* of Plato is being "twisted by knaves to make a trap for fools," it takes a near perfect act of self-deception to persuade ourselves that no such θεία τύχη exists today. And "by the dog that is god of Egypt," it can come as no consolation to the lazy that Socrates answers: "Yes!" No matter how ambiguous the words or the oath, the case I am making here would have been *closed* had Socrates said "No." Instead, the test continues:

> "I understand," he said; "you mean the city whose establishment we have described the city whose home is in the ideal [τῇ ἐν λόγοις κειμένῃ]; for I think that it can be found nowhere on earth [γῆς]." (592a9-10)

The CITY has finally found its rightful home: today in the *Republic* of Plato (ἐν λόγοις), yesterday in the soul of Glaucon, while tomorrow, it is Marcus Cicero who will constitute himself its first citizen. Glaucon here refuses to read the Πολιτεία as Cato did and as so many others after him will do. But the CITY is neither perfectionist program nor "Plato's Political Theory" (least of all "the Political Theory of Plato's Middle Period," later realistically revised in the *Statesman* and *Laws*). Glaucon grasps the essential distinction—the plateau dividing the Idea from the earth—and thinks no less of the ideal for his having done so. In short, Glaucon has embraced Platonism, and therefore ipso facto Justice (see section §32). Socrates therefore rewards him:

---

17. Quintus Cicero, who calls his brother "a Platonist" in his *Commentariolum Petitionis* 12, advises him to repeat as his daily mantra as he goes down to the Forum: "I am a New Man, I want to be Consul, this is Rome." By Rome, Quintus means *in faece Romuli.*

> "Well," said I, "perhaps there is a pattern of it laid up in heaven [ἐν οὐρανῷ ἴσως παράδειγμα ἀνάκειται] for him who wishes to contemplate it [τῷ βουλομένῳ ὁρᾶν] and so beholding to constitute himself its citizen [καὶ ὁρῶντι ἑαυτὸν κατοικίζειν]. But it makes no difference whether it exists now or ever will come into being. The politics of this city only will be his [τὰ γὰρ ταύτης μόνης ἂν πράξειεν] and of none other." (592b1-5)

Here then are the three characteristic moments of Justice: (1) the proleptic ascent toward the Idea (ἐν οὐρανῷ ἴσως παράδειγμα ἀνάκειται), (2) the vision of the Idea of the Good (τῷ βουλομένῳ ὁρᾶν), and (3) the basanistic return to the Cave (καὶ ὁρῶντι ἑαυτὸν κατοικίζειν). The ἀνά-κειται of the paradigm is answered by the κατ-οικίζειν of the citizen. The Just man doesn't wait for the perfect City to descend from the heavens: *that's his job*. No one practices Justice in a republic like ours, or Cicero's, in obedience to our native city's laws—although Frank Capra is great enough to make us believe otherwise at times—but as self-constituted citizens of Plato's CITY. And when we go back down into the Cave (and let's not forget that the τὰ in τὰ . . . πράξειεν refers to τά πολιτικὰ πράττειν), we do so, as Cicero did, as citizens of what another one of Cicero's disciples would later call *The City of God*. This, then, is the passage that inspired Cicero's "Dream of Scipio" and, through the lost *Hortensius*, was doubtless passed—as when a burning torch is passed by horsemen late at night—to Augustine of Hippo. North Whitehead's "footnotes to Plato" is beautiful but I prefer the λαμπάδια, especially because the torch of Justice continued on its way. It was an Augustinian friar named Martin Luther who rode into a Cave called "Worms"; no stranger he to "the shit-hole of Romulus." And his great namesake—the greatest American of my time and of a long time hence—descended from another mountaintop with an indelible dream imprinted in his soul.

Section 32. The Perfectly Bearable Lightness of Being

Even the exoteric surface of the *Republic*—the elegant isomorphism of City and Man (in accordance with the political mathematics of the Shorter Way)—is a thing of great beauty. But it is surpassed by the collapsing dualities of the Longer Way.

The first of these is Justice itself: on the Longer Way, Justice in the man is identical to justice in the City. To begin with, the same action that makes the philosopher Just—i.e., willingly practicing τά πολιτικά in the dangerous Cave—is precisely what would *realize* the just City, as demonstrated by the Third Wave of Paradox. With the ἐν οὐρανῷ παράδειγμα transference, the man and city become one not because there's a little City in the Man (as with the California Consultant) but because there's (1) a philosopher in the greatest CITY of all and (2) a great man *in Romuli faece*. These two become one thanks to being found simultaneously on either side of the Platonic plateau separating Being from Becoming.

But this reunification does not exhaust the elegance of Platonic Justice. In the previous section, I made the following strictly proleptic claim: that Glaucon's embrace of the distinction between Being and Becoming at 592a9-10—i.e., Platonism—means that he has ipso facto embraced Justice. I'd like to defend that claim now. To begin with, then: the inverse is clearly true. Platonic Justice entirely depends on the distinction between the Cave and the Idea of the Good, i.e., on the *Kluft* or χωρισμός between Being and Becoming. But, it will be justly objected, the philosopher may choose *not* to go back down, and thus my claim is false: the mere embrace of the distinction doesn't necessarily imply Justice. To which I respond: the vision of the Good is ipso facto an awareness that the philosopher is *already* necessarily below the Good in an ontological sense. The one who has escaped the Cave and seen the Idea of the Good is still existentially, ontologically, and ineluctably *down from the Good.*

Platonism is neither mysticism nor neo-Platonism: the soul does not become one with the Good. As suggested earlier, not the worst way to think of neo-Platonism is that it is a system in which it is *the Idea that goes down*—i.e., becomes immanent in the world *via* the world soul etc.—but not the philosopher. Neo-Platonism was probably just a rear-guard action against Christianity about which, in any case, Nietzsche was hardly wrong. The shame Plotinus experienced by "being in a body" (if Porphyry is to be believed) is the mark of his infinite distance from Plato, a distance made all the greater by the appropriated terminological and even philosophical similarities. Only in the body can we be Just. The mystic would escape into unity with the highest, the materialist finds her satisfaction, having negated the divine, down here below: neither has a place for Plato's plateau and both are merely monists in the end. "Going Back Down" is as much the recognition of an ontological truth as the implementation of an ethical "ought": such is the Idea of Justice. Remaining outside the Cave is therefore not only an act of cowardice, selfishness, bad faith with Plato, and Injustice: it is the result of a complete failure to maintain Platonic dualism *qua* Platonist (for whom alone this world of ours is a Cave) and therefore ipso facto impossible. The time for Neoplatonism is after death: in the meantime, the true Platonist has work to do and can only be a Platonist insofar as she voluntarily chooses to do it and therefore does so here (ἐνθάδε).

In this sense then, the philosopher's choice to Go Back Down into the Cave is simply an expression of the philosopher's awareness of Platonic ontology, of the plateau between Becoming and Being, and therefore of the truth without which there can be nothing false.[18] It is primarily the fact that the visible world is only the downside of something higher that makes it susceptible to our neces-

18. Obviously it is perfectly false to say: "It is true that there are no absolute, permanent, and abiding truths." There will always be room for philosophy as long as self-contradiction itself remains. This is why the poets with whom an American Platonist would quarrel today are all called "Walt Whitman." In the changing versions of the *Leaves of Grass*, he refutes himself repeatedly, and not only because, as he would say, "I contain multitudes."

sarily vain attempts to know it for what it is. Naturally we are all curious about where this world—with all its elegant symmetries and mysteries—came from and it is not for nothing that Plato will have us reading *Timaeus* next. The Idea's immanence is a tempting conception: one is tempted to say that it is a beautiful idea but neither "beautiful" nor "idea" really fit the case.[19] The essence of Platonism is precisely the Idea's transcendence: we can only be being tested when Plato, Timaeus or anyone else, leads us to hope that we can do more than catch sight of it from below. Our separation from it during our earthly existence—and its separation from the earth forever—is the plateau that defines Platonism. If God ever walked among us,[20] it is only because God came down. It is our distinctive glory to be able to do what even God cannot: to go *back* down, as Moses did. This ought to inspire us.

It seems quite similar to Pascal's wager, this Platonic question of what way of life we ought to choose. But there is no gambler in Plato: he counts on us to recognize the situation for what it is the instant we behold the Idea of the Good. We begin by asking: "Does some transcendent God exist?" We speculate about the existence of "the thing in itself," the Lord God, the transcendent Idea. *We never think to doubt our own existence.* Long before Descartes, we ourselves self-evidently *are*: the question is: "What else—aside from us, that is—is real?" As Plato teaches in the Second Part of the Divided Line, the assumption with which you begin necessarily entails the place you will also surely end. Modernity's unquestioned Hypothesis—and therefore the conclusion that its philosophers reach again and again—is the absolute certainty of the self. Is the itinerary of modern philosophy from Descartes to Heidegger—*via* Spinoza, Hegel, and Nietzsche (with no visit to old Immanuel Kant, but only Johann Georg Hamann in Königsberg)—anything more than a proof of this proposition? A Being-free

---

19. In the wake of Einstein and Heisenberg, it was perhaps inevitable that the failure of Quantum Mechanics to keep pace with what physicists actually know would be coincident with a second renaissance of Platonism. And it is, after all, to promote such a renaissance that this book is being written. For all of the dire warnings about the approaching Thrasymachean darkness, we are truly living in a Golden Age (see Section §3). This is visible in strictly material considerations: for example, this footnote. Word processing, the Internet, Perseus, e-mail, JSTOR, Barnes and Noble, all of these (and more) have recreated a true "republic of letters."

20. For a Christian Platonist interested in theology, the Holy Trinity could be presented as miraculous because in the creation, the incarnation, and the ministrations of the Holy Spirit, God *crosses the plateau*. In no case, however, would this render God permanently, implicitly, or intrinsically immanent in nature, mankind, or the Church. It will easily be seen why it was Neo-Platonism and Aristotelianism that the Church could embrace: the Renaissance revival could only lead to iconoclasm and the most important image shattered thereby was the Mediæval *Weltanschauung*. The Definition of Chalcedon (A.D. 452) offers a nice metaphor: the central conception of Mediævalism was the assumption that simply because the Christ is both man and God, both transcendent and immanent, that "the City of God" could be that as well. Naturally this ecclesiastical immanence, like its secularized Hegelian avatar, was sought for all-too-human reasons.

dualism is preserved but implicitly materialized in Descartes' Method, immediately collapsed by Spinoza, then blooms into German Idealism's Substance made Subject,[21] soon to be shorn of the pseudo-Trinitarian trappings of Hegelianism by the comparatively honest Nietzsche's anti-Platonism so that Martin Heidegger can find no external objection to joining the Nazis on May Day, 1933 or—thanks to burying what's left of himself in what's left of a Pre-Socratic—finding nothing to deplore about having done so afterwards. Away, then, with these fetid footnotes to Plato![22] *Mehr Licht!*

The esoteric teaching of Plato is really quite simple, as everything about Plato turns out to be in the end. The *self* is the Hypothesis that we must recognize as such: our radical finitude ought to clue us in to this fact. If the reader denies that this teaching is Platonic, then I'd like "the Self as Hypothesis" to be regarded as my own contribution to Platonism. Recognizing the apparently self-evident Self as mere Hypothesis originates in the First Part of the Divided Line: it is there that hypotheses are treated "οὐϰ ἀϱχὰς ἀλλὰ τῷ ὄντι ὑποθέσεις, οἷον ἐπιβάσεις τε ϰαὶ ὁϱμάς" ("not absolute beginnings but hypotheses in fact, approaches and spring-boards") in order to reach all the way up to the un-hypothetical ("μέχϱι τοῦ ἀνυποθέτου"). It is natural for us to think of our search for the Idea of the Good as *our* search. But there is something to be said for calling the un-hypothetical what I once heard it called in a Reggae song: "the over-I." It is easy to take the Hypotheses that Socrates is describing here as strictly mathematical. Beginning in chapter 3, I have argued for a broader application that encompasses what Plato himself is doing all along the Shorter Way. But the broadest application of a comprehensive understanding of the Second Part of the Line is to life itself as we live it. *The implicit methodology of our own existence is based on both Hypotheses and Images.*

The face whose Image we see in the mirror is taken to be ours even though it too is mere image (and a highly variable image at that): we *assume* ourselves to be the one our parents begot and named. The central Hypothesis on which our entire existence depends—and upon which all our questions (and therefore all our answers) depend—is the unquestionable and unquestioned existential reality of the Self. Its very complexity makes it all the more real to us. It is this fact that proves that the Self as Hypothesis is merely explication of Plato: he playfully

---

21. See Robert M. Wallace, *Hegel's Philosophy of Reality, Freedom, and God* (Cambridge UK: Cambridge University Press, 2005) for a thoughtful assertion of Hegel's infinite distance from Descartes (especially 294-46 and n9).

22. There is a natural tendency to apply Whitehead's dictum simply to what might be called "the problems raised by Plato." But it's another matter entirely to see—as in the case of the structures built on the unquestioned and strictly unhypothetical Cartesian self—that even the anti-Platonic solutions to these problems are prefigured in the dialogues. I have treated these matters more fully in an unpublished manuscript to which (original works of philosophy—to the severely limited extent to which a Platonist can write any such thing—being so difficult to publish) I will nevertheless refer the reader: "Toward a Theology of Self-Deception."

interweaves "self" and "hypothesis" through the principle of non-contradiction. After all, if there is anything on this side of the *Kluft* that proves that the law of non-contradiction is merely an Hypothesis, it is our complex and richly multi-formed "willy-nilly" of a Self: that which, for example, both believes and doesn't believe in "the over-I," "other minds," God, the Idea, the external world, the "thing-in-itself," or generally speaking the un-hypothetical. Only if we reverse the question e.g. "Do I believe in God?" into "From the perspective of the unchangeable, can I myself be meaningfully said to exist?" do we begin to convert the truly unquestioned Hypothesis—i.e., our Self—into what Socrates says all such unquestioned assumptions should be: approaches or impulses (ἐπιβάσεις τε καὶ ὁρμαί) toward something higher and infinitely more permanent.

We assume we are real despite the fact that we're here today and gone tomorrow. But when we begin to take our strictly hypothetical status seriously, we can come to grasp, thanks to the superior instruction offered in the Academy by Plato the Teacher, that the infinitude and unity for which our souls so obviously thirst—especially if we're frightfully ambitious, like Alcibiades and Hippias the Sophist —is perfectly real. And despite the fact that the Idea of the Good is realer than we are, we recognize the infinite value of our own existence—no longer a mere Hypothesis but, through our choice of Justice, an offspring of the Good—the moment we catch sight of its unearthly light. Our quest for that light is our love of the Beautiful. This then is our glory: moths are we, and moths do we remain. But there's no place for a mystic's flame-drunk self-immolation in Plato: it's light-years away, that Good we'd now reach, and our spaceships are far too slow for the journey. Such is this body-entombed life of ours for the Platonist. Above all, it's easy to forget that the realm of Becoming exists within you.

Of course I'm not saying it's only there. But it's terribly easy to lose sight of the fact that it's unquestionably more than "there as well." One of the details in the Cave that takes on vast importance for the pragmatic Platonist—and surely that is what any American Platonist must necessarily be—is Socrates' insistence that the Cavemen can see nothing of each other *or themselves* (515a5-8). They see only shadows. Whatever it is they are seeing, thinking, or feeling both without *and within* is therefore based entirely on shadows. Until the Platonic simplification that is philosophy (611d8), it is our richly complicated self—an indefinite plurality "stuffed with most excellent differences" and merely Imaged with the tripartite soul (588c7-e3)—that constitutes the most attractive and insistent of these shadows. Naturally, we Cartesians take ourselves to be fully and completely real. It is, moreover, perfectly easy to conceive of the Cave in strictly epistemological and in any case external terms (to say nothing of a purely sociological reading that insists that the shadows are what *they*—our society, for instance—do to us). But the Cave teaches more than our dependence on society or that nothing can be known with certainty through the senses. Socrates insists that it is the very fact of being (one must really say "becoming") in a body—of being the kind of Self that we are (but really *are not* because that Self cannot really be said *to be*)—that makes us Cavemen (519a7-b5). In short, Becoming inhabits both sides of the Cartesian dualism, not just the external or objective side. The Cartesian simplification—and it can't be denied that the Self of the *cogito* really is a monad—is the less adequate cousin of Plato's. But it is only when Freud reintroduces teeming diversity into that Self that the Platonic position becomes more persuasive to moderns like ourselves: up until the pres-ent we have been more inclined to follow the path of Spinoza than of Leibniz. We'd do far better to ponder the dialogues of Plato.

And that's simply because Plato offers a solution: purify yourself down to the Good-oriented Monad that you really are—the one that discovered your spiritual unity and your unity of purpose simultaneously with Justice itself—and you'll ipso facto construct a faster than thought-experimental spacecraft that will make the journey home in the smoothest of flashes; after virtuous toil, here too "smooth is the way" (364d1). Don't be ashamed that you are in the body: yearn for the day when you will be set—booster-propelled—free of it. And the best way to do that is to live not for yourself alone now: battling Thrasymachus amidst the shadows of the Cave will make you completely sure of where you'd much rather be. In the end, Justice is simply giving to both Becoming and Being what they are due: the world of Becoming's between your own ears and only Being is light.

Section 33. Coming Up and Going Down

Naturally it's easier to express such thoughts in a mythic form: the mystical spaceflight of the soul Monad is hardly the stuff of academic discourse. And it cannot be denied that there are parallels between the Myth of Er—where Plato himself expresses such outlandish thoughts—and "the Dream of Scipio," itself the first journey into outer space. On the other hand, it is the lesson of the Cave—which is to say the lesson of Plato's *Republic*—that is essential to both of them.

With the Myth of Er, Socrates offers an account of that which the censorship imposed by the sons of Ariston had prevented him from discussing earlier: the afterlife. The claim of Justice remains the same, and is hammered home in the last words of the Πολιτεία (621d1-3; translation mine): "καὶ ἐνθάδε καὶ ἐν τῇ χιλιέτει πορείᾳ, ἣν διεληλύθαμεν, εὖ πράττωμεν" ("Both here and in the thousand year journey through we which we've passed: let us do well!"). In other words, whether here (ἐνθάδε) or on the journey from here to there (τὴν ἐνθένδε ἐκεῖσε . . . πορείαν at 619e4), the lesson remains the same: εὖ πράττωμεν. This hortatory subjunctive is not simply (1) a word of "farewell"; it is a (2) an exhortation no less than (3) a program perfectly poised—on the plateau, as it were—between faith and fact. The basis for this primordial Platonic pun[23] is perfectly preserved in American slang: the colloquial response to "How

23. The reader was introduced to it in *Alc. I* 116b2-5.

ya' doin'?" is "I'm doin' good." To the extent that he has one, "Plato's ethical theory" revolves around the identity of doing and faring well. The notion that "virtue is its own reward" is a commonplace but it would hardly have become so without the help of Plato. But just because it's true both here and there doesn't mean that we'll fare well if there's no there.[24]

This last statement gives no ground to the atheist. It's not that "virtue is it's own reward" is false if there's no *there* (ἐκεῖ). It's rather a case of ethics collapsing into ontology: only if we acknowledge that there is a there while we're here can we practice Justice. Our mistake is to think of this dualism, as Cephalus does, in chronological terms (see section §6): it's not a question of the afterlife but of eternal and unchanging Being. It is something like: "Remember your Creator in the days of your youth." The churches are filled with old people and even the corrupt old Cephalus can try to make things right. In Platonism, everything depends on the ontological *there* of Being, not the chronological elsewhere of the afterlife. But it's only while we're here—indeed it's the recognition that where we are is simply Becoming's ἐνθάδε ("in this place here"), visible as such only in the light of Being's ἐκεῖσε ("to that place")—that "virtue is its own reward." And just because virtue is its own reward here, that doesn't negate the possibility that even greater rewards exist there. How well we do here depends on how much we yearn to be there. And how well we will be rewarded there, is (I suspect), in direct proportion to how little we care about those rewards while we're here.

In the Myth of Er, Socrates tells us of a heavenly instance—a mythical instance—of what the *Republic* has been about all along: the choice of lives. Although counseled to make an informed decision within the perfect leisure only school allows (κατὰ σχολὴν σκέψασθαι; 619c3), the first fellow chooses the life of a tyrant. Having "chosen unwisely," he does what we all do: "'For he did not blame himself [ἑαυτὸν] for his woes, but fortune and the gods and anything except himself [πάντα μᾶλλον ἀνθ' ἑαυτοῦ]'" (619c5-6). In the single-minded pursuit of our own good, we throw ourselves open to the influence of chance. And it's perfectly true that this tyrant was not the first to believe in the gods—if only to blame or bribe them—in order to reconcile himself to his own folly: as far as the *Republic* is concerned, the first to do so was Cephalus. While Just philosophers are busily doing both good and well in the Cave, the tyrant is enslaved to chance and fear, and even, at the very end, to the gods. And who is this tyrant? Is it Thrasymachus? No. It is simply the one who refused to Go Back Down into the Cave.

> "'He was one of those who had come down from heaven [ἐκ τοῦ οὐρανοῦ], a man who had lived in a well-ordered polity [ἐν τεταγμένῃ πολιτείᾳ] in his

24. Imagine how unreliable an indication of chronology of composition an avoidance of contraction could prove to be!

former existence, participating in virtue by habit and not by philosophy [ἔθει ἄνευ φιλοσοφίας ἀρετῆς μετειληφότα]'"[25]

Since Er's story is brought back from there, everything is reversed. The place to come down is here (ἐνθάδε): the time to go up is thence (ἐκεῖσε). But this we can only do if we've gone down here. The wrong choice is necessarily made by the one who has not done so. If we spend our entire lives ignoring our finitude, the truth comes as an awful shock. A life spent in pursuit of making our lives a heaven on earth comes a cropper in the end. And so the well-ordered Harmonious Man descended at last; the end of life brought him down ἐκ τοῦ οὐρανοῦ. His perfect internal harmonies now availed him nothing. If Plato's polity could be realized—if the *Republic* actually were Plato's dream of a just City—it would be a perfect disaster for its Guardians. Trained up to obedience by its founders, they would "go back down" at the age of thirty-five because they were told—had been born and bred in conformity with the Third Noble Lie (section §26)—to do so. Life in the Shorter Way's well-ordered City (ἐν τεταγμένῃ πολιτείᾳ)—a monastery, for example[26]—would be a perfect disaster for the Man: the streets of Calcutta are a better venue for her. This is why Katarina von Bora took a husband and Martin Luther took a wife.

"'and one may perhaps say that a majority of those who were thus caught were of the company that had come from heaven [τοὺς ἐκ τοῦ οὐρανοῦ ἥκοντας], inasmuch as they were unexercised in suffering [πόνων ἀγυμνάστους].'" (619d1-3)

The "race is not to the swift" and "the first shall be last";[27] small wonder is it indeed that it was only *Neoplatonism* that flourished in the years after the Septuagint and Christ: the Platonists proved Nietzsche right. Those who had suffered—i.e., those who had done well—now would fare well.

"'But the most of those who came up from the earth, since they had themselves suffered [αὐτούς τε πεπονηκότας] and seen the sufferings of others [πεπονηκότας ἄλλους τε ἑωρακότας], did not make their choice precipitately. For which reason also there was an interchange of good and evil [μεταβολὴν τῶν κακῶν καὶ τῶν ἀγαθῶν] for most of the souls as well as because the chances of the lot.'" (619d3-7)

---

25. 619c6-d1. Here again is the characteristically Platonic emphasis on the central importance of φιλοπονία.

26. Somewhere in the pages of E. K. Rand, the great mediaevalist, is to be found this perfect analogy.

27. "μήτε ὁ ἄρχων αἱρέσεως ἀμελείτω μήτε ὁ τελευτῶν ἀθυμείτω" (619b5-6): "'let neither the first be careless in her choice nor the last be despondent'" (translation mine).

Those who had gone down here were well prepared to go up there; such is the teaching of Er through Socrates, of Socrates through Plato. The just woman has nothing to fear from any μεταβολή. As far as Plato is concerned, there is only one thing to be done here: philosophize. And what is philosophy except the recognition that a more than human wisdom can neither be fully achieved nor completely denied but only loved, sought, and served with all our strength? It is somewhere hereabouts that is to be settled the old question: is Plato a skeptic or a dogmatist? The correct answer is that he is both: Plato's doctrine is poised on the plateau dividing skepticism (i.e., philosophy never arrives at the truth) and dogmatism ("I Plato am the truth").[28] Halfway between the mystic Plato, the oracle of Athens who knows (having fully experienced the truth in a flash of divine insight) and the skeptical Socrates who doesn't and hasn't, stands, inclining no more to one side than the other: Plato the Teacher. If he had ruled out access to the bright light of truth, or (conversely) if he had asserted: "I Plato am the Truth," philosophy would have died long ago. Philosophy is precisely the middle ground (μεταξύ) between skepticism and dogmatism; about this, every philosopher must be dogmatic. In other words, philosophy—in both its skeptical "love" (implying our distance from the truth) and its dogmatic assertion that there is unquestionably "wisdom" to be loved—is "Plato." Instead of dogmatists seeing Plato as a dogmatist and skeptics seeing Plato as one of them, both the skeptic who distrusts Plato as a dogmatist and the dogmatist who encounters in Plato a skeptic see more clearly the paths to which Plato points. The "sane love of Wisdom itself" is not only the best life for mortal men, it is itself the realization of that mortality and the crystal clarity of the plateau that makes this place where we all are nothing but *here*.

> "'Yet if at each return to the life of this world [ὁπότε εἰς τὸν ἐνθάδε βίον ἀφικνοῖτο] a man loved wisdom sanely [ὑγιῶς φιλοσοφοῖ], and the lot of his choice did not fall out among the last, we may venture to affirm, from what was reported thence [τῶν ἐκεῖθεν ἀπαγγελλομένων], that not only will he be happy here [οὐ μόνον ἐνθάδε εὐδαιμονεῖν ἄν] but that the path of his journey thither and the return to this world [καὶ τὴν ἐνθένδε ἐκεῖσε καὶ δεῦρο πάλιν πορείαν] will not be underground and rough but smooth and through the heavens [λείαν τε καὶ οὐρανίαν].'" (619d7-e5)

Yes, the Philosopher is certainly happy here (ἐνθάδε). But both from thence (ἐνθένδε) and on the journey thither (ἐκεῖσε) we will fare better yet (614a5-6). So Plato believed in spaceships after all, and they traveled smoothly homewards (τὴν . . . πάλιν πορείαν) at the speed of light.[29]

---

28. As Nietzsche put it in "The History of an Error"; *Götzendämmerung*.

29. Cf. Brittain, "Plato and Platonism," 535 (he is discussing the status of Platonism in the first-century A.D.): "The additional element required for the development of an overtly Platonist ideology was a theory that justify an *unqualified* return to Plato at this

Ending a second section on this oracular note is not to my taste. Therefore it is a pleasant task to refer an earlier passage that says much the same thing in a less mythic fashion and, moreover, in a fashion that reveals something more about Plato the Teacher. Indeed the necessity of the plateau is not only ontological but ultimately pedagogical as well: Plato refuses to rule out the truth (i.e., dogmatic skepticism is rejected) but likewise gives the student no reason to be in awe of the sage. Plato's awareness that some of his students were his spiritual superiors—and another proof-text for Justice—is found in a stunning passage that every teacher worthy of the name should ponder.[30] The context is the Allegory of the Cave, and the two types of blindness a philosopher can distinguish from the true blindness of those perpetual prisoners who can see the shadows with perfect ease.

> "But a sensible man [εἰ νοῦν γε ἔχοι τις]," I said, "would remember that there are two distinct disturbances of the eyes arising from two causes, according as the shift is from light to darkness [ἔκ τε φωτὸς εἰς σκότος μεθισταμένων] or from darkness to light [καὶ ἐκ σκότους εἰς φῶς], and, believing that the same thing happens to the soul too, whenever he saw a soul perturbed and unable to discern something, he would not laugh unthinkingly [οὐκ ἂν ἀλογίστως γελῷ]" (518a1-6)

Some souls are going up, some going down. It is the same imagery and the same message as Er's Myth except that it's all reversed: the Cave is here and the Sun is there. Because of this dualism, there is another dualism as well: going up and going down. And therefore the disoriented student—the one who is totally confused—may well be the wisest among those gathered in your classroom, and that includes yourself. Unable to grasp what you think is important—at best, after all, merely an image of reality expressed in speech—they appear to be laughably slow. But Plato the Teacher reminds us that there are two types of disorientation:

> "but would observe whether coming from a brighter life its vision was obscured by the unfamiliar darkness [ἐκ φανοτέρου βίου ἥκουσα ὑπὸ ἀηθείας ἐσκότωται], or whether the passage from the deeper dark of ignorance into a more luminous world and the greater brightness had dazzled its vision [ἐξ ἀμαθίας πλείονος εἰς φανότερον ἰοῦσα ὑπὸ λαμπροτέρου μαρμαρυγῆς ἐμπέπλησται]." (518a6-b2)

---

late point in the history of philosophy. . . . An unqualified return to Platonic wisdom was thus precisely what was required." Sounds good to me.

30. See Adam, *Republic of Plato*, on 518b f.: "Nothing that Plato has bequeathed to us is more valuable than his theory of education as developed in this part of the *Republic*, and there is probably nothing in the whole range of educational literature, ancient or modern, which takes so far-reaching and profound a view of the aim and scope of education, or is so well fitted to inspire the teacher with indomitable courage and inextinguishable hope."

Who can deny that it is better to be headed in the right direction than the wrong one? Surely "every man in the know"—the same noble fellow who would rather be benefited than benefiting others—can see that there is nothing better to leave behind than one's own ἀμαθία ("ignorance")! But such a one could never be a teacher: a teacher by definition would rather benefit others than be benefited by them. And since the teacher herself is grappling with the shadows in her students' minds without losing sight of the shadows in her own, it is probably only an empathetic readiness to recognize a kindred spirit—the one you were—that is really required.

> "And so he would deem the one happy [τὴν μὲν εὐδαιμονίσειεν] in its experience and way of life and pity the other, and if it pleased him to laugh at it [εἰ γελᾶν ἐπ' αὐτῇ βούλοιτο], his laughter [ὁ γέλως αὐτῷ] would be less laughable [καταγέλαστος] than that at the expense of the soul that had come down from the light above [ὁ ἐπὶ τῇ ἄνωθεν ἐκ φωτὸς ἡκούσῃ]." "That is a very fair statement," he said. (518b2-5)

A teacher's laughter at a student's *confusion* is never just; it is the student who is *certain* that involuntary self-contradictions like "everything's a matter of opinion" and "there are no absolute truths" (i.e., the "true lie" of 382a4) who earns the justified ridicule. But anyone's laughter at the one that's coming back down from up above (ἄνω-θεν) is to be laughed, put, and set down (κατα-γέλαστος) as the Injustice that it is. Plato teaches us to think with thoughts, not words. Whether up or down,[31] here or there, the Idea of Justice remains the same at all places and for all time, an Idea of whose eternal existence Plato merely reminds us in his mighty *Republic*.

Section 34. Plato the Imitator

It would require a Delian diver to get to the bottom of Book X:[32] likening it to a basanistic dialogue doesn't get the half of it. The (1) first half of the book consists of Socrates' defense of the exclusion of Homer (and the lesser imitative poets) from the City explicitly based from the start (595b1) on the tripartite

---

31. Socrates requires the reader to distinguish "the Being that is *truly* up" from what is "both in the middle and down" at 584e3-4. "οὐκοῦν ταῦτα πάσχοι ἂν πάντα διὰ τὸ μὴ ἔμπειρος εἶναι τοῦ ἀληθινῶς ἄνω τε ὄντος καὶ ἐν μέσῳ καὶ κάτω;"

32. Luckily, Burnet's successor at St. Andrew's dives deep indeed; in addition to Stephen Halliwell, *Plato:* Republic *10, with translation and commentary* (Warminster: Aris and Phillips, 1988) and *The Aesthetics of Mimesis: Ancient Texts and Modern Problems* (Princeton, NJ: Princeton University Press), especially 323-334, see his "Antidotes and Incantations," 244: "At the heart of my case will be the thesis that Book X offers not a simple repudiation of the best poets but a complicated counterpoint in which resistance and attraction are intertwined, a counterpoint which (among other things) explores the problem of whether, and in what sense, it might be possible to be a 'philosophical lover' of poetry."

soul[33] to which no allusion is made until 603d4-6. With that accomplished (608a5-b1), Socrates then (2) reopens the question of the soul and, after expressly rejecting the view that it has three parts (611a10-b3), is granted an opportunity to describe the rewards of Justice (beginning at 612d4-10) including those bestowed in the afterlife (614a5-8). In order to describe these, Plato (3) assumes the place of an even more imitative poet than Homer by representing Socrates as telling the Myth of Er, who like Odysseus in his Phaeacian Tale, reports on the doings of the dead. In other words, once the premise upon which (1) the banishment of Homer depends (2) is rejected, (3) Plato becomes Homer.

The central problem is a simple one. There is clearly something delightfully amiss when Plato—whose little *Ion* is a work of supreme artistry (to say nothing of his *Republic*) and who is unquestionably the greatest poet among philosophers—banishes the poets from his ideal City. When a divinely inspired honeybee of a Socrates—clearly no stranger to groves, rills, and springs (*Ion* 534a7-b3)—*proves* in inspired poetry that Ion's capacity to interpret Homer is completely irrational, when he makes his eloquent speech against rhetoric in the *Gorgias* (511c7-513c3), and when he insists on the rectitude of banishing imitators in *Republic* X immediately after he has just made indelible the image of the man, the lion, and the multi-headed beast all joined together in the outer form of a man in *Republic* IX (588b10-e3), we must surely realize that our leg is being pulled (cf. 393d7). Besides, Homer is scarcely banished from the *Republic*: he dominates a long section of it joining Books II and III, then reappears—even after being banished a second time—in Book X.[34] The answer is therefore very simple: Plato isn't really banishing the poets although he may well be supplanting the author of the *Odyssey* as the best of them. Plato regarded Homer as his competition (section §10) and it is a good thing for us that he did: it is most unlikely that his dialogues would be the beautiful works of art that they are had he not done so. To put it another way: Plato emulated Homer.

As I have been suggesting throughout, we are much too eager to embrace the view of writing presented by Socrates in the *Phaedrus* (*Phdr*. 276c7-d8) as Plato's own. It is Socrates who never wrote anything—excepting, perhaps, the versified Aesop with which he fulfilled an obligation in the *Phaedo* (*Phd*. 61b6-7)—not Aristocles son of Ariston. As a matter of principle, I categorically reject

33. 595a1-b1: "'And truly,' I said, 'many other considerations assure me that we were entirely right in our organization of the state, and especially, I think, in the matter of poetry.' 'What about it?' he said. 'In refusing to admit at all so much of it as is imitative [μιμητική]; for that it is certainly not to be received is, I think, still more plainly apparent now that we have distinguished the several parts of the soul.'"

34. 595b9-c4: "'I must speak out [ῥητέον],' I said, 'though a certain love [φιλία γέ τίς] and reverence [αἰδὼς] for Homer that has possessed me from a boy would stay me from speaking. For he appears to have been the first teacher and beginner of all these beauties of tragedy. Yet all the same we must not honor a man above truth [οὐ γὰρ πρό γε τῆς ἀληθείας τιμητέος ἀνήρ], but, as I say, speak our minds.'" Note the possible reference to διάνοια at 595b8.

the notion that Plato didn't know that his dialogues were works of towering genius that transcended the limitations of written speech he himself describes. If proof of this is required, the fact that Plato's *Republic* transcends those limitations with the Critical Ambiguity of its καταβατέον makes it self-evident that Plato knew that his *Republic* transcended those limitations. As far as *Phaedrus* goes, we need not make the mistake of assuming that all basanistic dialogues are necessarily ugly.

A useful way of thinking about Book X is to match each of its three parts to the proleptic, visionary, and basanistic typology that forms the analytical basis of *Plato the Teacher*. To be sure there are basanistic elements in the book's first half: first among these is the assault on the Idea of the Good in the Form (τὸ εἶδος) of a bed. I'd be interested to know the percentage of scholars who have taken the Bed—an artifact made by a φυτουργός (597d4) no less—as helping us to better understand Plato's Theory of Ideas *and then taken that Theory to be true*. Like Verity Harte (see section §25), I suspect the number is revealingly miniscule. As for "the bed by nature" (ἡ ἐν τῇ φύσει οὖσα [κλίνη]; 597b4-6), perhaps a momentary return to the City of Pigs is in order. The peaceful city Glaucon rejects is a place where there are neither beds[35] nor relish: the primitives were merely "bedding down upon well-spread strewings of both bed-straw and myrtles."[36] By excluding *beds* from the primitive city, Socrates undermines the claim that there is any such thing as an artifact by nature, least of all this particular artifact. But with respect to the coming *Timaeus*, the bed and its maker (597d8) are proleptic as well, although we are entitled to wonder who the real demiurge is around here.

But the real problem in Book X is "Plato the Imitator." Employing another Platonic triad, Socrates—himself merely present in the text as Plato's imitation of Socrates[37]—sharply distinguishes the following trio at 601d1-2: "That there

35. 372d5-e1: "'If you were founding a city of pigs, Socrates, what other fodder than this would you provide?' 'Why, what would you have, Glaucon?' said I. 'What is customary," he replied; "They must recline on couches [ἐπί τε κλινῶν], I presume, if they are not to be uncomfortable, and dine from tables and have made dishes and sweetmeats such as are now in use.'"

36. 372b4-5; translation mine of "κατακλινέντες ἐπὶ στιβάδων ἐστρωμένων μίλακί τε καὶ μυρρίναις." See the note of Adam, *Republic of Plato*, *ad loc.*: "The whole point of the passage is that instead of reclining on manufactured couches." Glaucon seems to be in on the joke at 597d6-7 (emphasis mine, although the "γε" really makes it Glaucon's as well): δίκαιον γοῦν, ἔφη, ἐπειδήπερ *φύσει* γε καὶ τοῦτο καὶ τἆλλα πάντα *πεποίηκεν* ("since it is *by nature* that he has *made*"). In fact, this entire passage forms a transition to the *Timaeus*: note the introduction of the (human) δημιουργὸς in Socrates' response.

37. Socrates has made room for himself being imitated since Book III (396c6-d2): "'A man of the right sort [ὁ . . . μέτριος ἀνήρ], I think, when he comes in the course of his narrative [ἐν τῇ διηγήσει] to some word or act of a good man [ἐπὶ λέξιν τινὰ ἢ πρᾶξιν ἀνδρὸς ἀγαθοῦ], will be willing to impersonate the other in reporting it, and will feel no shame at that kind of mimicry, by preference imitating the good man when he

are some three arts concerned with everything, the user's art [χρησομένην], the maker's [ποιήσουσαν], and the imitator's [μιμησομένην]."[38] Which of these embraces Plato's art? He is clearly imitating Socrates practicing Justice. But as Plato the Teacher (he who founded the Academy), to say nothing of the author of the *Republic*, he clearly knows himself to be able to create the moment of literary crisis in which his readers can recollect the Idea of Justice. And he can do this only by imitating Justice himself. In other words, these cleavages are no more absolute than are the tripartite soul's; indeed they are far less so. At the very least, Plato belongs among those he now calls "in truth the good poets" (although τῷ ὄντι should probably be taken far less colloquially here):

> "So we must consider whether these critics have not fallen in with such imitators and been deceived by them, so that looking upon their works they cannot perceive that these are three removes from reality, and easy to produce without knowledge of the truth. For it is phantoms, not realities, that they produce [φαντάσματα γὰρ ἀλλ' οὐκ ὄντα ποιοῦσιν]. Or is there something in their claim, and do good poets [τῷ ὄντι οἱ ἀγαθοὶ ποιηταὶ] really know the things about which the multitude fancy they speak well?" "We certainly must examine the matter," he said. (598e5-599a6)

This passage suggests an escape route for Plato the Imitator through ontology. Even if Plato's characters—Socrates, along with Glaucon and the rest—are mere φαντάσματα, there is still the Idea of the Good to be considered: i.e., the gateway and exemplar to whatever other ὄντα there may be.

But Plato the Imitator doesn't simply present himself as imitating the Idea: he needs Socrates to do that for him in his dialogues. He is therefore imitating Socrates imitating the Idea. But Plato's Socrates seems most ungratefully unimpressed with Plato: the Socratic εἴδωλον (i.e., the image of Socrates made by Plato) next proclaims, in anticipation of the basanistic *Phaedrus*, the paltry value of the Platonic dialogues that keep him alive and, moreover, constitute the sole grounds of his own—i.e., Socrates' own—existence.

---

acts steadfastly and sensibly [μάλιστα μὲν μιμούμενος τὸν ἀγαθὸν ἀσφαλῶς τε καὶ ἐμφρόνως πράττοντα].'"

38. Cf. the use of all three in close proximity in the Second Part of the Divided Line (510b4-8). "'By the distinction that there is one section of it which the soul is compelled to investigate by treating [χρωμένη] as images the things imitated in the former division [τοῖς τότε μιμηθεῖσιν], and by means of assumptions from which it proceeds not up to a first principle but down to a conclusion, while there is another section in which it advances from its assumption to a beginning or principle that transcends assumption, and in which it makes no use of the images employed by the other section, relying on ideas only and progressing systematically through ideas [εἴδεσι δι' αὐτῶν τὴν μέθοδον ποιουμένη].'" Notice that it is only along the Longer Way that true ποίησις is found. But obviously Plato uses all three throughout his *Republic*.

> "Do you suppose, then, that if a man were able to produce [ποιεῖν] both the exemplar [μιμηθησόμενον] and the semblance [τὸ εἴδωλον], he would be eager to abandon himself to the fashioning of phantoms [ἐπὶ τῇ τῶν εἰδώλων δημιουργίᾳ] and set this in the forefront of his life as the best thing he had?" "I do not." (599a7-b2)

In other words, Plato the δημιουργός imitates Socrates asserting some such thing as this: "If Plato could really make his students Just Men in the Academy, he never would have wasted his time creating *me*." Here the ventriloquist Plato is locked in battle with his own puppet: what a feast for the mind! But the paradoxes are the point. After all, the purpose of Platonic prolepsis is to awaken the mind to paradoxical possibilities. In addition, then, to the way in which the sea-god Glaucus is about to blow away the tripartite premise of the anti-imitation argument advanced in the first part of Book X,[39] Plato is already deconstructing Socrates' argument on the basis of *himself*, i.e., on the basis of Plato the Imitator. In fact, it might be said that it is in the following passage that Plato asserts his superiority to Socrates for the first time, at the very moment when his Socrates is basanistically negating the glory of Plato's dialogues:

> "But, I take it, if he had genuine knowledge [ἐπιστήμων εἴη τῇ ἀληθείᾳ] of the things he imitates [τούτων πέρι ἅπερ καὶ μιμεῖται] he would far rather devote himself to real things [ἐν τοῖς ἔργοις] than to the imitation of them [ἐπὶ τοῖς μιμήμασι], and would endeavor to leave after him many noble deeds and works as memorials of himself [πολλὰ καὶ καλὰ ἔργα ἑαυτοῦ καταλιπεῖν μνημεῖα], and would be more eager to be the theme of praise than the praiser [καὶ εἶναι προθυμοῖτ' ἂν μᾶλλον ὁ ἐγκωμιαζόμενος ἢ ὁ ἐγκωμιάζων]." (599b3-7)

A stunning text! As a first step, Plato was more than content to praise Socrates in his dialogues and clearly preferred praising (ἐγκωμιάζων) to being the one who is praised (ὁ ἐγκωμιαζόμενος). This is the third and last time—in addition to the City of Good Men Only and the Ship—that this crucial ethical distinction between active and passive verb forms arises in Plato's *Republic* (see sections §8 and §15). Plato's Socrates restates the selfish position of "the one in the know" who would rather be benefited than benefit others (i.e., being praised rather than praising), as Glaucon's response proves that Glaucon and Plato are

---

39. Charles Segal, "'The Myth Was Saved': Reflections on Homer and the Mythology of Plato's *Republic*," *Hermes* 106 no. 2 (1978), 315-336 at 332: "Plato uses a mythical legend of metamorphosis, the sea-change of Glaucus—a myth used by Dante in the *Paradiso* to express Christian transcendence of the earthly realm, *transumanar* (*Par.* 2.67-72)—in order to state the difficulty of seeing the immortal soul 'as it is when it becomes pure' (καθαρόν) and not with all its accretions of this life, 'just as those who see the sea-deity Glaucus would not easily see his ancient form and nature' (ἀρχαίαν φύσιν, X 611c-d)." So too must we learn to see Plato and then ourselves.

well aware.[40] And who will categorically reject the validity of Socrates' critique?[41] Plato will patiently grant his auditors all the time in the world to think about that one. But the best answer will always remain: "I will." It is only because of Plato that Socrates can make this argument against Plato. How perfectly Greek: it is likewise only because of Athenians that Sparta can shine forth in the historical record as superior to Athens. It is this text that must be weighed against the critique in *Phaedrus* and in truth that's to balance a single droning cicada with a champion's crown. It is Plato's thirty-five dialogues that are his many beautiful works (πολλὰ καὶ καλὰ ἔργα ἑαυτοῦ): mighty deeds and imitations of mighty deeds at one the same time. They are his memorials (μνημεῖα) and we were too hasty to think that just because he devoted his genius to praising Socrates that he didn't want to be praised as well. He imitates his own Socrates blaming him: he therefore compels the reader to come to his defense (cf. *Phdr*. 275e5). And when we do so, we will realize that it is not *qua* imitator that Homer is being challenged: it is as the unrivalled poet-philosopher (cf. 548b6-7) and indeed as the greatest educator who ever sang.

Section 35. Odysseus or Achilles?

Where Plato is concerned, this would hardly seem to be a difficult choice:[42] Plato's *Republic* ends with a myth that celebrates a choice made by Odysseus while

40. 599b8: "'I think so,' he said; 'for there is no parity [οὐ γὰρ ἐξ ἴσου] in the honor [τιμὴ] and the gain [ἡ ὠφελία].'" In the context of the previous line (599b7), the one who is praised gains τιμή whereas the one who praises confers a benefit (ὠφελία).

41. The immortal Quixote, in his most brilliant speech, admirably proved the superiority of deeds to words; i.e., it is not just the history of philosophy that constitutes "footnotes to Plato."

42. For a recent scholarly account of Plato's Odysseus, see Silvia Montiglio, *From Villain to Hero: Odysseus in Ancient Thought (*Ann Arbor: University of Michigan Press, 2011), 38-65. In offering a thoughtful and welcome response to the valorization of Odysseus as Platonic hero by the Straussians—Seth Benardete and Allan Bloom in particular (see below)—Montiglio makes only one interpretive error (57): "The only time the philosopher [sc. Plato] approvingly retains Odysseus as a concrete character acting concretely, in the Myth of Er, it is a novel Odysseus, Plato's own invention, the 'recantation' of his existing avatars who chooses the only action that can endow a character like Odysseus with Platonic heroism: withdrawal from politics." See section §15; cf. 620c6 and the "un-Socratic" Socrates of 496d6 (Brann, *Music of the* Republic, 255n11: "Furthermore, his [sc. Odysseus'] soul, disenchanted with ambition, chooses the perfectly private most un-Socratic life (620c6)"). Unfortunately, Montiglio goes farther than Brann where Brann is wrong: the opening κατέβην as Herculean descent to the underworld (Brann at 119-21, 215, and 244) becomes Odyssean at Montiglio, 55. But Montiglio's good sense prevails (52): "how could Odysseus be a model for the philosopher's redescent into the Cave, since he visits the Underworld not to guide others but to seek guidance himself?"

Book III repeatedly exposes the words and actions of Achilles to censure.[43] Allan Bloom has boldly summarized Socrates' literary criticism in this context: "Socrates brings Achilles to the foreground in order to analyze his character and ultimately to do away with him as *the* model for the young."[44] It is certainly noteworthy that the first passage from Homer that Socrates proposes to excise are the words of Achilles (386a6-c8); what makes this excision even more significant is that Socrates quotes the very same words of Achilles he proposed to excise in Book III once again while describing the moment of crisis within the Allegory of the Cave:

> "And if there had been honors and commendations among them which they bestowed on one another and prizes for the man who is quickest to make out the shadows as they pass and best able to remember their customary precedences, sequences, and coexistences, and so most successful in guessing at what was to come, do you think he would be very keen about such rewards, and that he would envy and emulate those who were honored by these prisoners and lorded it among them, or that he would feel with Homer and greatly prefer while living on earth to be a serf of another, a landless man, and endure anything rather than opine with them and live that life?" "Yes, he [Glaucon] said, I think he would choose to endure anything rather than such a life." (516c8-e2)

It would appear, then, that the decision to return to the Cave was un-Homeric and, more specifically, that Bloom's assessment is fundamentally correct: Socrates is rejecting the example of Achilles.

But there is a problem: these words of Achilles are found in the *Odyssey*, not the *Iliad*.[45] Achilles does not say them, Odysseus does: we are listening to Odysseus' Achilles. In the course of the long speech Odysseus makes to Alcinous, he describes—much as Socrates' Er will do in *Republic* X—his sojourn among the dead. Do we believe that he actually went there? Achilles' description of death, quoted twice by Socrates in Plato's *Republic*, is more accurately

---

43. The paradox inherent in this censure is indicated by Segal, "'The Myth Was Saved,'" 331: "He [sc. Socrates] begins his attack with myths of 'the terrors of Hades' (III 386b). Promoting the fear of death, these myths are the most harmful, for they inhibit the soul's upward yearnings. They pervert the power which myth has to help the soul know itself in the dimension of the eternal. They rob the soul of that Achillean 'heroism' which Socrates professes in the *Apology* (28b-c) and, implicitly, in the *Crito* (44d). They take away its wings."

44. Bloom, *Republic of Plato*, 354; consider also (354): "One of his [sc. Socrates'] principal goals is to put himself in the place of Achilles as the authentic representation of the best human type. One need only look to their physical descriptions ['Socrates is . . . making the ugly old man more attractive than the fair youth'] to recognize that they are polar opposites." A more un-Platonic statement it would be difficult to find but see Strauss, *Rebirth*, 164: "The abstraction characteristic of the *Republic* is the abstraction from the body." See Altman, *German Stranger*, 461n91.

45. *Odyssey* 11.487-503; references to Homer will be accordance with the Monro and Allen edition.

described as the description of death that *Odysseus* attributes to Achilles. And given that it is perhaps the central theme of the *Iliad* that Achilles voluntarily chose death in preference to the long and peaceful life of an idiot who minds his own affair,[46] it would appear that Achilles admits in the *Odyssey* that he made the wrong choice in the *Iliad*. As James Barrett has written: "we need first to appreciate that Achilles' reply to Odysseus at *Odyssey* 11.488-91 represents a striking departure from the characterization of Achilles in the *Iliad*. Here Achilles embraces a fundamentally Odyssean point of view."[47] This is an important insight, particularly because Odysseus was a notorious liar who is here narrating the words of his rival.[48]

In support of the view that Plato is fully aware that Odysseus is lying about Achilles, consider what his Phaedrus says about the son of Thetis in *Symposium*:

> "How different was the fate of Achilles, Thetis' son, whom they [the gods] sent with honors to the Islands of the Blessed, because, after learning from his mother that if he slew Hector he should die, while if he spared him he should end his days at home in the fullness of his years, he made the braver choice and went to rescue his lover Patroclus, avenged his death, and so died, not only for his friend, but to be with his friend in death. And it was because his lover had been so precious to him that he was honored so signally by the gods."[49]

It is not only Plato's Phaedrus who doubts the veracity of Odysseus on this point: Pindar also places the soul of Achilles in the Islands of the Blessed.[50] Leaving aside the question of Odysseus' veracity in general,[51] it is noteworthy

---

46. *Iliad* 18.94-104; this is the passage Socrates would quote during his trial (see below). Note that the passages about death Socrates excises at 386d4-387a3 are the various responses of Achilles to the death of Patroclus, not his own; a heroic indifference to death is a suitable pattern for poetry at 387c10.

47. James Barrett, "Plato's *Apology*: Philosophy, Rhetoric, and the World of Myth," *Classical World* 95 no. 1 (Autumn 2001), 3-30 at 22. Cf. Gregory Nagy, *The Best of the Achaeans: Concepts of the Hero in Archaic Greek Poetry*. Revised edition (Baltimore, MD: Johns Hopkins University Press, 1999), 35.

48. Cf. Glenn W. Most, "The Structure and Function of Odysseus' *Apologoi*." *Transactions of the American Philological Association* 119 (1989), 15-30 at 19: "Of course within the fiction of the Odyssey, the *apologoi* are described as true while the Ithacan tales are called lies: but why should their apparent truthfulness entail an anomaly in this particular regard? Thus, whatever *Homer* stands to gain by delegating this narrative to Odysseus at Phaeacia, we still do not know how *Odysseus* is likely to benefit."

49. *Smp.* 179e1-180a4 (translation by Michael Joyce);

50. *Olympians* 2.78-81; see Nagy, *Best of the Achaeans*, 166-67 and, for the Islands of the Blessed, 540b6-7.

51. See Hugh Parry, "The *Apologos* of Odysseus: Lies all Lies," *Phoenix* 48 no. 1 (Spring 1994), 1-20 (especially 12), Scott Richardson, "The Devious Narrator of the *Odyssey*," *Classical Journal* 101 no. 4 (April-May 2006), 337-359 and, most importantly, Scott Richardson, "Truth and Tales of the *Odyssey*," *Mnemosyne* 49 no. 4, 4th series (September 1996), 393-402; further bibliography can be found at 397n5 and 400n8.

that Homer himself contributes to our doubts in this specific instance: even on Odysseus' account, Achilles does not need to drink the blood in order to speak.[52] On the broader implications of this passage for Homer, Barrett puts it well: "it is more profitable to read this passage as the *Odyssey*'s polemical championing of its own hero against the hero of the *Iliad*."[53] And as Stamatia Dova has shown, even when Odysseus pronounces Achilles "most blessed" (μακάρτατος), he is really serving himself: "Odysseus manipulates the μακαρισμός to compare himself with Achilles and takes advantage of their encounter to promote his own epic agenda."[54]

We know from Plato's *Lesser Hippias* that there was an ongoing debate in antiquity about the comparative worth of Achilles and Odysseus (*Hp. Mi.* 363b1-c1). Plato's dialogue illustrates a transitional moment in that debate: the traditional choice for the highly principled Achilles was giving ground in imperial Athens to the claims of Odysseus, master of expediency and sea-borne self-interest. But the roots of this debate are likewise found in Homer. Before Odysseus begins his Phaeacian Tale in *Odyssey* 9, the blind singer Demodocus bookends his song of Aphrodite and Ares with two others in Book 8:[55] he sings first of *an otherwise unknown* strife in words between Achilles and Odysseus.[56] Next, commanded by its still undercover originator, Demodocus sings of the Trojan Horse (*Odyssey* 8.486-98). Since Odysseus is the inevitable hero of this final command performance,[57] Homer makes it easy for us to determine the winner of the first song for ourselves.[58] By forcing us to imagine "the Missing Song of Demodocus," Homer's *Odyssey* invites us—at the same moment that the blind bard has finally introduced himself—to consider his two epics as a pair and thus to choose between the rival claims of Achilles and Odysseus.[59] It is in the context of this quarrel that the words Odysseus places in the mouth of his

---

52. *pace* Jacob Howland, *The* Republic*; The Odyssey of Philosophy* (Philadelphia, 2004; originally published in 1993), 144; cf. *Odyssey* 11.465-72. Consider also the status of Heracles among the dead at *Odyssey* 11.601-4 (cf. *Iliad* 18.117-21).

53. Barrett, "Plato's *Apology*," 22; on the other side, see Robert Schmiel, "Achilles in Hades," *Classical Philology* 82 no. 1 (January 1987), 35-37.

54. "Who is μακάρτατος in the *Odyssey*?" *Harvard Studies in Classical Philology* 100 (2000), 53-65 at 61.

55. For the importance of the first song of Demodocus, see Nagy, *Best of the Achaeans*, 21-25.

56. *Odyssey* 8.75-82; see M. Finkelberg, "The First Song of Demodocus," *Mnemosyne* 40 no. 1/2, 4th series (1987), 128-132 and Clifford Broeniman, "Demodocus, Odysseus, and the Trojan War in *Odyssey* 8," *Classical World* 90 (1996), 3-13.

57. Cf. Broeniman, "Demodocus," 12: "His [sc. Odysseus'] specific invitation to Demodocus to sing the Trojan Horse song is a request to continue the earlier song. This new song will inevitably surpass the earlier song inasmuch as the actions of its hero will bring about the destruction of Troy, just as the *Odyssey* itself reveals an epic hero who eclipses the Iliadic hero."

58. For Homer's hints, cf. *Odyssey* 8.67 and 8.73 with *Iliad* 9.186 and 9.189.

59. Cf. Nagy, *Best of the Achaeans*, 25.

rival at *Odyssey* 11.488-91 must be understood: words to which Plato forcefully draws our attention by first deleting and then quoting again in the crucial context of the Return. If we take those words as an accurate report of what Achilles actually said, we will be inclined to see Odysseus as "the best of the Achaeans" (*Odyssey* 8.78) and Er's Odysseus as Socrates just man. But if we have committed ourselves to Justice and are already going back down into the Cave, we will know that Odysseus is lying and that the Myth of Er is testing us. As the basanistic dialogues that follow *Republic* will repeatedly prove, Plato did not think it was sufficient to be an altruist: an ability to see through bad guys was no less requisite. And indeed the process begins early, thanks to Homer: Plato's Socrates is being deeply Homeric when he states falsely in *Lesser Hippias* that Odysseus is never shown to lie in *Iliad* 9 (*Hp. Mi.* 369e5-370a1). In fact, Odysseus lies twice in "Litai," both in suppressing what Agamemnon actually said to the envoys and in falsely reporting to Agamemnon what Achilles actually replied to them.[60] Plato is fully aware of these lies and draws the student's attention to them: by the addition of Agamemnon (*Hp. Mi.* 370b2), Socrates indicates the first lie and once Agamemnon is recognized as the πρὸς αὐτὸν of 371a8, he indicates the second at 371a7-b1.[61] Χαλεπὰ τὰ καλά (*Hp. Ma.* 304e8; cf. 435c8) was proverbial among the Greeks and Plato had learned from Homer that preferring Achilles is difficult (*Hp. Mi.* 369d6-e3); Odysseus is easier for the audience to emulate.[62] The complicated rebel who dies for a noble cause having overcome savagery and acquired humanity, is a considerably less attractive role model than the cagey survivor who benefits his friends while harming his foes.[63] The contest silently sung by the blind Demodocus opens the door to the real Homer, Plato's Homer. We are put in the place of Agamemnon and are challenged to do what the knowledge-worshipping braggart Hippias could never do:[64] defend Achilles as "the best of the Achaeans" against Socrates' attack. It is

---

60. Particularly enlightening is Bernard Knox, "Achilles," *Grand Street* 9 no. 3 (Spring 1990), 129-150. See also Ruth Scodel, "The Word of Achilles," *Classical Philology* 84 no. 2 (April 1989), 91-99, particularly on the fact of Odysseus' deception at 97 and P. R. Coleman-Norton, "Odysseus in the *Iliad*." *Classical Weekly* 21 no. 10 (December 19, 1927), 73-78 at 76.

61. Cf. Nagy, *Best of the Achaeans*, 51-52.

62. James Arieti (email message to author, February 22, 2011): "Odysseus, like any good rhetorician, adopts what he says to his audience, and here he is speaking to the Phaeacians, a people who will perhaps be gladdened to learn that their style of life receives the stamp of approval in Hades."

63. Plato has already tested our loyalty to Odysseus in Book III: after telling us that the son of Laertes is "the wisest man" at 390a8, Socrates quotes a passage from *Odyssey* 9.8-10 at 390a10-b2 that might suggest that his description is ironic. He applies the word "wisest" to Achilles' teacher Chiron shortly thereafter at 391c1-2.

64. Hippias is the true ἀλαζών (*Hp. Mi.* 369e4; cf. 490a2) and thus like Odysseus (*Hp. Mi.* 370e10-11). Hippias' choice of Nestor as the wisest of the Greeks (*Hp. Mi.* 364c6) and indeed as preceptor to the son of Achilles (*Hp. Ma.* 286a8-b4) contains the

the fact that Socrates' attack is *deliberately deceptive* that makes it ultimately Homeric.[65] Although Odysseus attacks Achilles in the *Odyssey* and Socrates imitates him in *Lesser Hippias*, neither Plato nor Homer is best understood as celebrating Odysseus;[66] we are witnessing instead the Homeric origin and Platonic continuation of basanistic pedagogy.

By beginning an account of *Plato the Teacher* with "the crisis of the *Republic*," I have chosen to plunge *in medias res*, into the middle of things. The limitations of such an approach become particularly obvious when assessing Plato's attitude to Odysseus and Achilles and yet this also makes it a good place to end a story that has only just begun. Not only must account be taken of the early *Lesser Hippias*, but attention must also de directed to the end of the story, when Plato finally shows his hand in *Apology of Socrates*. Although Socrates quotes *Odyssey* 11.488-91 to suggest that returning to the Cave is the last thing that a sane man would do, the philosopher's return to the Cave as described in *Republic* VII is, on a literalist account of the City, a sanitized affair: compulsory (520a8), state-supported (520b1-c1), and strictly temporary (520c1 and 540b1-4). It involves none of the gruesome consequences of the choice of a just life as described by Glaucon in *Republic* II (361e1-362a1), the life of a just man who seems unjust (361b5-c1). But the trial and execution of Socrates present Justice in a more realistic light. The hero's fate, penultimate consequence of his decision to go back down into the Cave and do battle with the seeming wise,[67] occupies a middle ground between the sanitized and brutal extremes albeit one much closer to Glaucon's: if hemlock was painless compared to the torture stake and branding iron in the eyes (361e5-362a1), it was no less deadly. But as the paradigm of the philosopher who voluntarily goes back down into the Cave, Socrates did not live his life in the spirit of Er's Odysseus—had he done so, he would not have been put on trial—nor does he face death in the spirit of Odysseus' death-

---

seed of his inability to defend Achilles from Socrates' pedagogical and basanistic attack (consider the importance of σοφός at *Hp. Mi.* 366a4, 366d2, 367e2, 368b2, and 369d2).

65. Under the influence (252n27) of Seth Benardete, *The Bow and the Lyre: A Platonic Reading of the* Odyssey (Lanham, MD: Rowman & Littlefield, 1997), Laurence Lampert, "Socrates' Defense of Polytropic Odysseus: Lying and Wrong-Doing in Plato's *Lesser Hippias*," *Review of Politics* 64 no. 2 (Spring 2002), 231-259, while acknowledging that Socrates lies about Odysseus (244-45), fails to distinguish Socrates' ambivalent (cf. *Hp. Mi.* 372d7-e2 and 247-8) defense of lying in general from the pedagogical purpose that lying serves in *Prt.* (358a4-5), *Hp. Ma.* (288d1-5), and *Hp. Mi.*, i.e., to reveal the limitations of Hippias and the Sophists generally. The works of Roslyn Weiss are to be consulted on Socrates' nuanced approach to the Sophists, in particular, *The Socratic Paradox and its Enemies*.

66. When Odysseus deliberately lies about Achilles, he does it for his own benefit and in defense of his own kind of self-interested duplicity; when Homer, Socrates, and Plato deliberately lie about Odysseus and Achilles, they have another end in view: the education of their auditors.

67. 327a1, 357a2-b3, and 517a4-6: "And if it were possible to lay hands on and to kill the man who tried to release them and lead them up, would they not kill him?"

loathing Achilles but rather, as he tells the world in his *Apology*, in the dauntless spirit of Achilles himself:

> You are mistaken, my friend, if you think that a man who is worth anything ought to spend his time weighing up the prospects of life and death. He has only one thing to consider in performing any action—that is whether he is acting rightly or wrongly, like a good man or a bad one. On your view the heroes who died in Troy would be poor creatures, especially the son of Thetis. He, if you remember, made light of danger in comparison with incurring dishonor when his goddess mother warned him, eager as he was to kill Hector, in some such words as these, I fancy: My son, if you avenge your comrade Patroclus' death and kill Hector, you will die yourself—'Next after Hector is thy fate prepared.' When he heard this warning, he made light of his death and danger, being much more afraid of an ignoble life and of failing to avenge his friends. 'Let me die forthwith,' said he, 'when I have requited the villain, rather than remain here by the beaked ships to be mocked, a burden on the ground.' Do you suppose that he gave a thought to death and danger?[68]

As indicated by the choice implicit in the first word of Plato's *Republic*, Socrates chooses the life of Justice at the expense of death just as the noble Achilles did (*Iliad* 9.410-16). It is therefore Plato's use of basanistic pedagogy that accounts for the fact that it is not Achilles but the wily Odysseus who appears in *Republic* X: we must supply the son of Thetis for ourselves and thus show ourselves worthy to dream for ourselves the last dream of Socrates.

The culmination of the Myth of Er is the choice of lives; this makes it an appropriate place to bring *Republic* to a close. In the final pages, the words "choose" and "choice" multiply, and, as the following passage indicates, the context of this choice is Justice:

> "so that with consideration of all these things he will be able, having reasoned it out, to choose [αἱρεῖσθαι]—with his eyes fixed on the nature of his soul—between the better and the worse life, naming the worse life that which will lead it there, viz., to becoming unjust, but better, whichever will lead to the more just [τὸ δικαιοτέραν]. But all other considerations he will dismiss, for we have seen that both for the living and the dead, this is the best choice [αὕτη κρατίστη αἵρεσις]." (618d5-619a1; Shorey modified)

68. *Ap.* 28b5-d5 (translation Hugh Tredennick); see Bloom, *Republic of Plato*, 354-55 and 357-58 for an attempt to sever Socrates and Achilles; cf. Segal, "'The Myth was Saved,'" 320-21. Showing the decisive impact of Seth Benardete, "Some Misquotations of Homer in Plato," *Phronesis* 8 no. 2 (1963), 173-178 on this futile but self-revealing labor are Robert Metcalf, "Socrates and Achilles" in Patricia Fagan and John Russon (eds.), *Reexamining Socrates in the* Apology, 62-84 (Evanston, IL: Northwestern University Press, 2009), 71, David Lévystone, "La figure d'Ulysse chez les Socratiques: Socrate *polutropos*," *Phronesis* 50 no. 3 (2005), 181-214 at 208-9 and Klonoski, "The Preservation of Homeric Tradition," 268-270.

Schooled by disasters during his earthly journey, Odysseus isn't about to make the tyrant's mistake: according to Er, he takes his time in choosing his life.

> "'And it fell out that the soul of Odysseus drew the last [ὑστάτην] lot of all and came to make its choice, and, from memory of its former toils [μνήμῃ δὲ τῶν προτέρων πόνων] having flung away ambition, went about for a long time in quest of the life of an ordinary citizen who minded his own business [βίον ἀνδρὸς ἰδιώτου ἀπράγμονος], and with difficulty found it lying in some corner disregarded by the others, and upon seeing it said that it would have done the same had it drawn the first lot, and chose it gladly.'" (620c3-d2)

In accordance with the justice discovered on the Shorter Way, Odysseus makes the same choice as the just Man of Book IV. It is the idiot's choice, not the choice of a fool but the choice of the selfish "man in the know" who cares for nothing else except the harmonious arrangement of the three parts of his anything but immortal soul.[69] It is not only our long-term memory of the contrast between the Longer and Shorter Ways that is being tested; so too is our commitment to Book X's moment of vision: the revelation of unitary soul. Above all, it is we ourselves who are being tested and it requires a certain amount of wishful thinking on our parts to see the choice of Odysseus as described by Er in *Republic* X (620c3-d2; cf. 496e1-497a3) as embodying Plato's last word. But then again it requires the same kind of wishful thinking in Homer's auditors to supplant the hero of the *Iliad* on the basis of the *Odyssey*.[70] The choice made by Odysseus (as described by Er, the creation of Socrates, here being imitated by Plato) tests our knowledge of both Homer and Socrates: neither is committed to the comforting, self-serving, and therefore ultimately Unjust view that the just man minds his own idiotic affair. But by inviting the unwary to see Odysseus as the paradigm of the just choice, the end of Book X consummates a rapprochement between two peerless imitators, both of whose heroes seem to recommend minding our own affair and looking out for number one. The rapprochement between Plato and Homer requires us to recognize that Er's Odysseus is the antithesis of—and Homer's Achilles, the model for—Plato's Socrates.[71]

Just as Homer tests his audience's appreciation for the courageous self-sacrifice of Achilles by staging a poetic contest with Odysseus,[72] so too does

69. 443b9-444a2; cf. 611b9-612a6.

70. Cf. Hannah Hintze, "Gluttony and Philosophical Moderation in Plato's *Republic*" (doctoral dissertation, University of Chicago; 2009) at 302: "Odysseus chooses the life Achilles would choose now, if only he could choose again." See also Angela Hobbs, *Plato and the Hero, Manliness and the Impersonal Good* (Cambridge UK: Cambridge University Press, 2000), chapter 7.

71. Note that Socrates blames Homer for misconstruing Achilles at 388a5-6. Even in the midst of censure, Homer is praiseworthy at 404b11-c10, 405d9-406a3, and 407e5-408b2.

72. Consider Michelle Zerba, "Odyssean Charisma and the Uses of Persuasion." *American Journal of Philology* 130 no. 3 (Fall 2009), 313-339 at 318: "There are paral-

Plato use Odysseus to test his audience's willingness to imitate his own greatest imitation, the equally courageous son of Sophroniscus and Phaenarete. He does so for the same reason that he challenges his readers to discover for themselves the Idea of Justice he has deliberately hidden along the Longer Way, halfway between the Idea of the Good and the shadows of the Cave. In choosing to supplant Odysseus, Plato makes a deeply Homeric choice: Odysseus only *appears* to speak Homer's last word and laugh his last laugh. And so it is in the light of Plato's ongoing contest with Homer that his Socrates, while reciting the Myth of Er, proves himself Homer's disciple by tempting the reader, as Homer did, with the deceptive charms of Odysseus. Even while posing as Odysseus, Socrates isn't Odysseus: it is only his Er and not he himself who pretends to have traveled among the dead. This distinction makes Socrates more like Homer than Odysseus and this puts Plato exactly where Plato wants to be: he is now competing with the greatest of imitators. But he can only prove himself the greatest of educators (600a8) by imitating Homer's own pedagogy (cf. 606c1-5): if his Socrates, like Er's Odysseus, had truly minded his own business, he would not have compared himself with Achilles in *Apology*. It is therefore not as mere poet that Plato stages this immortal contest with Homer; there is no "art for art's sake" in the serious play of Platonism. The final showdown between Plato and Homer is staged in the context of the final basanistic test *for the reader*, exactly where that test needed to be from the start: the reader's own choice of lives. Only the student who rejects the example of Odysseus will ipso facto pass the test and thereby award Plato the crown he so clearly coveted in his contest with Homer. And on further consideration, this student will gradually come to realize why Plato, no less mindful of the example of Achilles, politely restores that crown to his master's brow by revealing through Er the selfish inferiority of Odysseus.[73] Even if there will never be a shortage of smart idiots, it bears repeating that it requires no brains to be selfish.

The *Odyssey* itself comes back home to the *Iliad* in Book 24: here Homer gives his own account of Achilles in Hades (*Odyssey* 24.15-98). Agamemnon, who presided over the quarrel between the best of the Achaeans in the Missing Song of Demodocus—a contest heard only by Homer's chosen audience (*Odyssey* 8.77-78)—here narrates the Funeral Games of Achilles or rather the divine ἄεθλα ("trophies") at stake (*Odyssey* 24.85-92). These disputed trophies are the

lels between the situation of Odysseus and the *Odyssey*-poet himself [note that the narrator is complicit in presenting the Phaeacian Tale as true; see Most, "Odysseus' *Apologoi*," 19n22], whose song by virtue of its oppositional stance to the *Iliad* . . . implies a world of poetic competition in which a space has opened for doubt and dissent." Given that the anti-unitarian approach to the two epics that Zerba takes for granted here was not available to Plato; in its absence, what I am calling "basanistic pedagogy" offers a plausible explanation for the phenomena that confirm her claims.

73. Cf. Segal, "'The Myth was Saved,'" 333: "The *Republic* is both a tribute to and a struggle against Homer because it is so deeply pervaded by the conviction that poetry exercises a compelling formative power on the human soul."

origin of the quarrel between Odysseus and Ajax (*Odyssey* 11.543-48), judiciously avoided by Achilles during the Funeral Games of Patroclus.[74] More importantly, Homer allows Agamemnon to crown first Achilles[75] and then Penelope, not Odysseus,[76] as the true heroes of his two epics.[77] The return to the *Iliad* continues above ground: the last book of the *Odyssey* implicitly contrasts Odysseus' shabby treatment of Laertes with Achilles' humane embrace of Priam (*Iliad* 24.507-551), image of his own father Peleus (*Iliad* 24.507 and 511), in the last book of the *Iliad*. Odysseus' decision to test Laertes (*Odyssey* 24.235-40) has troubled commentators because there is no motivation for it within the world of the *Odyssey*:[78] the suitors are dead, the danger is past, and Odysseus' Athena-sanctioned (*Odyssey* 13.294-95) deception is no longer necessary.[79] But this testing becomes both intelligible and necessary once we realize that it is not the pathetic Laertes but rather our own humanity that Homer, the creator of basanistic pedagogy, is testing here.[80] And when Achilles addresses Priam in the exact same words his wife Hecuba had used to persuade him not to trust Achilles,[81] when he makes it clear that it is not the ransom that compels him to turn over Hector's body,[82] and above all when he promises Priam—and the entire *Iliad* bears witness to the power of this particular promise—that he will prevent Agamemnon from attacking Troy until his son, the noble Hector, can be properly buried,[83] we become the privileged witnesses of a moral grandeur to which James Arieti[84] proves a peerless guide but Odysseus (to say nothing of his modern defenders) a perfect stranger.[85]

---

74. *Iliad* 23.733-7; see Roger Dunkle, "Swift-Footed Achilles," *Classical World* 90 no. 4 (March-April 1997), 227-234. Naturally Odysseus would not have won the footrace had Achilles competed, as Homer repeatedly reminds us at 23.749, 776, and 791-93. Cf. Dova, "Who is μακάρτατος," 55 n. 5.

75. *Odyssey* 24.92-94 (the last mention of Achilles).

76. *Odyssey* 24.192-98. Odysseus is blessed (24.192) in his wife; Achilles in his death (24. 36-37).

77. Cf. Dova, "Who is μακάρτατος," 59: "Achilles and Agamemnon are giving us a precious glimpse of a *Nekyia* without Odysseus."

78. See Ruth Scodel, "The Removal of the Arms, the Recognition with Laertes, and Narrative Tension in the *Odyssey*." *Classical Philology* 93 (1998), 1-17.

79. Scodel, "Removal of the Arms," 9.

80. On testing in Homer, see Ronald Knox and Joseph Russo, "Agamemnon's Test: *Iliad* 2.73-75." *Classical Antiquity* 8 no. 2 (October 1989), 351-358 and Erwin F. Cook, "Agamemnon's Test of the Army in *Iliad* Book 2 and the Function of Homeric *Akhos*." *American Journal of Philology* 124 no. 2 (Summer 2003), 165-198 at 184: "What then prevents Odysseus from sailing home?" For the beginnings of an answer, see 178, 190-92, and Benardete, "Some Misquotations," 173-74.

81. Cf. *Iliad* 24.203-5 and 24.519-21: the most sublime repetition in Homer.

82. *Iliad* 24.560-62, 580, and 588; cf. 19.198-214.

83. The last word of Achilles at *Iliad* 24.670 is exquisite.

84. James A. Arieti, "Achilles' Inquiry about Machaon: The Critical Moment in the *Iliad*," *Classical Journal* 79 no. 2 (December 1983-January 84), 125-130, "Achilles'

"The best of the Achaeans" was on Socrates' mind to the end: his forced return to Phthia on the third day[86] showed that he had made the same choice as Achilles and would return home only when an involuntary death, in accordance with the prohibition of suicide promulgated in *Phaedo*,[87] released him from further fighting in "Troy."[88] And despite attempts to present Socrates as a second Odysseus,[89] Richard Holway has pointed in a better direction by showing that just as Apollo caused the conflict between Achilles and Agamemnon at the start of the *Iliad*,[90] so also was it service to Apollo's oracle that brought Socrates into conflict with the sophists, true corruptors of the democratic city then as now. But it is Barrett who has done the best work on the question: he not only explains why Socrates includes Odysseus,[91] along with Sisyphus, among the seeming wise he looks forward to interrogating in Hades but also why he relishes the prospect of comparing notes there with Palamedes[92] and Ajax,[93] both victims of Odysseus.[94] Without Achilles to adjudicate as he did at the wrestling match in *Iliad* 23, Odysseus defeats Ajax and wins the god-made arms of Achilles; Odysseus also arranged the judicial murder of the unsung Palamedes,[95] who had ex-

---

Guilt," *Classical Journal* 80 no. 3 (February-March 1985), 193-203, and "Achilles' Alienation in *Iliad* 9," *Classical Journal* 82 no. 1 (October-November 1986), 1-27.

85. Presented as a singer of songs at *Iliad* 9.186-89, Achilles needs both the warlike and the peaceful modes of 399a5-c4; beginning with the Funeral Games (from 23.491 to 23.890-97), Achilles—past-master of the Dorian mode (19.420-23)—fleshes out and fulfils Socrates' description of the Phrygian (399b5-c1) in the interview with Priam (24.599-620; cf. 24.669).

86. *Cri.* 44a6-b4; see also Scott Kramer, "Socrates' Dream: 44a-b," *Classical Journal* 83 no. 3 (February-March 1988), 193-197.

87. Cf. *Phd.* 62a2-7, Xenophon *Apology* 7-9, Arieti, "Achilles' Guilt," 202, and Richard Holway, "Achilles, Socrates, and Democracy," *Political Theory* 22 no. 4 (November 1994), 561-590 at 563.

88. See Segal, "'The Myth Was Saved,'" 320-21.

89. There are at least two Odysseus-based readings of *Republic* in the Straussian tradition: Howland, *The Republic* and Patrick J. Deneen, *The Odyssey of Political Theory; The Politics of Departure and Return* (Lanham, MD: Rowman and Littlefield, 2000). Blondell, *Play of Character*, 85 and 159-162 suggests a more balanced approach.

90. Holway, "Achilles, Socrates, and Democracy," 564-65.

91. Barrett, "Plato's *Apology*," 8 including n22.

92. In addition to Xenophon, *Apology of Socrates* 26 (quoted below), see *Memorabilia* 4.2.33 and Barrett, "Plato's *Apology*," 9-15.

93. Barrett, "Plato's *Apology*," 8 n. 21; see also Diskin Clay, "Socrates' Mulishness and Heroism." *Phronesis* 17 no. 1 (1972), 53-60.

94. Barrett, "Plato's *Apology*," 8: "But in addition to being victims of unjust judgments, these two share the status of being victims of Odysseus." See also Montiglio, *From Villain to Hero*, 42-44, particularly 43: "By identifying himself with two distinguished victims of Odysseus' polytropic maneuvers [sc. Palamedes and Ajax], Socrates charges his accusers with Odysseus-like daring." And, of course, deceit.

95. "The name of Palamedes never appears in the Homeric epics" (164) at Susan Woodford, "Palamedes Seeks Revenge," *Journal of Hellenic Studies* 114 (1994), 164-169.

posed the cowardly imposture of Laertes' son.[96] Consider in this context the words of Socrates in Xenophon's *Apology of Socrates*:

> And I get comfort from the case of Palamedes, also, who died in circumstances similar to mine; for even yet he affords us far more noble themes for song than does Odysseus, the man who unjustly put him to death.[97]

Combined with the reference to Achilles' choice, these allusions emphasize Socrates' kinship with the son of Thetis while distancing him from Odysseus. Achilles' decision to remain in Troy and face certain death is the same choice Socrates will make to ignore Crito's plea and await hemlock in the jail-cell; Socrates is no Odysseus and he sets sail neither for Thessaly nor Crete[98] but rather defends his soaring soul's immortality while his body remains behind, shackled in Athens. But thanks to basanistic pedagogy, neither Plato nor Homer confines this kind of nobility to their respective heroes; the beloved Patroclus points in this direction by posing the crucial question to his conscience-stricken[99] friend: "How will another, some late-born one, be benefited by you if you don't defend the Argives from shameful ruin?" (*Iliad* 16.31-32; translation mine). Homer's

96. Cf. Howland, *The Republic*, 166n2 (ch. 8).

97. Xenophon, *Apology* 26 (translation O. J. Todd); for Palamedes as the inventor of number, see 522d1-8.

98. The notion that the Athenian Stranger is an escaping Socrates is found first in a letter from Leo Strauss to Jacob Klein (New York, December 12, 1938) in Strauss, *Gesammelte Schriften* 3, 562 (translation mine): "The *Laws* rests on the fiction that Socrates has escaped from the prison!" See also Strauss, *What is Political Philosophy?* 33; *The Argument and the Action of Plato's* Laws (Chicago, IL: University of Chicago Press, 1975), 2; and Thomas Pangle, *The* Laws *of Plato* (Chicago, IL: University of Chicago Press, 1980), 379. For the significance of this brilliant insight for understanding Strauss, see my *German Stranger*.

99. Arieti, "Achilles' Guilt," 200: "In so far as the death of Patroclus is an affront to himself—his own death—he must respond to the challenge in the traditional honorable terms: in so far as the death of Patroclus is the death of a loved comrade, he must feel 'awful' at not having helped him as much as he could. And what he feels for Patroclus he now extends to all the Greeks, of whom the comrade Patroclus was a representative. Torn and driven by this double motive, he feels a new feeling: no longer simply shame, but what we call guilt." Adkins, *Merit and Responsibility*, tactfully refuted here by Arieti, is wrong on the philosopher's return to the Cave for very similar reasons; see 291 (and section §18): "The philosophers would be more *eudaimon* if they remained aloof from politics: accordingly Plato can offer no real reason why they should go back. Admittedly the city would be better governed, and hence more *eudaimon*, if they went back; but Plato cannot explain why, if one's own *eudaimonia* is the end of life, one should prefer the city's—or anyone else's—*eudaimonia* to one's own."

Achilles, like a wheedled mother or a busy bird,[100] played his lonely part in answering Patroclus' question; so did Plato's Socrates.[101] Now it is our turn.

Unfortunately, it was not only Xenophon's noble cavalry officer that the machine gun negated as an ideal; the First World War made the heroic courage displayed by both Achilles and Socrates look like folly.[102] Plato has not recovered from Verdun and the Somme. In addition to a two-part Great War, the validation of much else in Thucydides has also been required to bring the citizens of these United States to the point where something worse than the mandragora of Thrasymachus is now being offered to us by those who appear to be unique in "taking Plato seriously." As I have been implying from the start, it is probably the political crisis of our own republic that now makes it possible to see with crystal clarity the decision that Plato the Teacher is challenging us to make for ourselves. Although it is in this greatest of dialogues that Plato jumps right out of the text—or, if you prefer, makes room for us on one of those comfortable couches in the home of Polemarchus in the refreshing cool of that most wondrous of Attic nights—Plato the Teacher has never for a moment lost sight of us and our concerns; he has been patiently awaiting the arrival of guests whose easy democratic circumstances, whose wealth and freedom, would allow them to hear him and to choose accordingly. Even if confined to that living room—or, if you prefer, to the text that contains it—Plato the Teacher makes sure to recreate the torchlight race through us. And of course it is not only a question of one text: having already awoken us before dawn to meet *Protagoras*, he will look us straight in the eye, soul to soul, and encourage us to pray for something worth praying for: both athlete and know-it-all can profit by being introduced by Plato to that irritating neighbor of Socrates who shows both the limits of measuring all things by human knowledge and the magic of divine inspiration. He will also make sure we know our Homer, especially the comparative worth of Odysseus and Achilles. After administering to us a quiz on chronology in order to determine if we are ready to find tragedy in *Symposium* (as well as the comedy that causes our unitary souls to soar)[103] we must then be tested in the wrestling

---

100. See Sophie Mills, "Achilles, Patroclus and Parental Care in Some Homeric Similes," *Greece & Rome* 47 no. 1, 2nd series (April 2000), 3-18.

101. I have already noted my debt to Andrew, "Descent to the Cave," 522 and 525: "In addition to Orpheus, lovers, such as Alcestis, Achilles or Codrus who, like Socrates, were willing to lay down their lives for their beloved, displayed, in the face of death, the extent of their love in order to win eternal fame from posterity (*Symposium* 208d)." It was this passage that set me to thinking about the true relationship between Socrates and Achilles. For recent work on this theme, see Metcalf, "Socrates and Achilles."

102. Cf. Bloom, *Republic of Plato*, 357: "When he [sc. Socrates] identifies himself with Achilles there [sc. in the *Apology*], he is trying to impress his audience with his dedication to philosophy; and nothing impresses the vulgar as much as a man who is willing to die for a cause."

103. Quite apart from the role of Beauty in Book V, two passages in Book III suggest the reader's prior familiarity with *Symposium*. The limitations of Adeimantus are on display when he gives his assent (395a6) to Socrates' words at 395a1-5; cf. *Symposium*

grounds of the Lyceum: will we be able to recognize the Idea of Beauty by its conspicuous absence in the puzzling *Lysis*? Will we still ask whether virtue is teachable after seeing it taught in *Euthydemus*? Will we have the courage Socrates displayed at Delium required to take on the likes of the slippery Critias in *Charmides*? Will *our* inner Callicles have what it takes to become "Plato" after hearing what Socrates said to his touchstone in *Gorgias*? Will we open ourselves to the divine spark that strangely dwelt in Socrates and seemed to burn most brightly in him only when beset by a charlatan like Meno or by the apt question of a student like Cleitophon? If so, we are finally ready for Plato's *Republic*.[104]

"I went down yesterday to the Piraeus with Glaucon, son of Ariston." Thus begins the middle—the positive, not (as in the case of Hegelian dialectics) the negative moment—of Plato's "Encyclopedia of the Philosophical Sciences." Unlike Hegel, Plato has no difficulty beginning his system or indeed any one of his dialogues. To be sure the beginning is always pregnant with the end: witness the κατέβην. But the real birth takes place in the student. Like Hegel's, "Plato's system" is both dialectical and triadic: the great tests will follow the moment of vision, itself carefully prepared by the proleptic anticipations of "the early dialogues." But as the simplicity of those early dialogues proves, it is also pedagogical and democratic. To be sure it isn't the relativism of "what you will," the truly anti-democratic teaching: democrats must know with absolute certainty that Hitler is wrong and that Plato has intentions. On the other hand, Plato's "dialogic system" makes no claim to containing the truth: dialectical in the true sense, the Beauty mirrored in the dialogues awaits its chosen auditors and does no more than point them up toward the Good so that they may thereafter light their way down by the torch of Justice. G. R. F. Ferrari has reminded us of the crucial role of "the beloved" in Plato's *Phaedrus*; this holds true for the readers of every Platonic dialogue and even more so for those who read the dialogues as a whole. But like *Phaedrus* itself, it is the dialogues that follow *Republic* that repeatedly refute the critique of writing Socrates offers us as a test in *Phaedrus*.

The opening question of Plato's *Timaeus* (17a1-3) announces that something is missing and commentators have duly noted that that the summary of the previous day's discussion of the state lacks vital features of *Republic*, to which it nevertheless deliberately appears to allude. Among those vital features, the Idea

223d3-6. This ironic or basanistic contrast is followed at 402d1-403c6 with a passage that reprises *Symposium*. Note the "the beautiful" at 403c6 and the "visionary" language of 402d4.

104. Cf. Hartmut Erbse, "Über Platons Methode in den Sogenannten Jugenddialogen." *Hermes* 96 no. 1 (1968), 21-40 at 39 (translation mine): "What one would like to say about all the works of this period—at least about the dialogues between *Protagoras* and *Republic*—applies as well to *Charmides*: they are not only written in order to communicate isolated philosophical discoveries but are also at the same time a curriculum constructed from psychagogic points of view [*ein nach psychagogischen Gesichtspunkten aufgebauter Lehrgang*] that pursues the goal of preparing the reader for apprehending the Ideas." Throughout his wide-ranging interests, this great scholar rewards attention.

of the Good deserves pride of place;[105] despite adopting the language of Being and Becoming,[106] Timaeus never mentions the Good, the Just, or the Beautiful. Indeed the entire cosmological project,[107] dependent as it is on a vision-based conception of philosophy,[108] runs afoul of the sharp division between Being and Becoming illustrated by the Cave. The wish Socrates expresses early in *Timaeus* to see his Guardians do battle (*Ti.*19c2-8; cf. 543a5) is gratified when his chosen readers take up arms[109] against Timaeus' fork-tongued[110] assault on the dualistic essence of Platonism and the resulting annihilation or at least concealment (*Ti.* 29e1-2) of its ethical center. The battle will continue when the reader meets the Athenian Stranger and the parricide from Elea.[111]

Parmenides—the third of Plato's teachers along with Homer and Socrates—set the crucial philosophical precedent in his epic poem: the otherworldly and

---

105. The absence of the Idea of the Good from *Philebus* is even more striking; see Gadamer, *The Idea of the Good*, 30-32.

106. *Ti.* 27d6-28a4. Note that the distinction is implicitly undermined from the start by the juxtaposition of ἔστιν and δόξα at *Ti.* 27a5. Thanks to the emphasis on αἰτία (*Ti.* 28a4), this juxtaposition blossoms into the full-blown contradiction of *Philebus* 26d8 (cf. the doubled use of γιγνόμενον at 585b11-c6), on which see Guthrie, *History of Greek Philosophy* V, 232 and Taylor, *Commentary on Plato's* Timaeus, 86 (on *Ti.* 31b3): "The words should be carefully noted. In the earlier Platonic dialogues (for example in *Rep.* V) γένεσις and οὐσία are placed in sharp antithesis to each other as indeed they are by Timaeus himself at *Timaeus* 27d6ff. In the *Philebus* we find a maturer doctrine according to which there is a *positive* relation between them." In opposition to developmentalism, upon which Taylor's "maturer" entirely depends, I propose reading the "late" dialogues as basanistic.

107. Cf. *Phd.* 114d8-115a3; the sense of word κόσμος here should not be restricted to e.g. cosmetics. For the anti-cosmological "cosmology" of *Phaedo*, see the brilliant analysis at Zuckert, *Plato's Philosophers*, 807-9.

108. *Ti.* 46e7-47b2. Note that it is with this passage that Cicero's translation of *Timaeus* ends, a translation that was to be placed in the mouth of the Pythagorean Nigidius; cf. *Orator* 8 (*neque oculis*) and 10 (*sub oculos ipsa non cadunt*) where Cicero finally speaks in his own name. Carlos Lévy, "Cicero and the *Timaeus*" in Gretchen J. Reydams-Schils (ed.), *Plato's* Timaeus *as Cultural Icon*, 95-110 (Notre Dame, 2003) ignores this distinction but when the reader supplies it, his argument is extremely important.

109. Cf. Kathryn A. Morgan, "Narrative Orders in the *Timaeus* and *Critias*" in Richard D. Mohr and Barbara M. Sattler (eds.), *One Book, the Whole Universe: Plato's* Timaeus *Today*, 267-285 (Las Vegas, 2010), 272.

110. Hence the need for διερμήνευσις at *Ti.* 19c7.

111. On my reading, the Eleatic Stranger *is* a parricide (*Sph.* 241d3; cf. 569b6) and the reader must come to the rescue of both "the great Parmenides" (*Sph.* 237a4-5; cf. 477a3) and "the late-learners" (*Sph.* 251b5-6; cf. 409b5): the merely Hypothetical mathematical One alone is truly one and only the Idea of the Good is good. As indicated by the quotation from Homer at *Sph.* 216c5 and 381d2-3, the passage from 380d1-383c5 prefigures the Stranger, who employs the divine against unchanging Being (*Sph.* 248e6-249a2; cf. 380e3-4), and applies to basanistic pedagogy generally; 382c7-d1 will reappear as an epigraph to the second volume of *Plato the Teacher*. For διαίρεσις in *Republic*, see 454a1-8.

immutable realm described in "Truth" was followed by an explicitly deceptive cosmology called "The Way of Opinion" (section §5). But the origin of basanistic pedagogy—the pedagogy that exposes the student to a deliberately contrived falsehood in order to test a fighting commitment to the previously revealed truth—is Homeric. Timaeus, the Eleatic,[112] and above all the Athenian Stranger on Crete play deceptive "Odysseus" to Socrates, Plato's version of Achilles. In a careful study of Odysseus' "Cretan Lies,"[113] Adele Haft has brought to light some important details bearing on the son of Laertes' ongoing attempt to surpass Achilles: in the lie to Athena, for example, the fictional "Odysseus" imagines himself defying a Cretan Agamemnon[114] after having killed the only character other than Achilles who is called "swift-footed" in Homer.[115] The "Lie to Athena" is particularly important not only because it allows the audience to realize the mixture of envy and hatred with which Odysseus continues to regard Achilles but also because it is the first time Homer explicitly states that a discourse of Odysseus is a lie (*Odyssey* 13.254). Since the "Cretan Lies" Odysseus tells Eumaeus and Penelope—the first further illustrates Odysseus' envy,[116] the second creates the basis for Plato's *Laws* and *Epinomis*[117]—are likewise false,[118] the auditor is challenged to revisit the Phaeacian Tale ("the Apology to Alcinous" at 614b2) to discover for themselves, as Plato had long ago discovered, that Odysseus lies about Achilles there. In short: Plato learned basanistic pedagogy from Parmenides and Homer. And just as his teachers would have been proud of him, so too he would have been proud of the apparently skeptical eclectic who called himself "Cicero" in the works he found time to write while fighting to the death on behalf of the Roman Republic. It is worth noting that it is a poor teacher who is not surpassed by his or her best student.

---

112. Cf. Benardete, "Some Misquotations," 177: "The [Eleatic] Stranger then is another Odysseus." Having created Er's Odysseus, Plato, following Homer, shows that he knows how an astute image-maker can create images of a bad man for the purpose of establishing a *good* polity in the reader's soul (cf. 605b5-c3).

113. Adele J. Haft, "Odysseus, Idomeneus and Meriones: The Cretan Lies of *Odyssey* 13-19," *Classical Journal* 79 no. 4 (April-May 1984), 289-306.

114. Haft, "Cretan Lies," 292: "In this first tale Odysseus, in an effort to win sympathy through common knowledge, emphasizes the theme of offended honor, revenge and alienation so reminiscent of the Iliadic conflict between Achilles and Agamemnon."

115. Haft, "Cretan Lies," 292n10.

116. At *Odyssey* 14.217, "Odysseus" appropriates another quality (ῥηξηνορίη) found elsewhere in Homer *only* as an epithet for Achilles.

117. Cf. *Odyssey* 19.178-79 and David Mulroy, "The Subtle Artistry of the *Minos* and the *Hipparchus*," *Transactions of the American Philological Association* 137 (2009), 115-131. *Odyssey* 19.203 (ψεύδεα πολλὰ ἐτύμοισιν ὁμοῖα) is a perfect description for the Athenian Stranger's discourse as I read it; see Altman, "A Tale of Two Drinking Parties," 247.

118. In the context of *Iliad* 9.312-13 and *Hp. Mi.* 369e2-370d6, consider Haft, "Cretan Lies," 299 particularly 299n10.

Not coincidentally, the part of Timaeus' discourse most discussed in antiquity involves blending Becoming and Being in a World Soul;[119] in the twentieth- century, attention has shifted to Timaeus' deliberately self-contradictory[120] description of "a third kind" (*Ti.* 52a8) or χώρα ("region") between them.[121] But it is only the philosopher's Return that joins the two realms on Platonic terms; it is the philosopher and not the Idea who goes back down in Platonism. In *Republic*, the empirical basis of astronomy is emphatically rejected (528e4-529c3) and the Idea of the Good alone is "beyond Being."[122] It is therefore the Battle Hymn of the *Republic* that must continuously ring in our ears as we proceed, sounded here for the last time:

> "And is not this true of the good likewise—that the man who is unable to define in his discourse and distinguish and abstract from all other things the Idea of the Good and who cannot, as if in battle, through all refutations emerging, not eager to refute by recourse to opinion but to essence, proceeding throughout in all of these with the discourse untoppled—the man who lacks this power, you will say, does not really know the good itself or any particular good but if

---

119. Taylor, *Commentary on* Timaeus, 109-36. Vying with Shorey's translation of *Republic* as the king of the Loeb Library in Greek Philosophy is Harold Cherniss, *Plutarch's* Moralia, volume 13, part 1 (Cambridge, MA: Harvard University Press, 1976); see his illuminating notes to "On the Generation of the Soul in the *Timaeus*."

120. *Ti.* 52b2-d1; cf. Taylor, *Commentary on* Timaeus, 614: "When we find T. [sc. Timaeus] falling into inconsistency we may suspect that his creator is intentionally making him 'give himself away.'" Cf. Sayre, "Multilayered Incoherence."

121. See Jacques Derrida, "*Khôra*" (1987; translated by Ian McLeod) in Jacques Derrida, *On the Name*, edited by Thomas Dutoit, 87-127 (Palo Alto, CA: Stanford University Press, 1995), at 103: "And yet, half-way through the cycle, won't the discourse on *khôra* have opened, between the sensible and the intelligible, belonging neither to one nor to the other, hence neither to the cosmos as sensible god nor to the intelligible god, an apparently empty space—even though it is no doubt not *emptiness*? Didn't it name a gaping opening, an abyss or a chasm? Isn't it starting out from this chasm, 'in' it, that the cleavage between the sensible and the intelligible, indeed between body and soul, can have place and take place?"

122. 509b8; see "Daydream" in John Sallis, *Platonic Legacies*, 47-60 (Albany: State University of New York Press, 2004) for a Derrida-inspired (48n1) meditation on the applicability of the words ἐπέκεινα τῆς οὐσίας to χώρα. This approach to Plato is analogous to dismissing Achilles' choice on the basis of *Odyssey* 11.488-91; see Benardete, *Bow and Lyre*, 2: "we are allowed to infer that Achilles would have accepted Calypso's offer and that Odysseus would have sailed home from Troy. Indeed, Achilles seems to tell Odysseus that he made the wrong choice (11.488-91), but we are not told that Odysseus had any regrets. . . . Homer possibly parts company with Odysseus [sc. on refusing Calypso's offer] and recovers a point of view as much beyond good and evil as he so readily assumed in the *Iliad*." Benardete's quarrel with Achilles is longstanding: see his "Achilles and the *Iliad*." *Hermes* 91 no. 1 (1963), 1-16 and "Some Misquotations," 174; on the latter (1963), note that Socrates places Achilles neither in Odysseus' company in Hades among those whose wisdom he would like to test (*Ap.* 41b5-7) nor among those wronged by Odysseus (*Ap.* 41b2).

> he joins himself in any way to some image he does so by opinion or reputation but not by knowledge." (534b8-d6; Shorey modified)

Today, for example, it is necessary for a Platonist to reject the Odyssean reading of Plato's *Republic*[123] emanating from the Straussian tradition and to see through the Continental deconstruction of Platonism[124] based on the χώρα in *Timaeus*. Because it points to the challenges that lie ahead, the Myth of Er is hardly the end of the story: we are following a considerably Longer Way. The battle will be a long one, not only because of the dialectical complexity of Plato's "late" dialogues, but also because many of the deliberately contrived falsehoods they contain have found articulate defenders willing to redefine what is truly Platonic on their basis. Paradoxically, these defenders will prove to be very useful in overcoming the daunting difficulties inherent in the dialogues themselves. But that is another story. At this early stage, the only certainty about the story's end is that by the time we have reached it, we will be filled with admiration for Plato the Teacher, he who created the most beautiful flute girls (*Prt.* 347d4-5) who ever danced, eternally interwoven, arm in arm.[125]

---

123. See the "revelation" of μῶλυ at *Odyssey* 10.305; originating with Leo Strauss, *History of Political Philosophy* (Chicago, IL: University of Chicago Press, 1987), 2-3, this approach flourishes in Benardete, *Bow and Lyre*, 80-90, particularly 84: "From every point of view, both intrinsically and extrinsically, this revelation [sc. of μῶλυ] is the peak of the *Odyssey*." See also an important commentary on 607b6-7 at David Janssens, "The Philosopher's Ancient Clothes: Leo Strauss on Philosophy and Poetry" in Pawel Armada and Arkadiusz Górnisiewicz (eds.), *Modernity and What Has Been Lost; Considerations on the Legacy of Leo Strauss*, 53-71 (South Bend IN: St. Augustine's Press, 2010). For a connection between Derrida and Strauss, see Altman, *German Stranger*, 391n181.

124. Cf. "the anti-Platonism at the heart of Platonism" (128) in Gilles Deleuze, *Difference and Repetition*, translated by Paul Patton (New York: Columbia University Press, 1994).

125. Cf. Pindar, *Olympian Odes* 2.70.

Bibliography

Adam, James (ed.). *The* Republic *of Plato.* Two Volumes. Cambridge, UK: Cambridge University Press, 1902.

Adkins, Arthur W. H. *Merit and Responsibility.* Oxford: Oxford University Press, 1960.

———. *From the Many to the One: A Study of Personality and Views of Human Nature in the Context of Ancient Greek Society, Values and Beliefs.* Ithaca, NY: Cornell University Press, 1970.

———. "ἀρέτη, τέχνη, and Sophists: *Protagoras* 316b-328d." *Journal of Hellenic Studies* 93 (1973), 3-12.

———. "Gagarin and the 'Morality' of Homer." *Classical Philology* 82 no. 4 (April 1987), 311-322.

Allen, Michael J.B. (ed.). *Marsilio Ficino: The* Philebus *Commentary.* Berkeley: University of California Press, 1975.

———."Ficino's Lecture on the Good?" *Renaissance Quarterly* 30 no. 2 (Summer 1977), 160-171.

———. "Marsilio Ficino on Plato, the Neoplatonists and the Christian Doctrine of the Trinity." *Renaissance Quarterly* 37 no. 4 (Winter 1984), 555-584.

Allen, R. E. "Participation and Predication in Plato's Middle Dialogues." *Philosophical Review* 69 no. 2 (April 1960), 147-164.

——— (ed). *Studies in Plato's Metaphysics.* New York: Humanities Press, 1965.

Altman, William H. F. "Leo Strauss and the *Euthydemus.*" *Classical Journal* 102 no. 4 (Winter 2007), 355-379.

———. "Exotericism after Lessing: The Enduring Influence of F. H. Jacobi on Leo Strauss." *Journal of Jewish Thought and Philosophy* 15 no. 1 (Spring 2007), 59-83.

———. "How to Interpret Cicero's Dialogue on Divination." *Interpretation* 35 no. 2 (Spring 2008), 105-121.

———. "Tullia's Secret Shrine: Birth and Death in Cicero's *de Finibus.*" *Ancient Philosophy* 28 no. 2 (Fall 2008), 373-393.

———. "Altruism and the Art of Writing; Plato, Cicero, and Leo Strauss." *Humanitas* 22 nos. 1-2 (August 2009), 69-98.

———. "Womanly Humanism in Cicero's *Tusculan Disputations.*" *Transactions of the American Philological Association* 139 no. 2 (Autumn 2009), 411-445.

———. "Catherine Zuckert's *Plato's Philosophers.*" *Polis* 27 n. 1 (Summer 2010), 147-150.

———. "The Problem of Time in Hegel's Philosophy of History." Doctoral dissertation, Universidade Federal de Santa Catarina, 2010.

———. "The Truly False Basis of Cicero's Platonism." *McNeese Review* 40 (2010), 37-56.

———. "A Brief Prehistory of Paraconsistency." *Principia* 14 (2010), 1-14.

———. "*Laches* before *Charmides*: Fictive Chronology and Platonic Pedagogy." *Plato: The electronic Journal of the International Plato Society* 10 (November 2010), 1-28.

———. "A Tale of Two Drinking Parties: Plato's *Laws* in Context." *Polis* 27 no. 2 (Winter 2010), 240-264.

———. "The Reading Order of Plato's Dialogues." *Phoenix* 64 nos. 1-2 (Winter 2010), 18-51.

———. *The German Stranger: Leo Strauss and National Socialism*. Lanham MD: Lexington, 2011.

———. "Laurence Lampert's *How Philosophy Became Socratic*." *Polis* 28 no. 1 (2011), 166-170.

———. "Why Plato wrote *Epinomis*; Leonardo Tarán and the Thirteenth Book of the *Laws*," forthcoming in *Polis* 28 no. 2 (2011).

———. "Reading Order and Authenticity: The Place of *Theages* and *Cleitophon* in Platonic Pedagogy," forthcoming in *Plato: The electronic Journal of the International Plato Society* (2011).

Andrew, Edward. "Descent to the Cave." *Review of Politics* 45 no. 4 (October 1983), 510-535.

Annas, Julia. "On the 'Intermediates.'" *Archiv für Geschichte der Philosophie* 57 no. 2 (1975), 146-166.

———. (ed. and trans.). *Aristotle's* Metaphysics, *Books M and N*. Oxford: Clarendon Press, 1976.

———. *An Introduction to Plato's* Republic. Oxford: Oxford University Press, 1981.

———. "Die Gegenstände der Mathematik bei Aristoteles" in Andreas Graeser (ed.), *Mathematics and Metaphysics in Aristotle/Mathematik und Metaphysik bei Aristoteles*, 131-147. Stuttgart and Bern: Paul Haupt, 1984.

———. "Plato's *Republic* and Feminism." Reprinted in Gail Fine ed., *Plato 2: Ethics, Politics, Religion, and the Soul*, 265-269. Oxford: Oxford University Press. 1999.

———. *Platonic Ethics, Old and New*. Ithaca NY: Cornell University Press, 1999.

———. "Politics in Plato's *Republic*: His and Ours." *Apeiron* 33 no. 4 (December 2000), 303-326.

———(ed.). *Cicero: On Moral Ends*. Translated by Raphael Woolf. Cambridge UK: Cambridge University Press, 2001.

Ardley, Gavin. "The Role of Play in the Philosophy of Plato." *Philosophy* 42 no. 161 (July 1967), 226-244.

Arieti, James A. "Achilles' Inquiry about Machaon: The Critical Moment in the *Iliad*," *Classical Journal* 79 no. 2 (December 1983-January 84), 125-130.

———. "Achilles' Guilt," *Classical Journal* 80 no. 3 (February-March 1985), 193-203.

———. "Achilles' Alienation in *Iliad* 9," *Classical Journal* 82 no. 1 (October-November 1986), 1-27.

Armstrong, A. H. "Plotinus" in A. H. Armstrong (ed.), *The Cambridge History of Later Greek and Early Medieval Philosophy*, 195-268. Cambridge, UK: Cambridge University Press, 1967.

Aronson, Simon H. "The Unhappy Philosopher—A Counterexample to Plato's Proof." *Journal of the History of Philosophy* 10 no. 4 (October 1972), 383-398.

Ausland, Hayden W. "On Reading Plato Mimetically." *American Journal of Philology* 118 no. 3 (Autumn 1997), 371-416.

———. "On a Curious Platonic Dialogue." *Ancient Philosophy* 25 (2005), 403-425.

Bailly, Jacques. *The Socratic* Theages*; Introduction, English Translation, Greek Text and Commentary*. Hildesheim: Georg Olms, 2004.

Bambrough, Renford (ed.), *New Essays on Plato and Aristotle*. London: Routledge & Kegan Paul, 1965.
Baracchi, Claudia. *Of Myth, Life and War in Plato's* Republic. Bloomington, IN: University of Indiana Press, 2001.
Barbera, André. "*Republic* 530C-531C: Another Look at Plato and the Pythagoreans." *American Journal of Philology* 102 no. 4 (Winter 1981), 395-410.
Barker, Ernest. *Greek Political Theory*. London: Methuen, 1918.
Barnes, Jonathan (ed). *The Complete Works of Aristotle*. The Revised Oxford Translation. Two Volumes. Princeton, NJ: Princeton University Press, 1984.
Barney, Rachel. "Eros and Necessity in the Ascent from the Cave." *Ancient Philosophy* 28 no. 2 (Fall 2008), 357-372.
———. "Platonic ring-composition and *Republic* X," in Mark L. McPherran (ed.), *Plato's* Republic: *A Critical Guide*, 32-51. Oxford: Oxford University Press, 2010.
Barrett, James. "Plato's *Apology*: Philosophy, Rhetoric, and the World of Myth." *Classical World* 95 no. 1 (Autumn 2001), 3-30.
Beatty, Joseph. "Why Should Plato's Philosopher be Moral and Hence, *Rule*?" *Personalist* 57, 132-144.
———. "Plato's Happy Philosopher and Politics." *Review of Politics* 38 no. 4 (October 1976), 545-575.
Benardete, Seth. "Achilles and the *Iliad*." *Hermes* 91 no. 1 (1963), 1-16.
———. "Some Misquotations of Homer in Plato," *Phronesis* 8 no. 2 (1963), 173-178.
———. *Socrates' Second Sailing*. Chicago, IL: University of Chicago Press, 1989.
———. *The Bow and the Lyre: A Platonic Reading of the* Odyssey. Lanham, MD: Rowman & Littlefield, 1997.
Benson, Hugh H. (ed.), *A Companion to Plato*. Malden, MA: Blackwell, 2006.
———. *Clitophon's Challenge: Platonic Dialectic & The Philosophical Method in Plato's Classical Dialogues* at http://www.ou.edu/ouphil/faculty/benson/benson.htm (forthcoming; accessed July 10, 2011).
Bett, Richard. "Socratic Ignorance" in Donald R. Morrison (ed.), *The Cambridge Companion to Socrates*, 215-236. Cambridge, UK: Cambridge University Press, 2011.
Blackburn, Simon. *Plato's* Republic*; A Biography*. London: Atlantic Books, 2006.
Blits, Jan. "Socratic Teaching and Justice: Plato's *Cleitophon*." *Interpretation* 13 no. 3 (September 1985), 321-334.
Blitz, Mark. *Plato's Political Philosophy*. Baltimore, MD: Johns Hopkins University Press, 2010.
Blondell, Ruby. *The Play of Character in Plato's Dialogues*. Cambridge, UK: Cambridge University Press, 2002.
Bloom, Allan. *The* Republic *of Plato*. New York: Basic Books, 1968.
———. "Response to Hall." *Political Theory* 5 no. 3 (August 1977), 315-330.
Blössner, Norbert. "The City-Soul Analogy" (translated by G. R. F. Ferrari) in Ferrari (ed.) *The Cambridge Companion to Plato's* Republic, 345-385. Cambridge, UK: Cambridge University Press, 2007.
Bluck, R. S. "Logos and Forms in Plato: A Reply to Professor Cross" in R. E. Allen (ed). *Studies in Plato's Metaphysics*, 33-41. New York: Humanities Press, 1965.
Bolton, Robert. 1998. "Plato's Discovery of Metaphysics: The New *Methodos* of the *Phaedo*" in Jyl Gentzler (ed.), *Method in Ancient Philosophy*, 91-111. Oxford: Clarendon Press, 1998.
Bowery, Anne-Marie. "Plato's Theory of Forms" in William A. Welton (ed). *Plato's Forms; Varieties of Interpretation*, 111-136. Lanham, MD: Lexington Books, 2002.

Boyle, A.J. "Plato's Divided Line: Essay II: Mathematics and Dialectic." *Apeiron* 8 (1974), 7-21.

Brann, Eva with Peter Kalkavage and Eric Salem. *The Music of the Republic: Essays on Socrates' Conversations and Plato's Writings*. Philadelphia, PA: Paul Dry, 2004.

Brentlinger, John A. "The Divided Line and Plato's 'Theory of Intermediates.'" *Phronesis* 8 no. 2 (1963), 144-166.

Brickhouse, Thomas C. "More on the Paradox of the Philosopher's Rule." *Personalist* 59 (1978), 304-306.

———. "The Paradox of the Philosopher's Rule." *Apeiron* 15 no. 1 (June 1981), 1-9.

Brickhouse, Thomas C. and Nicholas D. Smith. "Socrates' Gods and the *Daimonion*" in Nicholas D. Smith and Paul B. Woodruff (eds.), *Reason and Religion in Socratic Philosophy*, 74-88. Oxford: Oxford University Press, 2000.

Brisson, Luc. *Platon: Lettres. Traduction, introduction, notices et notes*. Paris: Flammarion, 1987.

Brittain, Charles. "Plato and Platonism" in Gail Fine (ed.). *Oxford Handbook to Plato*, 526-552. Oxford: Oxford University Press, 2008.

Broeniman, Clifford. "Demodocus, Odysseus, and the Trojan War in *Odyssey* 8." *Classical World* 90 (1996), 3-13.

Brown, Eric. "Justice and Compulsion for Plato's Philosopher Rulers." *Ancient Philosophy* 20 (2000), 1-17.

———. "Minding the Gap in Plato's *Republic*." *Philosophical Studies: An International Journal for Philosophy in the Analytic Tradition* 117 nos. 1-2 (2003), 275-302.

Brunt, P. A. "Three Passages from Asconius." *Classical Review* 7 nos. 3-4 (December 1957), 193-195.

———. "Plato's Academy and Politics" in *Studies in Greek History and Thought*, 282-342. Oxford: Clarendon Press, 1993.

Bruell, Christopher. *On the Socratic Education; An Introduction to the Shorter Platonic Dialogues*. Lanham, MD: Rowman & Littlefield, 1999.

Burkert, Walter. "Cicero als Platoniker und Skeptiker." *Gymnasium* 72 (1965), 175-200.

Burnet, John. *Platonis Opera*. Oxford: Clarendon Press, 1900-1907.

———. *Plato's* Phaedo. Oxford: Clarendon Press, 1911.

———. *Plato's* Euthyphro. Oxford: Clarendon Press, 1924.

Burnyeat, M. F. "Platonism and Mathematics. A Prelude to Discussion" in Andreas Graeser (ed.), *Mathematics and Metaphysics in Aristotle/Mathematik und Metaphysik bei Aristoteles*. Akten des X. Symposium Aristotelicum. Bern and Stuttgart: Paul Haupt, 1984.

———. "Sphinx without a Secret." *New York Review of Books*. May 30, 1985.

———. "Antipater and Self-Refutation; Elusive Arguments in Cicero's *Academica*" in Brad Inwood and Jaap Mansfield (eds.). *Assent and Argument: Studies in Cicero's* Academic Books, 276-310. Leiden: Brill, 1997.

———. "Plato on Why Mathematics is Good for the Soul" in Timothy Smiley (ed.), *Mathematics and Necessity: Essays in the History of Philosophy*, 1-81. Oxford: Oxford University Press, 2000.

Cairns, Douglas, Fritz-Gregor Herrmann, and Terry Penner (eds.). *Pursuing the Good; Ethics and Metaphysics in Plato's* Republic. Edinburgh: University of Edinburgh Press, 2007.

Campbell, Lewis. *The* Sophistes *and* Politicus *of Plato*. Oxford: Clarendon Press, 1867.

Cardini, Maria Timpanaro. *Pseudo-Aristotele,* De lineis insecabilibus. Milan: Instituto Editoriale Cisalpino, 1970.

Cary, M. "*Asinus Germanus*." *Classical Quarterly* 17 no. 2 (April 1923), 103-107.

Chayevsky, Paddy. 1971. *Hospital*. United Artists Films.

Cherniss, Harold. "The Philosophical Economy of the Theory of Ideas." *American Journal of Philology* 57 no. 4 (1936), 445-56.

———. *Aristotle's Criticism of Plato and the Academy*. Baltimore, MD: Johns Hopkins University Press, 1944.

———. *The Riddle of the Early Academy*. New York: Russell & Russell, 1945.

———. "Plato the Mathematician." *Review of Metaphysics* 4 no. 3 (March 1951), 395-425.

———. "*Timaeus* 38a5-b5." *Journal of Hellenic Studies* 77 part 1 (1957), 18-23.

———. "The Relation of the *Timaeus* to Plato's Later Dialogues." *American Journal of Philology* 78 no. 3 (1957), 225-266.

———. (translation and notes). *Plutarch's* Moralia. Volume 13, parts 1-2. Cambridge, MA: Harvard University Press, 1976.

Cherubin, Rose. "Light, Night, and the Opinions of Mortals: Parmenides B8.51-61 and B9." *Ancient Philosophy* 25 (Spring 2005), 1-23.

Christian, William. "Waiting for Grace: Philosophy and Politics in Plato's *Republic*." *Canadian Journal of Political Science / Revue canadienne de science politique* 21 no. 1 (March 1988), 57-82.

Crystal, Ian. "Parmenidean Allusions in *Republic* V." *Ancient Philosophy* 16 (Fall 1996), 351-363.

Ciholas, Paul. "Plato: The Attic Moses? Some Patristic Reactions to Platonic Philosophy." *Classical World* 72 no. 4 (December 1978-January 1979), 217-225.

Clay, Diskin. "Socrates' Mulishness and Heroism." *Phronesis* 17 no. 1 (1972), 53-60.

———. "Gaps in the 'Universe' of the Platonic Dialogues." *Proceedings of the Boston Area Colloquium in Ancient Philosophy* 3 (1987), 131-157.

———. "Reading the *Republic*." In Charles L. Griswold Jr. (ed.), *Platonic Writings, Platonic Readings*. University Park: Pennsylvania State University Press, 2002.

Cochrane, Charles Norris. *Christianity and Classical Culture: A Study of Thought and Action from Augustus to Augustine*. Oxford: Oxford University Press, 1940.

Cohen, Hermann. *Platons Ideenlehre und die Mathematik*. Marburg: G. E. Pfeil, 1878.

Coleman-Norton, P. R. "Odysseus in the *Iliad*." *Classical Weekly* 21 no. 10 (December 19, 1927), 73-78.

Cook, Erwin F. "Agamemnon's Test of the Army in *Iliad* Book 2 and the Function of Homeric *Akhos*." *American Journal of Philology* 124 no. 2 (Summer 2003), 165-198.

Cook Wilson, J. "On the Platonist Doctrine of the ἀσύμβλητοι ἀριθμοί." *Classical Review* 18 no. 5 (June 1904), 247-260.

Cooper, Craig. "Philosophers, Politics, Academics: Demosthenes' Rhetorical Reputation in Antiquity" in Ian Worthington (ed.), *Demosthenes: Statesman and Orator*, 224-245. London: Routledge, 2000.

Cooper, John M. "The Psychology of Justice in Plato." *American Philosophical Quarterly* 14 no. 2 (April 1977), 151-157.

Cooper, John M. (ed.) and D. S. Hutchinson. *Plato, Complete Works; edited with an Introduction and Notes*. Chicago, IL: Hackett, 1997.

Cooper, Neil. "The Importance of ΔΙΑΝΟΙΑ in Plato's Theory of Forms." *Classical Quarterly* (n.s.) 16 no. 1 (May 1966), 65-69.

Corlett, J. Angelo. "Interpreting Plato's Dialogues." *Classical Quarterly* n.s. 47 no. 2 (1997), 423-437.

Cornford, F. M. "Psychology and Social Structure in the *Republic* of Plato." *Classical Quarterly* 6 no. 4 (October 1912), 246-265.

———. "Mathematics and Dialectic in the *Republic* VI.-VII. (II.)." *Mind* n.s. 41 no. 162 (April 1932), 173-190.

———. "Parmenides' Two Ways." *Classical Quarterly* 27 n. 2 (April 1933), 97-111.

———. *Plato and Parmenides: Parmenides'* Way of Truth *and Plato's* Parmenides *translated with an introduction and running commentary.* London: Routledge, 1939.

———. *The Unwritten Philosophy and Other Essays*, edited with an Introductory Memoir by W. K. C. Guthrie. Cambridge, UK: Cambridge University Press, 1967.

Coxon, A. H. *The Fragments of Parmenides; A Critical Text with Introduction, Translation, the Ancient* testimonia *and a Commentary.* Assen/Maastricht: Van Gorcum, 1986.

Craig, Leon. *The War Lover.* Toronto: University of Toronto Press, 1994.

Cropsey, Joseph. *Plato's World: Man's Place in the Cosmos.* Chicago, IL: University of Chicago Press, 1995.

Cross, R.C. and A.D. Woozley. *Plato's* Republic*: A Philosophical Commentary.* New York: St. Martin's Press, 1964.

Dahl, Norman O. "Plato's Defense of Justice" in Gail Fine (ed.), *Plato 2:Ethics, Politics, Religion, and the Soul*, 207-234. Oxford: Oxford University Press, 1999.

Dakyns, H. G. (translator). *The Works of Xenophon.* Three Volumes in four. London and New York: Macmillan and Co., 1890-1897.

Dancy, Jonathan. "Harold Arthur Prichard." *Stanford Encyclopedia of Philosophy* (January 30, 2009) at plato.stanford.edu/entries/prichard/ (accessed August 5, 2011).

Danzig, Gabriel. "True Justice in the *Republic.*" *Illinois Classical Studies* 23 (1998), 85-99.

———. "Intra-Socratic Polemics: The *Symposia* of Plato and Xenophon." *Greek, Roman and Byzantine Studies* (2005)

Davies, J. C. "The Philosopher and the Cave." *Greece & Rome* 24 no. 1 (April 1977), 23-28.

Davis, Michael. "On the Intention of Plato's *Cleitophon.*" *Metis: Revue d'anthropologie du monde grec ancien* 13 (1998), 273-285.

———. *The Soul of the Greeks: An Inquiry.* Chicago, IL: University of Chicago Press, 2011.

Davis, Philip J. and Reuben Hersh. *Descartes' Dream: The World According to Mathematics.* Boston: Houghton Mifflin, 1987.

Dawkins, Richard. *The Selfish Gene.* Oxford: Oxford University Press, 1976.

de Burgh, W.G. Review of "Duty and Interest. An Inaugural Lecture delivered before the University of Oxford, on October 29, 1928. By H. A. Prichard." *Journal of Philosophical Studies* 4 no. 14 (April 1929), 259-261.

Deleuze, Gilles. *Difference and Repetition.* Translated by Paul Patton. New York: Columbia University Press, 1994.

Demetriou, Kyriakos. "Reconsidering the Platonic *Cleitophon.*" *Polis* 17 (2000), 133-160.

Demos, Raphael. "A Fallacy in Plato's Republic?" *Philosophical Review* 73 no. 3 (July 1964), 395-398.

Deneen, Patrick J. *The Odyssey of Political Theory; The Politics of Departure and Return.* Lanham, MD: Rowman and Littlefield, 2000.

Denyer, Nicholas. "Ethics in Plato's *Republic*" in Godfrey Vesey (ed.), *Philosophers Ancient and Modern*, 19-33. Cambridge, UK: Cambridge University Press, 1986.

———. (ed.) *Plato:* Alcibiades. Cambridge, UK: Cambridge University Press, 2001.

———. "Sun and Line: The Role of the Good." In G. R. F. Ferrari (ed.), *The Cambridge Companion to Plato's* Republic, 284-309. Cambridge UK: Cambridge University Press, 2007.

Derrida, Jacques. "*Khôra*" (1987; translated by Ian McLeod) in Jacques Derrida, *On the Name*, edited by Thomas Dutoit, 87-127. Palo Alto, CA: Stanford University Press, 1995.

De Vogel, C. J. "Platonism and Christianity: A Mere Antagonism or a Profound Common Ground?" *Vigiliae Christianae* 39 no. 1 (March 1985), 1-62.

de Vries, G. J. *Spel bij Plato*. Amsterdam: Noord-Hollandsche Uitg. Mij, 1949.

Dobbs, Darrell. "The Justice of Socrates' Philosopher Kings." *American Journal of Political Science* 29 no. 4 (November 1985), 809-826.

———. "Choosing Justice: Socrates' Model City and the Practice of Dialectic." *American Political Science Review* 88 no. 2 (June 1994), 263-277.

———. "The Piety of Thought of Thought in Plato's *Republic*, Book I." *American Political Science Review* 88 no. 3 (September 1994), 668-683.

———. "Plato's Paragon of Human Excellence: Socratic Philosopher and Civic Guardian." *Journal of Politics* 65 no. 4 (November 2003), 1062-1082.

Dodds, E. R. "The *Parmenides* of Plato and the Origin of the Neoplatonic 'One.'" *Classical Quarterly* 22 nos. 3-4 (July-October 1928), 129-142.

———. *The Greeks and the Irrational*. Berkeley: University of California Press, 1951.

———. *Plato,* Gorgias*; A Revised Text with Introduction and Commentary*. Oxford: Clarendon Press, 1959.

Dornseiff, Franz. "Platons Buch 'Briefe.'" *Hermes* 69 no. 2 (1934), 223-226.

Dorter, Kenneth. "Philosopher-Rulers: How Contemplation Becomes Action." *Ancient Philosophy* 21 (September 2001), 335-356.

———. *The Transformation of Plato's* Republic. Lanham, MD: Rowman & Littlefield, 2006.

Dova, Stamatia. "Who is μακάρτατος in the *Odyssey*?" *Harvard Studies in Classical Philology* 100 (2000), 53-65.

Douglas, A. E. (ed.). *M. Tulli Ciceronis,* Brutus. Oxford: Clarendon Press, 1960.

Drummond, John J. "Indivisible Lines and the Timaeus." *Apeiron* 16 (1982), 63-70.

Duff, Timothy E., *Plutarch's Lives: Exploring Virtue and Vice*. Oxford: Oxford University Press, 1999.

Dunkle, Roger. "Swift-Footed Achilles." *Classical World* 90 no. 4 (March-April 1997), 227-234.

Dunn, Michael. "The Organization of the Platonic Corpus Between the First and Second Century A.D." Ph.D. dissertation, Yale University, 1974.

———. "Iamblichus, Thrasyllus, and the Reading order of the Platonic Dialogues." in R. Baine Harris ed., *Studies in Neoplatonism: Ancient and Modern, Volume I*. Albany: State University of New York Press, 1976.

Edelstein, Ludwig. "Platonic Anonymity." *American Journal of Philology* 83 no. 1 (January 1962), 1-22.

Einstein, Albert. *Sidelights on Relativity*. London: Methuen, 1922.

England, E. B. *The Laws of Plato*. Two volumes. Manchester: At the University Press, 1921.

Erbse, Hartmut. "Platons *Politeia* und die modernen Antiplatoniker." *Gymnasium* 83 no. 3 (1976), 169-191.

———. "Über Platons Methode in den sogenannten Jugenddialogen." *Hermes* 96 no. 1 (1968), 21-40.

Evelyn-White, Hugh G. (trans.). *Hesiod, The Homeric Hymns and Homerica*. London: Heinemann, 1914.

Euben, J. Peter. *Corrupting Youth: Political Education, Democratic Culture, and Political Theory*. Princeton, NJ: Princeton University Press, 1997.

Fantham, Elaine. *The Roman World of Cicero's* De Oratore. Oxford: Oxford University Press, 2004.

Ferguson, John. "Sun, Line, and Cave Again." *Classical Quarterly* (n.s.) 13 no. 2 (November 1963), 188-193.

Ferejohn, Michael. "Knowledge, Recollection, and the Forms in *Republic* VII" in Gerasimos Santas (ed.), *The Blackwell Guide to Plato's* Republic, 214-233. Malden, MA: Blackwell, 2006.

Ferrari, G. R. F. *Listening to the Cicadas: A Study of Plato's* Phaedrus. Cambridge, UK: Cambridge University Press, 1987.

———. "Strauss's Plato." *Arion* 5 no. 2 (Fall 1997), 36-65.

———. *City and Soul in Plato's* Republic. Chicago, IL: University of Chicago Press, 2005.

———. (ed.). *The Cambridge Companion to Plato's* Republic. Cambridge, UK: Cambridge University Press, 2007.

Festugière, A.J. 1969. "L'ordre de lecture des dialogues de Platon aux Ve/VIe siècles." *Museum Helveticum* 26, 281-296.

Finck, Florian. *Platons Begründung der Seele in absoluten Denken*. Berlin: Walter de Gruyter, 2007.

Findlay, J. N. *Plato: The Written and Unwritten Doctrines*. London: Routledge & Kegan Paul, 1974.

Fine, Gail. "Forms as Causes: Plato and Aristotle" in Andreas Graeser (ed.), *Mathematics and Metaphysics in Aristotle/Mathematik und Metaphysik bei Aristoteles*, 69-112. Stuttgart and Bern: Paul Haupt, 1984.

———. *On Ideas: Aristotle's Criticism of Plato's Theory of Forms*. Oxford: Clarendon Press, 1993.

———. (ed.). *Plato 2: Ethics, Politics, Religion, and the Soul*. Oxford: Oxford University Press, 1999.

———. (ed.). *Oxford Handbook to Plato*. Oxford: Oxford University Press, 2008.

Finkelberg, M. "The First Song of Demodocus," *Mnemosyne* 40 no. 1/2, 4th series (1987), 128-132.

Fish, Stanley. *Surprised by Sin: The Reader in* Paradise Lost, second edition. Cambridge, MA: Harvard University Press, 1997.

Foster, M. B. "Some Implications of a Passage in the *Republic*." *Philosophy* 11 no. 43 (July 1936), 301-308.

———. "A Mistake of Plato's in the *Republic*." *Mind* (n.s.) 46 no. 183 (July 1937), 386-393.

———. "A Mistake of Plato's in the *Republic*: A Rejoinder to Mr. Mabbott." *Mind* (n.s.) 47 (April 1938), 226-232.

Frede, Michael. "Plato's Arguments and the Dialogue Form" in James C. Klagge and Nicholas D. Smith eds., *Methods of Interpreting Plato and his Dialogues*, 201-219. Oxford: Oxford University Press, 1992.

———. "Aristotle's Account of the Origins of Philosophy" in Patricia Curd and Daniel W. Graham (eds.), *The Oxford Handbook of Presocratic Philosophy*, 501-529. Oxford: Oxford University Press, 2008.

Frank, Erich. "The Fundamental Opposition of Plato and Aristotle." *American Journal of Philology* 61 nos. 1 and 2 (1940), 34-53 and 166-185.

Frank, Jill. "Wages of War: On Judgment in Plato's *Republic*." *Political Theory* 35 no. 4 (August 2007), 443-467.

Fuyarchuk, Andrew. *Gadamer's Path to Plato: A Response to Heidegger and a Rejoinder by Stanley Rosen.* Eugene, OR: Wipf and Stock, 2010.

Gadamer, Hans-Georg. *Dialogue and Dialectic: Eight Hermeneutical Studies on Plato.* Translated and with an introduction by P. Christopher Smith. New Haven, CT: Yale University Press, 1980.

———. *The Idea of the Good in Platonic-Aristotelian Philosophy.* Translated by P. Christopher Smith. New Haven, CT: Yale University Press, 1986.

———. *Plato's Dialectical Ethics: Phenomenological Interpretations Relating to the* Philebus. Translated by Robert M. Wallace. New Haven, CT: Yale University Press, 1991.

Gaiser, Konrad. *Platons ungeschriebene Lehre: Studien zur systematschen und geschichtlichen Begründung der Wissenschaften in der Platonischen Schule.* Stuttgart: E. Klett, 1963.

———. "Quellenkritische Probleme der indirekten Platonüberlieferung" in *Idee und Zahl: Studien zur platonishen Philosophie*, 31-84. Heidelberg: Carl Winter, 1968.

———. "Plato's Enigmatic Lecture 'On the Good.'" *Phronesis* 25 no. 1 (1980), 5-37.

———. "Platone come 'kolax' in una lettera apocrifa (13a Epist.)," *Sandalion* 4 (1981), 71-94.

Geffcken, Johannes. "Das Rätsel des *Kleitophon*." *Hermes* 68 no. 4 (1933), 429-439.

Gentzler, Jyl (ed.). *Method in Ancient Philosophy.* Oxford: Clarendon Press, 1998.

Gerson, Lloyd. *Aristotle and Other Platonists.* Ithaca, NY: Cornell University Press, 2005.

Gifford, Mark. "Aristotle on Platonic Recollection and the Paradox of knowing Universals: Prior Analytics B.21 67a8-30." *Phronesis* 44 no. 1 (February 1999), 1-29.

Gill, Christopher. "Review of *The Phaedo: A Platonic Labyrinth* by Ronna Burger." *Classical Review* (n.s.) 36 n. 1 (1986), 141-142.

Gill, Mary Louise. "Matter and Flux in Plato's *Timaeus*." *Phronesis* 32 no. 1 (1987), 34-53.

Glucker, John. "Plato in England; The Nineteenth Century and After" in Hermann Funke (ed.), *Utopie und Tradition; Platons Lehre vom Staat in der Moderne*, 149-210. Würzberg: Königshausen & Neumann, 1987.

———. "Socrates in the Academic Books and Other Ciceronian Works" in Brad Inwood and Jaap Mansfield (eds.). *Assent and Argument: Studies in Cicero's* Academic Books. Leiden: Brill, 1997.

Gonzalez, Francisco J. (ed.). *The Third Way: New Directions in Platonic Studies.* Lanham, MD: Rowman & Littlefield, 1995.

———. *Dialectic and Dialogue: Plato's Practice of Dialectical Inquiry.* Evanston, IL: Northwestern University Press, 1998.

———. "Nonpropositional Knowledge in Plato." *Apeiron* 31 no. 3 (1998b), 235-284.

———. "Plato's Dialectic of Forms" in William A. Welton (ed.), *Plato's Forms; Varieties of Interpretation*, 31-84. Lanham, MD: Lexington Books, 2002.

———. *Plato and Heidegger: A Question of Dialogue.* University Park: Pennsylvania State University Press, 2009.

Gooch, Paul W. "Socrates: Devious or Divine?" *Greece & Rome* (2nd series) 32 no. 1 (April 1985), 32-41.

Gosling, J. C. B. *Plato.* London: Routledge and Kegan Paul, 1973.

Gould, John. *The Development of Plato's Ethics*. Cambridge, UK: Cambridge University Press, 1955.

Greene, William Chase. "The Spirit of Comedy in Plato." *Harvard Studies in Classical Philology* 31 (1920), 63-123.

———. "The Paradoxes of the *Republic*." *Harvard Studies in Classical Philology* 63 (1958), 199-216.

Griswold, Charles L. Jr. "*E Pluribus Unum*? On the Platonic 'Corpus.'" *Ancient Philosophy* 19 (1999), 361-97.

———. "*E Pluribus Unum*? On the Platonic 'Corpus': the Discussion Continued." *Ancient Philosophy* 20 (2000), 195-97.

———. (ed.), *Platonic Writings, Platonic Readings*. University Park, Pennsylvania State University Press, 2002.

———. "Irony in the Platonic Dialogues." *Philosophy and Literature* 26 no. 1 (April 2002), 84-106.

Grote, George. *Plato and the Other Companions of Sokrates*. London: J. Murray, 1865.

Grube, G. M. A. "The *Cleitophon* of Plato." *Classical Philology* 26 no. 3 (July 1931), 302-308.

Gruen, Erich S. "P. Clodius: Instrument or Independent Agent?" *Phoenix* 20 no. 2 (Summer 1966), 120-30.

———. *The Last Generation of the Roman Republic*. Berkeley: University of California Press, 1974.

Guthrie, W. K. C. *The Greeks and their Gods*. Boston: Beacon Press, 1950.

———. *A History of Greek Philosophy*, Vol. II. Cambridge, UK: Cambridge University Press, 1965.

———. *A History of Greek Philosophy*, Vol. III. Cambridge, UK: Cambridge University Press, 1969.

———. *A History of Greek Philosophy*, Vol. IV. Cambridge, UK: Cambridge University Press, 1975.

———. *A History of Greek Philosophy*, Vol. V. Cambridge, UK: Cambridge University Press, 1978.

Hackforth, R. *The Authorship of the Platonic Epistles*. Manchester: At the University Press, 1913.

———. "Plato's Theism." *Classical Quarterly* 30 no. 1 (January 1936), 4-9.

Haft, Adele J. "Odysseus, Idomeneus and Meriones: The Cretan Lies of *Odyssey* 13-19," *Classical Journal* 79 no. 4 (April-May 1984), 289-306.

Hahn, Robert. "On Plato's *Philebus* 15b1-8." *Phronesis* 23 no. 2 (1978), 158-172.

Haldane, E. S. and Frances H. Simson (trans.). 1955. *Hegel's Lectures on the History of Philosophy*. London: K. Paul, Trench, Trübner, & Co., 1892-1896.

Hall, Dale. "The Philosopher and the Cave." *Greece & Rome* (2nd series) 25 no. 2 (October 1978), 169-173.

Halliwell, Stephen. *Plato:* Republic *10, with translation and commentary*. Warminster: Aris and Phillips, 1988.

———. *The Aesthetics of Mimesis: Ancient Texts and Modern Problems*. Princeton, NJ: Princeton University Press.

———. "Antidotes and Incantations: is there a Cure for Poetry in Plato's *Republic*" in Pierre Destrée and Fritz-Gregor Herrmann (eds.), *Plato and the Poets*, 241-266. Leiden: Brill, 2011.

Hamilton, Edith. *The Greek Way*. New York: W. W. Norton, 1930.

Hamilton, Edith and Huntington Cairns (eds.). *The Collected Dialogues of Plato*. Princeton, NJ: Princeton University Press, 1961.

Hans, James S. *Socrates and the Irrational*. Charlottesville: University of Virginia Press, 2006.

Hardie, W. F. R. *A Study in Plato*. Oxford: Clarendon Press, 1936.

Hare, R. M. *The Language of Morals*. Oxford: Clarendon Press, 1952.

———. "Plato and the Mathematicians" in Renford Bambrough (ed.), *New Essays on Plato and Aristotle*, 21-38. London: Routledge & Kegan Paul, 1965.

Harman, John D. "The Unhappy Philosopher: Plato's *Republic* as Tragedy." *Polity* 18 no. 4 (Summer 1986), 577-594.

Harte, Verity. "Review of *Plato's Philosophy of Mathematics* by P. Pritchard." *Journal of Hellenic Studies 118* (1998), 227.

———. "Plato's Metaphysics" in Gail Fine (ed.), *Oxford Handbook to Plato*, 191-216. Oxford: Oxford University Press, 2008.

Harward, J. "The Seventh and Eighth Platonic Epistles." *Classical Quarterly* 22 nos. 3-4 (July-October 1928), 143-154.

———. *The Platonic Epistles, Translated with Introduction and Notes.* Cambridge, UK: Cambridge University Press, 1932.

Heath, Thomas L. *The Thirteen Books of Euclid's* Elements; *translated from the text of Heiberg with Introduction and Commentary.* Three Volumes. Second Edition. New York: Dover Books, 1956.

Heidegger, Martin. *An Introduction to Metaphysics.* Translated by Ralph Manheim. New Haven, CT: Yale University Press, 1959.

Heidel, W. A. *Pseudo-Platonica.* Baltimore, MD: Johns Hopkins University Press, 1896.

Heinaman, Robert. "Why Justice Does Not Pay in Plato's Republic." *Classical Quarterly* (n.s.) 54 no. 2 (2004), 379-393.

Herrmann, Fritz-Gregor. *Words and Ideas; The Roots of Plato's Philosophy.* Swansea: Classical Press of Wales, 2007.

———. "The Idea of the Good and the Other Forms in Plato's *Republic*" in David Keyt and Fred D. Miller (eds.), *Freedom, Reason, and the Polis: Essays in Ancient Greek Political Philosophy*, 202-230. Cambridge UK: Cambridge University Press, 2007.

Hicks, R. D. (translator). *Diogenes Laertius*, Lives of Eminent Philosophers. Two Volumes. London: Heinemann, 1925.

Highet, Gilbert. *The Classical Tradition.* Oxford: Oxford University Press, 1947.

Hintze, Hannah. "Gluttony and Philosophical Moderation in Plato's *Republic.*" Doctoral dissertation, University of Chicago; 2009.

Hobbs, Angela. *Plato and the Hero, Manliness and the Impersonal Good.* Cambridge, UK: Cambridge University Press, 2000.

Holway, Richard. "Achilles, Socrates, and Democracy," *Political Theory* 22 no. 4 (November 1994), 561-590.

Hösle, Vittoriano. "On Plato's Philosophy of Numbers and Its Mathematical and Philosophical Significance." *Graduate Faculty Philosophy Journal* 13 no. 1 (1988), 21-63

Howland, Jacob. "Re-Reading Plato: The Problem of Platonic Chronology." *Phoenix* no. 3 (Autumn 1991), 189-214.

———. *The* Republic*; The Odyssey of Philosophy.* Philadelphia, PA: Paul Dry, 2004.

———."The *Republic*'s Third Wave and the Paradox of Political Philosophy." *Review of Metaphysics* 51 no. 3 (March 1998), 633-657.

Huard, Roger. *Plato's Political Philosophy: The Cave.* New York: Algora, 2007.

Hyland, Drew A. "Against a Platonic 'Theory' of Forms" in William A. Welton (ed.), *Plato's Forms; Varieties of Interpretation*, 257-272. Lanham, MD: Lexington Books, 2002.

Inwood, Brad and Jaap Mansfield (eds.). *Assent and Argument: Studies in Cicero's* Academic Books. Leiden: Brill, 1997.

Irwin, Terence. *Plato's Moral Theory*. Oxford: Oxford University Press, 1977.

———. *Plato's Ethics*. Oxford: Oxford University Press, 1995.

———. "The Platonic Corpus" in Gail Fine (ed.), *Oxford Handbook to Plato*, 63-87. Oxford: Oxford University Press, 2008.

Jackson, Henry. "On Plato's *Republic* VI 509 D sqq." *Journal of Philology* 10 (1882), 132-150.

Jaeger, Werner. *Aristotle; Fundamentals of the History of his Development*. Translated by Richard Robinson. Second Edition. Oxford: Oxford University Press, 1934.

Janssens, David. "The Philosopher's Ancient Clothes: Leo Strauss on Philosophy and Poetry" in Pawel Armada and Arkadiusz Górnisiewicz (eds.), *Modernity and What Has Been Lost; Considerations on the Legacy of Leo Strauss*, 53-71. South Bend, IN: St. Augustine's Press, 2010.

Johansen, Thomas K. "The *Timaeus* on the Principles of Cosmology" in Gail Fine (ed.), *Oxford Handbook to Plato*, 463-483. Oxford: Oxford University Press, 2008.

Jowett, Benjamin. *The Dialogues of Plato, Translated into English with Analyses and Introductions*. Four Volumes. Oxford: Clarendon Press, 1871.

Joyal, Mark. *The Platonic* Theages. Stuttgart: Franz Steiner, 2000.

Kahn, Charles H. "Did Plato Write Socratic Dialogues?" *Classical Quarterly* (n.s.) 31 no. 2 (1981), 305-320.

———. "Plato's *Charmides* and the Proleptic Reading of Socratic Dialogues." *Journal of Philosophy* 85 no. 10 (1988), 541-549.

———. "Proleptic Composition in the *Republic*, or Why Book 1 Was Never a Separate Dialogue." *Classical Quarterly* (n.s.) 43 no. 1 (1993), 131-142.

———. *Plato and the Socratic Dialogue: The Philosophical Use of Literary Form*. Cambridge UK: Cambridge University Press, 1996.

———. "Response to Griswold." *Ancient Philosophy* 20 (2000), 189-193.

———. "Plato on Recollection" in Hugh H. Benson (ed.), *A Companion to Plato*, 119-132. Malden, MA: Blackwell, 2006.

Kalkavage, Peter. *Plato's* Timaeus. Newburyport, MA: Focus, 2001.

Karasmanis, Vassilis. "Plato's *Republic*: the Line and the Cave." *Apeiron* 21 no. 3 (1988), 147-171.

Kaufmann, Walter (ed.). *The Portable Nietzsche*. New York: Vintage, 1954.

Keyt, David and Fred D. Miller (eds.), *Freedom, Reason, and the Polis: Essays in Ancient Greek Political Philosophy*. Cambridge, UK: Cambridge University Press, 2007.

King, Peter (trans. and ed.). *Augustine,* Against the Academicians *and* The Teacher. Indianapolis, IN: Hackett, 1995.

Kirwan, Christopher. "Glaucon's Challenge." *Phronesis* 10 no. 2 (1965), 162-173.

Klagge, James C. and Nicholas D. Smith (eds.). *Methods of Interpreting Plato and his Dialogues*. *Oxford Studies in Ancient Philosophy*; Supplementary Volume, 1992.

Klein, Jacob. *A Commentary on Plato's* Meno. Chicago, IL: University of Chicago Press, 1965.

———. *Greek Mathematical Thought and the Origin of Algebra*. Translated by Eva Brann. Cambridge, MA: M. I. T. Press, 1968.

Klonoski, Richard J. "The Preservation of Homeric Tradition: Heroic Re-Performance in the *Republic* and the *Odyssey*." *Clio* 22 (1993), 251-271.

Knox, Bernard. "Achilles," *Grand Street* 9 no. 3 (Spring 1990), 129-150.

Knox, Ronald and Joseph Russo, "Agamemnon's Test: *Iliad* 2.73-75." *Classical Antiquity* 8 no. 2 (October 1989), 351-358.

Konstan, David. "Altruism." *Transactions of the American Philological Association* 130 (2000), 1-17.

Knox, T. M. (trans. and ed.). *Hegel's* Philosophy of Right. Oxford: Clarendon Press, 1942.

Krämer, Hans Joachim. *Arete bei Platon und Aristoteles*. Heidelberg: C. Winter, 1959.

———. "Über den Zusammenhang von Prinzipienlehre und Dialektik bei Platon; Zur Definition des Dialektikers *Politeia* 534 B-C." *Philologus* 10 (1966), 35-70.

———. "ΕΠΕΚΕΙΝΑ ΤΗΣ ΟΥΣΙΑΣ; Zu Platon, *Politeia* 509 B." *Archiv für Geschichte der Philosophie* 51 (1969), 1-30.

Kramer, Scott. "Socrates' Dream: 44a-b," *Classical Journal* 83 no. 3 (February-March 1988), 193-197.

Kraut, Richard. "Reason and Justice in Plato's *Republic*" in E. N. Lee, A. P. D. Mourelatos, and R. M. Rorty (eds.). *Exegesis and Argument*, 207-224. Assen/Maastricht: Van Gorcum, 1973.

———. "Egoism, Love, and Political Office in Plato." *Philosophical Review* 82 no. 3 (July 1973), 330-344.

———. (ed.) *The Cambridge Companion to Plato*. Cambridge, UK: Cambridge University Press, 1992.

———. "The Defense of Justice on Plato's *Republic*" in Richard Kraut (ed.), *Plato's Republic; Critical Essays*. Lanham, MD: Rowman & Littlefield, 1997.

———. "Return to the Cave: *Republic* 519-521" in Gail Fine (ed.), *Plato 2: Ethics, Politics, Religion, and the Soul*, 235-254. Oxford: Oxford University Press, 1999.

Kremer, Mark. "Socratic Philosophy and the *Cleitophon*." *The Review of Politics* 62 no. 3 (Summer 2000), 479-502.

———. *Plato's* Clitophon*: On Socrates and the Modern Mind*. Lanham, MD: Rowman & Littlefield, 2004.

Kung, Joan. "Mathematics and Virtue in Plato's *Timaeus*" in John P. Anton and Anthony Preus (eds.), *Essays in Ancient Greek Philosophy*, Vol. 3, 309-339. Albany: State University of New York Press, 1989.

Lachterman, David. "What Is 'The Good' of Plato's *Republic*." *St. Johns Review* 39 (1989-1990), 139-171.

Lamb, W. R. M. (translator). *Plato,* Charmides et al. London: Heinemann, 1927.

Lampert, Laurence. "Socrates' Defense of Polytropic Odysseus: Lying and Wrong-Doing in Plato's *Lesser Hippias*." *Review of Politics* 64 no. 2 (Spring 2002), 231-259.

———. *How Philosophy Became Socratic: A Study of Plato's* Protagoras, Charmides, *and* Republic. Chicago, IL: University of Chicago Press, 2010.

Lamm, Julia. "Schleiermacher as Plato Scholar." *Journal of Religion* 80 no. 2 (April 2000), 206-39.

Lear, Jonathan. "Aristotle's Philosophy of Mathematics." *Philosophical Review* 91 (1982), 161-192.

Lee, E. N., A. P. D. Mourelatos, and R. M. Rorty (eds.). *Exegesis and Argument*. Assen/Maastricht: Van Gorcum, 1973.

Lennox, James G. "Aristotle, Galileo, and 'Mixed Sciences'" in William Wallace (ed.), *Reinterpreting Galileo*, 29-51. Washington D.C.: Catholic University of America Press. 1985.

Lévy, Carlos. "Cicero and the *Timaeus*" in Gretchen J. Reydams-Schils (ed.), *Plato's* Timaeus *as Cultural Icon*, 95-110. Notre Dame, IN: University of Notre Dame Press, 2003.

Lévystone, David. "La figure d'Ulysse chez les Socratiques: Socrate *polutropos*," *Phronesis* 50 no. 3 (2005), 181-214.

Lloyd, G. E. R. "Plato as a Natural Scientist." *Journal of Hellenic Studies* 88 (1968), 78-92.

———. "Plato and Archytas in the Seventh Letter." *Phronesis* 35 no. 2 (1990), 159-174

Lodge, Rupert Clendon. "Private and Public Spirit in Platonism." *Philosophical Review* 34 no. 1 (January 1925), 1-27.

Long, A. A. "The Principles of Parmenides' Cosmology." *Phronesis* 8 no. 2 (1963), 90-107.

———. "Plato's Apologies and Socrates in the *Theaetetus*" in Jyl Gentzler (ed.), *Method in Ancient Philosophy*, 113-136. Oxford: Clarendon Press, 1998.

———. "Socrates in Later Greek Philosophy" in Donald R. Morrison (ed.), *The Cambridge Companion to Socrates*, 355-379. Cambridge, UK: Cambridge University Press, 2011.

Lovejoy, A. O. and George Boas. *Primitivism and Related Ideas in Antiquity*. Baltimore, MD: Johns Hopkins University Press, 1935.

Mabbott, J. D. "Aristotle and the χωρισμός of Plato." *Classical Quarterly* 20 no. 2 (April 1926), 72-79.

———. "Is Plato's *Republic* Utilitarian?" *Mind* (n.s.) 46 no. 184 (October 1937), 468-474.

———. "Is Plato's *Republic* Utilitarian?" Revised for Gregory Vlastos (ed.), *Plato: A Collection of Critical Essays* II, 57-65. Garden City, NJ: Anchor Books, 1971.

Mackie, John. *Ethics: Inventing Right and Wrong*. New York: Penguin, 1977.

MacQueen, Bruce. *Plato's* Republic *in the Monographs of Sallust*. Chicago, IL: Bolchazy-Carducci, 1981.

Mahoney, Timothy A. "Do Plato's philosopher-rulers sacrifice self-interest to justice?" *Phronesis* 37 no. 3 (1992), 265-282.

Mann, Thomas. *The Magic Mountain*. Translated by H. T. Lowe-Porter. New York: Alfred A. Knopf, 1927.

Mansfeld, Jaap. *Prolegomena: Questions to be Settled Before the Study of an Author, or a Text*. Leiden: Brill, 1994.

Mara, Gerald M. "Politics and Action in Plato's *Republic*." *Western Political Quarterly* 36 no. 4 (December 1983), 596-618.

———. *Socrates' Discursive Democracy:* Logos *and* Ergon *in Platonic Political Philosophy*. Albany: State University of New York Press, 1997.

Marciano, M. Laura Gemelli. "Images and Experiences: At the Roots of Parmenides' *Aletheia*." *Ancient Philosophy* 28 (Spring 2008), 21-49.

May, James M. and Jakob Wisse, *Cicero:* On the Ideal Orator *(De Oratore)*. New York and Oxford: Oxford University Press, 2001.

McCabe, Mary Margaret. *Plato and His Predecessors; The Dramatisation of Reason*. Cambridge, UK: Cambridge University Press, 2000.

McClain, Ernest G. *The Myth of Invariance*. York Beach, ME: Nicolas-Hays, 1976.

———. *The Pythagorean Plato: Prelude to the Song Itself*. Stony Brook, NY: Nicolas Hays, 1978.

McNeill, David N. *An Image of the Soul in Speech: Plato and the Problem of Socrates.* University Park: Pennsylvania State University Press, 2010.

McPherran, Mark L. (ed.). *Plato's* Republic: *A Critical Guide.* Cambridge, UK: Cambridge University Press, 2010.

Meinwald, Constance. "The *Philebus*" in Gail Fine (ed.), *Oxford Handbook to Plato,* 484-503. Oxford: Oxford University Press, 2008.

Merlan, Philip. *From Platonism to Neoplatonism.* The Hague: Martinus Nijhoff, 1953.

———. "Greek Philosophy from Plato to Plotinus" in A. H. Armstrong (ed.), *The Cambridge History of Later Greek and Early Medieval Philosophy,* 14-192. Cambridge , UK: Cambridge University Press, 1967.

Metcalf, Robert. "Socrates and Achilles" in Patricia Fagan and John Russon (eds.), *Reexamining Socrates in the* Apology, 62-84. Evanston, IL: Northwestern University Press, 2009.

Miles, Murray. "Plato on Suicide (*Phaedo* 60c-63c)." *Phoenix* 55 nos. 3-4 (Autumn-Winter 2001), 244-258.

Miller, Mitchell. "Platonic Provocations: Reflections on the Soul and the Good in the *Republic*" in Dominic J. O'Meara (ed.), *Platonic Investigations,* 163-193. Washington D.C.: Catholic University of America Press, 1985.

———. *Plato's* Parmenides*: The Conversion of the Soul.* University Park: Pennsylvania State University Press, 1986.

———. *The Philosopher in Plato's* Statesman *together with "Dialectical Education and Unwritten Teachings in Plato's* Statesman*."* Las Vegas, NV: Parmenides, 2004.

———. "Beginning 'The Longer Way.'" In G. R. F. Ferrari (ed.), *The Cambridge Companion to Plato's* Republic, 310-344. Cambridge, UK: Cambridge University Press, 2007.

Mills, Sophie. "Achilles, Patroclus and Parental Care in Some Homeric Similes." *Greece & Rome* (2nd series) 47 no. 1 (April 2000), 3-18.

Mishima, Teruo. "Clitophon's Challenge and the Aporia of Socratic Protreptic." Paper presented at the SAAP, Cambridge University, September 21, 2010.

Mitchell, Basil G. and J. R. Lucas. *An Engagement With Plato's* Republic*: A Companion to the* Republic. Aldershot and Burlington, VT: Ashgate, 2003.

Mittelstrass, Jürgen. "On Socratic Dialogue" in Charles L. Griswold Jr. (ed.), *Platonic Writings, Platonic Readings.* University Park, Pennsylvania State University Press, 2002.

Mohr, Richard D. "The Number Theory in Plato's *Republic* VII and *Philebus.*" *Isis* 72 n. 4 (December 1981), 620-627.

Monoson, S. Sara. *Plato's Democratic Entanglements: Athenian Politics and the Practice of Philosophy.* Princeton, NJ: Princeton University Press, 2000.

Montiglio, Silvia. *From Villain to Hero: Odysseus in Ancient Thought* (Ann Arbor: University of Michigan Press, 2011.

Moore, Christopher. "Socrates and Clitophon in the Platonic *Clitophon.*" Unpublished Draft of May 4, 2010 athttps://webspace.utexas.edu/crm697/www/clitophon.pdf (accessed July 10, 2011).

Moors, Kent. "Equality and Cognition in Plato's Divided Line." *Quaderni Urbinati di Cultura Classica* 16 no. 1 (1984), 147-157.

———. "The Argument Against a Dramatic Date for Plato's *Republic,*" *Polis* 7 no. 1 (Spring 1987), 6-31.

Morgan, Andrew S. *Plato.* Durham: Acumen, 2010.

Morgan, Kathryn A. "Narrative Orders in the *Timaeus* and *Critias*" in Richard D. Mohr and Barbara M. Sattler (eds.), *One Book, the Whole Universe: Plato's* Timaeus *Today*, 267-285. Las Vegas, NV: Parmenides Press, 2010.

Morris, C. R. "Plato's Theory of the Good Man's Motive." *Proceedings of the Aristotelian Society* (n.s.) 34 (1933-1934), 129-142.

Morrison, Donald R. "The Happiness of the City and the Happiness of the Individual in Plato's *Republic*." *Ancient Philosophy* 21 (2001), 1-24.

———. "The Utopian Character of Plato's Ideal City" in G. R. F. Ferrari (ed.) *The Cambridge Companion to Plato's* Republic, 232-255. Cambridge, UK: Cambridge University Press, 2007.

Morrison, J. S. "Two Unresolved Difficulties in the Line and Cave." *Phronesis* 22 no. 3 (1977), 212-231.

Morrow, Glenn R. *Plato's Cretan City: A Historical Commentary on the* Laws. Princeton, NJ: Princeton University Press, 1960.

———. *Plato's Epistles*; A Translation with Critical Essays and Notes. Indianapolis, IN: Bobbs-Merrill, 1962.

Most, Glenn W. "The Structure and Function of Odysseus' *Apologoi*." *Transactions of the American Philological Association* 119 (1989), 15-30.

Mourelatos, Alexander P. D. "Plato's "Real Astronomy": *Republic* 527D-531D" in John P. Anton (ed.), *Science and the Sciences in Plato*, 33-73. New York: EIDOS, 1980.

———. *The Route of Parmenides*, revised and expanded edition. Las Vegas, NV: Parmenides Press, 2008.

Mueller, Ian. "Review of *Aristotle's* Metaphysics, *Books M and N* by Julia Annas." *Philosophical Review* 87 (1978), 479-485.

———. "On Some Academic Theories of Mathematical Objects." *Journal of Hellenic Studies* 106 (1986), 111-120.

———. "Mathematical method and philosophical truth" in Richard Kraut (ed.), *The Cambridge Companion to Plato*, 170-199. Cambridge, UK: Cambridge University Press, 1992.

———. "Platonism and the Study of Nature (*Phaedo* 95e ff.)" in Jyl Gentzler (ed.), *Method in Ancient Philosophy*, 67-89. Oxford: Clarendon Press, 1998.

Mulroy, David. "The Subtle Artistry of the *Minos* and the *Hipparchus*." *Transactions of the American Philological Association* 137 (2009), 115-131.

Murphy, N. R. "The 'Simile of Light' in Plato's *Republic*." *Classical Quarterly* 26 no. 2 (April 1932), 93-102.

———. *The Interpretation of Plato's* Republic. Oxford: Clarendon Press, 1951.

Murray, Gilbert, Cyril Bailey, E. A. Barber, T. F. Higham, and C. M. Bowra (eds.), *The Oxford Book of Greek Verse*. Oxford: Clarendon Press, 1930.

Nagy, Gregory. *The Best of the Achaeans: Concepts of the Hero in Archaic Greek Poetry*. Revised edition. Baltimore, MD: Johns Hopkins University Press, 1999.

Nails, Debra. "Plato's 'Middle' Cluster." *Phoenix* 48 no. 1 (Spring 1994), 62-67.

———. "The Dramatic Date of Plato's *Republic*," *Classical Journal* 93 no. 4 (April-May 1998), 383-396.

———. *The People of Plato; A Prosopography of Plato and Other Socratics*. Indianapolis, IN: Hackett, 2002.

Nehamas, Alexander. "Plato on the Imperfection of the Sensible World." *Philosophical Quarterly* 12 no. 2 (April 1975), 105-117.

———."Self-Predication and Plato's Theory of Forms." *American Philosophical Quarterly* 16 no. 2 (April 1979), 93-103.

Neu, Jerome. "Plato's Analogy of State and Individual: *The Republic* and the Organic Theory of the State." *Philosophy* 46 no. 177 (July 1971), 238-254.

Nichols, Mary P. "The *Republic*'s Two Alternatives: Philosopher Kings and Socrates." *Political Theory* 12 no. 2 (May 1984), 252-274.

Nicol, A. T. "Indivisible Lines." *Classical Quarterly* 30 no. 2 (April 1936), 120-126.

Nightingale, Andrea Wilson. *Genres in Dialogue; Plato and the Construct of Philosophy.* Cambridge, UK: Cambridge University Press, 1995.

———. *Spectacles of Truth in Classical Greek Philosophy.* Cambridge, UK: Cambridge University Press, 2004.

Novotný, Franciscus. *Platonis Epistulae commentariis illustratae.* Brünn: Opera Facultatis Philosophicae Universitatis Masarykianae Brunensis, 1930.

Nussbaum, Martha C. *The Fragility of Goodness: Luck and Ethics in Greek Tragedy and Philosophy.* Cambridge, UK: Cambridge University Press, 1986.

Oates, Whitney J. and Eugene O'Neill Jr. (eds.). *The Complete Greek Drama.* Two Volumes. New York: Random House, 1938.

O'Neill, William (ed.). *Proclus:* Alcibiades I*; A Translation and Commentary.* The Hague: Martinus Nijhof, 1965.

Orwin, Clifford. "The Case against Socrates: Plato's *Clitophon.*" *Canadian Journal of Political Science / Revue canadienne de science politique* 15 no. 4 (December 1982), 741-53.

Owen, G. E. L. "The Place of *Timaeus* in Plato's Dialogues." *Classical Quarterly* (n.s.) 3 no. 1-2 (January-April 1953), 79-95.

———."A Proof in ΠΕΡΙ ΙΔΕΩΝ." *Journal of Hellenic Studies* 77 (1957), 103-111.

———."Eleatic Questions." *Classical Quarterly* (n.s.) 10 no. 1 (May 1960), 84-102.

Palmer, John A. *Plato's Reception of Parmenides.* Oxford: Clarendon Press, 1999.

———. "Melissus and Parmenides." *Oxford Studies in Ancient Philosophy* 26 (2004), 19-54.

———. *Parmenides and Presocratic Philosophy.* Oxford: Oxford University Press, 2009.

Pangle, Thomas L. (ed.). *The* Laws *of Plato.* Chicago, IL: University of Chicago Press, 1980.

———. *The Roots of Platonic Political Philosophy: Ten Forgotten Socratic Dialogues, Translated, with Interpretive Essays.* Ithaca, NY: Cornell University Press, 1987.

Parry, Hugh. "The *Apologos* of Odysseus: Lies all Lies," *Phoenix* 48 no. 1 (Spring 1994), 1-20.

Parry, Richard D. *Plato's Craft of Justice.* Albany: State University of New York Press, 1996.

Penner, Terry. "Platonic justice and what we mean by 'justice.'" *Plato* 5 (2005) at www.nd.edu/~plato/plato5issue/Penner.pdf (accessed August 6, 2011).

———. "What is the Form of the Good the Form of? A Question about the Plot of the *Republic*" in Douglas Cairns, Fritz-Gregor Herrmann, and Terry Penner (eds.). *Pursuing the Good; Ethics and Metaphysics in Plato's* Republic, 15-41. Edinburgh: University of Edinburgh Press, 2007.

———. "The Good, Advantage, Happiness and the Form of the Good: How Continuous with Socratic Ethics are Platonic Ethics" in Douglas Cairns, Fritz-Gregor Herrmann, and Terry Penner (eds.). *Pursuing the Good; Ethics and Metaphysics in Plato's* Republic, 93-123. Edinburgh: University of Edinburgh Press, 2007.

Peterson, Sandra. *Socrates and Philosophy in the Dialogues of Plato.* Cambridge, UK: Cambridge University Press, 2011.

Planeaux, Christopher. "The Date of Bendis' Entry into Attica," *Classical Journal* 96 no. 2 (December 2000-January 2001), 165-192.

Plass, Paul. "'Play' and Philosophic Detachment in Plato." *Transactions of the American Philological Association* 98 (1967), 343-364.

Plax, Martin J. "Socrates' Silence in the *Cleitophon* and his *Apology* Speech." Paper presented at the Annual Meeting of the Midwest Political Science Association, April 18, 2006.

Plochmann, George Kimball. "Socrates, the Stranger from Elea, and Some Others." *Classical Philology* 49 no. 4 (October 1954), 223-41.

Pocock, L. G. (ed.). *A Commentary on Cicero* in Vatinium (1926). Reprinted Amsterdam: Adolf M. Hakkert, 1967.

Post, L. A. *Thirteen Epistles of Plato, Introduction, Translation and Notes.* Oxford: Clarendon Press, 1925.

Poster, Carol. 1998. "The Idea(s) of Order of Platonic Dialogues and Their Hermeneutic Consequences." *Phoenix* nos. 3-4 (Autumn-Winter 1998), 282-298.

Powell, J. G. F (ed.). *Cicero: On Friendship and the Dream of Scipio.* Oxford: Oxford University Press, 1990.

———(ed.). *M. Tulli Ciceronis;* De Republica, De Legibus, Cato Maior De Senectute, Laelius De Amicitia. Oxford: Clarendon Press, 2007.

Press, Gerald A. "Principles of Dramatic and Non-dogmatic Plato Interpretation" and "Introduction" to Press (as ed.), *Plato's Dialogues: New Studies and Interpretations.* Lanham, MD: Rowman & Littlefield, 1993.

———. (ed.), *Who Speaks for Plato? Studies in Platonic Anonymity.* Lanham MD: Rowman & Littlefield, 2000.

———. *Plato: A Guide for the Perplexed.* London: Continuum, 2007.

Prichard, H. A. *Kant's Theory of Knowledge.* Oxford: Clarendon Press, 1909.

———. "Does Moral Philosophy Rest on a Mistake?" *Mind* (n.s.) 21 no. 81 (January 1912), 21-37.

———. "Duty and Interest" (1928), reprinted in H. A. Prichard, *Moral Writings*, 21-49. Edited by Jim MacAdam. Oxford: Clarendon Press, 2002.

Pritchard, Paul. *Plato's Philosophy of Mathematics.* Sankt Augustin: Academia Verlag, 1996.

Raaflaub, Kurt A. "Politisches Denken und Krise der Polis: Athen im Verfassungskonflikt des späten 5. Jahrhunderts v. Chr." *Historische Zeitschrift* 255 (1992), 1-60.

Rand, E. K. *The Founders of the Middle Ages.* Cambridge, MA: Harvard University Press, 1928.

Reale, Giovanni. *Plato and Aristotle.* Edited and translated by John R. Catan. Albany: State University of New York University Press, 1990.

———. *Toward a New Interpretation of Plato.* Translated by John R. Catan and Richard Davies. Washington D.C.: Catholic University of America Press, 1997.

Recco, Greg. *Athens Victorious; Democracy on Plato's* Republic. Lanham, MD: Lexington Books, 2007.

Reeve, C. D. C. *Philosopher-Kings.* Princeton, NJ: Princeton University Press, 1988.

Reich, Klaus. "Kant and Greek Ethics." *Mind* (n.s.) 48, nos. 191-192 (July and October 1939), 338-354 and 446-463.

Renault, Mary. *The Last of the Wine.* New York: Pantheon Books, 1956.

Richardson, Scott. "Truth and Tales of the *Odyssey.*" *Mnemosyne* 49 no. 4, 4th series (September 1996), 393-402.

———. "The Devious Narrator of the *Odyssey,*" *Classical Journal* 101 no. 4 (April-May 2006), 337-359.

Rist, John M. "The Order of the Later Dialogues of Plato." *Phoenix* 14 no. 4 (Winter 1960), 227-221.

Roberts, Alexander and James Donaldson (eds.). *The Ante-Nicene Fathers; Translations of the Writings of the Fathers down to A.D. 325*. Reprint of the 1885 Edition. Edinburgh: T&T Clark, 1989.

Robinson, Richard. *Plato's Earlier Dialectic*. Oxford: Oxford University Press, 1953.

Roochnik, David L. "The Riddle of the *Cleitophon*." *Ancient Philosophy* 4 (1984), 132-145.

———. "Socrates' Rhetorical Attack on Rhetoric." In Francisco J. Gonzalez (ed.), *The Third Way: New Directions in Platonic Studies*, 81-94. Lanham, MD: Rowman & Littlefield, 1995.

———. *Beautiful City; The Dialectical Character of Plato's Republic*. Ithaca, NY: Cornell University Press, 2003.

Rosen, Stanley. *Plato's* Republic*: A Study*. New Haven, CT: Yale University Press, 2005.

Ross, David. *Aristotle's Metaphysics*. Two Volumes. Oxford: Clarendon Press, 1924.

———. *Plato's Theory of Ideas*. Oxford: Clarendon Press, 1951.

———. (ed). *Aristotelis Fragmenta Selecta*. Oxford: Clarendon Press, 1955.

Rowe, Galen O. "Two Responses by Isocrates to Demosthenes." *Historia* 51 n. 2 (2nd Qtr. 2002), 149-162.

Rowe, Christopher. *Plato and the Art of Philosophical Writing*. Cambridge, UK: Cambridge University Press, 2007.

Rudebusch, George. "Neutralism in Book I of the *Republic*" in Douglas Cairns, Fritz-Gregor Herrmann, and Terry Penner (eds.), *Pursuing the Good; Ethics and Metaphysics in Plato's* Republic, 76-92. Edinburgh: University of Edinburgh Press, 2007.

Rutherford, Richard. *The Art of Plato: Ten Essays in Platonic Interpretation*. London: Duckworth, 1995.

Ryle, Gilbert. "Plato's 'Parmenides' (II.)." *Mind* (n.s.), 48 no. 191 (July 1939), 302-325.

———. *Plato's Progress*. Cambridge, UK: Cambridge University Press, 1966.

Sachs, David. "A Fallacy in Plato's *Republic*." *Philosophical Review* 72 no. 2 (April 1963), 141-158.

Sallis, John. *Platonic Legacies*. Albany: State University of New York Press, 2004.

Santos, Gerasimos. "The Form of the Good in Plato's *Republic*" in John P. Anton and Anthony Preus (eds.), *Essays in Ancient Greek Philosophy*, Vol. 2, 232-263. Albany: State University of New York Press, 1983.

———. (ed.). *The Blackwell Guide to Plato's* Republic. Malden: Blackwell, 2006.

———. *Understanding Plato's* Republic. Chichester: Wiley-Blackwell, 2010.

Saxonhouse, Arlene. *Athenian Democracy: Modern Mythmakers and Ancient Theorists*. Notre Dame, IN: University of Notre Dame Press, 1996.

———. "Democracy, Equality, and *Eidê*: A Radical View from Book 8 of Plato's *Republic*." *American Political Science Review* 92 no. 2 (1998), 273-284.

———. "The Socratic Silence in Plato's *Cleitophon*." *Polis* 22 no. 1 (2005), 128-135.

———. *Free Speech and Democracy in Ancient Athens*. Cambridge, UK: Cambridge University Press, 2006.

Sayre, Kenneth M. "A Maieutic View of Five Late Dialogues" in James C. Klagge and Nicholas D. Smith (eds.), *Methods of Interpreting Plato and his Dialogues*, 221-243 *Oxford Studies in Ancient Philosophy*; Supplementary Volume, 1992.

———. *Plato's Literary Garden*. Notre Dame: University of Notre Dame Press, 1995.

———. "Do Forms Have a Role in *Philebus*?" in William A. Welton (ed.). *Plato's Forms; Varieties of Interpretation*, 169-192. Lanham, MD: Lexington Books, 2002.

———. "The Multilayered Incoherence of Timaeus' Receptacle" in Gretchen J. Reydams-Schils (ed.), *Plato's* Timaeus *as Cultural Icon*, 60-79. Notre Dame, IN: University of Notre Dame Press, 2003.

Schiller, Jerome. "Just Men and Just Acts in Plato's *Republic*." *Journal of the History of Philosophy* 6 no. 1 (January 1968), 1-14.

Schindler, D. C. *Plato's Critique of Impure Reason; On Goodness and Truth in the* Republic. Washington D.C.: Catholic University of America Press, 2008.

Schmiel, Robert. "Achilles in Hades." *Classical Philology* 82 no. 1 (January 1987), 35-37.

Schofield, Malcolm. *Saving the City; Philosopher-Kings and other classical paradigms.* London: Routledge, 1999.

———. "Approaching the *Republic*" in Christopher Rowe and Malcolm Schofield (eds.) in association with Simon Hornblower and Melissa Lane, *The Cambridge History of Greek and Roman Political Thought*, 190-232. Cambridge, UK: Cambridge University Press, 2000.

———. "Plato and Practical Politics" in Christopher Rowe and Malcolm Schofield (eds.) in association with Simon Hornblower and Melissa Lane, *The Cambridge History of Greek and Roman Political Thought*, 299-302. Cambridge, UK: Cambridge University Press, 2000.

———. "Plato in His Time and Place" in Gail Fine (ed.), *Oxford Handbook to Plato*, 36-62. Oxford: Oxford University Press, 2008.

Scodel, Ruth. "The Word of Achilles," *Classical Philology* 84 no. 2 (April 1989), 91-99.

———. "The Removal of the Arms, the Recognition with Laertes, and Narrative Tension in the *Odyssey*." *Classical Philology* 93 (1998), 1-17.

Scolnicov, Samuel. *Plato's Metaphysics of Education.* London: Routledge, 1988.

Scott, Dominic. "Metaphysics and the Defense of Justice in the *Republic*." *Proceedings of the Boston Area Colloquia in Ancient Philosophy* 16 (2000), 1-20.

———. *Recollection and Experience; Plato's Theory of Learning and its Successors.* Cambridge, UK: Cambridge University Press, 1995.

———. "The *Republic*" in Gail Fine (ed.). *Oxford Handbook to Plato*, 360-382. Oxford: Oxford University Press, 2008.

Scott, Gary Alan. *Plato's Socrates as Educator.* Albany: State University of New York Press, 2000.

Sedley, David. "Plato's *Auctoritas* and the Rebirth of the Commentary Tradition" in Jonathan Barnes and Miriam Griffin (eds.), *Philosophia Togata II: Plato and Aristotle at Rome*, 110-29. Oxford: Oxford University Press, 1997.

———. "Platonic Causes." *Phronesis* 43 no. 2 (May 1998), 114-132.

———. "The Ideal of Godlikeness" in Gail Fine (ed.), *Plato 2: Ethics, Politics, Religion, and the Soul*, 309-328. Oxford: Oxford University Press, 1999.

———. *Plato's* Cratylus. Cambridge, UK: Cambridge University Press, 2003.

———. "Philosophy, the Forms, and the Art of Ruling" in G. R. F. Ferrari (ed.), *The Cambridge Companion to Plato's* Republic, 256-283. Cambridge, UK: Cambridge University Press, 2007.

Seel, Gerhard. "Is Plato's Conception of the Form of the Good Contradictory?" in David Keyt and Fred D. Miller (eds.), *Freedom, Reason, and the Polis: Essays in Ancient Greek Political Philosophy*, 168-196. Cambridge, UK: Cambridge University Press, 2007.

Segal, Charles. "'The Myth Was Saved': Reflections on Homer and the Mythology of Plato's *Republic*." *Hermes* 106 no. 2 (1978), 315-336.

Shields, Christopher. "Forcing Goodness in Plato's *Republic*" in David Keyt and Fred D. Miller (eds.), *Freedom, Reason, and the Polis: Essays in Ancient Greek Political Philosophy*, 21-39. Cambridge, UK: Cambridge University Press, 2007.

———. "Plato and Aristotle in the Academy" in Gail Fine (ed.), *Oxford Handbook to Plato*, 504-525. Oxford: Oxford University Press, 2008.

Shorey, Paul. *De Platonis idearum doctrina atque mentis humanae notionibus commentatio.* München: Theodor Ackermann, 1884.

———. "The Idea of the Good in Plato's *Republic*; A Study in the Logic of Speculative Ethics." *The University of Chicago Studies in Classical Philology* (1895), 188-239.

———. *The Unity of Plato's Thought.* Chicago, IL: University of Chicago Press, 1903.

———. "Ideas and Numbers Again." *Classical Philology* 22 no. 2 (April 1927), 213-218.

———. *Republic* (as translator). Two Volumes. Cambridge, MA: Harvard University Press, 1930 and 1935.

———. *What Plato Said.* Chicago, IL: University of Chicago Press, 1933.

Silverman, Allan. *The Dialectic of Essence: A Study of Plato's Metaphysics*. Princeton, NJ: Princeton University Press, 2002.

———. "Philebean Metaphysics" in Welton, William A. Welton (ed.), *Plato's Forms; Varieties of Interpretation*, 193-220. Lanham, MD: Lexington Books, 2002.

———. "Ascent and Descent: The Philosopher's Regret" in David Keyt and Fred D. Miller (eds.), *Freedom, Reason, and the Polis: Essays in Ancient Greek Political Philosophy*, 40-69. Cambridge, UK: Cambridge University Press, 2007.

Singpurwalla, G. K. "Plato's Defense of Justice in the *Republic*" in Gerasimos Santos (ed.), *The Blackwell Guide to Plato's* Republic, 263-282. Malden: Blackwell, 2006.

Slaveva-Griffin, Svetla. "Of Gods, Philosophers, and Charioteers: Content and Form in Parmenides' Proem and Plato's *Phaedrus*." *Transactions of the American Philological Association* 133 no. 2 (Autumn 2003), 227-253.

Slings, S. R. *Plato:* Clitophon. Cambridge, UK: Cambridge University Press, 1999.

———. *Platonis* Rempublicam. Oxford: Clarendon Press, 2003.

Smith, Nicholas D. "The Objects of *Dianoia* in Plato's Divided Line." *Apeiron* 15 no. 2 (1981), 129-137.

———. "Plato's Divided Line." *Ancient Philosophy* 16 (1996), 25-46.

———. "Return to the cave," in Mark L. McPherran (ed.), *Plato's* Republic: *A Critical Guide*, 83-102. Cambridge, UK: Cambridge University Press, 2010.

Snyder, H. Gregory. *Teachers and Texts in the Ancient World; Philosophers, Jews and Christians*. London: Routledge, 2000.

Solmsen, Friedrich. "Parmenides and the Description of Perfect Beauty in Plato's *Symposium*." *American Journal of Philology* 92 no. 1 (January 1971), 62-70.

Souilhé, Joseph. *Platon; Oeuvres Complètes*, Volume 13.1. Paris: Budé, 1949.

Spariosu, Mihai. *The Wreath of Wild Olive: Play, Liminality, and the Study of Literature*. Albany: State University of New York Press, 1997.

Spelman, Elizabeth V. *Inessential Women: Problems of Exclusion in Feminist Thought.* Boston: Beacon Press, 1988.

Stahl, W. H. (ed. and trans.). *Macrobius,* Commentary on the Dream of Scipio. New York: Columbia University Press, 1990.

Stallbaum, Gottfried. *Platonis Opera Omnia*. Gotha: Hennings, 1858-1859.

Stangl, Thomas (ed.). *Ciceronis Orationum Scholiasticae*. Hildesheim: G. Olms, 1964.

Stern, Paul. "The Philosophic Importance of Political Life: On the "Digression" in Plato's *Theaetetus*." *American Political Science Review* 96 no. 2 (June 2002), 275-289.

———. *Knowledge and Politics on Plato's* Theaetetus. Cambridge, UK: Cambridge University Press, 2008.

Stewart, J. A. *Plato's Doctrine of Ideas.* Oxford: Clarendon Press, 1909.

Stocks, J. L. "The Divided Line of *Plato Rep. VI.*" *Classical Quarterly* 5 no. 2 (April 1911), 73-88.

Stokes, Michael C. *One and Many in Presocratic Philosophy.* Washington D.C.: Center for Hellenic Studies, 1971.

Strasburger, Hermann. *Caesars Eintritt in die Geschichte* (1938), reprinted Darmstadt: Wissenschaftliche Buchgesellschaft, 1966.

Strauss, Leo. "Fârâbî's Plato." *Louis Ginzberg Jubilee Volume*, 357-393. New York: American Academy for Jewish Research, 1945.

———. "On a New Interpretation of Plato's Political Philosophy." *Social Research* 13 no. 3 (September 1946), 326-367.

———. *Persecution and the Art of Writing.* Chicago: University of Chicago, 1952.

———. *Natural Right and History.* Chicago, IL: University of Chicago Press, 1953.

———. *Thoughts on Machiavelli* (Chicago, IL: University of Chicago Press, 1958.

———. *What is Political Philosophy?* Glencoe, NY: The Free Press, 1959.

———. *The City and Man.* Chicago, IL: University of Chicago Press, 1964.

———. *Liberalism Ancient and Modern.* Chicago: University of Chicago, 1968.

———. *The Argument and Action of Plato's* Laws. Chicago, IL: University of Chicago Press, 1975.

———. *Studies in Platonic Political Philosophy.* Chicago, IL: University of Chicago Press, 1983.

———. "Plato" (1963) in Leo Strauss and Joseph Cropsey (eds.), *History of Political Philosophy*, third edition. Chicago, IL: University of Chicago Press, 1987.

———. *The Rebirth of Classic Political Rationalism.* Edited by Thomas Pangle. Chicago IL: University of Chicago Press, 1989.

———. *Philosophy and Law; Contributions to the Understanding of Maimonides and His Predecessors.* Translated by Eve Adler. State University of New York Press: Albany, 1995.

———. *Gesammelte Schriften.* Ed. Heinrich u. Wiebke Meier. Stuttgart: J. B. Metzler, 1997 and 2001.

Szlezák, Thomas A. "Unsterblichkeit und Trichotomie der Seele im zehnten Buch der Politeia." *Phronesis* 21 no. 1 (1976), 31-58.

———. "Notes sur le débat autour de la philosophie orale de Platon." *Les Études philosophiques* no. 1 (January-March 1998), 69-90.

———. *Reading Plato.* Translated by Graham Zanker. London: Routledge, 1999.

Tait, W. W. "Noesis: Plato on Exact Science" in D.B. Malament (ed.), *Reading Natural Philosophy: Essays in the History and Philosophy of Science and Mathematics*, 11-30. Chicago and LaSalle, IL: Open Court, 2002.

Tarnopolsky, Christina H. *Prudes, Perverts, and Tyrants: Plato's* Gorgias *and the Politics of Shame.* Princeton, NJ: Princeton University Press, 2010.

Tarrant, Harold. *Thrasyllan Platonism.* Ithaca, NY: Cornell University Press, 1993.

Taylor, A. E. *A Commentary on Plato's* Timaeus. Oxford: Clarendon Press, 1928.

———. *Plato: The Man and his Work*, third edition. London: Methuen, 1929.

———. "The Right and the Good." *Mind* (n.s.) 48 no. 191 (July 1939), 273-301.

Taylor, C. C. W. "Plato and the Mathematicians: An Examination of Professor Hare's View." *Philosophical Quarterly* 17 (1967), 193-203.

———. "Forms as Causes in the *Phaedo.*" *Mind* (n.s.) 78 (1969), 45-59.

Taylor, John Hammond. "St. Augustine and the *Hortensius* of Cicero." *Studies in Philology* 60 no. 3 (July 1963), 487-498.

Tejera, Victorino. "The Hellenistic Obliteration of Plato's Dialogism." In Gerald A. Press (ed.), *Plato's Dialogues: New Studies and Interpretations.* Lanham, MD: Rowman & Littlefield, 1993.

———. "The Dialogism of Plato's *Parmenides*" in Francisco J. Gonzalez (ed.), *The Third Way: New Directions in Platonic Studies*, 211-221. Lanham, MD: Rowman & Littlefield, 1995.

———. *Plato's Dialogues One by One; A Dialogical Interpretation.* Lanham, MD: University Press of America, 1999.

Thesleff, Holger. "The Interrelation and Date of the *Symposia* of Plato and Xenophon." *Bulletin of the Institute of Classical Studies* 25 (1978), 157-170.

———. *Studies in Platonic Chronology.* Helsinki: Societas Scientiarum Fennica, 1982.

Tigerstedt, E. N. *Interpreting Plato.* Uppsala: Almquist & Wiksell, 1977.

Tulli, Mauro. *Dialettica e scrittura nella* VII Lettera *di Platone*, preface by Graziano Arrighetti. Pisa: Giardini, 1989.

———. "L'esortazione di Parmenide al sapere." *Materiali e discussioni per l'analisi dei testi classici* 31 (1993), 35-50.

———. "Il rapporto di Parmenide con i πολλοί" in Graziano Arrighetti (ed.), *Ricerche di Filologia Classica IV: Poesia Greca*, 171-187. Pisa: Giardini, 1995.

———. "Esiodo nella memoria di Parmenide" in Graziano Arrighetti (ed.), *Litteratura e Riflessione sulla Letteratura nella Cultura classica*, 65-81; Atti del Convegno, (June 7-9). Pisa: Giardini, 1999.

Vernezze, Peter. "The Philosopher's Interest." *Ancient Philosophy* 12 (1992), 331-349.

Vlastos, Gregory. "Review of Hans Joachim Krämer, *Arete bei Platon und Aristoteles.*" *Gnonom* 35 n. 7 (November 1963), 641-655.

———. "Degrees of Reality in Plato" in Renford Bambrough (ed.), *New Essays on Plato and Aristotle*, 1-19. London: Routledge & Kegan Paul, 1965.

———. "The Argument in the *Republic* that 'Justice Pays.'" *Journal of Philosophy* 65 no. 21 (November 7, 1968), 665-674.

———. "Justice and Psychic Harmony in the *Republic*." *Journal of Philosophy* 66 no. 16 (August 21, 1969), 505-521.

———. (ed.) *Plato.* Volume 2. New York: Anchor Books, 1971.

———. *Plato's Universe.* Seattle: University of Washington Press, 1975.

Wallace, Robert M. *Hegel's Philosophy of Reality, Freedom, and God.* Cambridge, UK: Cambridge University Press, 2005.

Wallach, J. R. *The Platonic Political Art: A Study of Critical Reason and Democracy.* University Park: Pennsylvania State University Press, 2001.

Walsh, W. H. *Philosophy of History: An Introduction.* New York: Harper & Row, 1960.

Waterfield, Robin (trans.). *Plato,* Republic. Oxford: Oxford University Press, 1993.

Waterlow, Sarah. "The Good of Others on Plato's Republic." *Proceedings of the Aristotelian Society* (n.s.) 73 (1972-1973), 19-36.

Watson, Walter. "Dogma, Skepticism, and Dialogue." In Francisco J. Gonzalez (ed.). *The Third Way: New Directions in Platonic Studies*, 189-210. Lanham, MD: Rowman & Littlefield, 1995.

Wedberg, Anders. *Plato's Philosophy of Mathematics.* Stockholm: Almqvist & Wiksell, 1955.

Weingartner, Rudolph H. "Vulgar Justice and Platonic Justice." *Philosophy and Phenomenological Research* 25 no. 2 (December 1964), 248-252.

Weiss, Roslyn. "The Hedonic Calculus in the *Protagoras* and the *Phaedo*." *Journal of the History of Philosophy* 27 no. 4 (October 1989), 511-529.

———. *Virtue in the Cave; Moral Inquiry in the* Meno. Oxford: Oxford University Press, 2001.

———. *The Socratic Paradox and its Enemies*. Chicago, IL: University of Chicago Press, 2006.

Welton, William A. (ed.). *Plato's Forms; Varieties of Interpretation*. Lanham MD: Lexington Books, 2002.

White, Michael J. "Plato and Mathematics" in Hugh H. Benson (ed.), *A Companion to Plato*, 228-243. Malden, MA: Blackwell, 2006.

White, Nicholas P. *A Companion to Plato's* Republic. Indianapolis, IN: Hackett, 1979.

———. "The Classification of Goods in Plato's *Republic*." *Journal of the History of Philosophy* 22 no. 4 (October 1984), 393-421.

———. "The Ruler's Choice." *Archiv für Geschichte der Philosophie* 68 (1986), 22-46.

Whitehead, David. *The Demes of Attica*. Princeton, NJ: Princeton University Press, 1986.

Wild, John. *Plato's Theory of Man*. Cambridge, MA: Harvard University Press, 1946.

———. "Plato and Christianity: A Philosophical Comparison." *Journal of Bible and Religion* 17 no. 1 (January 1949), 3-16.

Williams, Bernard. "The Analogy of City and Soul in Plato's *Republic*" in E. N. Lee, A. P. D. Mourelatos, and R. M. Rorty (eds.). *Exegesis and Argument*, 196-206. Assen/Maastricht: Van Gorcum, 1973.

Wohl, Victoria. "Plato Avant la Lettre: Authenticity in Plato's Epistles." *Ramus* 27 (1998), 60-93.

———. *Love Among the Ruins: The Erotics of Democracy in Classical Athens*. Princeton, NJ: Princeton University Press, 2002.

Wood, Robert E. "Structure and Content: On a Passage in Plato's *Republic*." *Review of Metaphysics* 40 no. 3 (March 1987), 495-514.

Woodford, Susan. "Palamedes Seeks Revenge," *Journal of Hellenic Studies* 114 (1994), 164-169.

Wörle, Andrea. *Die politische Tätigkeit der Schuler Platons*. Darmstadt: Kümmerle, 1981.

Yu, Jiyuan. "Justice in the *Republic*: An Evolving Paradox." *History of Philosophy Quarterly* 17 no. 2 (April 2000), 121-141.

Zadorojnyi, Alexei V. "Cato's Suicide in Plutarch." *Classical Quarterly* 57 no. 1 (May 2007), 216-230.

———. "The Ethico-Politics of Writing in Plutarch's *Life of Dion*." *Journal of Hellenic Studies* 131 (2011), 147-163.

Zehl, Donald J. "Plato and Talk of a World in Flux: *Timaeus* 49a6-50b5." *Harvard Studies in Classical Philology* 79 (1975), 125-148.

Zerba, Michelle. "Odyssean Charisma and the Uses of Persuasion." *American Journal of Philology* 130 no. 3 (Fall 2009), 313-339.

Zetzel, James E.G. *Cicero.* De Re Publica*: Selections*. Cambridge, UK: Cambridge University Press, 1995.

Zuckert, Catherine H. *Postmodern Platos: Nietzsche, Heidegger, Gadamer, Strauss, Derrida*. Chicago, IL, University of Chicago Press, 1996.

———. "Plato's *Laws*: Postlude or Prelude to Socratic Political Philosophy?" *Journal of Politics* 66 (2004), 374-395.

———. *Plato's Philosophers: The Coherence of the Dialogues*. Chicago, IL: University of Chicago Press, 2009.

Index

absence. *See* "conspicuous by its"
absolute truths, there are no, 368n18, 376-77
abstraction, human capacity for, 277
abyss between Athenian ideals and practice as origin of Platonism, 53
"academics," 13, 107n70
academics and athletics, 106
Academy, xiv, xix, 4, 7, 11, 12, 36n-105, 81, 83, 106, 106n69, 178, 180, 184, 249, 267, 268, 275, 282n85, 296, 318, 335, 339, 340-41, 345, 348, 380; "open spaces of" (Cicero), 4, 180; two kinds of students in, 83; women in, 296n6
academy (as elite secondary school), 106
"Achaeans, best of the," *see* Demodocus, "Missing Song" of
Acharnae, trees of, 61, 62n70
Achilles, 41, 231n194, 382-98; as "best of the Achaeans," 386, 392; as Odysseus' rival, 385-87, 397; choice of, 384, 393, 398n122; needs both Dorian and Phrygian Modes, 391-92n85; Odysseus on, 41, 383-86, 385n57, 397; Patroclus' question to, 393; promise to Priam, 391, 391n83, 392n85; self-sacrifice of, 389; Socrates and, 392-93
Achilles : Troy :: Socrates : jail-cell, 393
Acropolis, 48
active/passive verb forms, 93, 94, 167, 381; in City of Good Men only (Book I), 93-94, 381; in the Ship (Book VI), 167, 381; on imitation (Book X), 381-82
Adam, James, 13, 13n40, 25n76, 27-28, 40n6, 42n9, 44n14, 50, 55, 55n48, 62n71, 82n10, 90, 121n18, 129n-35, 130-31, 131n39, 133n49, 134n53, 208n56, 281n79, 293, 303n20, 314n60, 376n30, 379n36; and the torch, 42n9; loyalty to Platonism, 208n56; missing Introduction of, 42n9, 55n48, 62n71; on Intermediates in Plato, 129n35, 130-31
Adeimantus, 5n16, 6, 31, 42, 42n8, 52, 56n50, 58, 62n72, 65-67, 78n, 83, 105-9, 113, 122, 127, 141, 157-59, 160n107, 163, 165, 172, 206, 207, 209, 215n94, 237, 240n234, 245, 250, 254, 265n32, 296, 348-50, 394n103; accepts politically quiescent philosopher, 159; and oligarchy, 109, 109n76, 348; as musical, 106, 108n72, 109; as well-read, 105, 109, 348; Bloom on, 108n72; c omes nobly to the aid of Socrates, 109; comparatively obtuse, 107, 109, 394n103; most beautiful literary conceit entrusted to, 42; parallel to Xenophon's Glaucon, 108, 159; psychobiography of, 108; speech of, 105- 9; adumbrates Longer Way, 107; introduces Guardians, 108; seeks Justice, 108; with Nicias and Thrasymachus, 348
Adkins, Arthur W. H., 213-15, 213-15nn84-93, 217-19, 218n114, 221, 221n134, 223-24, 393n99
Adrasteia, 82n10
advantage of the stronger (Thrasymachus on justice), 53, 89, 159, 236
Aeschylus, 53, 82n10
Aesop, 378
afterlife, 96, 105, 180 ("that purer world"), 347n137, 372, 378

Agamemnon, 386, 390-91, 391n77, 397, 397n114
Agathon, 39n5, 231n199, 297n10
"Age of Heroes," 349-50, 352, 354-55, 363; as philosophy's golden age, 349; and reader, 352; corresponds to Democracy, 349, 363; followed by tyranny, 354-56; fourth age in Hesiod, 349
Ajax, 390, 392, 392n94
akra physeos, 230n187
Albinus, xvi
Alcestis, 231n194, 393n101
Alcibiades, xviii, 26n79, 53n38, 106, 161, 179n12, 241, 242n236, 336, 371
Alcibiades Major, xvi, xvii-viii, xviiin-13, xviiin15, xviii, xxii, 20n66, 30n89, 44n14, 53n38, 83-84, 88n25, 92, 95, 95n51, 106n68, 121n18, 160n105, 161, 161nn109-10, 179, 256, 336, 338, 394 ("soul to soul"); "too Platonic," xviiin14
Alcibiades Minor, xxii, 20n66, 30n89, 84, 88n25, 179, 394 ("worth praying for")
Alcinous. *See* Odysseus, Phaeacian Tale of
Alcoholics Anonymous, 25
Alexander Aphrodisiensis, 314n64
Alexander, Samuel, 131n41
Alexander the Great, 249n5, 275n65
Alexandria, 285
Allen, Danielle S., 23n73, 35-36n105
Allen, Michael J. B., 280n75, 281n81, 325nn89-90
Allen, R. E., 276n67
Allen, Thomas W., 383n45
allusions, inter-dialogue, 238n230, 239, 240
altruism, 93, 96, 97, 100, 103n62, 167-68, 167n121, 181, 195n34, 219, 219n115, 223nn144-45, 224, 229, 236, 236n223, 253, 275, 286, 364, 386; and maieutic pedagogy, 286; rewards of, 236, 236n223; Adkins, Strauss, and Bloom on, 224; and Justice, 97; and "other-regarding aspect of justice" (Singpurwalla), 217n105, 235; basanistic repudiation of, 168; insufficient, 386; native to humanity, 100 , 294; noble and good, 92; reduced to self-interest (Dawkins), 223n144
"Altruism" (Rudebusch), 222-23, 222n-144, 223n147, 225, 225n158, 229, 229n182, 232n202, 235 (author's reading)
Ambrose, 282
"Am I Guardian material?," 86; qualifications, 86n20
anachronism, 49
Anaxagoras, 26n79, 208n57
Andrew, Edward, 230, 230-31nn193-94, 393n101
Anglo-American analytic Plato scholarship, 12-13, 16-18, 26n78
Annas, Julia, xixn22, 9n25, 13n40, 28-29n81, 106n69, 125n26, 133n49, 134n52, 142n74, 208n59, 225n-159, 227-28, 227nn174-176, 228nn179-80, 232n201, 234n214, 234n216, 250n6, 296n7, 305n25, 318n75, 320n78
anonymity, *see* Platonic anonymity
anticlimax (justice), 44, 113, 133, 141; justice identical with the grounding Hypothesis of the City, 133
anti-dualism and anti-dualists, 197n38, 197-98
Antiochus, 283n93, 360n6
Antipater, 9n24
anti-Platonism, 20, 399n124; Straussian and Anglo-American, 20
Anton, John P., 129n34, 155n91, 287n106, 305n24, 334n116
Anytus, 301n16
Aphrodite, 385
Apollo, 26n79, 392
Apology of Socrates, xvi, xvii, xxii, 9, 17, 26n79, 31n89, 60n65, 81, 160n106, 237-40, 237n227, 279, 341n129, 360, 383n43, 387-88, 394n102
aporetic dialogues, 33, 34
aporia, 83, 83n11, 140
appearance/reality, 86, 89, 102, 104
Arcesilaus, 9
Archytas, 268-69, 269nn46-49
Ardley, Gavin, 44n13

Ares, 385
Arginusae, 160
Arieti, James, 386n62, 391, 391n84, 392n87, 393n99
Aristides, 301n17
Aristocles, 1, 36, 68, 68n79, 95, 106, 162, 299, 353, 378; becomes "Plato," 162, 353
Ariston, 1, 36, 48, 58, 65, 160, 162
Ariston, son of, 65-77, 108n74, 160, 161, 178, 242, 299
Ariston the Argive, 67-68, 86, 100, 107, 142n75, 162
Aristophanes, 53, 58, 59n61, 78n2, 163-64, 163nn112-13, 164n117, 242n236, 299; attacks Democracy and Socrates, 163; *Birds*, 242n-236; *Frogs*, 163, 163n112; *Knights*, 59n61, 78n2, 163-64, 163n113, 164n117, *Lysistrata*, 299
Aristotle, 10, 28, 70, 75-76, 75n102, 84, 85n18, 92n41, 95n50, 96n53, 129-31 134n52, 136n60, 137n62, 144, 148, 161n108, 166n119, 167n121, 179, 196, 196n35, 197n38, 198, 203n-40, 220, 225n-158, 230n188, 249n5, 275-77, 276n67, 276-77nn69-70, 287n104, 300, 305-27 *passim*, 327n98, 331n107, 332-33nn113-14; dualism as "separability in thought," 197n-38; explanation of his confusion on Plato's mathematics, 306-7, 316n69, 318-19, 322; Jaeger on, 315n65; "man" and "three" of, 277, 322; methodology with respect to, 309, 322; misunderstood Plato's dialectical pedagogy, 306, 308-9, 310-11, 315, 316n69, 318; on Ideal Numbers, 321-22. *See* "Incomparable Numbers"; on Intermediates in Plato, 129-31, 130n37, 277, 277n70, 311, 314, 319-22. *See* Intermediates; on mathematical objects, 311-12, 311n49, 312n50, 320; on Parmenides, 75-76, 316n69; on Plato's identification of the Good and the One, 305, 305n25; on Plato's mathematics, 305-324 *passim*; on (Pythagorean) Plato, 306, 315-17, 321, on the Good, Beautiful, and Just in *Metaphysics*, 316, 316n68, 317, 325n92; "Platonism" (early) of, 315n65, 316-17, 319, 321, 324, 324n86; polemical purpose of, 309, 309n39, 311-12, 314, 318, 322; rejects Pla tonic dualism, 196, 305; restored Problem of the One and the Many, 329n103; self-reference by?, 317n70; speaks for himself, 323; why cited on liberality and altruism, 167n121
Aristotelianism, 180, 324n86, 369n20; origins of, 324n86
arithmetic, 314, 321n80, 325-26, 329-36, 342, 348; "how forcefully upwards does it lead the soul!," 335
Arjuna, 285
Armada, Pawel, 399n123
Armstrong, A. H., 329n104
Aronson, Simon H., 221-22, 221n132, 222nn141-43, 224-25, 224n156, 225n162, 247n2
Arrighetti, Graziano, 73n89, 264n30
ars amatoria, 297n10
Asconius, 362n10
asking for votes, 243
Aspasia, 297, 297n9; represents basanistic element, 297n9
astronomy (Book VII), 26n79, 155, 155n91, 209, 314, 334, 334n116, 340, 398
atheism, 71, 77
Athena, 49, 53, 53n39, 391
Athenian Laws, speech of, xivn3
Athenian Stranger, 17, 84n17, 98, 154n89, 155, 162, 206, 206n48, 251, 273n59, 347, 353, 393n98, 396-97, 397n117; and "One out of Many," 154n89, 155; as escaping Socrates, 393n98; as "Odysseus," 397; hates boys, 84n17
Athens, 49-54, 53n38, 78n3, 151, 178n-10, 180, 242n236, 273, 279n70, 297n10, 336, 350, 353, 353n148, 355, 385, 393; and Jerusalem, 282n85; and the United States, 50; and Venice, 178n10; and Victorian/Edwardian Britain, 50; schools of, 54; as "bazaar of constitutions,"

351; as democracy, 51, 51, 273; as empire, 49n27, 51-53, 385; as excellent place to discover timeless truth, 53; as "school of Hellas," 350-51; democrats of, 61n69
athetizing dialogues, 84n16
Atlantis, xvn6
Attica, 51, 58, 58n58, 61
Attic Greek, 14, 27
Attic nights, 394
Attic Tragedy, 228
"Atomic Lines." *See* "Indivisible Lines"; as deliberate self-contradiction, 136n60, 154n88
Atomists, 329n103
Augustine, 282-83, 282-83nn89-95, 360n6, 367; *City of God*, 367, 369n-20; exoteric anti-Platonism of, 283
Augustus, 1, 275n65, 283n95, 355
Aulus Gellius, 82n9
Ausland, Hayden, 20n65, 30n85, 32n94
authenticity of Platonic dialogues, xvii-ix, xxii, 18, 20, 21n67, 27, 29, 30, 154, 156; and "unity of Plato's thought," 154, 156
autostereogram, 73
auxiliaries, 100
avatars (of Thrasymachus), 169, 236
Axiothea of Phlius, 296n6

Babette's Feast, 168n122
Bailey, Cyril, 262n25
Bailly, Jacques, 21n67, 32n94, 237n229
"bald-headed tinkers," 71
Bambrough, Renford, 276n68
Baracchi, Claudia, 183n21
Barber, E. A., 262n25
Barker, Ernest, 6n20
Barnes, Jonathan, 308n33, 360n6
Barney, Rachel, 38n3, 270n52
Barrett, James, 384-85, 384n47, 392, 392nn91-94
basanistic element, xx, xxi, 21-22, 91, 93, 96-100, 108, 145, 154-56, 154n-88, 160, 165, 165n118, 167-68, 193-94, 197-200, 208n56, 246-47, 260, 329, 332, 336-37, 339, 344-47, 346n134, 365, 367, 377, 379, 390, 394n103, 395n106; and Adam, 208n56; and active/passive verb forms, 93; and *Epinomis*, 155-56; and Firesticks, 246-47; and Parmenides, 22, 74, 75n103, 154n88, 165n118; and *Phaedrus*, 99n58, 142n77, 379-80; and *Philebus*, 197-98; and Seventh Letter, 259-60; and Shorter Way, 145; and the Tübingen School, 99n58; tests grasp of visionary teaching, xxi, 91, 98 (Justice); causes teaching to leap, xxi; causes recollection of higher truth, xxi; confirms the teacher, 91, 91n38; contradicts visionary teaching, 98; essential to reconstruction of the Reading Order, 344; falling prey to, 345; leads to firm possession of the truth, 98, 272n57; reflected in true/false questions, 10n29, 260; use of fraudulent discourses, 193; vs. (slavish) literalism, 93. *See also* basanistic pedagogy
basanistic pedagogy, xxi, 8, 15, 100, 103, 108, 154n88, 193-94, 200, 208n56, 213n81, 272, 323, 353n150, 387, 387n64, 390n72, 393, 396n111, 397; Homeric origin of, 387, 390n-72, 391, 396-97; Parmenides and, 396-97; points to reader, 393
"Battle Hymn of the *Republic*," 21-22, 68-69n82, 198, 336, 345-47, 398; requires student to distinguish the Good "from all other things," 346n135
"bazaar of constitutions." *See* Democracy, as
Beast, multi-headed (Bk. IX), 5, 201-2, 378
Beatty, Joseph, 223n147, 224n155, 225-26, 225-26n163, 234n216, 250n6
Beautiful, the and Beauty, 71n83, 96n53, 192, 252, 315n66, 316, 316n68, 328, 371, 394n103; and the base, as two, 328
"beautiful things are difficult," 83, 103, 386
Beauty, Idea of, 179, 198, 236, 277-89 *passim*, 299, 302, 302nn18-19, 395;

draws the soul upward from Becoming and the body, 279, 395
"beauty in the eye of the beholder," 88, 241; as bacillus of sophistry, 88
Becoming, 19, 25, 72-73, 104, 144, 152-53, 157, 181n18, 201, 276, 293, 280n74, 301-3, 303n21, 331, 371-72; and "pseudo-dyadic indistinctiveness," 331; as indefinite plurality, 201, 276, 302; cannot be said to truly exist, 135, 276, 276n68, 277, 302; hypothetical, 277; infinitely divisible, 72; on both sides of Cartesian dualism, 372; within us, 371-72; without integrity, 73, 152. *See also* Being and Becoming
beds/couches, 47, 64n74, 203, 276-77, 379, 379nn35-36; as artifact by nature, 379
Bedford Falls/Pottersville, 287
bees, 177n9, 294
Beethoven, Ludwig van, 107, 278
Being, 19, 22, 24-26, 72-73, 76, 104, 152-53, 157, 181n18, 185, 196, 276, 280n74, 301-3, 303n21, 344, 372; and Idea of the Good, 196; and unity, 152; bearable lightness of, 372; exclusive existence of, 79; gender-neutral, 303, 303n21; "is what it is," 276; not of visible world, 276; truly and necessarily is, 76; unchanging, 396n111. *See also* Being and Becoming
Being and Becoming, 19, 48, 72-73, 86, 103-4, 153, 181n18, 184, 195-98, 207, 209, 275-76, 293, 301-3, 302nn20-21, 315, 332, 339, 342-45, 347, 367-68, 372-73, 395-97, 395-96n106; and Justice, 184; and Platonic dualism, 153, 184, 195; and Problem of the One and the Many, 153; and Reading Order, 339, 342-45; "definite dyad" of, 332; distinction between, 48, 86, 345; divided by plateau, 72, 196, 367; mathematical μεταξύ between, 104; proleptic introduction of (Book IV), 153
Benardete, Seth, 55, 55n46, 56nn51-52, 197, 382n42, 387n65, 388n68, 391n80, 396n112, 398nn122-23
Bendis, 52n34, 53n39
"benefiting friends and harming enemies," 85, 85n18; and structure of the *Republic*, 85; and Xenophon, 85
benefiting/being benefited, 94, 167, 177, 181, 284, 377, 382n42, 393. *See also* active/passive verb forms
benefit others, 92, 101, 168, 168n122, 242, 284, 377; the city and friends, 242; teachers and other decent human beings will beg to, 168n122, 377. *See also* altruism
Ben-Hur, 241n235
Benson, Hugh H., 30n84, 129n36, 300n15
Bett, Richard, 9n27
"beyond Being," 24-26, 25n76, 26n79, 195, 274, 280n74, 289, 314n61, 320n78, 336, 398, 398n122; and non- or anti-Platonists, 320n78; application to χώρα, 398n122; as "above Being," 195; if One exists, Good is, 336; interpretation should not be the defining basis of "Platonism," 26
Bhagavad Gita, 285
Bible, 105
Bildungsroman, *Republic* as, 86
Blackburn, Simon, 233n206
Blits, Jan, 29n83
Blitz, Mark, 17n55
Blondell, Ruby, 40n7, 81n8, 392n89
Bloom, Allan, 54, 55n47, 56nn51-52, 62n72, 108, 108nn72-73, 108n75, 215n93, 216-17, 216-17nn101-3, 218n117, 221, 221n134, 229-31, 229-30nn185-92, 231n194, 231nn197-98, 234n216, 250n6, 382n42, 383, 383n44, 388n68, 394n102; on impressing the vulgar, 394n102; on Glaucon vs. Adeimantus, 62n72, 108; on two jobs for one man, 217
Blössner, Norbert, 179-80n15, 247n2
Boas, George, 48n25
Bodhisattva, 285
von Bora, Katarina, 374
Bowe, G. S., 30-33, 30nn85-89, 31n93, 32n95, 32n97, 33nn100-1
Bowery, Anne-Marie, 286n103

Bowra, C. M., 262n25, 263n27
Brann, Eva, 37n2, 133n50, 136n61, 307n30, 330-31n107, 382n42
"breaking the frame," 35, 86, 232, 232n204, 235, 285n102. *See* "crisis of the *Republic*"
Brecht, Bertold, 363n14
Brentlinger, John A., 113-14n5, 129n35
Brickhouse, Thomas C., 225-26, 226nn164-65, 237n228
"bridle of Theages" (physical disability preventing political activity), 240, 240-41n234, 299, 352
"bridle of Theages/champion of justice" speech (496e11-e3), 237-38, 239, 240, 242, 292n4; alludes to *Theages*, 238n230, 240; foreshadows *Apology*, 240
Brisson, Luc, 264n30
Brittain, Charles, 283n92, 360n6, 375-76n29
Broad, C. D., 349n138
Broeniman, Clifford, 385n56
Brown, Eric, 226n166, 233-34, 233-34nn207-14
Browning, Robert, 178b10
Bruell, Christopher, 29n83, 31nn91-92
Brunt, P. A., 35n105, 362n10
Brutus, 275n65
Buddha, 285
Burger, Ronna, 18n56
deBurgh, W. G., 210n65
Burkert, Walter, 3n13, 214n85
Burnet, John, xiiin1, xviin14, 13, 13n40, 50, 112n3, 137n64, 157n99, 160n106, 183, 296n6, 377
Burnyeat, Myles, 9n24, 42-44, 43nn10-11, 129n36, 277n70, 285n102, 307n32, 310n42, 313n57, 313n59, 319n76, 320n78; on Intermediates in Plato, 129n36, 277n70
"Burnyeat's Question," 43, 278-79
Bury, R. G., 13n40
"by nature," 295, 297-301, 304. *See also* Cavemen; Equality of the Sexes; *and* Two Jobs for the Just

Cadmus, 293, 356
Caesar, C. Julius, 1, 13, 275n65, 355, 359, 361, 362n10, 363, 363n14
Cairns, Douglas, 1n2, 222n144
"California Consultant." *See* Harmonious Man as
Callias, xviiii, 39n5, 231n199
Callicles, 36, 50, 50n31, 91, 95, 95n51, 98, 223n145; as touchstone, 91, 98
Callipolis, 207n52, 229n184
Calypso, 398n122
Cambridge Companion to Plato, 28, 206nn45-46
Campbell, Lewis, 13n40, 344
Capra, Frank, 287, 367
Cardini, Maria Timpanaro, 322n85
Cary, M., 361n9
Cassius, 13
Catan, John R., xiiin2
Catiline, 1, 355-56, 362n10
Cato (of Utica), 359, 359nn1-4, 361, 363n14, 366
Catullus, 1, 363n14
Cave, xx, 2, 35, 41-42, 44-45, 48-49, 53, 80, 103-4, 127, 144, 153, 159, 171, 179, 184-85, 237, 250-51, 281, 281n80, 284, 300, 303n22, 304, 335, 359, 367-68, 371-72; all of us born in?, 179, 371-72; as Becoming from perspective of Being, 153; demotes the physical world to shadows, 184; foreshadowing of, 45, 103; mathematics and, 335; no awareness of without the Idea of the Good, 184; no Justice without, 184
Cave, Allegory of, 3, 3n13, 5, 12n38, 13, 37, 39-40, 42, 45, 86, 103, 127, 140, 157n100, 158, 162, 165, 167-68, 173-74, 181, 195, 223n146, 246, 279, 286, 371-72, 376-77, 383; as movie theater, 286; epistemological and sociological readings of, 371; essential for understanding both Myth of Er and ""Scipio's Dream," 372; linked with Line and Sun, 127, 158, 173; necessary part of any well-educated person's training, 178; third of three key passages, 246; women and, 286
Cavemen, 40-41, 89n26, 181, 195, 255, 371-72; as Cartesians, 371; born into time and physicality, 255; cannot see themselves, 371-72; not by nature,

255; would kill returning philosopher if they could, 181
censorship, 5n16, 78, 304, 372
centrality of *Republic*, xv, xix, xxii, 13n40, 24, 28, 29n81, 86n21, 194; links Justice to Plato's ontology, 181
Cephalus, 54, 58, 77-81, 82, 85, 146-47, 160, 180n16, 263n29, 350-51, 373; and the Cave, 80; and "the meaning of life," 81; arms contractor, 54, 77; as "Christian," 80; as "Platonist," 79, 373; "charming," 77-79; dreams of, 80; insurance policy of, 78; loses himself, 80
Cervantes, Miguel de, 251n7
chariot (Parmenides, *Phaedrus*), 22, 72
"Charlie," 78. *See* Cephalus
Charmides, xviiin18, xxii, 21, 101n59, 115n8, 121, 179, 339, 394, 395n104
Chayevsky, Paddy, 89n28
Cherniss, Harold, 209n59, 305n25, 3067nn28-30, 321n81, 332n113, 397n119
Cherubin, Rose, 75n100
"chicken or the egg?," 286
Chiron, 386n63
Chora (χώρα), 397-99, 398nn121-22
Church, 369n20
Church and State, 213n80
Churchill, Winston, 159, 354
Christianity, 25, 104n65, 105, 157, 194, 213, 213n78, 213n83, 218, 229n182, 233n206, 280-83, 281n80, 284n100, 368-69, 381n39
Christian humanism, 281n78
Christian theology, 280, 282n87
Christian, William, 281n77
Christmas, 105
"chronology of composition" (Poster), xvi, xvin8, 16, 27, 91, 302, 373n24; agnosticism toward, xvi; intra-textual pretensions of, 91
Church Fathers, 281-83
Cicero, Marcus Tullius, xx, 1-11, 2nn4-9, 9n24, 11n32, 13, 28, 35, 35n105, 38-39, 72n84, 93n43, 104n65, 161n-108, 179n14, 200, 208n57, 242n237, 269, 274n63, 275n65, 281, 281n78, 283, 283nn93-94, 298n12, 355, 355n152, 357, 359-67, 360nn5-6, 362-63nn13-14, 366n17, 396n108, 397; and "Cicero," 9, 9n25, 397; and the CITY, 200, 360; as *conservator rei publicae*, 365; as "eclectic copyist," 360, 397; as (with Plato) "first Christian humanists" (Rand), 281n-78; as philosopher and statesman, 2, 361; as Platonic feminist, 298n12; as Platonist, 359-61, 360n6, 366n17; as Plato's best student, 1, 361, 397; as Plato's rival (*aemulus*), 1, 2n4, 275n65, 361, 397; did not survive death of the Roman Republic, 360, 360n5; distinguishes Anaxagoras and Socrates, 208n57; Herculean labors of, 355; influence on United States, 2, 362; interpretation of *Republic* embodied in his life, 360; mantra of, 366n17; never-ending fight of, 357; recognized by Augustine as true lover of Plato, 283; returned from "Athens," 360; use of rhetoric, 2; works of: *Academica*, 9, 9n24, 9n26, 9n28; *Brutus*, 35n105, 179n14; *De Inventione*, 2n7; *De Finibus*, 2n9, 9n25, 93n43, 269n48; *De Natura Deorum*, 10; *De Republica*, 2, 243n237; *De Officiis*, 2n4, 4nn15-16, 38; *De Oratore*, 2n6, 4n15, 10, 179n14, 274n63; *Hortensius*, 283n94, 367; *In Catilinam* IV, 347; *Orator*, xx, 4, 179n14, 396n-108; *Philippics* II, 363n14; "Somnium Scipionis," 2, 3, 5n16, 35n104, 360, 367, 372; *Timaeus* (translation), 396n108; *Tusculan Disputations*, 2n9, 10, 208n57, 281, 298n12
Ciceronian Platonism, 18
Cicero, Quintus, 366n17
Ciholas, Paul, 281n82, 282n84, 282nn87-88
city (actual, like U.S., Athens or Rome), 247, 392; as "Troy," 392; as "pasturage of poisonous herbs," 258-59, 351n145
City, 2, 4-7, 15, 39, 78, 106, 111, 119, 122-25, 133, 138-41, 158, 158n101, 162-63, 172-77, 176n8, 200, 204-5, 224, 229, 231n195, 245-50, 256, 258, 292n4, 294, 328n102, 331,

334n118, 340, 350, 352, 367, 374, 377-78, 387; and Divided Line, 141; as a monastery, 374, 374n26; as geometrized Athens, 141; as imaginary, 2, 172; authoritarian/regulated, 151, 351, 353n146, 365n16; based on one man/one job principle (Hypothesis), 113, 133, 139, 142, 153n87, 176n8, 328n102; compulsion in, 200, 226n166; degenerates, 200, 334n118; fictional, 177; first ruler of, 106; founder(s) of, 173, 175-77, 204, 352; functions like geometrical diagram, 138; hazardous to long-term spiritual health, 351, 374; Hypotheses and Images in, 139-41; hypothetical and/or imaginary, 39, 139n68; immanent vs. Idea transcendent, 64; intelligible Image of visible thing, 138; its four, three, two, and ones, 141; justice in based on founding Hypothesis, 133; justice in (trivial), 44; made intelligible, 111; necessary for Justice, 140-41; non-existent, 39, 200; philosopher-king and, 258; realized by Justice, 367; realization of, 55, 58-59, 82, 258, 367; Return sanitized in, 387; three classes/four metals in, 122, 125, 142; unity of, 328n102, 331

CITY, 200, 360, 366-67; as Plato, 350; as Plato's *Polity*, 200; distinguished from City, 200; "Dual Citizenship" in, 200, 361; no compulsion in, 200; philosopher in, 367

City and Man, 78n3, 119-25, 142, 151, 186, 201, 220, 245-50, 253, 279, 367, 374; analogy between, 120, 122n22; analogy, direction of, 120n16; and Second Part of the Divided Line, 123; based on an Image, 122; based on series of Hypotheses, 119-25, 120-21n18, (1) things called same name are the same, 119, 120-21, (2) just Man will not differ *qua* just from just City, 119, 120-22, 142, 186, 246 (3) City was just (*et al.*) from each of three classes doing their own job, 119-22, 142, 149, 205, 245, (3a) City has three classes, 121-22, 142, (3b) justice can be found by process of elimination, 120n18, 121-22, 121n19, 124, (3b) there are four virtues, 120-21n18, 121-22, 142. *See* virtue, (4) Man will likewise be just in this tripartite way, 119, 121, 149; friction between, 254; hypothesizing principle of non-contradiction necessary for "(4)," 120, 124. *See also* non-contradiction; incongruence between, 253. *See also* Key Passage, I. Firesticks; numbering system for assumptions: four virtues, three parts of soul/classes, City and Man, and one man or part/ one job, justice in City identical to justice in Man, 125, 125n25; triangular congruence, 142, 149, 253. *See also* "isomorphism (elegant)"

City in the Man, 144-45, 363, 367. *See also* Harmonious Man

City of Good Men Only, 5, 90, 92, 96-100, 106, 162, 166-68, 177, 248, 364; and Ship, 166-68; as microcosm of proleptic, visionary, and basanistic elements, 96-99; good men desire neither money nor honor, 90, 90n30, 364; penalty does not exist there, 92, 167, 248; points to Idea of Justice, 99-100; selfishness in, 168; "why would good men rule in it?," 99

City of Pigs, 5, 47-48, 64-65, 64nn74-75, 85n19, 108, 162, 246, 292n4, 379, 379n35

classic, 48

Clay, Diskin, xv, 238n230

Cleisthenes, 161n108

Cleitophon, 31-32, 36, 38, 42, 79, 160, 160-61n108, 171, 237, 239, 296, 301n16; any given, 36; as first-order imaginary audience for Plato's *Republic*, 32, 35, 38; as opposed to "Cleitophon," 32-33, 32-33nn98-99, 89; political career of, 160-61n108

Cleitophon, xv, xvn6, xviii, xviiin-16, xix, xxii, 17, 20-21, 21n67, 27, 29-36, 101n59, 115n8, 150, 179, 237, 300n15, 301n16, 338, 395; as introduction to *Republic*, xviii, 21; as

inauthentic, 21n67, 29-30; as "un-Platonic," 29; "Cleitophon's Challenge," 30-35; riddle of, 29, 29n82, "Socrates' Silence," 29-30, 32
"Cleitophon's Question," 35-36, 38-39, 42, 47, 100, 171, 237, 301n16
Clement of Alexandria, 282, 282n86
Cleon, 61n69
Clodius, 1, 361n9, 362n13
Cochrane, Charles Norris, 283n95
Codrus, 231n194, 393n101
Cohen, Hermann, 137n65
Coleman-Norton, P. R., 386n60
comedy, 45
communism and community of women and children, 292, 304, 328n101
"Complex, the" (One, Dyad, Ideal Numbers), 317-20, 323, 325n90; and Aristotle's intellectual development, 324n86; and *Philebus*, 325n90; easily refutable, 318; as "Platonic," 324; inconsistent with Intermediates, 317; once taken seriously by Aristotle, 319; refuted by Aristotle, 323
"conspicuous by its absence," 38, 92, 145, 163, 168, 206, 352, 365n16
contradiction, art of, 292n4
Cook, Erwin F., 391n80
Cook Wilson, J., 129n34, 210n65, 306n28, 307n29, 310n42, 314n63, 318-19n76, 321n80
Cooper, Craig, 35n105
Cooper, John M., xviin15, 34n103, 224-25, 225n158, 232n201
"Copernicanism," 148, 204-5, 215n93; *see also* Justice : Copernicanism
Corcyra, 52
Corinth, 52
Corlett, J. Angelo, 16n51
Cornford, F. M., 14nn40-41, 43n11, 49-50, 50n29, 120n16, 120-21n18
cosmology, xv, 3, 22, 73, 76, 208-9, 208nn55-56, 275, 396, 396n107; depends on vision, 396, 396n108
courage, 243, 287-88
Coxon, A. H., 284n96
Craig, Leon, 56n50, 59n60
Crassus (*de Oratore*), 10
Crassus (*triumvir*), 359, 361, 362n10
Cratylus, 75
Cratylus, xxii, 13n39, 22, 195n34; Justice, the sun, and altruism in, 195n34, 270
credit cards, 356
"Cretan Lies," 397
Crete, 393, 397
crisis (κρίσις), 8, 81, 103, 258, 276, 294
"crisis of the *Republic*," xiv, xix, xxii, 6-8, 10, 38, 45, 103, 176-77, 180, 204, 210n67, 236, 248, 253, 294, 339, 343, 352, 380, 383, 387, 394; and "intuitionism," 210n67; avoiding it requires conceiving Guardians as real, 294; personal, 236. *See* Critical Ambiguity
Critias, xvn6, xxii, 22, 29-30, 30n89, 162, 338
Critical Ambiguity, 176-79, 180, 241, 243, 252, 258, 294, 340, 351-52, 379; and Browning's "A Toccata of Galuppi's," 178n10; and reader's sovereign choice, 180
Crito, xivn3, xvi, xxii, 84n16, 237n227, 279, 341n129, 383n43
Cronos, 349
Cropsey, Joseph, xxn25, 17n52, 197n37
crucifixion and Crucifixion, 104-5, 104-5n65, 217n108, 281, 285
Cross, R. C., 132n24
Crystal, Ian, 74n94, 75n99
Ctesippus, 8,
Curd, Patricia, 309n39
Cyrus, 85

Daedalus, 207n52
Dahl, Norman O., 210n66
Dakyns, H. G., 13n40
Dancy, Jonathan, 210n66
Dante, 381n39
Danzig, Gabriel, 21n69, 82n9
Davies, J. C., 229, 229nn181-82
Davies, Richard, xiiin2
Davis, Michael, 31n91, 32-33n98, 71n83, 103n62
Davis, Philip J., 136n59
Dawkins, Richard, 223n144
Definition of Chalcedon, 369n20

"deflationary readings," compulsion applied to Guardians (Return), 226n-166, 233, 234n215, 235, 236n-222
déjà vu, 72n84
Deleuze, Gilles, 399n124
Delian League, 49nn27-28, 51
deliberate falsehood, xxi, 8, 9-10, 10n29, 160, 387, 387n66, 399
deliberate self-refutation, 162
Demetriou, Kyriakos, 20n65, 30n85, 239n232
demiurge, 203, 379, 379n36
Democratic Man, 351, 354
Democracy, 51, 62, 258, 273, 291, 292n4, 294n5, 340, 348-58; and Glaucon, 348; and City, 292n4; and education, 291-92, 301; and imperial arrogance, 51; and those "by nature free," 351, 353, 353n147; and United States, 355-56; and Tyranny, 354-56; as Age of Heroes, 294n5, 349. *See* "Age of Heroes"; as "bazaar of constitutions," 350-54; civil strife ("Thebes") and, 357, 357n155; condition for the possibility of Pla to's *Republic* and Justice, 350-51; contains seed of its own destruction, 355; description of as "first real test contained in Plato's *Republic*," 357-58; foreign wars ("Troy") and, 356, 357n166; freedom/license in, 350-54; freedom from compulsion to hold office, 352; good of as "indefinite plurality" (freedom), 353; misogyny and, 358n159; not the City, 351, 351n145; philosophy in, 354-55; praised in Book VIII, 348-58; *Republic* as evidence of its excellence, 355
Democritus, 72, 75
Demodocus, "Missing Song" of, 385, 385nn55-58, 390; as Homer, 385-86
"Demos of the Pnyx." *See* Ship
Demos, Raphael, 143-44n78, 217nn105-6, 218n112, 219n117, 224, 232n201
Demosthenes, 2n10, 35-36n105, 82n10, 179, 179n14, 249n5, 275n65, 264, 360n5; as Plato's auditor, 35n105, 179n14, 360n5
Deneen, Patrick J., 392n89
Denniston, J. D., 27
Denyer, Nicholas, xviin15, 12-13n38, 88n25, 129n36, 133n49
Derrida, Jacques, 196n36, 398nn121-22, 399n123
Descartes, René, 136, 335, 369-72, 370nn21-22; and number line, 335; *cogito* as monad, 372
Desmoulins, Camille, 2n8
Destrée, Pierre, 139n68
developmentalism, xvi, xxi, 16, 19, 20, 197, 302, 396n106; presupposes that Plato's conception of the unchanging changed, 302; rejects unchanging Being for a Plato who becomes, 344-45. *See also* "Plato's Development"
De Vogel, C. J., 281n80
diachronicity vs. timelessness, 81
dialectic, 14-15, 37, 79, 136, 143, 171, 202, 248, 249n4, 287, 292n4, 307, 310, 310n47, 330, 343, 343n131; and the word "γενναῖος," 292n4; and deliberate self-contradiction, 307; within dialogues, xix, 7, 171n1, 343; between dialogue and reader, xix, 7, 343; between dialogues, xix, 343; between Plato and the student, xxii, 7, 41; "doing away with hypotheses," 310n77; methodological, 8, 136; necessary for unmasking Shorter Way, 143, 248; number three constitutive of (two speakers and topic), 143; "text-imminent," 171n1; transitional form of, 343. *See* self-contradiction, deliberate
dialectical pedagogy, 96, 98-99; and basanistic element, 98; transforms written texts, 99
Dicaearchus, 296n6
Diels-Kranz, 22n71, 78n3
Dillon, John, 275n65
Diogenes Laertius, 58n56, 58n58, 67-68, 67n80, 106, 156n95, 296, 296n6, 325n88
Dion, xiv, 261-63, 259, 263n27, 265, 267, 267n40, 270, 270n53, 273n59, 275n65; and Justice, 263; epitaph of, 262-63, 263n27
Dionysius of Halicarnassus, 28-29, 36

Dionysius of Syracuse, 261-62, 263n-29, 264, 267n40, 268, 270-71, 273-74
Dionysius (Plato's teacher), 67, 106
Diotima, 179, 226n168, 227-28, 232n201, 279, 296n6, 297, 297n10, 299, 302n19, 304n23; and visionary element, 297n10; as spokesman for Idea that has no body, 299
Divided Line, 5, 14, 22, 33n102, 43n11, 111, 113-41, 157n100, 158, 173, 181n17, 181-86, 190, 200-3, 231n195, 245-46, 248, 250, 265, 269, 277, 287-88, 307, 309n42, 310, 313, 319n76, 320, 321n80, 324, 327, 329-30, 343, 369-71, 380n38; "Intermediates" in, 43n11, 113n5, 133, 307, 309n42, 319n76, 321n80. *See* Intermediates in Plato; linked with Cave and Sun, 127, 158, 173; pedagogical, 137; problem of objective correlates, 132; reveals methodological limitations, 122; scholarly attention to, 129n34; second of three key passages, 246; self-transcending aspect of, 136; shows how to divide Shorter and Longer Ways, 245; First Part: dialectical method :: Second Part : methods used in Books II-IV, 126, 137, 182; First Part : Going Back Down into the Cave :: Second Part : one man/one part of soul doing its natural job, 182; First Part : emancipation from Second Part :: Second Part : emancipation from "pseudo-dyadic indistinctiveness," 330; First Part : Justice :: Second Part : justice, 137, 182; First Part : Longer Way :: Second Part : Shorter Way, 126, 137, 182, 245
Divided Line, First Part of (fourth in order of presentation), 5n17, 115, 126, 129, 132, 181-85, 200, 202, 265n33, 277, 287-88, 310, 313, 330, 343, 370; deduces other Ideas from the un-hypothetical, 184, 287, 343; describes dialectic, 182; dialectical method of, 343; discloses the un-hypothetical, 130, 248, 313; distinct from Second, 43n11, 132, 133n49, 182; does away with hypotheses by bringing dialectical objections, 310n47, 313; emancipation of νόησις from διάνοια, 330; elucidation depends on prior elucidation of the Second Part, 182; infinitely more important than Second Part, 182; links Justice to Plato's ontology, 182-85; objects are intelligible, 114, 132, 133; objects radically distinct and fully emancipated from sensibles, 132-33, 135, 184; treats Hypotheses of Second Part as mere hypotheses, 182
Divided Line, Second Part of, 5-6, 5n17, 14, 14n41, 113-141, 182, 201-3, 231n195, 265n33, 277, 287-88, 307, 313, 343, 369-71, 380n38; and Book IV, 14; and Book X, 380n38; and City, 231n195; and Divided Line itself, 118; and mathematics, 5, 14, 114, 116; 129n35, 313. *See also* mathematics, objects of; and methods (pursuits) of Shorter Way, 141, 343; and principle of non-contradiction, 117; and Shorter Way, 5, 6, 22, 114, 122-28, 136, 201-3; circularity, method leads to, 133, 141, 182, 369; depends on diagrams, 135; describes any Hypothesis-bound in quiry that is compelled to employ sensible objects as Images, 117, 132; διάνοια in, 130. *See Index verborum*; "form of inquiry," 113-14; emancipates soul from sensibles, 133; geometry and arithmetic as examples, 116-17; Hypotheses (assumptions) in, 5, 14,113-28, 114n5, 119n15, 122, 132-33, 137, 182, 200, 202-3, 313, 370-71; Images in, 5, 14, 115, 116n10, 117, 122, 129-141, 200-2, 370; intelligible objects, 5, 114, 132, 133; necessary, 136; no intrinsic connection between use of Images and Hypotheses, 126n29; objects not fully emancipated from objects of sense, 134, 184; objects of inseparable from method that creates them, 132; One as grounding hypothesis in, 132, 201-2. *See* One

(mathematical); third in order of presentation, 5n17, 113; three speeches devoted to, 115; useful for dividing Shorter from the Longer Way, 111, 113-14, 116n10, 118, 124; useful pedagogical step toward Ideas, 133; verbal parallelism with City/Man analogy, 120, 120n17
Divided Line, Third Part of, 130, 132-34, 265n33; equal in length to Second, 133, 133n49, 134-36, 135n56
divine inspiration, 249
Divine Love, 196
"Do I exist?," 371
"Do the difficult!" (Tunberg), 241
Dobbs, Darrell, 234-35, 234-35n218, 289n109
Dodds, E. R., 50, 50n31, 91, 91n37, 214n85
dogmatism and dogmatists, 10, 375
Donaldson, James, 282n83, 282n86,
Dorian Mode, 242-42, 249, 252, 365, 391n85
Dornseiff, Franz, 266, 266nn34-37, 269n49, 270
Dorter, Kenneth, 37n1, 96n55, 233n210, 234n216
Douglas, A. E., 35n105
Dova, Stamatia, 391n74, 385, 385n54, 391n74, 394n77
"dramatic chronology" (Post), xv, xvi, xvii, xviii, 17, 84, 84n16
dramatic connections between dialogues, xviii, xxii
Drang nach Einheit (G. "quest for unity"), 73, 76, 153, 208, 329
"Dream of Scipio," *see* Cicero, "Somnium"
dreams, 71-72n84
Drummond, John J., 309n38
Dual Citizenship, 200
dualism, 73, 79, 184, 196, 396
Duff, Timothy E., 360n5
Dunkle, Roger, 390n74
Dunn, Michael. xvin10
Dutoit, Thomas, 398n121
duty, 2, 212, 212n76, 214, 214n87, 223, 223n146, 232n201, 236
dyads, i.e., paired Platonic dialogues, 30, 30n89, 158, 162
Ecclesiates, 80
Echecrates, 296n6
Edelstein, Ludwig, 20n64, 266-67n39
Edwardian Britain, 50
egalitarianism, 292, 299
"Egoism" (Rudebusch), 3n14, 222, 222-23n144, 224, 225, 225n158, 229, 232n201
Egypt, 285, 296
Einstein, Albert, 126n29, 369n19
Eleatic Stranger, xxin28, 81n8, 98, 112n3, 162, 251, 273, 344, 347-48, 396-97; as "another Odysseus" (Benardete), 396n112; as parricide, 81n8, 396n11
elitism, 158n103, 164, 213, 245, 247n2, 293, 301, 304n23; democratic, 301; how to refute, 158n103, 301; Plato's, 301
empiricism and empiricists, 180
England, E. B., 333n113
Epicureans, 106n69, 258
Epinomis, xxii, 20n66, 30n89, 155-56, 158, 156nn93-95, 162, 208, 315n65, 338, 397; "basanistic dialogue par excellence," 156
equality of Second and Third Parts of Divided Line. *See* Divided Line, Third Part
Equality of the Sexes, 87n23, 292, 294-304, 304n23; and Diotima, 299; and Justice, 295, 298; and "the same nature," 304; and timeless Idea, 298; as corollary to pedagogical revolution, 300; compliment to males, 299; counter to convention but not nature, 297; learned on the plateau, 299; necessary component of what we call "justice," 298; rejection of the most common type of caste system (second "Genetic Fiction"), 304; revolutionary proposal, 295
Erastai, xxii, 20n66, 33n102, 67, 67n80, 84, 106, 106n68, 179, 179n-12, 339, 394 ("both athlete and know-it-all")
Erbse, Hartmut, 121n18, 395n104
Er, Myth of, 3. *See* Myth of Er
eristic, 292n4

eros, 15n44, 47n24, 56, 77n1, 371; as tyrant, 77n1
Estiénne, Henri (Stephanus), 1n1, 270
eternity, 81, 180
ethical truths, most important of, 93
Euben, J. Peter, 350n143
Euclid, 28, 131, 308n35, 320n78, 332
Eumaeus, 397
Euripides, 49, 53, 58, 63, 208, 208n57, 296; fr. 92, 208n57; *Medea*, 296n8; *Trojan Women*, 49, 58
Euthydemus, xxii, 8, 8n23, 17, 142n75, 179, 301n17, 394
Euthyphro, 81n7
Euthyphro, xvi, xvii, xxii, 17, 31n89, 78n3, 81, 81n8, 84n16, 237n227, 279, 341n129
Evelyn-White, Hugh G., 350n141, 356n154, 357n157
"exemplification," 223-24, 223n148
Exodus, Book of, 25, 285
exoteric surface of Plato's text, 11-12, 236
"expressivist" readings of the Return, 233, 233n213, 235, 235n221

Fagan, Patricia, 388n68
falsehood, *see* deliberate
Fârâbî, 9-10n30, 19n63
Favorinus, 325n88
feminism, Platonic, 298n12, 304n23
Ferejohn, Michael, 284n98
Ferguson, John, 129n34
Ferrari, G. R. F., 15n43, 16, 26n78, 46n21, 129n36, 179n15, 207n52, 209n60, 234n214, 395
Festiguière, A. J., xvin12
Ficino, 30n87, 280, 280n75, 325nn89-90
"fictive chronology," 17. *See* "dramatic chronology"
Findlay, J. N., 12n37, 305n25
Fine, Gail, 21n67, 204n41, 210n66, 217n104, 278n71, 283n92, 296n7, 316n67, 322n84, 360n6
Finkelberg, M., 385n56
"fire and earth," 75, 75n 103
Firesticks, 8. *See* Key Passage: Part I
Fish, Stanley, 7n22, 171n1
Five Cities (Books VIII and IX), 142, 339-40, 354-58; and nuptial number; 348; connection to Hesiod, 349, 356-57; connection to interlocutors, 348; Democracy arrests progressive decline, 349; Democracy as alternative to Tyranny, 355; Democracy as test, 348, 357-58; Democracy as Age of Heroes, 349. *See* Age of Heroes; Democracy/Glaucon, 348
Foley, Richard, 135-36, 135nn55-56, 136n58
"footnotes to Plato" (Whitehead), 370, 370n22, 382n41
force/persuasion, 46, 46n22
form/content distinction, 112-13
"forms and politics" (Kraut), xxin27
Foster, M. B., 211, 211n71, 212-3, 212-13nn74-83, 217, 217n108, 218, 224, 229n182; refused to accept implications of self-sacrificing Return on Christian grounds, 213n83, 218
Fowler, Harold North, 297n10
Frank, Erich, 196n35, 268n42, 274n62
Frank, Jill, 51n32, 358n159
"fraudulent synthetic unity," 145. *See* One out of Many
Frede, Michael, xxn25, 11n32, 16n51, 309n39
Frege, Gottlob, 312n50
Freud, Sigmund, 72n84, 363, 372
friends and enemies, 85, 85n18, 86-87, 236; Justice renders each their due, 236
Funke, Hermann, 50n30
Fuyarchuk, Andrew, 197n38

Gadamer, Hans-Georg, 26n80, 196, 196n36, 197, 197n38, 325n91, 395n105; and *Philebus*, 197
Gagarin, Michael, 213n84
Gaiser, Konrad, 99n58, 266n38, 325n91
Galileo, 312n53
Gallienus, 6
Gallupi, Baldassaro, 178n10
Gandhi, Mohandas, 287
"Gap" (Brown), 221n130, 233-34, 233-34nn207-214, 235; as provocation, 221n130; deliberate, 235; "gap-

filling strategy," 233; celebration of, 234, 235; necessary but not sufficient moment, 234; pedagogical purpose of, 235; unbridgeable, 235. *See also* Brown, Eric
Gay, R. K., 75n102
"Genetic Fiction," 293-94, 300, 304; *see also* Noble Lie(s); as "Phoenician Tale," 293
genetics, 293
Geffcken, Johannes, 29n82
"geometrical fiction. *See* point, as
geometry, 196-97, 310, 314, 321n80, 332-34, 332n113; and "Plato's door," 332, 332n113; objects of, resemble the One, 333. *See* point
"German Platonic-Aristotelian synthesis". *See* neo-Neo-Platonism
Gerson, Lloyd, 312n52, 313n55, 313n58
gerundives, 38
Gibbon, Edward, 54n41
Gifford, Mark, 287n104
Gill, Christopher, 18n56
"give [back] justice," 79
Glaucon, 5n16, 6, 26n79, 27, 32, 33-34n102, 35-39, 42, 44, 47, 54-65, 66-67, 82-83, 86, 101-5, 113-17, 121n20, 137n65, 139n71, 143, 146-48, 158, 172-73, 180-81, 189, 189n-30, 207, 215n94, 217, 217n108, 247n2, 261, 265n32, 285n102, 292n4, 293, 295-98, 328, 330, 348, 350-52, 357n158, 365-66, 379nn35-36, 380, 387; and Athens, 65; and Democracy, 348, 351; and three parts of the soul, 55n47, 56n50; as γενναῖος, 292n4; as hero of the *Republic*, 348, 351; as spirited, 55, 55-56nn45-50; as philosophic, 56n50 attitude towards war, 52, 55-56, 55n47, 56n51, 58n57, 64; birds and dogs of, 293, 298; beautiful and good, 65; boyhood home of, 61-62; chooses Justice, 351, 366. *See* "Glaucon's Choice"; decides to remain in the Piraeus, 64; embraces Platonism, 366; failure of, 247n2; ideal student, 65; imposes heroic labor on Socrates, 351. *See* "Glaucon's Challenge"; love life of, 47n24, 55; misunderstands *Republic*, 55n46; moral sensibilities of, 328; not Xenophon's Glaucon, 108-9; Plato's older brother, 47, 47n23; Plato's favorite brother, 56n50, 103, 180; real, 47, 59, 59n60; recognizes and chooses Justice, 6, 180-81; secret tears of, 65; skewers Socrates, 102; statues of, 103, 105; vs. Adeimantus, 62n72, 108, 207; war hero, 52, 65, 82
Glaucon's Challenge, 102-5, 109, 220, 281, 351; third part of, 103,
Glaucon's Choice, 38-39, 41-42, 103, 138, 253, 351
Glaucon's Defense of the Guardians, 172-73; Justice as unjust, 172
Glaucon's Description of the Just Man, 104, 217n108, 218n110, 280-81, 387
Glaucon's interruptions, 47-48, 55-64, 89-90, 94, 102-5, 172; Book I, 89-90, 94; challenges reader to interrupt, 94; Book II (speech), 90, 102-5; proleptic, 103; three parts of, 102-3; Book II (City of Pigs), 47-48, 64-65; Book V, 55-63, 82; provoked by Socrates in three ways, 56-57, 63; Book VII, 172
"Glaucon's misunderstanding," 295-97, 304
"Glaucon's statue," 218n110. *See* "Glaucon's Description"
Glaucus, 254-55, 255n11, 381, 381n39; contrast with Cave (subject vs. object), 255-56
Glucker, John, 9n28, 50n30
Go(ing) back down into the Cave, 12n38, 35, 37-38, 43, 79, 92, 100-1, 158-59, 161, 171-81, 184, 194, 200, 221n130, 222n141, 224, 239, 241, 243, 248, 365, 368; as idea?, 184, 204-36; attempts to prove just, 204-36; expression of Platonism, 368; in our native city, 200; maxim of, is Justice, 100, 204, 236; obligation to, for Guardians only, 224. *See* "Singularism"; paradigmatically Just action, 204; philosopher's choice to, 171;

refusal to do so as Injustice, 368; requires going up, 194; teaching may instantiate, 241; "to not wish to," 174; unwillingness to, 43; voluntary decision, 37, 38, 174-76
God, 3, 24-25, 105, 191n31, 194, 369, 371; "an unknown God," 187-88n26, 194; *causa sui*, 25; "does God exist?," 369; Judeo-Christian-Muslim, 194, refuted?, 371
gods and God, two laws relating to (Book II), 186-87, 191n31, 198, 249; identified with Ideas, 187, 187n25; third law (monotheism)?, 186, 187n26, 249
Goethe, Johann Wolfgang von, 370
Gonzalez, Francisco J., 14-15, 14n42, 15nn45-46, 16n51, 19n60, 34n103, 84n16, 121n18, 141n73, 274n63, 284n98, 345-46n134
Good, Idea of, xx, xxii, 1n2, 3, 4n15, 12, 12n38, 14n41, 15n44, 19, 24-27, 40-41, 43, 48, 64, 68, 68-69n82, 79, 86, 92, 96, 100, 126n28, 127-28, 129n34, 134, 144, 173, 179, 179-80n15, 183-86, 188-203, 218n112, 220n126, 223-24, 223n148, 224n-152, 232, 235, 235n221, 236, 252, 258, 260n16, 274-89 *passim*, 280n-74, 299, 302, 305-7, 313-17, 317n73, 319-20, 320n78, 323-25, 328, 332, 335-36, 339, 343, 345-47, 346n135, 350, 353-54, 353n149, 357, 357n-158, 367, 368, 370, 371, 379, 380, 395, 396n111, 398; absolving from diminution, 194; analogous to sun, 192-93; and Justice, 184, 195, 325; and Longer Way, 127-28; and Plato's lecture, 325. *See* Plato's Lecture on the Good; and "Plato's Theory of Ideas," 188, 190, 193, 198, 302; and mathematical objects, 129n34; and Reading Order, 339, 345-47; and sexual differences, 299; and "the Battle Hymn of the *Republic*," 345-47; and the One, 328; and the sun, 191-94; anti-immanent, 196; antithesis (logical) of the One (mathematical), 324; approached by Sun, Line, and Cave, 173; ἀρχή of Platonism, 305; as center of dialogue's solar system, 204-5; as center of dialogues as a whole, 205; as central core of Platonism, 185, 188, 193, 198, 206, 314; as heart of Platonism, 68-70, 185, 198; as most important Idea, 188; as only Idea?, 188; autonomy of, 313, 319; begetter of physical sun?, 194-95; beyond Being, 320n-78. *See* "beyond Being"; causal agency of, 41, 195, 317, 317n73, 323; χωρισμὸς-cleaving majesty of, 335; everything else equally not, 69; fully emancipated from objects of sense, 134, 184; generous grandeur of, 235; highest, 196; in *Sophist*, 396n111; introduced, 188-89; mentioned five times in *Republic*, 185; moral implications of, 211, 211n69; more sun-like, 191; no better or best without, 69, 299; not immanent, 195; not the One, 305-336 *passim*; orbited by Justice, 204-5; otherwordly, 196; priority of, 302, 323; "suntan" from, 258; tested with, 345; transcendent, 48, 69, 190, 196, 209, 325; un-hypothetical, 126n28, 134, 190, 200, 248, 277, 302, 314, 324-25; unitary, 205
Good, pluralizing the, 194, 205-9, 220n126, 221n131; and Kraut, 205-6, 220n126; and Vlastos, 220n126, 221n131; as "downwards ascent," 194; as variety of Forms, 194, 205-7, 207n52, 208n58, 209; "cosmos of forms," 209; needed to bridge gap between Harmonious Man and political activity in Cave, 205
Good, the, 93n46, 114n5, 173, 215n93; as philosophizing (Adkins and Bloom), 215n93
"good things are difficult," 103, 160
good will, preexisting, 96
Golden Age, 49, 349, 369n19
Gooch, Paul W., 281n77
Gorgias, 301n17
Gorgias, xx, xxii, 10, 21, 23, 36, 50n31, 91, 91n38, 93-96, 93n45, 95n51, 101, 101n59, 112n1, 115n8, 160n105, 179, 208n58, 236, 242n-236, 263, 267, 272, 274, 274n63,

278, 296, 300n15, 338, 378, 394-95; and *Phaedrus*, 112n1
Górnisiewicz, Arkadiusz, 399n123
Gosling, J. C. B., 234n215
Gould, John, 14n41, 120n18
Graeser, Andreas, 285n102, 316n67, 319n76
Graham, Daniel W., 309n39
Great Fleet, 51
Great War, 52, 52n33, 394. *See also* World War One; *and* World War Two
Greek Anthology, 263n27
Greene, William Chase, 44n13, 242n236, 249n4
Griffith, Miriam, 360n6
Griswold, Charles L. Jr., 17n53, 18n58, 20n64, 84n13, 275n64
Gropius, Walter, 363n14
Grosz, George, 363n14
Grote, George, 30-31n89
Grube, G. M. A., 310n43
Gruen, Erich S., 361nn8-9, 362-63, 362-63nn11-14
Guardians, 1, 15n44, 35, 78, 82, 85, 100, 102, 106-8, 138-41, 150, 171-81, 203-4, 212, 223n149, 223n151, 224, 227-28, 233, 235, 241, 243, 278, 280, 294, 334n118, 340, 343-44, 348, 351-52, 357, 365n16, 374; and "islands of the Blessed," 357; and Just philosophers, 140; as hunting pups 86-87nn22-23, 102, 140; as hypothesized, 1; as inconsistent, 228; both fierce and mild, 85; compelled to behold Idea of the Good, 203; compelled to go back down, 174-75, 233, 235, 241; education of, 82, 85, 106-7, 150; fictional, 177, 241; gentle to friends and terrible to foes, 85n19; imaginary, 39, 172, 176n8, 228; introduced by Adeimantus, 108; memories of, 44n14, 175, 175-76n8; primary education of, 186; self-sacrifice of (Foster), 212; self-sacrifice of (White), 223n151; soldiers, 85; speech to, 171-81, 235; true, 100, 168 ("Plato's chosen reader"), 193-94; voluntary Return of, 227
Gundert, Hermann, 325n91
Guthrie, W. K. C., xviin14, xixn20, 14n40, 25n76, 50, 50n29, 52n34, 58n55, 59n60, 74, 74n90, 76n104, 84n12, 88n25, 128n32, 136n60, 153n88, 156n95, 223n146, 259n12, 264n31, 268n41, 278n72, 395n106
Guthrie, Woody, 164n115
Gyges, 103, 103n62
gymnastics, 107n70. *See* music and gymnastics

Hackforth, R., 8, 50, 264n30, 267n40
Hades/Underworld, 37n2, 382n42, 383 383n43, 386n62, 390, 398n122; descent to the dead, 378, 383
Haft, Adele, 397, 397nn113-15, 397n118
Hall, Dale, 229-30, 229nn183-86, 230nn188-91
Halliwell, Stephen, 139n69, 377n32
Halper, Edward, 324n86
Hamann, Johann Georg, 369
Hamilton, Edith, 353n148
Hans, James S., 236n226
Hardie, R. P., 75n102
Hare, R. M., 129n34, 210n66, 312n52
Harman, John D., 230-31, 230n192
Harmonious Man, 3n14, 96, 141-59 168-69, 175n7, 176, 204-5, 204n42, 207, 216n100, 217-21, 226-27, 227n170, 250, 252, 258, 328, 331, 363-64; adultery and, 148; aerobic exercise and, 151; and Thrasymachus, 147, 149, 151, 159; and twenty-first century Americans, 151; as "California Consultant," 150-51, 151n85, 175n7, 176, 205, 207, 255, 217n106, 242, 366, 367; as Plato's version of just man, 148; as "One out of Many," 154-56; a unity, 142; "best craftsman of his own work," 151; defense of, 148, 151-52; depends on "soul as harmony," 142; "does his own thing," 151; does not go back down onto the Cave, 142-43, 145-46, 148-49, 162; doesn't do much, 143, 145-46, 147, 226; embezzling and, 147-48, 151; ethical or political shortcomings, 145-152, 168; harmonious unity is justice of,

142; has "gotten it together," 151; internal/external action/inaction, 146; "looks out for number one," 145, 151; mathematical or metaphysical shortcomings of, 145-46, 152-58, 168; methodological shortcomings of, 142, 145, 152, 156, 168. *See also* City and Man; music in, 142, 150; necessary and basanistic counterpart to the returning philosopher, 145; necessary moment in the reader's recognition of Justice, 228; not wicked, 148; origins of, 151; parents of, 148; permits victory of Thrasymachus, 159; piety of, 148; "p-justice" (Irwin) of, 227n170; politically quiescent, 145, 150-51, 158, 159; proleptic introduction to Being and Becoming, 158; requires to be benefited, 169; sacrilege and, 147; self-absorption of, 227; self-interest and, 151; theft and, 146-48
Harris, R. Baine, xvin10
Harte, Verity, 275, 275n66, 278n71, 379
Harward, J., 259-72 *passim*, 262n26, 264n30, 291
Havelock, Eric, 214n85
Heartfield, John, 363n14
Heath, T. H., 13n40, 308n35, 309n41, 310n45, 320n78, 333n114
Hector, 388
Hecuba, 391, 391n81
Heiberg, J. L., 308n35
Heidel, William A., xviin14
Heisenberg, Werner, 363n14, 369n19
Hegel, G. W. F., 14, 144-45, 150, 228, 228n178, 249n3, 278, 352n146, 369-70, 369-70n20-21, 395; *Absolute Wissen* and the Idea of the Good, 249n3; and Plato, 144-45, 228, 249n3, 395; as dialectical and triadic, 145, 395; author on, 352n- 146; dualism as "moment" for, 144, 197n38; sublates dualism with dialectical synthesis, 144; synthetic unity in, 145, 150
Hegelians, 180
Heideggerians, 196, 197n38
Heidegger, Martin, 93n42, 105, 197n38, 328n100, 330n106, 369-70
Heinaman, Robert, 234, 234n217
"He knows if you've been sleeping," 105
Helen, 356
Helicon, 273
hemlock, 101, 387
Heraclitus, 75, 76n104, 79, 153, 153n88, 316; influence on Plato, 75, 316; vs. Parmenides, 76n104
Hercules/Heracles, 355, 382n42, 385n52
hermeneutic isolationism, *see* isolationist
Hermann, Karl Friedrich, 91n35
[*Hermocrates*], xvn6
Herodotus, 103n62, 267n40
Herrmann, Fritz-Gregor, 1n2, 139n68, 185n23, 222n144
Hersh, Reuben, 136n59
Hesiod, 23, 105, 122, 122n21, 294, 294n5, 349, 349nn139-40, 355-57; and Thrasymachus, 356, 356n154; Homer's *first* rival, 294; *Works and Days*, 105, 122, 349-50, 349n140, 355-57, 356n154
Higham, T. F., 262n25
Higher Education (Book VII), 150, 154, 202, 241, 303, 305, 307, 325-6, 326n93, 330-36, 339-347, 348; and cosmology, 330; and nuptial number, 348; as child's play, 330, 333-34, 342, 348; as prelude to the prelude of "the song itself," 303, 330, 348; depends entirely on the mathematical One, 325-26, 330, 342; dialectical unity of mathematical sciences contained in, 324; emancipates soul from "pseudo-dyadic indistinctiveness," 330; five parts of, 334; furnishes three principles on which reconstruction of the Reading Order of Plato's Dialogues will be based, 339, 342. *See* Reconstruction Project; Hypotheses and Images in, 342; must be guided by synthetic investigation that connects the five, 342, 342n130; principal principle of, 326n93; purpose of, 330; five-year

program, 241; guide to what Plato taught in Academy, 339; sublime simplicity of, 305
Highet, Gilbert, 2n8
Hintze, Hannah, 389n70
Hipparchus, xxii, 20n66, 31n89
Hippias, 301n17, 371, 386, 386n65
Hippias Major, xxii, 20n66, 30n89, 84, 86n21, 87n24, 179, 386-87nn64-65, 394 ("That irritating neighbor of Socrates")
Hippias Minor, xxii, 30n89, 84, 87n24, 385-87, 386-87nn64-66, 394 ("know our Homer")
Hippocrates, 111
Hippolytus, 30n88
Hitler, Adolph, 356, 363n14, 395
Hobbs, Angela, 389n70
von Hofmansthal, Hugo, 363n14
Holway, Richard, 392, 392n87, 392n90
Homer, 23, 41, 57n53, 105-6, 149n83, 213n84, 352, 377-78, 381n39, 382-98, 396n112; as creator of basanistic pedagogy, 391; as preceptor of Hellas, 352; basanistic pedagogy and unitarianism, 390n72; chosen audience of, 390; most sublime repetition in, 391n81; not banished from City, 149n83, 377-78; on Achilles and Penelope, 391, 391n76; Plato's, 378n34, 386, 389-90
homo sapiens as mammal, 286
Horace, xiii, 106n69, 387u
Hornblower, Simon, 1n2, 264n30
Hösle, Vittoriano, 144n79
Hospital, The (Chayevsky), 89
Howland, Jacob, xvin8, 231n196, 385n52, 392n89, 392n96
Huard, Roger, 233n206
humanity, 292
Hume, David, 10
Hutchinson, D. S., xvn15, 34n103, 53n38, 67n81
Hyland, Drew A., 25n76
Hypotheses, 114-15n8. *See also* Divided Line, Second Part
Iamblichus, xvin10
"I am that I am," 25, 285
iconoclasm, 369n20
Idea, eternal, 50, 302
Idea of the Good : un-hypothetical :: mathematical objects : hypothetical, 307
"Idea," word uses (21), 185-203, 185n23; appearances distributed by books, 185; appear in triads, 186, 188, 199, 199n39; Book II (Idea of gods or God), 186-87, 198; Book II singleton introduces the Hypothesis on which the Image of the Shorter Way depends, 198; Books II, VI, and VIII (the structural singletons), 186, 193, 198, 199-200; Books V and VI (introduction of the Idea of the Good), 188-89, 198-99; Book VI (the Theory of Ideas), 190-94, 198, 199, 337; Book VII (the Idea of the Good), 194-98, 199; Book VIII singleton, 199-200; Book IX (the Beast-Lion-Man Image), 199n39, 201-2; Book X (the Idea of Bed), 199n39, 201-3
Idea of the Good. *See* Good, Idea of
Ideal Line, 309. *See* "Indivisible Lines"
Ideal Numbers, 131, 131n39, 144n79, 305-6n26, 306, 306n28, 318n75; term less than ideal, 306n26. *See* "Incomparable Numbers"
Ideas, Platonic, 19, 180, 203; not Hypothesized Images of visible things, 203. *See* "Plato's Theory of Ideas"
"idiot" and "idiotic," etymology of, 149, 149n84, 364, 384, 389-90
Iliad, 57n53
images (visible of intelligible) of Books VI and VII, 158, 158n100, 173; why not Images, 158n100
Images, use of. *See* Divided Line, Second Part
"imitationist" readings of the Return, 233-34, 234n214, 235, 235nn219-20
immanence of God, 369n20
immanence of the Idea, 368-69
Immortality of the Soul, 19, 254, 389
"Incomparable Numbers," 306-7, 306n28, 311, 314-24, 322, 324n86, 330; and "Indivisible Lines," 322-23, 330; arise in polemical context, 322; as consequence of hypothesis, 318, 321; as deliberately self-con-

tradictory, 306n28, 318, 322; as dialectical objection brought against the One as absolute ἀρχή, 318, 322-23; as easily refutable, 318, 322; as *modus tollens* on the One as absolute ἀρχή, 321; generated by One and the Indefinite Dyad, 317n72, 323, 324n86; not found in Plato, 322. *See* "Complex, the"; *and* Plato's Numbers, Problem of

inconsistency, deliberate, dialectical, and pedagogical, 19. *See* self-contradiction, deliberate

Indefinite Dyad, 12, 76, 268, 307, 314-324, 314n64, 317n72, 323, 324n86, 326-29, 331n109, 332; and phenomenology of νόησις, 327; and Tübingen School, 327; archeological, 326; as δύο κεχωρισμένα (524c1), 327; as "pseudo-dyadic indistinct tiveness," 327-30; as second Platonic principle in Aristotle's account of Plato, 326-28; as "the great and the small," 317n72, 319, 319n77, 327, 327nn97-98; demoting, 328; identified with matter, 317n72, 324n86; indefinite plurality, 92, 324n86; infects sense-based epistemology, 328; in *Philebus*, 325n90, 326n94, 327n97; in *Republic* IV, 326n94, 327-29; in *Republic* VII, 326-27; introduces/gives way to the mathematical One, 326, 327; negative role of, 327, 332; not ἀρχή in *Republic* VII, 326; not "definite dyad," 327; Ross on, 321n80

"Indivisible Lines," 136n60, 137n62, 154n88, 306, 306n28, 307-11, 313, 318, 322, 325, 330; and "Incomparable Numbers," 322-23, 330; and "indivisible magnitudes," 318n74; arise in polemical context, 309, 322; Aristotle on, 309. *See* Aristotle; as deliberately self-contradictory, 136n-60, 306n28, 308-11, 322-23; as dialectical objection to the (un-hypothetical) point, 310-11, 310n44, 310n47, 313, 318, 323. *See* point, as "geometrical fiction"; as joke, 308, 325; easily refutable, 309, 318, 322; emphasizes part-less purity of point *qua* One, 308; not found in Plato, 309, 322

"Indivisible Lines" : denying the point is "a geometrical fiction" :: "Incomparable Numbers" : affirming that the One is a metaphysical principle, 307, 315, 323

Infinitesimal Calculus, 136, 136n60, 322, 322n85

injustice, 21, 71, 89; artist, craftsman, or technician of, 89, 104; more shameful to inflict than to suffer (*Gorgias*), 21, 94, 263, 275

Injustice and Unjust philosophers, 240, 258, 368, 377, 389

"inside and outside the text," 7-8

"Intellectual History of the Return, *Leitmotiv* of" (sc. Plato's critics identify a real problem but fail to realize Plato created it deliberately; Plato's defenders reach correct conclusion for the wrong reason), 222n141, 227-28 ("the same peculiar dialectic")

Intermediates in Plato, 43n11, 113n5, 129nn35-36, 129-37, 130nn37-38, 277, 305-25 *passim*, 306-7n29, 307, 314, 317, 318, 319-20, 319n76, 321n80; and Forms as numbers, 320; Anglophone assault on, 321n80; in consistent with "the Complex," 317; not Ideas, 277; Ross on, 321n80; separable *qua* intelligibles but not *qua* Ideas, 318. *See also* Plato's Numbers, Problem of

"intuitionism" (Prichard), 210, 210n67, 236

Inwood, Brad, 9n24, 9n28

Ion, 236

Ion, xxii, 23, 105, 105n67, 179, 236, 339, 378, 385-87, 386-87nn64-65, 394 ("magic of divine inspiration")

Iran, 49

Iron Age, 50, 122n21, 349, 355-56

Irwin, Terence, 16, 21n67, 26n78, 85n-18, 180n16, 218n112, 226-28, 226-27nn167-74, 228n177, 229n182,

231n194, 232n201, 233n208, 236n224
Islam, 25
Islands of the Blessed, 109n77, 357, 357n158, 384, 384n50
Isocrates, 35n105, 54, 54nn41-42
isolationist (approach to dialogues), 16, 29, 30-31, 85, 197
"isomorphism (elegant)" between City and Man, 142, 201, 206, 220, 220n128, 253, 367
Israel, 195
Isthmian Games (Plato wrestled at), 67, 87
It's a Wonderful Life, 286-87
"I went down," 3, 28, 35, 79, 144, 388

Jackson, Henry, 114n7, 129n34, 319n76, 321n80
Jaeger, Werner, 315n65, 321n82, 325n90
Janssens, David, 398n123
Jehovah's Witnesses, 105
Jesus Christ, 105, 188n26, 218, 281-83, 282n83, 282n86, 283n91, 284, 285, 287, 369, 369n20, 374; as Platonist?, 283; "descended into a perfectly recognizable Cave," 281; did not go *back* down, 369; impaled on a torture stake, 105, 218, 281n77; proof of Plato's prior discovery of Justice, 284
Joannes Philoponus, 332n113
"jocks and egg-heads," 107
Jowett, Benjamin, 13n40, 24, 49-50, 223n146; and intellectual history, 223n146
Joyal, Mark, 237n229
Joyce, Michael, 384n49
Judaea, 285
Judaism, 25, 194
Judeo-Christian-Muslim God, 194, 276. *See also* God; belief in refuted?
Judeo-Christian West, 285
"jumps right out of the text," 86, 100, 232, 394. *See* "breaking the frame"
just acts, 145
justice, 5-6, 14, 27, 37, 44, 113-15, 142, 153, 171, 204-9, 218, 224, 235, 245, 259, 386, 389; along the Shorter Way, 113, 142-43; cannot motivate Return, 218; circularity of discovery, 113, 115-17, 133, 141; depends on a "one" that is many, 153; distinguished from Justice, 5, 6, 44, 145, 153, 171; does not require sacrifice, 259; exemplified by Er's Odysseus, 386, 389; hunting imagery in search of, 44-45, 45n15; Hypothesis-based Image of, 143; in the City, 44, 113, 245; in the soul, 205. *See* Harmonious Man; praised only with regard to happiness (Prichard), 218; present from the start (one man/one job), 113, 142; "psychic" or "psychological" (Vlastos and Irwin), 219n120, 220, 226, 226-27nn169-70, 233, 235; scarcely fulfils the demands of "vulgar justice" (Sachs), 218; "social" (Vlastos), 219n120, 220-21; to the advantage only of the one who practices it (Adkins), 218; three-falls victory of, 142, 253
Justice, 2-8, 12-13, 15, 27, 37-38, 40-42, 44-45, 48, 50-51, 53, 79, 89, 92, 96-97, 100, 108, 114, 136, 138, 140-41, 143-44, 153, 158-59, 162-63, 167-68, 171-85, 189n30, 194-95, 195n34, 218n113, 228, 235n221, 235-36, 239, 242-43, 245-50, 258-59, 263, 265, 268, 274, 277, 279, 283-89, 294, 299, 304, 348, 350-52, 355-58, 360, 365, 368-72, 373, 376, 378, 386, 388, 390; "action freely chosen," 243; adamantine commitment to, 259; advantage of the stronger *and* the ruled, 101, 159, 236; and Achilles, 386, 388; and City, 143-44; and Democracy, 351-52; and self-interest, 222; and women, 286, 299; as action and choice, 181, 248; as altruism, 100, 144; as "another's good," 236; as εἶδος, 248. *See* Justice, Idea/Form of; as great exception in Plato's *Republic* (Foster), 218; as human virtue, 289; as idealism, 144; as liberal spirit of a freeman, 100; as *mandatum novum*, 100; as maxim of going back down into the Cave, 100, 204, 236,

287; as moral excellence, 284; as "obligatory choice," 235n221; as "offspring of the Good," 27, 184, 193-95, 235n221, 277, 371; as *noblesse oblige*, 95; as philosopher's free decision to go back down into the Cave, 245, 358; as "realm-connecting synthesis," 195; as unwritten doctrine of the Seventh Letter, 274; as "upwards descent," 194; as "voluntary duty," 352; basanistically negated on Shorter Way, 145, 158, 218; basis in Plato's ontology, 181, 368; between the Idea of the Good and the Cave, 184, 368, 390; can only be practiced in a body, 368, 372; choice for must be free, 174, 181; choosing, 6, 174; compulsion to practice depends on its intrinsic moral excellence, 236; consequences of (ugly), 104-5; conspicuous by its absence, 92, 145; dangers confronted by philosopher who practices, 356-57; denied three times in Book VI, 163; depends on freedom, 175; depends on philosophy, 92, 92n40; depends on Platonism, 368; depends on reader, 171-72; dialogue's principal concern, 37, 204; discovered in an unjust place, 53, 54; freely chosen, 79, 95, 97, 100, 175, 181; Harmonious Man a necessary moment in the reader's discovery of, 228; hidden revelation of, 175; human expression of the Good, 235n221; intrinsic excellence of, 236; joins Plato the Teacher to Plato the Philosopher, 304; like dialectic, 144; moral grandeur of, 236; "next step freely taken," 243; no Academy or *Republic* without Plato's practice of, 184, 304; no pre-experiential awareness of Being without Plato's, 185; no teacher of the Good or the Cave without, 184; only practicable in the context of others, 144; premonition of, 89; present from the start (κατέβην), 45, 113, 204; proof-texts for, 171-81, 376-77; requires (1) philosopher, (2) others, (3), Idea of the Good, 144; reached by reading that passes through negativity of Annas en route to Irwin's sunny conclusions, 228; recognition of, requires a non-singularist reading, 180-81; rewards and consequences of, 5, 78, 96, 365, 378; sun-like, 195, 195n34; teaching may instantiate, 241; tested in Book VIII, 357-58; tested in Book IX, 365-67; tested in Book X, 388-90; this world as arena of, 79, 368-69; three instantiations of, (active political life, life of Socrates, life of Plato the Teacher), 242; three moments of, 367; torch of, 42; Thrasymachus, defeated by, 100-1, 236; why choice-worthy, 46; "win-win" (not counting Thrasymachus), 101, 103, 158-59

Justice and justice, 180-81n17, 204-36 *passim*, 250, 246n1, 278; difficulty of proving the paradigmatically Just action (going back down into the Cave) just, 204-5, 204n42; "gap" between, 221n130. *See* "Gap"; only if justice is a harmonious cosmos of forms can Return be shown to be just, 209; planetary metaphor, 204-5; methodology and discovery in Books IV and VII, 180-81n17, 246n1; "Plato's inconsistency" alleged. *See* "Plato's error"; Plato's pedagogy requires student to discover that Justice is not justice, 218-19; problem created by Plato deliberately, hence value of Sachs, 218; Shorter Way inadequate for Justifying Justice, 218; textual evidence for Justice noted by Mabbott, 218n113; Justice : Copernicanism :: justice : Ptolemaic epicycles, 204-5; Justice : One :: justice : "One out of Many," 153; justice, form of, 119

Justice, Idea/Form of, xxii, 3, 6, 42-44, 43n11, 90, 100, 184-86, 245-50, 253-54 274, 277-89 *passim*, 302, 345, 368, 372, 377, 380, 390, 395; both ethical and ontological, 368; empirical basis of, 287; matrix of other Ideas, 287. *See* virtue(s), "tran-

scendental deduction" of; sends the soul back down, 279, 395. *See* Beauty, Idea of; timeless, unchanging, and universal, 285; universally recognized as moral excellence by simple people everywhere, 284; written in the souls of Plato's readers, 285
"justice, everyday," "vulgar," or "what we call," 204n42, 217-18, 218n112, 219, 219n117, 219n119, 227n169 ("c-justice" of Irwin), 233, 233n208, 298
"justification of injustice" (Strauss on *Republic*), 11n34, 216, 229; and Bloom, 229n185
Justinian, 54n41
Justin Martyr, 281-82, 282nn83-84
just life, the (Strauss), as "the retired life par excellence, the life of the philosopher," 216n98
Just man, 104
just man happier than tyrant, 142. *See* seven-hundred twenty-nine times
just tuning and "the well-tempered clavichord," 334-35n119

Kafka, Franz, 105
Kahn, Charles H., xixn21, xxn23, 18, 18n58, 90, 90-91nn32-35, 96, 97n57, 106n68, 114-15n8, 139n70, 268n42, 300n15
Kalkavage, Peter, xxin29, 37n2, 75n103
Kantianism, 24, 210, 211n68, 210n67, 211n70, 213n84, 214nn86-87; Plato and, 210n67
Kant, Immanuel, 10, 24, 96n54, 210, 211n67, 211n79, 219, 307-8n32, 369; as secret Platonist, 213n79; why five and seven?, 307-8n32
Karasmanis, Vassilis, 130n38
καταβατέον ("it is necessary to go back down"). *See Index verborum*; temporal and modal elements of, 174
κατέβην ("I went down"), *see Index verborum*
Key Passage (434d1-435d4), first of three (along with Divided Line and the Allegory of the Cave), 245-46, 246n1, 248, 254, 258, 278, 303n22, 334n119; located between discovery justice in the City and the search for justice in the Man, 4, 118n13, 245; returning to, 258, 303n22
Key Passage, Part I: The Firesticks (434d1-435a4), 139n71, 181n17, 245-250, 252-54, 256, 258-60, 259n12, 267-68, 269n47, 278-79; and Divided Line, 248; and Seventh Letter. *See* Seventh Letter; and unitary soul, 256; as moment of extreme negativity, 278; for whom they blaze, 252-53, 256; dialectical antithesis implicit in, 278; leads to synthetic epiphany, 278; methodological import of, 250; philosophy and politics, conflict between, 253; scholarly attention to, 247n2; third method of, 248-50; unlocks the door to Idea of Justice, 250, 278
Key Passage, Part II: Inadequate Methods and the Longer Way (435c9-d4), 112n4, 114n6, 116n10, 118-19, 118n13, 123-24, 125n27, 126; first mention of Longer Way, 118, 246; first use of "method," 116n10; highly proleptic, 118; "method" used in sense [III], 118n13. *See also* method; unlocks structure of *Republic*, 118
Keyt, David, 185n23, 226n166, 234n215
King, Martin Luther, Jr., 287, 367
King, Peter, 282-83nn89-91, 360n6
Kipling, Rudyard, 366
Kirwan, Christopher, 218n110
Klagge, James C., xxn25, 284n99
Klein, Jacob, 11n34, 216, 216n100, 230n191, 270n51, 307n30, 309-10n42, 332, 393n98
Klimt, Gustav, 363n14
Klonoski, Richard J., 37n2, 388n68
Kluft (G. "cleft"), 49, 196, 197, 207, 276, 277, 287-89, 334n116, 368; as primordial "crisis" in Plato's thought, 276; basis for "the separation of Forms" (Aristotle), 276
knowledge and opinion, 86n21
knowledge of ignorance, 9
Knox, Bernard, 386n60
Knox, Ronald, 391n80

Knox, T. M., 228n178
Konstan, David, 219n115
Krämer, Hans Joachim, 11, 11n33, 12n36, 24n75, 29n81, 99n58, 330n106, 346n135; Plato's secret teaching revealed by, 346n135
Kramer, Scott, 392n86
Kraut, Richard, xxi, 132n47, 186n24, 204-9, 204nn41-42, 205n44, 206nn45-46, 206-7nn49-51, 207n53, 208n58, 220n126, 221-22, 221-22nn133-41, 224, 225n161, 233-34
Kremer, Mark, 29n83, 31n90, 31n93
Kung, Joan, 155n91

Laches, xviiin18, xxii, 58n57, 81, 101, 101n59, 179, 339, 394 ("displayed at Delium")
Lachtermann, David, 188n27, 324n87, 328n100
Laertes, 386n63, 391-92, 397
Lamm, Julia, 156n96, 239n232
Lampert, Laurence, xviiin18, 12n35, 52n34, 53n39, 82n10, 88n25, 187n25, 231n197, 387n65
Lane, Melissa, 1n2, 264n30
Lang, Fritz, 363n14
Lastheneia of Mantinea, 296n6
Laws, xvi, xxii, 6, 6n21, 7n22, 17, 22, 30n89, 84, 84-85nn16-17, 102, 112n3, 154n89, 156, 156n96, 162, 254, 273n59, 304n23, 315n65, 333n114, 338, 366, 393n98, 397. *See also* Athenian Stranger
"leaping spark," 7, 10, 99, 267-68
Lear, Jonathan, 311-12nn49-50, 312n53
Lee, E. N., 120n16, 221n133, 247n2
Leibniz, G. W., xiii, 372
Lennox, James G., 312n53
Leontius, son of Aglaion, 256
Letters, 20n66, 112n3, 259-75; and epistolary fraud, 264; and *Republic*, 265, 273. *See also* Seventh Letter; and "Syracusan short-cut," 268, 261, 263-65, 267 (reductio ad absurdum on); and Third Wave of Paradox, 260-61, 263-64, 267, 273; arrangement of, 264; as historical documents, 265-66, 268; as integrated work of art, 265-66, 270, 273; authenticity of, 264-65, 270; education must precede political action in, 274; emphasize the Academy's role, 267; Justice in, 263, 265, 268; must be read dialectically, 268; pedagogical purpose of, 267, 273; place in the Reading Order (between *Republic* VI and VII), 264-65, 273-74; ring-composition in, 270, 270n52; rule of law in, 262-63, 273; (self-) presentation of Plato in, 266-67; First, 266-67, 267n40, 270; Second, 270, 272, Third, 270, 274; Fourth, 270; Fifth, 270; Sixth, 270; Seventh, as pivot, 270. *See* Seventh Letter; Eighth, 266n26, 270, 271, 272, 273n59; Ninth, 269, 270; Tenth, 269n49, 270, 272n57; Eleventh, 270, 274; Twelfth, 270; Thirteenth, 266, 266n38, 270, 272-73
"Let us do well!" (last words of *Republic*), 372-74; as "primordial Platonic pun," 372
Lévy, Carlos, 396n108
Lévystone, David, 388n68
liberality, 167n121
Liddell, H. G., xiiin1, 13, 27, 50, 111, 112nn2-3
"Light!, Let there be," 195, 203
line (geometrical), 322, 333, 333n114; as flux of a point, 333n114; as "ideal line" (indivisible), 322; as infinitely divisible, 333; one-dimensional, 333
"Litai" (*Iliad* 9), 386
literalism, 93, 191, 193
Lloyd, G. E. R., 269, 269nn46-47, 272n58, 336n121
Lodge, Robert Clendon, 92-93n42
Logical Positivists, 258
"logographic necessity" (*Phaedrus*), 341n129
Lombardi, Vince, 88
Long, A. A., 9n27, 22n71
Longer Way, 4-5, 8, 12, 12n35, 14n41, 15, 27, 44-45, 96, 100, 107, 109, 116n10, 118, 119n14, 127-28, 137, 140, 143-44, 150, 157-58n100, 158-59, 180, 181n17, 182, 200, 205, 207,

245-49, 289, 303n22, 343, 348, 367, 380n38, 389-90, 399; and Idea of the Good, 27, 343; and Justice, 137, 390; and Shorter Way, 5 (good reading must distinguish), 111, 113, 116n10, 118, 159, 180-81n17, 200, 207 (chasm dividing), 245, 246n1, 343, 389; collapsing dualities of, 367-68; triadic and dialectical, 144
Long Walls, 51, 58, 59n58, 279n73
"looking out for number one," 89, 389
Lovejoy, A. O., 48n25
Lowe-Porter, H. T., 52n33
Löwith, Karl, 215n95
Lucian, 105n65
Lucretius, 363n14
Luther, Martin, 367, 374
Lutoslavski, Wincenty, 90
Lyceum, xix
Lysias, 23, 54
Lysis, xviii
Lysis, xviii, xix, xxii, 17, 86n21, 179, 338, 394

Mabbott, J. D., 211-13, 211-12nn72-3, 218n113; recognized Justice, 212, 218n113
MacAdam, Jim, 210n62
Mackie, John, 210n66
Macrobius, 35n104
MacQueen, Bruce, 355n152
Mahayana Buddhism, 285
Mahler, Gustav, 363n14
Mahoney, Thomas A., 226n166, 232n204, 233n213, 234n215
maieutic pedagogy, 286, 297n9
Maimonides, 10n29
Malament, D. B., 129n34
mandragora, 169, 394
Manheim, Ralph, 197n38
"man in the know, every," 92-94, 98, 101-2, 167, 177, 377, 381, 389
Man, justice in the, 4, 119, 122-25, 158, 389. *See also* Harmonious Man
"manliness and virtue," 242, 252
Mann, Thomas, 52n33
Mansfeld, Jaap, xvin12, 9n24, 9n28
Mantinea, 296n6, 297n10
Mara, Gerald M., 231n195, 350n143
Marathon, 49, 51
Marciano, M. Laura Gemelli, 72n86
materialism and materialists, materialism, 79; 180, 368; and cosmology, 73
mathematical sciences, dialectical unity of, 324; as prelude, 324, 324n87
"mathematicals," 130, 314. *See* mathematics, objects of
mathematics, 43n11, 104, 134-37, 231n195, 335; as crutch, 134; humble monad of, 335. *See* One (mathematical); intermediate place in Platonic pedagogy, 137; necessary but insufficient means to reality, 136; prolegomenon to philosophy, 135
mathematics, objects of, 116-17, 130-37, 184, 287n106, 305-39 *passim*; Aristotle on, 311-12, 320; between the sensible objects of the Third and the *exclusively* intelligible objects of the First Part of the Divided Line, 132-33, 320; by definition divisible if resting on monad and point, 323; dialectical objections brought against making them un-hypothetical, 323; existential status of, 135-37, 313, 320; fictional?, 137, 137n62, 311n-49, 313nn57-58. *See* point; geometrical and arithmetical, 116-17, 135, 320, 323; hypothetical, 116, 307, 313n58, 320; : Ideas :: must be hypothesized : only things that truly exist, 320; identical to each other, 307n29, 311, 319-20; intelligible, 133, 313, 320; intelligible Images of visible objects, 133, 334; intermediate status of, 130, 132-33, 319-20. *See* Intermediates; One as ἀρχή of, 305; One as hypothetical basis of, 130, 132; inseparable from the method that creates them, 132, 311; rest on unproven existential Hypotheses, 137; : un-hypothetical Good :: shadows : physical objects, 314, 314n60
Matthew, 105
Maundy Thursday, 100
Maya, 285
May, James M., 2n6
maxim of an action, Justice as, 100, 204, 236, 287

McClain, Ernest, 334n117, 334n119
McLeod, Ian, 398n121
McNeill, David, 14n41
McPherran, Mark L., xixn22, 270n52
Mediævalism, 369n20
Meier, Heinrich and Wiebke, 11n34
Megara, 52, 52n35, 58n57
Melissus, 74, 75n101
Melos, 49, 49n28, 58, 58nn54-55, 61, 61n69, 63, 65; nuking, 49
Menexenus, xviii, 3
Menexenus, xviii, xix, xxii, 23n74, 179, 297n11, 394 ("quiz on chronology")
Meno, xxii, 19n62, 21-22, 101, 179, 101n59, 114-15n8, 137, 160n105, 297n9, 299-300, 300n15, 301n16, 330n105, 338-39, 395
Merlan, Philip, 329n104
Metcalf, Robert, 388n68, 394n101
method, 111-141; coined by Plato, 111, 115n9; defined in LSJ ([I] and [2]), 112, 116n10, 118n13, 119, 126n28, 342n130; dialectical, 112, 115n9, 116n10, 126n28; etymology suggests "pursuit," 111, 112n2; first encountered in *Republic* IV, 111n1, 118-19; importance of sense [2], 112, 118; instances in *corpus* (26), 112n3, 116n10; instances in *Republic* (8), 112, 112n4, 126n29; third meaning; *see* "methods"
methodology, 8, 14-15, 111-17, 122, 129, 132, 136, 140, 152, 154, 158n100, 182, 201-3, 235, 245, 250, 343, 370; explains difference between Longer and Shorter Ways, 113; Hippocrates : method :: Plato : methodology, 111; invented by Plato, 111-12
"methods" ([III]), 112, 116n10, 118-19, 118n13, 125, 125-26n27, 126n29, 137, 141, 182, 182n19; applies to Shorter Way, 119
Millay, Edna St. Vincent, 334
Miller, Fred D., 185n23, 226n166, 234n215
Miller, Mitchell, 7n22, 15, 15n43, 39n5, 46n21, 231-33, 231-32nn198-203, 233n205, 235, 247n2, 251n8, 287n105
Mills, Sophie, 393n100
Milton, John, 7n22, 171n1, 242n236
Minos, xxii, 20n66, 31n89
Minucius Felix, 25n77
Mishima, Teruo, 30n84
misogyny, 304n23, 358n159
"missing thirds," 187n26, 248-49; third law of theologizing, 187n26, 249; third motive for descent to Piraeus, 248-49; third musical mode, 187n26, 243, 243n237, 249; Third Noble Lie, 187n26, 249, 374; third Way, 187n-26, 245, 248, 249
Mittelstrass, Jürgen, 20n64
modern science, 136
Mohr, Richard D., 310n42, 396n109
Momus, 93
monism and monists, 73, 79, 180, 368; mystics and materialists as, 368
monochord, 334
Monoson, S. Sara, 350n142
monotheism in Plato, 186, 187-88n26
monotheism, 24,
Monro, David B., 383n45
Montiglio, Silvia, 382n42, 392n94
Moore, Christopher, 30n85
Moors, Kent, 46n20, 47n23, 135-36, 136n 57, 279n73, 341n129
Morgan, Andrew S., 223n145
Morgan, Kathryn A., 396n109
Morris, C. R., 211nn69-70
Morrison, Donald R., 9n27, 26n78, 234n216
Morrison, J. S., 133n49
Morrow, Glenn, 264n30, 266n38
Moses, 281n82, 282n84, 285, 287, 369
Most, Glenn W., 384n48, 389n72
motherhood, 97, 286, 296, 299
Mother Theresa, 374
Mount Horeb, 285
Mourelatos, Alexander P. D., 22n71, 72n85, 73, 73n85, 120n16, 153-54n88, 221n133, 247n2, 334n116
Mueller, Ian, 132n47, 305n25, 325n88
Mulroy, David, 397n117
multiplex (many-leveled), Platonic dialogues as, 4, 8, 162
Murphy, N. R., 229n182
Murray, Gilbert, 262n25
Muses, 106, 107n70

music, 107n71, 334, 340, 342, 348
music and gymnastics, 106-7, 106-7nn68-71; skill in defined Athenians, 106
music of the spheres, 2, 243n237, 330, 334; and Higher Education, 330, 334; as "one out of many," 330
Musil, Robert, 363n14
mystics and mysticism, 73, 178, 368
Myth of Er, 372-76, 378, 382n42, 383, 386, 388, 390, 399; and chance, 373, 374n27; and the choice of lives, 373, 388; and the City, 373-74; and the Harmonious Man, 374; as test, 386; up and down reversed in, 374, 376
Mytilene (Debate), 58, 58n55, 61n69, 63

Nagy, Gregory, 384n47, 384n50, 385n55, 385n59, 386n61
Nails, Debra, xvin9, 17n54, 52n34, 58n55, 66n78, 84n14
Napoleon, 50
nationalism, 291
nature, and art, 251; and convention, 297. *See also* "by nature"
Neanthes, 67, 68
"negative moment," 235. *See also* "Plato's error"
Nehamas, Alexander, 203n40
neo-Neo-Platonism, 198
Neo-Platonism, xvin10, xvii-viii, 196, 234n215, 305, 332n113, 368, 374; Christian, 332n113; Idea, not the philosopher, goes down in, 305, 368, 398; identification of the Good and the One as a boundary dividing Platonism from, 305; rear-guard action against Christianity?, 368
Neo-Platonists, xvi, xvii, 6, 10, 280n75
Neo-Pythagoreans, 306n27
Nestor, 387n65
Neu, Jerome, 120n16, 121n19, 122n22, 128n33, 247n2
"Neutralism" (Rudebusch), 222, 224, 225n159, 232n201
New Academy, 282
Niceratus, 58, 58n57, 60, 160n107
Nichols, Mary P., 231, 231n195, 234n216, 250n6
Nicias, 58, 58n57, 60-61, 63, 160, 160n107, 348
Nicol, A. T., 136n60, 137n62, 154n88
Nietzsche, Friedrich Wilhelm, 31n90, 50, 50n31, 71, 73, 82n10, 87, 163n-112, 196n36, 197n38, 213-14, 214n-85, 215n95, 273n60, 276, 368-70, 374, 375n28; Christianity as vulgar Platonism, 368, 374; dualism as body-hating, 197n38; honest enough to hate Platonism, 73, 276, 370
Nightingale, Andrea Wilson, 97n56, 156n93, 224n155, 250n6
Nigidius, 396n108
nihilism and nihilists, 71, 180, 230; in Socratic garb, 230
Nirvana, 285
Noble Lie(s), 164, 291-94, 349; and the Ship, 164, 292n4; and three Waves of Paradox, 292; as "genetic fiction," 164n114, 293, 349; as lie, 291, 349; First, 291-92, 291n1, 305. *See* Waves of Paradox, Second; Second, 291, 291n2, 294, 304, 349; *see* Waves of Paradox, First; Second derived from Hesiod, 349; two, in consistent with each other, 291n2; "what is true if these are false?", 291, 293; what polity lacks?, 164; *see also* Third Noble Lie; *and* Genetic Fiction
noblesse oblige, 95, 97, 364; and True Ruler, 97
non-contradiction, principle or law of, 117, 117n12, 120, 124-25, 140, 142, 150, 163, 202, 254, 310n46, 371; and the Self, 371; basis for City/Man analogy, 124, 142. *See also* City and Man; first Hypothesis identified as such, 163; hypothesized in accordance with Second Part of Divided Line, 117, 124-25; if it is shown to be false, invalidates all that rests on it, 125; subject to dialectical objections, 125; used to validate tripartite soul and resulting justice in Man, 124, 142, 202, 254

non-singularist reading, 229-30, 231n194. *See* "Singularism"
Novotný, Franciscus, 264n30
"nuke Melos," 49
number, 304-336 *passim*; Palamedes as inventor of, 393n97. *See* Plato's Numbers, Problems of; as number of monads, 326; as divisible, 326n93; can be added, 318
"Number One," 145. *See* "One out of Many"
Nuptial Number, 200, 334, 334-35nn118-19, 348
Nussbaum, Martha C., 298n12

obligation (to return), 38, 176-78, 212n75, 218, 225, 236, 258; and Prichard's "intuitionism," 210; and White's "singularism," 224; self-imposed, 218
Odysseus, 41, 149n83, 231n194, 378, 382-98; and justice, 389; as Achilles' rival, 384-87, 397; as "best of the Achaeans," 386; as liar, 384, 384n-48, 384n51, 386, 386n60, 392n94; as "man in the know," 389; as (Straussian) hero, 382n42, 391, 392n89; character of, 385-86; choice of (in Myth of Er), 382n42, 389, 389n70; "Cretan Tales" of, 397; enemy of Ajax, 390, 392, 392n94; enemy of Palamedes, 392-93, 392n94; Er's, 382n42, 387-89, 396n112; in Book III, 386n63; Ithacan tales of, 384n48, 397; Phaeacian tale of, 378, 383, 385, 384n48, 385, 386n62, 397; Plato's, 382n42; lies about Achilles, 384-85
Odyssey, 378, 390-91; comes home to the *Iliad*, 390
Oedipus, 356
Oedipal Complex, 72n84
"offspring of the Good," 26-27, 26n79, 184, 190-94, 1901n31, 235, 235n-221, 277, 337
oligarchy and "oligarchic man," 340, 353-55,
O'Meara, Dominic J., 7n22
omega, 76, 255n11
one man/one job, 44-45, 85n19, 113, 119, 139, 140n72, 142, 149, 154, 182, 187n26, 219, 228n180, 234n-216, 250-52, 250n6, 258, 278; and philosopher-king, 250-51, 250n6, 258; justice as, 44, 182; leads to circular process, 113, 182; opposite of Justice, 250, 278
One and the Many, Problem of the, 76, 152-58, 152n86, 153nn87-88, 157nn97-98, 326, 329, 329n103, 330n105, 331-32nn109-10, 331-33, 335; and "all things are one," 329; and *Drang nach Einheit*, 76, 329; arises from *Drang nach Einheit*, 333; Aristotle's restoration of, 329n103; composite substances and, 329; frontline of interpretive battle in post-*Republic* dialogues, 329; Heraclitus and, 153; origins in physics, 76, 329; proleptic appearance of, 153n87; Plato's solution, 76, 152n86, 329, 329n103, 331-33, 335; *see* One (mathematical)
[1.a]. *See* Third Wave of Paradox
[1.b]. *See* Third Wave of Paradox
one-half, 326n93
"One is not a number," 152, 307n30, 326, 335
One (mathematical); also "mathematical unit" and "monad," 116n11, 130-37, 152-58, 152n86, 201-3, 276-77, 305-336 *passim*, 305n26, 307n29, 396n111; "absolute, multiplicity-excluding unity of the true Monad," 154; accounts for priority of arithmetic in Higher Education, 307, 314; and Cartesian number-line, 335; and *Parmenides*, 333, 333n115; and point as "geometrical fiction," 311-12; and "pseudo-dyadic indistincttiveness," 327-31; antithetical to "One out of Many," 154; ἀρχή of mathematical objects, 305, 323, 334; as basis of arithmetic, 130, 276, 323, 334; as basis of Becoming and the Good conceived as unities, 276; as basis of geometry, 276, 326; as basis of "mathematics," 130, 132, 323, 326, 335; as Hypothesis on which

mathematics depends, 132, 154, 201, 323, 325, 329; as Hypothesis on which hypostatization depends, 132, 202. *See also* "Plato's Theory of Ideas"; as hypothetical Image of each individual thing, 132, 134, 202-3, 329; as (strictly) hypothetical monads, 307n29, 323, 333n115; as identical/infinitely repeatable, 307n29, 311, 319-20, 326; as image of body-less soul, 335; as intelligible Image of every visible object, 133, 134, 326, 335; as "Intermediate," 325; most accessible of intelligibles, 335-36; as partially emancipated intelligible, 134; as pedagogical, not metaphysical gateway to Being, 331; as principal principle, 326n93; as shadow of truly transcendent objects, 134; as singularity of each thing, 202; as solution to the Problem of the One and the Many, 329, 332; as thought-atom, 332, 335; as "total inverse of the dialectical One" (Brann), 330-31n107; atomic, 154, 326; basis for deconstructing Shorter Way, 154; contains no parts, 326, 332; dimensionless, 320; emancipates soul from Becoming, 331; Euclid on, 320n78; existential status of, 307, 313-14, 333n115; frees soul from objects of sense, 329; geometrical resemblances of, 333; identical because hypothetical, 311, 320; individual, 324n86, 326n93; indivisible, 152, 152n86, 307, 320, 326; in *Sophist*, 396n111; made possible *qua* intelligible by the Good, 335; makes the Many *many*, 329; necessary for freeing us from contradictions of perception, 330; not a number, 152, 326; not emanation of the One (metaphysical), 330; not many, 153; not numbered among "the things that exist," 320n78; not the One (metaphysical), 326, 329, 330; not the Idea of the Good, 329; only true One, 329; origin of legend about Plato's door, 332; origin of number, 152, 326, 329; phenomenology of (Book VII), 137; plurality-excluding, 201, 203, 326; plurality of cannot be generated from unity, 333; pre-arithmetical, 307n30, 311; prior to geometrical point, 307, 314, 326; protects the fortress of Platonic ontology, 332; root of Platonic play, 335

One (metaphysical principle), 12, 26, 76, 156, 268, 305-6, 314-26, 317n72, 322-23, 324n86, 325-26, 328-30, 330-31n107, 332; and Indefinite Dyad, 76, 268, 317, 317n72, 326, 324n86; and Tübingen School, 156, 268, 305-6; as alternative to the truth taught in Divided Line, 329; as "beyond Being," 326; as "the dialectical One which as the Whole is the source of Being" (Brann), 330, 330n107; a ἀρχή of emanationist monism, 326; as οὐσία?, 317n72, 324n86; as the Good, 325, 328-29, 332; basanistic alternative to the Good, 329; bridge to protology of the "unwritten doctrines," 306; bridge to "Ideal Numbers," 306, 319, 319n77; cosmogonical, 329; hypostatizes the One (mathematical) as ἀρχή, 332; identified (erroneously) with the Idea of the Good, 305-6

"One out of Many," 145, 150, 152-58, 201, 203, 205-6, 276n66, 328-29; and conclusions of the Shorter Way, 154; and G. *Einklang*, 329; demotion of, 329; fraudulent, 153, 328-29; harmonious, 329; in *Republic*, 328-29; makes Many one, 329; metaphor for Becoming, 153; must be deconstructed on Longer Way, 154; negative sense of, 329, 332; not "unwritten," 329; seductive, 328-29; sham unity, 203; synthesis of plurality within unity, 150; three is one, 158; unity is plural, 158. *See also* One and the Many, Problem of

"one's own business, doing," 149, 149n83

Ones, three kinds, 131n39. *See also* One (mathematical), One (metaphysical principle) *and* "Incomparable Numbers"

O'Neill, William, xviin13
ontology (bastard) and politics (tyrannical), xxi, xxin27, 158, 162, 368; *Laws/Epinomis*, 162; *Sophist/Statesman*, 158, 162; *Timaeus/Critias*, 162
ontology, Platonic, 25, 46, 48-50, 196, 212n77, 276, 313-14; austerity of, 313; center of, 314; dualistic, 196, 212n77
ontology vs. historical circumstances, 49
opinion, 304, 313; objects of do not really exist, 313
Orpheus, 231n194, 393n101
"original intent," 161n108
Orwin, Clifford, 29n83, 31n92, 31n94, 32n97
Otanes, 267n40
"outside the text," 42; reader and the Good, 27
"Over-I," 370
Ovid, 1, 1n3, 2, 2n10, 251n7
Owen, G. E. L., 22n71, 75n100, 137n65, 165n118, 276n67

Palamedes, 392-93, 392nn94-95, 393n97
Palmer, John, 72n85, 74-75, 74nn91-93, 74-75nn95-101, 76n104; "modal interpretation" (Parmenides) of, 74; on Heraclitus and Parmenides, 76n104
Panegyricus (Isocrates), 54
Pangle, Thomas, 11n32, 18n57, 154n89, 393n98
pantheism and pantheists, 180
Paradise Lost, 7n22, 171n1
Parmenides, 22-23, 22n71, 72-76, 81n8, 86, 137n65, 153-54n88, 238n230, 283-84, 316n69, 344, 347, 396n111, 396-97; and definition of philosophy (Book V), 74, 86n21; and *Timaeus*, 22; as "generous monist," 74; basanistic/dialectical pedagogy of, 22, 74, 75n103, 154n88, 165n118, 316n69, 344, 397; "contingent being" in, 74; cosmology in, 73, 76 ("on the other side of 'Truth'"); division between "Truth" and "Opinion," 73, 75-76; "the great," 396n111; "Truth," 22, 72-73, 75-76, 396; "Way of Opinion," 22, 73, 75n99, 75n103 (prototype for *Timaeus*), 154n88 (archetype for basanistic pedagogy), 165n117, 347, 396; well-rounded sphere of, 72
Parmenides, xxii, 17, 22, 84, 84n16, 203n40, 238n230, 276n67, 284n96, 278, 322n84, 330n105, 331nn109-110, 333, 333n115
parricide, 81, 81n8. *See* Eleatic Stranger; Athens as, 81
Parry, Hugh, 384n51
Parry, Richard D., 235, 235nn219-221, 287n105
Parthenon, 48-49
Pascal, Blaise, 369
Patroclus, 384n46, 388, 390, 393, 393nn99-100
Patton, Paul, 399n125
Paul, 283n91
"pay the penalty," 61n69, 77. *See also* "give [back] justice"
"pedagogical order" (Post), xv, xvi, xviii, 17, 106n68
Peleus, 391
Peloponnesian War, 50, 52, 54, 57-63, 299
Penalty (Book I), 90, 90n31, 92, 273, 364
Penelope, 391, 397
Penner, Terry, 1n2, 3-4n14, 4n15, 38n4, 211n69, 222n144, 305n24
"periagogy" (a turning around of the soul), 303
Pericles, 48, 48-49nn26-27, 50-51, 53, 53n38, 297n11, 301n17, 350, 351n145, 353n148
Perrin, Bernadotte, 48-49nn26-27, 360n5
Perseus, 369n19
Persian Gulf, 52
Persian War, 50, 51
Peterson, Sandra, 33-34n102
Phaeacia, 384n48. *See* Odysseus
Phaedo, xv, xvi, xvii, xx, xxii, 6n18, 17, 67, 79, 84n16, 97, 112n3, 142, 197, 237n227, 254, 271, 278n71, 278, 281, 283, 315, 316n67, 322n84,

341n129, 345n134, 359, 378; condemnation of suicide in, 359, 359nn2-3, 392n87; "soul as harmony" rejected in, 142
Phaedrus, 384, 384n49
Phaedrus, xxi-xxii, 8, 12, 22, 31n89, 72, 72n87, 111, 111-12n1, 112n3, 143, 172, 270, 274, 274-75n64, 277, 284n97, 341n129, 378, 380, 382; analogous to *Gorgias*, 112n1; as basanistic, 172; criticisms of writing in, xxi-xxii, 274, 274-75n64
Phaenarete, 48, 297, 297n9, 299, 304n23, 390; represents proleptic element, 297n9; son of, 299. *See* Socrates
Phalerus, 279n73
phenomenal/physical world, 26, 44n13, 72, 184, 276; visible world of Becoming, 72, 276; infinitely diverse and divisible, 72
Phidias, 53
Philebus, 102
Philebus, xxii, 22, 102, 131, 197-98, 205, 208n58, 211n69, 269-71, 269n47, 315n65, 321n80, 325n90, 326n94, 327n97, 331nn109-10, 347, 395-96nn105-6
Philip of Macedon, 179, 275n65
Philip of Opus, 156n93
Philo Judaeus, 285
Philo (*mechanicus*), 105n65
Philo (the Academic), 283n93, 360n6
[*Philosopher*], xvn6, 158
philosopher(s), *passim*; and just Man (Book IV) not distinguished in Book VI, 158, 163; and "the political life" (Strauss followed by Bloom), 216, 230, 230n191; and statesman, 2; as "bald-headed tinkers," 258; as moth, 252, 256, 371; as mountain-dwelling sage, 258; as philosopher-king, 90; as reader, not imaginary Guardian, 174n3, 176; choice of, redeems *Republic*, 236; of Book VI, do not return, 158; of Book VII, are compelled to behold Idea of the Good, 203; of Book VII, are compelled to return, 174-75, 215n97 (Strauss); other than Platonic, 180; Platonic, 178, 180, 203 (us); returns to the Cave, 144, 158, 179-81, 181 (faces murderous Cavemen), 253; true, 252-53, 346; unjust. *See* Injustice; would not Return, 229; would not *wish* to Return, 253; philosopher-king/-ruler, xiv, xivn4, 234nn216-17, 251
philosophy, *passim*, 53, 79, 86, 86n21, 163, 177, 255-56, 299, 328; and self-contradiction, 368n18; and sexual differences, 299; and unitary soul, 255-56, 280; as dogmatism ("I, Plato, am the truth"), 375; as skepticism ("philosophy never arrives at the truth"), 375; as the middle ground between skepticism and dogmatism, 375; as understood by physicists and Euripides, 208n57; defined, 86n21, 177, 180; love of what truly is, 299; preferable to ruling, 92, 92n40
philosophy of history, speculative, 349, 349n138
Phlius, 296n6
"Phoenician Tale." *See* "Genetic Fiction"
Phrygian Mode, 242-43, 249, 256, 392n85
Phthia, 392
physicists and physics, 72-73, 75, 208n57, 329-30, 369n19
piety, xix, 25, 78n4, 121n18, 128n33, 288-89, 288-89nn108-9; and Justice, 289; as fifth virtue, xix, 78n4; Platonic, 289
Pindar, 78, 78n4, 80, 384, 384n50, 399n125
Piraeus, 39n5, 42, 46-47, 50-54, 58, 78, 78n2, 81-82, 88, 180, 231n199, 242, 248, 256, 279n73, 298, 365; as Hades/Underworld, 37n2, 382n42; basis of Athenian power, 51; piety, curiosity, and Justice in, 248-49
pity, 41-42, 195
Planeaux, Christopher, 52n34
Plass, Paul, 44n13
Plataea, 262

"plateau," 71-73, 76, 196, 200, 287, 288, 299, 301-2, 304, 366-67, 368-72, 369n20, 375, 376; and dualism, 76, 184; and "Plato," 76, 302; as boundary between Being and Becoming, 302, 367; basis of Plato nism, 76, 368; crystal clarity of, 375; north of (Being), 200, 287, 302; pedagogical necessity of, 376; south of (Becoming), 72, 287-89, 302; south side (as mathematical mirror), 72-73; transgressed, 73

Plato, *passim*, 58, 65-76, 109; accessible to all, 353n149; and Achilles, 389, 389n71; and free Academy, 353n149; and "late-learners," 396n111; and philosophy, 375; and Socrates, 65, 97, 353, 353n149; and teachability of virtue, 301n17; and the Good, 69-70; and women, 294-304, 353n149; anti-tyrannical teaching of, xiv, 179; as aristocrat, 66, 69n82; as dualist, 144, 276; as educator, xiv, 7, 168n122, 178, 270-73, 271. *See* Plato the Teacher; as elitist, 303, 304, 349; as empiricist, 272, 272n58, 336; as excellent teacher, 301, 376-77, 397 as hero, 266; as "high-minded fanatic," 225n158; as "Homer's rival," 105, 352, 378, 378n34, 382, 389, 389n71, 390; as idealist, 336; as imitator, 378-82; as immortal, 178, 180; as Kantian, 210n67; as innovator, 353n149; as musician, 252, 382; as paranoid, 336; as Parmenidean, 73-76, 74n99, 316n69; as patient genie, 172; as "plateau," 76, 196, 276; as Platonist, xxii, 276; as playful. *See* "playful Plato"; as poet, 201, 258, 378, 382; as politician, xiv, 260, 260n18; as preceptor of Hellas, 352; as Pythagorean, 76, 268-69, 269n47, 271, 306, 306n27, 315n65, 316, 316n69; as smiling and Phrygian, 256; as stern and Dorian, 252, 271; as sympathetic, 271; as "twice the genius," 251-52; as ventriloquist, 381; as "we," 177; as world-class culture hero, 294; as wrestler, 55, 67, 69n82; austerity of, 134,135n54, 313, 336; benefited by Socrates, 160; caught sight of the Idea of Justice, 283-85; chosen readers/auditors of, 395-96; compared with Hegel, 144-45, 228, 249n3, 395; consistency of, 252; conversion of, 66-67, 76; craves no temple, 180; creates something beautiful, 103, 109; dialogues of, *see* Plato's Dialogues *and individual dialogues*; democracy, attitude toward, 66, 273, 292, 349, 350nn142-43, 352-55, 353n149; democracy, indirect praise of, 354-55; denies entry to un-geometrical, 332; dialectical humor of, 319, 325; dialogue form, use of, xx, xxn25, 11, 20, 232n200; duty of, 243; enables Socrates to benefit others, 160; esoteric teaching of ?, 370. *See* "Self as Hypothesis"; family pride of, 59n60; family's role in prosecution of Socrates?, 162; has kept philosophy alive, 178, 375; independently wealthy genius, 92; intends Socrates to be our model, 241; intentions of, 395; invented "academics," 178; in the middle, 178; knew Aristotle was coming, 198; knew his dialogues transcended the limitations described in *Phaedrus*, 379; literary genius of, 48-49, 378-79; name of, 66-76; neither skeptic nor mystic, 178; New Testament and, 282; never wavered on the Good, 345; not an "ethical egoist," 221; Old Testament and, 282, 282n-84; philosophical loyalty of, 198; poised on plateau dividing skeptic cism and dogmatism, 375; proper pride of, 178; purpose of, 40, 41, 236; reveals what Justice is, 180; self-assurance and humility of, 271; self-criticism of, 266-67, 376; self-portrait of, 161-62, 292n4; synoptic reading of, 343; taught women, 296, 296n6; tears of com passion of?, 252; the Athenian, 151, 353; two most important things we know of (other than writings), 66, 68, 353; uses images of bad men to create a

good polity in the reader's soul, 396n112; valued hard work, 270, 353n149, 374n25; wanted reader to know Socrates intended to go back down into the Cave, 239
"Plato," 162-63
Plato and Aristotle, synthesis of, 282
"Plato" (name), 66-68, 71, 345; as division sign, 71; as plateau, 71, 76; as true form of the Socratized version of "the son of Ariston," 76
"Plato, a secret" (rejects the Idea of the Good), 71; as Aristocles, 71
Plato : Reader :: Socrates : Glaucon, 37, 39
Plato scholars and scholarship, xvi, 10, 27-28, 84, 275, 280, 299n13; female, 299n13; few are believers in the Forms, 275; dominated by professors not high-school teachers, 84; latest chapter of a long history, 280
Platonic anonymity, 20, 267n39
Platonic pedagogy, xix, xxii, 23, 85, 88n25 (previous scholarly attention to), 92, 167n121, 179n13, 181, 234, 235-36, 243, 297nn9-11, 301-3, 340-42, 345; and Reading Order, 340-42; as "periagogy," 303, 342; as "synagogy," 342, 344; dead center of, 181, 345; depends on plateau, 301; dialectical reading and, 234; egalitarian with respect to student, 300-1; elitist with respect to teacher, 301; first lead out, then send back, 243; from easier to more difficult, 85; Homeric origin of, 386-87; "natural slave" and, 301; revolutionary, 300, 303; supplants noble birth, 301; self-interest is slavish in, 92; two distinct moments of reorientation in, 302; Parmenidean basis of, 23
Platonic revival, 19, 269n19, 275-76n29
Platonism, xviin14, xx, xxii, 2n9, 7, 10, 18-19, 24-27, 64, 67-76, 80-81, 97, 106n69, 155n91, 156, 188, 195-96, 208n55, 212n77, 227, 230n188, 252, 274, 275-89 *passim*, 276n67, 299, 301-3, 313-17, 319n76, 320, 325, 332, 335, 347n136, 354, 359, 366-72, 366n17, 390, 398; and causes of physical things/change, 315-17, 315n65; and Christianity, 281n80; and Idea of the Good, 302, 320; and egalitarianism, 299-300; and Justice, 212n77, 368; and Problem of the One and the Many, 76; and Renaissance, 369n20; and "Self as Hypothesis," 370; as division, 71, 276; as "plateau," 72, 76, 196, 301; as Pythagorean, 18n60, 76, 315n65; as traditionally understood, 19, 212n77; attack on, 230n130; austere, 188, 313, 320; battleground of, 208; Brittain on, 360n6, 375-76n29; categories of, 302; Cicero vs. Cato on, 359; citadel of, 332; Cook Wilson and, 319n76; deconstruction of, 399, 399n124; delineated, 68-76; depends on "plateau," 76; dualism in, 73, 76, 184, 195, 212n77, 396; *Epinomis* as perversion of, 156; ethical dimension of, 73, 76; ethics collapse into ontology in, 373; heart of, 68-69, 185; history of, 280, 329, 329n-104; larger the number of "Forms," the easier to refute, 275, 312; means never confusing Ideas with heavens, 208n55; not mysticism or Neo-Platonism, 368; ontological radicalization of the afterworld, 80; ontology of what truly is, 25, 272, 276, 299, 313; origins of, 53, 73; otherworldly, 19n61, 69, 71, 73, 320; Parmenidean, 73, 76; revival of, 19, 269n19 ("second renaissance"), 375-76n29; *sine qua non* of, 196; Stoic deformation of, 106n69, 360n6; textual basis of, 301-2
"Platonism" (exaggerated), 133n49, 309, 309-10n42, 313. *See* "Plato's Theory of Ideas
"platonist" (mathematical), 133n49, 318n75
Platonist(s), 28, 70, 108, 156, 178, 236n225, 370-72, 370n22; American, 368n18, 370n22, 371; and unity with God, 208, 371; author as, 70, 156; challenges facing, 398-99; Christian, 280, 284; dialectal, 108,

156; Greco-Roman, 285; know not everybody is going to become one, 70; pragmatic, 371; revere Plato as their teacher, 178
"Plato's Big Idea," 196, 344, 366. *See* also "plateau," *Kluft*, and (in *Index verborum*) χωρισμός
Plato's Burning Question, 180
"Plato's Development," xvii, 13, 16, 27, 321n80; Aristotelian origins of, 321n80
Plato's Dialogues, *passim*; always say the same thing?, xxii; as a whole, 205, 394-95; as "flute girls," 399; as pedagogical treasure, 178; basanistic, 347; early, xvi, xx, 20, 83, 341, 395; dialectical unity of, xx, xxi, 395; following *Republic*, xx, xxi, xxii, 206, 260, 341, 343, 346, 395 ("the great tests"); late, xvi, xx, xxi, 22, 83, 198, 396n106, 399; middle, xvi, xvin9, xx, xxi, 19, 22, 83; must have played a part in academic pedagogy, 341; paltry value of, 380; preceding *Republic*, xx, xxii, 22, 395; three kinds of, xx; to be read synoptically, 343; what they are designed to teach, 302
Plato's exotericism, 11-12, 219, 219n-115. *See* basanistic pedagogy
"Plato's Ideal City," *Republic* as program for, 6, 7, 27, 35. *See also* "Plato's political theory"
"Plato's error," 4n15, 213, 215; according to Adkins ("scandalous"), 215n-90; according to Annas ("results are very ugly"), 228n179, 228; according to Aronson ("conflict between two senses of justice"), 222; according to Foster ("confusion"), 213n81; according to Heinaman (argument "breaks down"), 234, 234n217; according to Irwin (no need for compulsion), 227, 227n173; according to Penner ("unresolved tension"), 4n15; according to Sachs ("wrecks the *Republic's* main argument"), 218, 218n111; according to Vlastos ("the error"), 220n125, 219-21; deliberate, 222n141, 226n163; dialectical necessity of recognizing, 234; Guardians are inconsistent, not Plato, 228; "negative moment," 234-35. *See also* basanistic pedagogy, deliberate falsehood, *and* self-contradiction, deliberate
Plato's Lecture on the Good, 305n25, 317n71, 325, 325nn88-89, 325n91; as test, 325, 325n91; did Aristotle pass?, 325, 325n88, 325n91; parallel with Ficino, 325n89
Plato's Numbers, Problem of, 305-336 *passim*; Aristotle on, 321n81, 306-7n29; dilemma (Intermediates vs. Ideal Numbers), 306n26, 306-7n29, 317; Forms as numbers (Aristotle), 321, 321n81; number of numbers?, 306-7n29; numbers as Ideas, 307n-30, 314n62, 319n76; numbers (Ideal) in, 306, 307n29, 318n75, 319n76, 320, 321n81. *See* "Incomparable Numbers"; numbers (mathematical or "Intermediates") in, 307n29, 311, 318n75, 318-19, 320n78, 320, 321n-81. *See* One (mathematical) *and* Intermediates in Plato; numbers ("popular" or "vulgar") in, 306, 307n29, 311, 321n81; ones, how many in?, 305-6, 305-6n26, 306-7n29
"Plato's philosophy has a central core," assumption that, 185
"Plato's Political Theory," 111, 138, 141, 143, 149n83, 245, 252, 359, 366; reading *Republic* as, waned since World War II, 111
Plato's *Polity*, 1, 200, 360. *See also* CITY
"Plato's psychology," 143
"Plato's *Republic*," 1, 2, 3n14, 360; Ciceronian reading of, 3, 359-60
"Plato's Theory of Education," 376n30
"Plato's Theory of Ideas (Forms)," 25n76, 27, 122n22, 131-133, 184, 186, 188-89, 191-93, 198, 201-9, 275-77, 276n69, 314n62, 315-17, 379; and the Idea of the Good, 188, 190, 198; as "second world," 275; defined as "the theory that Plato regarded the existence of many Ideas as the central core of his philoso-

phy," 189; easily refuted, 203n40, 275; few believe in, 275, 278, 379; "form of apple," 134-35; "Ideas" as causes of physical things/change/ becoming, 315-17, 317n72; "Ideas" as hypostatized concepts, 131-32 (Shorey), 133, 192, 322 (Aristotle); "Ideas" as Hypothetical intelligible Images, 202-3. *See also* Divided Line, Second Part; "Ideas" as Hypothesized Images of visible things, 203; "Ideas" as intelligible Images of visible things, 188, 275, 277; "Ideas" as result of dianoetic process, 192; "Ideas" depend on mathematical monad, 132-33, 192; "Ideas" not Ideas, 133; indefinite plurality of, 275; more entangled with sensibles, the less separate, 315-16; passage that supports "plurality of Forms," 206; passages that support "Ideas," 189, 190-94; Platonic argument against, 203n40; substance of, 302; unity and plurality in, 192

"Plato's Thought, Unity of," 154, 156-57; "dialectical, inclusive, and comprehensive," 156

"Plato's unwritten doctrines," 11, 267-69, 268n43, 273-74, 305n25, 328-29, 332, 334, 344; as Reading Order of Plato's Dialogues, 344; as written in *Republic*, 273-74, 328-29, 332

Plato the Teacher, *passim*, xix, xx, 6-7 10n31, 17, 23, 28, 53n38, 70, 81, 85-86, 94-97, 106, 114, 125, 141, 146, 148, 177-78, 185, 197-98, 203, 203n40, 236, 242, 249, 252-54, 267, 270-73, 277, 283-84, 295-304, 326n93, 335, 344, 375-77, 394, 399; Adam on, 376n30; admiration for, 399; always in search of a touchstone, 344; and adolescent males, 354; and basanistic pedagogy, 97-98, 197, 213n81, 272-73; and child's-play, 300, 335; and *discere docendo*, 298, 304; and one-half, 326n93; and Plato the Philosopher, 304; and the One, 335; and "virtue cannot be taught," 301n17; and "Theory of Ideas," 203n40; as author of dialogues, 271; as egalitarian, 299-300, 301; as elitist, 301, 303; challenges freedom-loving reader to prove him wrong, 354; challenges the reader to question assumptions (Book IV), 125; charges no tuition, 81, 83; compared with Hegel, 144-45, 228; deliberately exposes student to false hood, 98; dialectical pedagogy of, 96, 98, 306-7, 316n69, 318; dialectical process employed by, 228; discovered best route to the Good, 277; effective pedagogy of, 354; heart of (*Plato the Teacher*), 301n17, 315n-65; halfway between "skeptical Socrates" and "the oracle of Athens," 375; intends that "you" should go back down into the Cave, 146; life-altering counsel of, 236; *noblesse oblige* of, 95; nurtures the philosophical nature, 253; on teaching, 358n159; our obligation to, 177-78, 236; peerless, 7; persuades philosophical nature to learn the political art, 253; playful, *see* "playful Plato"; proof-text of, 295; proud of professsion, 271; purpose of, 97; regarded his life as Just (?), 242; revered by Platonists, 178; self-description, 106n69; students of, 11, 70, 83 (boys interested in sex and war), 84-85n17, 85, 253; "secret teaching" of, 11-12, 278; self-criticism of, 267; surpassed by his best student, 397; teaches his readers how to teach, 114, 117; teaches meaning of "method," 254; teaching of, xix, 10, 154; testing by, 272-73; two types of disorientation recognized by, 376-77

Plax, Martin, 29n83

"playful Plato," 44, 44n13, 46, 149n84, 178, 189, 204, 238, 250, 256, 304, 325, 333-36, 349, 349n140, 351, 390

play within a play, 48, 85-86

pleasure and pain, 255n10

Plochmann, George Kimball, 112n3

Plotinus, 6n19, 7, 368

Plutarch, 2n5, 2n10, 28, 48, 48-49nn26-27, 263n27, 267n40, 270n53,

275n65, 281, 359-60nn2-5, 361 363n14; and Plato, 360n5; on Plato and Cicero, 275n65, 360n5
Pocock, L. G., 361n9
point (geometrical), 307-23 *passim*, 332-34; as "extremity of a line," 308-10, 314; as "indivisible line," 308. *See* "Indivisible Lines"; as "geometrical fiction," 136n60, 137n62, 307-8, 309-10, 309n41, 311, 315, 318, 320, 322-23; as "monad with position added," 308, 308n35, 320, 320n79, 326; as moving, 310, 333, 333n114; Euclid on, 332; existential status of, 310-11, 313, hypothetical, 310-11; identical/ indistinguishable because hypothetical, 311, 320; in equally imaginary space, 333; logically posterior to monad, 307. *See* One (mathematical); logically prior to figures and angles, 310, 310n46; no dimensions of, 333-34; relation to line, 308, 310, 310n45
Polemarchus, 42, 47, 78, 82-88, 106, 160n107, 296, 298, 348, 350, 394; and Thirty Tyrants, 83, 160n-107; and timocracy, 348; and Xenophon, 82, 348; house of, 78; important character, 82; initiates Book V re volt, 82; interruption of compelled (Lampert), 82n10
"political things, stern and inevitable logic of," 252
Pompey, 361, 363n14
popular sovereignty, 164. *See* Ship
Porphyry, 6n19, 368
"possession for eternity," Plato's dialogues as, 23-24
Post, L. A., xivn3, 260-272 *passim*, 264n30, 280n74,
post-developmentalism, 17
post-God heresies, 24
Poster, Carol, xv, xvn7, xvin8
potency (δύναμις), 300, 324n86,
Potidaea, 52
Powell, J. G. F., 3n12
praising/being praised, 381-82. *See also* active/passive verb forms
pragmatism, 13, 371
prejudice/animus, 281, 285; anti-theological, 25, 187, 281, 285; Judeo-Christian, 281
Press, Gerald A., xxn26, 16n51, 17n54, 18n60, 20n64, 84n14, 84n16, 106n-68, 156n96
Preus, Anthony, 129n34, 155n91, 287n106, 305n24
Priam, 391
Prichard, H. A., 209-13, 210-11nn62-69, 212n75, 217-18, 221, 221n134, 223-24
primitivism, 48, 48n25, 379
Prinzipienlehre (Tübingen), 12, 76, 268, 330, 346n135
Pritchard, Paul, 275n66, 307nn29-30, 309n42, 312n51, 313n55, 321n81
process of elimination (Book IV), 121-22, 120-21nn18-19, 124
Proclus, xvii, xviin13, 333n114
Prodicus, 258
projection, 71, 71n83
prolepsis, *see* proleptic element
proleptic element, xix, xx, xxii, 8 ("expressive but obscure language"), 10 ("intimations of hidden depths"), 18, 45, 90-91, 90-91nn32-35 (Kahn), 93, 96-99, 118-19, 140, 144, 154, 158, 179, 184, 186, 193, 198-99, 258, 279, 297n9, 327, 338, 346, 367, 379, 381, 395; and paradox, 96-97; awakens mind, 381; confuses reader, 96; discovered by Kahn, 90-91, 96; represented by Phaenarete, 297n9; whets appetite for vision, 96
proleptic, visionary, and basanistic (as triad), 96-99, 112n1, 154, 198-99, 338, 367, 379; in Book II, 96-99; in Book IX, 367; in Book X, 379; in *Gorgias*, *Republic*, and *Phaedrus*, 112n1
Prometheus, 82n10
prophecy, 72n84
propositional calculus, 13
Protagoras, xviii, 214n84, 289, 301n17
Protagoras, xv, xviii, xix, xxii, 22, 23, 53n38, 87n24, 88n25 (Guthrie's comment on), 115n8, 127-28, 179, 270, 301n17, 336, 338, 351n145, 387n65, 395n104; and *Republic* VI,

128; reveals inadequacy of Shorter Way, 127-28; to be heard first, 88n-25; "from whence," 87-88, 351n145
Protarchus, 325n90
protology, 12, 268, 268n43, 274-75
provocations, Platonic, 7, 7n22, 9, 10, 12, 15, 29, 39, 41, 221n130, 231-32, 235; identified by Miller, 7n22, 232
Pseudo-Aristotle, 322, 322n85
"pseudo-dyadic indistinctiveness," 327; *see* Indefinite Dyad, as
psychological politics, 144, 357n155, 364. *See* City in the Man
psychologism, 312n50, 312n53
Pythagoras and Pythagoreans, 75-76, 136, 296n6, 306n27, 307-8, 329n-103, 333n114, 396n108. *See also* Plato, as Pythagorean

Quintilian, 2n4, 275n65, 361
Quixote, 382n41

Raaflaub, Kurt A., 160-61n108
"radical ontology," 81. *See* Platonism
Raeder, Hans Henning, 90, 156n95
Rand, E. K., 281n78, 372n26
reader(s), *passim*, 6-7, 27, 32n96, 34n102, 37, 39, 41, 48, 94, 138, 157-58, 159, 168, 171-72, 176-81, 204, 228, 232-33, 233n205, 236, 285n-102, 294, 351-52, 390, 394-95; and Going Back Down into the Cave, 233n205, 241; and Harmonious Man, 159; and relativism, 171-72, 395; as hero of the *Republic*, 352; as metaphor, 50; as re-reader, 157; as "the beloved," 395; as true Guardian, 194; author's interpretation and, 171-72; birth takes place in, 395; brought into dialogue, 171; catch sight of Justice, 236; challenged, 232, challenged to interrupt, 94, 143; challenged to question, 125, 143; challenged to revolt, 175; choice of lives, 390, 394; comes to Plato's defense, 382; democratic, 352, 394-95; final basanistic test for, 390; free not to apply Socrates' directive, 172, 241; Idea of Justice written in the souls of, 285; in Milton and Plato, 171n1; invited to wonder, 158; obligation to Plato of, 177-78, 180; Plato's chosen, 168, 181n17; resolution of inconsistency takes place in, 228; response of, 7, 12, 180; second-order audience for Plato's *Republic*, 32n96; willing to undergo a spiritual revolution, 180
reading order hypothesis, xix, 29-30, 33, 35, 197, 237, 239-40, 240n-233; confirmed if *Theages* is genuine, 240
Reading Order of Plato's Dialogues, xiv, xv, xvn5, xvi, xviii, xviiin19, xxii, 17, 20, 23, 29, 44n14, 78n4, 83, 90, 94, 101n59, 106n68, 115n8, 121, 125, 127, 144, 156, 158, 179, 193, 237-40, 237n227, 240n233, 271-73, 300n15, 302, 336-47; and inter-dialogue allusions, 238n230, 239, 240; and "logographic necessity," 341n129; and Platonism, 302; *Apology* follows and *Theages* precedes *Republic* in, 249; as "one out of many," 338, 345n134; Book I : II-VII :: early dialogues : *Republic*, 93; center of, 273; de facto, 237n227; evolving, xvi, 302; five years required to complete?, 179, 345n133; Higher Education as adumbration of, 339-347; in *Letters*, 271-72; other authors included in, 23, 53, 160n106; proving the existence of, 239-40; reconstruction of, xvi, xvii, 17, 29, 90, 101n59, 195n34, 302. *See also* Reconstruction Project; *Republic* best place to introduce, 338; synoptic, 343, "well-ordered pedagogical program," 17, 34; why *Alcibiades Major* precedes *Erastai*, 106n68
Reagan, Ronald, 231n198
Reale, Giovanni, xiiin2, 11n33, 12n36, 268n43, 269, 269n45, 271n54, 273n61, 325n90, 328n101
reception studies, 264n30
Recco, Greg, 350n143
Recollection, 19, 21, 137, 167n121, 236, 287n104, 284, 297n9, 300,

300n15, 353n149, 377, 380; in *Republic*, 300n15
Reconstruction Project, 339-347; analogy between Higher Education of the Guardians (a, b, c) and reconstruction of the Reading Order of Plato's Dialogues (1, 2, 3), 339-40; "dialectical connections" between dialogues, 343; dramatic connections between dialogues, 340, 342-43; kinship between dialogues, 342; possibility of analogy discussed, 340-41; pivot of, 345, principles of (three), 339; student must (re)discover systematic order of their studies (1), 339-42. *See* sequential order in Books VII-IX; student is tested with respect to Being and Becoming (2), 339, 342-45; student must fight for the Idea of the Good (3), 339, 345-47; thematic connections between dialogues, 340, 342-43
reductio ad absurdum, 12nn35-36, 168, 267; Lampert on Strauss, 12n35; Szlezák on Tübingen, 12n36
reductio ad injusticiam, 169, 172
Reeve, C. D. C., 56n50, 222-23n144, 310n43
Reggae, 370
Reinhardt, Max, 363n14
relativism, 171, 303-4, 395; as "every thing is a matter of opinion," 304; as the mandragora of Thrasymachus, 304; as the truly anti-democratic teaching, 395
Rémond, Nicolas, xiii
Renaissance, 280-81, 369n20
Renault, Mary, 14n40, 60n66, 178n10
Republic, passim, xxii, 24, 29, 33, 97; allowing it to become real, 47; an educational tale about education, 85; and *Cleitophon*, 20-21, 29-36; and "open society," 292; and reading order question, 338; and *Symposium*, 279n73; and *Theages*, 20-21, 237-40; as *Bildungsroman*, 86; as central visionary dialogue, 194, 273; as exoteric text with Shorter Way as its surface, 219, 278-79, 367; as middle of Plato's "Encyclopedia of the Philosophical Sciences," 395; as multiplex, 162; as "possession for eternity," 54; as proof of Democracy's excellence, 355; as σύγγραμμα he claims he would never write, 279; as war story, 85; best joke in, 250-51; book divisions in, 265n32; bridges gap between easy/early and difficult/late dialogues, 83, 338; center of Platonic dialogues, 194, 205; constructive answer to "Cleitophon's Challenge," 33; contains "central core" of Plato's philosophy, 185, 315n65; contains no definition of Justice, 181; contextualizing, 53; dialectical reading of, 228; dramatic date of, 52n34, 58n55, 61n67; examines us (Miller), 233n205; filming, 47; follows preparation, 338; good interpretation of, must be embodied in a life, 360; good reading of, 5; inconsistency in, 228; key to author's reading of, 113-14; literary integrity of, 127; looks forward and back, 338; meaning of, 171; microcosm of Platonic dialogues, xv; most important passage in, 175; Odysseus-based readings of, 392n89, 398, 398-99n-123; philosopher's choice redeems, 236; portrait of Socrates practicing Justice, 181; practical vs. theoretical, 35; principal/sole concern, 37, 204; product of Plato's practice of Justice, 181, 184; provides student with doctrine that must be preserved, 338; purpose/goal of, 37, 97, 180, 236; *Republic* : Platonic dialogues as a whole :: Sun, Line, and Cave :: *Republic*, 127, 194; safest guide to Platonism, 315n65; "sound-bite" of, 252; stern message of, 240-41; Strauss on, 11n34, 216; structure of, unlocked. *See* Key Passage, Part II; succinct summary of, 181; sweetest moment of, 181; time it would take to read aloud, 46, 46n20; two rival interpretations of, 359; ten separate books of: I, 32-33, 39, 45, 64, 83 (as separate dialogue), 85, 87, 89 (as *Thrasymachus*), 90, 93, 96,

101-2, 107, 166-67; as proleptic prelude, 102, 253, 327; II, 31, 38, 46, 64, 90, 101-2, 107, 109, 113, 122-23, 125-26, 141, 176, 186-87, 327, 351, 378; III, 93n45, 107, 109, 123, 125, 126, 141, 150, 291, 327, 349, 353n-150, 378, 382-83, 386n63, 394n103; IV, 4-6, 8, 14n41, 21, 27, 44-45, 90, 107, 109, 111n1, 112-15, 123, 125-26, 133, 141-42, 154-56, 158, 187, 204, 217, 224, 246n1, 249-50, 253, 255n10, 259, 265, 327-28, 331, 389; V, 55, 58, 64, 74, 74n94, 74n99, 82, 86, 104, 158, 177, 192n33, 198, 246n1, 255n10, 265, 273, 276-77, 292, 299, 304, 328, 331, 348, 351, 363, 394n103; VI, 5, 25, 78n3, 82, 104, 111, 112n4, 124, 126, 127, 158, 165, 168, 173, 198 (three images of), 176, 177, 184, 209, 239, 265, 273, 276, 277, 363n15; VII, xix, 4, 4n15, 25, 37, 39, 45, 82, 87, 90, 96, 103, 104, 112n4, 127, 130, 137, 150, 153-56, 155n91, 158, 165, 168, 176, 184, 195-98, 209, 235, 246n1, 253, 258-59, 265, 276-77, 302-3, 305, 326-27, 339-40, 348; VIII, 61, 142, 177n9, 198, 253, 287, 339-40, 348-49, 355-58, 363n15; IX, 77n1, 142, 198, 253, 339-40, 348, 363, 378; X, 47, 79, 112n4, 198, 254, 276, 377-82

Return (to the Cave), xx, 14, 40, 43, 80, 89, 90, 100, 148, 158, 168, 171-81, 204-36, 258-59, 274-75, 280, 283-89, 352, 357-58, 369, 382n42, 383, 386, 387, 398; and Harmonious Man, 148, 222; as un-Homeric, 383; "expressivist" and "imitationist" (Brown) approaches to, 233-34; George Bailey's, 286-87; George C. Scott's, 89n28; discussion of ignores Glaucon's description, 217n108, 280-81; involuntary, 46n22, 242-43; in the self-interest of the philosopher/Harmonious Man (Kraut et al.), 222, 225; joins Being and Becoming, 398; not mentioned by Christian Platonists, 280-81; only obligatory for Platonists, 179-80; only possible when Democracy is giving way to Tyranny, 258; philosopher's, 43, 90, rejected by Adkins, 214, 215n93; rejected by Bloom, 216n102, rejected by Strauss, 215n97; sanitized in the City, where it is compulsory, state-supported, and temporary, 387; self-sacrifice of, undermines Plato's position (Aronson), 222; selfless, 234; "self-sacrificing duty of the," 218; terrifying in direct proportion to necessity, 258; voluntary, 2n4, 14, 37, 38, 39, 41, 168, 174-75, 236, 242-43, 275; vs. compelled, 39, 46n22, 174-75, 215n97 (Strauss)

"reveals and conceals," 161. *See* "conspicuous by its absence"

Revelation, 24, 194; Judeo-Christian-Muslim, 25, 194

rewards of justice, 78, 96

Reydams-Schils, Gretchen, 309n38, 396n108

Richardson, Scott, 384n51

Rigg, Diana, 89n28

right conduct of life, 65, 101-2, 101n60, 258, 275

Roberts, Alexander, 282n83, 282n86

Robinson Crusoe, justice not applicable to, 143

Robinson, Richard, 123n34, 315n65

Robinson, T. M., 266-67n39

Roman Empire, 275n65

Roman Republic, 1, 51, 355, 359-67

Roochnik, David L., 29n82, 30n86, 31n92, 32n97, 274n63, 350nn142-43

rooster, 46

Rorschach, Hermann, 99

Rorty, R. M., 120n16, 221n133, 247n2

Rosen, Stanley, 197n38, 231, 231n197

Ross, W. D., 129n35, 130n37, 133n49, 137n62, 305n25, 306n26, 308n33, 309n41, 310n47, 312, 312n50, 314nn63-64, 315n66, 315n69, 317nn70-71, 318, 318n75, 319nn76-77, 321, 321n80, 325nn88-89

Rowe, Christopher, 1n2, 16, 16n47-48, 19n61, 20n66, 26n78, 237n227, 264n30

Rowe, Galen O., 35n105

Rudebusch, George, 222, 222n144, 288, 288n107

Russell, Bertrand, 132n45
Russo, Joseph, 391n80
Russon, John, 388n68
Rutherford, Richard, 32n94

Sachs, David, 143n76, 217-19, 217-18nn104-12, 219, 219n116, 220n-124, 220n126, 221, 221n133, 224, 227n169, 231n198, 233n208, 280n-76, 284n101
Salamis, 49, 51
Salem, Eric, 37n2
Sallis, John, 308n122
Sallust, 355n152, 363n14
Santas, Gerasimos, 129n34, 217n105, 284n98, 287n106, 299n13, 305n24
Sassoon, Siegfried, 58n57
Sattler, Barbara M., 396n109
Saxonhouse, Arlene, 29n83, 30n88, 350n142
Sayre, Kenneth M., 99n58, 309n38, 397n120
Schadewalt, Wolfgang, 325n91
Schiller, Jerome, 217n106
Schindler, D. C., 232n204
Schlegel, Friedrich, 239n232
Schleiermacher, Friedrich, 156, 156n96, 239n232
Schmiel, Robert, 385n53
Schnitzler, Arthur, 363n14
Schofield, Malcolm, 1n2, 264n30
scholarly literature, *see* Plato scholars and scholarship
"school," etymology of, 149n84
Scipio Africanus, 2, 3
Scodel, Ruth, 386n60, 391nn78-79
Scolnicov, Samuel, 88n25
scorched-earth policy, 59-63, 59n59
Scott, Dominic, 15n44, 39n5, 157n100, 217n104, 253n9, 303n22
Scott, Gary Alan, xviin15, 88n25
Scott, George C., 89, 89n28
Scott, Robert, xiiin1, 13, 27, 50, 112, 112nn2-3
Sedley, David, 13n39, 68n77, 66n79, 360n6
Segal, Charles, 381n39, 383n43, 388n68, 390n73, 392n88
"Self as Hypothesis," 370-72; self as Good-oriented monad, 372
self-contradiction, deliberate, 9, 10n29, 11, 136n60, 154n88, 195n34, 222n-141, 226n163, 304n23, 307, 308n33, 310, 322-23, 325, 375; dialectical purpose of, 307, 310
self-contradiction, involuntary, 216, 284n101, 377; as "true lie," 377
selfishness, 3, 89, 92-94, 98, 101, 167-69, 216, 232, 275, 286, 364 (self-centered), 368, 381, 389-90; both bad and base, 93; of "the man in the know," 98, 101; slavish, 92, 92n41, 93-94; takes no brains, 89, 390; unjust (Strauss), 216
(self-)sacrifice, 212, 219, 222-23, 223n-151, 232, 259, 263, 284, 288, 389
sense, making, 12, 12n37, 19, 276
sense, objects of, 132-35; are not individual, integrated, unitary, 135; do not unqualifiedly exist, 134
Septuagint, 374
Seriphos and the Seriphian, 78, 78n3;
seven-hundred and twenty-nine times, 142-43, 253, 334, 334n117
Seventh Letter, xiv, xv, 8, 242n236, 259-70, 269n47, 273-74, 278-79, 291; and Firesticks, 259-60, 273-74, 278-79; and *Republic*, 259-61, 268 ("symbiotic relationship between, similar to Firesticks"); and Tübingen School, 267-69; as central, 264, 266, 270, 273; "philosophical digression" in, 259-60, 269n47, 273-74. *See* *Letters*
sequential order in Books VII-IX, 339-42, 348; analogous to Reading Order, 339, 340-41. *See* Reconstruction Project; five cities (Books VIII and IX), 339-40, 348. *See* Five Cities; five mathematical sciences (Book VII), 339, 341n129, 348; not taught in sequence, 340-41; sequence must pre-exist, 340-41; student must rediscover, 339, 341-42
"sewer of Romulus," 359, 367. *See* Rome; as arena of Justice, 367
Sextus Empiricus, 137n65, 306n27
shadows (of the Cave), 3, 45n17, 49, 80, 107, 158-59, 194-95, 248, 251,

361, 363, 371-72, 377, 390; and Cicero, 361, 363
Shakespeare, William, 11n32, 12, 13, 62n70, 67, 81, 178n11, 195, 274, 354n151, 371
shame, 95, 95n49, 354
Shields, Christopher, 226n166, 234n215, 276n69
Ship (Bk. VI), 5, 162-69, 173, 177; and City of Good Men Only, 162, 166-68; basanistic negation of Justice, 162-63, 165, 168; basanistic with respect to City of Good Men Only, 168; "Demos of the Pnyx" as Ship-owner, 163-64, 163n113, 168, 292; Few and Many in, 166, 168; honor and money in, 167n120, 168; influence of Aristophanes on, 163-64; Penalty in, 167-68; popular sovereignty and, 164; proleptic with respect to Cave, 168; rich and poor in, 165-66, 168; "Sausage Seller" and, 164, 164n117; "True Steersman" of, 164. *See* True Steersman
Ship : Adeimantus :: Cave : Glaucon, 165; Ship : Cave :: Shorter Way : Longer Way, 165 (obrigado, Paulo de Tarso)
Shorey, Paul, vii, xiii, 1, 16n50, 30n87, 40n6, 44n14, 47, 64, 80, 82n10, 93n-45, 104, 104n65, 116n11, 118n13, 123, 127n30, 131-32, 131-32nn39-44, 132n46, 147, 150, 153-56, 155n90, 172, 175n8, 177n9, 183, 183n20, 191n31, 208n55, 217n-108, 241, 266n39, 280n76, 281, 306n29, 322, 327n97, 330n105, 331nn109-110, 333n115, 354n151, 363, 397n-119; on Ideal Numbers, 131, 131n39, 306-7n29; on Ideas as hypostatized concepts, 131-32, 322; on Intermediates, 131, 131n43, 132n46, 307n29, 314n62; on "offspring of the Good," 191n31; on "unity of Plato's thought," 154
Shorter Way, 4, 5, 12, 15, 15n44, 22, 27, 44-45, 96, 108, 111-169 *passim*, 113-14, 117-18, 126, 127-28, 133, 136-37, 140-43, 145, 148-49, 152-54, 162, 165, 169, 172, 176, 180-81n17, 182, 200, 204-9, 218, 235, 245-49, 256, 258, 273, 288, 342-43, 367, 370, 374, 389; Adeimantus content with, 108; and basanistic dialogues following *Republic*, 209; and Book IV definitions, 5, 389; and Harmonious Man, 162; and Problem of the One and the Many, 152-54; and Thrasymachus, 162; as exoteric surface of *Republic*, 219; cannot Justify Return, 218; central Hypothesis of, 246; circularity of, 113, 117, 133, 141; conclusions depend on "One out of Many," 154; linked to Second Part of Divided Line, 5, 114, 117, 136, 137, 154 (isomorphic but not identical); methodological unmasking of, 143; methods of, 27, 154, 342, 343; never named, 5, 114n6, 116n10; neither Plato nor Socrates exist along, 162, necessary, 96, 127, 136, 140, 143, 149; not a joke but funny, 143; unsatisfactory, 128; piety absent on, 148; political and psychological geometry of, 149; self-contradictory essence of, 162; uses both Hypotheses and Images, 126n27, 154; victory of justice in, 142-43; wreck of, 258
Sicilian Expedition, 51, 60n66, 61, 61n68
Sicily, xiv, 51, 52
Sierra Club, 242
Sign of Socrates, 237-40; apotreptic, 237-39, 240; in *Apology of Socrates*, 237; in *Republic*, 237-38; in *Theages*, 238-39; prevented Socrates from entering politics, 236-40; we can't use that excuse, 240, 242
Silverman, Allan, 64n75, 133n48, 234n215
Simplicius, 325n88
Singpurwalla, G. K., 217n105
"Singularism" (sc. Return applies only to Guardians), 15n44, 174n3, 224, 224n153, 224n155, 227-29, 228n-179, 231n194, 235, 236n222, 299n-13; abandoning, 235, 299n13
singularity/plurality, 202-3, 205. *See* "one out of many"

skeptic and dogmatist readings, 18n59, 178, 375
skepticism, 178, 375-76
slavery, 95, 161
Slaveva-Griffin, Svetla, 72n87, 284n97
slavish literalism, 93-94; appropriate to unresponsive text (*Phaedrus*), 94
slavishness, 92-93, 100-1
Slings, S. R., xiiin1, 1n1, 21n67, 26n-80, 30n87, 116n11, 177n9, 183
Smiley, Timothy, 43n10
Smith, Nicholas D., xxn25, 129n35, 133n49, 137n64, 224n154, 237n228, 238n231, 284n99
Smith, P. Christopher, 26n80, 197n38
Smythe, Herbert Weir, 27, 60n64
Snyder, H. Gregory, xvin11
Socrates, *passim*, 9n27, 58n57; and Achilles, 383, 387-89 ("model for"), 392-93; and Ajax, 392, 392n94; and Athenian Stranger, 393n98; and ethical definitions, 316; and Odysseus, 382n42, 387, 389 ("antithesis of"), 392-93, 392n94; and Palamedes, 392-93, 392n94, aporetic and constructive, 33, 33n99, 33n102; as benefactor, 94; as "champion of justice," 160, 163, 240; as Charlie McCarthy, 381; as Clarence, 287; as expert on love matters, 297n10; as hero, xvii, 351; as Homer's disciple, 390; as model/paradigm, 241-42, 387; as "one of the self-styled advocates of justice," 172; as overseer of the Guardians, 172, 176; as Plato's "Socrates," 379-82; as pre-Socratic physicist, 330; as second Odysseus, 392; as "wily old bear" pursued by hounds, 102; benefited Athens?, 160; benefited Plato, 160; Christ "partially known" by (Justin Martyr), 282; claims City is needed because it is bigger than Man, 143; conventional agent vs. Plato, 65, 103, 173; crown of, 219; defends immortality of the soul while body remains in Athens, 393; descent of, 41, 51, 231n197, 231n199; fate of, 240; "has spent his life going down into the cave" (Miller), 231n199; hedonism of, 114n8; instantiation/image of Justice, 40, 279, 283; intended to go back down into the Cave, 239; knows a considerable amount about "the greatest thing to learn" (the Idea of the Good), 189; knows that he knows nothing, xx, 9, 10n31, 11, 16, 19, 19n62; last dream of, 388, 392, 392n86; lies, 101, 254, 387n66; makes same choice as Achilles, 392; midwifery of, 297n9; moment of victory of, 181; practices Justice?, 236-37, 380; preaches Justice, 236; presents Justice as dangerous, 40, 387, 387n67; returns to the Cave to fight Thrasymachus, 100, 105, 387; *see also* Thrasymachus, making friends with; sandals of, 105; self-portrait (basanistic) of, 159-61, 163, 242; Sign of, 237. *See* Sign of Socrates; son of Sophroniscus (and Phaenarete), 48, 390; successor of Cephalus, 80; trial, imprisonment, and death of, 6, xxn25, 160, 160n105, 162, 195n34, 279, 301n16, 387; unique? 40n7, 241, 283; war-hero, 60n65; warms up, 107, 109; willingly endures being wronged, 94; willing to lay down his life for his be loved, 231n194; Xenophon's, 9
"Socrates," 162
Socrates' Speech to the Guardians, 171-81, 177n9, 258, 278, 351; and "Plato's burning question," 180; "crucial ambiguity" in, 176. *See* Critical Ambiguity; delivered by fictional founder, 177; possibility that Plato is speaking, 258-59; Justifies Justice, 172-73, 176; most important passage in *Republic*, 175; response to "Glaucon's Defense," 172-73, 278, 294; second part of, 176-78, 180; two parts of, 173, 175-76
Socratic Ignorance, 53n38
Socratic revolution in ethics, 301
"son of Ariston," 65-76, 81n7
"song itself, the" (531d7), 303
Sophocles, 53, 77, 77n1

Sophist, xvii, xxii, 17, 22, 30, 31n89, 81n8, 112n3, 158, 162, 205, 238n-230, 270, 271, 320n78, 341n129, 344, 360. *See also* Eleatic Stranger
Sophists and Sophistry, 87-89, 214n84, 236, 387n65, 392; *bacillus* of, 88; necessary for Socrates, 87
Souilhé, Joseph, xviiin17, 237-38n229
soul (unitary), 254-56, 280; undermines Shorter Way, 256
soul/body distinction, 67-68, 67n81, 255, 255n10, 304n23
soul, three parts of. *See* tripartite soul
"spaceflight" (Platonic), 371-72, 375
Spariosu, Mihai, 214n85
Sparta, 51-52, 58, 59n61, 61, 63, 351n145, 382
Spelman, Elizabeth V., 304n23
Speusippus, 7, 67, 325n88
Sphacteria, 59n61
Spinoza, 369-70, 372
springboards, xx, xxi, 14-15, 98-99, 370-71
Stahl, W. H., 35n104
Stallbaum, Gottfried, 56n50, 134n53
Stangl, Thomas, 362n10
Star Trek, 109n77, 352
Statesman, xvii, xxii, 6, 17, 22, 30, 31n89, 112n3, 158, 162, 197, 205, 260n16, 270, 271, 273, 360, 366. *See also* Eleatic Stranger
Stenzel, Julius, 331n110
stereometry, 334, 340, 341n129
Stewart, J. A., 284n99
Stobaeus, Joannes, 157
Stocks, J. L., 133n49
Stoics, 106n69, 360n6
Stokes, Michael C., 329n103
Stone, I. F., 66
Strasburger, Hermann, 275n65, 361n9
Strauss, Leo, xxn25, 8n23, 9-10n29, 10n31, 11-12, 11n32, 11n34, 12n35, 16, 16n49, 18n56, 19nn62-63, 31n-92, 54-55, 54-5nn43-45, 55n49, 56n-50, 59, 62n72, 63, 154n89, 196n36, 212n75, 214n87, 215-16, 215-16nn-94-100, 224, 229, 229-30n187, 230n191, 230n193, 231n197, 269n-45, 270, 270n51, 273n60, 294n5, 349, 383n44, 393n98, 398-99n123; all serious students of Plato in his debt, 294n5; and Tübingen School, 11-12n34, 265n45; attention to dramatic details, 54; developmentalism questioned, 54; discovery of connection between Democracy and Age of Heroes, 294n5, 349; exotericism, 11, 212n75, 216n99; influenced by Nietzsche, 54, 54n44, 215n95; involuntary self-contradiction in, 216; *see* "justification of injustice"; post-Straussian alternative to, 219n115; "spurious" dialogues restored by, 54, 54n43; "text-immanent" exotericism of (Szlezák), 99n58
Straussian(s), 10n29, 16, 18-19, 55-56, 62n72, 63, 219, 229-31, 231n194, 232n202, 339n128, 382n42, 392n89; and Odysseus, 231n194; approach of, of considerable dialectical value, 230; reject singularism, 229; reject the City, 229, 229n184; reject the Return, 229; "taking Plato seriously," 394
Stresemann, Gustav, 363n14
strong rule the weak, 52
stylometric analysis, xvi, 344; limitations of, xvi, 373n24
Sun (Book VI), 127, 158, 173, 248, 302; linked with Line and Cave, 127, 158, 173
Sun, Line, and Cave (Books VI and VII), 127, 158, 173; and excerpting editor, 127, 127n30
sun (physical/visible), 26, 40-41, 190-92, 194, 317; analogous to Idea of the Good, 192; inside the Cave, 194;
Symposium, xix, xx, xxii, 17, 26n79, 31n89, 41, 51, 84n16, 86n21, 97, 179, 189, 198-99, 218n112, 226n-168, 227, 227n171, 232n201, 233, 270, 279n73, 338, 360, 394, 394n103
synoptic reading of Plato, 343
Syracuse, 65, 264, 267-68, 273, 275; quarries of, 65
system, Platonic dialogues as, xiii, 144, 395; both dialectical and triadic (like Hegel's), 395
Szlezák, Thomas A., 12n36, 99n58

Tait, W. W., 129n34
Tarán, Leonardo, 156n94
Tarnopolsky, Christine, 95n49
Tarrant, Harold, xvin10
Taylor, A. E., 14n40, 22n72, 30n87, 60-61n67, 75n103, 395-96n106, 397nn119-20
Taylor, C. C. W., 312n52, 316n67
Taylor, John Hammond, 283n94
teaching and teachers, 97, 397
Tejera, Victorino, 18n60, 84n16, 156n96
temperance, 243, 287
Tertullian, 282, 282n85
tests and testing, xx, xxi, 21, 149, 159, 193, 198, 203, 247, 249, 251, 256, 272-73, 292n4, 332, 337, 344-47, 348, 351n145, 353n140, 357-58, 369, 386, 389-91; child's play compared to politics, 251, 348; in Book III, 353n140; in Book VII, 344-47, 351n145; in Book VIII, 348, 357-58, 363; in Book IX, 363, 365-67; in Book X, 381-82, 386; in Homer, 389, 391, 391n80
Thälmann, Ernst, 363n14
Theaetetus, 320n78
Theaetetus, xvii, xxii, 6n18, 13n39, 17, 112n3, 238n230, 297n9, 341n129
Theages, 237-40, 238n230; muscular dystrophy (?) of, 238
Theages, xviiin16, xxii, 20-21, 20n66, 21n67, 27, 51-52, 81, 101n59, 115n-8, 160n105, 179, 237-41, 238n230, 297n10, 395 ("divine spark"); and reading order hypothesis, 240; authenticity of, 237n229, 239-40, 239-40nn232-33
Thebes, 356
Themistocles, 51, 77, 78n2, 301n17
theology and theologians, 187, 187-88n26, 191, 191n31, 280; strongest theological claim in *Republic*, 191
"theoretical and metaphysical order" (Poster), xvi, xviii
"Theory of Ideas." *See* "Plato's Theory of Ideas"
Theramenes, 160-61n108
Thessaly, 393
Thetis, 388-89
"thing in itself" (Kant), 24, 369
"Third Man," 203, 276n67, 286n103, 322
"Third Method of the Firesticks," 248-50
Third Mode, 243n237, 249
Third Noble Lie, 249, 292, 294; philosophers bred to rule, 294
Third Reich, 197n38, 273n60
"third for the savior," 265-66, 379
Third Wave of Paradox, xii, xivn4, xxi, 2, 13, 64, 64n73, 106, 231n196, 257-59, 260-61, 263-64, 294, 328, 367; and Third Noble Lie, 294; converting kings to philosophy [1.b], 257, 260n19, 263, 267. *See* Plato, *Letters*; crux is relationship between philosophy and politics, 294; four separate elements of paradox, 257; philosophers who refuse to participate in politics excluded [2.b], 13, 257-58, 267; philosophers become rulers [1.a], 257, 260-61, 260n19, 267; selfish philosophers and, 258
"Third Way" (Gonzalez), 15-16, 345n133; modified, 16; Straussians and Analysts, 16, 18; Unitarians and Isolationists, 16-17
thirty-five dialogues, xiii, xv, xvi, xviin15, 20n66, 271, 341, 345n133; linked to thirty-five year old Guardians?, 341
thirty-five-year-old Guardians, 37, 174, 241, 341, 344, 374
Thirty Tyrants, 83, 160n107, 273
"This Side of Paradise," 109n77
Thrasyllus, xvi, xvin10, xvi-viii, xviin15, 20n66, 21, 29, 30-31n89, 31; tetralogies of, xvn6, xvi; First, xvii, Eighth, 29, 31n89
[*Thrasymachus*], 89
Thrasymachus, 11n34, 32, 32n94, 48-50, 50n31, 52, 52n37, 54, 58n55, 71, 78-79, 85-90, 85n18, 92n41, 100-3, 147, 158-60, 168-69, 180, 206-7, 215-16, 222, 223n145, 232, 236, 251-53, 292n4, 301n17, 304, 348-51, 355, 372- 73, 394; Adkins on, 215n-92; Aronson on, 222; and Thrasy-

macheanism, 71; and Tyranny, 348, 350, 355; as "bad guy," 87; as sophist, 87-88, 236; blushes, 90; correct about Justice, 101, 253; defeated outside the text, 253; defines justice, 87-89; friends of, 236n225; making friends with, 158-59, 162, 163, 168-69, 206; mandragora of (relativism), 169, 304, 394; many justices of, 79, 87-88, 100' modern avatars of, 169, 236; not harmed, 236n225; on perfectly unjust city, 90, 90n29; prevented from ruling, 158, 158n102, 236n225; slavish nature of, 100; sweats, 107; Thracian, 53n39, 100, 236; victory of, 159; war with, 87, 372; wrestling with, 100-1; three-falls victory over, 142, 142n75
Thrasymachean Platonists, 304
Thucydides, 23-24, 49-50, 49n28, 52-53, 52nn35-36, 59n59, 60n63, 61nn68-69, 63, 65, 160n107, 161n-108, 292n4, 350-51, 351nn144-45, 353n148, 394; grim-eyed, 53
Thucydides, father of Melesias, 301n17
thumos, 55-56, 56n50, 96, 109n77, 231n195; Captain Kirk as embodiment of, 109n77. *See also Index verborum*
Tigerstedt, E. N., 20n64
Timaeus, xxin28, 98, 206, 206n48, 273, 347, 396-97, 397n120; fork-tongued assault on Platonic dualism of, 396; well-rounded sphere of, 72, 76n104
Timaeus, xv, xvn6, xxi, xxin29, xxii, 22, 22n72, 29-30, 30n89, 63, 72, 75-6nn103-4, 136, 162, 185, 191n31, 203, 209, 234n215, 260n16, 268-69, 271, 269n47, 277, 283n91, 304n23, 309n38, 315n6, 338, 369, 379, 379n-36, 395-96, 395-96n106, 396nn108-10, 397-99; and Parmenides, 22, 75n103; basanistic world of, 203; missing fourth in, 309n38; tempting half-truths of, 209
Timocracy, 348, 353
Todd, O. J., 393n97
Tone, Octave, Fifth, and Fourth, 243n237
Torch of Justice, 248-50, 253, 345, 367, 394-95; depends on reader's response, 180; friction and, 248-50, 258-59; passing the, 42, 42n8, 180, 245; most beautiful conceit, 42
touchstone, 91, 98, 273, 344; Socrates : Callicles :: Plato : Reader, 98
Toynbee, Arnold, 223n147
Tredennick, Hugh, 388n68
Triads (Platonic), 102, 121, 142n75, 179n13, 248-49, 265-66, 292, 379, 381. *See also* Trinity (Platonic) *and* "third for the savior"; arithmetic basis of, 179n13; City of Good Men Only, the Ship, and "Plato the Imitator" among, 381
Trinity (Holy), 157, 280, 280n75, 369n20; Platonism and, 279, 369n20
Trinity, Platonic (Beauty, Justice and the Good), 265n33, 278-80, 288, 302, 303n21, 361, 395; one on the way up, three on the way down, 280; *see* soul (unitary), transcends mathematical monad?, 279
tripartite soul, 56n50, 72n84, 90, 96, 111n1, 119, 141-42, 149, 205-6, 208-9, 245, 253, 254-56, 371, 377-78, 378n33, 380-81
triremes, 51
Triumvirate, 281, 359
Trojan Horse, 385, 385n57
Trojan War and Troy, 356, 385n46, 388, 391, 398n122
true/false questions, xxi, 10n29, 291
True Ruler, 97, 106
True Steersman, 164-69, 177, 206, 252; *see also* Ship, does not go back down into the Cave, 165; Harmonious Man *qua* philosopher on the Ship, 168; must be begged to benefit others, 167-69, 177; penalty ignored by, 168; scans the starry heavens, 165, 169; spoiled brat, 166
Tübingen School, xiiin2, 11-12 11n34, 24, 26, 26n80, 29n81, 76, 99n58, 180n15, 264n30, 267-68, 273-74, 305, 325n91, 327-28, 328n100, 331n107, 344, 346n135; and Aristotle's testimony, 11, 76, 305; and Heidegger, 328n100, 330n106; and

Phaedrus, 11-12, 99n58; and Plato's Lecture on the Good, 325n91; and Seventh Letter, 11, 267-69; and Leo Strauss, 11-12n34, 265n45; Krämer as greatest intellectual force of, 346n135; protology or *Prinzipien-lehre* of, 12, 76, 268; wrong to identify the Idea of the Good with the One, 30 Plato's unwritten doctrines
Tullia, 360nn5-6
Tulli, Mauro, 72n86, 73n89, 264n30, 356n153
Tunberg, Karl, 241n235
[2.b]. *See* Third Wave of Paradox
two differentiae/four possibilities, 70, 239-40, 251
Two Jobs for the Just, 2, 217, 249-50, 250-59, 364; and philosopher-king, 258; discovered by Bloom, 217, 250n6; for which is the philosopher by nature suited?, 251-53, 256, 364; practiced by Cicero, 2
"two worlds," 276
Tyranny, 2, 49, 50, 177n9, 258, 273, 275, 292n4, 340, 348-49, 353-57; "hymnists of," 49
tyrant, 142-43, 179, 232n202, 357n156, 373, 388; endless wars and, 357n156

Uncle Sam, 275
unitarian reading of Plato, 16
United States, 1-2, 49-50, 178, 275, 366, 394; as "the other city," 178, 180; as republic, 1-2, 50, 180, 275; as republic in crisis, 180, 258, 366, 394 369n19 ("Thrasymachean darkness"); and Great Britain, 50; and "republic of letters," 369n19
"universe" of Platonic Dialogues (Clay), xv
un-Platonic, 383n44
"us" (existential status of), 277, 371

verbal adjectives, 38, 64, 174n3, 210-11, 236, 361n7
Verdun, 394
Vernezze, Peter, 226n166, 233n213
Vesey, Godfrey, 12n38
veterans, 60
Victoria/Victorian Britain, 50, 50n30
Vienna (pre-War), 363n14
violet-crowned city, *see* Athens
Virgin Goddess, *see* Athena
virtue(s); four, xix, 114n5, 119, 120-21n18, 121-22, 124-25, 127-28n31, 127-28; five, xix, 127-28; may not have parts, xix, 128; "transcendental deduction" of, 287-89
visible vs. intelligible, 64
visible world, 72. *See* phenomenal
visionary element, xx, xxi, xxii, 96-97, 154, 167, 179, 189, 194, 197-99, 236, 297n10, 338, 367, 389, 394n103, 395; embodied in *Symposium*, *Republic*, and *Phaedo* (Kahn), 97, Idea of the Good, 189, pure Platonism, 97, represented by Diotima, 297n10, unitary soul, 389, view from the mountain, 97
Vlastos, Gregory, 12n38, 16, 99n58, 120n18, 142n74, 212n73, 218n112, 219-21, 219-21nn116-31, 224, 225-26n163, 276n68
de Vries, G. J., 44n13

Wallace, Robert M., 197n38, 370n21
Wallace, William, 312n53
Wallach, J. R., 350n143
Walsh, W. H., 349n138
Waterfield, Robin, 285n100
Waterlow, Sarah, 224-25m 225nn159-60, 232n201
Watson, Walter, 18n59, 345n134
Waves of Paradox; First, 56, 294-304; Second, 56-57, 57n53, 255n10, 292, 328; as "one out of many," 328. *See* Third Wave of Paradox
Wedberg, Anders, 137n63, 305-6n26, 306-7n29, 321n81
Weimar Republic, 363n14
Weingartner, Rudolph H., 218n112, 219n117, 224
Weiss, Roslyn, 16, 39n5, 115n8, 121-22n20, 387n65
Welton, William, 25n76, 286n103
"what is Plato trying to say here," 12, 71, 220-21
"What Plato Taught," 302
"whistling a tune on the way down to Piraeus" (is philosopher's descent

voluntary?), 242-43; both modes required, 243. *See* Dorian *and* Phygian
White, Michael J., 129n36
White, Nicholas P., 145n80, 218n110, 223-24, 223-24nn148-53, 225n157, 236n222
Whitehead, A. N., 180, 198, 367, 370n22
Whitehead, David, 58n58
Whitman, Walt, 368n18
"who are his sons?", 301, 353n149
"Whole, the," 73
Wilamowitz-Möllendorff, Ulrich, 90
Wild, John, 284n100
Williams, Bernard, 120n16, 247n2
Will to Power, 71
wisdom, 287
Wisse, Jakob, 2n6
Wittgenstein, Ludwig, 137n65, 363n14
Wohl, Victoria, 53n39, 270, 270n50
women, Plato's, 297, 299; superiority of, 286, 296, 299
Woodhead, W. D., 91n39
Woodruff, Paul B., 237n228
Woolf, Raphael, 9n25, 269n48
Woozley, A. D., 132n45
world soul, 368, 397, 397n119
World War One, 50, 223n147, 285, 394; Plato not recovered from, 394
World War Two, 111
Wörle, Andrea, 179n14
Worms (diet of), 367
Worthington, Ian, 35n105
"would Plato be pleased?" 13

Xenocrates, 136n60, 325n88
Xenophon (son of Gryllus), 9, 53, 57n54, 82, 82n9, 85, 108, 159-60, 160n106, 166n119, 269n45, 292n4, 348, 353n148, 392-94, 392n87, 392n92, 392n97; *Apology*, 392-93; *Cyropaedia*, 82, 82n1, 85, 161n109; *Hellenica*, 160n106; and machine gun, 394; and Odysseus, 393; and Plato, 82n9, 85, 108-9; as finest product of Athenian democracy, 353n148

"yesterday," 46-52, 88, 105, 151-52, 158-59, 180, 298-99
Ypres, 52
Yi, Jiyuan, 234n216
"you" (Book VII), 99n58, 146, 177-78, 252, 352, 366; as us/we, 176-78; what prevents "you" from going into politics?, 240-41, 366

Zadorojnyi, Alexei J., 263n27, 359n3
Zanker, Graham, 12n36
Zeller, Eduard, 319, 319n77
Zeno, 74
Zerba, Michelle, 389-90n72
zetetic, 339n129
Zetzel, James E. G., 3n12
Zeus, 82n10, 349
Zuckert, Catherine H., xviiin18, 16, 17nn54-55, 22n72, 31n91, 76n103, 84n13, 84n15, 156n96, 196n36, 206n48, 231n197, 396n107

Index *verborum*

ἀγαθόν (τὸ μέγιστον), 328, 346n135
ἀδικεῖν, 94, 175
ἀδικεῖσθαι, 94
αἴσχιον, 93n45, 94
αἰτία, 194-95, 315-16, 395n106
αἴτιος, 40-41
ἀλαζών, 386n64
ἄλλο τι, 246
ἀλλοτριόν ἀγαθόν, 93, 101, 209n61, 236
ἀναβαίνειν, 173
ἀναγκαστέον, 38
ἀνάκεισθαι, 367
ἀναλογίζεσθαι, 80, 330
ἀνάλογος, 191, 192
ἀνασχινδυλευθήσεται, 104n65, 281n77
ἄνθρωπος, xiii, 43n12, 296
ἄνοδος, 194-95
ἀντεραστής, 179n12
ἄνω ἀνάβασις, 194-95
ἄνωθεν, 377
ἄπειρα τὸ πλῆθος, 331n109
ἁπλῶς, 312n50
ἀποβλέπειν, 363-64
ἀπορία (and verb), 83, 140, 331
ἀριθμοί οὐ σύμβλητοι, 129n34, 306n28, 311, 318, 321, 323
ἄρτι, 158
ἀρχαί νέων, 241
ἄρχεσθαι, 166, 167
ἀρχή, xii, xv, 70, 129n34, 179n13, 182, 305, 316, 318, 321, 323, 326-28, 326n93, 327n98, 346n135
ἄρχων (τῷ ὄντι ἀληθινὸς), 93-94, 97, 166, 167
ἀτόμους γραμμάς, 136n60, 137n62
αὐτοκράτωρ, 267n40
βασανίζω, 91, 91n36, 103, 246, 249, 251, 344
βασανιστέον, 38, 241, 345n133
βασάνος, 91, 91n36, 98, 272
βλοσυρός, 338n125
γελοῖον, 295, 337
γένεσις, 26n79, 104, 104n63, 196-97, 303n20, 303n21, 332, 345, 396n106
γενναῖος, 164, 164n114, 292-93, 292n4, 351n145
γεννᾷν, 191, 293
γίγνεσθαι, 152, 153, 187, 188, 189, 201, 293
γιγνομένον, 301-2, 302n20, 395n106
γῆν τέμνειν, 59n59
γνῶσις, 137n65, 192n32
γράμματα, 122, 123n23, 138, 138n67
γράφειν, 123n23, 138-39
γραφική, 140n72
δημουργός, 89n27, 134n51, 203, 379n36, 381
δημοσίᾳ, 364
διαβολή, 207, 207n54
διαίρεσις, 396n111
διάκρισις, 325n90
διαλεκτικὴ μέθοδος, 112, 343n131
διαλεκτικός, 343, 344
διαμάχεσθαι, 308, 310n44
διαμηχανήσασθαι, 303-4
διανοηθῆναι, 135n54
διάνοια, 5n17, 14n41, 104n64, 130, 134n51, 134-35n54, 135, 138, 140n72, 189n29, 198, 206, 309n42, 321n80, 323, 329-332, 331n109, 378n34
διά παντός, 153n88
διάστασις, 103-4
διατρίβειν, 43n12
διερμήνευσις, 396n110
διευλαβητέον, 336-37, 340
δίκαια πράττειν, 201
δίκαιον, xiv, 123n24, 127n30, 181, 188, 195n34, 212n75, 218n113

δικαιοσύνη, 43, 103, 127-28n31, 247, 261-62, 284n100
δικαιότερον, 6n18
δίκη (ἥ), 336-37
δίκην διδόναι, 61n69, 77, 79
δόγμα γεωμετρικόν, 137n62, 308, 309n41, 313
δόξα, 347, 395n106
δουλοπρεπής, 95-96
δριμύτης, 338n126
δύναμις, 300
δύο ἀχώριστά, 326-27
δύο κεχωρισμένα, 326-27
δύσβατός, 45
δυσδιερεύνητος, 45, 175n6
δυσσύμβολός, 166n119
ἐάνπερ, 364-65
ἐθέλειν, 174, 364-65, 365n16
ἕκαστος, 300
ἔκγονος τοῦ ἀγαθοῦ, 27, 190, 191, 193
ἐγκωμιάζων/ἐγκωμιαζόμενος, 381
ἐκεῖ, 79, 208n55
εἶδος, 3, 42, 119, 130, 131, 187, 188n26, 200, 201, 202, 245, 248-50, 319-20, 319-20n77, 345, 379
εἴδωλόν, 250, 347, 361, 362, 380-81
εἰκών, 114n6, 125n27, 138, 140, 201-2
εἰς Πειραιᾶ, 51-54
ἐκβαίνειν, 187, 187n26
ἐκεῖσε, 372-73, 374, 375
ἐκτός, 147
ἐλέγχειν, 346-47
ἐλευθέριοι (ἀν-), 92n41, 96n53, 166n119
ἐλεύθερος φύσει, 353, 353n147
ἐλευθεροπρεπής, 95n52
ἐλευθεριώτατον, 97
ἐλευθεριώτερον, 92n41, 95
ἕν, 152, 153, 155, 202, 246, 318, 326, 327n98, 330n106, 331, 331n109, 346n135
(ἕνα) ἕκαστον ἓν, 113, 130, 131
ἓν ἑκάτερον, 326-28
ἕν ἐκ πολλῶν, 152-53
ἐνθάδε, 79, 372-73, 374, 375
ἐνθένδε, 375
ἐνοῦσα, 300
ἐν τεταγμένῃ πολιτείᾳ, 373-74
ἐντός, 147
ἐξ ἀρχῆς, 113
ἐπάνοδος, 303n22
ἐπανιόντες, 246, 247, 251,
ἐπέκεινα τῆς οὐσιας, 24, 27, 398n122
ἐπιβάσεις τε καὶ ὁρμαί, 370-71
ἐπιεικέστατοι, 163, 165, 167n120
ἐπιθυμητικὸν, 72n84
ἐπίσκιος, 45n17
ἐπιτρέπειν, 173, 174
ἐρωτικά (τὰ), 297n10
εὐήθης, 88
εὐλαβεῖσθε, 190, 337, 337n122,
εὖ πράττωμεν, 201, 372, 374
εὑρετικός, 295
ἐφεξῆς, 348
ζητεῖν, 115, 123, 138, 186, 331
ζήτημα, 122-23
ζήτησις, 122-23, 123n24
ζητητικός, 339n128
ἡ ἄλλη πόλις, 177, 178
ἡμεῖς, 177
ἡ τοῦ ἀγαθοῦ ἰδέα, 188, 189, 189n28, 194, 195, 196, 332, 345
ἡ τοῦ διαλέγεσθαι δύναμις, 344
ἡ τοῦ ὄντος φύσις, 340
θεία μοίρα, 261
θεία τύχη, 366
θεῖος, 207, 271, 281n79, 288n108
θεός, 53n39, 186, 187n26, 194
θεὸς που, 194
θυμός, 55, 56, 56n50, 96
ἰδέα, 185n23, 186-203, 188n26, 323
ἰδέα πολιτείας, 200
ἰδεῖν, 201
ἰταμότης, 338-39n126
καθ᾽ ὅσον ἀνθρώπῳ, 288n108
καιρός, 81
καλλωπίζεσθαι, 93n45
καλόν (τὸ), 188, 189, 189n28, 192, 192n33
κατά (and κατα-) 118n13, 189-90n30, 247, 250, 300, 377
καταβαίνειν, 37, 103, 173-74, 183, 188n26, 246
καταβὰς, 39, 40, 174
καταβατέον, 35, 38, 172, 173, 177, 179, 210, 211n70, 218n113, 247,

249, 251, 278, 285, 303n22, 340, 352, 361, 379
κατέβην, 35, 36, 37-45, 76, 79, 113, 173, 251, 274, 278, 345
καταβιβαστέον, 38, 174, 241, 344n133
κατὰ δόξαν, 346-47
καταμένειν, 174
κατοικίζειν, 367
κατ᾿ οὐσίαν, 346-47
κάτω βλέπειν, 206, 209
κήδησθαι, 364, 366
κίβδηλος, 108, 190, 191, 192, 193, 337n122
κλίνη, 47, 64n74, 203, 379, 379n35, 379n36
κοινά, 159, 159n104, 269n49, 260
κοινωνία, 342, 343
κόσμιός, 207, 208, 272
κοσμός, 76n103, 208n56, 396n107
κρίσις, 8, 103
κτῆμά ἐς αἰεὶ, 23-24, 54, 60n64
κύριος, 195
λαμπάδια, 42, 42n8, 367
λογιστικὸν, 96
λόγος, vii, xiv, 34, 36, 72n84, 89n27, 129n34, 190, 191, 193, 271, 274, 281n79, 346, 347n136, 366
λόγῳ, 312
μαθήματα, 202, 271, 338n124, 338n126, 340, 341
μαθηματικὰ, 130
μάθησις βέβαιος, 342, 343
μάθησις (ἡ περὶ τὸ ἓν), 155, 331
μανθάνειν, 340
μέγα καὶ (σ)μικρόν, 327, 327n98
μεγαλοπρέπεια, 339n128
μέθοδος, 112, 112nn3-4, 114n6, 115 115n9, 116n10, 118, 118n13, 119, 119n14, 126n28, 126n29, 139n71, 186, 202, 250, 342, 380n38
μέν, 100-1
μενετέον, 64
μέσον, 179n13
μεταβολή, 374-75
μεταξύ, xiii, 1, 104, 130, 319-20, 375
μετὰ ταῦτα (τὸ and ὁ λόγος), 34
μετέχειν, 188n27
μέτρον, 330n106
μιμεῖσθαι, 380, 380n7, 380n38, 381
μονάς, 131n39, 320n78, 323
νόησις, 14n41, 130, 132, 135, 309n42, 314, 326n95, 327, 329-32
νοούμενα (τὰ), 191, 193
νοσοτροφία, 238
νῦν, 47, 62n71, 64
-ὁδός, 118, 119n14, 139n71, 157-58n100, 250, 271-72
οἰκεῖα, 342, 343
οἰκειότης, 340
ὁμοίως, 299
ὁμολογουμένως, 113, 116
ὄντα, 153
ὄν (τὸ) also τὸ ἐόν, 155n92, 189n29, 196, 284n95, 301-2, 303n20, 303n21, 331, 332, 344, 345
ὁρώμενα (τὰ), 191, 193
οὐκ ἄρα, 364-65
οὐσία, 26n79, 104, 196, 303n20, 303n21, 312, 317n72, 327n98, 331, 332, 345, 363-64, 363-64n15, 396n106
οὐσίᾳ, 312
ὄφελος, 166, 167
ὄψον, 47
παιδεία, 300
πάλιν, 38, 39, 183, 241, 247, 249, 251
πάλιν καταβαίνειν, 173-74, 174n5, 183-84, 184n22
πάντα, 153
παράδειγμα, 367
πᾶς ὁ γιγνώσκων, 92-94, 98
πάσχειν, 148n82, 262-63
πεῖρα, 272, 325n91, 343, 344
πέρας, 308
περιαγωγή, 303, 303n22, 343n131
περιακτέον, 301-2, 340
περίοδος, 303n22
πίστις, 130
πλάττειν, 138-39, 142n75, 201-2
πλατύτητα τῆς ἑρμενείας, 67-68
Πλάτων, 76
ποιεῖσθαι, 380n38
πόλις (ἐν λόγοις κειμένη), 200
πολιτεία, vii, 1, 111, 161n108, 199, 200, 273, 336-37, 359n1, 360, 363
πολιτικὰ (πράττειν), 200, 201, 236, 237, 238, 239, 260, 364-65, 367

πολλά (ἀντὶ μιᾶς), 328
πολλάκις, 44n14, 309, 325
πόνος (and verbs), 271, 340n127, 374
πορεία, ἡ πάλιν, 375
πρᾶγμα (πᾶν τὸ), 271-72
πρακτέον, 35, 150
πράττειν, 43n12, 148n82, 150, 238, 365, 380n37
πράττειν (τὸ) τὰ αὑτοῦ, 269, 269n49
προθυμούμενος, 346-47
προτρέπειν, 34, 173n2, 238
σκοτεινός, 45, 45n16, 361, 361n7,
σκύλαξ, 87n23, 102
σπουδαιότερον ἐπαίζομεν, 337
συγγένεια, 342, 343
σύγγραμμα, 271n54, 278-79
συμφέρον, τὸ αὑτῷ, 93-96, 167
συνακτέον, 340, 341, 344
συνεθιστέον, 361, 361n7, 363
σύνοψις, xiii, 54, 340, 341, 342, 343, 347n136
συνοπτικός, 343, 344
σχήματα, 134n51, 192n33
τελεώτερον, 177-78, 179n13
τελευτή, xiii, xv
τέλος, 179n13
-τέον, 38
τίθημι (LSJ B.6), 113, 139-40, 192, 202, 203, 308, 310, 312, 313, 325
τιμή, 374, 382n40
τί τοὐντεῦθεν, 35, 36, 100, 150, 172
τραγήματα, 47
τρία ὄντα (συναρμόσαντα), 152, 157
τρίβειν, 247, 260
τριττὰ εἴδη, 116, 120
τῷ ὄντι, 380
ὕλη, 317n72, 327n98
ὑμεῖς, 177
ὑπογραφή, 139n69
ὑποθέμενοι (ὑποτίθεσθαι), 116, 117, 124, 202, 313n58
ὑπόθεσις, 113, 114n6, 115, 116, 125n27, 129n34, 370
ὑπομνήματα, 271
φαντάσματα, 380
φεύγειν, 6n18
φιλοπονία, 339n127, 352n149, 374n25
φύλαξ, 87n23, 102
φύσις, 379n36
φύσεως ἄκρα καὶ πρῶτα, 269 269n45, 274
φυτουργός, 379
χαλεπὰ τὰ καλά, 103, 160
χθές, 46-50, 78n3
χρῆσθαι, 2, 118n13, 123, 125n27, 138, 261-62, 380, 380n38
χύδην, 340-41
χώρα, 398, 398nn122-23
χωρισμός, 49, 67, 196, 207, 276, 368
ὥσπερ ἐν μάχῃ, 346
ὠφελία, 382n40
ὠφελῶν/ὠφελεῖσθαι, 93-94, 96-97, 167
ὠφέλιμον, 92n41, 93n46

Index *locorum*

Aristophanes

Frogs
937, 163n112

Knights
40, 163n112
214-15, 164n117
814-16, 78n2

Aristotle

Constitution of Athens
29.2-3, 161n108
34.3, 161n108

De Anima
409a4-5, 310n45
409a6, 307n32

Eudemian Ethics
1218a20, 305n25

Fragmenta (Ross)
55.20, 314n64
(112), 317n71
151.8 (117), 325n88

Metaphysics
987b14-18, 130, 277n70
987b14-22, 319
987b19-22, 317n72, 327n98
990b2-4, 276n67
990b5-6, 315
990b18-22, 317n70
991a9-11, 315
991b3-4, 315n66
991b24-992a1, 311n48
992a19-24, 308
992a20, 310n47
992a20-23, 137
992a24-29, 315
1028b19-21, 321n81
1076a36-37, 311
1076a38, 311
1076b12, 311
1077a36-b2, 312n54
1077b17, 312
1077b33-34), 312
1078a22-23, 312
1078a31-32), 325n92
1078b13-17, 316
1078b17-19, 316
1078b31-32, 316
1078b33-34, 322
1079a1-2, 315
1079a14-19, 317n70
1079b12-15), 315
1080a2-3, 315n66
1080a12-14, 316
1080a30-32, 319n76
1080b9-10, 318n75
1080b11, 319n76
1081a5-16, 323
1081a8-17, 321n81
1082b23-32, 321n81
1083a17-20, 321n81
1083a28-30, 318
1083a34-b1, 318
1083b12-16, 318n74
1084a12-17, 321n81
1084a18-21, 321n81
1084a21-25, 321n81
1084b27, 320n79
1086b5-12, 276n69
1088b1-3, 324n86
1088b18-20, 324n86
1089a3, 324n86
1089a27-31, 324n86
1089b3, 324n86
1089b16-32, 324n86
1089b29, 324n86
1091b19-24, 316n68
1093b26-29, 316

N. Ethics
1120a11-13, 148n82
1120a13-15, 95n50, 166n119
1120a21-23, 92n41
1120a23-25, 96n53
1120b4-6, 167n121
1178b8-17, 144

Physics
188a18-23, 75
206a16-17, 309n40

Posterior Analytics
93b24-25, 312n52

Topics
141b15-22, 308n34

[Aristotle] *On Indivisible Lines*
968a9-11, 322

Aulus Gellius

Noctes Atticae
14.3, 82n9

Augustine

Contra Academicos
3.17.37-41, 282n89
3.18.41, 283n93, 360n6
3.18.41.21-23, 272n90
3.19.42, 282-83

Confessions
3.4.7, 283n94

Cicero

Academica
1.16, 9
1.45, 9
2.74, 9, 9n26

Ad Atticum
2.1.8, 359

De Divinatione
1.61-63, 72n84

De Inventione
1.1-5, 2n6

De Finibus
2.45, 269
2.118, 93n43

De Natura Deorum
2.30, 10
2.46, 10
2.77, 10

De Officiis
1.23, 4n14
1.28, 2n4, 38
1.29, 4n14

De Oratore
1.47, 10

De Republica
6.12, 5n16
6.16, 3
6.17, 3
6.19, 3
6.22, 3, 243n237
6.25, 3
6.33

In Catilinam
4.22, 357

Orator
8, 396n108
10, 396n108
12, xxn24, 4

Philippics
2.116, 363n14

Tusculan Disputations
2.41, 281
5.11, 10

Quintus Cicero
Commentariolum Petitionis
12, 366n17

Clement of Alexandria
Stromata
1.5, 282n86

Diogenes Laertius

Lives of Eminent Philosophers
3.1, 58n56
3.4, 67
3.6, 58n58
3.37, 325n88
3.46, 296n6

Dionysius of Halicarnassus
De Compositione Verborum
3.16, 28

Euripides

Fragmenta (Nauck)
902, 208n57
Medea
248-251, 296n8

Greek Anthology
7.99, 263n27

Herodotus

3.83, 267n40

Hesiod

Works and Days
156-60, 349-50
162-165, 356
167-73, 357
182-196, 356n154

Homer

Iliad
9.186, 385n58
9.186-89, 391n85
9.189, 385n58
9.312-13, 397n118
9.410-16, 388
16.31-32, 393
18.94-104, 384n46
18.117-21, 385n52
19.198-214, 391n82
19.420-23, 391n85
23.491, 391n85
23.733-37, 390n74
23.749, 391n74
23.890-97, 391n85
24.203-5, 391n81
24.507, 391
24.507-551, 391
24.511, 391
24.519-21, 381n91

24.560-62, 391n82
24.580, 391n82
24.588, 391n82
24.670, 391n83
24.599-620, 392n85
24.669, 392n85
24.776, 391n74
24.791-93, 391n74

Odyssey
8. 5-82, 385n56
8.67, 385n58
8.73, 385n58
8.77-78, 390
8.78, 386
8.486-98, 385
9.8-10, 386n63
10.305, 398n123
11.487-503, 383n45
11.488-91, 384, 398n122
11.543-48, 390
11.601-4, 385n52
13.254, 397
13.294-95, 391
14.217, 397n116
19.178-79, 397n117
19.203, 397n117
24.15-98, 390
24.36-37, 391n76
24.85-92, 390
24.92-94, 391n75
24.192, 391n76
24.192-98, 391n76
24.235-40, 391

Isocrates

Panegyricus
4.7, 54

Lysias

Against Eratosthenes
12, 54
19, 54

Macrobius

Commentary on the Dream of Scipio
1.1-2, 3n12

Minucius Felix

Octavius
18.8-10, 25n77

Ovid

Amores
1.2, 1n3
Tristia
4.10, 2n10

Parmenides (Mourelatos)

B1.32, 153n88
B8.43-44, 72n85
B8.52, 22, 76n103
B8.52-59, 75n99
B8.56, 75n103
B8.57-60, 75n99
B8.59, 75n103
B8.60, 22

Pindar

Olympians
2.70, 399n126
2.78-81, 384n50

Plato

Alcibiades Major
103a4, xviii
105b5-c6, 161n109
106d4-5, 53n38
107e5-6, 55
108c7-d8, 106n68
109e1-110c11, 53n38
111a1-3, xviii
111a1-4, 53n38
116b2-5, 372
121e6-122a, 121n18
122a2, 121n18
127a14-c7, 44n14
129e3-130a4, 67n81
131e4, 297n9
132c7-133c16, 256
134c4-6, 95n52
134c10-11, 95n52
135c2-d1, 161n109
135e6-8, 160n105

Apology of Socrates
21d3-6, 9
21d7, xx
26d1-3, 26n79
28b5-d5, 388
28e1-3, 60n65
31c7-d6, 237
31d3-4, 237
31d5, 237
33e7, 237
41b5-7, 398n122
41b2, 398n122

Charmides
160d1-2, 139n70
161b6, 121
171d2-3, 313n56
172c8-9, 313n56

Cleitophon
408c2-4, 34
408c4, 34
408c9, 34
408d1-4, 34
408d4-e2, 173n2
408d5-6, 34
408d7, 34
408d7-e2, 35
408e1-2, 100
410a7-b1, 85

Cratylus
412c6-b5, 195n34
428a3-5, 195n34
431c4-d2, 138n67
431c10-11, 138n67

Crito
44a6-b4, 392n86

Epinomis
991e5, 155
992b6-7, 155

Erastai
132c5, 179n12
132d1-2, 106n68
133b3, 179n12

Euthydemus
297d1-2, 8, 252
303a6, 8

Euthyphro
4a6, 81n8

Gorgias
448e2-7, 101n59
459d1-2, 278
461b6, 278
481c3, 272
482d8, 94, 95n51
485b7, 95n51
485e1, 95n51
486c3, 95n51
486d1-7, xx
486d2-5, 91
486d2-7, 91, 272
486d3-487e2, 91n36
486e5-6, 91n38
487e1-3, 344
492d3-5, 101n60
511c7-513c3, 378
518a2, 95n51
521d6-8, 236

Hippias Major
283b3-e2, 87n24
286a8-b4, 386n64
286d8, 86n21
288d1-5, 387n65
304e8, 103, 386

Hippias Minor
363b1-c1, 385
364c6, 386n64
366a4, 386n64
366d2, 386n64
367e2, 386n64
368b2, 386n64
369d2, 386n64
369d6-e3, 386
369e2-370d6, 397n118
369e4, 386n64
369e5-370a1, 386
370b2, 386
370e10-11, 386n64
371a7-b1, 386
372d3-7, 87n24

Ion
530b9-10, 105n67
534a7-b3, 378
534d4-7, 23
540d1-6, 236

Laches
185a3-5, 101n60
190b8-c2, 101n59
200d1, 58n57

Laws
808d4-7, 84-85n17
894a1-5, 333n114
965c2, 154n89

Letters
309b2-3, 267
309b6-8, 270
312c8, 272
312d7, 274
312e1-3, 274
312e1-4, 280n74
313c7-d3, 272
313d1-3, 272
313d2, 272
314a1-b5, 272
314a6, 272
314b1, 272
314c3-4, 270, 271
314c4-6, 270
316c7-d1, 272
319c1-2, 274
323a1-2, 272
323d3, 274
324b9, 159n104, 260n18, 269n49
324b9-c1, xiv
324d7-8, xiv, 273
325a7-b1, xiv, 260
325b1, xiv, 159n104
325b1-5, 273
325b5-d1, 273
325c6, 260n18
325d1-2, xiv
325d1-326a7, xiv
325d2-4, xiv
325d3-4, xiv
325d4-5, xiv, 267
325e1-2, xiv, 260n18
326a7-b4, 260, xiv, 261
327a1-4, xiv
327a3-4, 260n18
327a4-5, xiv
327a6, xiv
327a6-7, xiv
327a7, 271
327b1, xiv, 271
327e1-2, xiv
328a4-b1, 261
328a6-b1, xiv
328b3-5, 271
328c2-3, 265
328d4-329a5, xiv
328d6-e1, xiv
329b1-2, 271
331a5-b4, 270
332c7-d2, 274
332d6-e1, 274
334c6-7, 262, 273
334c8-d1, 262
334b1-4, 273
334d5-6, 262
334d7, 266, 142n75
334d7-e1, 262
334d8-e1, xiv
334e3-5, 263
334e5-335a2, 263
335a2-7, 263
335a7-c1, 263
335b1-2, 263n29
335c2, 263
335c2-d1, 261
335d1-3, 262
335d1-e2, 261

335d3-5, 262
336c1, 142n75, 266
336d6-7, 273
336e3-337a3, 263
337a6-8, 263
337c4-d2, 263
339b2-4, 269
339d1-3, 269
340a3-4, 142n75, 266
340b1-341b3, 271
340b3, 259n13
340b4-345b7, 273n61
340b5, 272
340b7-d1, 271-72
340b8, 271
340b8-c1, 272
340c1, 271, 338n127
340c2-3, 271
340c3, 271
340c5, 271
340d6-341a3, 272
340d8, 271
340e1-2, 271
341a2, 271
341a3, 271
341a5, 338n127
341a7, 271
341b3, 272
341b3-c5, 267-68
341c1-2, 274, 278
341c4-d2, xxi, 8, 99n58, 259, 278
341c7-8, 10n30
341c7-d1, 7, 268
341d1-2, 99
342a7-344c1, 265n33
342a7-344d2, 269n44
342c2-3, 265n33
342d3-8, 265n33
342d4-5, 278
342d4-7, 288
344a2-b1, 260n14
344b1-3, 260, 291
344b3-c1, 260
344c7-8, 274
344d3-7, 268-69
344d4-5, 268
344d5, 269n46
344d9-e2, 270
344a1-2, 270
344a2-b1, 270
345c1-2, 274
346a1-4, 263
350c1-6, 273
351a5-c1, 273
351c6-7, 263, 288
352e1-2, 270
353b3, 267n40
354b8-c7, 273
354c5-6, 263
354d1-e3, 273
354e3-5, 273
354e5-355a1, 273n59
355a8-357d2, 273n59
355c5-8, 272
356d5-7, 271
357e6-358a3, 269
358a6-b3, 273
358a7, 269n49
358c7-8, 273
359b1-3, 274
359c6, 271
359d6-e1, 270, 271
359e1-2, 270
360b7-8, 271
360b8-e3, 273
360d6-e3, 271
362d1-e1, 267n40
363a5-7, 271
363c9-d1, 271
363d2-5, 271

Lysis
203a1, xix
204b8-c2, 297n10
219d1, 86n21

Menexenus
236a8-b6, 297n11

Meno
71b3-4, 101n59
74a5, 339n128
81a5, 297n9
81a10, 297n9
81c5-d5, 300n15
81e1, 339n128
82b4, 299
86d3-6, 101n59
86e3, 114n8
88a8, 339n128
93c7-8, 301n16
94d6-8, 301n17

Parmenides
130b7-8, 278
131a1-2, 322n84
132a2-b3, 322n84
137e3-4, 308n37

Phaedo
57a7, 296n6
61b6-7, 378
61e5-62c8, 359n3
62a2-7, 392n87
63e8-64a2, 80
64c6, 313n55
65c5-e5, 135n54
65d4-7, 278
65d4-12, 322n84
65d4-e5, 278n71
65e3, 135n54
67d9, 49, 67
79e3, 112n3
97b6, 112n3
98e3-5, 315n66
98e5-99a4, 5n14
100d5-8, 283
100d7-e3, 315n66
100e5-6, 322n84
114d8-115a3, xv, 396n107
118a17, 283
118e7-8, xix

Phaedrus
247d5-4, 72
249b6-c1, 277
264b7-e2, 341n129
270c1-e1, 111
275d4-9, 143n77
275d4-e5, xxi, 12, 99n58

275d6, 8
275e5, 382
276c7-d8, 378

Philebus
11c7-8, 102
23d9-e1, 325n90
26d8, 395n106
56d9-e3, 307n29

Protagoras
309a1, 88n25, 351n145
310a8, xix
327e3-328a1, xviii, 53n38
337a-c3, 258
347d4-5, 399
349b1-3, xix
349b2-3, 128
358a4-5, 387n65

Republic
327a1, 35, 145, 387n67
327a2, 53n39
327a2-3, 249
327b1, 249
327b4-5, 82
327c2, 58n57, 160n57
327c7-9, 42
327d7-9, 64
328a1-328b3, 42n8
328b2, 64
328b4, 78
329c4, 77n1
329e4, 363n15
329e6-330a2, 78n3
330c3, 363n15
330d2, 363n15
330d4-e2, 77
330e1, 263n29
330e2-4, 80
330e4-331a1, 80
331a4, 78n4, 289n108
332d4-334b9, 85
333a13-14, 166n119
334a1, 108
334c1-3, 86
334b7, 83
335b6, 158n102
335c4, 288, 289
335e5-6, 158n102
336e3-9, 279
336e7, 65, 101n60
337b2-4, 307n32
337e4-7, 19n62
338e1-339a4, 87
339a2-3, 94
339c1-2, 89
340b6-7, 89n26
340d6-e7, 89
340e1-3, 89n27
341c5-8, 89
342e7-11, 89, 94n48
343c3, 93, 100, 253
344b3-4, 147
344c2, 94n48
344c5-6, 92n41, 95
344d1, 102
344e1-2, 275
344e1-3, 65 101n60, 279
345b5-8, vii
345d6-e1, 94n48
345e6-346a1, 94n48
346e3-7, 90
347a3-5, 89
347a5, 364
347a6, 89, 94
347a6-8, 365
347a6-b4, 167n120
347b1-c3, 90n30
347b6-7, 364
347b6-c2, 168
347c3-d2, 90n31, 355
347d2-6, 5
347d2-8, 91-92, 97
347d4-6, 97
347d4-8, 93
347d5-6, 167
347d6-8, 8, 10, 87, 93n44, 167
347d7, 167
347d8-e2, 100
348c12, 88, 292n4
349c6, 90n29
350d3, 90
351a7-b5, 52n37
351b1, 90n29
351b1-5, 58n55
351b4-5, 216n98
351d3, 357n155
351e1, 357n155
351e4-352a4, 90
352a2, 357n155
352a9, 357n155
352a9-353e12, 145n81
352d5-6, 279
352d6-7, 65, 101n60
353b2-3, 145n81
354a10-11, 53n39
354c1-3, 101n59
357a1-b2, 102
357a2-b3, 387n67
357d4, 46
358a1-3, 6, 46n19, 365
358b6-7, 105
358d3, 108
359a2-7, 104
359a5, 364n15
359c1, 104n64
359c7-360b3, 103
359d5, 103
360d8, 8
360d8-e2, 103
360d8-362c6, 103
360e1-3, 6
360e3, 103
361a5-b8, 104
361a6-d3, 86
361b5, 104, 364n15
361b5-c1, 387
361b7, 292n4
361c4-d3, 6
361c5-6, 104
361c6-7, 103
361d5, 8, 103
361d7, 10
361e1-362a6, 104
361e4-362a1, 281n77
361e5-362a1, 387
362d5, 107

363a8, 292n4, 349n140
363a8-b4, 349n139
364c8-d2, 349n139
364d1, 372
364d3, 107
365a7, 161
365c4, 107
365d4-5, 46n22
366b5, 108
366d5-367a4, 109
366d7-e1, 172
367a4, 108
367b3-6, 6
367b5, 108
367c3, 253
367d2, 108
367d7-e1, 78n5
367e1-5, 5n16
368a3, 52, 58n57, 60n65
368b7-c8, 289n108
368c7-369a5, 123
368c8-369a4, 123
368d3-5, 138
368d6-8, 123
368e1, 123n24
368e2-369a4, 142
368e7-369a4, 186
369a1-369a8, 6
369a3, 45
369a4, 200
369c9, 113
369e3, 45, 113
369e3-370a4, 85n19, 142
369e3-370b7, 113
371d4, 104n63
371e12, 104n63
372a5-c2, 5
372b3, 292n4
372b4-5, 379n36
372b5, 64n74
372b7-8, 64n75
372c3, 47, 64
372c3-376d3, 141
372c5-d4, 47
372d5, 47, 108
372d5-e1, 379n35
372d7, 47
372d7-e1, 86n19
372d8, 203
372d8-e1, 47
372e1, 47, 62n71, 66
373e3, 85n19
373e6-8, 104n63
374a5, 138
374a4-6, 138
374b6-d6, 85n19
374c7-10, 141
374e7-9, 141
375a2, 292n4
375a2-3, 86n22, 140
375c10-11, 108
375c10-d1, 140
375d3-5, 140
375d4-5, 141
375d11, 292n4
375e8-10, 140
376b9, 86n22
376b12-c3, 140
376c9, 141
376d4-5, 141
376d4-398c1-5, 108
376e1, 85n19
377b4, 78n6
377e6-378a6, 187n26
379b1, 191n31
379b3-7, 158n102
379b11, 93n46, 191n31
379c2-7, 191n31
379b5-c4, 191n31
379c4, 191n31
380c7-9, 187n26
380c7-10, 186
380d1-e2, 187
380d1-383c5, 396n111
380e3-4, 396n111
381d2-3, 396n111
382a4, 377
382b1-4, 87n24
382c7-d1, 396n111
383c1-5, 288n108
386a6-c8, 383
386d4-387a3, 384n46
387c10, 384n46
388a5-6, 389n71
389c4-d5, 163n111
390a8, 386n63
390a10-b2, 386n63
390e4-391a2, 57n53
391c1-2, 386n63
392c7-9, 113
393c10-d1, 267n39
393d7, 37
394e3-4, 153n87
394e8-9, 153n97
395a1-5, 394n103
395a6, 394n103
396c6-d2, 379-80n37
397b7, 248
397d9-e3, 153n97
398a1-b4, 87n24
398a8, 135n54
399a5-c4, 242-43, 391n85
399b5-c1, 392n85
399c2, 46n22
400e3, 140n72
400e5-6, 140n72
401a1, 140n72
401b2-8, 140n72
401b9, 259, 351n145
402d1-403c6, 394n103
402d4, 394n103
403c6, 394n103
404b11-c10, 389n71
404d8, 93n45
404e3-5, 93n45
404e3-405c6, 93n45
405a2-3, 93n45
405b5, 93n45
405b8, 93n45
405c1-3, 93n45
405c5, 93n45
405c6, 93n45
405d9-406a3, 389n71
407e5-408b2, 389n71
408e4, 104
409a1-c1, 351n145
409b5, 396n111

409c1, 292n4
410e5-9, 153n97
411a5-c3, 107n71
411c4-e2, 107n70
412a4-b1, 241
412a4-b2, 106n69
412d9-c4, 353n150
412e5, 338
413a1, 46n22
413c5-414a4, 353n150
413e1, 353n150
413e6, 353n150
414b7-c7, 293
414b8, 292n4
414d1-e5, 291n1
415a1-7, 122
415a2-7, 291n2
415a6-7, 122n21
416a2-6, 140
417b9, 265n32
419a1, 108, 265n32
420b8-c1, 123
421c1, 151
422e1-423c4, 398n102
423d3-6, 398n102
423e5-424a3, 82
424a5-10, 334n118
425d3-c4, 273n59
426e3-7, 355
427c6-7, 108n74
427c6-d7, 108
427d6-7, 108n74
427d8-e1, 289n108
427e1-2, 127n31
427e9-10, 127n31
427e9-428a1, 124
429a5-432b6, 142
430c8-el, 121n20
430d3-4, 121n20
432b8-d4, 246n1
432c8, 45
432c8-9, 45n15
432c9, 175n6, 361n7
432c9-d4, 45n15
432d2-4, 245
432d8, 139
432d8-9, 113
432d8-e2, 45n18
432e7-433b1, 44n14
433a1, 139
433a1-6, 113, 139, 313n56
433a5-6, 1
433a8-9, 4
433a8-b4, 149n83
433b1-2, 245
433b4, 269n49
434a9-10, 122n21
434b8, 122n21, 142
434b8-c2, 245
434c7-10, 245
434d1-435a4, 245-50, 259
434d1-435a4, 8, 247n2
434d1-435d4, 246, 246n1, 250, 255, 334n119
434d2, 3
434d3-4, 247
434d4, 247
434d5-e4, 246
434e1, 253
434e3-435a3, 278
434e4-435a1, 246
434e4-435a4, vii, 10, 99n58
435a1, 251, 279
435a1-2, 10n30
435a1-3, xxi, 8
435a1-435a2, 247
435a2, 260
435a2-4, 247
435a3-4, 99
435a5, 250
435a5-6, 123
435a5-c2, 120, 123
435a6-8, 119
435b1-2, 119
435b4-7, 119
435b9-c2, 119
435c4-6, 119
435c4-d4, 118
435c5, 120
435c8, 103, 386
435c9-d2, 10
435c9-d4, 4, 118n13, 123, 124, 154, 246
435d1, 112n4, 116n10, 118, 119, 123, 126n27, 126n29 186, 250
435d1-2, 141
435d1-4 245-46
435d2-3, 10, 114n6, 126
435d3, 4, 141, 157n100
436b9, 117
436b9-10, 117n12, 120, 140, 142, 310n46
437a3-8, 117 125, 310n46
437a5, 124
437a5-8, 124
438a7-c4, 326n94
439a6-7, 138n66
439e7, 256
440c1, 292n4
440d1, 292n4
440e3-4, 357n155
440e8-441a4, 142, 142n74
441a5-6, 250
441c4-e1, 126n25
441c5-6, 142n74
441c11-d2, 121n20
442d8-9, 250
442e4-443a2, 146
442e4-443a10, 146
443a3-4, 147
443a4, 146, 149n84
443a6-10, 147
443b1-2, 124
443b4, 250
443b9-444a2, 389n69
443c4-5, 250
443c5-7, 126n25

443c5-d1, 4
443c9, 250
443c9-10, 149
443c9-444a2, 95, 146, 149, 363
443c9-444a6, 3n14
443c11-d3, 149
443d1, 147
443d3-5, 150
443d3-6, 157n97
443d5-e2, 150, 152
443d6, 157n98
443e1-2, 156
443e2, 157n97
443e2-3, 150
443e3, 363
443e3-4, 150
443e4-7, 151
443e7-444a2, 151
444a5-6, 8
444c11, 145
445c4-7, 326n94
445d2, 142
449a7-b1, 348
449b1-6, 82
449b1-450a6, 348
449c4-5, 82
451a4, 82n10
451a6-7, 278
451d4-9, 87n23
451d10-11, 298
454a1, 292n4
454a1-8, 292n4
452a7, 295
452b4-5, 295
452e4-453a4
454a1-8, 396n111
455b4-c3, 295
455c4-6, 296
455c5-7, 296
455d2-5, 297
455d3-5, 296n7
455d6-e4, 298
455e5-7, 298
456a1-3, 298
456a4-6, 299
456a7-12, 304
456c1-3, 297
456e7-457a1, 89
457d6-8, 328n101
457d6-9, 57
457e1, 57
457e7-458b7, 56
458e1-2, 289n108
459a1-10, 292-93
459a3, 292n4
459a6, 292n4
460d1, 255n10
460d9, 140
461a4, 289n108
461d5-e1, 292n3
462a2-b3, 328n102
462c10-11, 255n10
462d1-5, 255n10
462e2, 255n10
463d5, 289n108
464a1-b4, 255n10
464b1-6, 328n101
464d2-4, 255n10
464d7-8, 255n10
466d4-6, 63
466d5-7, 57
466d8, 57
467d10-e4, 60n66
468b13-e4, 47n24
468c2-3, 47n24
469b5-471c2, 57
469b5-471c4, 57n53
469b8-c1, 58
470a5-b1, 59
470a5-6, 62
470a5-7, 59
470a8, 59
470a9-b2, 60, 61
470b4-d2, 57
470b4-471c2, 60n62
470c7-d2, 60
470d1, 60
470e4-5, 60
470e6, 60
471a1-2, 60
471a4, 61
471a6-7, 61
471a9-10, 62
471a9-b5, 58, 61n69
471a11-b1, 58n55
471b1, 58n55, 61n69
471b2-3, 62
471b4-5, 61n69
471b6-8, 62
471b8, 62n71
471c1-2, 59n59, 62
471c3, 64, 82, 258
471c3-e4, 55
471c4, 57, 63, 64
472a3-4, 13
473c6-7, 257
473c11-d3, 13, 257
473c11-d1, xiv, 2
473d3-5, 10, 13
473d3-6, 257
474c1-2, 2
474c2-3, 47n24
475e6-476a9, 328
476a10-b7, 134n51
476b4-7, 192n33
476b6-7, 86n21, 135n54
476c1, 86n21
476c2-4, 192n32
476c7-d2, 188n27
476d4-5, 86n21
476e7-479e5, 74
477a3, 396n111
477b11-12, 25
478b5-c3, 86n21
478c3, 86n21
478c12-13, 75n99
478c12-d3, 86n21
478e3, 86n21
479a1, 189, 198
479a1-2, 189n28
479a7, 289n108
479c7, 86n21, 363
479d6, 86n21
484b4-487a5, 86n20
485b2, 104
485d10-e1, 255n10
486a4-10, 208n57
486c7-8, 175n8
486d7-487a2, 189n29
486d10, 189, 198
487a6, 93

487b1, 108, 163
487b7-c3, 258
487d3-5, 163, 165
487e4-489d9, 163
488a2, 163
488a6, 163n112
488a7-8, 163
488a7-489a2, 5
486b6-8, 166n119
488c1-2, 164
488c2-5, 164
488c4, 164,
292n4
488c5, 164
488c5-7, 168
488d4-8, 165
489a4-e2, 165
489b3-5, 165
489b5-8, 165
489b5-c3, 93n44
489b8-c3, 165
489c3, 167
490a2, 386n64
491c1-4, 279
492e5-6, 289n108
494c4-6, 161
494c4-495a1, 163
494c6, 292n4
494c7-d3, 161
496d4-5, 160
494d5-8, 161
494d10-e1, 162
494e1-495a1, 162
495a2-3, 162
495e5, 71, 258
496a10-e2, 163
496a11-b7, 237, 237n229, 240
496a11-496e3, 161, 240
496b2, 292n4
496b3-5, 78n3
496b6-7, 240
496b7-c5, 238
496c1, 238n230
496c2, 237, 238
496c7-d3, 159, 240
496d1, 242
496d5, 159
496d5-e3, 159
496d6, 382n42
496e1-497a3, 389
497a1-2, 108, 159
497a3-5, 159
498c9-d1, 206
498d1-2, 158 159, 163, 169
499c7-d6, 134, 178n11
499d8-500a8, 109n76
500b8-c5, 207
500b8-c7, 206, 207
500c1, 209
500d1, 208
500d1-3, 207
500d2, 289n108
501c2-3, 289n108
502c9-d3, 340
503a1-2, 353n150
503a1-7, 353n150
503a6, 353n150
504a4, 120n17
504a7-8, 175n8, 127n30
504b1-b4, 124, 127
504b1-d3, 44
504b1-505b1, 27
504b2, 5, 114n6, 139n71, 157n100, 206, 303n22
504b4-c4, 128
504c2-3, 128
504c9, 126
504d6, 139n69
505a1-b3, 191
505a2, 188, 189, 191, 193, 206, 277
505a2-b3, 188-89
505b3, 277
505d5, 277
506a4-5, 278
506d1, 64, 108
506d1-e1, 189
506d7, 357n158
506e2, 26, 26n79, 190
506e2-3, 27
506e2-507a4, 190, 191
507a4-6, 190, 337n122
507b1-6, 192n32
507b2-508c2, 337
507b4-508a2, 193
507b5, 192
507b8-11, 192n33
507b12-c2, 191
507b19, 192
507d1, 193
507e5, 192, 193
507e5-508a2, 193
508a4-508d3, 158
508b12-13, 193
508d10-e2, 317n73
508d10-509a5, 193, 302n18
508e1-2, 193, 200
509b2-10, 26n29
509b3, 26n29
509b8, 24, 26n79, 320n78, 398
509c1-2, 26n79
509d6-8, 5
509d9, 133n49
510b4, 123, 135
510b4-8, 5, 114, 117,135n54, 380n38
510b4-511b2, 5
510b4-511c2, 115
510b4-511d5, 307
510b5, 123
510b6-8, 114n6
510b8, 112, 112n4, 126n29, 139n71
510b9, 114
510b9-c1, 116n11
510b9-d3, 116n11
510c1, 4, 5, 115
510c1-2, 184
510c1-d3, 115
510c2-5, 310
510c2-511a2, 4
510c4-5, 120
510c4, 134n51

510c5, 112, 112n4, 118n113, 129n29, 139n71
510c6-d3, 313n56
510d1-3, 113
510d2-3, 141
510d5, 115, 123
510d5-511a2, 123n23, 135, 138
510e2, 138, 139
510e2-3, 202
510e2-511a1, 201
510e3, 123, 141
511a4, 115
511a4-a9, 5, 115, 126n27
511a5, 123
511a5-7, 113
511a7, 123
511a7-8, 135
511a8-9, 134n53
511b2, 115
511b2-5, 182
511b2-c2, 15, 182
511b5, 98, 248
511b5-7, 182-83
511b6, xx
511b6-c1, 183, 343
511b7-8, 184n22
511c1, 123, 265n33, 277
511c1-2, 287
511d8-e1, 5n17, 14n41, 113, 130, 188
511e1, 135
511e2-4, 133n49
514a2-517a6, 4
515a5-8, 371
515a7, 45n17
515b9, 45n17
515c2, 45n17, 89n26
515c6-d7, 80
515e7, 45
516b4-c6, 40
516b6, 274
516b8-c2, 41
516c4-6, 40, 41
516c8-d4, 41, 174
516c8-e2, 383
516d4-e2, 41
516d4-7, 41, 174
516e3, 184n22
516e3-4, 174
516e3-6, 41
516e3-517a7, 39
516e4, 45n16
516e7-517a2, 41
517a2-4, 41
517a4-5, 281n79
517a4-6, 41, 181, 387n67
517a5-6, 41
517a8, 172
517a8-b6, 246n1
517a8-b7, 194
517b3, 40
517b4, 196
517b7-c4, 194-95
517b8, 198
517b8-c1, 41
517b8-c4, 43, 317n73
517c6-d3, 43n12
517d4-5, 289, 365n16
517d4-e2, 43
517d7-8, 279
517d7-e1, 40
517d8-9, 279
518a1-6, 376
518a6-b2, 376
518b2-5, 377
518b7-c3, 300
518c4-7, 300
518c7-d2, 301
518c8, 92
518d3-7, 303
519a7-b5, 371
519c5-6, 357n158
519c8-d2, 173
519c9, 174n3
519d2-7, 174
519d3, 173
519d4-5, 174, 184n22
519d4-7, 173
519d8-9, 35, 175
519e1-520a4, 175n7
520a6-b1, 176
520a7-8, 35
520a8, 387
520b1-3, 176
520b1-c1, 387
520b3-5, 177
520b5-6, 99n58
520b5-c1, 10
520b5-c3, 177
520b5-d5, 177n9
520b6-7, 294
520c1, 10, 35, 38, 148, 172, 178, 181n17, 387
520c1-3, 45n16
520c1-5, 237, 361
520c5, 278
521c6, 180
520c6-d5, 252
520d7-9, 180
520e1, 6, 81n7 181, 218n113, 247, 351
520e4-521a2, 92n40, 181, 252
521b1-5, 179n12
521b5, 179n12
521c5-8, 303n22
521d4-5, 303n20
522d1-8, 393n97
523a3, 363n15
523a7-8, 91, 344
523a8, 344
523e1-524a3, 331n109
524b1-6, 326n95
524b3-526c7, 307, 320n78
524b7-c2, 326
524c1, 443
524c3-9, 327
524d1-d8, 329-30
524d8-e2, 331
524d9-526c7, 152
524e2-525a3, 331n109
525a2-3, 155
525a4-6, 331n109
525b3, 181n18, 303n20, 363n15
525c8-e3, 152n86
525d5-8, 335
525d6, 131

525d8-e3, 332
525d8-e4,
326n93, 331n110
525d8-526a4, 203
525d9-e3, 154
526a1-5, 130
526a3-4, 307n29
526d7-e8, 345
526d7-e9, 196,
332
526e2, 198
526e7, 363n15
526e7-8, 181n18
527b4-5, 303n20
527b8, 292n4
528a6-b3,
341n129
528d8, 112,
112n4, 126n29
528e4-529c3, 398
529a7, 209
529a9-10, 26n29
529b3-5, 155
529d7-e3,
334n116
530b7, 26n80
531c5-7, 302n18
531c9-d3, 126n28
342, 343
531c9-d8, 324n87
531c10, 112
531d1, 126n29
531d6-7, 324n87
531d7, 303n20
531d8, 126n28
532a1-d1, 26n80
532a6, 135
532c2, 26n80
532d7, 324n87
533b2, 112
533b3, 126n29
533c3-6, xiii
533c8, 112,
126n28, 126n29
533c8-d6,
343n131
534b8-c1, 346
534b8-d1, 336
534b8-d2, 21-22,
68-69n82, 198
534b8-d6, 398
534b9-c1, 198
534c1-3, 346-47
534c4-d6, 347
534d6-8, 347n137
535a3-536a8, 336
535a6-536a7, 338
535b1-3, 351n45
338n125
535b2, 338n126
535b5-6, 338n126
535b6-9, 338n124
535b8, 338n127
535c1, 338n127
535c3, 338n127
535c6-9, 339
535d1-7,
338n127, 339
535d5, 339n128
535d9-e5, 339
536a3, 339n128
536a4, 339
536b1-7, 336
536b8-c7, 337
536d4-537a1, 335
537b6-c3, 340
537b7-c3, 342
537b7-540a2, 91n36
537c2, xiii
537c4-7, 342-43
537d3, 37, 271
537d3-8, 344
538a7, 344
538a9, 344
538b7, 344
538d7-e4, 278
539e2-3, 37, 174
539e2-540a5, 179
539e2-540a6,
344n133
539e3, 184n22,
271
539e3-4, 174
539e3-6, 241
539e3-540a2, 38
539e5, 242n236
539e6-540a2, 241
540a4-5, 37
540a6-9, 38n3
540a6-b1, 174n3
540a6-b7, 357
540a8, 203, 364
540a8-9, 203
540b1-4, 387
540b6-7, 384n50,
357n158
540c3-9, 299n13
540c5-9, 241
541a1-7, 83
543a5, 396
544b4, 142n75
544c1-7, 142
544c6, 292n4
544c8, 200
545b1-2, 158, 355
546a1-547a5, 334n118
546b4-d3,
334n119
546b5, 200
547a1, 349
548b6-7, 382
548d8-576b9, 108
550c6, 142
551b3, 363n15
552c2-3, 177n9
553b5, 363n15
554c4-10, 36n105
554d3, 363n15
555b7, 8
556a9-b4, 354
557c4-9, 358n159
557d2-5, 350
557d2-d7, 350
557e1-3, 352
558b1-8, 351n145
558b8, 292n4
559b6, 351
559e9-560a2, 1
560b6-7, 79
561c1-2,
353n147,
353n150
561c6-d3, 354
561d3-8, 354
561e5, 358n159
562b10-c2, 353
562c2, 175, 351
563a5-7, 358n159
563b5-10,
358n159

563d1-2, 61
564c1-5, 177n9
564d6-e2, 1
565b9-c1, 164
566a1-2, 1, 355
566a11-b2, 1
566c9-d2, 1n2
566e8-9, 357n156
567a5-8, 357n156
568b8, 49
569b6, 396n111
569b7, 72n84
571d1, 72n84
571d7-572a9, 71-72n84
573a8-b7, 1n2
573b6-7, 77n1
576c5-d1, 119n15
577d1, 119n15
580b1-c2, 81n7
580b9, 47
580c1-5, 119n15
580d2-4, 119n15
583b2-3, 142n75, 266
584c3-5, 255n10
584e3-4, 377n31
585a3-4, 197
585b9, 326n94
585b11-c6, 395n106
585c9-d3, 188n27
587c5-588a5, 142
587d3-588a5, 334n117
588b6-8, 201
588b9-11, 201
588b10-e3, 378
588c1-6, 201
588c7-d1, 5
588c7-d2, 201
588c7-e3, 371
588d2-e3, 202
588d5, 279
590d1-3, 159
590e2-591a3, vii
591c1-4, 338n124
591e1-4, 363
591e5-592a4, 364
592a5, 201
592a5-6, 364
592a5-8, 174n5
592a7-8, 366
592a9-10, 366, 368
592a10, 200
592b1-2, 200
592b1-5, 367
595a1-b1, 378n33
595b1, 377
595b8, 378n34
595b9-c4, 378n34
596a5-9, 203
596a10-b2, 203
596b1-9, 203
595b9-c3, 105n67
596a5, 118n13
596a5-8, 134
596a6, 112, 112n4, 126n29
597d4, 379
597b4-6, 379
597d6-7, 379n36
597d8, 379
598e5-599a6, 380
599a7-b2, 381
599b3-7, 381
599b5-7, 93n44
599b8, 382n40
599b7, 382n40
600a8, 390
601d1-2, 380
602e8-9, 117n12
603d4-6, 378
604a5-7, 144n78
605b5-c3, 396n112
606c1-5, 390
607b6-7, 397n123
608a5-b1, 378
609d4-7, 288
610a9, 12
611a10-b3, 378
611a10-b4, 254
611b5-8, 254
611b9-c4, 254
611b9-612a6, 389n69
611c4-d6, 255
611c5, 24
611c7, 254, 255n11
611d6, 255n11
611d6-8, 255
611d8, 280, 371
611d8-612a3, 256
612a3-7, 256
612d4-10, 378
613a1-2, 67
613a7-b1, 289n108
614a5-6, 375
614a5-8, 378
614b2, 397
615b1-2, 161
615b6, 289n108
616b4-c2, 194
617b6-8, 3
618d5-619a1, 388
619b5-6, 374n27
619c3, 373
619c5-6, 373
619c6-d1, 351, 373-74
619c7-8, 351n145
619d1-3, 374
619d3-7, 374
619d7-e5, 375
619e4, 372
620c3-d2, 389
620c6, 149n84, 382n42
620d1, 149n83
621d2-3, 95, 145, 201, 372

Sophist
216c5, 396n111
237a4-5, 396n111
238a10-11, 320n78
241d3, 81n8, 396n111
248e6-249a2, 396n111
251b5-6, 396n111
Statesman
293c7-d1, 347
311a6-9, 338n126
311a7, 338n126

Symposium
172c3, 189
177d6-7, 297n10
179e1-180a4, 384
180b4-5, 41
201d1-8, 297n10

210b2, 86n21
211a1-2, 302n19
211b1-2, 86n21
220b6, 285
220d4-5, 26n79
223d3-6, 394n103
223d10, xix

Theaetetus
143a1, 271
144c5-8, 62
149a1-4, 297n9
150b7-8, 286
176b1, 5n14
183e6, 81n8

Theages
125e8-126a4, 241
128b2-6, 297n10
128d2-5, 238
129c8-d2, 51, 52

Timaeus
17c1-19b2, 64n73
19c2-8, 396
19c7, 396n110
21a2, 53n39
22c1-3, 23
27a5, 395n106
27d6-28a4, 395n106
28a4, 395n106
29e1-2, 396
31a3-5, 134n51
31b3, 395n106
31b6-8, 75n103
33b4-5, 72
46e7-47b2, 396n108
52a8, 398
52b2-d1, 397n120

Plutarch

Life of Caesar
4.4, 363n14

Life of Cato
30.6, 359n4
68.2, 359n2

Life of Cicero
4.1-2, 2n4
20.4, 361
32.5, 2
48.3, 281

Life of Demosthenes
3.3, 2n10, 360n5
5.5, 360n5

Comparison of Demosthenes and Cicero,
3.4, 360n5

Life of Pericles
12.1-2, 49n27
13.3, 48
13.6, 61n68

Life of Dion
13, 267n40
16.1, 267n40
19.3, 267n40

Porphyry

Life of Plotinus 12, 6n19

Quintilian
Education of the Orator
10.123, 2n4, 361

Sextus Empiricus

Adv. Mathematicos
10.261, 306n27

Tertullian

De praescriptione haereticorum
7, 282n85

Thucydides

1.1, 60n63
1.22.4, 23, 24, 54
1.72.2, 52n36
1.88, 52
2.23, 59n59
2.31.3, 52n35
2.39.1, 351n145
2.41.1, 350-51
3.48, 61n69
5.84, 61n69
5.116.4, 49
7.86, 61n68
8.97.2, 161n108

Xenophon

Apology
7-9, 392n87
26, 392n92, 393

Hellenica
2.2.3, 58n54

Memorabilia
2.6.3, 166n119
3.6, 109, 159
4.2.33, 392n92

About the Author

Having been persuaded by Plato's *Republic* that justice requires the philosopher to go back down into the Cave, **William H. F. Altman** has devoted his professional life to the cause of public education, presently as a Latin teacher at E. C. Glass High School in Lynchburg, Virginia. Born in Washington D.C. where he was educated at the Sidwell Friends School, and with degrees in Philosophy from Wesleyan University, University of Toronto, and the Universidade Federal de Santa Catarina, he has been a public high school teacher in Vermont, California, Massachusetts, Connecticut, and Virginia and has taught Social Studies, History, Philosophy, English, Drama, and Latin as well as offering extracurricular instruction in Ancient Greek. He began publishing scholarly articles in Philosophy, Intellectual History, and Classics in 2007; his *The German Stranger: Leo Strauss and National Socialism* was published by Lexington Books in 2011.